Active Server Pages™

Stephen Walther

201 West 103rd Street
Indianapolis, IN 46290

UNLEASHED

Copyright © 1998 by Sams.net Publishing

FIRST EDITION

International Standard Book Number: 1-57521-351-6

Library of Congress Catalog Card Number: 97-68015

2000   99   4   3

Interpretation of the printing code: the rightmost double-digit number is the year of the book's printing; the rightmost single-digit, the number of the book's printing. For example, a printing code of 97-1 shows that the first printing of the book occurred in 1997.

Composed in AGaramond and MCPdigital by Macmillan Computer Publishing

Printed in the United States of America

Trademarks

Publisher	*Joe Wikert*
Executive Editor	*Christopher Denny*
Managing Editor	*Jodi Jensen*
Brand Director	*Alan Bower*

Acquisitions Editor
Christopher Denny

Development Editor
Fran Hatton

Software Development Specialist
John Warriner

Production Editor
Robin Drake

Indexer
John Sleeva

Technical Reviewer
Bryan Morgan

Editorial Coordinators
Mandie Rowell
Katie Wise

Technical Edit Coordinator
Lynette Quinn

Resource Coordinator
Charlotte Clapp

Editorial Assistants
Carol Ackerman
Andi Richter
Rhonda Tinch-Mize
Karen Williams

Cover Designer
Sandra Schroeder

Book Designer
Gary Adair

Copy Writer
Eric Borgert

Production Team Supervisor
Andrew Stone

Production
Jeanne Clark
Cyndi Davis-Hubler

Part II   Markup and Scripting Languages

Part VI Using Microsoft Visual Studio

25 Using Visual InterDev   631

Acknowledgments

I'd like to thank my smarter younger sister, Sue Walther, for reading and commenting on every page of this book (including this page) when she should have been finishing her novel. This book is much more readable because of her efforts.

I am also grateful to my parents, who have always been supportive of the strange new twists and turns my life has taken.

I would also like to thank John Pyrovolakis. I owe John a debt of gratitude for awakening me from my dogmatic slumbers and getting me involved in the World Wide Web.

I am also grateful to Andy Rebele for patiently giving me time to work on this book while we were creating the CityAuction Web site. Andy wrote Chapter 30, "Web Site Promotion and Marketing."

Thanks also to Ruth Johnson for her help with the HTML appendix.

Finally, I want to thank Fran Hatton and Robin Drake for putting up with the blunders of a new author. Thanks for your patience!

About the Authors

Stephen Walther

Stephen Walther received his B.A. from the University of California at Berkeley. He was a Ph.D. candidate in Linguistics and Philosophy at the Massachusetts Institute of Technology when he became involved with the World Wide Web. Formerly the chief technical officer of Collegescape, where he designed and managed the implementation of the original Collegescape Web site (www.collegescape.com), he is currently the chief scientist at CityAuction (www.cityauction.com). He can be contacted at Swalther@aol.com.

Mike Culver

Mike Culver is CEO of Extencia, Inc., a software firm in Redmond, Washington, that specializes in electronic commerce Internet applications. Extencia's focus grew from Mike's lifetime of experience in the wholesale distribution industry, where huge databases are the norm—but no one was connecting them to the Internet in a secure manner. (Extencia's Web site is located at www.extencia.com.) Born in Madison, Wisconsin, Mike has a BBA in Finance from the University of Wisconsin–Madison. In the late eighties he moved to the Seattle area, and now lives near Microsoft's campus. With almost 15 years of professional computer experience, he still spends almost all his time in front of the computer. However, his real passions are sailboat racing and soaring.

J. Simon Hancock

Originally from Sarasota, Florida, J. Simon Hancock studied computer science at the University of Maryland, University College, in College Park, Maryland. He began his computing career at the age of 12, writing software for his paper route. Currently a Microsoft Certified Systems Engineer (MCSE), Simon is pursuing the Microsoft Certified Solution Developer (MCSD) title as well. As a former cooperative education student, he is a strong believer that experience is the best teacher. Simon currently is developing CTI solutions for Nabnasset Corporation in Boston, Massachusetts. He can be reached at JSimonH@acm.org.

William Kenney

William Kenney is a corporation partner and Web consultant for General Systems Software. He designed and developed several SQL Server Web databases for Fortune 500 clients, and is on the board of directors of IPIPE, Inc., an Internet service provider for Web hosting. He is a Microsoft Solution Provider and Microsoft Certified Product Specialist.

Andy Rebele

Andy Rebele worked leasing industrial real estate in Houston in 1987 (the year of the see-through buildings), and, after stints as a high school rowing coach and bartender, got his MBA at MIT in 1994. He was an evangelist and then manager of Internet business development at General Magic, working to put GMI's agent and handheld platform technologies on the Internet. From there he went to Interactive Imaginations, where he did business development, working on the Riddler game site and the Commonwealth Network Web site advertising network. Now Andy works on business development, marketing, and hype at CityAuction (www.cityauction.com).

Noelani Rodriguez

Noelani Rodriguez is a Microsoft Certified Trainer, public speaker, and contributing author for Que's *Using Systems Management Server*. She is also Webmaster for the Microsoft Certification Exam resource page on the Web.

Eleanor Sparks

Eleanor Sparks has been managing and directing multimedia and Internet projects for the past five years. She has worked in Web site development since the earliest days and has produced many online and hybrid applications. As a director of Virtually Perfect, the company she started with her husband, Grant, Eleanor currently works primarily on Active Server Pages and training new recruits to the frenzied world of content production.

Charles Williams

Charles Williams, a Microsoft Certified Systems Engineer, specializes in the security and development of Internet and local area network-based information systems. When he's not stuck in front of his computer, "Jade" (named by his wife), Chuck enjoys mountain biking, walking, travel, the stock market, investigating new technology, and spending quality time with his wife and inspiration, Lisa. Chuck can be reached at ab831@detroit.freenet.org.

Tell Us What You Think!

As a reader, you are the most important critic and commentator of our books. We value your opinion and want to know what we're doing right, what we could do better, what areas you'd like to see us publish in, and any other words of wisdom you're willing to pass our way. You can help us make strong books that meet your needs and give you the computer guidance you require.

Do you have access to the World Wide Web? Then check out our site at http://www.mcp.com.

As the team leader of the group that created this book, I welcome your comments. You can fax, e-mail, or write me directly to let me know what you did or didn't like about this book—as well as what we can do to make our books stronger. Here's the information:

Fax: 317-817-7070

E-mail: cdenny@mcp.com

Mail: Christopher Denny
          Comments Department
          Sams.net Publishing
          201 W. 103rd Street
          Indianapolis, IN 46290

Introduction

Active Server Pages is Microsoft's solution to building advanced Web sites. You can use Active Server Pages to create anything from a simple home page to a very advanced, large-scale, commercial Web site. You will find this book a valuable resource no matter how simple or advanced your Web project may be.

Using Active Server Pages, you can

- **Create dynamic Web pages.** An Active Server Page can display different content to different users or display different content at different times.
- **Process the contents of HTML forms.** You can use an Active Server Page to retrieve and respond to the data entered into an HTML form.
- **Add a hit counter to a Web page.** Using an Active Server Page, you can display the number of times a particular Web page has been requested.
- **Store and retrieve information from a database.** An Active Server Page can insert new data or retrieve existing data from a database such as Microsoft SQL Server.
- **Detect the capabilities of different browsers.** An Active Server Page can detect whether a browser can use frames or background sound and can display content appropriately.
- **Track user sessions.** You can use Active Server Pages to store information about users from the moment they arrive at your Web site until the moment they leave.
- **Read and write to files.** You can use Active Server Pages to gain complete control over a computer's file system.
- **Integrate custom ActiveX components into your Web site.** You can extend your Active Server Pages with custom ActiveX components written in such languages as Visual Basic or Java. This means that there's no limit to what you can do with an Active Server Page.

Why You Should Buy This Book

- This book covers the latest version of Active Server Pages and Internet Information Server (version 4.0). There are many important changes in this version of Active Server Pages, including a number of completely new components.
- This book contains four valuable appendixes that offer references for the Active Server Pages objects and components, VBScript, JScript, and HTML.

■ This book teaches you how to use scripts written in both VBScript and JScript within your Active Server Pages.

■ This book teaches you how to program using SQL and how to integrate SQL commands into your Active Server Pages. Using SQL, you can store and retrieve data from a database, creating database-driven Web sites.

■ This book explains how to create Active Server Pages Web sites using Visual InterDev. Visual InterDev provides an easy-to-use interface for writing Active Server Pages scripts and managing the files on a Web site.

■ This book teaches you how to create your own custom ActiveX Active Server Page components in both Visual Basic and Java.

How This Book Is Organized

After reading this book, you will have a thorough mastery of Active Server Pages. To exploit the full power of Active Server Pages, you need to be able to work with a number of different server applications and programming languages. This book covers them all.

There are eight parts to this book:

Part I, "Preparing for Active Server Pages," discusses all the server applications that you need to set up a Web site and run Active Server Pages. You learn how to install and configure NT Server, Internet Information Server, SQL Server, and Exchange Server.

Part II, "Markup and Scripting Languages," covers the three languages that you will weave together to create your Active Server Pages. This part includes a thorough guide to HTML, including advanced features such as frames and cascading style sheets. Both the VBScript and JScript scripting languages are also described. These are the languages that will make your Active Server Pages active.

Part III, "Working with Data: SQL," discusses the single most important topic for creating advanced commercial Web sites: database access. In this part of the book, you learn how to use SQL, the standard language of databases, to manipulate the data in a SQL Server database.

Part IV, "Creating Active Server Pages with Objects and Components," explains how to use ActiveX objects and components within your Active Server Pages. You learn how to use all the built-in and installable objects that are bundled with Active Server Pages.

Part V, "The Database Component," discusses how to use a very special set of objects—the ActiveX Data Objects—to issue SQL commands within your Active Server Pages. The ActiveX Data Objects act as the interface between your Web site and SQL Server.

Part VI, "Using Microsoft Visual Studio," explains how to use the Visual Studio programs Visual InterDev, Image Composer, and Music Producer to create the elements of a Web site. This part also contains a very important and interesting chapter on creating custom ActiveX components for your Web site.

Part VII, "Bringing It All Together," discusses how to build a complete sample Web site from start to finish. You learn how to create the Active Server Pages Job Site. This part also contains a chapter on the very important topic of how to promote and make money from your Web site.

Part VIII, "Appendixes," contains four quick references for the Active Server Pages objects and components, VBScript, JScript, and HTML. When you need to quickly locate the syntax for a command, look here.

Who Should Read What

This is a long book. It's a comprehensive book. It's not expected that every reader of this book will read each and every chapter from start to finish. Different readers will have different needs.

If you're completely new to creating Web sites and Web pages, you should start with the chapters on HTML in Part II of this book. Once you have a thorough understanding of HTML, you can begin to create Web pages and move forward to more advanced topics.

If you're new to using Active Server Pages but have experience using other scripting languages (such as Allaire's Cold Fusion), begin by reading the chapter on VBScript in Part II and the chapters on the Active Server Pages objects and components in Part IV.

Finally, if you've used earlier versions of Internet Information Server and Active Server Pages, you should jump immediately to Chapter 13, "Building Active Server Pages." Also, you should familiarize yourself with Internet Information Server 4.0 by reading Chapter 2, "Installing and Using Internet Information Server."

Conventions Used in This Book

Names of commands, objects, methods, and so on appear in a `special monospace typeface`. Long code lines, blocks or snippets of code, and scripts are placed on separate lines at the margin for easy readability.

Occasionally, command lines are so long that they must wrap to following lines to fit within the margins of this book. In those cases, a special code-continuation arrow (➡) appears at the beginning of succeeding lines, to indicate that the command should or must be typed on a single line, as in the following example:

```
MyDictionary.Item("A Sentence")="This is a very long
➡sentence that must appear on one line"
```

Placeholders or variables appearing within code lines or text appear in *`italic monospace`*. In the following example, you would substitute the appropriate information for *`name@domain`* to complete the address:

```
<FORM ACTION="MAILTO:name@domain.com">.
```

In syntax examples, some command elements may be optional. In these cases, the optional element appears in brackets. In the following example, there may be multiple arguments for the `function` command, a single argument, or no arguments at all:

```
functionfunctionname([argument1[,argument2[,...argumentn]]])
{
statements
}
```

For consistency, names of elements in JScript, VBScript, and so on follow the capitalization appropriate for each language, and some sentences thus may begin with lowercase letters. (For example, "`for...next` statements are closely related to `for...in` statements.")

Good Luck

I hope you'll find this book to be a valuable resource. To receive the most up-to-date information on the material in this book, visit the ASP Web site at `http://www.aspsite.com`.

PART

I

Preparing for Active Server Pages

Installing and Using Windows NT Server

IN THIS CHAPTER

CHAPTER 1

Welcome to Active Server Pages, featuring Windows NT! This chapter discusses relevant pre-installation issues concerning system hardware, software, networking, and security policies. Next, we go through an actual NT installation from start to finish and subsequently assist you in configuring networking components to meet your requirements.

Hardware Considerations

This section discusses many of the issues involved with the specification and configuration of your computer and networking components. Investing in the appropriate technology will improve the performance and scalability of the Web server and its associated systems.

Scalability Concerns

The Internet is the fastest growing phenomenon in the computer industry today. To be sure, part of the reason you're embarking on the Internet journey is to capitalize on this new frontier with a system that embraces the Internet and its associated technologies (including Active Server Pages).

With all computer systems, it's important to find that perfect balance of cost versus performance. Because not everyone has the capital resources of Bill Gates, we must make smart purchase decisions and procure equipment that's *scalable*. Scalable equipment has the capability to grow to meet your future needs. For example, a single-processor system may meet your needs initially, but the system should be able to eventually support symmetric multiprocessing (more than one processor).

Fault Tolerance Features

When procuring server resources, make an effort to buy systems that are fault tolerant. *Fault tolerance*, simply put, indicates that the server components are built and configured with the capability to recover safely from some type of failure, without an interruption in service. Common examples of this technology are servers with dual power supplies and systems that support *Error Checking and Correcting (ECC) memory*. If the system being implemented is mission critical, investing in highly fault-tolerant server equipment is worth the extra money.

The most important component of any server, of course, is the data stored on it. As such, a highly critical feature of any server should be its fault-tolerant drive subsystem. This fault tolerance is achieved most commonly through hardware, utilizing a RAID array controller. *RAID*, which is an acronym for *redundant array of inexpensive disks*, provides a level of data redundancy across two or more drives, thereby minimizing the potential for loss of data. This technology is present in most high-end server systems. For those without the means to purchase a hardware-based RAID implementation, Windows NT provides administrators the ability to implement RAID via software. This feature is integrated in Windows NT and is relatively easy to configure. *RAID 1*, or *disk mirroring*, is an inexpensive way to provide a heightened level of fault tolerance. RAID 1 is also the simplest method to configure; the only requirements are two physically separate disks, with enough space on each to mirror the partition that requires mirroring.

But RAID is just one of several types of protection available. The simplest method of protection, which should be performed regardless of the level of fault tolerance implemented, is a tape backup or other type of offline storage. Of course, one problem with using tape backup as your only method of protection is the downtime involved in recovering from a disk failure. Depending on the type of system and amount of data lost, a system recovering from tape can be unavailable from one hour to several days.

New technology is currently available that will enable Windows NT systems to be "hardware mirrored"—thereby providing administrators the ability to create hot spare servers that take over should the original (master) server fail. This upcoming technology will prove to be a significant weapon in the fault tolerance arsenal. Two popular products are Vinca's StandbyServer and the upcoming Microsoft "Wolfpack" technology—included in the upcoming Windows NT Server Enterprise Edition, due in late 1997.

x86 versus RISC

The abbreviation *x86* stands for Intel's line of microprocessors, with the just-released Pentium II leading the way. *RISC* is a generic term that stands for *reduced instruction set computing.* Current RISC-based processors supported by Windows NT are DEC Alpha, Motorola PowerPC, and the MIPS platform—but not for long. Microsoft has announced that it plans to stop support for all but the DEC Alpha platform.

All processor platforms should meet the performance needs of all but the most strenuous operating environments. The x86-versus-RISC decision should be made based on the existing operating environment.

> **NOTE**
>
> To benefit the largest possible audience, this chapter details both x86- and RISC-based installations of Windows NT.

Network Connectivity Issues

For most Web servers today, the primary system bottleneck is network bandwidth. Unfortunately, it's also usually the largest expenditure in a Web server system, due to the high costs of networking hardware and monthly charges for Internet access. For this reason, it's important to make smart purchasing decisions when choosing your network connection.

Appropriately scaling network bandwidth involves buying enough bandwidth to meet existing need, as well as possessing enough scalability to meet anticipated requirements. The following sections discuss methods to measure your anticipated throughput requirements and associated costs.

Measuring Bandwidth Need

Measuring bandwidth requirements is a difficult task. The number of variables involved—several being outside an administrator's control—make it impossible to precisely calculate requirements. Fortunately, guidelines are available to assist in *estimating* your anticipated bandwidth requirement.

First and foremost, it's important to determine the role that the system will play in the Internet environment. Systems that support relatively mundane tasks, such as serving e-mail (SMTP, POP3) or supporting Telnet connections, require fewer system resources than more intensive tasks such as video, streaming audio, or even transmitting complex HTML pages. Supporting several Internet functions compounds the system requirements.

Another important measure is response time. If users expect prompt response, the system must be able to support the expected level of service. Less critical tasks, such as batch-mode processing, are less time critical, and can wait in any service queues created due to a surge in requests.

The final measure—number of concurrent users or requests—is often most difficult to estimate. Calculating these factors may require preliminary testing, performing a pilot test, or querying other systems on the Internet that perform a similar function.

Using the Bandwidth Algorithm

Before estimating the necessary bandwidth, you must understand the subtle differences between the different TCP/IP connection methods. Take the following FTP and HTTP transfer scenarios:

- Transferring a 100KB file via FTP
- Transferring a graphically intense Web page, containing nine graphic images, whose total size equals 100KB

In this example, the FTP download requires only TCP connection, which remains open for the duration of the transfer. The HTTP download, however, requires the negotiation of one TCP connection for every component located on the Web page (graphic, applet, and so on). These TCP connections, while usually taking less than a second to negotiate, have an impact on performance as the connection volume increases. If the connection latency is 250 milliseconds (approximately the latency of today's Internet), downloading 10 components of a Web page theoretically amounts to approximately 7 seconds of latency (10×250 ms for the requests, 10×250 ms for the server's responses, and 10×250 ms for the connection to be closed). This doesn't even account for the time necessary for the data to be transferred or for the Web browser to render the Web page.

Luckily, early browser developers anticipated this problem and designed browsers to perform multiple HTTP requests at once. This solution, while certainly a help, is still affected by the available bandwidth at the client's end. A 28.8 modem connection can easily be fully saturated by a few concurrent requests.

It should be of comfort to most readers to learn that the next version of the HTTP standard, HTTP/1.1, enables pages and their incorporated graphics to be *streamed* to the client over one persistent HTTP connection. This new standard should significantly reduce roundtrip latency.

You can use a simple algorithm to help estimate an Internet server's bandwidth requirements. The only variables associated with this estimate are the estimated number of concurrent user connections and the average size of the documents being transferred. The formula is as follows:

(Average document size in kilobytes × (8 bits data + 4 bits overhead)) × (connections per day / seconds per day)

Now let's plug in the following variables:

Average document size: 112KB

Average connections per day: 9,000

With those numbers, we arrive at the following:

$(112 \times 1024 \times (8 + 4)) \times (9,000 / 86,400)$

The estimate totals 1433KB, or approximately one T1 connection.

Remember that 1KB isn't 1000 bytes—it's 1024 bytes. Also, 86,400 is 24 hours × 60 minutes × 60 seconds. Although it's true that "the Internet never sleeps," this number may need to be reduced in an effort to reflect peaks in utilization during "normal business hours."

Available Connection Types

Table 1.1 lists the types of Internet connections that are commercially available through most Internet service providers (ISPs). The data in this table varies depending on location (U.S. or abroad). It's simply intended to provide an estimated relative measure of cost versus performance. Several new technologies, including the cable modem and xDSL (which operates over existing telephone lines) promise to provide significantly greater throughput—in excess of 10 Mbps—at a greatly reduced cost. Until these new technologies become mainstream, several options still exist.

Table 1.1. A comparison of Internet connection types.

Transmission Method	Throughput	Approximate Cost
28.8 modem	28.8 Kbps (best case)	Varies widely; less than $50/month
ISDN	64 to 128 Kbps	$30/month and higher—not including local telephone company charges
Fractional T1	56 to 512 Kbps	$100/month and higher
Full T1	1.54 Mbps	$1,000/month and higher
T3	45 Mbps	Highly dependent upon availability

One recommended bandwidth strategy this author considers noteworthy provides an adequate amount of initial bandwidth and affords excellent scalability. This solution, the fractional T1 line, enables Webmasters to begin with a lower-cost solution while possessing the potential to scale to a full T1 line.

NOTE

The new 56K modem technology, while providing excellent improvements for those downloading information from the Internet, isn't a good solution for an active Web server connection. The 56K technology improves throughput only when downloading information; uploading of information stills takes place at 28.8 or 33.6 and is sensitive to telephone system mishaps.

If Requirements Exceed Capacity

Imagine that the new Web server is more popular than initially expected and connection throughput can't meet the growing demand. Several avenues are available to reduce the system's disparity:

- The simplest (and often most effective) solution is to increase the available bandwidth via a fractional-T1-to-full-T1 upgrade, as discussed earlier, or by adding additional lines. Either option results in increased cost, because connectivity and bandwidth are not cheap.

- Another alternative is to reduce the services provided by the server. Removing e-mail, Usenet news, Gopher, or FTP services can help reduce the system's load. This option should be executed only if existing capacity is far outmatched by demand and no additional resources are available to upgrade the system. This solution is similar to the preceding one in that the goal is to reduce the system's load, not increase the system's capacity. This strategy may help in the short term, but is usually counterproductive. The goal should be to maximize the system's usability, not reduce it.

- A third alternative is to reduce the possible number of concurrent remote clients. Microsoft Internet Information Server (IIS) has the capability to restrict the number of concurrent client connections. Lowering this threshold prevents additional clients from connecting to IIS, and should be used only as a last resort. The system should be scaled to meet the demands of your users, and lowering this threshold may cost you the system's most precious commodity—customers.

- A relatively easy way to improve the customer's perceived performance is to reduce the complexity or size of the graphic files transmitted from the server. Reducing graphic complexity requires knowledge of the type of information sent by the server. Simple, computer-generated graphic images should be saved in GIF (Graphical

Interchange Format), ideally utilizing 4-bit (16 color) depth. This standard provides good quality and keeps the graphic small. Continuous-tone images, such as photographs, should be saved in JPEG (Joint Picture Experts Group) format. JPEG is a *lossy* compression method, which means that some picture quality is lost during the process, but it provides the best compression ratio. High-color images should be saved in JPG format if they're necessary on the server. See Chapter 5, "Basic HTML," for more information about the creation of efficient graphic images.

Your Upstream Provider

An *upstream provider* (or ISP) is the company from which you're buying Internet connectivity. This provider usually in turn buys Internet connectivity from a major communications company, such as AT&T, MCI, Netcom, and so on. Choosing the right provider is often more important than choosing the right computer hardware. That is to say, your network response is dependent to a large degree on the quality of your network, which is affected by your upstream provider's provider.

Several criteria should be considered when choosing an ISP:

- Redundancy of Internet connections and supporting hardware
- Throughput of Internet connections
- Level of support provided (responsiveness)
- Current or past client references
- Price
- Willingness to work with your support staff

All of these issues should be considered before making your selection.

Some ISPs also provide additional services that can be of significant benefit. These services include hardware leasing, disk space leasing (hosting), providing preliminary advertising for your site, providing hit statistics, and so forth. Inquiring about these "value added" services may help you get better value for your money.

In that regard, I recommend selecting providers with the network capacity, support, and knowledge to meet your needs.

Software Considerations

Now that we've discussed some important hardware issues, let's move on to the exciting world of software! This section discusses the importance of software compatibility and transaction logging programs.

Compatibility

Ensuring software compatibility—on both the server and the client—is crucial in today's environment of complex, heterogeneous systems. Extensive testing of new server-based software should be performed before adding it to the production environment. It's not uncommon for software packages to make configuration changes to the system that can affect its reliability or security. As such, it's very important that all new software components be tested thoroughly on a non-production system.

In addition, many Web browsers today support advanced features that are specified to that particular browser. Before posting any new Web page, ensure that it's compatible with the various browsers available on the market today.

Logging of Data

Tracking the transactions (hits) on the system is an important part of maintaining an Internet system. These log files can be used to help detect potentially malicious activity, calculate server usage to help predict growth, and examine statistics describing which users are connecting to the system.

IIS provides extensive logging capability that enables you to track the number of clients accessing the site, what they attempt to access, where the request originates from, and how much data was sent during the transaction. This information is stored in a text file by default, but IIS can be configured to log directly to a database.

The data files in their native format are difficult to interpret. Several third-party software packages are available that examine the IIS log files and provide comprehensive data reporting and analysis. These packages are well worth the expense; purchasing one is recommended.

Security Considerations

This section discusses some pertinent security issues associated with running an Internet-connected Web server. Although several items are discussed, new issues are being discovered all the time. Part of being a good administrator includes being well educated about the numerous risks present in the Internet environment.

Network Security

Keeping a site secure from unauthorized network-based access is one of the most critical—and difficult—responsibilities of supporting an Internet-based Web server. Attempts are regularly made to compromise networked computers. Some do it simply for fun or the challenge, and others for more insidious reasons.

Although no system or methodology provides 100% protection, you can take several steps to keep the risk at a minimum. Several common precautions are discussed in this section.

NOTE

This text provides valuable information about the mitigation of security risks, but it shouldn't be considered a comprehensive source of security information. New security issues are discovered on a regular basis. It's your responsibility to be aware of these new risks when they're discovered and take action accordingly. Up-to-date security information is available at the Microsoft Web site (www.microsoft.com) or the CERT Web site (www.cert.org).

Data Encryption

Data transmitted between Web browsers and Web servers using TCP/IP is susceptible to unauthorized interception. To protect sensitive data, the most common and most viable method of protection is data encryption.

Secure Sockets Layer (*SSL*) provides a high level of data privacy, integrity, and user authentication between a Web server and its client. This technology utilizes public-key and symmetric-key cryptography, in addition to digital signature and certificate technology. This enables the client and server to communicate in an encrypted fashion, while guaranteeing that each participant is authentic and who it claims to be.

SSL can protect only certain types of Internet communication. This protection is available only during an HTTPS transaction. HTTPS is the secure alternative to the HTTP protocol, which is used when most Web pages are transmitted to and from Web servers. Two protocols that don't have secure alternatives are FTP and Gopher. For security reasons, all communication using these protocols should be assumed to be vulnerable to unauthorized access.

Various levels or strengths of encryption are available when using SSL. The highest level of protection available today uses 128-bit encryption. 128-bit SSL includes an encryption key that's one of 2^{128} possible combinations (higher than your calculator can count). Experts have deemed this level of encryption "theoretically impossible" to breach. Due to the high level of protection that 128-bit SSL provides, the U.S. government has classified it as munitions, which makes it illegal to export out of the country. But 40-bit SSL, which provides adequate protection for most data, can be exported to other countries. Although 40-bit encryption has been compromised in the past, the efforts necessary to achieve this breach are prohibitive. In one case, breaking a single 40-bit SSL-encrypted HTTP transmission took over 31 hours of raw computing time. As a rule, 40-bit encryption is safe enough for all but the most sensitive secure transactions.

NOTE

Recently the U.S. government has approved the export of 128-bit encryption technology in certain applications and circumstances. Because of the legal implications and the ever-changing rules, it's recommended that you check the latest federal export restrictions on encryption technology.

One of the problems associated with using SSL is the system overhead associated with it. In addition to the additional encryption and synchronization data transferred over the Internet, significant processor time is required. During an SSL communication, the data is encrypted in real time, with each 40-bit or 128-bit key being created on-the-fly. The larger the encryption key being used, the greater the strain on the processor. If significant amounts of data will be encrypted from your site, be sure to anticipate the increased bandwidth and processor requirements.

About SYN Attacks

Many potentially harmful methods are available to foil an Internet-based Web server. One method that's easily detected is the *SYN attack*. A SYN attack utilizes the SYN (synchronizing character) of the TCP/IP handshake. During the normal initiation of a TCP/IP connection, communication is initiated by sending a SYN, or synchronization request. This request is responded to with a SYN-ACK, which is sent back to the client. If a SYN is sent with an incorrect return address, the server's response won't reach the client, and the connection will remain half open.

The SYN attack prevents the availability of service by flooding the server with numerous invalid requests. These requests result in an equal number of half-open TCP connections. Once the server has reached the maximum number of allowable TCP connections, additional connection attempts are refused. These refused connections usually result in authorized end users receiving an error stating that their connection with the server has been reset.

While there is no way to prevent a SYN attack without additional firewall or proxy server equipment, the damage from these attacks can be mitigated by extensive system monitoring and prompt action.

Monitoring an Internet-based server is one of the critical tasks undertaken by systems administrators. Measuring system load, responsiveness, and capacity, and tracking the clients that access the system, are all statistics that can be captured by a properly configured Windows NT system. Monitoring the TCP connections will provide assistance in detecting SYN attacks.

The NETSTAT utility is available to view the existing TCP connections. To use NETSTAT, open a command prompt and type

```
NETSTAT -n -p TCP x
```

where x is the interval for which you would like the TCP statistics updated (in seconds). For example, if you want a continuously updating set of statistics detailing the current TCP connections, type this:

```
NETSTAT -n -p TCP 1
```

This command will initiate NETSTAT and update the display every second. To get a one-time view of the TCP statistics, omit the time interval:

```
NETSTAT -n -p TCP
```

Using NETSTAT will help determine the occurrence of a SYN attack by detailing an unusually high number of SYN_RECEIVED status connections. Refer to Microsoft's Web site for additional information and software patches to help resolve this problem.

NetBIOS over TCP/IP

Windows NT provides exceptional support for remote server administration via a TCP/IP network. With a properly configured LMHOSTS file and the necessary administrative password, an individual can connect to a server, map drives, utilize the administrative utilities (User Manager, Server Manager, and so on), and start or stop system services. This support has obvious drawbacks on an Internet-connected system. Savvy hackers, just like savvy administrators, know exactly how to configure their systems to gain server access. Preventing this inherent support for remote administration in Windows NT 4 is relatively easy. It involves blocking certain data transfers at the protocol level.

Windows NT supports remote administration and WAN connectivity by encapsulating NetBIOS information in TCP/IP packets. In effect, this enables the use of network resources as if the end user was located on the local area network. To eliminate the associated risks, it's necessary to restrict Windows NT's capability to receive NetBIOS-based data. You can achieve this either by restricting the TCP and UDP ports that are reserved for receiving NetBIOS information, or by removing the link or "binding" between NetBIOS and TCP/IP.

The TCP and UDP protocols communicate with other systems through *ports*. These ports define the type of communication being initiated, and certain applications listen to which specific ports respond when requests are sent. For example, the HTTP protocol utilizes TCP port 80, and the FTP protocol uses TCP port 21. Attackers commonly use a technique called *port scanning* in an effort to determine what types of services are installed on an Internet system. This port scan reveals whether a system is running an FTP service, WWW service, and so forth. The NetBIOS-over-TCP/IP implementation communicates over TCP and UDP ports 139, 137, and 138. It's a good idea to block all traffic using nonessential TCP and UDP ports to reduce the risks associated with port scanning, specifically blocking the ports utilized by NetBIOS. Blocking these ports eliminates the risks associated with unauthorized remote administration.

Blocking unnecessary TCP and UDP ports can be performed through the IP Address page in the Network Control Panel applet. Click the Advanced button to bring up the Advanced IP Addressing dialog box. Then check the Enable Security box and click the Configure button to bring up the TCP/IP Security dialog box, where the specific TCP and UDP ports can be enabled (see Figure 1.1).

Another method to remove the risks associated with remote administration is to disable the binding between TCP/IP and the NetBIOS interface. This is accomplished through the Bindings page in the Network Control Panel applet. The Bindings page displays the binding between Windows NT network components (see Figure 1.2). Disable the NetBIOS-to-TCP/IP interface by expanding the NetBIOS bindings (click the plus icon next to the NetBIOS Interface listing), highlighting the WINS Client (TCP/IP) item, and clicking the Disable button. The binding will provide visual feedback when bindings are disabled. Click OK to complete the configuration.

FIGURE 1.1.
Enabling IP security.

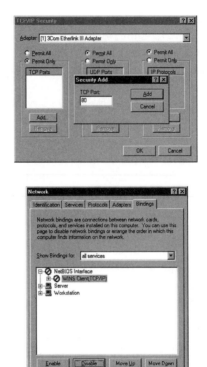

FIGURE 1.2.
Disabling network bindings.

Disabling CMD and BAT Mappings

Most computer systems support the use of batch files or scripts, which are used to automate frequently performed tasks. These batch files are executed by the server, and can be used maliciously. It's possible to call a batch file by referencing it through a standard WWW URL, because IIS contains file mappings that instruct the server to execute files with the .BAT and .CMD file extensions.

You can disable these file mappings so that the NT command interpreter won't execute these types of files. Do this manually by choosing Start | Run and entering **REGEDIT.EXE**. The file-mapping keys are under this setting:

```
HKEY_LOCAL_MACHINE/SYSTEM/CurrentControlSet/Services/W3SVC/Parameters/Script Map
```

Delete the keys that start with .BAT and .CMD and then restart IIS. If the .BAT and .CMD keys are not present, the mappings don't exist, and no modification is necessary.

> **NOTE**
>
> The Registry editor, REGEDIT.EXE, is a very powerful tool. Improper modification of the Windows NT Registry can cause significant problems, including complete system failure. Extreme care should be taken whenever modifying the system Registry.

Don't Install the FTP and Gopher Services

Installing the FTP and Gopher services provides more opportunities for malicious attackers. These software components can assist attackers in various ways, such as supplying potentially harmful information about the system's configuration, or providing opportunities to crack user ID/password combinations using brute force methods. For example, Windows NT's FTP service announces itself as a Windows NT service during logon. This provides hackers the ability to easily detect the type and revision of operating system you're using. Figure 1.3 shows how the Windows NT FTP Service displays system information to any connecting user.

FIGURE 1.3.
The Windows NT FTP prompt.

Rename Unnecessary and Dangerous Applications

Several applications are installed by default during the Windows NT installation. These applications can assist potential attackers in compromising system resources. Executables such as RCP.EXE (remote copy) and FTP.EXE (the FTP client application) should be renamed to prevent execution. For example, renaming RCP.EXE to RCP.APP prevents this application from being launched through a malicious batch file or execution command.

Computer Configuration Security

Proper server configuration can mean the difference between developing a system that resembles Fort Knox or one that is as secure as a used paper bag. Windows NT Server provides several integrated features to help protect sensitive information and detect suspicious activity.

File System and Disk Partitions

Windows NT supports two types of file systems: FAT and NTFS. While FAT provides a compatibility advantage (it can be read from Windows 95 or DOS), NTFS provides a significant security advantage.

NTFS, an abbreviation for *new technology file system*, provides several advantages over the traditional FAT (file allocation table) file system:

- NTFS is *recoverable* because it tracks all directory and file updates. This enables the system to recover should a hardware or power failure occur while data modification is taking place.

- NTFS supports *hot fixing*. Hot fixing aids in the instant recovery of data when a write attempts to store data on a bad sector of the physical disk. NTFS enables the operating system to salvage the data intended for the bad sector and write it to a different location on the same volume.

- NTFS meets POSIX.1 standard requirements. A POSIX.1-compliant file system enables case-sensitive naming of files, provides an additional time stamp of when the file was last accessed, and supports *hard links*, which allow two different filenames to point to the same data.

- NTFS supports the Windows NT security model, which enables file-level auditing and access permissions.

- NTFS supports larger partition sizes, up to 64 exabytes. This is probably more than you'll ever need.

- NTFS supports filenames up to 255 characters in length, including extensions. In addition, NTFS preserves case, but is not case-sensitive.

- File fragmentation is reduced on NTFS partitions. The NTFS algorithm always attempts to locate a contiguous block of hard disk space that's large enough to store the entire file.

- Files on NTFS volumes can be compressed using NTFS compression. This compression algorithm is efficient, providing performance similar to commercial compression programs.

These improvements do incur a certain cost. NTFS partitions require an additional amount of overhead to store file security and auditing characteristics; therefore, Microsoft recommends that NTFS partitions be at least 50MB in size.

Segregating system and data files is necessary to maximize security on an Internet-based system. The best way to accomplish this setup involves creating a separate partition to store data that will be transmitted to users over the Internet. This configuration facilitates the restriction of unauthorized access to system files by using the NTFS file-level security at the partition level. This partition-level configuration also makes the system easier to manage. See the later section "Installation" for additional instructions.

Auditing of System Events

One of the most effective tools to detect and prevent unauthorized access of system resources is Windows NT Server's extensive auditing feature, which assists in the detection of suspicious activity.

To get the greatest benefit from Windows NT's auditing capabilities, you must perform periodic reviews of the audit log files. After all, what good is auditing if the logs are never analyzed and used to your advantage? All WWW-, FTP-, and Gopher-related data requests are stored in text files created by IIS. All Windows NT system-specific events, such as file access, privilege changes, and so on, are logged in the Windows NT Event Viewer. For additional information on using the Event Viewer, see the later section "The Event Viewer." For additional information about the IIS log files, see Chapter 2, "Installing and Using Internet Information Server."

Using Windows NT auditing, you can track almost every system action—even at the process level. Performing such a highly detailed level of auditing creates significant amounts of log data. The Event Viewer logs have a finite maximum size and can quickly be filled. Therefore, it's generally a good idea to limit the audit's scope to a manageable level.

Following are some suggestions for events to audit using the Event Viewer:

- Logon and logoff failure
- File and object access failure
- Failed attempts to exercise user rights
- User and group management success and failure
- Security policy change success and failure
- Restart, shutdown, and system security success and failure

Although cryptic, the IIS log files contain detailed information about every transaction performed by IIS. You should examine the log files frequently for "suspicious activity," using an ordinary text editor such as Notepad. Suspicious activity includes activities such as these:

- Multiple failed command attempts
- Attempts to access CMD or BAT files
- Unauthorized upload success or failure
- Excessive requests from a single IP address

NOTE

Several third-party software packages are available to assist in reviewing the IIS log files. These packages read the cryptic log files and present the information in reports that make the data easier to filter and comprehend.

Revoke the Access from Network Right

Revoking the Access from Network right is an integrated feature of Windows NT that prevents users from accessing file, print, and administrative services through the network. This doesn't affect the capability of IIS to transmit—or the end user's ability to receive—data transmitted via the World Wide Web, FTP, or Gopher, however, because of the method by which IIS responds to end-user requests. During interaction with IIS, the remote user actually logs on locally to Windows NT.

Users' Account Policies

As an administrator, one way that you can protect your system from danger caused by users is by limiting their access to the system. This section suggests a number of ways that you can provide good account security.

Limiting Risk from Built-in Windows NT Accounts and Groups

During installation, two accounts are created by default. These accounts, Administrator and Guest, provide a great opportunity for a malicious remote user to hack away at these accounts in hopes of guessing the correct account password.

Fortunately, you can take several steps to mitigate the risks associated with the built-in Windows NT user accounts. The Administrator account is a necessary component of Windows NT and can't be deleted, but it can be renamed to a less obvious name—"George," perhaps. The Administrator account can be renamed using the User Manager, as shown in Figure 1.4.

FIGURE 1.4.

Renaming the Administrator user ID.

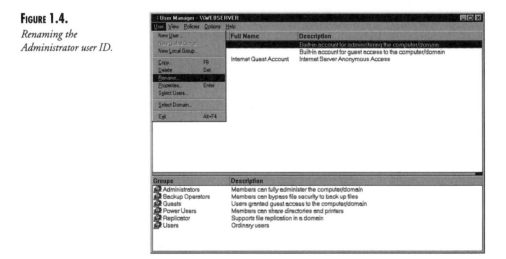

The Guest account, as the name implies, is designed for users requiring guest access to system resources. Providing guest access to the server is a big no-no. It eliminates your ability to track who is accessing the server and to place liability on an individual should a malicious act occur. The Guest account should never be provided for use and should in fact be disabled. Guest can be disabled using the User Manager; check the Account Disabled box in the User Properties dialog box (see Figure 1.5) and then click OK.

FIGURE 1.5.
*Disabling the Guest
user ID.*

Account Policies

As the old adage says, a chain is only as strong as its weakest link. This is especially true in the world of system security. Usually the weakest link in the security chain is the end-user password. The average authorized user doesn't understand the importance of passwords. User passwords commonly refer to the spouse, kids, dog, Social Security number, and so on, and hackers realize this.

It's no coincidence that this weak link is often exploited by malicious remote users. Password-cracking programs are available that perform exhaustive searches at compromising passwords. Some programs are even designed to use every word found in English and foreign-language dictionaries! Fortunately, ways exist to reduce the risks associated with authorized user passwords.

First and foremost, it's important that authorized end users understand the purpose of passwords and the risks present in today's computing environment. In this regard, a little education goes a long way toward keeping the system safe.

Next, strong password and account policies can help protect systems, should other options fail. Most competent account policies contain the following stipulations:

- Users can't share IDs or passwords.
- Passwords must be changed at regular intervals.
- Passwords must be *password-cracking resilient* (not easily cracked).
- User accounts must be disabled after a specified number of incorrect password attempts.
- Sufficient password history must be kept to prevent the reuse of system passwords.
- All passwords must be a minimum password length and, optionally, must contain a combination of letters and numbers.

Implementing a password policy with these guidelines helps reduce the risk in this area.

Statement of Acceptable Use

In addition to a strong password/account policy, you must inform users of what's considered acceptable use of the computer system. Acceptable use policies vary widely from system to system; it's important that these acceptable use expectations be known and understood by all authorized end users.

Should the unfortunate circumstance arise where a system is breached and criminal prosecution or civil litigation follows, the presence of a published and acknowledged acceptable-use policy may mean the difference between success and failure.

Physical Security

Protecting the system from network-based attack is half the job. Ensuring the system's physical security is equally important. Some common practices can reduce the likelihood of unauthorized system access:

- Ensure that the system is stored in a secure area, unavailable to access by end users. Ideally, place the system in a restricted-access computer facility. This facility should also possess systems to provide protection from fire, electrical power surges, and excessive heat or humidity.

- If this level of protection isn't available, keeping the server in a locked closet can help prevent unauthorized tampering. Extra precautions, such as locking the floppy drive, reduce the chances of an unauthorized user stealing information stored on the system.

C2 Security

The *C2* security guideline was developed by the Department of Defense in the 1980s and has become a means to measure system security. The C2 definition is one of many levels of security defined in the DOD's Trusted Computer System Evaluation Criteria, or *Orange Book*. Although C2 isn't the most secure specification detailed in the Orange Book, it's the one most often embraced by companies and computer manufacturers.

It's interesting to note that Windows NT is C2 compliant only as a standalone workstation. When connected to a network, it no longer meets the DOD's C2 requirements. Microsoft developed a C2 compliance checker called *C2CONFIG* to assist in the evaluation of Windows NT systems (see Figure 1.6). C2CONFIG examines the server's configuration and details which components don't meet C2 specifications or good security practices. This utility is available in the Windows NT Resource Kit, which is a very valuable resource. The NT Resource Kit is available at many bookstores and can be purchased for a modest fee (approximately $125 U.S.).

FIGURE 1.6.

The C2 Configuration Manager interface.

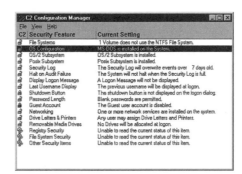

The following list describes various components included in the C2 security standard:

- Owners of system resources (files, processes, and so forth) must be able to control access to those resources.

- The operating system must prohibit the unauthorized reuse of system objects. These system objects include memory, disk space, and so on. The purpose of this requirement is to disallow any attempt to utilize data that was stored in these system resources before they were released. For example, files located on an NTFS partition can't be undeleted.

- Every user must be authenticated to the system through the use of a unique user ID/password. The system must be able to use this user ID/password combination to track the activities of the user.

- The system must support the ability to audit security events. This audit data must be restricted from unauthorized end users.

- The physical configuration must support protection from external tampering. Examples of this protection include locking the floppy drive, power switch, and so on.

Domain Considerations

Before beginning installation, it's important to complete the configuration checklist. This checklist includes details about the system's network configuration, specifically what role the server will play in the network environment. The server can be configured as a domain controller (primary or backup) or as a standalone server. It's very important to make the correct decision in this area, because Windows NT can't be changed from a domain controller to a standalone server or vice versa without a complete reinstallation of the system. Due to the nature of the Web server and its role in the networking environment, configuring the system as a standalone server is usually a wise choice. This setup reduces the security risks associated with supporting domain-level authentication, and improves system performance.

Configuration Checklist

This checklist should be completed before performing the installation. It will ease installation by consolidating all the information you may need.

Hardware Specification

System type and serial number: _____

_____

Amount and type of RAM installed: _____

_____

Network card(s)

    Type: _____

    IRQ / base memory address: _____

    MAC address: _____

    PCI slot (if applicable): _____

    Media type (10BaseT, coax, and so on): _____

Disk subsystem

    RAID/SCSI controller model and firmware revision: _____

    Physical disk information (disk types and locations): _____

    RAID configuration (RAID 0, 1, 5; hardware or software, and so on): _____

    System partition's number and size: _____

    WWW data partition's number and size: _____

Network Configuration

Host name: _____

Domain: _____

Workstation (NetBIOS) name: _____

Workgroup/domain name: _____

IP address(es): _____

Subnet mask(s): _____

Default gateway(s): _____

Domain name server(s): _____

User Information

Administrator ID and password: _____

Installation

Installing Windows NT is a relatively easy exercise. The Setup program bears strong resemblance to the Windows 95 installer. Microsoft provides extra flexibility by supporting the beginning of installation from both DOS and Windows NT. The DOS-based installer is named `WINNT.EXE`, and the Windows NT-based installer is named `WINNT32.EXE`. For purposes of this chapter, we'll assume that installation is being performed from DOS. To perform the same installation from Windows NT, simply replace the `WINNT` with `WINNT32` in commands. If you forget this caveat, don't worry. The DOS-based setup program (`WINNT.EXE`) won't work in the 32-bit Windows NT environment.

Installation Options

You can choose among three different methods for installing the software:

- **Creating boot floppies.** What? Lost your boot floppies? No problem—the Windows NT installation program supports creation of setup boot floppies. Simply change to the install directory that reflects the hardware of the machine on which NT will be installed (`i386` for Intel, `Alpha` for DEC Alpha, and so on) and type `WINNT /OX`. This command starts the Setup program and prompts you to insert the appropriate floppies so the data can be copied.

- **Installing from CD-ROM.** Windows NT can be installed without floppy disks. This method of installation is faster, but requires more initial disk space (the boot files must also be copied). To begin this installation, simply place the Windows NT installation CD in the CD-ROM drive, change directories according to the processor version of NT you'll be installing (`i386` for Intel x86 machines, `MIPS` for MIPS-based systems, `ALPHA` for DEC Alpha systems, or `PPC` for PowerPC systems) and type `WINNT /B` to begin the "floppyless" installation method.

■ **Installing from shared media.** Installing Windows NT from a location on the network is also possible. Performing this is very similar to the CD-ROM installation described in the preceding paragraph. Map a drive to the Windows NT source located on the network, change to the directory containing the installation files appropriate for your processor type, and type `WINNT /B`.

Installation Procedure

For purposes of this chapter, we'll install Windows NT using the three installation floppy disks. If one of the other two installation methods is desired (CD-ROM or network), simply replace the beginning installation steps with the `WINNT /B` command. The remainder of the installation process is identical using either the floppy or floppyless methods.

Beginning with a complete, error-free set of boot floppies, simply insert the Setup Boot disk into the system and reboot. This action starts the Windows NT Setup program and begins the installation procedure.

When Setup Disk 2 has been copied, Windows NT loads its protected-mode NT kernel. You can detect this by a sudden flicker of the screen and the Windows NT blue screen. After this occurs, the Welcome to Setup screen is presented. This screen provides several options, which can be selected by pressing the appropriate key:

F1	To learn more about Windows NT
Enter	Set up Windows NT
R	Repair a damaged Windows NT Installation
F3	Quit Setup

Assuming no incomplete or corrupt installation of Windows NT exists, press the Enter key.

The next screen describes how Windows NT detects mass storage devices. This is a very important step because it's critical that Windows NT accurately and completely detects all the mass storage devices present in the system. Windows NT Setup automatically detects all floppy and ESDI/IDE-based hard disk controllers—it's the SCSI controllers that can cause concern. The following options are available:

Enter	Continue with mass storage device detection
S	Skip mass storage device detection

Unless Windows NT has inaccurately detected a mass storage device previously, the suggested course of action is to press Enter.

The next screen prompts the installation of Setup Disk 3. Replace Setup Disk 2 with Setup Disk 3 and press Enter.

Next, Windows NT Setup will copy and load common mass-storage device drivers and test for the presence of that type of adapter. There's a noteworthy change in the mass storage devices supported by the Windows NT 3.5x Setup program versus the Windows NT 4.0 Setup program.

Beginning with Windows NT 4.0, Microsoft stopped the automatic support of the following device drivers:

- Always IN-2000 (`always.sys`)
- Data Technology Corp. 3290 (`dtc329x.sys`)
- Maynard 16-bit SCSI adapter (`wd33c93.sys`)
- Media Vision Pro Audio Spectrum (`tmv1.sys`)
- Trantor T-128 (`t128.sys`)
- Trantor T-130B (`t13b.sys`)
- Ultrastor 124f EISA Disk Array Controller (`ultra124.sys`)

If one of the listed devices is being used in the system, the appropriate driver can still be installed, but it must be installed using a floppy (or you must have memorized its location on the Windows NT CD-ROM).

The procedure to create a driver disk is quite simple:

1. Prepare a blank, formatted 3½-inch floppy disk.
2. Copy all files from \drvlib\storage\retired*processor*, where *processor* corresponds to the type of CPU used in the server to be upgraded (MIPS, i386, or Alpha).

After Windows NT Setup has finished the detection process, the discovered devices are listed. At this point, Windows NT Setup provides the capability to add any unlisted or outdated drivers that support devices not automatically detected. The following options are available:

Enter	All devices have been detected; continue with Setup
S	Additional device drivers need to be loaded manually

If everything was detected properly, press Enter. Windows NT Setup copies the additional drivers necessary to detect and use the system's components. These drivers include support for ESDI/IDE hard disk controllers, support for NTFS, and so on.

The next step requires agreement to the Windows NT License Agreement. This is an important step. The license agreement should be completely read and understood before continuing. Pressing the Page Down key displays the remaining pages of the license agreement. At the agreement's end, Windows NT Setup provides the following options:

F8	Agreement with the license and continuation of Setup
Escape	Declining acceptance of the agreement. This will cause Windows NT Setup to quit. You must agree to abide by the license requirements before continuing installation.

Complying with the conditions of the license agreement is necessary to prevent the violation of federal law.

Assuming that the license agreement is acceptable, press F8.

Next, Windows NT Setup searches for existing installations of Windows NT. If a previous version or installation of Windows NT exists on the system, Setup provides the opportunity to upgrade or reinstall that existing installation. Upgrading an existing installation preserves any existing user account information and may preserve certain application settings. If an existing installation is present, Setup provides the following options:

Enter	Upgrade an existing installation
N	Install a fresh copy of NT

If Windows NT is being installed on a clean disk partition, Setup doesn't present this option. For this installation, we'll assume no previous installations of Windows NT exist.

Next, Setup displays a list of detected devices in the system's configuration. You can change the type of computer, display, keyboard, keyboard layout, and pointing device. If any of these settings require modification, use the up-arrow and down-arrow keys to select the item in question; you can view a list of alternative choices by pressing Enter. If no changes are required, Setup will continue once the Enter key is pressed.

The next step of the Windows NT installation is the definition of the system partition and its file system. If partitions already exist on the disk media, Setup displays a list from which to select. If no partitions exist, Setup detects the physical disks present and provides an opportunity to define partitions from the available disk space. Assuming that disk partitions already exist, Setup provides the following options:

Enter	Install Windows NT on the selected partition
C	Create a partition from unutilized disk space
D	Delete the existing highlighted partition

If the system partition has been created in advance, highlight it by using the up-arrow and down-arrow keys, and press Enter. If the system partition hasn't yet been defined, press C and define a partition of the appropriate size. The partition should be created to accommodate anticipated need. This need will depend highly on what system-based resources will be added to Windows NT (tape backup software, defragmentation software, and so on). A golden rule is not to skimp on system partition disk space. Enlarging this partition after Windows NT has been installed is a *very* troublesome event and likely will involve taking the system offline for an extended period of time.

The next step involves formatting the selected system partition. For purposes of this installation, assume that an existing partition is already present and has been formatted with the FAT file system. Based on this, Windows NT Setup provides the following options:

- Format the partition using FAT
- Format the partition using NTFS
- Convert the partition to NTFS
- Leave the current file system intact

Because the system should utilize the features of NTFS (hot fixing, security, auditing, and so on), the recommended option is to convert the existing partition to NTFS. Using the up-arrow and down-arrow keys, highlight the option to format the partition using NTFS or to convert the partition to NTFS and press Enter.

The next step of Windows NT Setup involves specification of the system directory. In an effort to maximize the level of security, it's recommended that the installation directory be changed from the default of \WINNT to any logical alternative. Changing the system directory's name can prevent a malicious script or batch file that affects files or data in the system directory from executing.

Windows NT Setup next provides the opportunity to examine the installation partition for errors. It's recommended that you continue installation by pressing Enter.

After the disk examination is complete, Setup begins copying system files necessary for installation. When the file copying is complete, Setup gives notice that the current portion of Setup has completed successfully. For Setup to continue, you must press Enter.

> **NOTE**
>
> Make sure that the floppy disk has been removed from the drive!

When the system restarts, Windows NT Setup continues installation in GUI mode.

The GUI mode of installation involves the following steps: gathering information about your computer, installing Windows NT networking, and finishing setup. To proceed, click the Next button.

During the next few steps of installation, Windows NT Setup requires certain information in order to continue. To prepare for this, please have the configuration worksheet (created earlier) and the installation CD-ROM available for reference. Then go on to the following sections.

User Identification

Windows NT Setup asks for the name and organization of the person installing the software. Enter your name and organization in the appropriate fields and click Next.

Entering the License Information

Windows NT Setup requires that you enter the licensing key. This key can typically be found on the Windows NT CD-ROM media or on the Windows NT software license agreement. Enter the CD key in the appropriate boxes and click Next.

Selecting the Desired Licensing Mode

Windows NT Setup now prompts for the type of licensing mode desired. Two options are available: per-server and per-seat licensing. *Per-server licensing* is designed to support the licensing of a specified number of clients that connect to the particular server. The number of allowable client connections depends, of course, on the number of licenses that were purchased for the server. *Per-seat licensing* is different in that the licensing focus is on the client computer. Per-seat licenses are purchased to enable a client computer to utilize resources on as many Windows NT 4 servers as necessary. Again, the number of clients that can legally utilize NT 4 resources depends on the number of purchased Windows NT 4 client licenses.

No easy way exists to determine which method of licensing is better; it depends completely on the specific operating environment in question. The best course of action is to create two pricing scenarios—one for per-server licensing and one for per-seat licensing—and select the one most appropriate to the situation. In doing this, be sure to account for future needs. If the number of Windows NT servers being utilized will increase in the future, be sure to account for this in the pricing model.

If per-server licensing is the method to be used, click the Per Server option and enter the number of licenses purchased. If per-seat licensing has been selected, click the Per Seat option. After the correct option has been selected, click the Next button to continue.

> **NOTE**
>
> Depending on the CD-ROM being used to install Windows NT Server, a confirmation dialog box may appear requesting confirmation of the license agreement. Click the I Agree check box and then click OK to continue.

Selecting the Computer Name

The computer name will be used to uniquely identify the system on the network. As such, the computer name can't be the same as an existing computer, workgroup, or domain name and must be fewer than 16 characters. (Note that this computer name isn't necessarily the name your system will be known by on the Internet. This name, called the *hostname*, is configured in a later phase of installation.) Enter an appropriate computer name in the text box and click Next.

Determining the Server Type

During this phase of installation, Windows NT Setup needs to know whether the system will be used as a standalone server, backup domain controller, or primary domain controller. (Refer to the earlier discussion of standalone server versus domain controller, if necessary.) Select the most appropriate option. Because the majority of Web servers won't be used for other LAN-based activities, the choice most often recommended is standalone server mode. For the purposes of this installation, assume that the Web server will be standalone in configuration. Click the Stand-Alone Server option button, and then click Next to continue.

Setting the Administrator Account Password

Windows NT Setup creates the Administrator account (among others) automatically during installation. For security purposes, Windows NT Setup requires the Administrator password to be defined during installation. The Administrator password can be up to 15 characters long and is case-sensitive. Enter the Administrative password in the Password and Confirm Password text boxes and click Next to continue.

Creating an Emergency Repair Disk (ERD)

The *emergency repair disk (ERD)* is a very important component should the Windows NT installation become corrupted in some way. It stores the current computer configuration and can be used to restore these settings.

Updating the ERD is critical every time the system is configured. Changes such as adding a hard disk, changing partition sizes, adding device drivers, updating the system with a Service Pack, and so on require the ERD to be updated. This can be accomplished after installation by executing the RDISK.EXE application. RDISK updates an existing ERD or creates a new one if necessary.

To create the initial ERD, click the Yes option, and click Next to continue.

Selecting Additional Components

During this step, Windows NT Setup allows the installer to select the components to be installed during the installation. The major component groups are listed in the Components window. To see a detailed list of the available components, highlight the desired component group and click Details. Once the desired components have been selected, click Next to continue the installation process.

> **NOTE**
>
> In the event that the list of desired components is unknown or your needs change, Microsoft provides the capability to add or remove components after installation is completed. This can be accomplished through use of the Add/Remove Programs Control Panel applet.

Installing Network Components

During this phase of Windows NT Setup, the desired networking components are installed and configured. To continue, click Next.

Defining Windows NT Network Participation

In this step of the installation, Windows NT Setup requires specification of the type(s) of network connection that will be utilized in the system. The available options are Wired to the Network and Remote Access to the Network.

For most installations, the Wired to the Network box should be checked. For many, depending on the presence of a modem and a desire to use Remote Access Service (RAS), the Remote Access to the Network check box should also be checked. And for a select few who will be using a modem to provide Internet connectivity (using an ISP that provides a static IP address, for example), the Remote Access to the Network box should be the only box checked.

Although RAS provides several beneficial features (remote administration via modem, and so on), it also is a security risk. If installing RAS and configuring RAS to accept dial-in calls, ensure that appropriate security measures have been taken to prevent unauthorized access to system resources.

Because a majority of installations shouldn't involve a modem, the Wired to the Network box will be the only box checked in the sample installation. Ensure that the Wired to the Network box is checked and click Next to continue.

> **NOTE**
>
> If Remote Access Service is required at a later date, RAS support can be installed through the Network Control Panel applet.

Installing Internet Information Server (IIS)

This step provides the installer the opportunity to select Microsoft Internet Information Server (IIS) for installation. If you leave the box checked, Windows NT Setup will automatically install IIS with default settings. It's recommended that you *not* install IIS during Windows NT installation, because the default configuration settings don't provide strong enough security, nor does the installation process provide the opportunity to customize disk partition settings prior to installation. Once the Windows NT installation is complete, IIS should be installed and configured to meet specifications.

If the appropriate disk partitioning and configuration have been performed prior to beginning Windows NT Setup, it's okay to specify IIS for installation.

Detecting Network Adapters

In this step, Windows NT Setup performs a search for existing network interface cards that are installed in the system. To continue, simply click the Start Search button to begin the search for installed network cards. If Windows NT Setup successfully detects the appropriate network adapter(s) in the system, click Next to continue. If Setup detects the installed card incorrectly, or doesn't detect a card at all, the adapter can be added manually by clicking the Select from List button and choosing the adapter that matches the installed card. Assuming that the adapter is correctly detected, ensure that the check box by its description is checked, and click Next to continue.

NOTE

It's unusual for Windows NT Setup to incorrectly detect or identify installed network adapters. If Setup doesn't detect the installed network adapter, the adapter may be configured incorrectly and conflicting with another device in the system or may be malfunctioning in some way. If Setup doesn't detect the adapter, attempt to specify the adapter manually using the Select from List button. If this doesn't solve the problem, be prepared to change the network card.

Selecting Network Protocols

In this step, Windows NT Setup requires the specification of the network protocols that will be installed. The available default protocols are TCP/IP, IPX/SPX, and NetBEUI. TCP/IP is required for communication on the Internet and should be installed. IPX/SPX and NetBEUI are protocols designed for LAN-based communication and can be installed if required—although this isn't recommended for security purposes. Using an Internet-based Web server for other LAN-based functions isn't recommended and can significantly increase the security risk. Select the desired protocols by checking the boxes next to their descriptions and click Next to continue.

Selecting System Services

During this step, Windows NT Setup requires the installer to specify which system services will be installed. The default services for Windows NT Server are the RPC Configuration service, NetBIOS Interface service, Workstation service, and Server service. Additional services can be added by clicking the Select from List button and selecting the appropriate service. The services that should be of most interest in a Web server environment are the Microsoft DNS Server service and perhaps the Simple TCP/IP Services service. For purposes of this installation, the DNS Server service and Simple TCP/IP Services service will be added. Once the appropriate services have been added, click Next to continue.

Verifying and Installing Network Components

In this step, Windows NT Setup asks the installer to verify the network, protocol, and service selections previously made. If all the selections are correct, click Next to continue. Setup will begin to install the specified components of Windows NT.

Supplying Configuration Information

During this stage of installation, Windows NT Setup asks for additional information about the components that have been selected for installation. It's important to have your configuration checklist handy during this stage. If the checklist was completed accurately, all the required information should be located there. If information is requested that isn't readily available, changes can be made to the system after the installation is complete.

Assuming that the installation guidelines were followed and only the recommended components were specified for installation, you can expect the following requests for information. Note that the following steps vary depending on the components selected for installation.

> **NOTE**
>
> The configuration advice provided here is the bare minimum necessary to complete the Windows NT installation. Additional configuration (the addition of services, protocols, and so on) may be required, depending upon your specific requirements.

Windows NT Setup should first request additional information about the network adapter detected in the previous phase of Setup. Depending on whether the adapter is based on ISA, PCI, or Microchannel (gasp!), the request will ask for an IRQ, base memory address, and perhaps a media connection type or PCI slot number. It depends totally on the network adapter being used. After verifying the information, click OK.

Next, Setup asks whether this system should utilize DHCP (Dynamic Host Control Protocol), which is used to assign IP addresses to computers on a network that has a DHCP server. Because a Web server should have one or more static IP addresses, not dynamic addresses, using DHCP isn't appropriate for this system. Click the No button.

Setup then displays the TCP/IP Properties dialog box. This tabbed dialog box is the primary interface through which configuration of TCP/IP-based properties is performed.

The IP Address page requires that you provide the following information: IP address, subnet mask, and default gateway. This is some of the fundamental information necessary for the system to communicate on any TCP/IP network, including the Internet. Enter the information detailed on the configuration checklist into the appropriate text boxes.

The next page, DNS, requires additional information about the system's Internet connections. The Host Name text box will by default contain the name that was specified in an earlier step. Note that this name doesn't necessarily have to be the same as the computer's machine name (which applies to NetBIOS naming), and can be changed if required. The system will be known on a TCP/IP network by its hostname, so assign the name as appropriate. The Domain text box defines the system's name suffix, or domain name. This name is registered with the InterNIC and is used to identify the computer on a TCP/IP network. For example, if a system's hostname is WWW and the domain is ADOMAIN.COM, the system could be contacted by using WWW.ADOMAIN.COM. Note that this isn't the only name that can be used to identify the server. Domain Name Service supports the use of aliases, which allows a system to be contacted using a variety of names.

Below the Host Name and Domain text boxes is an area that can be used to define the domain name servers that will be used by the system. These IP addresses should be provided by your ISP and can be added by clicking the Add button in the DSN Service Search Order area. Usually, more than one DNS server should be defined to provide an increased level of redundancy. These DNS servers can be prioritized by using the up arrow and down arrow next to the text area. Once this preliminary information has been entered, click OK.

Reviewing Protocol Bindings

In this step, Windows NT Setup enables you to change the priority of the protocol bindings. This essentially enables you to define the priority in which these protocols are given by Windows NT. The higher the priority, the better the service. If TCP/IP was the only protocol selected, there's no need to adjust bindings, because there's only one protocol. If more than one protocol was installed, adjusting bindings may be necessary. As a general rule, it's better to leave the protocol bindings in their default priority. Once the bindings have been reviewed or modified, click Next.

Starting the Network

This step prepares the user for starting the networking components of Windows NT. If the system is misconfigured, an error message will be provided and reconfiguration will be necessary. To continue, click Next.

Adding the System to a Workgroup or Domain

Provided that the networking components are properly configured, Windows NT Setup requires you to define the system's location in a workgroup or domain. Note that the system can create its own workgroup, be added to an existing workgroup, or be added to an existing domain. For purposes of this installation, the system will be added to a workgroup called WEBSERVICES. If the system is being added to an existing domain, an Administrator-equivalent ID and password should be known. Windows NT Setup is unable to add the computer to an existing domain if administrative rights aren't available. For this example, select the Workgroup option and type **WEBSERVICES** in the Workgroup text box. Then click Next.

Finishing Setup

During this stage of Setup, Windows NT is installed, using the specifications defined by your earlier input. Begin this installation by clicking Next.

If Microsoft IIS was specified for installation, Setup requests information necessary to install and configure the IIS files. Referring to the configuration data determined prior to installation, install the IIS system files and WWWROOT directory on the partition defined for those purposes. In addition, select or deselect product installation options based on your system needs. If Gopher or FTP services aren't required, don't install them, as they will only provide potential holes in system security. Once IIS has been properly configured, click OK.

Next, Setup copies all the necessary system files to complete the installation and creates the system's Registry. During this step, you have the options of installing the SQL Server ODBC driver, defining the system's time zone, setting the display adapter options (screen flickering may occur), creating the emergency repair disk, and saving the system's Registry.

After you have successfully restarted Windows NT and the system appears to be operating properly, you must begin preparations to install Microsoft IIS. The IIS WWW data should be located on its own Web partition, to minimize the risk of unauthorized system file access. If the WWW partition hasn't yet been created or formatted, do so now using the Disk Administrator. After the partition has been created and formatted using NTFS, you can continue the installation of IIS. You will notice a shortcut placed conveniently on the system's desktop that points to the IIS Setup program. The IIS system files are located on the Windows NT Server CD-ROM, so it must be available before installing IIS. Double-clicking the IIS Setup shortcut launches the IIS Setup program. Select only the product options that are necessary, and select an appropriate destination directory located anywhere on the WWW partition. IIS Setup then installs and configures the necessary software.

Active Server Pages (ASP) was still being developed when Microsoft released IIS 2.0 and Windows NT 4.0. Therefore, the Active Server Pages Setup application must be downloaded. ASP is available at the Microsoft Web site, and is included with the Microsoft TechNet subscription.

Finally, after installing all the necessary components, be sure to apply the latest Service Pack distributed by Microsoft. This will ensure that all the latest bug fixes and feature enhancements are present in the Web system.

Management Tools

This section discusses some of Windows NT Server's system management tools that come bundled with the server software. These tools provide an excellent interface for performing administrative functions.

The User Manager

The User Manager is the tool used to modify the Windows NT user database. It provides a simple interface to assign users to groups, reset passwords, enable auditing, configure account restrictions, and so on (see Figure 1.7). It's located in the Administrative Tools folder on the Start menu.

The Event Viewer

The Event Viewer is used to monitor all system, application, and security events. It provides extensive event-filtering capabilities to assist the user in reviewing the event logs (see Figure 1.8). The Event Viewer is also used to define how the event logs are captured and retained.

The Disk Administrator

The Disk Administrator controls the hard disks located in the computer. Using the Disk Administrator, an authorized user can create and delete partitions, define software-based fault-tolerant RAID configurations, and assign drive letters to data volumes (see Figure 1.9).

FIGURE 1.7.

The Windows NT User Manager.

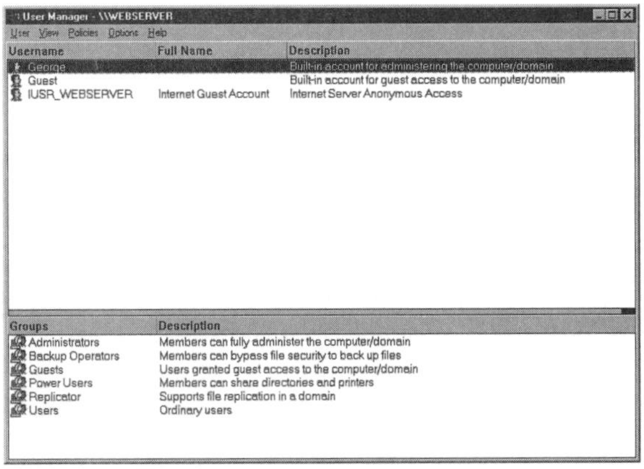

FIGURE 1.8.

The Windows NT Event Viewer.

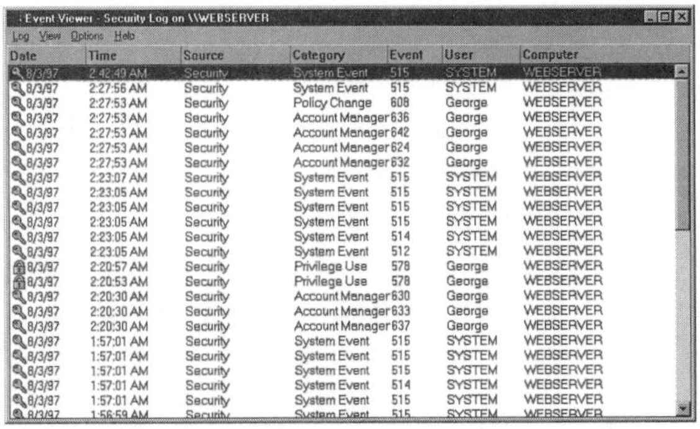

FIGURE 1.9.

The Windows NT Disk Administrator.

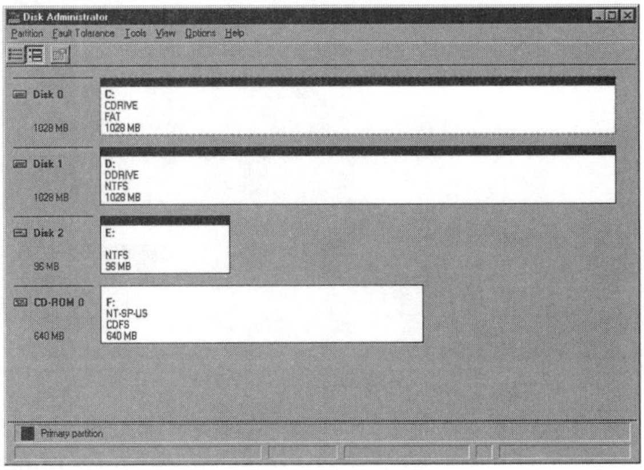

The Server Manager

The Server Manager enables authorized users to review and modify the set of currently connected users and resources in use, to create and delete share points, to start and stop services, and to configure server replication (see Figure 1.10).

Figure 1.10.

The Windows NT Server Manager.

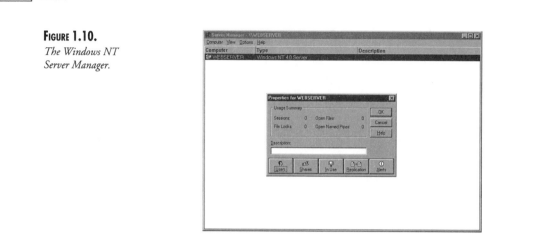

The Performance Monitor

The Performance Monitor may be the tool used most often. It can track a variety of system resources and display the data in various ways (see Figure 1.11). See Chapter 8 in the *Windows NT Server 4.0 Concepts and Planning* reference for a complete description of the Performance Monitor's features and functionality.

Figure 1.11.

The Windows NT Performance Monitor.

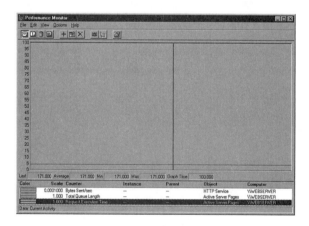

Summary

This chapter provides the information necessary to get your system up and running on the Internet. Be sure to continue proper maintenance and monitoring once the system is online. Best of luck in the new frontier!

Installing and Using Internet Information Server

IN THIS CHAPTER

CHAPTER 2

Internet Information Server (IIS) is the core Windows NT service that provides Internet services. NT ships with IIS on the CD, but you should download the latest version from the Microsoft Web site at www.microsoft.com/iis. The Web site has information about the latest patches and Service Pack requirements. Be certain to read the release notes and install whatever updates are suggested.

Installation is self-guiding, and uses Microsoft's usual wizard approach. The only key decisions are where you want to install the software and which components you want to include. We recommend installing all components, and using the largest NTFS volume available. Avoid DOS partitions if at all possible—or risk serious performance and security degradation if DOS partitions are used.

> **NOTE**
>
> Why does Microsoft post so many patches? Every operating system is in a constant state of flux, but the Internet makes it difficult for even Microsoft to keep up.
>
> In actual fact, Microsoft posts very few patches when compared to commercial UNIX systems. Better yet, Microsoft doesn't charge for the upgrades! These patches represent a mixture of performance upgrades, security patches, and operating system enhancements.

What Exactly Does IIS Do?

Microsoft has a wide variety of products designed for Internet connectivity. In fact, so many choices are available that differentiating between them is difficult. Internet Information Server is the underpinning that provides information-publishing capabilities on the Internet. Microsoft provides other vehicles for *personal* content publishing—such as Personal Web Server—but Internet Information Server is Microsoft's engine for departmental and enterprise-level publishing. IIS is the engine that runs large Web sites such as microsoft.com, msn.com, and investorsedge.com.

IIS is now in its fourth revision. IIS 1.0 became available in 1995, but it was IIS 3.0 that really caught on in the summer of 1996. IIS 4.0 became available as a public beta in June 1997. With IIS 4.0, Microsoft introduces a number of new features, outlined in Table 2.1.

It's fair to say that IIS 4.0 makes the Internet into a serious applications-development environment. Many of the applications for IIS 4.0 will be hardcore C++ components held together by VBScript. Developers are still able to use the old VBScript/HTML mixture that IIS 3.0 introduced, but serious developers will take advantage of the new architecture.

Table 2.1. New features in IIS 4.0.

Feature	Description
MMC	Microsoft Management Console is an integrated server management tool. Although it appears as part of IIS 4.0, Microsoft has announced that MMC will be a native component in NT 5.
Bandwidth control	Bandwidth can be controlled on a site-by-site basis. A big plus for Web presence providers!
Certificate Server	Microsoft now supports X.509 digital security certificates for use with Secure Sockets Layer (SSL).
Command Line Admin	IIS responds to commands issued from script files.
Debugging	Integrated debugging is available for the first time.
HTTP 1.1	Most but not all portions of the HTTP 1.1 standard are implemented in IIS 4.0. Missing components of the standard were left out because no browsers support all the 1.1 features.
Index Server 2.0	Index Server allows searches of the NT file system using SQL commands. Searches can be called from scripts, VB, C, Java, and JavaScript.
MTS integration	Microsoft Transaction Server (MTS) has been called Microsoft's next OLE. While MTS *per se* is a separate product, integration means that developers are able to leverage its power. MTS has two core features from a Web developer's perspective: Single-user apps scale to multiuser apps without any special tweaking, and complex transactions are possible—even when those transactions take place across multiple computer systems.
Process isolation	Rogue components won't hang all IIS processes, as long as the component is marked to run in its own separate memory space.
Replication	Content replication between servers is implemented as part of Internet Information Server.
Web site tools	Microsoft Site Analyst creates comprehensive content analysis and link management, and Usage Analyst allows Webmasters to create custom reports.

IIS is far more than the average Web server platform. At its core are several publishing protocols, described in Table 2.2. Microsoft also bundled Microsoft Transaction Server (MTS), although MTS isn't technically part of IIS. MTS represents the most powerful feature of IIS, however: extensibility, limited only by your imagination and your ability to write add-in components that enhance and extend IIS functionality.

Table 2.2. Internet Information Server protocols.

Protocol	Description
FTP	File Transfer Protocol. Publishes files in a directory format. Commonly used as a mechanism to both distribute and receive files.
WWW	World Wide Web. This is the protocol that most people associate with the Internet (although certainly not the only one).
NNTP	Commonly referred to as News. A mechanism to publish newsgroups. Note that newsgroups are a derivative of mail, and aren't really "hosted" by any one site. Multiple sites can each have a news server, and those servers can talk peer-to-peer so that a news posting at site A will be replicated to site B.
SMTP	Simple Mail Transport Protocol, usually known as "mail." This is a standard mail implementation that's extremely useful for sites that use mail as a messaging engine for communications. This implementation *does not* include POP (Post Office Protocol). Popular e-mail clients such as Eudora and Microsoft Outlook use POP.

The following example illustrates why MTS is such a powerful tool. An electronic commerce site sells gift shop items to visitors. Before a transaction is completed, several distinct actions must be completed—on separate computer systems. These transactions (in order of completion) are as follows:

1. In Los Angeles, check inventory availability on the corporate mainframe, which runs an Oracle database.
2. Allocate inventory.
3. Validate credit card info with a service bureau in New York.
4. Submit the completed order via EDI to an order pipeline system.
5. If any one of these steps fails, roll back the entire transaction. MTS not only makes rolling back an easy operation for the programmer—it also handles the remote communications to the bank!

For IIS 4.0, the vision is defined as an alphabet soup known as COM, DCOM, and MTS. COM and DCOM stand for *component object model* and *distributed component object model*, respectively. COM is the single most powerful feature of IIS. To see why, an explanation of its predecessor is required.

Traditional Web servers use a programming language known as *CGI (Common Gateway Interface)* to provide dynamic content. A typical CGI application might receive a request to look up a database record, then return that record to the Web server for publication in a Web page. Such a CGI script is functionally equivalent to opening a DOS box under Windows NT, starting a script, retrieving the answer, and closing the box. This is known as an *out of process* way of doing things, meaning that a separate process is spawned for each request.

IIS components built to the component object model operate *in process*. That is, they're built as a DLL and simply sit there, waiting for the next request to come along. When the request is received, a new thread starts to process the request and return an answer.

For these reasons, CGI applications don't scale well to large sites, while IIS applications usually grow without creating problems. Chapter 28, "Extending Active Server Pages," shows you how to build IIS components in Visual Basic and Java. If you're comfortable with either language, building components is as easy as writing VBScript.

Using the Service Manager

Microsoft introduced a new management tool with IIS 4.0, known as the *Microsoft Management Console* (*MMC*). MMC is more of a framework that hosts *snap-ins*, such as IIS, than it is a program *per se*. As Microsoft moves forward to NT 5, more snap-ins will be designed for MMC.

MMC is used to manage IIS, not to install it. As Figure 2.1 indicates, MMC uses a familiar Explorer-like interface, complete with an expandable tree view control. It isn't integrated with Explorer in the same way as Control Panel and Internet Explorer 4.0, but anyone familiar with the Windows interface will find MMC intuitive.

FIGURE 2.1.

The Microsoft Management Console uses a tree view interface that most users find familiar.

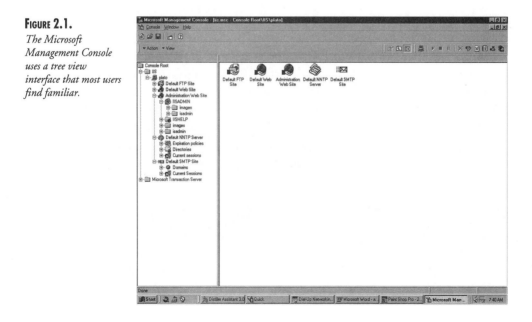

By default, IIS sets up one or two sites when you install it—a default site and an optional HTML administration site. To create a new site, start the MMC and right-click your machine name, as illustrated in Figure 2.2. This will start the New Web Site Wizard and walk you through the steps to create a normal Web site.

FIGURE 2.2.

New Web sites are set up via the MMC, which invokes a wizard to set properties.

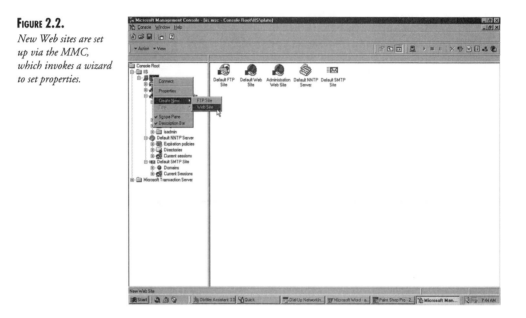

Site Wizard Makes Setup Easy

The New Web Site Wizard steps you through the most common (and important) choices in setting up your site. The first choice is the site name. This name need not be the same as the URL, although the name should be meaningful. We'll use a site about soaring (gliders) as an illustration in this chapter. We'll enter **soaring** as a site name, and later refer to the URL as www.ssa.org, in which ssa stands for Soaring Society of America. (The site is real, and runs under IIS. Check it out!)

Are you setting up separate sites that map to distinct IP addresses? If so, the second wizard step is where you specify the relationship, as indicated in Figure 2.3. In this instance, we've set a specific IP address.

> **NOTE**
>
> IIS 4.0 introduces a neat new feature that allows you to map URLs to separate physical directories, without burning up an IP address for each URL. But the scheme has its limits. You need a registered URL, so test sites can't use the feature.

FIGURE 2.3.
Choose the IP address that will map to your site.

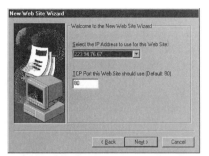

CAUTION

There is almost never a reason to change default port 80 to another value. If you want to hide your site from public view, consider using either a firewall or user authentication. Simply changing the port number is *security by obscurity*, which is analogous to hiding your car keys on top of the front tire.

Each Web site defined in the console requires a root (home) directory. This directory may contain only one file, or it may contain a large portion of the site. You must specify this relationship between the physical location and URL. For example, `http://www.ssa.org` might map to `e:\Soaring\root`.

There are many options for the way that a site is set up, but we'll set ours up as shown in Figure 2.4. The Soaring site will have only one file in the root directory: `default.asp`. All other script files will be located in `e:\Soaring\scripts`, and artwork will be in `e:\Soaring\images`.

FIGURE 2.4.
The www.ssa.org *site contains three virtual directories. These directories are not subdirectories of each other, which eliminates security concerns caused by inherited permissions.*

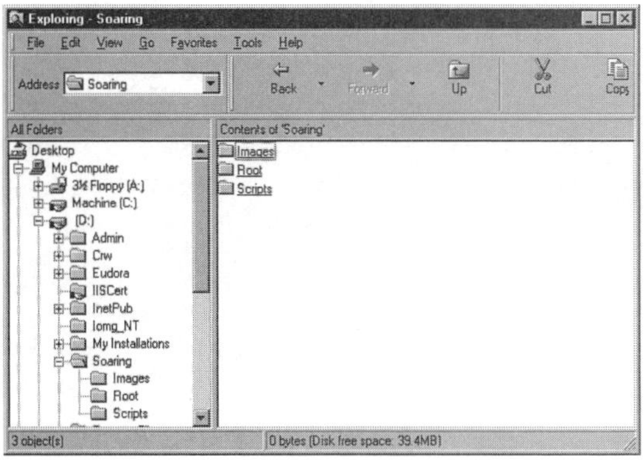

The Internet Information Server Setup program creates a special account named IUSR_*MACHINE*, where *MACHINE* is the name of your computer. All Web access uses this special account name and password to log onto the computer and read Web files. The option to allow anonymous access, which appears on this screen, shouldn't be used, because it will allow hackers to have a party at your expense.

Another method is available to restrict access to your site via a password screen. Change directory permissions via Explorer to only allow authorized users or groups access. Guests will be prompted with a Windows NT challenge/password screen each time they visit. Test the NT security approach carefully, however—a number of problems have been reported with older Netscape browsers, causing authentication failure.

Your site can be tailored to behave in almost any manner imaginable. Fortunately, Microsoft brings almost all these options together in one place, as Figure 2.5 illustrates. The settings controlled by the screen in the figure can also be set directly in the Registry and a special database called the *metabase*. An extensive set of tables at the end of this chapter describe how to do that. In fact, not every attribute of the root directory is exposed via the user interface. Some obscure settings *require* that you set them directly.

FIGURE 2.5.

Microsoft provides a rich array of options that affect how the root directory behaves.

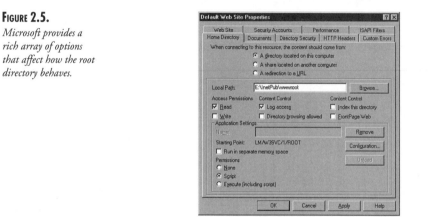

NOTE

It's not just Web surfers who need to be paranoid. As a site administrator, you should be aware that the physical path to your files is transmitted in the header packet that each Web site response sends to visitors. Hackers can use this information to help formulate an attack strategy against your Web site.

Take the time required to learn about this important issue. You can find more information about firewalls and hacker threats in general by subscribing to the firewalls mailing list sponsored by Great Circle Associates. Visit http://www.greatcircle.com for subscription details.

Configuring Read/Execute Privileges

Permissions are a fundamental underpinning of Internet Information Server's security model. The next wizard screen sets one or more of the permissions described in Table 2.3. Make certain that these permissions are set correctly; incorrect permissions can cause your site not to work, or even display your source code on a visitor's browser.

Table 2.3. Directory privileges.

Protocol	Description
Allow Read Access	Files can be read directly by a browser, without preprocessing by ASP.DLL. Set this permission for images and directories that contain read-only HTML. Never set this permission for script directories.
Allow Script Access	Files are preprocessed by ASP.DLL if the file extension is flagged as an ASP file. Other files are treated as though they don't exist.
Allow Execute Access	Includes Allow Script Access. Used primarily for custom components that your pages call.
Allow Write Access	Just what it sounds like. If you have scripts that upload user files to your Web site, this permission is appropriate. Otherwise, it's extremely dangerous!
Allow Directory Browsing	Allow FTP browsers to see your site's organization. Because FTP protocols are embedded in Web browsers, anyone who types ftp://www.*yoursite*.com will have the ability to browse your directory tree. Do not use this permission under normal circumstances!

Two key concepts are important:

- All site visitors impersonate an NT user and log on as IUSR_*MACHINE*. Make certain that this special user is granted access to just the appropriate directories and files.
- NT reads security profiles in top-to-bottom order. If the first entry in a security list is Deny All, NT never reaches the second entry, no matter what it says. This point represents one of Microsoft's top technical support call issues.

Configuring Password Authentication

There are three basic approaches to security: none, normal IUSR_*MACHINE* authentication, and protected site areas. Other options also exist in the form of Microsoft Membership Server and smart hardware cards, but they're beyond the scope of our discussion here.

Setting security to none is accomplished either by using the setup wizard or by right-clicking the site name and choosing the appropriate permissions.

By default, IIS sets up IUSR_*MACHINE* as a user with correct permissions to log onto the site. Each Web request is then turned into an impersonation of this special user, and the appropriate security tests determine how the site behaves.

> **TIP**
>
> You can change the Web user name, and in fact it's a worthwhile exercise to make the change. Hackers assume that your Web account follows the standard naming convention just described. Because your machine name is returned in the HTTP header, all they have to figure out is the password. Change the name by right-clicking the site name and choosing the Security Accounts page. If you have more than one site, each virtual site must be changed separately.

Multi-Homing

Multi-homing means that the server has more than one network card, often with each card connected to a separate physical network. These networks are commonly called the *external* and *internal* networks, for obvious reasons.

This scheme is most often used when the NT server is also configured to be a firewall or proxy server. Software running on NT determines what traffic is permitted to pass from one network segment to the other. Multi-homing is also used in high-traffic environments to balance network loads. In this case, both cards may be on the same network.

> **CAUTION**
>
> Hackers seem to favor Web servers as targets. If you run other services such as a proxy server on the same system as your Web site, be prepared to keep your site up-to-date with Microsoft's latest patches. Better yet, use a separate machine (this philosophy also applies to UNIX sites).

Configuring a Multi-Homed System

A common problem is mis-defined default gateways. Make certain that the gateway is on the external side of the machine only! The Network applet in Control Panel controls this setting, as illustrated in Figure 2.6. The internal card must have a blank entry for Default Gateway. This setting has caused many people hours of frustration because it's not well documented.

> **CAUTION**
>
> The Routing tab on the Protocols page controls whether IP packets are forwarded from one card to the other. Make certain that the setting represents the behavior you want. Unchecked, it prevents traffic from passing, but if it's checked traffic will bypass any firewall software installed on the server. (Firewall software controls packet forwarding within its own program logic.)

FIGURE 2.6.
*The default gateway
must be blank for the
internal network.*

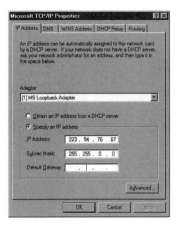

Logging

IIS 4.0 introduced robust new logging features. You can control logging at the site and directory levels, and you can also determine whether the log will be written to a flat file or ODBC data source. (ODBC is an industry standard protocol invented by Microsoft that links to a wide variety of data sources, including Microsoft SQL Server, Oracle, Microsoft Access, and others.)

Ask yourself the following questions to decide how logging can be optimized for your site. Keep in mind that the average site is interested in who visited, when they visited, and what they did while visiting.

- Is my site a high-volume site? Don't use ODBC logging for high-volume sites (per Microsoft).
- Are the contents of this directory worth logging? Directories that contain page elements (such as GIF files) aren't worth logging.

NOTE

IIS doesn't provide logging granularity all the way down to the file level. At first this appears to be a shortcoming, but in fact the overhead required for that level of granularity is too costly for a production site. Keep this restriction in mind when you organize your site.

Allowing Directory Browsing

Directory browsing is a bad idea for most sites. If enabled, FTP can be used to examine site structure. There's no valid reason to expose your files in this manner, and if browsing is absolutely required you should consider setting up the directory as an FTP-accessible area.

If you absolutely must allow browsing, enable it by right-clicking your Web site name and choosing Properties. In the Properties dialog box, select the option Directory Browsing Allowed on the Home Directory page, as illustrated in Figure 2.7.

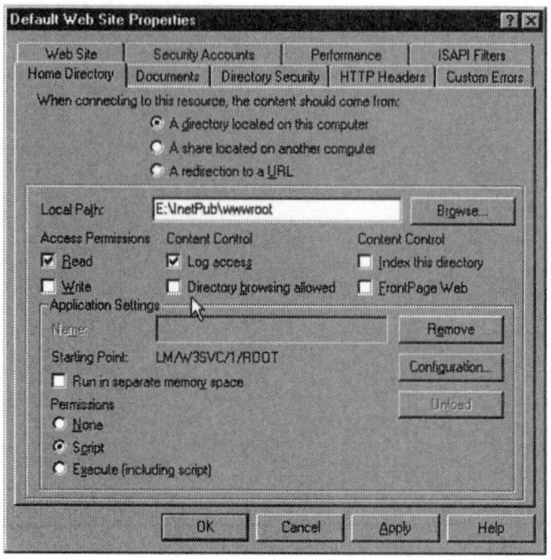

FIGURE 2.7.

Directory browsing is enabled on the Home Directory page of the Properties dialog box. Make certain it's disabled for most sites.

Setting the Default Page

IIS needs to know what Web page is the default, so that requests such as `http://www.ssa.org` translate to `http://www.ssa.org/default.asp`. Start the MMC, then right-click the directory that you want to set. Choose Properties, which displays the dialog box shown in Figure 2.8. Finally, click the Documents tab to display default documents.

FIGURE 2.8.

Default documents can be named whatever you choose, and can be different for each virtual directory.

IIS first looks for default.asp followed by default.htm, in that order, unless you modify the settings. Because the default page can be set for each virtual directory, it's possible to have a variety of default page names. Standardize on a single scheme; using many different names may cause confusion later.

> **NOTE**
>
> If you modify the Registry so that some extension other than .ASP is handled by ASP.DLL, remember to modify this setting as well. The Registry settings are in the following location:
>
> `\HKEY_LOCAL_MACHINE\System\CurrentControlSet001\Services\W3Svc\Parameters\`
> `➥ScriptMap`

Using the Secure Sockets Layer

Secure Sockets Layer—commonly known as *SSL*—is an industry standard encryption methodology. SSL encrypts data as it's transmitted over the wire from server to client and back. Server digital IDs allow Web sites to identify themselves and enable secure communications with customers. In fact, a server digital ID is necessary to establish SSL connections. These IDs are issued in the form of a server certificate by an issuing agency such as VeriSign.

Following is a simplified description of the authentication process. When a secure session initiates, a conversation starts between the browser and server. The browser retrieves the server's ID and address, then verifies them with the certificate authority. If the certificate authority validates the ID, it issues an encryption string, and the SSL session starts.

> **NOTE**
>
> Key Manager (discussed in the next section) only administers the server's digital ID used for SSL encryption, which is not in and of itself user authentication. Several security "certificates" are in use. This chapter discusses server certificates (also known as *site certificates*).
>
> The following are two common forms of client certificates, and have nothing to do with Key Manager:
>
> - Microsoft Certificate Server is a proprietary protocol used for client authentication.
> - VeriSign's personal certificates function in concert with the server digital ID to perform user authentication.

Certificates are available from commercial vendors such as VeriSign. They typically cost several hundred dollars the first year, and approximately $100 per year thereafter. If you run more than one site on the same machine, a separate certificate is required for each site.

> **TIP**
>
> The restriction on 128-bit encryption raises an interesting issue. If you need military-strength encryption for use both outside and inside the United States, make certain that you acquire the technology from a nation that has no such restrictions. The two best countries of origin for encryption are Israel and Singapore.
>
> While 40-bit encryption is usually strong enough, there are many legitimate reasons to use stronger security measures. On June 17, 1997, someone broke the 56-bit DES key, which is used as the standard for global financial transactions. Since 40-bit and 48-bit keys were broken some time ago, stronger measures are appropriate.
>
> If your secret is important enough, someone will try to intercept it! Do you want to explain to the chairman of the board why a new competitor knows your secret formula for your company's most popular product?

Using the Key Manager

The Key Manager is used to request a site certificate and then install it. Be careful to consider all information and options before ordering your certificate, because changes are difficult and expensive.

Two steps are involved: requesting a certificate, and installing the certificate. We cover the certificate request here; certificate installation procedures vary depending on how you requested the certificate, and follow an intuitive set of steps.

To request a certificate, start the Key Manager from MMC by right-clicking the site involved and choosing Properties. In the Properties dialog box, click the Directory Security page, and then click Edit Secure Communications. Yet another dialog box appears, where you must click Key Manager to start the Key Manager program.

Next, choose Key | Create New Key. This invokes a wizard to collect information. The first wizard step asks you to decide between a real-time certificate request and a text file that can be sent later (see Figure 2.9). If you're not already connected to the Internet, the batch approach is your only choice.

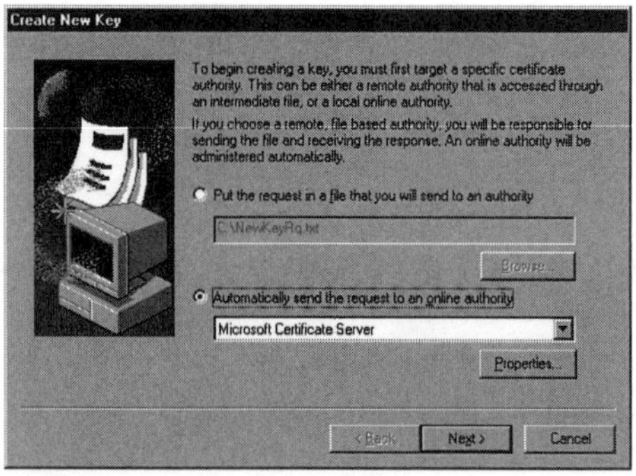

FIGURE 2.9.

Choose between automatic online certificate request submission or a text file to e-mail later.

Step two of the Key Wizard asks for a key name, password, and key size (see Figure 2.10):

- The key name is for your convenience only, and helps provide a friendly name to find the key request later.

- The password is extremely important. Choose one that combines both numbers and letters, and that you don't use for anything else. This password will be used each time the certificate is accessed in future years, so write down the password and store it in a safe place.

- Default key-bit length is 512 bits. Choose the highest value offered in the dialog box.

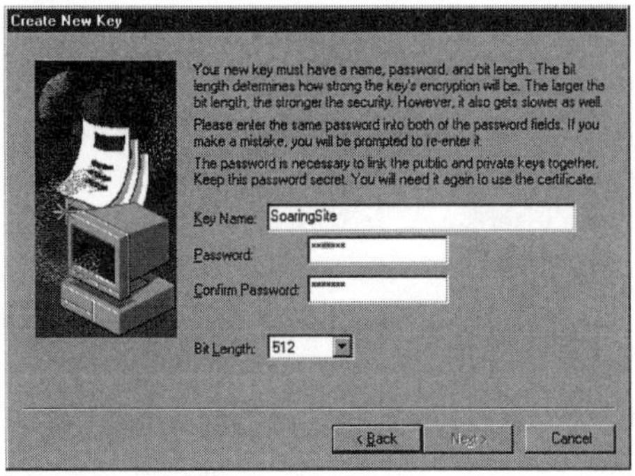

FIGURE 2.10.

The second wizard step asks important information that affects certificate operation.

Step three asks for organization name, organization unit, and common name. We'll fill in Soaring Society of America as the organization, Internet Development as the unit (department), and www.ssa.org as common name. The term *common name* refers to the common name on the Internet; if your server is intranet only, use the machine name.

Step four asks for country, state, and city. For country and state, use two-letter abbreviations such as US for United States and WA for Washington. Our example uses Redmond for the city.

After answering these questions, you're ready to send the request to the appropriate authority. The request is automatically sent if you chose a real-time connection with the authority. If you chose a certificate file, the wizard asks for your name, e-mail address, and telephone number.

Application Development Settings

Thus far, this chapter has discussed how to implement and configure IIS by using the user interface. But sometimes the user interface isn't an appropriate tool, so the rest of this chapter is devoted to a description of the behind-the-scenes settings that control the IIS operation.

There are two common reasons why these settings are controlled directly:

- Some settings are not exposed via the user interface. These are typically settings that could adversely affect IIS performance if changed inadvertently.

- You are an application developer, and need to change settings from another program.

The discussion that follows assumes that your interest is application development. The tables are divided into logical sections that control distinct sections of IIS operations, such as global settings, WWW services, or FTP services. A few settings are used for more than one section; these are noted in the tables involved.

Application development is an iterative process. IIS programmers build a component, then test it by embedding it in an ASP page. If the component operates incorrectly, the development cycle starts over.

Several important settings affect development operations:

- Set the ASP cache size to zero (0). In theory, each edit you make to the ASP source code will be detected by Internet Information Server, but in real life you may experience problems if the cache isn't set to zero. Right-click the directory involved in MMC's tree view Explorer and choose Properties | Home | Configuration to display the dialog box shown in Figure 2.11. Finally, click the Active Server Pages tab, and set the ASP File Cache Size setting to 0.

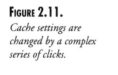

FIGURE 2.11.

Cache settings are changed by a complex series of clicks.

- Turn on script debugging. (Don't use this feature on a production machine, however, because performance will be terrible if you do.) Right-click the directory in MMC Explorer and choose Properties | Home | Configuration to display the dialog box shown in Figure 2.12. Click the ASP Debugging tab, and select Enable ASP Server-Side Script Debugging. (Client-side debugging is not available in this release of IIS.)
- Some components are untrustworthy. If you suspect that a component is unstable, run it in its own address space. Use MMC Explorer to find the directory that the component is in. Right-click the directory and choose Properties. Then select the Run in Separate Memory Space option (see Figure 2.13). All components in the directory will then exhibit this behavior.

FIGURE 2.12.
Enable script debugging in a development environment only.

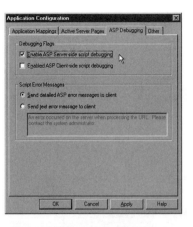

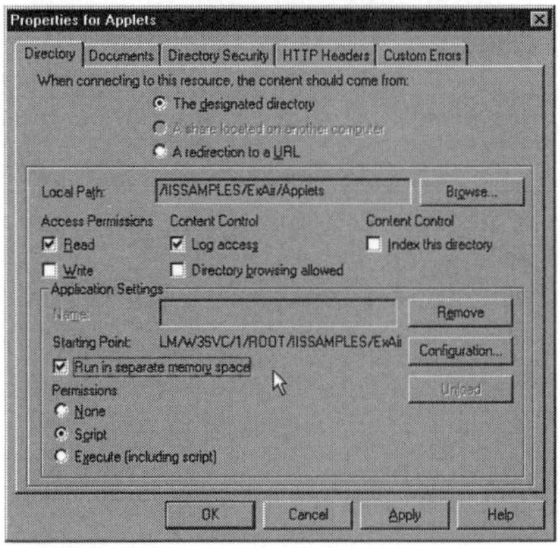

FIGURE 2.13.
Running applications in separate memory space is enabled at the directory level.

You can set this behavior at the file level by setting the `AppIsolated` parameter in the metabase. Unfortunately, this parameter is not exposed in the property sheet; programmatic manipulation of the metabase is required. (See the metabase entries at the end of this chapter.)

Working Directly with the IIS Registry and Metabase Entries

Some of Internet Information Server's settings are kept in the Windows NT Registry, along with settings for virtually every other NT service and program. But many IIS settings have been moved to a new database—known as a *metabase*. Entries that are part of the Registry are there either because they're used to start IIS itself, or for backward compatibility.

The metabase has two advantages: it's hierarchical, and it's faster. Microsoft is gradually moving many of its Registry entries into metabases, which makes sense because the Registry is oriented toward the operating system *per se*.

CAUTION

The Registry contains settings that affect computer operation and performance. It's possible to render your computer completely useless by changing a few settings. Make certain that you have a current backup and emergency repair disk before editing the Registry.

The following entries are listed for your convenience. The settings can also be found in the online documentation that ships as part of Internet Information Server.

Invoke the Registry Editor by choosing Start | Run, typing `RegEdit`, and pressing Enter.

Global Registry Entries

When IIS 3.0 was introduced, the Registry contained settings about virtually every aspect of IIS. IIS 4.0 moved many of these settings to metabases (see the preceding section), but a number of entries in the Registry remain in order to allow IIS to "bootstrap" itself. Table 2.4 lists the global settings.

This is the Registry path:

```
HKEY_LOCAL_MACHINE\SYSTEM
\CurrentControlSet
 \Services
  \InetInfo
   \Parameters
```

Table 2.4. Global Registry entries.

Name	Range	Default	Description
CacheSecurityDescriptor	0, 1	1	Enables security descriptors for objects. 1 is enabled.
DisableMemoryCache	0, 1	0	Disables memory caching. Can be set via `RegEdit` only.
ListenBackLog	1-250	15	Number of active connections to hold in queue.
MaxConcurrency	0-0xFFFFFFFF	0	Number of threads per processor. When set to 0, IIS decides.
MaxPoolThreads	0-0xFFFFFFFF	10	Number of pool threads per processor. Pool threads monitor network requests.
PoolThreadLimit	0-0xFFFFFFFF	2/MB	Max number of pool threads. Defaults to 2 per MB of physical memory. Must be greater than or equal to `MaxPoolThreads`.

Name	Range	Default	Description
MinFileKbSec	1-8192	1000	Timeout before server aborts the file transfer. Setting is in bytes, not KB.
ObjectCacheTtl	0-0xFFFFFFFF	30	Time to live for the object in the cache (in seconds).
ThreadTimeout	0-0xFFFFFFFF	1 day	Length of time (in seconds) that I/O threads should be maintained after the last request.
UserTokenTtl	0-0x7FFFFFFF	10 minutes	Length of time (in seconds) that user tokens are cached. These tokens are used when a logon is required.

Service-Specific Registry Entries

Table 2.5 lists Registry entries specific to individual IIS services. Once again, these entries are "bootstrap" settings, and many more settings are controlled by entries in the metabase. (Metabase parameters are described beginning with Table 2.8.)

The Registry path is as follows:

```
HKEY_LOCAL_MACHINE\SYSTEM
\CurrentControlSet
 \Services
  \ServiceName (W3SVC or FTP)
   \Parameters
```

Table 2.5. Service-specific Registry entries.

Name	Range	Default	Description
AcceptByteRanges	0, 1	1	If set, HTTP server processes inbound requests that have "Range: bytes=" in the header. This is related to a new HTTP extension that was recently implemented as a standard. (WWW)
AllowGuestAccess	0, 1	1	Allows Guest logons. Turn off for best security. (FTP, WWW)

continues

Table 2.5. continued

Name	Range	Default	Description
AllowSpecialCharsInShell	0, 1	0	Permits characters [¦ (, ; % < >] in command strings. Don't enable this if you value your computer, because hackers will exploit it. (WWW)
AnnotateDirectories	0, 1	0	Enables custom messages when changing directories. Annotations are stored in a file named *~ftpsvc~.ckm*. (FTP)
EnablePortAttack	0, 1	0	Allows connection to reserved ports below *IP_PORT_RESERVED*. Don't enable this if hacking is a concern. (FTP)
EnableSvcLog	0, 1	1	Enables discovery by Internet Service Locator. (FTP, WWW)
LogErrorRequests	0, 1	1	Enables error logging. (WWW)
LogSuccessfulRequests	0, 1	1	Enables activity logging. (WWW)
LowerCaseFiles	0, 1	0	Enables case sensitivity when files are requested. (FTP)
SSIEnableCmdDirective	0, 1	1	Enables #exec directive. Not in the Registry by default (but still set to 1). (WWW)
TryExceptDisable	0, 1	0	Disables exception caching. Enabling this causes miscreant ISAPI apps to stop the server. Use it only for debugging! (WWW)
UploadReadAhead	0-0x80000000	48KB	The default amount that the server will read from a client before passing control to the app. The app must then read the remaining data. (WWW)
UsePoolThreadForCgi	0, 1	1	Use pool thread for CGI apps. Slow apps may exhaust the pool. See MaxPoolThreads. (WWW)

Language Engine Registry Entries

Internet Information Server is incredibly flexible, especially when scripting languages are involved. If you prefer to script in FORTRAN, simply develop a scripting version of the language and tell IIS about it here. Table 2.6 describes the setting used to add new languages.

Several scripting languages are in common use, including PerlScript, which is available for download at www.hip.com.

Note that this key is not installed by default. Use RegEdit to create it.

Here's the Registry path:

```
HKEY_LOCAL_MACHINE\SYSTEM
\CurrentControlSet
 \Services
  \W3SVC
   \ASP
    \LanguageEngines
     \LanguageName
```

Table 2.6. Language engine Registry entries.

Name	Range	Default	Description
LanguageEngines	String	N/A	Specifies scripting languages that are not native to IIS.

Metabase

The metabase is similar to the Registry, except that it's faster and supports inheritance. This file is located in \WINNT\system32\inetsrv\MetaBase.bin.

There is no equivalent to RegEdit that allows direct manipulation of the metabase database. However, it can be configured through the MMC, Microsoft Active Data Services Interface (ADSI), or IIS Administration Base Object. All of these methods require programming, except MMC. Examples in C++, Java, and Visual Basic are all shown in the online documentation that ships with IIS.

Namespace

The namespace specifies metabase property locations, and is similar to file system directories or the Registry's hive structure.

Table 2.7 (shown on the following page) describes how the namespace components are assembled in a string. The formal structure is required for a hierarchical relationship such as the metabase.

Table 2.7. Key to namespace variables.

Name	Key	Example
`LM`	Local machine	`LM`
`Service`	`W3SVC` (WWW) or `MSFTPSVC` (FTP)	`W3SVC`
`Website`	Web site	`Soaring`
`Root`	Reserved keyword	`Root`
`virtual directory`	Virtual directory	`wwwroot`
`dir`	Directory	`e:\Soaring\wwwroot`
`file`	File	`default.asp`

Once assembled, the components fit together as follows:

`LM/Service/Website/Root/Virtual directory/dir/file`

The right-hand column of Table 2.7 contains examples that relate to the soaring site we've used in this chapter. So the examples become

`LM/W3SVC/Soaring/Root/wwwroot/e:\Soaring\wwwroot`

Inheritance

Internet Information Server is designed so that if most attributes aren't explicitly defined, the program will "walk the tree"—that is, look to higher levels until an attribute value is found.

> **TIP**
>
> Inheritance is a very powerful concept, because administrators need not specify the same setting over and over again.

Tables 2.8 through 2.14 are provided for your convenience. This information is also in the online documentation that ships with Internet Information Server.

Table 2.8. Metabase settings for computer LM.

Name	Range	Default	Description
`MaxBandWidth`	`0-0xFFFFFFFF`	`0xFFFFFFFF`	Maximum bandwidth. The default means "no restriction."
`MemoryCacheSize`	`0-0x7FFFFFFF`	10%	Physical memory in bytes.

Table 2.9. Metabase settings for LM/W3SVC.

Name	Range	Default	Description
DownlevelAdminInstance	1	1	Server instance to administer for IIS 2.0 Service Manager. (Only this setting also applies to FTP.)
AspBufferingOn	0, 1	0	If set, output is buffered and sent to the client. `Response.Buffer` overrides the default setting.
AspLogErrorRequests	0, 1	1	Enables error logging. (Note that the Registry has a similar setting.)
AspScriptErrorSent ↪ToBrowser	0, 1	1	Enables full error reporting (such as line number) in the browser output.
AspScriptErrorMessage	N/A	See desc	The default is `An error occurred on the server when processing the URL. Please contact the system administrator.`
AspScriptFileCacheSize	1-0xFFFFFFFF	-1	Cache size in bytes for precompiled scripts. `0` disables caching; `-1` means "cache all."
AspScriptEngineCacheMax	0-0xFFFFFFFF	30	Maximum number of language engines the system will cache.
AspScriptTimeout	0-0xFFFFFFFF	90	Maximum script run time in seconds.
AspSessionTimeout	1-0xFFFFFFFF	20	Minutes after the last access before a session times out. `Server.ScriptTimeout` overrides this value.
AspEnableParentPaths	0, 1	1	Enables use of two periods (..) as a directory path.
AspAllowSessionState	0, 1	1	Controls use of the session state. If disabled, also disables `Session_OnStart` and `Session_OnEnd`.

2

INSTALLING AND USING IIS

continues

Table 2.9. continued

Name	Range	Default	Description
AspScriptLanguage	N/A	VBScript	Default script language.
AspStartConnectionPool	0, 1	0	Enables ODBC connection pooling.
AspAllowOutOfProc ➥Components	0, 1	0	Enables out-of-process DLLs.
AspExceptionCacheEnable	0, 1	0	Enables exception catches by ASP. Set to 1 for debugging.
AspCodepage	Any	0	Default code page. Use %@Codepage=*nnn*% to override.
AppAllowDebugging	0, 1	0	Enables debugging. Do not turn on for production sites.
AppAllowClientDebug	0, 1	0	Enables client-side debugging.
InProcessIsapiApps	N/A	N/A	Name of ISAPI apps that must run in-process with WWW server.

Table 2.10. Metabase settings for LM/*Service*/*Website*.

Name	Range	Default	Description
AllowAnonymous	0, 1	1	Allows anonymous connections. (FTP)
AllowPathInfoFor ➥ScriptMappings	0, 1	0	Allows the client to specify script mappings. *Do not* turn this on if you value your source code, because it enables a well-documented hacker feature that relates to multiple periods in the URL! (WWW)
AnonymousOnly	0, 1	0	Only anonymous connections are permitted. (FTP)
ExitMessage	N/A	Blank	Message that's sent to the client when it executes the quit command. (FTP)
FrontPageWeb	0, 1	0	Enables FrontPage Manager by creating special extension files. (WWW)

Name	Range	Default	Description
GreetingMessage	N/A	Blank	Welcome message displayed when the user connects. (FTP)
LogAnonymous	0, 1	0	If set, logs anonymous connections. (FTP)
LogNonAnonymous	0, 1	0	If set, logs non-anonymous connections. (FTP)
MaxClientsMessage	N/A	Blank	Message sent to the client when ServerMaxConnections is exceeded. (FTP)
MaxEndPointConnections	0-0xFFFFFFFF	No Max	Number of simultaneous connections a particular network endpoint is allowed. (FTP, WWW)
MSDOSDirOutput	0, 1	1	Specifies DOS-style directory listings. If turned off, UNIX format is used at the expense of CPU overhead. (FTP)
NetLogonWorkstation	0-2	0	Controls contents of the logon field when the NT logon security dialog box is displayed. 0 = empty, 1 = IP address, 2 = DNS-friendly name. (WWW)
PasswordCacheTtl	0-32768	10	Time in minutes for which a password is held in memory. (WWW)
PasswordChangeFlags	0-2	0	Determines password change behavior. 0 = Change unsecure, 1 = Change disable, 2 = Advance notify disable. (WWW)
PasswordExpiredNotify ➥UnsecuredUrl	N/A	Blank	URL of the non-secure page that notifies users that their password has expired. (WWW)
PasswordChangeUrl	N/A	Blank	Specifies a URL that notifies users to change their password via IIS. (WWW)

continues

2

INSTALLING AND
USING IIS

Table 2.10. continued

Name	Range	Default	Description
PasswordExpireNotifyUrl	N/A	Blank	URL of the page that notifies users that their password has expired. (WWW)
PasswordExpire ➥PrenotifyDays	0-32768	14	Warns users of impending password expiration. (WWW)
PasswordExpired ➥UnsecureUrl	N/A	Blank	URL to which the user is redirected if the password has expired. This is used only if passwords are required for unsecure portions of the site.
PasswordExpiredUrl	N/A	Blank	Specifies a URL where a user can change his password, if it's expired at login. (WWW)
ProcessNTCRIfLoggedOn	0, 1	1	Enables Challenge/Response authentication. (WWW)
SecureBindings	0-65535	See desc	Port that the remote connections bind to. The default is blank if no SSL, else ":443:". See also ServerBindings. (WWW)
ServerConnectionTimeout	0-0x80000000	900	Time in seconds before the server drops the connection (after the last activity). Note: Most browsers don't maintain a persistent connection, so this applies more to FTP. (FTP, WWW)
ServerMaxConnections	0-0xFFFFFFFF	No Max	Number of simultaneous connections to this service. (FTP, WWW)
ServerAutoStart	0, 1	1	Enables automatic server start when NT boots. (Same as the setting in the Services Control Panel applet.) (FTP, WWW)

Name	Range	Default	Description
ServerBindings	N/A	":80:"	Port number that the service runs on (":21:" for FTP). You can set per IP address in the form "192.192.192.1:80:". (FTP, WWW)
ServerComment	N/A	N/A	Comment that appears in MMC. (FTP, WWW)
ServerListenTimeout	0-120	120	Time in seconds before the server drops open clients that haven't sent data. (FTP, WWW)
ServerSize	Small, Medium, Large	Medium	Site size in hits per day—less than 10,000, 10,000 to 100,000, or greater than 100,000. (FTP, WWW)
ServerState	See desc	Started	Read-only state of the server. Possible values are Starting, Started, Stopping, Stopped, Paused, Continuing. (FTP, WWW)
ServerCommand	See desc	N/A	Passes command to the server. Valid commands are Start, Stop, Pause, Continue. (FTP, WWW)
UseHostName	0, 1	0	If set, returns the host name from the DNS or machine name (if the DNS entry is blank). By default, IIS returns IP address. (WWW)

2

INSTALLING AND USING IIS

Table 2.11. Metabase virtual directory settings for LM/*Service*/*Website*/Root/*Virtual directory*.

Name	Range	Default	Description
AppCommand	See desc	N/A	Passes commands to WAM (Web Application Manager). Valid commands are None,

continues

Table 2.11. continued

Name	Range	Default	Description
			Get Status, Create, Create In Process, Create Out of Process, Change to In Process, Change to Out of Process, Delete, Unload.
AppErrorCode	N/A	N/A	Returns more specific information about Error in AppStatus.
AppIsolated	0, 1	0	Forces the app to run in its own process.
AppLastOutprocId	N/A	N/A	Returns the last out-of-process MTS package ID.
AppPackageId	N/A	N/A	Package ID of MTS (Microsoft Transaction Server).
AppPackageName	N/A	N/A	Name of the MTS package. Read-only.
AppRoot	N/A	/LM/W3SVC	URL that's the root of the application namespace.
AppStatus	See desc	N/A	Read-only WAM status. Possible responses are Error, Created, Deleted, Unloaded, Killed, Running, Stopped, NoApplication. Not valid unless AppCommand is called first.
AppWamClsId	N/A	N/A	CLSID of the WAM (Web Application Manager).
ContentIndexed	0, 1	0	Enables indexing by Microsoft Index.
DirBrowseFlags	See desc	See desc	Sets display attributes of directories. Also controls use of EnableDefaultDoc. This is an *XAND* bitwise mask that uses the following constants: EnableDirBrowsing, DirBrowseShowDate*, DirBrowseShowTime*, DirBrowseShowSize*, DirBrowseShowExtension*,

Name	Range	Default	Description
			`DirBrowseShowLongDate`, `EnableDefaultDoc*`. The asterisk denotes the default value. (Doesn't apply to the root directory.)
`Path`	N/A	N/A	Path of the virtual directory.
`UNCAuthentication` `➥Passthrough`	0, 1	0	If the authentication scheme allows delegation, this setting enables it.
`UNCUserName`	N/A	N/A	User name when calling UNC virtual roots.
`UNCPassword`	N/A	N/A	Password when calling UNC virtual roots.

Table 2.12. Metabase file settings for LM/*Service*/Website/Root/*Virtual directory*/*dir*/*file*.

Name	Range	Default	Description
`AccessFlags`	See desc	`AccessRead`	Read-only. Indicates access rights for files. Possible values are `AccessRead`, `AccessWrite`, `AccessScript`, `AccessExecute`.
`AccessSslFlags`	See desc	`AccessRead`	Read-only. Indicates access rights for files. Possible values are `AccessRead`, `AccessWrite`, `AccessScript`, `AccessExecute`.
`AdminAcl`	N/A	N/A	Who can access metabase.
`AllowKeepAlive`	0, 1	1	Enables keep-alive negotiation with client. Don't disable this without good reason, or performance will degrade.
`AnonymousUserName`	N/A	See desc	Local name for the anonymous user. Defaults to `IUSR_MACHINE`. Security-conscious sites may want to change to a non-default name. Remember to set up the new name in the NT user database.

continues

Table 2.12. continued

Name	Range	Default	Description
AnonymousUserPass	N/A	Random	IUSR's password.
AuthFlags	See desc	See desc	Possible NT authentication schemes. Three possible values: AuthAnonymous, AuthBasic, AuthNTLM. AuthAnonymous is the default.
AuthPersistence	0-2	2	Determines whether authentication persists between connections. 0 = disabled, 1 = No, 2 = Yes, except for proxy server requests, which are never persistent.
CacheISAPI	0, 1	1	ISAPI DLLs are not unloaded after running. Disable for debugging if you need to call a new revision of the DLL after each test.
CGITimeout	10-0x80000000	15	Maximum time (in minutes) that the server will wait for a CGI script to complete.
CreateCgiWithNewConsole	0, 1	0	Start each CGI with a new console. Don't enable this without good reason, for performance issues.
DefaultDocFooter	N/A	N/A	Custom file sent to the browser at the end of the data stream. Must enable EnableDocFooter.
DefaultLogonDomain	N/A	Blank	Specifies the default domain, if filled in. If not filled in, the domain name is used if a domain controller, else the machine name is used.
DontLog	0, 1	0	Turns off logging for individual files.
EnableDocFooter	0, 1	0	Enables use of DefaultDocFooter.

Name	Range	Default	Description
EnableReverseDns	0, 1	0	Turns on reverse DNS look-ups. These lookups take up to 30 seconds each, so don't enable this without a really good reason.
HttpCustomHeaders	N/A	None	Custom headers that will be sent to the browser.
HttpErrors	N/A	N/A	Custom error string sent to the browser (HTTP 1.1 or later only).
HttpExpires	N/A	0xFFFFFFFF	Sets expiration time (in seconds) in the HTTP header. The default is never. Can be overridden at run time by Response.ExpiresAbsolute.
HttpPics	N/A	None	Sets PICS rating in the header. (PICS is a self-imposed industry rating system, designed to protect children from objectionable content.)
HttpRedirect	N/A	Blank	URL to which visitors are redirected.
IPSecurity	Binary	None	IP restrictions for an individual file. Can be set for individual computers on up to entire domains.
LogonMethod	0-2	0	Clear-text logon method. 0 = interactive, 1 = batch (user fills in the information on the client, then transmits it), or 2 = network (requires network access rights).
MimeMap	N/A	Blank	MIME file extensions. If not set, the extensions are inherited from the /LM/MimeMap entry in the metabase.

2

INSTALLING AND
USING IIS

continues

Table 2.12. continued

Name	Range	Default	Description
Realm	N/A	Blank	Realm value when the server asks the client to validate via a certificate via clear-text authentication. It appears in the user's Password dialog box.
ScriptMaps	N/A	Blank	List of the file extensions that are script mapped.
SsiExecDisable	0, 1	0	Disables #exec in server-side include statements.

Table 2.13. Metabase file settings for LM/W3SVC/*Website*/Filters/ (local filters) and LM/W3SVC/ Filters/ (global filters).

Name	Range	Default	Description
FilterDescription	N/A	N/A	Description of an ISAPI filter.
FilterLoadOrder	N/A	N/A	Load order stored in a comma-delimited string.
FilterEnabled	0, 1	N/A	If entered into the database, turns the filter on or off. (The default is N/A because by default there are no filters.)
FilterFlags	N/A	N/A	Flags in which a particular ISAPI DLL is interested.
FilterPath	N/A	N/A	Full path to the filter DLL.
FilterState	See desc	N/A	Read-only value. Possible values are Loaded, Loading, Unloaded, Unloading.

Table 2.14. Metabase file settings for SSL keys LM/W3SVCSSLKeys/IP:Port | IP | Port | Default.

Name	Range	Default	Description
SSLKeyPassword	Binary	Blank	Password used to generate the private key from the public/private key.
SSLPrivateKey	Binary	Blank	Private key associated with an IP address.
SSLPublicKey	Binary	Blank	Public key associated with an IP address.

Summary

This chapter described IIS configuration and administration, as well as providing a reference that lists the "under the hood" settings that control Internet Information Server. You learned how to set up a Web site up by using the Microsoft Management Console, explored multi-homed systems, and are now familiar with the Secure Sockets Layer (SSL). You also examined just how the metabases are arranged.

The power and flexibility of IIS, especially all the options and settings, make this service one of the most robust ever developed for Windows NT. As you read the rest of this book, you'll learn how to build on this foundation to produce world-class sites.

2

INSTALLING AND
USING IIS

Installing and Using SQL Server

CHAPTER

3

The Microsoft SQL Server 6.5 database has been selected as the database of choice for the Internet Information Server and Active Server Pages sample applications in this book. Microsoft SQL Server's price performance as well as its easy integration with Windows NT Server make it the obvious choice.

This chapter discusses how to install and maintain Microsoft SQL Server. The first section provides a step-by-step overview of the installation process. In the second section, you learn how to create database devices, databases, and tables. The final section gives an overview of how to maintain your databases.

> **NOTE**
>
> This chapter focuses on how to install SQL Server. To learn how to use SQL, the language of SQL Server, see Part III of this book, "Working with Data: SQL." To learn how to integrate SQL Server with Active Server Pages, see Part V, "The Database Component."

Installation and Setup

Before you can begin installation of SQL Server, you need to know the basic system requirements. For SQL Server 6.5, the requirements are as follows:

- Disk space required is 60MB for SQL Server 6.5. If you're going to install Books Online, 15MB more is required. In planning your server, keep in mind that the data storage space is only part of the equation. Log files, indexes, and backup devices also take up drive space, so a good rule of thumb is to double the drive space you think you'll need for data storage, and that should handle the database.

- 25MB is required for the master database.

- Microsoft's documentation says 16MB of system memory is the minimum. Don't even think about going with the minimum. 32MB is a starting point. For a Web server, I would recommend that the server contain at least 64MB of memory.

- Windows NT 3.51 or later.

> **WARNING**
>
> Do *not* install SQL Server on a primary domain controller (PDC) or a backup domain controller (BDC). These servers are involved in resource-intensive maintenance tasks. They're constantly replicating and validating user database information. The PDC is responsible for authenticating all logons to the NT domain. You should plan to install SQL Server on its own server.

Several steps are involved in the installation of SQL Server 6.5. Before you install SQL Server, you'll need to gather some information and make a few decisions:

- The NT server name
- The NT Server account that SQL Server will use on startup
- The security model (standard, Windows NT Integrated, mixed)
- Location and size of the `master` database
- Character set
- Sort order
- The network protocol that SQL Server will use (named pipes, TCP/IP sockets, IPX, and so on)
- The number of concurrent users who will have access to the server (licenses purchased)
- User groups set up for access to SQL Server databases

The following sections provide a step-by-step guide to installing SQL Server. Here's a quick overview of what you'll need to do:

1. Run Setup.
2. Choose a licensing mode.
3. Specify the installation path and master device.
4. Select configuration options.
5. Specify a logon account.

Running Setup

Restart NT Server and log on with a user account that has the proper permissions to create files and directories on the server. If the account doesn't have the proper permissions, the installation process will be halted with the message `Can't create directory`.

Install the SQL Server 6.5 CD-ROM in the CD-ROM drive. Find the proper subdirectory on the CD-ROM for your server. At the command line, type the appropriate command:

Intel x86 processor	`E:\I386\Setup`
MIPS processor	`E:\MIPS\Setup`
DEC Alpha APX machines	`E:\ALPHA\Setup`

Alternatively, you can use Explorer, find drive `E:` and the proper subdirectory, and double-click the `setup.exe` file (see Figure 3.1).

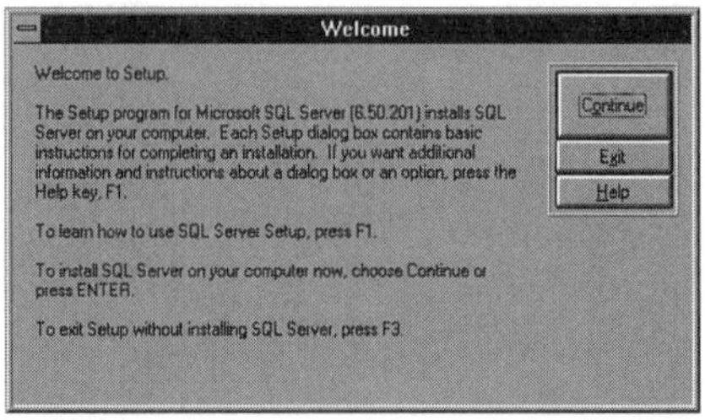

Figure 3.1.

The first SQL Server setup dialog box.

Answer all the questions on the screens relating to the name of your organization and the product ID. The SQL Server options dialog box will then appear (see Figure 3.2). Select the option Install SQL Server and Utilities and click Continue.

Figure 3.2.

SQL Server options.

Choosing the Licensing Mode

After you specify the type of installation and click Continue in the Options dialog box, the Choose Licensing Mode dialog box appears (see Figure 3.3). When you buy SQL Server, you choose to buy a certain number of client licenses. You can choose one of two types of client licenses: Per Server or Per Seat. If you choose per-server licensing, you pay Microsoft for each concurrent connection made to the database. If you choose per-seat licensing, you pay Microsoft for each computer that will connect to the database. Your choice of licensing modes doesn't affect the server's performance in any way. The choice only affects Microsoft's calculation of how much you owe them.

> **NOTE**
>
> As of this writing, Microsoft requires that you purchase an Internet database connection license if you want to use SQL Server on the Internet. The cost is $2,995 for the Internet connection (added to the purchase of SQL Server). The license can be purchased at any authorized Microsoft reseller.

Specifying the Installation Path and Master Device

The next step in the installation process is to choose the directory where the SQL Server files will be located. The directory name must not be longer than eight characters and can't include spaces (no long names). By default, the SQL Server files will be placed in the MSSQL directory.

After you have selected the SQL Server directory, you are asked to specify the location and size of the master device. The *master device* is used to hold all the system databases. For example, it holds both the master and tempdb databases. By default, the size is 25MB. However, you should make it larger to improve server performance (for example, 50MB), space permitting.

Figure 3.3.

License settings.

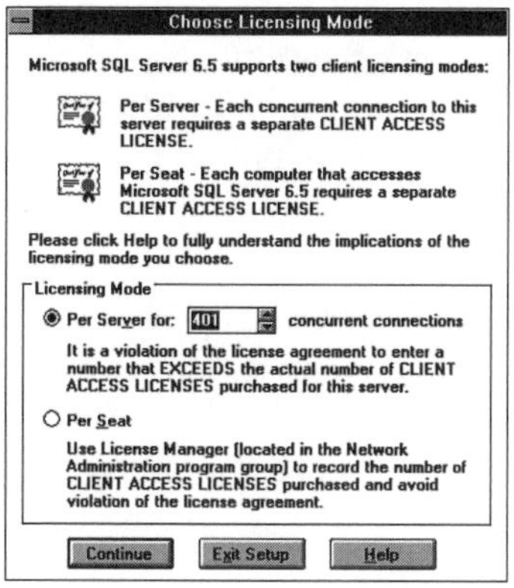

Setting Books Online and Installation Options

The next set of screens asks whether you want to put Books Online on the hard disk. If disk space is limited, choose the Run from CD option or the Do Not Install option. Loading Books Online on the hard disk speeds up access to the help files.

If you choose not to install the help files on the disk, you must use the CD-ROM to search the help files. Most SQL Server installations *do not* install the help files on the server. The administrator's workstation (PC) is the place to install the help files and the SQL administrative tools.

The Installation Options dialog box appears next. The character set, sort order, and network support can be changed here:

■ **Character Set.** The default character set is the ISO 8859-1 (Latin 1 or ANSI) character set. This character set is compatible with the ANSI characters used by Microsoft Windows NT and Windows. I recommend using this character set for Web-based applications. The other character sets are as follows:

   ■ Code page 850 (Multilingual). This character set includes characters for languages of North American, European, and South American countries.

   ■ Code page 437 (U.S. English). This character set includes many graphics characters not usually stored in databases.

■ **Sort Order.** The following sort options are available:

   ■ Dictionary order. Case-insensitive is the default setting—with this setting, case doesn't matter.

- Binary sort order. Every character is sorted in ascending order by its binary representation.

- Dictionary order, case-insensitive. Uppercase sorts first.

- Several other sort orders based on language; case and accents are available. (See SQL Books Online for a complete list. Search the keywords **sort order**.)

- **Additional Network Support.** The default for this option is Named Pipes. You'll want to change this option to the Multi-Protocol selection because Multi-Protocol allows almost any network protocol to communicate with the SQL Server database.

  - Multi-Protocol. Gives the server the capability to access other databases and other clients the capability to access the database. Multi-Protocol is the latest protocol developed by Microsoft and increases server performance to the user over the other protocols. Multi-Protocol also allows for the use of integrated security.

  - NWLink. This protocol is used to interface to a Novell network.

  - TCP/IP Sockets. Standard Windows sockets protocol.

- **Auto Start SQL Server at Boot Time.** This option should be selected. NT automatically starts SQL Server when NT is rebooted. There's no need to log on to NT and start SQL Server.

- **Auto Start SQL Executive at Boot Time.** This option should also be selected for the same reasons as the preceding option.

Specifying the Logon Account

The Setup program displays a dialog box asking for the logon account for SQL Executive to use. SQL Executive runs as a service. The default logon for this service is Local System Account. There's no need to change the default unless you need to use features of SQL Server that depend on network access (for example, replication, SQL Mail, or generating Web pages over the network using the SQL Server Web Assistant).

If you choose to change the account under which the SQL Executive service runs, there are some requirements:

- The account must meet the same requirements as the account used for the SQL Server service. For this reason, it makes sense to use the same account for both services.

- The account must belong to the Administrators local group on the SQL Server computer.

- The account must have the Log On as a Service privilege.

- The account must have its Password Never Expires option selected.

After you have installed SQL Server, you can change the account used by the SQL Executive and SQL Server services by choosing Settings | Control Panel | Services. The SQL Executive service is listed as SQLExecutive and the SQL Server service is listed as MSSQLServer. In other words, specifying a logon account during setup doesn't irrevocably commit you to anything.

The SQL Server Setup program now copies the required files to your hard disk. The Registry is also updated at this time. When the installation process is complete, you'll be asked to reboot the computer.

Setup Review

Most of the setup options can be left with the default settings. For Web server access, it's important that the following options be set:

- Network Protocol: Multi-Protocol
- Auto Start SQL Server
- Auto Start SQL Executive

Registering the Server

After you reboot the server, choose Start | Programs | SQL65 | SQL Enterprise Manager. You'll be asked to register a new server (see Figure 3.4). Type the name of the server (the NT machine name) or select it from the drop-down list box. The name of the server can be found in the Control Panel under the Network option.

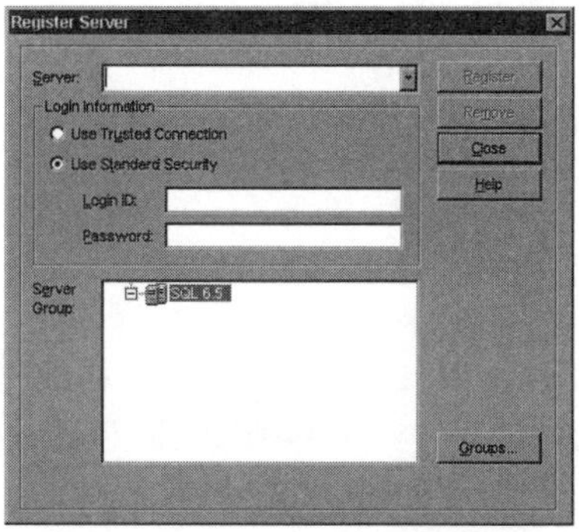

FIGURE 3.4.

The SQL Server Register Server dialog box.

You're also required to enter a username and password. For trusted security, the username and password are not required because SQL Server is using NT security for its user and password validation. The default administrator user for SQL server 6.5 is sa. When you enter **sa** as the username, no password is required (the default setting). It is highly recommended that the password be changed. The user name sa can't be deleted, so make sure you change the password.

> **NOTE**
>
> To change the password for sa, select the name of your server within the Enterprise Manager and then select Manage | Logins from the menu. The Manage Logins dialog box should appear. Select sa from the Login Name drop-down list. You can now enter a new password.

After this step is completed, the server name appears in the SQL Enterprise Explorer. (The Explorer is the graphic display of the objects in the SQL Enterprise Manager.) Click the server name; several server objects should appear. Your setup was successful.

If you're unsuccessful in logging on to SQL Server, the setup process wasn't completed properly. Try to isolate the problem. If all else fails, reinstall SQL Server.

> **WARNING**
>
> Most errors in logging on occur because the network protocol isn't set properly. Make sure you have selected Multi-Protocol.

Creating Database Devices, Databases, and Tables

In this section, you learn how to add three types of objects to SQL Server: database devices, databases, and tables. You should create all three types of objects before you start using the server to store data.

When you store data in SQL Server, you store that data in tables. Tables, in turn, are stored in databases. Finally, databases are stored in database devices.

When you installed SQL Server, you created the *master database device.* The master database device contains all the system databases used internally by SQL Server, such as the master and tempdb databases. You can add your own databases to the master device and your own database tables to the master database. However, this is not recommended. Instead, you should create a database device and database of your own.

> **NOTE**
>
> Storing your own tables in the master database is a bad idea for a number of reasons. For example, it makes backing up your database inconvenient because your database objects will be mixed together with system objects.

Creating A Database Device

A *database device* is the allocation of disk space for use by a database and its contents (tables, indexes, stored procedures, triggers, and users). When you create a device, SQL Server asks for the amount of disk space you want to reserve for that device. For example, if you name your device test and tell SQL Server to reserve 50MB of space, SQL Server creates a directory entry (file) called test.dat and sets the test.dat file size to 50MB. This space is now reserved for device test.

> **NOTE**
>
> The current version of SQL Server (version 6.5) can contain a maximum of 256 devices. Each database device can have a maximum size of 32 gigabytes.

More than one database can reside in a device. For example, you can create the device called test and then create several databases that use the device's disk space. When you create a new database, SQL Server asks for the name of the device in which to create the database, as well as the size of the database. Again, SQL Server is allocating the space for your database.

Because you have to allocate space when you create your database, it's important to plan your database carefully *before* creating any data devices or databases. You can go back and resize the database if you need to do so, but it's always better to size it properly the first time. Otherwise, you may risk data loss from a database becoming filled.

There are two ways to create database devices. The first way is to write SQL queries using system procedures to create the devices. Because this can become tedious and confusing, we'll concentrate on the second way to create these devices—using the SQL Enterprise Manager. Microsoft developed the SQL Enterprise Manager as a GUI front end to make it easier for the SQL administrators to maintain a database.

Here are the steps for creating a new database device:

1. Choose Start | Programs | SQL65 | SQL Enterprise Manager.
2. Click the name of your database server to select it and then select Manage | Database Devices from the menu. The Manage Database Devices window appears.
3. Click the New Device button on the toolbar. The New Database Device dialog box appears, as shown in Figure 3.5.
4. Fill in the name, default directory, and size of the device. The dialog box displays a graphic of the available storage space on all drives. You can't enter a device size larger than the storage space on the specified drive.

FIGURE 3.5.

Setting up a new database device.

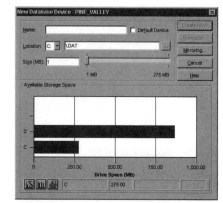

> **NOTE**
>
> If you decide to mirror the device you're creating, you'll need twice the storage space. *Mirroring* is just that—making a "carbon copy" of the device. Mirroring a data device allows for nonstop recovery of data if the mirrored device becomes unusable.

5. After you have completed all the selections, click the Create Now button. SQL Server creates the data device on your hard disk and SQL Enterprise Manager displays the device under the Database Devices folder.

Now that you have created a database device, you're ready to create a new database where you can store your data. In the next section, you learn how to create a new database of your own.

Creating a Database

When you create tables, you create them within a database. To create a new database, follow these steps:

1. In the SQL Enterprise Manager, select the name of your server.
2. Choose Databases from the Manage menu. The Manage Databases window appears.
3. Click the New Database button on the toolbar. The New Database dialog box appears, as shown in Figure 3.6.

> **NOTE**
>
> The current version of SQL Server (version 6.5) can contain a maximum of 32,767 databases. Each database can have a minimum size of 1 megabyte and a maximum size of 1 terabyte.

3

INSTALLING
AND USING
SQL SERVER

FIGURE 3.6.

The New Database dialog box in SQL Enterprise Manager.

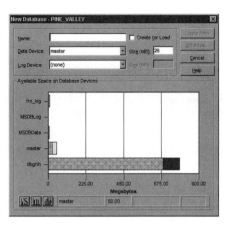

4. Fill in the name that you want to use for the database. (No spaces here.) Next, fill in the data device in which you want the database to reside (for example, the database device you created in the previous section). The New Database dialog box displays a graphic of all the data devices and the used/unused space in each.

5. When you're creating a database, you have the option to create the *transaction log*. To create a transaction log, a *log device* needs to be identified. In the New Database dialog box, open the drop-down list box labeled Log Device, and choose a data device and a size for the log.

NOTE

Each database has its own transaction log, which records requests to modify, insert, or delete records in the database. The log is an internal audit trail of the processes of the database. It allows a process to execute updates, inserts, or deletes on records, thereby enabling you to "roll back" those update, deletes, or inserts if the need arises. Transaction logs are also useful if the system halts or resets without the proper shutdown—SQL Server will use the transaction log to restore data when you reboot.

NOTE

The transaction log is truncated when you dump the transaction log to a dump device for backup. You can also force the transaction log to be truncated. If you want advanced information on the transaction log, search the SQL Books Online and use the keywords `transaction log`.

---

6. When you're finished answering all the questions in the New Database dialog box, click the Create Now button. Your database is displayed under the `Databases` folder.

Creating a Table

To store data in the database, you need to create some tables with fields in them. The tables in SQL Server are much the same as files in dBASE or tables in Microsoft Access.

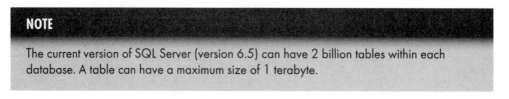

NOTE

The current version of SQL Server (version 6.5) can have 2 billion tables within each database. A table can have a maximum size of 1 terabyte.

To create a new table, use the following steps:

1. In the SQL Enterprise Manager, select the name of your database server.
2. Select the name of a particular database (for example, the database you created in the preceding section).
3. Choose Tables from the Manage menu. The Manage Tables window appears (see Figure 3.7).

FIGURE 3.7.

Creating tables.

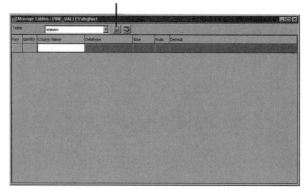

Save Table button

4. Create the desired field names. Remember that SQL Server doesn't allow spaces, hyphens, or commas in field names.

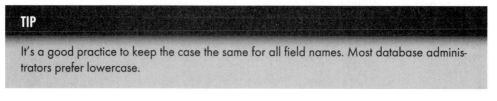

TIP

It's a good practice to keep the case the same for all field names. Most database administrators prefer lowercase.

5. Define the datatype for each field (char, date, money, int, to name just a few).
6. If desired, define the default value for each field.

7. After you have created the fields you want, click the Save Table button and name your table. You now have a table ready to store data.

> **NOTE**
>
> A very significant limitation of the current version of SQL Server (version 6.5) concerns the maximum size of a table row. The combined column size of a table can't exceed 1962 bytes (excluding text and image columns). A table also can't have more than 250 columns. If you really need larger tables, consider using an Oracle database.

Understanding SQL Server Security Options

SQL Server provides three security options, referred to as *login options*:

- Standard security
- Windows NT Integrated security
- Mixed security

The following sections describe the three options.

Standard Security

The *standard security* option is the default login option. When using standard security, SQL Server itself determines who has the right to access the server. With this option set, you have to create user login IDs for all processes that access the database.

When you use standard security with Internet Information Server and Active Server Pages, you should create a login ID other than the sa account. If Internet users are allowed to access the database with the sa login ID, they have full permission to change anything within your database. This is extremely dangerous. To get around this problem, you should create a new login ID associated with more restricted permissions (permissions are discussed in the later section "Groups, Users, and Permissions").

You can give any name to the login ID for Internet users. For example, you can name it **webusers**. To create a new login ID, select Manage | Logins from the Enterprise Manager menu. The Manage Logins dialog box appears. Next, select <New User> from the Login Name drop-down list box. Enter the name that will be used by Internet users. You also need to specify a password and the databases that the Internet users should be allowed to access. Once you have specified this information, click Add and the new login ID will be added.

Integrated Security

The *integrated security* option is the option of choice for using SQL Server. With integrated security you will *passthrough* NT security accounts. That is, Windows NT accounts can be used with SQL Server.

The advantage of using integrated security is that you don't have to worry about maintaining two systems of security. You can create a new user with appropriate rights and permissions only once within the security framework of NT. Once the user is created for NT, the user can be mapped to a login ID using SQL Security Manager. (To learn how to do this, see the later section "The SQL Security Manager.")

You need to perform a few steps to activate this security option:

1. After SQL Server is installed, choose Start | Programs | SQL65 | SQL Enterprise Manager.

2. Choose Server | SQL Server | Configure to open the Server Configuration/Options dialog box (see Figure 3.8). Then click the Security Options tab (see Figure 3.9).

Figure 3.8.

The server configuration menu option.

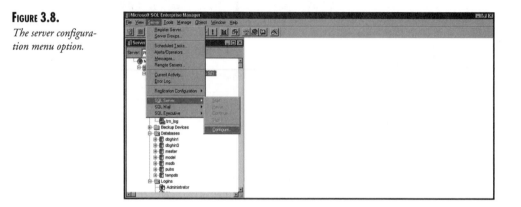

Figure 3.9.

Security options for SQL configuration.

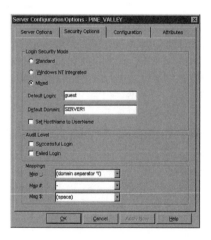

3. Select the Windows NT Integrated security option.

4. For the Default Domain option, specify the domain where the user accounts exist. If you're not part of a domain, supply the name of the NT machine where SQL Server resides.

5. For the Default Login option, indicate the default login you want to use. The default login option is used for all users who don't have a valid login ID.

6. If desired, select the Set HostName to UserName option. When selected, this option displays the user's machine name when the sp_who stored procedure is run.

7. Set the Mappings options as necessary. These options enable you to reassign invalid characters (* - # /).

8. After the appropriate options are selected, exit SQL Server and reboot the server.

PLANNING USER NAMES

If you have decided to use integrated security, plan your usernames carefully. Decide on a naming convention and stick to it. SQL Server doesn't accept certain characters (such as - # @ * / \) that are acceptable to NT. SQL Server enables you to map these characters to acceptable characters. From a practical standpoint, keep the names simple and avoid unacceptable characters—for example, John Propeller could be PropellerJ, but the SQL Security Manager would require you to map Propeller-J to Propeller_J. The hyphen (-) would raise an error.

The Security Options page in the Server Configuration/Options dialog box contains the map selections (refer to Figure 3.9).

Mixed Security

Mixed security offers the advantages of both standard and integrated security. You can mix accounts between NT groups and users local to SQL Server. You can add login IDs directly on SQL Server as well as grant rights to NT user groups via the SQL Security Manager (see the later section "The SQL Security Manager").

The only difference between mixed and integrated security is the NT user account. With integrated security, a user *must* have an account and be a member of a group to have access to the SQL server. You can't add logins to SQL Server with integrated security. Mixed security enables you to add logins directly to the SQL server. Users with accounts in the NT user database as well as any logins you created in SQL Server can have access to the databases. The mixed security option is preferred because of its flexibility while maintaining NT login validation.

Groups, Users, and Permissions

In the preceding section, you learned how to create login IDs. Login IDs provide a very coarse level of security. They work much like passports into SQL Server. They determine who has access to SQL Server, but not what users can do once they have access. To specify more fine-grained permissions, you must define permissions for users and groups.

Each SQL Server database, stored procedure, and table has an associated set of permissions. Only certain users or certain groups of users have permission to access each object or perform particular actions with the object. Properly configuring object permissions is especially important when using SQL Server with the World Wide Web.

For example, suppose you have a table named CreditCards that contains the credit card numbers collected from people who have bought products from your Web site. You wouldn't want any stranger from the Internet to have access to this table. You need to configure the permissions on this table carefully to prevent the information from falling into the wrong hands.

In the case of the credit card table, you need to set the permissions in such a way that users from the Internet can insert new data but not retrieve any data. You need to allow users to insert their credit card numbers but not read the credit card numbers of others. How can you do this?

Permissions are not associated with login IDs. Permissions are associated with groups or users. Therefore, the first thing you need to do is to create a new user and associate it with the login ID being used by your Web site's visitors. These are the necessary steps:

1. Select the database where the CreditCards table is located. A user is defined relative to a particular database.
2. Choose Manage | Users. The Manage Users dialog box appears (see Figure 3.10).
3. Enter a new user name. This name can be anything you want. For example, it could be **Webvisitor**.
4. From the Login drop-down list, choose a particular login ID. Doing this maps the user to the login ID.
5. Click OK to create the new user.

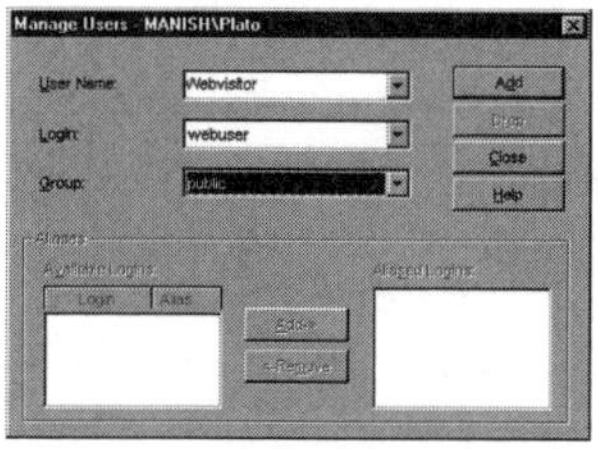

FIGURE 3.10.

*The Manage Users
dialog box.*

Now that you have created a new user, you can specify the permissions associated with the user. You have a choice: You can specify permissions either by user or by object. Here are the steps for configuring permissions by object:

1. Select the CreditCards table by clicking the name of the table.
2. Choose Object | Permissions. The Object Permissions dialog box appears (see Figure 3.11).

3. Choose the tab labeled By Object. A list of users and groups appears.

4. Check the Insert box next to the Webvisitor user. By checking this box, you are granting the Webvisitor user permission to insert data into this table.

5. Make sure that the Select box next to the Webvisitor user is unchecked. If Select isn't checked, Webvisitor doesn't have permission to retrieve data from the table with a SELECT statement.

6. Click the Set button. Clicking this button actually sets the new permissions.

7. Click Close to close the dialog box.

FIGURE 3.11.

The Object Permissions dialog box.

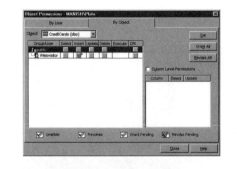

TIP

When developing an application, it's often easier to simply remove all permission restrictions from a user or group. To do this, click Grant All in the Object Permissions dialog box. Next, click Set. Grant All grants all permissions to a user or group.

Instead of specifying permissions for users one by one, you can also specify a set of permissions for a group of users. For example, you can create one group of trusted Web users and another group of suspicious Web users. You can then specify permissions in such a way that the former group has permission to access anything but the latter group has permission to access hardly any database objects at all.

To create a new group, follow these steps:

1. Select the name of a database. Groups are defined relative to a particular database.

2. Choose Manage | Groups. The Manage Groups dialog box appears.

3. Enter a name for the new group.

4. Using the Add button, add the users you want included as members in the new group.

5. Click Add (the second Add button on the upper right of the screen) to add the new group to the database.

You specify the permissions for a group of users in the same way as you specify the permissions for a particular user: Click the name of the group and choose Object | Permissions. You can then specify the objects that the group has permission to access and the actions that members of the group are allowed to perform.

The SQL Security Manager

The purpose of the SQL Security Manager is to set up the passthrough security from Windows NT to SQL Server (see Figure 3.12). The program maps user groups from Windows NT to login IDs in SQL Server. SQL Security Manager works only if mixed or integrated security was selected in SQL Enterprise Manager under the Server | SQL Server | Configure menu option. You won't be able to use this program to add individual accounts, but you can grant NT groups certain rights to your database.

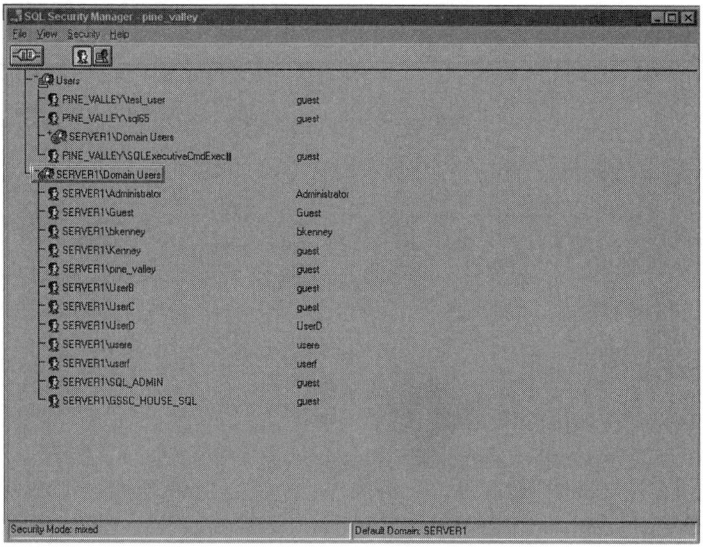

FIGURE 3.12.

The SQL Security Manager.

Following are the steps required to map Windows NT users who are part of the Administrator group to the SQL Server sa login ID:

1. To access the SQL Security Manager, choose Start | Programs | SQL65 | SQL Security Manager. The login screen appears.

2. Use the sa password here and click Connect. The System Administrator Privilege dialog box is displayed.

3. Choose the menu selection Security | Grant New. The Grant System Administrator Privilege dialog box appears (see Figure 3.13). If you're part of a domain, select the Groups on Default Domain option to display all the administrator groups on the default domain. Otherwise, leave the default, Local Groups, selected.

4. Click the Grant button. SQL Server Manager assigns all granted NT accounts the sa privilege. (The sa login has full control over SQL Server.) This setting gives any NT user who is part of the Administrator group full access to all the functions in SQL Server. (Remember that giving full access to a user is extremely dangerous because the user can intentionally or unintentionally destroy all the data in the database.)

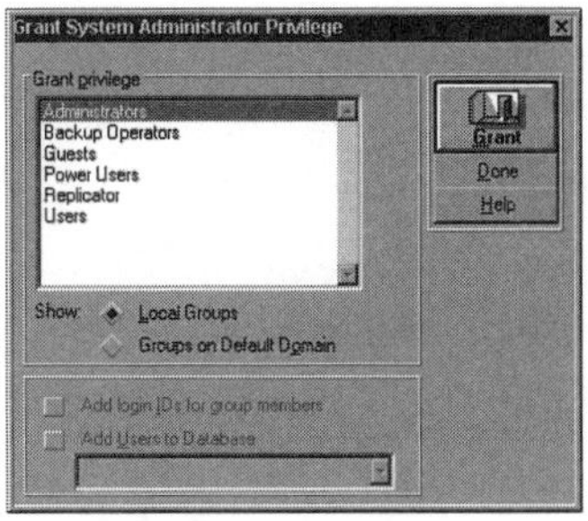

FIGURE 3.13.

Granting system administrator privileges.

To grant particular users access to SQL Server, the SQL Server Manager grants entire NT groups access to SQL Server. All users in those groups are added as logins in the SQL Server Logins folder. You can grant or revoke rights and access using SQL Security Manager.

These are the steps for mapping Windows NT user groups to SQL Server login IDs:

1. To access SQL Security Manager, choose Start | Programs | SQL65 | SQL Security Manager. The login screen appears.

2. Use the sa password here and click Connect. The System Administrator Privilege dialog box is displayed.

3. Select the User Privilege button or choose View | User Privilege. The Users screen appears.

4. Select Security | Grant New. The Grant User Privilege dialog box is displayed.

5. Choose the group for which you want to provide login IDs from the list of user groups. You have the choice of viewing either local groups or groups on the default domain.

6. Click the Grant button. SQL Server Manager automatically generates a SQL Server login ID for all granted NT accounts.

Remember, when a user account is modified in Windows NT it also affects the SQL databases to which the integrated account has access. Before you delete a user account from the User Manager in Windows NT, you need to revoke the user's rights to SQL Server with the SQL Security Manager. You accomplish this from the Users screen in the SQL Security Manager. Click the user account to revoke, choose Security | Account Detail, and click the Drop Login button. You have removed the user login from SQL Server. If you deleted the user from NT first, you would have to delete the login from SQL Server by using the SQL Enterprise Manager. The user account would have to be deleted for all databases and the Logins folder. Make sure you use SQL Security Manager to remove logins before deleting them from the Windows NT User Manager.

Maintaining SQL Server Databases

This section shows you how to maintain your database. First you learn how to create alerts, and then how to back up your data. Finally, you're introduced to the SQL Server Database Maintenance Plan Wizard (often just called the "Maintenance Wizard").

Creating Alerts

SQL Enterprise Manager enables you to create system alerts based on error codes or certain conditions on the database. These alerts can be in the form of e-mail or pager requests. The alert engine enables you to enter the people to contact and the method of contact.

One of the main benefits of the alert system is the ability to maintain the database proactively instead of reactively. The goal of a good maintenance strategy is to minimize downtime if a failure occurs, and to have enough warning that a failure is about to occur. The alert system enables you to design this type of warning system.

To use alerts, a mail service must be installed on the same server as SQL Server. The alert system uses e-mail for paging as well as e-mail. If you're planning to use the paging feature, make sure that your mail system supports paging.

Follow these steps to enable SQL Mail:

1. In the Enterprise Manager, choose Server | SQL Mail | Configure. The SQL Mail Configuration dialog box appears.
2. Enter the e-mail account information requested (the appearance of this dialog box depends on the mail system in use on your server). For example, if you're using Exchange, enter the name of a valid Exchange profile. The profile must be assigned to the same Windows NT domain account under which SQL Server itself is running.
3. Click OK to save the SQL Mail configuration information.
4. Choose Server | SQL Mail | Start. This should start the SQL Mail service.

After SQL Mail is functioning, you can specify operators who will receive e-mail messages from SQL Server. To create a new operator, follow these steps:

1. In SQL Enterprise Manager, choose Server | Alerts/Operators. The Manage Alerts and Operators window appears, as shown in Figure 3.14.
2. Click the Operators tab. Next, click New Operator to create a new operator (the button looks like a firefighter's hat). The New Operator dialog box appears.
3. Type a name for the operator. Next, enter an e-mail address for an e-mail account or pager. The e-mail address specifies the location where alerts will be sent for this operator. You can test whether the e-mail address is functioning correctly by clicking the button labeled Test.

FIGURE 3.14.

Managing alerts and operators.

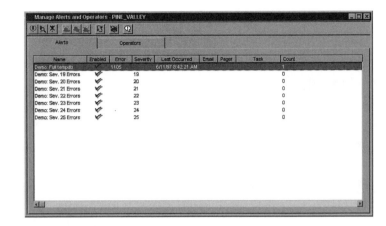

4. Click OK to save the definition of the new operator.

The operator is now prepared to receive an alert. To create the alert, follow these steps:

1. In SQL Enterprise Manager, choose Server | Alerts/Operators. The Manage Alerts and Operators window appears (refer to Figure 3.14).

2. Click the New Alert button. Next, enter a name for the alert in the New Name text field. This name will be used when displaying the alert in the Alerts/Operators window.

3. Specify the error or type of error that will trigger the alert. For example, you can specify that an alert will be triggered by any fatal error caused by a hardware error. To do this, check the box labeled Severity and choose 024: Fatal Error: Hardware Error from the drop-down list.

4. Specify whether to e-mail or page an operator. Remember, *operators* are associated with e-mail accounts that will receive the message (alert) when the alert condition is fired off.

5. Finally, click OK to save the new alert.

NOTE

Most digital paging systems allow you to access the pager via an Internet e-mail message.

You can also set up alerts in conjunction with the NT Performance Monitor. Performance Monitor can monitor any SQL Server processes and run the SQL Server alert engine, thus firing off an alert, which will send an e-mail. The most widely monitored process is the tempdb storage space. You can have Performance Monitor alert the SQL Server alert engine when the

3

INSTALLING
AND USING
SQL SERVER

`tempdb` is 50% full, 60%, 70%, and so on. This gives you time to clear it before the server is halted. Filling up `tempdb` can halt the server and, if allowed to persist, can cause damage to the `master` database.

Backing Up Data

Planning a thorough backup-and-recovery procedure minimizes downtime should disaster strike. You should keep several things in mind when planning a backup procedure:

- Keep all backup devices in the same directory. Keeping them in one subdirectory makes it easier for the server to back up the devices to tape.
- Always back up the `master` database after completing a new installation of SQL Server.
- Always back up the application databases before backing up the `master` database.

Back up the `master` database after any of the following occurrences:

- You add or drop a device.
- You create or change the ownership of a database.
- You add or change user IDs, login IDs, or remote login IDs.
- You run `sp_configure`.

If you lose the `master` database, you could lose all other databases. In any event, it's a painful process to have to rebuild the `master` database. *Back it up often!*

Back up the transaction log files as needed.

The SQL Enterprise Manager makes scheduling backups easy. To schedule backups, the first thing you have to do is create a backup device. Follow these steps:

1. Open SQL Enterprise Manager and select the name of your server.
2. From the Tools menu, choose Database Backup/Restore.
3. Choose New Backup Devices. The New Backup Device dialog box appears, as shown in Figure 3.15.
4. Enter the name of the device and the location of the backup device. You also can specify whether to back up to disk or tape.
5. Click Create.

To schedule backups, follow these steps:

1. Choose Tools | Database Backup/Restore. The Database Backup dialog box appears (see Figure 3.16).
2. Select the database to back up from the Database Backup drop-down list box.
3. Select the backup device you want to use.

FIGURE 3.15.
*The New Backup
Device dialog box.*

FIGURE 3.16.
*Scheduling database
backups.*

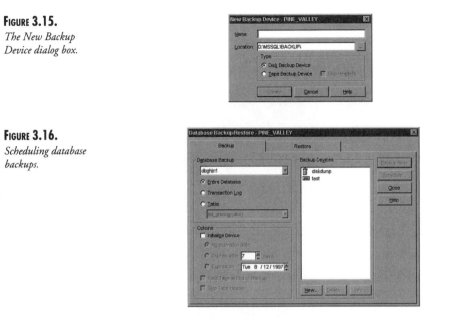

4. The first time you create or schedule a backup, you need to *initialize* the device (create it). If you choose the Initialize Device option for subsequent backups, the backup overwrites the previous backup. The other option would be an incremental backup. If the Initialize Device option is not selected, the system defaults to an incremental backup.

5. Click the appropriate button—Backup Now or Schedule (to schedule the backup for a specific time).

Restoring the data from a backup is also very easy to accomplish. Follow these steps:

1. Choose Tools | Database Backup/Restore. The Database Backup/Restore dialog box appears.

2. Click the Restore tab in the Database Backup/Restore dialog box. Select the backup device to restore as well as the database to restore to (see Figure 3.17, shown on the following page).

3. Click Restore Now.

The Database Maintenance Plan Wizard

The Database Maintenance Plan Wizard was designed to make it easy to perform maintenance tasks on your database (see Figure 3.18). The Database Maintenance Plan Wizard schedules data consistency checks, checks data linkage, checks index linkage, checks data allocation, and checks index allocation. (These are a few of the maintenance options available. For a complete list, search the Books Online, using the keyword **Wizard**.) The wizard determines the best maintenance plan for you, based on the series of questions you answer in the wizard dialog boxes (see Figure 3.19). In reality, all the wizard does is write SQL scripts and execute them. The wizard turns an arduous task into a fairly simple one. The only downside is that the wizard doesn't recommend its use on databases of over 400MB.

FIGURE 3.17.

Restore from a backup device.

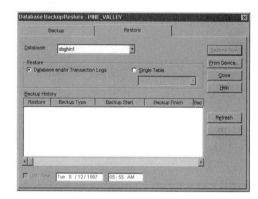

FIGURE 3.18.

The Database Maintenance Plan Wizard.

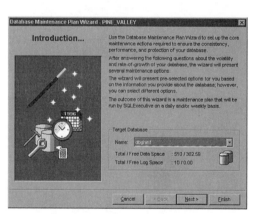

FIGURE 3.19.

Database Maintenance Plan Wizard questions.

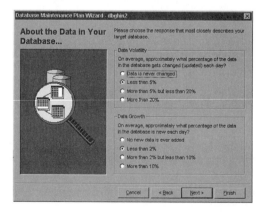

Summary

Microsoft SQL Server is one of the easiest database engines to install and maintain. The server is robust enough to handle most data requirements you will have.

Several commercial Web servers use SQL Server to dynamically store Web pages in the server database. In planning your Web layout, you can store some or all of the HTML code to your pages in a database table and retrieve it with a simple lookup query from an Active Server Page. SQL Server enables you to store all the fonts, HTML color codes, and so on. This option makes maintaining your pages really easy. Suppose all the text in your Web pages changes twice a week. You'll be well served if you keep the text in a database and use your Active Server Pages to retrieve the text. You can then change the text with a simple word processor such as Microsoft Word. Microsoft Query or Microsoft Access can also be used to update the text in the database.

The main use of SQL Server on the Internet is to store and retrieve large amounts of data. You'll find the response time of SQL Server as a Web database more than adequate. One Web site in the Northeast downloads 1.5 million records from a mainframe database to SQL Server once a week. It takes 40 minutes for the download, and after that, the response time is approximately 1 second to retrieve 1 record of data from the Web. Not bad.

Exchange Active Server, Index Server, and NetShow

CHAPTER 4

Unparalleled progress has been achieved in the world of Microsoft technology and its easy integration with the World Wide Web. In almost no time, we have acquired the ability to access Exchange Server content over the Web and to view mail and other content using browsers—via Active Server Pages with no HTML programming. With Index Server, we can search all the Web sites we host with rich functionality. With NetShow, we can share multimedia data in a multicast fashion simultaneously with many users.

Never has developing for the Web been such an easy proposition. And the best news is that the price is right. Active Server for Exchange ships with Exchange 5.0, and Index Server and NetShow are both free and downloadable. They're also available on the Windows NT Server 4.0 Service Pack 2 and 3 CD-ROMs.

This chapter covers these three products in the following order:

- **Exchange 5.** The chapter begins with an overview of Web features of Exchange that are new with Exchange 5. Through Active Server Pages, all Exchange content—including mail and discussion folders—is available to Internet clients that have browsers. The text also discusses the advent of popular Internet standards that provide Internet mail, newsgroup, and address book functions.

- **Index Server.** Next is a discussion of Index Server, a high-level search engine component for large production Web sites. Index Server comes with a programming interface to customize its functions.

- **NetShow.** The final segment of the chapter is an exploration of NetShow, a server-side and client-side component that multicasts live multimedia content in a bandwidth-efficient manner, offering multimedia content on demand.

Microsoft Exchange 5.0 Web Features

Microsoft Exchange has been updated to allow it to serve your Web site more fully. The following list describes some new Web features of Microsoft Exchange Server 5.0:

- **POP3 Server services.** Microsoft Exchange Server now has POP3 Server services so that any commonly available POP3 client—such as Eudora, Netscape Mail, or the Microsoft Exchange Inbox with Internet Mail client services—can be used to send and receive e-mail.

- **Newsgroup protocol support.** Network News Transfer Protocol (NNTP) enables users to access Microsoft Exchange public folders using any NNTP newsreader. Usenet newsgroups can be downloaded to Microsoft Exchange public folders, and data can be accessed using a standard NNTP newsreader or Web browser such as Explorer, using Internet Mail and News client software.

- **SMTP protocol support.** Microsoft Exchange Server can connect to and communicate with other Simple Mail Transfer Protocol (SMTP) systems as of release 4.0. This service, along with POP3 Server, allows Web clients to browse their Exchange mail in Exchange 5.0.

- **Internet Mail Wizard.** The wizard provided for configuring the Internet Mail Service (IMS) enables administrators to set up and configure the Internet Mail Service at the server step by step, allowing Exchange to send and receive SMTP mail and Internet Mail to and from SMTP clients.

- **Newsfeed Configuration Wizard.** The Newsfeed Configuration Wizard helps an administrator automatically set up and configure NNTP connections between Internet newsgroups and a Microsoft Exchange server.

- **Microsoft Exchange Active Server Components.** Active Server components enable users running Microsoft Internet Explorer, Netscape Navigator, or other Web browsers to have read/write access to Microsoft Exchange servers. They can now send and receive mail, browse the directory, and access private and public folders—using just a browser. Skilled developers and unsophisticated users alike can create Active Server Pages to create Web applications for Exchange—such as discussion applications, employee lookup applications, and others.

POP3 Overview

Why is the POP3 server feature such an important addition to Microsoft Exchange 5.0? SMTP was originally designed for transmitting messages between hosts that are continuously accessible in a network. Because there is no guarantee of continuous connection on the Internet, the Post Office Protocol (POP) was developed. The POP3 service can be characterized as a "mail drop" service, which can hold mail at the server until client software retrieves it to the user's workstation. The current version is the third; it's called POP3 and is described in RFC 1939.

POP is simple in design and only provides support for reading messages. SMTP is used to send messages. These two protocols together provide the support needed to pick up Exchange mail, Public Folder info, and so on from a browser. POP3 is a basic client/server protocol for extracting messages from a mail drop. With POP3 support on Microsoft Exchange Server, any commonly available POP3 client—such as Eudora, Netscape Mail, or the Microsoft Exchange Inbox in Windows 95 with Internet Mail client service—can be used to access mail.

> **NOTE**
>
> POP3 is somewhat limited in its functionality; it will "dump" mail where you are, no longer storing it for you at the server level once you retrieve it. Also, POP3 can't read encrypted mail or mail stored in folders other than your Exchange Inbox.

POP3 support is enabled by default when you install Microsoft Exchange Server 5.0, so POP3 clients can retrieve their mail right away. POP3 administration is fully integrated with Microsoft Exchange Server administration, providing a single interface for POP3 and Microsoft Exchange Server administration. Administration options are provided to easily restrict POP3 access on a per-mailbox, server, or site basis.

> **NOTE**
>
> POP3 is enabled on the server level by default in Exchange. However, you can disable it, and you can also turn it on or off at the mailbox level. If you disable POP3 at the server level, all mailboxes will have POP3 disabled by default.

Microsoft Exchange provides a high-performing, more scalable platform than competing products. For example, on a mid-level server platform running Windows NT (dual-Pentium 166, 130MB RAM), Microsoft Exchange can support over 2,500 active mail users, each sending and receiving over 22 messages in a typical 8-hour day.

To enable or disable POP3, go to the site object, select `Configuration\Protocols`, and then select the POP3 protocol object (see Figure 4.1).

FIGURE 4.1.

Enabling/disabling POP3.

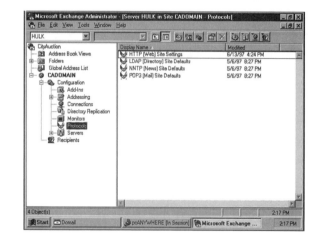

Internet Mail Service Overview

Whereas POP3 is a mail drop service that enables you to read mail from the server, the Internet Mail Service is required for clients to send and read SMTP mail. Both POP3 and Internet Mail Service allow the Microsoft Web client to run.

The Internet Mail Service is an NT service that allows Exchange to send SMTP mail. SMTP mail is the standard for the Internet. The Internet Mail service allows the following:

- Any two Exchange servers to connect using the Internet as a backbone
- Any two mail servers that "talk" SMTP to connect
- Exchange Server to deliver SMTP mail to any SMTP mailbox on the Internet

On the server level, the Internet Mail service runs as a service, allowing Exchange Mail to be converted to SMTP. On the client level, the Internet Mail and News services enable you to retrieve and deliver Internet (SMTP) mail.

Let's look at an example. You have just connected to your company's Internet Web site and looked up an employee link, and now you want to send mail to this employee. Through your internal e-mail system with Exchange you would send mail through your Inbox, but on the Web site the Internet Mail service on your client would be used to push SMTP mail through the Web link.

Exchange Internet Mail Service is easier than ever to configure with the Internet Mail Wizard. The wizard takes you through the following configuration steps (see Figure 4.2):

1. At the Welcome page, the wizard explains tasks, gathers information, and then installs the Internet Mail Service. You are asked to specify on which Exchange server you want to install the Internet Mail Service. There's also a check box that allows Internet mail through a dial-up connection.

2. If you selected the option to allow Internet mail through a dial-up connection, you're asked to select a phone book entry from the Remote Access Service (RAS) phone book.

3. Next you specify how the Internet Mail Service will send mail. You can select DNS for mail routing, or specify another host by entering the hostname or its TCP/IP address.

4. If you like, you can limit which address(es) a particular Internet Mail Service can send mail to. The option All Internet Mail Addresses is the default. Mail can be limited to a specific set of Internet mail addresses, for example *.edu for only the .edu domain on the Internet.

5. You're asked to specify the site address used to generate the e-mail address for clients. For example, entering XYZCorporation.com as the site address would set the user e-mail address for a Microsoft Exchange user named Administrator to Administrator@XYZCorporation.com. This dialog box appears only if this is the first Internet Mail Service in the Microsoft Exchange site.

6. Next you specify the Postmaster account—the administrator mailbox to which to send notification of non-delivery reports. If the mailbox option exists, the wizard shows Use. If the administrator mailbox doesn't exist, the site shows Create.

7. When Finish is selected on the Install page, the Internet Mail Wizard installs the Internet Mail Service.

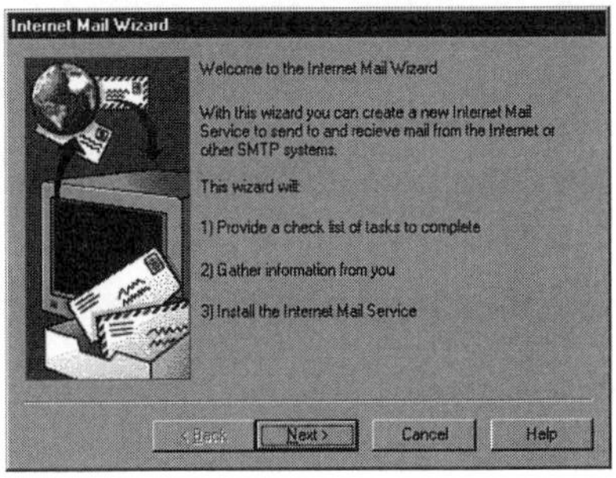

FIGURE 4.2.

Using the Internet Mail Wizard.

4

EXCHANGE ACTIVE
SERVER, INDEX
SERVER, NETSHOW

Using Internet Mail to See Your Exchange Mail Through Your Browser

With the Microsoft Exchange Web client, users can access mail or public data on a Microsoft Exchange Server computer using an Internet browser (see Figure 4.3).

FIGURE 4.3.

Viewing Exchange mail over the Web.

The Microsoft Exchange Web client enables you to do the following:

■ Open a mailbox.

■ Access a public folder.

■ Allow anonymous users to read/post to public folders.

■ Look for recipients in the address book.

■ Look at schedule info.

Users can publish information on the Internet without having to manually convert documents to HTML format, thanks to the Web client's functionality. Microsoft Exchange Server data is translated by Active Server Pages into HTML and transmitted to the browser using HTTP. Through the Microsoft Exchange Server Administrator program, you can control browser access on a per-user basis or make access available to any anonymous user.

The "Web client" isn't actually a client. It's a server-side application that renders Microsoft Exchange data as HTML code and delivers that HTML code to clients' Web browsers. The Web client uses files of these types:

■ .asp files. Active Server Pages complete with scripts.

■ .gif files. Graphic image files common on the Internet.

■ .htm or .html files. HTML files.

How Active Server Works with Exchange

The Active Server essentially makes Exchange Services available to HTTP clients. The Active Server is a component of NT Server 4.0 and is configured using the Microsoft Exchange Server Administrator program. Users don't have to use Hypertext Markup Language (HTML) to publish information on the Internet.

The Web client is a good example of an Active Server application. The initial login form is an ASP file, and after authentication the server presents the user with a list of links matching the top level of the user's mailbox folder hierarchy. Selecting one of the links runs another ASP script that generates a page listing subfolders or message subject lines. Selecting a message line runs a script that generates a page containing that message's text. One of the top-level folders is `Calendar`. When selected, the script generates a list of the user's current appointments ranked by day or by the names of the people who scheduled them. Additional links could cause the script to reorder the list by appointment title, or restrict the list to appointments for the current day. This can be used by virtually all Web browsers.

What Is Active Messaging?

Active Messaging ships with Microsoft Exchange 5.0 and takes the form of both Active Server Pages and Active Server DLL files that interpret content into HTML. Active Messaging acts as an interpreter between Exchange and IIS, so that users running Web browsers can access Microsoft Exchange data—such as messages, public folders, and global address books. Active Server Pages applications can access not only Exchange but also SQL and SNA data by using the SQL and SNA Active Server components.

Among the key components of Active Messaging are two dynamic link library (DLL) files installed by Exchange Server onto an IIS 3.0 system. One of the functions of those DLLs is to use the Messaging Application Programming Interface (MAPI) to access Microsoft Exchange information and convert it into HTML for display on the Web. Developers write applications that use Microsoft Active Server Pages, another component of IIS 3.0 that processes scripts. A user, using a browser, calls a URL that points to an `.asp` file. That file contains scripts that call the Active Messaging DLLs. Content from the server is then interpreted into HTML for the browser.

For example, you might have an Active Server Pages file that obtains the subject lines of all new posts in a discussion folder, translates those lines into HTML, and delivers them to the client. The HTML code could make each subject line a link to the body of the posting; when the user selects one of the subject lines, another script can retrieve the body of that post, convert it to HTML, and display it for the user.

The ASP files can contain scripting commands written for any of several scripting environments, including Visual Basic Scripting Edition (VBScript) and JScript. It also supports other scripting languages such as REXX and Perl through optional Active Scripting plug-ins. In addition, developers can use ActiveX components developed in C++, Visual Basic, Java, and COBOL.

You can think of Active Messaging as a translation mechanism. Existing content in Exchange Server can be translated into HTML by using the Active Server Pages included with NT 4.0. Because the output of the Active Server Pages is HTML, users with any type of computer and any type of browser can access and benefit from the Active Server data.

Any two directories can contain identical files, or files with the same name but different content.

Active Messaging offers a solution whenever an organization needs to add e-mail, public folders, or directory access to a Web-based application. The Exchange application farm, available on the `Microsoft.com` site or on the TechNet CD, now includes copious Active Server scripts that can be incorporated by Webmasters. For instance, Active Server scripts for employee restaurant reviews, customized employee discussion folders, new employee application forms for business cards, new meeting request forms, and so on can be adapted easily for your Web site.

Active Platform is a development platform that provides developers with an easy way to build applications that take advantage of the best of the Internet and the best of the PC. Active Platform is based on three core technologies: Active Desktop, Active Server, and ActiveX. For the first time, developers can now target a consistent, unified platform from client to server in order to build a wide variety of Web-based applications quickly.

A new generation of programs is sure to result quickly, including database access, financial updates, form processing, file access, classified ads, and other applications. Figure 4.4 shows the Active Server version of threaded discussion folders.

FIGURE 4.4.

Sample site demonstrating Active Messaging for threaded discussions.

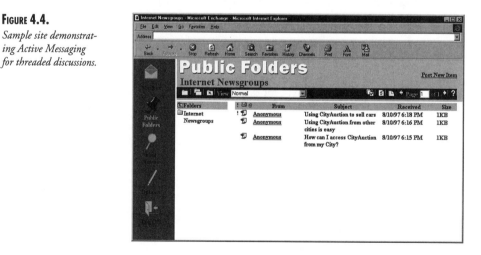

Through *Exchange Form Designer*, businesses have been able to add messaging and groupware functionality to their intranet or Internet Web sites with little or no coding involved. Now they can create Active Server Pages through HTML and script coding, or by using FrontPage and Active Server Extensions. Existing Exchange applications can be extended to all platforms that support Web browsers, and current Web pages can be enriched with new levels of functionality.

In summary, Active Messaging is an Active Server component and is part of Microsoft's Active Platform. Users and developers alike can write ASP applications that use Active Messaging to access functionality in Microsoft Exchange Server. Active Platform with Active Messaging has become a catalyst for the development of a new generation of business applications that combine Web technologies with the power and reliability of Microsoft Exchange Server.

Sample Active Server Application

Users wanting to know more about Active Server applications can see The Microsoft Exchange Community Discussion Forum sample, found on the Microsoft Exchange Application Farm available on the Web at the following URL:

```
www.microsoft.com/syspro/technet/boes/bo/mailexch/exch/tools/appfarm/default.htm
```

You can also get this sample on the TechNet CD. Static HTML files and GIF graphic files have been altered to customize the page, but the scripting files are unchanged. If you direct your Web browser to `www.exchangeserver.com`, select Interaction, then Peer Discussions, then Application Design, you will see the type of screen shown in Figure 4.5.

FIGURE 4.5.
Discussion sample application.

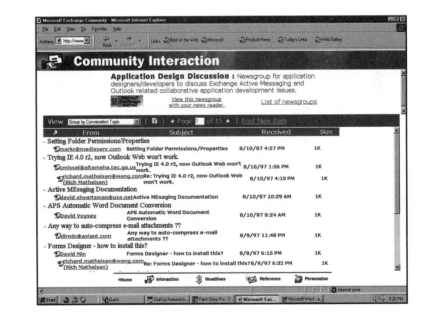

This site provides any frames-based Web browser with anonymous, read-and-write access to a Microsoft Exchange public folder.

These frames display several kinds of content:

- **Static HTML code.** The navigation bars are written in HTML, as well as text describing the Application Design Discussion at the top.
- **GIF graphics.** The yellow "Post" icons are GIF files.
- **Dynamically-created HTML code.** The code extracts text from messages stored on a Microsoft Exchange server, and renders the text into HTML code.

By viewing the source code, you can learn more about the way pages like these have been authored.

In summary, Exchange Server 5.0 not only offers the benefits of the Microsoft Exchange Web client to users, giving users access to e-mail, but it also adds the comprehensive capabilities of Active Messaging for translation of content into HTML and Active Platform for a new, quick, and easy development environment.

Microsoft Index Server

Microsoft Index Server helps provide the popular function that you see on a lot of Web sites: "Search this Web site." Microsoft Index Server provides comprehensive content indexing and searching for servers running Internet Information Server (IIS). You can formulate queries such as "Search for pages containing the words Index and Internet." The Index Server can also index documents in different languages.

What if documents are formatted, as is the case with Word and Excel documents? These documents can also be indexed—which is a good function for employees searching for internal documents that aren't necessarily published on the Web.

The indexing tools that make these searches possible traditionally have involved expensive proprietary equipment and are difficult to set up. Microsoft Index Server is a free, downloadable component of Windows NT Server version 4.0. This means that if your organization has NT 4.0, it can access all its documents directly on your intranet in their original format, without converting everything to HTML.

> **NOTE**
>
> For additional information and to download, see the Microsoft Web site at
> www.microsoft.com/windows/common/contentNTSI.

One of the key features of Index Server is Automatic Maintenance. Once it's set up, Microsoft Index Server is designed for 24-hour operation. It runs in the background to optimize resources, update indexes when files change, and recover if there's a power failure.

Using Index Server involves doing a query. Users fill out a simple query form stating what directories they would like to search, what they would like to search for, and so on.

This list describes some of the query features that Index Server includes:

- **Full-text indexing.** Search for a whole sentence or paragraph.
- **Query by properties.** Search for only .htm files created by a certain date, with a certain file size, and so on.
- **"Fuzzy" queries.** Use wildcards or terms such as LIKE to find something you know the approximate name for.
- **Advanced searches.** Use NEAR (indicating proximity for words near other words), numeric operators (<, =, >), and Boolean operators (AND, OR, NOT) in your query.
- **Security observed.** Users are shown only documents that they have permission to view.
- **Administration tools.** The administration tools for NT Server integrate with Index Server, so you can monitor how many queries are happening, the performance of the server, and so on.

How Does Index Server Work?

How does Index Server work? The administrator configures a scope of documents to be searched. These documents can be in one directory or can span many directories on the network. This body of documents is called a *corpus*. Index Server scans the corpus for documents, then pulls text from them. For instance, a formatted Microsoft PowerPoint presentation would be filtered for just its text. The filtered output then goes through what's called a *word breaker*. This is a common function of many Web search engines. The output is filtered for *noise words*— that is, words that have little meaning, such as *a, an, the, is,* and so on.

A *catalog* is the largest organizational unit, containing master indexes, secondary indexes, and cache instructions. An Index Server query can't span multiple catalogs. Indexes are built from directory lists and are administered by Index Server on a per-directory basis. Indexes can be refreshed so they'll pick up changes to a directory, but Index Server doesn't need to index all documents to pick up the changes.

Basic Query Features

Each query consists of three elements: where to search, what to search for, and what information to view.

A *query scope* specifies the scope of documents to be searched. An IIS Web site corresponds to a virtual root, which in turn corresponds to a physical storage place for documents—such as a directory or list of drives and directories. /Spreadsheets and /Documents are two examples of virtual roots on the server.

Index Server packages query hits into result sets that are returned to the client. For example, a 200-item result set may be retrieved by the client in 10 pages of 20 hits each. The form may allow the client to specify the number of hits to retrieve per page.

Index Server can also create document *abstracts*, which may also be returned in a result set. An abstract is simply a document summary to give the client some idea of what a particular document is about. You often see them with search results in Yahoo! or other Internet search engines.

`Microsoft.com` utilizes Index Server. Go to `www.microsoft.com` to see their search engine in action. Figure 4.6 shows the result set generated by a query.

FIGURE 4.6.

Sample query results.

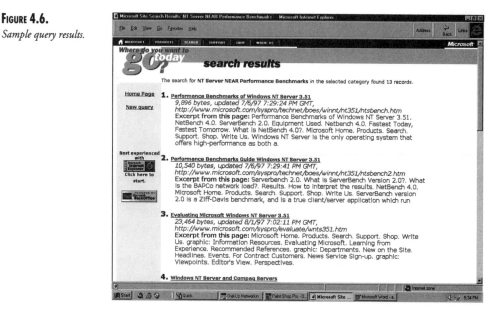

The Indexing Process

The indexing process consists of three main steps: filtering, word breaking, and normalization.

When the system begins to operate on a document, it determines the document's type and uses the appropriate content filter in a process known as *filtering*. A *content filter* can be thought of as a little version of an application that only knows how to read its own files. The filter extracts text chunks from the document and passes them to Index Server in a format that the system recognizes.

In addition to extracting text chunks, another important function of the content filter is to recognize language shifts in documents. Some document formats indicate the language used for a particular chunk of text. If these tags exist, the content filter emits the tag with its corresponding text chunk. For example, the filter may emit a chunk of text that corresponds to a paragraph written in French. This chunk of text will be tagged by the filter as `French`. Index Server uses the language tag to load the appropriate word breaker and normalizer for the language (described shortly).

Index Server indexes not only the text in a Word document, but any text in a Microsoft Excel spreadsheet that's embedded in the Word document.

Because there are thousands of different programs and data formats, and document formats change frequently, the programmatic interface used to implement content filters has been standardized by Microsoft in the open standard IFilter Interface. This standard interface between the Index Server and the rest of the world specifies how content filters will be used, allowing other companies to write content filters for their data. It also means that those people most familiar with the data format are the ones to write the content filter for that format.

After filtering, the next major task is *word breaking*. Index Server indexes words rather than just characters, so it must be able to identify the words within the character stream. It's easy for people to look at a sequence of characters and identify words, but that's a difficult task for a computer. Different languages treat words and the breaks between words very differently. Many languages use white space and punctuation to indicate word breaks. Other languages, such as Japanese, don't use white space to indicate word breaks.

Index Server provides language-specific word breakers that understand how to break a stream of characters into valid words. These modules understand a particular language's structure and syntax, and they analyze the text to identify words. Index Server provides word breakers for the following languages: English, French, German, Spanish, Italian, Dutch, and Swedish.

Like content filters, word breakers are modular components. Independent software vendors can create their own word breakers using the open standard, and plug them into the system. This enables third parties to provide linguistic utilities for languages not currently supported by Index Server.

The final stage of indexing is *text normalizing*. Normalizing cleans up noise words in the word breaker output. The normalization process also handles things like capitalization and punctuation, creating a smooth output for Index Server's indexes.

Fault Tolerance

Fault tolerance is critical with a Web server. If a system has a hardware failure and goes down in the middle of indexing many hundreds of documents, it isn't efficient to be forced to begin re-indexing the entire body of documents. Index Server's design includes recoverability. When a system comes up after a failure and disk integrity is verified, Index Server can do a full integrity check on all indexes, using the same kind of logging and recoverability mechanism that the NT file system uses.

Index Server and Database Connectors

Index Server interfaces with IIS in a manner very similar to SQL Server (if you're familiar with SQL and the ISAPI layer). Index Server uses its own database connector rather than ODBC.

Instead of using IDC (Internet Database Connector) files, as SQL does, Index Server uses IDQ files. These have a very similar structure and format. Index Server also uses HTX files, to format results.

Every query in Index Server references a particular IDQ file or index file. This data is then converted into a proper query that it can execute against the indexes.

One of the lines in the IDQ file specifies an HTX file, which is used to format the output. Then, using the query results and format specified by the HTX file, Index Server builds a results page in HTML. This is then sent back to the IIS server, which in turn forwards it to the browser.

Query Form Syntax

Figure 4.7 shows a simple query form. In the HTML code for the query form is a reference to the IDQ files, as follows:

```
<FORM ACTION="/Indexes/Index1.idq?" METHOD="POST">
```

When the user clicks the Execute Query button, the form data is sent to IIS and processed. The IIS server locates the specified IDQ file and passes the form data and the IDQ file to the Index Server program.

FIGURE 4.7.

Simple query form for HTML.

Future versions of Index Server will feature something called *hit highlighting*, which will enable the user to view hits of queries not only from HTML but also Word, Excel, or PowerPoint documents. Also, you should be able to use Index Services in conjunction with Internet News Services to search newsgroup articles not only on your intranet but on the Internet as well.

Executing a Query

Figure 4.8 shows an example of a query form. In this sample query, the user is searching the entire Web site for all documents that contain the phrase NT Server near the phrase Performance Benchmarks. To execute this query, the user clicks the Search Now! button.

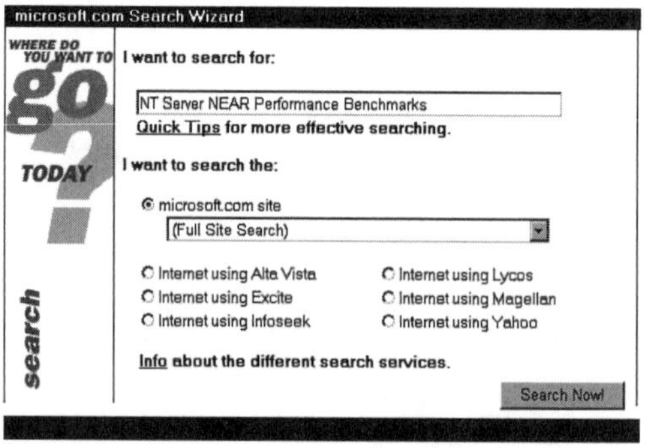

FIGURE 4.8.

Sample query form.

Configuring Index Server

You can run Index Server on an NT server or NT workstation. On a workstation, you'll need a minimum of 16MB of RAM. On a server, you'll want 16MB of RAM above the 16MB needed for the operating system.

> **NOTE**
>
> You must have IIS 2.0 or later and Windows NT 4.0 to install Index Server. You can also install Microsoft Peer Web Services (PWS) on Windows NT 4.0 instead of IIS.

The program files for Index Server require a mere 3 to 12MB, depending on how many languages you install. However, a lot of disk space is required—as much as 40% of the size of the corpus you intend to query on during peak disk space usage. Average disk space usage will be less than 30% of the corpus.

Installation of Index Server is straightforward; double-clicking the file `idxsveng.exe` installs the English version of Index Server. You will merely be asked to indicate to what directory your indexes should be written. However, we suggest that when prompted you install the sample query pages and sample query scripts to use for your first queries.

For More Information

Refer to Microsoft's Web site for more information on Index Server, downloads, and so on:

Microsoft home page   `www.microsoft.com`

Index Server home page   `www.microsoft.com/ntserver/search`

Microsoft NetShow

Microsoft NetShow is a software component of NT 4.0 for clients and servers that supplies two main functions: NetShow Live with live streaming audio; and NetShow On-Demand with streaming audio, illustrated video, and audio available on demand.

Suppose you want to get information out to employees in a creative way. Maybe you're having a release party at your record company for a new CD. With NetShow, you can spend a minimum of money because the client for NetShow is free and downloadable. You can also use your existing hardware if your clients have a multimedia 486 PC.

You can turn to existing videotape to capture frames for illustrated audio .asf files and for Internet- and intranet-bandwidth video .asf files. You can use the existing video editing tools to capture frames and to edit the video.

> **NOTE**
>
> NetShow is codec-independent. You can use any PCM/ACM codec for audio or video as long as the user's computer has the same codec.

NetShow Live enables you to multicast live from the release party to every employee, partner, or customer's desktop. All any user needs to receive the multicast audio is the NetShow client. But what about viewing the demonstrations and training? Use the demonstration and training portion of the videotapes to create various ActiveX streaming (.asf) files. As opposed to forcing users to download huge video files, NetShow streaming enables users to watch video files with no download time—even during peak viewing hours. The NetShow client is free, so you don't have to worry about the user not having the client.

How NetShow Works

Microsoft NetShow exploits two key technologies to enhance users' networked multimedia experience, while reducing the impact on the network's throughput:

- **Multicasting.** The bulk of the traffic on today's networks is *unicast*: A separate copy of the data is sent from the source to each client that requests it. *Multicasting* sends a single copy of the data to those clients that request it. Multiple copies of data are not sent across the network, nor is data sent to clients that don't want it. Multicasting within NetShow uses a standard that minimizes the demand for bandwidth.

- **Streaming media.** Normally, when accessing networked multimedia content, users have to wait for an entire file to be transferred before they can use the information. *Streaming* allows users to see or hear the information as it arrives, without having to wait. With NetShow, Microsoft has developed an open streaming platform capable of high performance under demanding network conditions.

NetShow will change the way people share multimedia information, by enhancing an organization's ability to distribute live and on-demand audiovisual presentations efficiently. Typical scenarios include the following:

- **Meetings.** Everyone in an organization can listen in live to important organizational briefings, regardless of their geographic location. If they miss the meeting, they can see and hear a stored version later, on demand.

- **Training.** NetShow lends itself well to live training or on-demand applications. Existing video and/or audiotape can be converted into NetShow training content.

- **Online tours.** Certain subjects lend themselves to audio or image content, such as real estate tours, tours of corporate facilities, previews of motion pictures, video products, and so on.

NetShow Live versus NetShow On-Demand

NetShow Live can deliver a stream of live audio to Internet users. NetShow uses a protocol for real time called *Real Time Protocol* (*RTP*), which is an industry standard and allows for one-to-many transmission without sending copies of everything to each individual user.

Think of a NetShow Live production as a slide show with live audio and with slides, graphics, and URLs all transmitting in sync with the audio track.

Configuring NetShow

Requirements for NetShow are divided into server and client components. NetShow On-Demand servers must be at least Pentium 90s with 32MB RAM and 16-bit sound cards, running NT 4.0 and IIS 2.0.

Clients running the On-Demand Player must have at least 486s with 16-bit sound cards, 28.8 modems, Windows 95 or NT Workstation 3.51, and Internet Explorer 3.0 or Netscape Navigator 3.0. A neat thing about the NetShow On-Demand Player is that it can be embedded in Web pages for users to use, rather than downloaded.

On the server, you can install a couple of optional components:

- **ActiveX Streaming Format (ASF) Editor.** This editor assembles video or audio files into a single ASF file and compresses the ASF file for streaming in the low- to mid-bandwidth range. You can also use the ASF Editor to add command strings and URLs to a presentation. To get more information on the ActiveX Streaming Format Editor, see the ActiveX Streaming Format Editor Help file (`Winase.hlp`).

- **Conversion tools and utilities.** These tools include `VidToAsf` and `WavToAsf`, which are command-line utilities that you can use to convert `.mov`, `.avi`, or `.wav` files to the `.asf` format.

To install the NetShow On-Demand Server or the Live Server, use the setup program available from the Microsoft NetShow On-Demand Web site at `www.microsoft.com/netshow//`.

First, make sure you have IIS and Internet Service Manager installed. From the Windows NT Start menu, choose Programs | Microsoft Internet Server (Common).

`Nsosrv.exe` is the downloadable self-extracting file that installs the Microsoft NetShow On-Demand Server. `Nslsrv.exe` installs the NetShow Live Server. Once the Setup program is extracted, installation is very straightforward. Be sure to select the check box for installing the administration tools. Figure 4.9 shows the setup screen for the On-Demand Setup.

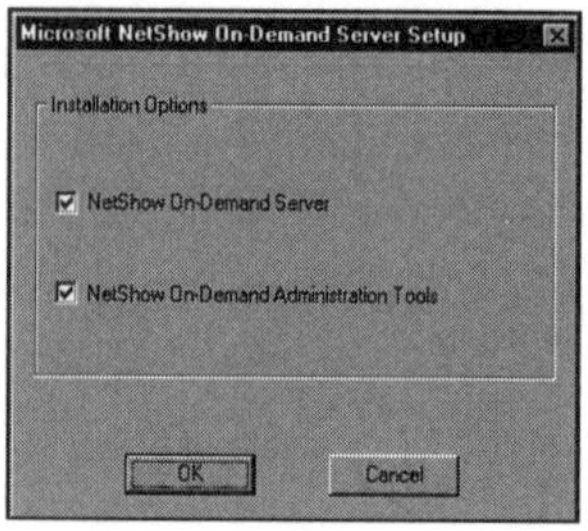

FIGURE 4.9.

Check the option for the administration tools during On-Demand Server setup.

Microsoft On-Demand Player

Microsoft NetShow On-Demand Player is downloadable from Microsoft's Web site. This player is similar to a Real Audio player or the Media Player in Windows 95. You can fast forward, rewind to the beginning, and so on. It's a very simple tool for viewing On-Demand information.

NetShow On-Demand Administration Tools

The On-Demand administration tools are similar to the IIS tools. IIS offers two choices for administration: any Web browser, or the Internet Service Manager for both Windows NT and Windows 95. The Internet Service Manager gives you the unique ability to monitor the status of all your servers on all machines.

NetShow and the Windows NT Performance Monitor are integrated to let you conduct performance comparisons, analyses, and capacity planning of all your Web servers using Performance Monitor. This integration also enables security auditing through the Windows NT Event log. Performance Monitor contains an SNMP agent for reporting to a standard network management console.

How to Learn More About NetShow

You can download the NetShow client or server components from the Microsoft Web site. You can also use the client with some of Microsoft's NetShow On-Demand sample presentations on the Microsoft Web site, or download demos of NetShow.

Microsoft NetShow 1.x is available for download over the Internet at no charge. NetShow can be downloaded from the Microsoft Web site at `microsoft.com/netshow/`.

Summary

This chapter covered the Web features of Exchange 5, including Active Server for Exchange, which offers Web access to Internet Mail, newsgroup, and address book functions. You learned that Index Server creates a body of documents to scan, creating a search index, and comes with a programming interface to customize its functions. Finally, the chapter discussed NetShow, and how this component offers multimedia content on demand. NetShow can be embedded into your Active Server Pages so that clients don't have to download NetShow to see multimedia content.

II

PART

Markup and Scripting Languages

Basic HTML

IN THIS CHAPTER

CHAPTER 5

After reading this chapter, you'll understand the basics of Hypertext Markup Language (HTML), the language of the World Wide Web. You learn how to create your own Web pages with colors, page and text formatting, hypertext links, and images.

If you're already familiar with HTML, you may want to skim or even skip this chapter and move immediately to the next part of this book. If you don't have a firm grasp of HTML, however, stay where you are, don't turn a page. A mastery of the material covered in this chapter and the next is crucial for effective Active Server Pages programming.

In this chapter, you learn everything you need to know to create simple Web pages. While reading, don't be afraid to experiment with the techniques discussed. Playing with a new computer language is always the most effective way of learning it.

What Is an HTML File?

An *HTML file* is what a Web browser uses to generate a Web page. At its heart, the World Wide Web is nothing but a vast collection of HTML files residing on the hard drives of computers spread throughout the world, and a transport protocol for transferring these files from computer to computer. These HTML files, in turn, are simply text files—files that can be easily read and understood by human eyes.

Web browsers, such as Netscape Navigator or Microsoft Internet Explorer, interpret HTML files in order to display Web pages. This is the main function of a Web browser. Whenever you use a browser to view a page on the World Wide Web, the browser has converted that Web page from an HTML file.

To see an example of an HTML file, start your favorite Web browser and visit the Active Server Pages Web site by typing `http://www.aspsite.com/hello.htm` into the address bar of your Web browser. (You need to be connected to the Internet to get there.) After the hello page loads, choose the View Source command from your Web browser's menu bar. A new window should pop up on your screen and display some curious-looking text. The text that you see is an HTML file.

An Introduction to HTML Tags

HTML files are different from other text files because they include special codes called *HTML tags*. If you look closely at the HTML file that you just revealed with the View Source command, you can identify the HTML tags by searching for expressions surrounded by the two angle bracket characters (< and >). This is a characteristic of HTML tags in general. Here's an example of an HTML tag and some text that it modifies:

```
<B> This is bold</B>
```

In this example, `<B>` is an HTML tag used for making text bold. If you surround a piece of text with `<B>` and `</B>`, the text will be boldfaced when displayed in a Web browser. This illustrates another general feature of HTML tags: Most HTML tags come in pairs and act as *containers*.

In this example, the `<B>` tag tells the Web browser when to start displaying text as bold and the `</B>` tag tells the browser when to stop displaying the text as bold. Because it functions in this way, the `<B>` tag is called a *container tag*.

> **NOTE**
>
> Different browsers may interpret particular HTML tags in different ways—and sometimes not at all. For example, not all browsers can interpret the `<FONT>` tag. See the later section "The HTML Standard" for details.

Following is an example of a slightly more complicated HTML tag:

```
<FONT COLOR="RED"> I am red </FONT>
```

When interpreted by a Web browser, the sentence I am red is displayed in the color red. The COLOR attribute of the `<FONT>` tag tells the browser which color to use when displaying the text. This tag illustrates yet another feature of HTML tags in general: Most HTML tags have one or more attributes that determine how the tag will behave. The COLOR attribute is only one of many attributes of the `<FONT>` tag. The next example uses another attribute:

```
<FONT COLOR="GREEN" FACE="ARIAL"> My name is Arial and I am green </FONT>
```

In this example, the sentence appears as green, in the Arial typeface. Both COLOR and FACE are attributes of the `<FONT>` tag. The two expressions "GREEN" and "ARIAL" are the values of the two attributes. The COLOR attribute determines the color of the contained text, and the FACE attribute determines the typeface of the contained text.

The order in which attributes appear in an HTML tag is unimportant. Also, you can generally type the value of an attribute with or without the quotation marks. So the two sentences in the following fragment of an HTML file will be displayed by a Web browser in exactly the same way:

```
<FONT COLOR="GREEN" FACE="ARIAL"> My name is Arial and I am green </FONT>
<FONT COLOR=GREEN FACE=ARIAL> My name is Arial and I am green </FONT>
```

You should get in the habit of always including the quotation marks, however, because they can make a difference in a few rare cases.

> **NOTE**
>
> When does the presence or absence of quotation marks around the values of attributes make a difference? In two cases.
>
> *continues*

continued

First, when you need to include spaces in an attribute's value, you must use quotation marks. Consider the following example:

```
<INPUT TYPE=SUBMIT VALUE=Submit Me!>
```

If you want the words `Submit Me!` rather than the single word `Submit` to appear on this form button, you need to place quotation marks around the expression like this:

```
<INPUT TYPE=SUBMIT VALUE="Submit Me!">
```

The second case concerns possible ambiguities that could arise with the ASP script tag. For example, the following innocent-looking piece of HTML code would be misinterpreted by ASP:

```
<HR WIDTH=100%>
```

The problem is that the expression `%>` has a special meaning for ASP. The expression `%>` would be interpreted by ASP as the tag that's used for ending a server-side script. Just surround the attribute value in quotation marks and the problem goes away:

```
<HR WIDTH="100%">
```

HTML tags are not case-sensitive. This means that you can type the characters that make up an HTML tag without worrying about whether they are uppercase or lowercase. The following example displays the text in exactly the same way as the examples shown earlier:

```
<FoNt FaCe="Arial" cOLor="GREeN"> My name is Arial and I am green </fOnT>
```

Of course, the case of the text contained within the HTML tag *does* matter. If you type `MY NAME IS ARIAL AND I AM GREEN`, all in uppercase, the browser will display the text in uppercase.

In HTML, one space is the same as two or twenty. Web browsers ignore extra spaces in HTML files. This is a difficult aspect of HTML for beginners to grasp. Consider the following fragment of HTML:

```
<B> I am compact </B>
<B> I    am    spread    all    the    way    across    the    page    </B>
```

The second sentence is lying. When displayed in a Web browser, both sentences appear without any extra spaces, like this:

I am compact I am spread all the way across the page

Take a look at Figure 5.1 to see it in the Netscape browser.

Of course, to say that one space is as good as two or twenty doesn't mean that the initial space is without importance. You can make the first sentence of the preceding lines into a liar by adding extra spaces. Consider this HTML fragment:

```
<B> I a m com pact </B>
```

FIGURE 5.1.

Web browsers ignore extra spaces in HTML files.

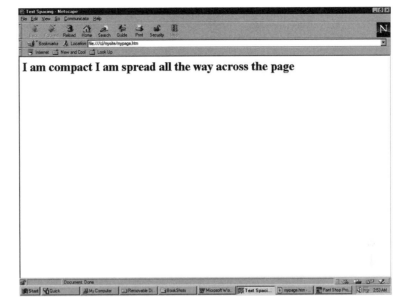

When it's displayed in a browser, you'll get something like this (see Figure 5.2):

`I a m com pact`

FIGURE 5.2.

Web browsers don't ignore all spaces in HTML files.

Notice the extra spaces. They appear exactly where you would expect them to appear. If you added even more spaces immediately following these spaces, however, the additional spaces would be ignored.

Web browsers also ignore carriage returns and tab characters in HTML files. You can include as many blank lines and tab characters in an HTML file as you like; the browser will never display them to the world. However, you should avoid using tab characters because, in a future version of HTML, they may be given a special meaning.

The fact that Web browsers ignore extra spaces and carriage returns is useful for making your HTML files more readable. You can feel free to format your HTML file with spaces and blank lines in a way that makes the file easy for you to understand.

The HTML Standard

In the best of all possible worlds, every Web browser would display every HTML file in exactly the same way. Ideally, every HTML tag should have exactly the same effect when interpreted by any browser on any computer. Sadly, however, our actual world has three defects.

First, HTML is an evolving standard. Over time, more and more HTML tags have been added to the official specifications for HTML. For example, the <FONT> tag is an example of a new HTML tag. Older browsers will fail to understand it and will simply ignore it.

When creating your Web pages, you can't expect everyone in the world to be using a Web browser that's compatible with the latest official HTML standards. For example, the version of the Microsoft browser that was included with the original version of Windows 95 (Microsoft Internet Explorer 2.0) can't properly interpret all the HTML tags included in the latest official HTML specification. People using this browser—and no doubt there are quite a few—see a less interesting version of the Web. You must always keep these unfortunate people with early versions of Web browsers in mind when you design your Web pages.

> **NOTE**
>
> The World Wide Web Consortium (W3C) is the official keeper of standards for HTML. At the time of this writing, the standard endorsed is HTML version 3.2. HTML is evolving very rapidly, however, so expect a new version of HTML to become the standard soon. To find out the latest version of the official HTML standard, visit the W3C Web site at `http://www.w3.org`.

Even if everyone owned a browser that could interpret the latest official version of HTML, however, a problem would still exist. Microsoft and Netscape keep ignoring Web standards. With each new version of their Web browsers, they add their own HTML tags.

Malevolence is not their motivation. Both Microsoft and Netscape want to dominate the browser market, and the Web browser that will dominate will be the one that can display the most HTML tags. The end result of this competition to control the browser market is tags that are browser-specific and not part of the official HTML specification. Some HTML tags work only with Netscape Navigator; some work only with Internet Explorer. This fact makes things more difficult for the designer of Web pages.

Finally, even if everyone in the world used the latest version of Netscape Navigator and no other browser to view Web pages, there still would be a problem. Every computer is unique. Computers use different operating systems and have different screen display characteristics. If you view the same Web page with the same version of Netscape on a UNIX computer and on a Windows computer, you'll see a number of subtle differences in the way the Web page appears. The background colors of text boxes, as one example, will appear different when viewed on the two computers. This is an unavoidable difference caused by the method by which the two operating systems draw screen elements.

A much more significant difference concerns the display types of different computers. In theory, Web pages should display the same way on a screen of any size. In practice, however, if your computer monitor has a higher resolution than mine, you and I will see the Web in different ways. Consider all the different types of computer displays in the world. Some people are browsing the Web using large 30-inch monitors, while some people are viewing the very same Web pages on the LCD screens of hand-held computers. A Web page that fits on one screen simply won't fit on the other.

Furthermore, computer monitors often display colors in different ways. Some monitors display only 256 colors; others can display over 3 million. Also, people have adjusted their individual monitors to display the same colors with different tints. Even if you own the same brand of monitor as I do, you probably have it adjusted with different settings than mine. Finally, Macintosh computers display colors in a very different way than Windows computers.

So three general problems prevent Web pages from being displayed in the same way in all browsers and on all computers:

- Older browsers can't interpret all the HTML tags that are part of the latest official HTML standard.
- Netscape and Microsoft have introduced their own browser-specific tags.
- Computers using different operating systems and monitors display the same Web pages in different ways.

What should a good Web designer do? Presumably, if you have gone to all the time and effort to design a Web page, you want everyone in the world to be able to see it the same way as you do. With the problems just discussed in mind, how can you guarantee this? The short answer is that you can't.

Some fanatical purists out there refuse to use *any* HTML tags except those supported by very early versions of Web browsers. They refuse to use any tags that aren't part of the official HTML standard, including any Netscape- or Microsoft-specific tags. Although this approach to Web design may provide you with a greater psychological sense of control, it also can result in boring Web pages.

No easy answer exists to the question of which HTML tags to use. You should consider the target audience of the Web site you plan to create and the browsers that your intended audience will most likely be using. You should also decide on the HTML tags that you can't live without. After reading the next few chapters, you'll have a better understanding of the tradeoffs involved in using different HTML tags.

In general, it's usually a good idea to design Web pages that will function on the greatest number of browsers. The most popular browsers, by far, are Netscape Navigator, Internet Explorer, and the America Online browser. If you design your Web pages to display correctly on recent versions of these browsers, you're probably pretty safe.

Most monitors have a horizontal display of at least 640 pixels. Some Web pages are optimized for this screen resolution; other Web pages won't appear correctly unless displayed on screens with a horizontal resolution of no less than 800 pixels. Again, you must decide on your intended audience, and predict the type of monitor that they'll most likely be using.

Creating a Basic Web Page

The best way to learn how to create Web pages with HTML is to start with a very simple page. The following listing includes the bare minimum of HTML needed to create a functional Web page:

```
<TITLE>Minimal Web Page</TITLE>
Hello World!
```

To create this HTML file, start the Windows program Notepad and enter these two lines of text. After entering the text, save the file you've created on your local hard drive with the name mypage.htm. Next, start your favorite Web browser (for example, Netscape Navigator or Internet Explorer) and type the full path of the file in the address bar of the Web browser. For example, if you saved the HTML file as c:\mypage.htm, you can load the file into your Web browser by typing the text **c:\mypage.htm** in the address bar. You should see the Web page shown in Figure 5.3.

No one would deny that this is a very boring Web page. All that appears is the text Hello World! However, the process of creating it does illustrate a number of important points.

First, notice that you didn't need to be connected to the Internet to create the HTML page or to view the resulting Web page in your Web browser. Web browsers work just as well with files residing on your local hard drive as they do with files residing anywhere else on the Internet. A Web browser will attempt to interpret any page you load into it, without caring about where the page came from.

FIGURE 5.3.
Your first HTML file!

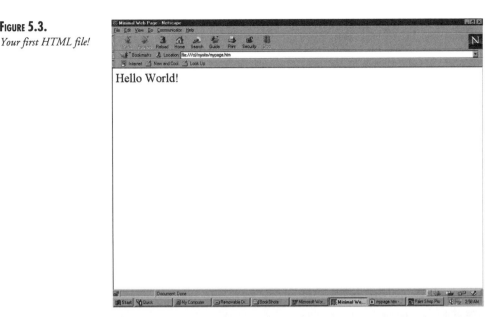

> **NOTE**
>
> Technically, our minimal Web page is incomplete. According to the official reference specification for HTML, every HTML file must start with a <!DOCTYPE> declaration tag that identifies the version of HTML being used. This HTML tag doesn't affect the page, however, and most Web authors simply leave it out (due to laziness). See Appendix D, "Quick HTML Reference," for more information on how to use this tag.

Second, notice the name of the file you created. You named the file mypage.htm. All HTML files must end with the extension .htm or .html. This book uses the convention of saving files with the .htm extension. You can save an HTML file with almost any name you like, as long as you don't use spaces in the name.

Third, notice the words <TITLE> and </TITLE> that appear in the first line of the HTML listing. Now, look at the line at the very top of your Web browser. You should see the text Minimal Web Page. This is the text that you typed between the container tags <TITLE> and </TITLE>. The <TITLE> tag does just what the name implies—the tag provides your Web page with a title. This title is used when people bookmark your Web page and search engines index your Web site (two things you hope will happen often).

Most HTML files are a little more complex than the one just discussed. Consider the HTML listing that's shown on the following page.

5

BASIC HTML

```
<HTML>
<HEAD>
<TITLE> Less Minimal </TITLE>
</HEAD>
<BODY>
Hello World!
</BODY>
</HTML>
```

This listing introduces three additional HTML tags: the <HTML>, <HEAD>, and <BODY> tags. If you display this HTML file in a browser, you see the same thing as in the previous example. So what do these three new tags do? The only purpose of these tags is to act as containers for other tags.

The <HTML> container tag identifies the file as a whole as an HTML file. It contains the HTML file. Officially, this tag isn't really necessary, but you should always include an <HTML> tag at the beginning of your HTML file and a </HTML> tag at the end to ensure compatibility with older browsers.

The <HEAD> container tag contains all the HTML tags that occur in the head of your HTML file. HTML tags that occur in the head of your HTML file are not displayed in the main screen area of a Web browser. For example, the text contained between the <TITLE> and </TITLE> tags appears on a Web browser's title bar and not on the Web page itself.

The <BODY> tag contains the main body of your HTML file. All the text and all the HTML tags that actually will be displayed in your Web page should be contained here. For example, Hello World! is contained here, because you want this sentence to be displayed. The bulk of your HTML page is almost invariably contained between the <BODY> and </BODY> tags.

Before ending this section, one final tag should be discussed. It's often useful to add comments to your HTML files that aren't displayed in the browser. For example, you might want to include a comment at the top of your HTML file describing the purpose of the file, so in the future you can remember why you made it. Here's an example of an HTML file with some comments added:

```
<!-- I am ignored by everybody -->
<HTML>
<HEAD>
<TITLE> Commented </TITLE>
</HEAD>
<BODY>
<!-- I am a three line comment which
     explains that this document displays
     the text 'Hello World!'   -->
Hello World!
</BODY>
</HTML>
```

The sentence I am ignored by everybody will never appear in a browser because it's enclosed in the comment tags (`<!--` and `-->`).

> **CAUTION**
>
> Don't ever put genuinely private information in a comment tag, because people can always view your comments by using the View Source command on their browsers.

You can place comments anywhere in an HTML file, and your comments can span multiple lines. When your HTML files begin to get very large, it's usually a good idea to start adding plenty of comments to label what you're doing in various sections of your file. (Trust me, some day you'll forget what you were doing.)

Adding Color to Your Web Page

Many of the HTML tags discussed in this chapter have attributes that can be set to different colors. For example, by default the background color of your Web page is either gray (if you're using Internet Explorer) or white (Netscape Navigator). Suppose you want to change this background color to another color of your own choosing. Here's an example of how to do it:

```
<HTML>
<HEAD>
<TITLE> Background Color </TITLE>
</HEAD>
<BODY BGCOLOR="lime">
Hello World!
</BODY>
</HTML>
```

When this HTML file is displayed in a Web browser, the background color of the Web page will be lime green. Notice that you changed the color of your Web page by including the BGCOLOR attribute of the <BODY> tag.

According to the official HTML specification, you can use any of the colors in Table 5.1 when specifying any HTML tag's color attribute.

Table 5.1. Color names and their RGB values.

Color	RGB Value
Aqua	#00FFFF
Black	#000000
Blue	#0000FF
Fuchsia	#FF00FF
Gray	#808080

continues

5

BASIC HTML

Table 5.1. continued

Color	RGB Value
Green	#008000
Lime	#00FF00
Maroon	#800000
Navy	#000080
Olive	#808000
Purple	#800080
Red	#FF0000
Silver	#C0C0C0
Teal	#008080
White	#FFFFFF
Yellow	#FFFF00

You should notice two odd things about this table of colors. First, they're a strange selection of colors. These colors were chosen for historical reasons—they were the colors supported by early Windows machines that had a VGA graphics card. In reality, if you're willing to violate the official HTML specification, you're not limited to these color names. Recent versions of both Netscape Navigator and Internet Explorer recognize dozens of color names. (For a list of these colors, see Appendix D.)

The second odd feature of this color table concerns the strange numbers that appear after each color. Colors can be represented either by name or by RGB value. If you want to guarantee that every browser will be able to display the colors you select, you should specify colors using their RGB values instead of their names.

NOTE

Computers represent each color internally by three numbers—the color's red, green, and blue values (the RGB value). Each of these numbers can take a value between 0 and 255. The color black, for example, is represented by all zeros, because black is the absence of any red, green, or blue. If you want the background color of your Web page to appear in the color black, you can specify the BGCOLOR attribute like this:

```
<BODY BGCOLOR="#000000">
```

In this example, the first two zeros are the color's red value, the second two zeros are the color's green value, and the last two zeros represent the color's blue value. The number sign (#) tells the browser that you're specifying the color with a number rather than by name.

What makes things slightly more complicated is that computers think using the hexadecimal number system rather than the decimal system. Even though both computers and humans have the same number of numbers, computers use 6 more numerals to represent them. So, for a computer, the number 16 is represented by the numeral F and the number 255 is represented by the numeral FF. To create a white background, you do it like this:

```
<BODY BGCOLOR="#FFFFFF">
```

Using RGB values, you can represent 16,777,216 colors (over 16 million colors). Of course, the fact that you can represent all these colors doesn't mean that every computer monitor can display every one of them. Some monitors are physically capable of displaying only 256 colors (or less).

Basic Page Formatting with HTML

This section explains how to control the spacing and general layout of the text that appears in a Web page. You learn how to break a line of text into more than one line, and how to align text within the browser window. Finally, you learn how to break text apart by using horizontal rules.

Creating New Lines of Text

As discussed earlier, browsers ignore extra spaces and carriage returns in HTML files. To a browser, one space is as good as two or twenty. Consider the following listing:

```
<HTML>
<HEAD>
<TITLE> Two Lines of Text </TITLE>
</HEAD>
<BODY>

I am the first line of text.
I am the second line of text.

</BODY>
</HTML>
```

If you display this HTML code in a Web browser, you won't see what you expect. The browser ignores the carriage return separating the two lines of text, and you see the following:

```
I am the first line of text. I am the second line of text.
```

So how do you introduce line breaks into your Web page? An HTML tag exists specifically for this purpose. The <BR> tag is used for breaking a line of text, as in the following example (continued on the next page):

```
<HTML>
<HEAD>
<TITLE> Two Lines of Text </TITLE>
</HEAD>
<BODY>
```

```
I am the first line of text.<BR>
I am the second line of text.

</BODY>
</HTML>
```

A Web browser interprets this HTML code in the way you expected from the earlier example—the two lines of text appear on separate lines. Notice that the <BR> tag isn't a container tag. In other words, there's no such thing as the </BR> tag; it doesn't make sense to specify when a line break ends (they just happen without any lingering effects).

Creating New Paragraphs

More than one way is available to break a line of text. You can also use the <P> tag to achieve this purpose. The <P> tag is called the *paragraph tag* because it's used to create paragraphs, as in the following examples:

```
<HTML>
<HEAD>
<TITLE> Two Lines of Text </TITLE>
</HEAD>
<BODY>

    I am the first line of text.<P>
    I am the second line of text.

<P> I am the first line of text.</P>
<P> I am the second line of text. </P>

</BODY>
</HTML>
```

The first <P> tag in this listing has almost the same effect as the <BR> tag used in the earlier example. It separates the first two lines of text, but with a little more space between the lines than created by the <BR> tag. It creates a new paragraph, but the paragraph can contain as little text as you want.

The second pair of sentences also appear on two different lines when interpreted by a Web browser. However, notice that the <P> tag is being used as a container tag in this case. The <P> tag can be treated as either a container tag or in the same way as a non-container tag (such as <BR>). When used to break lines of text into different paragraphs, most Web authors simply leave out the closing </P> tag.

> **NOTE**
>
> In some cases, the ending tag </P> is required. For example, if you are using the ALIGN attribute or using the <P> tag with cascading style sheets, you need to mark both the beginning and end of a paragraph. See the next section for more information on using the <P> tag to align text. See Chapter 7, "Advanced HTML," for more information on cascading style sheets.

Aligning Text

The <P> tag has a useful attribute. You can use the <P> tag to align text at the left, center, or right side of a screen. The alignment attribute is illustrated in the following HTML listing:

```
<HTML>
<HEAD>
<TITLE> Aligned Text </TITLE>
</HEAD>
<BODY>

<P ALIGN="LEFT"> I am left.</P>
<P ALIGN="CENTER"> I am center. </P>
<P ALIGN="RIGHT"> I am right. </P>

</BODY>
</HTML>
```

By default, the <P> tag aligns text at the left side of the screen, so you would normally never need to use <P ALIGN="LEFT"> in an HTML file.

You should be warned that not all browsers recognize the ALIGN attribute of the <P> tag. Versions of Netscape Navigator and Internet Explorer before version 3.0 simply ignore this attribute and align all text at the left. If you want to center text using earlier versions of these browsers, you need to use the <CENTER> tag. There is no simple way to right-align text without the <P> tag.

Creating Preformatted Text

Another HTML tag that you can use to position text is the <PRE> tag. Suppose you have some text that you want to format precisely, and you want every space to appear exactly as you typed it. Normally, HTML ignores precise spatial formatting, but you can get a Web browser to recognize your spaces. There are better and worse ways to do this. Here's an example of one of the worst:

```
<HTML>
<HEAD>
<TITLE> Three Lines of Text </TITLE>
</HEAD>
<BODY>

<PRE>
I am the first line.
  I am the second line.
    I am the third line.
</PRE>

</BODY>
</HTML>
```

The <PRE> tag is used to contain preformatted text. Text that occurs within this tag will appear in a browser precisely as you type it, spaces and all. This would seem to be a very useful tag, and in some cases it is. However, most of the time Web authors don't use it because of some of the tag's significant drawbacks.

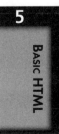

First, when the text that occurs in the <PRE> tag is displayed in a browser, the browser displays it with an ugly fixed-pitch font. Your text won't be pleasant to read. Also, unlike other text that occurs in an HTML file, text contained in the <PRE> tag won't wrap to a new line. A long line of preformatted text will simply go off the right edge of the browser screen.

The <PRE> tag violates the basic reasoning behind HTML. The language was designed to allow people to view Web pages on computers with different screens of any size. While in practice this design goal usually doesn't work—because Web pages are usually optimized for displays with particular screen dimensions—the <PRE> tag *guarantees* that it won't work. So, if you can, try to avoid the <PRE> tag. People using monitors with small screen resolutions will thank you.

Creating Horizontal Rules

The final tag considered in this section is the <HR> tag. It's used to create horizontal rules—lines that can be used to break up the text on a screen. Following is an example of how this tag is used:

```
<HTML>
<HEAD>
<TITLE> Horizontal Rule </TITLE>
</HEAD>
<BODY>

I am the first line of text.
<HR>
I am the second line of text

</BODY>
</HTML>
```

When this HTML code is displayed in a browser, a line separates the first and second lines of text (see Figure 5.4).

FIGURE 5.4.

Text separated by a horizontal rule.

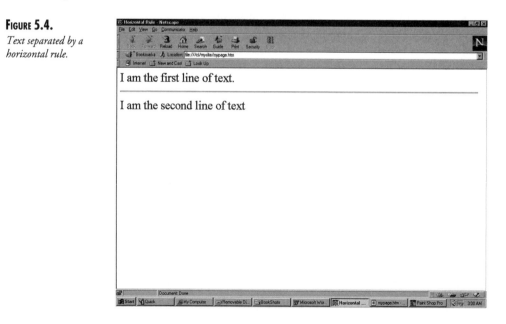

The <HR> tag has a number of useful attributes. (For a complete list of attributes, see Appendix D.) As in the case of the <P> tag, you can use the ALIGN attribute to align a horizontal rule at the left, center, or right side of the screen. You can also specify the amount of screen width that the horizontal rule occupies, by setting the WIDTH attribute.

When you specify the value of the WIDTH attribute, you can specify the width in pixels or as a percentage of the screen. Consider the following HTML listing:

```
<HTML>
<HEAD>
<TITLE> Horizontal Rules </TITLE>
</HEAD>
<BODY>

<HR WIDTH="640">
<HR WIDTH="100%">

</BODY>
</HTML>
```

If you display this HTML file on a computer with a horizontal screen resolution of 640 pixels (a typical screen resolution for a low-end Windows computer), the two horizontal rules appear to be almost the same width. But if you display the very same HTML file on a computer with a horizontal screen resolution of 1024, the first line appears significantly shorter than the second. Most of the time, it makes much more sense to use percentages rather than precise pixel values (when given the choice).

Basic Text Formatting with HTML

A Web page containing only plain text would be boring. To create a more attractive page, you need to control such things as the size, color, and typeface of the text that you display. In this section, you learn how to control these features.

Working with Fonts

The <FONT> tag was briefly discussed earlier in this chapter. The <FONT> tag has three attributes: SIZE, COLOR, and FACE. The following example uses the SIZE attribute:

```
<HTML>
<HEAD>
<TITLE> Font Sizes </TITLE>
</HEAD>
<BODY>
<FONT SIZE=1> I am small. </FONT>
<P>
<FONT SIZE=7> I am big! </FONT>
<P>
<FONT SIZE=+1> I am a little bigger than the base font </FONT>
<P>
<FONT SIZE=-1> I am a little smaller than the base font </FONT>
</BODY>
</HTML>
```

You specify the size of a font by setting the SIZE attribute to a number between 1 and 7, in which 1 is the smallest size and 7 is the largest. This is a way to provide absolute sizes, but you can also provide relative sizes. If you look closely at the third example of the SIZE attribute in this listing, you'll see that the value of the SIZE attribute is set to +1. This tells the browser to make the font one size larger than the base font.

The size of the base font is determined by the <BASEFONT> HTML tag. You're under no obligation to use this tag, however. If you leave it out, as in this example, the base font will be set by the browser.

The <BASEFONT> tag works exactly like the <FONT> tag, except that it applies to the document as a whole. The <BASEFONT> tag should be used only once in a document, and should appear before any <FONT> tags. Following is an example of how this tag is used:

```
<HTML>
<HEAD>
<TITLE> Base Font </TITLE>
</HEAD>
<BODY>
<BASEFONT SIZE=6>
I am big.
<P>
<FONT SIZE=+1> I am bigger! </FONT>
</BODY>
</HTML>
```

The sentence I am big. appears in the size specified by the <BASEFONT> tag, so its size is 6. The sentence I am bigger! appears one size larger than the base font, so its size is 7.

You can't guarantee that your fonts will appear in the absolute sizes that you specify. The size of the fonts that appear in a browser can be set by the user of a browser, and the user has the final word. So, when your Web page is displayed in a browser, everything may appear larger or smaller than you expect.

You can control the color of the text that appears in your Web documents by specifying the value of the COLOR attribute of the <FONT> tag, as in this example:

```
<HTML>
<HEAD>
<TITLE> Color Fonts </TITLE>
</HEAD>
<BODY>
<FONT COLOR="GREEN"> I am green. </FONT>
<P>
<FONT COLOR="RED"> I am red. </FONT>
</BODY>
</HTML>
```

The first sentence in this example appears in green and the second sentence appears in red. Using color names is a very easy way to specify the color of fonts. However, to guarantee compatibility with all browsers, you should use RGB colors instead. (See Appendix D for a full list of colors and RGB color codes.)

The <FONT> tag has one more useful attribute. By using the FACE attribute, you can specify a font's typeface. Here's an example of how to do it:

```
<HTML>
<HEAD>
<TITLE> Font Face </TITLE>
</HEAD>
<BODY>

<FONT FACE="Courier"> I am Courier </FONT>
<P>
<FONT FACE="Arial,Courier">  I am Arial, but if that does not work,
   I am Courier </FONT>

</BODY>
</HTML>
```

When this HTML file is displayed in a browser, the first sentence is displayed in the Courier typeface and the second sentence in the Arial typeface.

Well, maybe.

The browser will do the best it can with the computer on which it's running. Not all computers have the same typefaces. For example, if the computer doesn't have the Arial typeface, the browser attempts to use the next typeface specified in the FACE attribute. In this example, the browser uses the Courier typeface instead. You can list as many alternative typefaces as you want.

Personally, I use the <FONT> tag quite often. However, you should be warned that it has some serious drawbacks. When using it, be aware of issues of both backward and forward compatibility.

The <FONT> tag is relatively new. It won't work on older browsers. For example, although Netscape Navigator version 2.0 understands the SIZE and COLOR attributes of the <FONT> tag, it doesn't understand the FACE attribute. Other browsers fail to interpret the <FONT> tag at all.

Also, while the <FONT> tag is part of the current official HTML specification, the FACE attribute isn't. Furthermore, the <FONT> tag as a whole may be dropped from the official HTML specification in the near future. All the functions of the <FONT> tag can be replaced by using cascading style sheets (explained in Chapter 7). Keep these compatibility issues in mind when using this very useful tag.

Creating Big and Small Text

If you don't want to use the <FONT> tag to control the size of your text, you can use the <BIG> and <SMALL> tags to make your text big or small. In case you haven't guessed, the <BIG> tag makes your text slightly bigger than the normal size, and the <SMALL> tag makes your text slightly smaller, as in the following example.

```
<HTML>
<HEAD>
<TITLE> Big and Small </TITLE>
</HEAD>
<BODY>

<BIG>  How big of you. </BIG>
<P>
<SMALL>  How small of you. </SMALL>

</BODY>
</HTML>
```

Working with Headings

Headings are useful for breaking up paragraphs of text into smaller sections. They also can be used to control the size of the text that appears in your Web page (as yet another alternative to using the SIZE attribute of the <FONT> tag). Following are some examples of headings using the <H> tag:

```
<HTML>
<HEAD>
<TITLE> Headings </TITLE>
</HEAD>
<BODY>
<H6> I am a small heading </H6>
<H4> I am a medium heading </H4>
<H1> I am a large heading </H1>
</BODY>
</HTML>
```

You specify headings of different sizes by assigning different numbers to the headings. There are six different levels of headings. Text contained within an <H1> tag, for example, would appear very large in a browser; text within the <H6> tag would appear very small.

Notice that you don't need to use the <P> tag to break up the sentences into separate lines. The first text that appears outside an <H> container automatically appears on a new line. Therefore, a <P> tag is not required.

Technically, the <H> tags specify the importance of the contained text, rather than its size. In theory, a browser could represent the importance of a heading in a different way than size (using brighter and darker colors, for instance). However, in practice, every browser that I have ever used has interpreted <H> tags as size tags.

Bold, Italic, Underlined, and Strikethrough Text

The <B> tags, as mentioned earlier, make text bold. To make text italic, contain the text in the <I> tags. You can underline text by using the <U> tags. Finally, if you want strikethrough text (text that appears with a line through it), use the <STRIKE> or <S> tags. Here are some examples (Figure 5.5 shows how this code would appear in a browser):

```
<HTML>
<HEAD>
<TITLE> Text Formatting </TITLE>
```

```
</HEAD>
<BODY>

<B> To boldly go where no.... </B>
<P>
<I> Really? Really? Are you sure? </I>
<P>
<U> I am not a hypertext link. </U>
<P>
<S> Strike One! </S>
<P>
<STRIKE> Strike Two! </STRIKE>

</BODY>
</HTML>
```

FIGURE 5.5.

Bold, italicized, underlined, and strikethrough text.

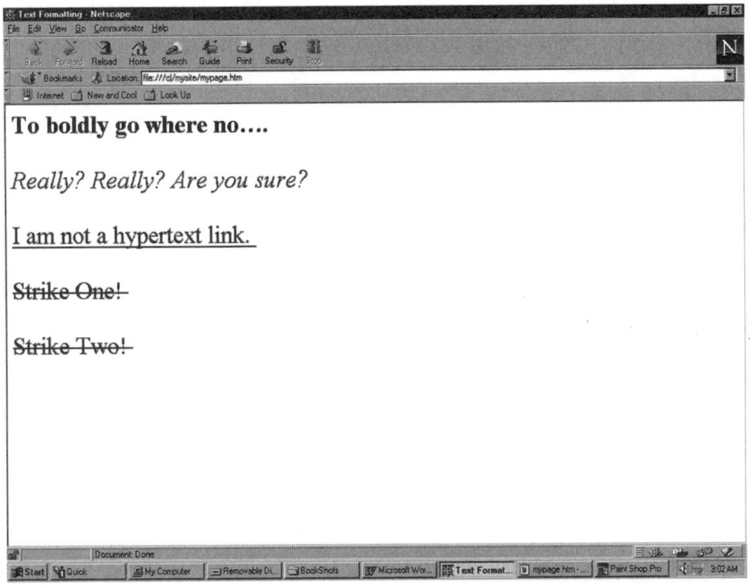

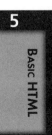

The `<STRIKE>` tag is being phased out in favor of the `<S>` tag. If you want to maintain compatibility with older browsers, use the `<STRIKE>` tag. If you want to guarantee that your page will appear properly in the future, use the `<S>` tag.

NOTE

It's morally wrong for you to use the `<U>` tag. Please never use it in your HTML documents—underlined text on a Web page normally means that the text is a hypertext link. Using the `<U>` tag can only lead to confusion. If you want to emphasize text, use the `<I>` tag instead.

5

BASIC HTML

Superscripts and Subscripts

On rare occasions, you may need to create superscript and subscript text (text that appears above and below the normal text line, such as $E=mc^2$ and H_2O). You can do this with the <SUP> and <SUB> container tags. Here's an example of how these two tags work:

```
<HTML>
<HEAD>
<TITLE> Superscript and Subscript </TITLE>
</HEAD>
<BODY>

<SUP> I'm feeling high. </SUP>
<P>
<SUB> I'm feeling low. </SUB>

</BODY>
</HTML>
```

Blinking Text

No single HTML tag is as universally reviled as the <BLINK> tag. People will hit their browser's Back button the moment they lay eyes on it. The only browser that supports this tag is Netscape Navigator. It isn't part of the official HTML 3.2 Reference Specification, and Microsoft refused to support it in Internet Explorer. With great reluctance, here's an example of the <BLINK> tag:

```
<HTML>
<HEAD>
<TITLE> Blinking Text </TITLE>
</HEAD>
<BODY>

<BLINK> Blink, blink </BLINK>

</BODY>
</HTML>
```

Use this tag with great caution if you want people ever to return to your Web site.

Adding Special Characters

Sometimes you need more characters than your keyboard can produce. For example, you may need to include the copyright and trademark symbols, or use foreign accent symbols. You can include these special characters in your Web pages by using special character codes, as in the following examples (see Figure 5.6):

```
<HTML>
<HEAD>
<TITLE> Special Characters </TITLE>
</HEAD>
<BODY>

I am copyrighted &copy;
<P>
```

```
I am a registered trademark &reg;
<P>
My name is Kurt G&ouml;del
</BODY>
</HTML>
```

FIGURE 5.6.

The copyright, registered trademark, and umlaut characters.

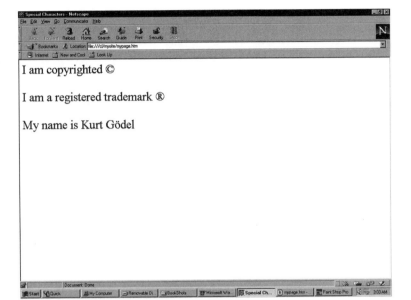

In this listing, the expression © creates the copyright symbol, the expression ® creates the registered trademark symbol, and the expression ö creates the German umlaut symbol over the lowercase letter *o* (for a complete list of these special characters, see Appendix D).

When using these special character expressions, you need to be careful about typing all the characters in lowercase. Using Netscape Navigator (versions 3 and 4), for example, the expression &Copy; won't create the copyright symbol, but instead will display the actual code for the symbol.

Another practical application of these special characters is in creating the greater-than and less-than symbols (< and >). You may wonder why you need special characters for these symbols, since they appear on your keyboard. The problem is that if you include these characters in your HTML files, the browser will attempt to interpret them as HTML tags rather than actual characters. For this reason, you need to use special characters as shown in the following code lines (continued on the next page):

```
<HTML>
<HEAD>
<TITLE> Special Characters </TITLE>
</HEAD>
```

5

BASIC HTML

```
<BODY>

HTML Lesson 1:
<P>
How to use the &lt;BR&gt; tag.

</BODY>
</HTML>
```

In this example, you use the < and > expressions to create the less-than and greater-than signs (see Figure 5.7). If you want to mention an HTML tag in your Web page rather than use it, you need to use these two special expressions.

FIGURE 5.7.

Mentioning HTML tags.

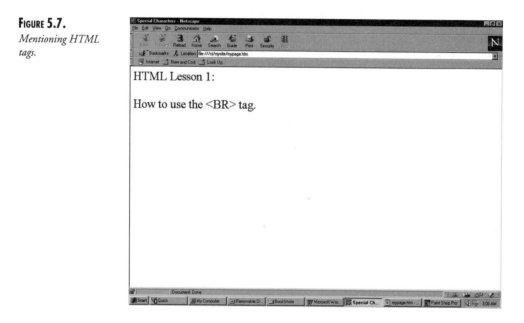

One final special character worth mentioning is the non-breaking space character. Suppose you want to indent the first sentence in a paragraph. One way to do this would be to use the special expression . Here's an example:

```
<HTML>
<HEAD>
<TITLE> Creating Space </TITLE>
</HEAD>
<BODY>
     I am the first sentence in this paragraph
and I am indented.<BR>
I am the second sentence and I am flush left.
</BODY>
</HTML>
```

By placing five non-breaking space characters in a row, you can create an indentation of five characters.

Be cautious in using special characters. Although they all work in recent browsers, when you try to use them with a browser that doesn't understand them you get *worse* than the normal results. Normally, when a browser doesn't understand an HTML tag, it just ignores it without displaying it. However, because these special characters aren't really HTML tags, when a browser doesn't understand them it displays the actual codes on the screen. This looks particularly ugly.

Linking HTML Pages

The World Wide Web would not be a Web if not for the existence of *hypertext links*. Hypertext links enable you to link one HTML document to another. They allow you to move from one Web page to another with the effortlessness of a single mouse click. In this section, you learn how to link your Web pages into the global Web. However, first you need to understand how Internet addresses work.

Understanding Internet Addresses

You can visit the HotWired Web site by typing `http://www.hotwired.com` into the address bar of your Web browser. When you type `http://www.hotwired.com`, you're typing a *Uniform Resource Locator* (*URL*). URLs can be thought of as addresses for Web pages, although they can be addresses for many other types of files as well.

> **NOTE**
>
> Typically, *URL* is pronounced "You are Elle," and not *earl*.

For the purposes of this discussion, a URL has three important parts.

The first part of the URL tells the browser what type of *protocol* you want to use to access whatever you're trying to get over the Internet. When using a Web browser, you almost always use the Hypertext Transfer Protocol (HTTP), because normally you're retrieving HTML documents. HTTP is a protocol for transferring HTML files from one computer to another.

The second part of the URL provides the *domain name* of the resource you're attempting to access. For example, because HotWired is registered on the Internet with the domain name `www.hotwired.com`, you can transfer the home page of this Web site to your computer by typing `http://www.hotwired.com` into the address bar of your browser.

However, the HotWired Web site has more than one Web page. In fact, most commercial Web sites have dozens or hundreds of Web pages, organized into various subdirectories. If you need to access a particular Web page on the HotWired Web site other than the home page, you need to provide additional address information. In the third part of the URL, you specify the location of the particular HTML file that you're interested in retrieving.

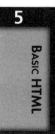

Suppose you want to access a file called new.htm from the HotWired Web site. In that case, you could type **http://www.hotwired.com/new.htm** in the address bar of the browser to retrieve that particular HTML file. The last part of this URL specifies the particular HTML file that you're interested in retrieving.

Usually, HTML files are organized on a Web site in subdirectories. For example, the HotWired Web site might have two subdirectories called new and old, each containing multiple HTML files. To access an HTML file called new.htm in the new subdirectory, you would type the address **http://www.hotwired.com/new/new.htm**. If this file was located in the old subdirectory, you would type **http://www.hotwired.com/old/new.htm**. As you can see, Internet addresses can quickly become very long. This is one of the main reasons why hypertext links are so useful.

Linking Between Web Sites

To link your Web page to any other page on the World Wide Web, you use something called a *hypertext anchor*. To create a hypertext anchor, you use the <A> HTML tag. Here's an example of how you would link a Web page to the HotWired Web site:

```
<HTML>
<HEAD>
<TITLE> Inter-site Anchor </TITLE>
</HEAD>
<BODY>

<A HREF="http://www.hotwired.com"> HotWired </A>

</BODY>
</HTML>
```

Notice that the <A> tag is a container tag. The text that it contains becomes a hypertext link. In this example, the text HotWired is displayed in a browser with an underline. This tells the viewer of the page that the text is a hypertext link. If you click the word HotWired, the home page of the HotWired Web site is loaded into your browser.

You supply the Web address as the value of the HREF attribute of the <A> tag. This address can be the URL of any page on any Web site in the world. You can link your Web page as easily to a Web site located in Hong Kong as to a Web site located in California.

NOTE

By convention, you don't need to ask permission from the owner of a Web site to add a hypertext link from your Web site to theirs. Most Webmasters want as much Web traffic as they can get. By providing links from your site to theirs, you increase the number of potential users of their Web site.

An HTML file can have as many hypertext links as you want. For example, if you want a Web page that displays links to some major Internet search engines, you could use the following HTML file:

```
<HTML>
<HEAD>
<TITLE> Inter-site Anchor </TITLE>
</HEAD>
<BODY>

<A HREF="http://www.yahoo.com"> Yahoo </A>
<P>
<A HREF="http://altavista.digital.com">Alta Vista</A>
<P>
<A HREF="http://www.excite.com">Excite</A>

</BODY>
</HTML>
```

Linking Within a Web Site

Your Web site probably will have more than one page, and you'll want the users of your Web site to be able to move easily from one page to another. To allow this, you need to add hypertext anchors that link your Web site's pages together. You create links within your Web site in the same way that you create links between Web sites. Listings 5.1 and 5.2 show two HTML files, named `this.htm` and `that.htm`, respectively, that are linked to one another by using the <A> tag.

Listing 5.1. Listing for `this.htm`.

```
<!-- This -->
<HTML>
<HEAD>
<TITLE> Inter-site Anchor </TITLE>
</HEAD>
<BODY>

<A HREF="that.htm"> That </A>

</BODY>
</HTML>
```

Listing 5.2. Listing for `that.htm`.

```
<!-- That -->
<HTML>
<HEAD>
<TITLE> Inter-site Anchor </TITLE>
</HEAD>
<BODY>
```

continues

5

BASIC HTML

Listing 5.2. continued

```
<A HREF="this.htm"> This </A>

</BODY>
</HTML>
```

If you save these two files in the same directory with the names this.htm and that.htm, you can click That to get to This and This to get to That.

Notice the values given to the HREF attributes of the <A> tags. These are not full Internet addresses, as they merely provide the name of an HTML file without specifying a protocol or a domain name. A full Internet address is called an *absolute URL*; a partial address, as in this example, is called a *relative URL*.

You can always use an absolute URL to specify an HTML file. However, if you're linking to an HTML file located on the same computer or Web site, it's better to use a relative address. Not only are relative URL addresses easier to type, they also make it easier to move your HTML files into new subdirectories if you need to do this at a later time.

Imagine that your Web site has a directory called maindir, and two subdirectories of this directory named subdir1 and subdir2. Now suppose this.htm is located in subdir1 and that.htm is located in subdir2. Using the following absolute and relative URL addresses, you can create hypertext links between this.htm and that.htm:

```
<!-- This -->
<HTML>
<HEAD>
<TITLE> Inter-site Anchor </TITLE>
</HEAD>
<BODY>

<A HREF="http://www.yourdomain.com/maindir/subdir2/that.htm"> That </A>
<P>
<A HREF="/maindir/subdir2/that.htm"> That </A>
<P>
<A HREF="../subdir2/that.htm"> That </A>

</BODY>
</HTML>
```

All three of the URL addresses in this example link to the correct file. The first anchor uses an absolute address for that.htm. It will work, and continue to work, only if the file that.htm remains in the subdir2 subdirectory of maindir.

The second anchor uses a relative URL address. Because that.htm is located on the same Web site as this.htm, there's no need to specify the domain name. In fact, if the domain name of the Web site ever changes, or you transfer these HTML files from one Web server to another, the link between these two files won't be broken.

The third anchor also uses a relative URL address. The two periods (..) in the relative address `../subdir2/that.htm` mean "ascend one directory level above the current file." Because the parent directory of `this.htm` is `maindir`, the URL is translated to mean `/maindir/subdir2/that.htm`, which is the correct URL of `that.htm`.

Relative URL addresses are almost always better than absolute URL addresses because they allow for significant changes in the directory structure of a Web site without resulting in broken links. If you rename the `maindir` directory to something else, the third anchor will still work correctly. This anchor will also continue to work if you move the `maindir` directory and all its subdirectories into a new directory. When you can, use relative URL addresses.

Linking Within a Web Page

Sometimes it's useful to have hypertext links that take you to a particular location within a page. For example, if you have a table of contents at the top of a Web page, you may want the users of your Web page to be able to click different parts of the table of contents to arrive at particular sections of your document. You can use the <A> tag to create this type of hypertext link as well. Listing 5.3 shows an example.

Listing 5.3. Linking from a table of contents.

```
<HTML>
<HEAD>
<TITLE> Linking Within A Web Page </TITLE>
</HEAD>
<BODY>

<H1> Contents </H1>
<A HREF="#section1"> Section I </A>
<BR>
<A HREF="#section2"> Section II </A>
<P>
<A NAME="section1"> Section I </A>
<BR>
This is the first section.
<P>
<A NAME="section2"> Section II </A>
<BR>
This is the second section.

<A HREF="that.htm"> That </A>

</BODY>
</HTML>
```

In this example, the top of the Web page has a table of contents that lists two sections. If you click either section, you'll arrive at that section of the document (see Figure 5.8).

FIGURE 5.8.

Linking from a table of contents.

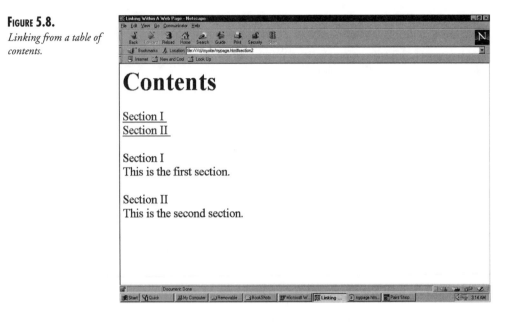

FIGURE 5.8.

Linking from a table of contents.

You create named locations within a document by using the NAME attribute of the <A> tag. When you use the NAME attribute, instead of creating a hypertext link you create a target for a hypertext link. You can create as many named locations within a Web page as you want, and you can name a location anything you please.

To create a hypertext link that refers to the named location, you use an anchor's HREF attribute as usual. However, you must include the number character (#) before the name of the location to which you want to link. In the preceding example, the tag <A HREF="#section1"> links to the location in the document named section1.

If you want, you can have multiple hypertext links that refer to the same location. This is useful when you have a long Web document and you want to provide the user with an easy way to get back to the top of the document. Here's an example of how you would do this:

```
<HTML>
<HEAD>
<TITLE> Multiple Links Within A Web Page </TITLE>
</HEAD>
<BODY>

<A NAME="TOP"> Welcome </A>

…some long text…

<A HREF="#top"> Back To Top </A>

…some more long text…

<A HREF="#top"> Back To Top </A>
```

```
</BODY>
</HTML>
```

You can also use the <A> tag to create a hypertext link to a named location within another document. For example, suppose you've created a location in the HTML file that.htm with the name there_in_that. You can create a hypertext link to this named location by using the following tag in the this.htm file:

```
<A HREF="that.htm#there_in_that"> Go There </A>
```

When someone viewing this.htm file clicks the hypertext link Go There, the person will arrive in the that.htm file at the location named there_in_that.

You can think of the expression #there_in_that as an extension to a normal URL address. It extends a normal URL address by specifying a particular location within the same or another HTML file. The file that contains the named location may be located on the same Web site or anywhere else on the World Wide Web.

Controlling the Color of Links

At least in the case of Netscape Navigator, prior to the first time a hypertext link is clicked the text of the link appears in a bright blue color. After the link is clicked and the destination has been visited, the color of the hypertext link changes to purple. Finally, while the mouse button actually is being held down on the hypertext link, the text appears red.

You can change these colors if you prefer. The three attributes that control the color of a hypertext link are the LINK, VLINK, and ALINK attributes. All three of these are attributes of the BODY tag. Here's an example:

```
<HTML>
<HEAD>
<TITLE> Link Colors </TITLE>
</HEAD>
<BODY LINK="lime" VLINK="lime" ALINK="lime" >

<A HREF="http://www.yahoo.com"> Yahoo </A>

</BODY>
</HTML>
```

In this example, the hypertext link Yahoo appears with the color lime green before, during, and after you click the link. The LINK attribute determines the color of links that have yet to be visited. The VLINK attribute determines the color of visited links, and the ALINK attribute determines the color of links that are actively being clicked. You can use any color name or RGB value to set the link color attributes.

Adding Images

Web sites on the Internet can be divided into two types: those that use a lot of pictures and those that don't. At one extreme, at Web sites such as HotWired, every page is dominated by various graphical elements. The design of the HotWired Web site provides a very definite style and attitude (see Figure 5.9).

At the other extreme are Web sites such as Amazon books. The Amazon Web site uses barely any pictures at all. Almost every page contains nothing but plain text. This makes the Web site fast and functional at the expense of visual appeal (see Figure 5.10).

FIGURE 5.9.

The HotWired Web site uses plenty of images.

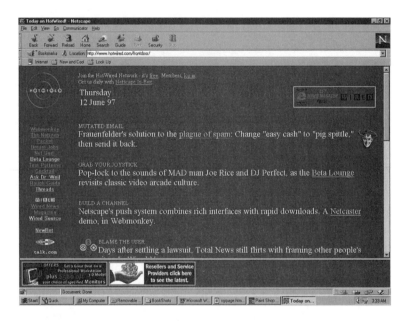

FIGURE 5.10.

The Amazon Web site uses almost no images.

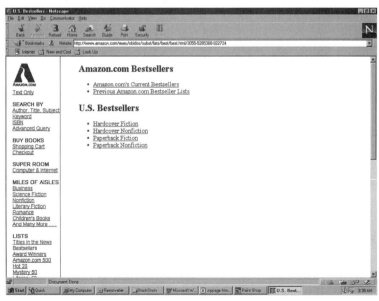

Which approach makes more sense? It depends on the purpose of your Web site. HotWired has an interest in projecting a particular image to the world. Therefore, it makes perfect sense for the makers of this Web site to include a multitude of eye-catching images. On the other hand, the purpose of the Amazon Web site is to sell books. If a user of this Web site has to wait too long for a Web page to load, that person might decide to walk to Borders to purchase the book instead.

When designing your Web site, you can find a middle ground between these two extremes. There are better and worse ways to include images in a Web page. If you choose your images carefully, you can create Web pages that are both visually appealing and fast to load. In this section, you learn how to do this.

GIFs and JPEGs

The most popular image format on the World Wide Web is the *Graphical Interchange Format* (*GIF*). You can use GIF images in your Web pages for just about anything, including banner logos, page dividers, and hypertext links. GIF images have a number of useful properties that you should know about:

- First, GIF images can have different color palette sizes. The maximum number of distinct colors that can appear in any GIF image is 256. However, it's often better to create images with even smaller palettes. Reducing the palette size of a GIF image can dramatically decrease the size of the image file, and the smaller the image file the faster it will load into a Web browser.

- GIF images can have transparent colors. If you don't want your image to appear in the shape of a rectangle, you can set one color to be transparent and make the border of the image appear to be any shape you want. Transparent colors are also useful if you want the background graphic or color of your Web page to show through your image.

- GIF images can be *interlaced*. When a browser loads an interlaced GIF, the browser will begin to show the image even before it's fully loaded. This creates the psychological effect of the image loading faster. For this reason, you should always create interlaced GIFs rather than non-interlaced GIFs.

- Finally, GIF images can be animated. You can create GIF images that cycle through a series of images instead of only one.

> **NOTE**
>
> You can pronounce the word *GIF* with either a hard or a soft g.

GIF images are not the only type of images used on the World Wide Web. A second format, the *Joint Picture Experts Group* (*JPEG*) format, is also widely used. Images that use the JPEG format typically end with the extension .jpg.

Why have two image formats? Each format is best at displaying a particular type of picture.

> **NOTE**
>
> You pronounce *JPEG* as "jay peg."

In general, the JPEG format is a better format to use for displaying photographs on a Web page—JPEG works well with images that have a lot of color variation. The JPEG format is better for this type of image than GIF for two reasons:

- Unlike GIFs, JPEG images aren't limited to only 256 distinct colors. A JPEG image can contain millions of distinct colors. Of course, this doesn't mean that every monitor will be able to display all those colors.

- The second reason that the JPEG format is better than the GIF format for displaying most photographs concerns the way in which the two image formats compress pictures. If you format a picture with a lot of color variation as a GIF file, the resulting file will be much larger than if you format it as a JPEG file. This is important because smaller files load faster into a Web browser.

In the majority of cases, you'll use GIF to create graphics for your Web site. GIF files are typically smaller and therefore load faster. They also have useful features, such as transparency, that JPEG files don't have.

> **NOTE**
>
> A third image format is not widely used at this time, but may be in the near future. The PNG (pronounced *ping*) format is being pushed by the World Wide Web Consortium, among others, as a replacement for GIF. One problem with the GIF format is that it isn't in the public domain; it was originally developed by CompuServe. Even though the GIF format is proprietary, you can use GIF images in your Web pages without paying any fees.

Finding Images for Your Web Pages

Before learning how to include images in your Web pages, you need to know how to get the images in the first place. In general, there are four sources for images:

- Hire a Web design company to create the images for you. This can be very expensive, especially for a large Web site. For professionally drawn images, you should expect to pay between $50 and $100 for each image. Web design companies normally charge even more for images such as navigator bars, animated images, and banner logos. For a medium-size Web site, it's not unreasonable to pay $5,000 or more.

If you can afford it, and you can find a good Web design company, this is the best source for images to use on your Web site. No other aspect of your Web site will affect its viewers' perception of its quality more than the quality of the images it contains. If you can, pay for good images. It makes a big difference.

■ Buy collections of images on CD that have been specially created for use on Web sites. You can either use these images without modification or individualize them for your particular Web site needs. For example, the Microsoft Visual Studio CD is packaged with hundreds of images that you can use on your Web site without paying any royalties.

■ Download images from the World Wide Web from a number of free and commercial image banks. One good commercial source of images for Web pages is PhotoDisc, located at http://www.photodisc.com. When downloading images for use in your Web site, make sure that you're licensed to use them. It's both illegal and morally objectionable to copy an image from the Web and use it without the consent of the author of the image.

■ Create the images for your Web site yourself, by using a paint program. Even if you acquire images by any of the methods described earlier, you'll probably need to make certain modifications to the images in the future yourself. To do this, you'll need a paint program compatible with the image formats used on the Web.

TIP

You can't use the Paint program that's part of the Windows NT or Windows 95 operating system to make images for your Web pages; this paint program won't work with either GIF or JPEG files. Chapter 26, "Using Microsoft Image Composer," shows you how to use the Image Composer program (packaged with Microsoft Visual Studio) to create Web graphics. If you don't have Visual Studio, you can use the shareware program Paint Shop Pro (available at http://www.jasc.com). Alternatively, if you want to purchase a quality commercial paint program, some good choices are Adobe's Photoshop or Fractal Design Painter.

Adding Images to Your Web Page

Adding images to your Web page is easy. To add an image, use the <IMG> HTML tag, as in the following example (continued on the next page):

```
<HTML>
<HEAD>
<TITLE> Image Example </TITLE>
</HEAD>
```

```
<BODY>

<IMG SRC="myimage.gif">

</BODY>
</HTML>
```

In this example, the image myimage.gif will be displayed in a Web browser. The SRC attribute of the <IMG> tag indicates the source of the image file. You can use any absolute or relative URL address to refer to an image file. The image file doesn't even need to be located on your computer; it can be located anywhere on the World Wide Web.

For example, if you're connected to the Internet, you can use the following code to display an image from the Active Server Pages Web site on your own Web page:

```
<HTML>
<HEAD>
<TITLE> External Image </TITLE>
</HEAD>
<BODY>

<IMG SRC="http://www.aspsite.com/testimage.gif">

</BODY>
</HTML>
```

The <IMG> tag has a number of useful attributes. Using the WIDTH and HEIGHT attributes, for example, you can warn a browser about the size of an image before the image is actually loaded. Although specifying the width and height of an image doesn't make the image itself load any faster, specifying these values does allow the browser to preserve space for the image on a page while the image loads. This results in the final Web page being displayed faster because the Web browser doesn't have to recalculate the position of all the page elements that surround an image a second time, after the image is loaded.

TIP

Always use the WIDTH and HEIGHT attributes of the <IMG> tag because using them results in Web pages that are displayed faster.

Another useful attribute of the <IMG> tag is the ALT attribute. Using the ALT attribute, you can specify text that will appear as an alternative to the image specified in the tag. Some people (although I admit that I've never met any of them) are claimed to have turned off all graphics on their Web browsers. When these mythical people view a Web page, instead of seeing images, they see the text specified as the value of the ALT attribute.

The ALT attribute can also be used to create a bubble of text that pops up over an image when you position the mouse pointer over it. This works with both Internet Explorer versions 3 and 4 and Netscape Navigator version 4. This is an example of how to use the ALT attribute:

```
<HTML>
<HEAD>
<TITLE> Image With An Alternative </TITLE>
</HEAD>
<BODY>

<IMG SRC="myimage.gif" WIDTH=10 HEIGHT=12 ALT="This is my image!">

</BODY>
</HTML>
```

Yet another useful attribute of the <IMG> tag is the BORDER attribute. This attribute has different effects when used with the Netscape and Microsoft browsers. With Netscape Navigator, the BORDER attribute can be used to create a black border around an image. This can be useful when you want the image to appear within a frame (see Figure 5.11).

FIGURE 5.11.

Image with border and white space in Netscape Navigator.

When used with Internet Explorer, on the other hand, the BORDER attribute creates a transparent border around the image (see Figure 5.12 on the following page). In theory, this would be useful for ensuring that other page elements surrounding the image appear at some distance away from the image. However, given the BORDER attribute's effect on the Netscape Navigator, it's best to use the following two tags to do this instead.

The HSPACE and VSPACE attributes create horizontal and vertical white space around an image. These two attributes work with both the Microsoft and Netscape browsers. This next example uses the BORDER, HSPACE, and VSPACE attributes with an image:

```
<HTML>
<HEAD>
<TITLE> Image Attributes </TITLE>
</HEAD>
```

```
<BODY>

<IMG SRC="myimage.gif" WIDTH=10 HEIGHT=12 ALT="This is my image!"
 BORDER=5 HSPACE=10 VSPACE=10>
This is some text.

</BODY>
</HTML>
```

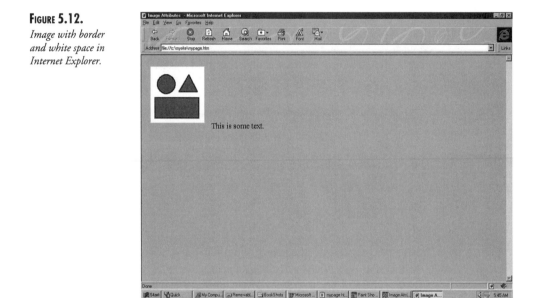

Notice that the text This is some text. appears ten pixels to the right of the border of the image. In Netscape Navigator, the text appears ten pixels to the right of a black frame. In Internet Explorer, the text appears ten pixels to the right of a transparent frame.

A final useful attribute of the <IMG> tag is the ALIGN attribute. The ALIGN attribute of the <IMG> tag is used to position an image relative to the baseline of text. Officially, this attribute can be set to five different values: top, middle, bottom, left, and right. Here's an example of an image with no alignment and each of the five different values of the ALIGN attribute (see Figure 5.13):

```
<HTML>
<HEAD>
<TITLE> Image Alignment </TITLE>
</HEAD>
<BODY>

<IMG SRC="myimage.gif"> This image is not aligned
<P>
<IMG SRC="myimage.gif" ALIGN="top"> This image is top aligned
<P>
<IMG SRC="myimage.gif" ALIGN="middle"> This image is middle aligned
<P>
<IMG SRC="myimage.gif" ALIGN="bottom"> This image is bottom aligned
<P>
```

```
<IMG SRC="myimage.gif" ALIGN="left"> This image is left aligned
<P>
<IMG SRC="myimage.gif" ALIGN="right"> This image is right aligned

</BODY>
</HTML>
```

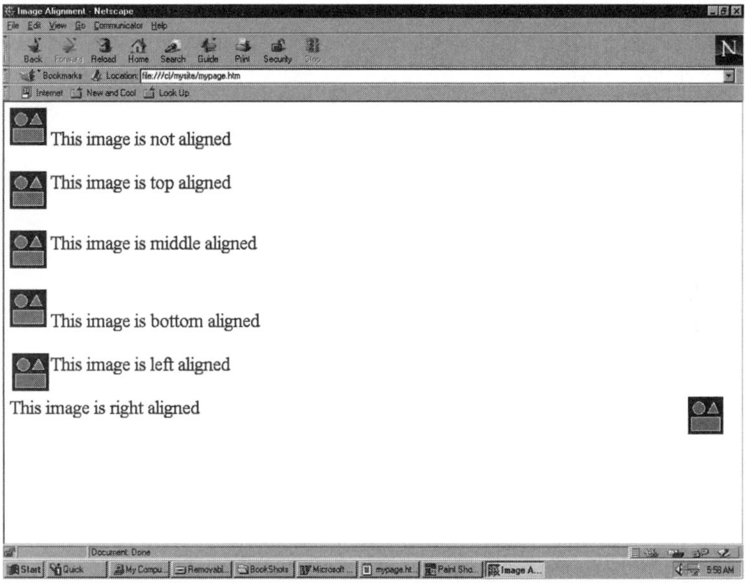

FIGURE 5.13.

Images aligned in various ways.

For these five values, the ALIGN attribute works in exactly the same way for both the Netscape and Microsoft browsers. The images are aligned relative to the baseline of the text. When the ALIGN attribute is specified as "top", for example, the image is aligned with the top of the text that appears on the same line as the image.

> **NOTE**
>
> Netscape has introduced some additional values for the image's ALIGN attribute. However, it's not a good idea to use these values, because they only work reliably with the Netscape Navigator. See Appendix D for more information.

Creating Links with Images

You can create links between Web pages just as easily with images as with text. Normally, when you create a hypertext link, you use the <A> tag to contain the text that you want to act as a link. However, you can also place an image within the <A> tag, as in the next example (shown on the following page).

```
<HTML>
<HEAD>
<TITLE> Image Attributes </TITLE>
</HEAD>
<BODY>
<A HREF="http://www.yahoo.com"><IMG SRC="myimage.gif"></A>
</BODY>
</HTML>
```

In this example, if someone clicks the image myimage.gif, the Yahoo! home page will be loaded (see Figure 5.14).

Figure 5.14.

An image that works as a link.

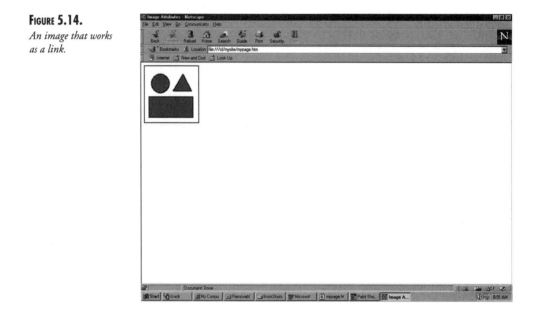

Notice the border that appears around the image when it's used as a link. The color of this border can be controlled like the color of hypertext links can be controlled—by using the LINK, VLINK, and ALINK attributes of the <BODY> tag (see the earlier section "Controlling the Color of Links"). Most of the time, however, you probably won't want a border to appear around your image. To get rid of the border, set the width of the border to 0, using the BORDER attribute of the <IMG> tag.

Using Images as Backgrounds

You can change the appearance of your Web page dramatically by using a background image. Background images are tiled across the back of your Web page screen, appearing beneath all the other page elements. The smaller the image, the more times the image is repeated. Look at this example:

```
<HTML>
<HEAD>
<TITLE> Background Image </TITLE>
</HEAD>
<BODY BACKGROUND="mylittleimage.gif">
Hello World!
</BODY>
</HTML>
```

When this HTML file is displayed in a Web browser, the image `mylittleimage.gif` is tiled repeatedly, both vertically and horizontally (see Figure 5.15). If you use a larger image, however, the image wouldn't appear to be tiled (see Figure 5.16). You can see examples of both effects in the figures.

> **CAUTION**
>
> Be careful when selecting a background image for a Web page. A poorly selected background image can make any text that appears above it impossible to read. If a Web page includes a large section of text, it's often better not to use a background image at all.

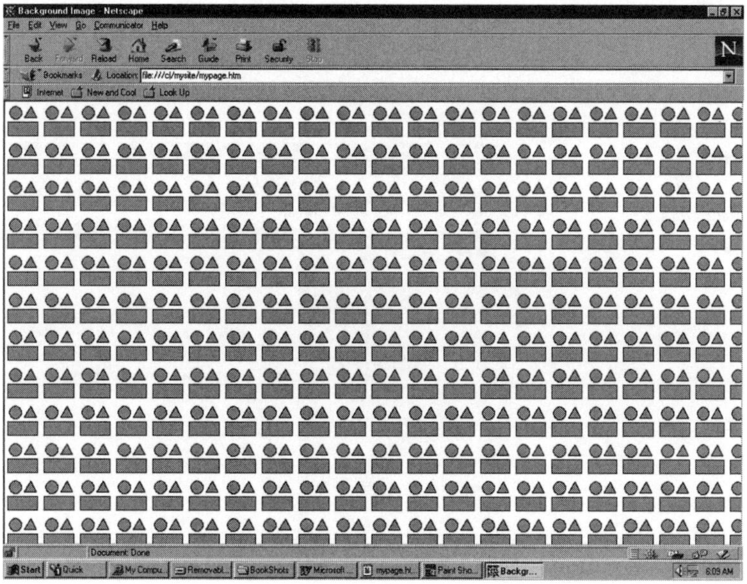

FIGURE 5.15.
Window tiled with small image.

5

BASIC HTML

FIGURE 5.16.

Window tiled with large image.

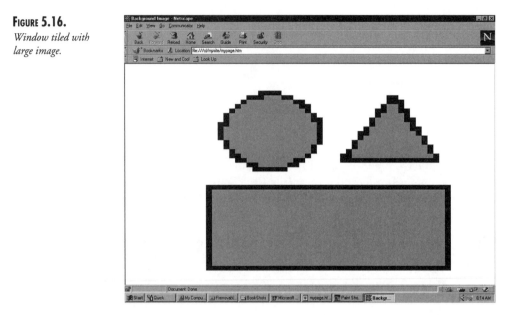

One interesting effect that you can get with a background image is a Web page with a color column running down its left margin. This effect is achieved by using an image with a height of a single pixel and a width of 1200 pixels, in which the first 300 pixels are one color and the remaining pixels are another color. When the image is tiled in the browser, it's only tiled vertically because of its width (see Figure 5.17).

FIGURE 5.17.

Two-color column background.

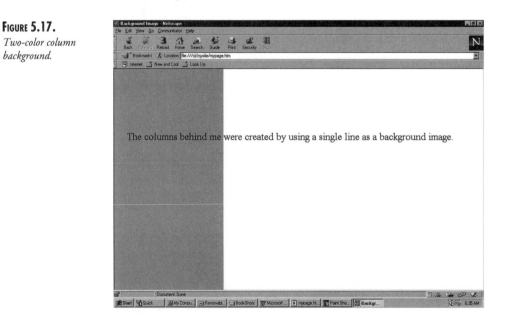

Microsoft has added an attribute to the <BODY> tag that works only with Internet Explorer. Normally, when you scroll down through a Web page with a background image, the background image scrolls as well. However, sometimes you may want the background image to remain fixed. You can create this effect by using the BGPROPERTIES attribute of the <BODY> tag. For example, if you want the image myimage.gif to remain fixed, you use the following tag:

```
<BODY BACKGROUND="myimage.gif" BGPROPERTIES="fixed">
```

For a short Web page, this additional attribute makes no difference. If your page is long enough to be scrolled, though, you'll notice that the background image doesn't scroll.

Even if you use a background image, you still should use the BGCOLOR attribute of the <BODY> tag to set the color of your Web page's background. Like all images, background images take some time to load. While the background image is loading, the background color appears until the image is finished loading.

Creating Fast-Loading Web Pages with Images

The tradeoff to using images in a Web page is the speed at which the Web page loads. This tradeoff doesn't need to be as extreme if you use images properly in your Web pages. Try to follow these tips for making fast-loading Web pages with images:

- Try to use the same image repeatedly in your Web pages. When a browser loads an image, it saves a local copy of the image in its browser cache. If you use the same image on multiple pages, the browser won't have to reload the image across the Internet each time it loads a page. Make sure the SRC attribute of the <IMG> tag is exactly the same on each page where you load the same image file.

- Reduce the color palette size used with an image. Most paint programs allow you to specify the size of the palette used with a GIF image. Use the smallest palette of colors possible. Notice that this isn't the same as reducing the number of colors that appear in an image. For example, you can make a really inefficient image by using a full 256-color palette with only two colors actually being used in the image.

- Always use the WIDTH and HEIGHT attributes of the <IMG> tag. If you don't use these attributes, the browser won't know how much space on a page to reserve for an image. In that case, the browser has to redraw the whole Web page again after the image is actually loaded. Furthermore, if you have multiple images, the Web page has to be redrawn again and again for each image.

- Always interlace your GIF images. Interlaced images seem to appear on a Web page faster because they begin to appear even before the whole image is transferred to the browser. This psychological trick is effective. You should always use it.

- When you can, choose images that don't have a lot of color variation. An image that has large blocks of the same color will transfer faster. All things being equal, the more variation in an image, the more information that needs to be transferred. Often, simple graphics have more impact than complex graphics anyway.

■ Don't use too many distinct images in a Web page. In certain circumstances, a browser needs to make a separate request to the server of a Web page for each distinct image that appears on a page. It's better to combine multiple images that appear adjacent to one another into one large image than to transfer each of these images separately. In general, when you can combine separate images into one, do it.

Summary

A lot of information has been covered in this chapter. You learned all the basic tags of HTML. You should now understand how to create your own Web pages.

You learned how to use color, and how to use HTML tags to perform page formatting and text formatting. You also learned how to use hypertext links to link your Web pages to others. And you now understand how to use images effectively in your Web documents.

By this point, you should have an appreciation for the flexibility and power of HTML. Using nothing more than the HTML tags introduced in this chapter, you can create very sophisticated Web pages. More exciting tags are coming, however. In the next chapter, you learn how to include forms, lists, and tables in your Web pages.

Intermediate HTML

IN THIS CHAPTER

This chapter extends your knowledge of the basic tags of HTML by showing you how to work with forms, lists, and tables. Using forms, you can create Web pages that interact with the visitors to your Web site. This chapter also shows you how to use the HTML tags needed to format lists of information. After reading this chapter, you'll even be able to create Web pages with advanced layouts by using HTML tables.

Working with HTML Forms

To create a genuinely interactive Web site, you need to use *HTML forms*. HTML forms enable you to gather and respond to the information provided by the visitors to your Web site. Using forms, you can create such things as check boxes, radio buttons, and text areas.

ASP

A mastery of forms is crucial to effective Active Server Pages programming. One of the main functions of ASP scripts is to respond to the information entered in HTML forms. Therefore, you should think of forms as the primary user interface to your ASP applications.

To create HTML forms, you use the <FORM> tag. This tag works as a container tag, enclosing other form elements and specifying, through its attributes, what should be done with the information gathered within the form. Here's an example of a very simple form:

```
<HTML>
<HEAD>
<TITLE> Simple Form </TITLE>
</HEAD>
<BODY>

<FORM>
<INPUT>
</FORM>

</BODY>
</HTML>
```

When this HTML file is displayed in a Web browser, a single three-dimensional box appears (see Figure 6.1). You can type whatever text you want into this box. However, as it stands, nothing happens after you enter the text. This form is too simple to be useful.

The first problem with this example is that the form doesn't know when you're finished entering information. To rectify this problem, you need to add another form element: a *submit button*. Here's the same form, with the addition of a submit button:

```
<HTML>
<HEAD>
<TITLE> Simple Form </TITLE>
</HEAD>
<BODY>

<FORM>
<INPUT>
<INPUT TYPE=SUBMIT VALUE="Submit Me!">
</FORM>

</BODY>
</HTML>
```

FIGURE 6.1.
A simple HTML form.

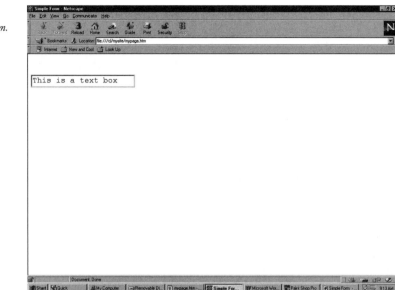

When you display this modified HTML file, a button appears with the words Submit Me! By clicking the Submit Me! button, you indicate that you're finished entering information in the text box. This lets the browser know that it must now do something with the information.

Currently, however, the form has no idea what to do with the information that it has gathered. You have to tell the form how to handle the information, by using the ACTION attribute of the <FORM> tag. The ACTION attribute determines what action the form will take with the form information. The following example shows how this attribute is used:

```
<HTML>
<HEAD>
<TITLE> Simple Form </TITLE>
</HEAD>
<BODY>

<FORM ACTION="MAILTO:billg@microsoft.com">
<INPUT>
<INPUT TYPE=SUBMIT VALUE="Submit Me!">
</FORM>

</BODY>
</HTML>
```

When you fill out and submit this form, the ACTION attribute tells the form that the information should be sent immediately to Bill Gates at Microsoft. You can have form information sent to any Internet address by using this syntax:

```
<FORM ACTION="MAILTO:name@domain.com">.
```

However, you'll rarely need to send form information to an e-mail address. In most cases, you want the form information to be sent back to your Web site to be processed. Chapter 15, "Working with More Than One Active Server Page," explains how to create Active Server Pages scripts that can process form information. To send form information to an Active Server Page, you use the following HTML lines:

```
<HTML>
<HEAD>
<TITLE> Simple Form </TITLE>
</HEAD>
<BODY>

<FORM ACTION="/somedirectory/mypage.asp" METHOD="POST">
<INPUT>
<INPUT TYPE=SUBMIT VALUE="Submit Me!">
</FORM>

</BODY>
</HTML>
```

In this example, the attributes ACTION and METHOD specify that the form information should be posted to an Active Server Page named mypage.asp to be processed. The ACTION attribute gives the path to the Active Server Page. The METHOD attribute indicates how the form information should be sent. In this case, the form information that's entered in the text box is *posted* to the Active Server Page.

In almost all cases, your <FORM> tag will have the same general characteristics as in this example. You'll specify an Active Server Page that will process the form by using the ACTION attribute, and you'll specify that the form information should be posted by using the METHOD attribute.

One final addition needs to be made to our form example to make it useful. When you include form elements such as text boxes, you need to give each form element a name. You do this with the NAME attribute of the <INPUT> tag. This example has two different text boxes named text1 and text2:

```
<HTML>
<HEAD>
<TITLE> Simple Form </TITLE>
</HEAD>
<BODY>

<FORM ACTION="/somedirectory/mypage.asp" METHOD="POST">
<INPUT NAME="text1">
<INPUT NAME="text2">
<INPUT TYPE=SUBMIT VALUE="Submit Me!">
</FORM>

</BODY>
</HTML>
```

In this example, information entered into the text box named text1 will be associated with the name text1 when it's sent to the Web site for processing. This will distinguish the text entered into this first text box from any information entered into any other form element.

Form information is sent to the destination specified in the ACTION attribute in name and value pairs, separated by an ampersand (&) character. For example, if you enter **your first name** in the first text box and **your last name** in the second text box, the information sent to be processed would look like this:

```
text1=yourfirstname&text2=yourlastname
```

Actually, prior to being sent, the form information will be URL-encoded. When text is URL-encoded, certain characters are replaced with others. For example, the space character is replaced with a plus sign (+). So if you enter the text **This is textbox1** in the first text box and the text **This is textbox2** in the second, the following text would be sent for processing:

```
text1=This+is+textbox1&text2=This+is+textbox2
```

When you learn how to develop your ASP scripts in Chapter 15, you'll also learn how to work with form information that has been URL-encoded.

Mixing Forms with Other HTML Tags

You can use just about any HTML tag inside the <FORM> tag that you would normally use in the body of your document. This feature is useful for creating labels for your form elements. For example, if you have a number of text boxes, you could label them like so:

```
<HTML>
<HEAD>
<TITLE> Simple Form </TITLE>
</HEAD>
<BODY>

<FORM ACTION="/somedirectory/mypage.asp" METHOD="POST">
<BR><B>First Name:</B> <INPUT NAME="firstname">
<BR><B>Last Name:</B> <INPUT NAME="lastname">
<INPUT TYPE=SUBMIT VALUE="Submit Me!">
</FORM>

</BODY>
</HTML>
```

In this example, the text box named firstname is labeled (in bold) with the text First Name: and the text box named lastname is labeled (also in bold) with the text Last Name: (see Figure 6.2). If you really wanted to, you could use images next to your text boxes as well. By using images, you can add more interesting labels to your form elements with pictures and specialized text.

Sadly, one thing that you can't do is use HTML tags to alter the text that's displayed in form elements. For example, you can't use HTML to make the text Submit Me! on the submit button appear bold. Also, you can't control the appearance of the text that's entered into a text box. This is a current weakness of HTML; your forms will always appear with gray buttons and black text (unless you use images, which are discussed shortly).

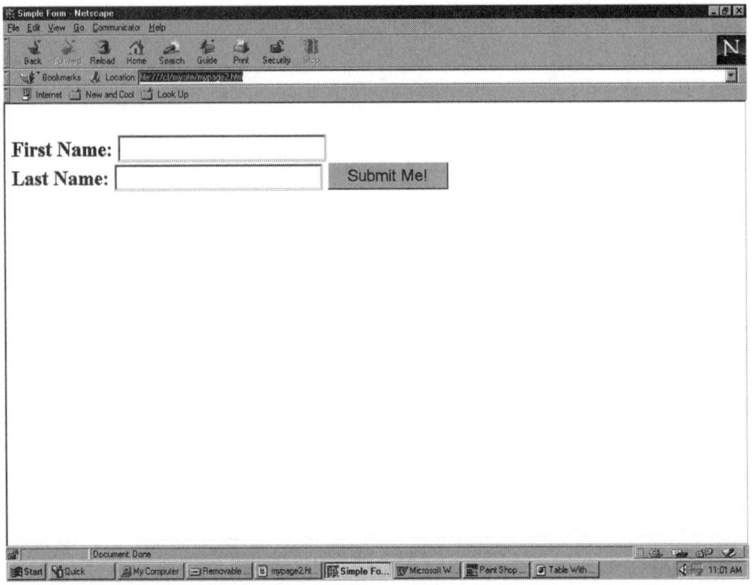

FIGURE 6.2.
An HTML form with labels.

NOTE

Although you can't use standard HTML tags to control the appearance of text within form elements, you can use cascading style sheets to do this with Netscape Navigator 4.0 and Internet Explorer 4.0. See the next chapter to learn how to use cascading style sheets.

You can place your <FORM> tags anywhere in the body of an HTML document. Also—and you'll often find this necessary—you can have multiple forms in the same HTML document. This is useful when you need to invoke different Active Server Pages scripts to process different form information. Just make sure that your forms don't overlap or contain one another. For example, the following HTML code is illegal:

```
<HTML>
<HEAD>
<TITLE> Bad Form </TITLE>
</HEAD>
<BODY>

<FORM ACTION="/somedirectory/mypage.asp" METHOD="POST">
<INPUT NAME="textbox1">
<INPUT NAME="textbox2">
<BR><INPUT TYPE=SUBMIT VALUE="Submit Me!">

<FORM ACTION="/someotherdirectory/myotherpage.asp" METHOD="POST">
<INPUT NAME="anothertextbox1">
<INPUT NAME="anothertextbox2">
<BR><INPUT TYPE=SUBMIT VALUE="Submit Me Also!">
</FORM>
```

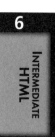

```
</FORM>

</BODY>
</HTML>
```

This HTML code won't work because one `<FORM>` tag is embedded in another. If you ever find yourself in a situation where one of your forms doesn't work as it should, check to make sure that you haven't accidentally overlapped your `<FORM>` tags or forgotten to close one of your forms.

Text Boxes

The most basic form element is a *text box* (see Figure 6.3). You can create a text box with nothing more than the tag `<INPUT>` with no attributes. However, to create a useful text box, you need to include the NAME attribute. The next example includes two text boxes named `text1` and `text2`:

```
<HTML>
<HEAD>
<TITLE> Simple Form </TITLE>
</HEAD>
<BODY>

<FORM ACTION="/somedirectory/mypage.asp" METHOD="POST">
<INPUT NAME="text1" TYPE="text">
<INPUT NAME="text2">
<INPUT TYPE=SUBMIT VALUE="Submit Me!">
</FORM>

</BODY>
</HTML>
```

FIGURE 6.3.

Text boxes.

Notice that the first text box has its TYPE attribute set to `"text"`. You can include this attribute for a text box if you prefer, but it really has no effect; the `<INPUT>` tag defaults to TYPE=`"text"` anyway.

You can also use the VALUE attribute of the `<INPUT>` tag to specify the default text that will appear in the text box before the user makes any changes. For example, suppose you have a text box in which users can enter the name of their country. If you expect most of your users to originate from the United States, you can make the default country USA by using the tag `<INPUT NAME="country" VALUE="USA">`.

Another useful attribute of the `<INPUT>` tag is the SIZE attribute. Using the SIZE attribute, you can control how wide a text box will appear. The value you provide to the SIZE attribute is the number of characters that you want the text box to display.

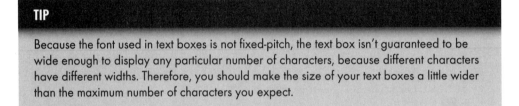

TIP

Because the font used in text boxes is not fixed-pitch, the text box isn't guaranteed to be wide enough to display any particular number of characters, because different characters have different widths. Therefore, you should make the size of your text boxes a little wider than the maximum number of characters you expect.

A final, very useful attribute of text boxes is the MAXLENGTH attribute. Normally, you can keep typing more text into a text box forever, because the text box will just keep scrolling horizontally to let you type more. This can be bad for two reasons:

- First, in principle, a malicious user of your Web site could stuff a text box with so many characters that it could seriously burden your Web site to process it. You need to set boundaries on the actions of your visitors. Just to be safe, include the MAXLENGTH attribute to put a boundary on how much information a user can enter.

- Second, sometimes you want to force a user to enter information of a certain length. For example, you might want to force a user to enter a five-digit ZIP code and not the full nine-digit version. Again, use the MAXLENGTH attribute to do this.

Form Buttons

Three types of buttons are typically used in HTML forms. You've already been introduced to the first type of button—the *submit button*. When you click the submit button, the form is processed by whatever program is referred to in the ACTION attribute of the `<FORM>` tag. The syntax of the submit button is as follows:

```
<INPUT TYPE=SUBMIT VALUE="Do it!">
```

The VALUE attribute determines the text that appears on the button.

The *image button* has almost exactly the same effect as the submit button. This type of button, however, appears as an image instead of the typical ugly gray rectangle (see Figure 6.4). Following is an example of how to use an image button:

```
<HTML>
<HEAD>
<TITLE> Simple Form </TITLE>
</HEAD>
<BODY>

<FORM ACTION="/somedirectory/mypage.asp" METHOD="POST">
<INPUT NAME="textbox1">
<INPUT NAME="textbox2">
<BR><INPUT TYPE=IMAGE SRC="myimage.gif" BORDER=0>
</FORM>

</BODY>
</HTML>
```

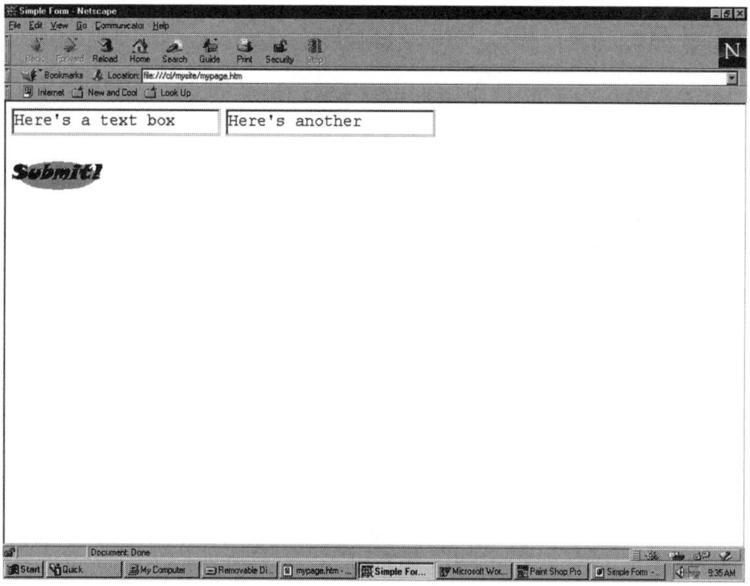

FIGURE 6.4.

An image button.

As in the case of images used for links, you should set the BORDER attribute to zero to hide the border that appears around images on browsers such as Netscape Navigator. In some cases, the extra image border can be distracting. You can use any of the other attributes of the <IMG> tag with image buttons as well. (See Chapter 5, "Basic HTML.")

NOTE

An interesting aspect of the image button is that when clicked it not only submits the form data, it also submits the exact coordinates of where the image was clicked. For example, if you click dead center on an image button that has a width and height of five pixels, the x,y coordinates of 3,3 are passed with the rest of the form information.

This feature of form buttons is useful if you need to combine the function of a form with that of an image map (image maps are discussed in the next chapter). A normal image map doesn't allow you to pass the contents of form fields.

The final type of button is the *reset button*. When a user of a form clicks the reset button, all the form fields are returned to their initial state. For example, text boxes with no default value will be cleared; those with their VALUE attributes set will be reinitialized to the specified value. As in the case of the submit button, you specify the text that appears on a reset button by supplying a VALUE attribute, as in the next example:

```
<HTML>
<HEAD>
<TITLE> Simple Form </TITLE>
</HEAD>
<BODY>

<FORM ACTION="/somedirectory/mypage.asp" METHOD="POST">
<INPUT NAME="textbox1">
<INPUT NAME="textbox2" value="mydefault">
<BR><INPUT TYPE=SUBMIT VALUE="Submit Me!">
<BR><INPUT TYPE=RESET VALUE="Clear Me!">
</FORM>

</BODY>
</HTML>
```

In this example, when a user of the form clicks the button labeled Clear Me!, all the form fields are cleared back to their initial state.

You aren't restricted to using any of these three buttons only once within a particular form. This can be valuable, particularly in the case of the submit button. Sometimes it's useful to have several submit buttons so that the user can send the form information while indicating how the information should be used.

For example, suppose your Web site has a registration page, and you want the users of your Web site to be able to specify whether they want their registration information kept private or made public. On the one hand, you could add an additional form field where the user can select a preference. On the other hand, you could simply create two submit buttons, one labeled Register Private and one labeled Register Public. In the latter case, users can make their preference known simply by clicking one of the two buttons.

To use multiple buttons, you need to supply the NAME attribute for the buttons. Look at this simple example:

```
<HTML>
<HEAD>
<TITLE> Simple Form </TITLE>
</HEAD>
<BODY>

<FORM ACTION="/somedirectory/mypage.asp" METHOD="POST">
<BR><INPUT name="YES" TYPE=SUBMIT VALUE="yes!">
<BR><INPUT name="NO" TYPE=SUBMIT VALUE="no!">
</FORM>
</BODY>
</HTML>
```

Here, clicking either yes! or no! will invoke the same form action. However, when the form is processed, the user's vote can be determined. (Exactly how the user's vote can be determined is covered in Chapter 10, "Basic SQL," and Chapter 11, "Intermediate SQL.")

Just to reiterate, in this section you've learned how to use the three types of buttons most commonly used in HTML forms:

- **Submit buttons.** Used to submit the contents of a form to the server for processing or to e-mail a form to a particular e-mail address.
- **Image buttons.** Used for the same purpose as a submit button, but contains an image instead of text.
- **Reset buttons.** Reinitializes all the elements of a form to their initial state.

Password Boxes

Suppose you want the visitors to your Web site to register before they can use it. Using standard text boxes, you could create an HTML form that demands the user's name and password. However, you wouldn't want people to have to enter their passwords in plain view of others who might be looking over their shoulders. To protect the user's password, you need to use a *password box* (see Figure 6.5). A password box works like a text box except that when information is entered, it's hidden. Here's an example:

```
<HTML>
<HEAD>
<TITLE> Simple Form </TITLE>
</HEAD>
<BODY>

<FORM ACTION="/somedirectory/mypage.asp" METHOD="POST">
Please enter your name and password:
<BR> Name: <INPUT name="username">
<BR> Password: <INPUT name="password" TYPE=PASSWORD>
<INPUT TYPE=SUBMIT VALUE="Continue">
</FORM>

</BODY>
</HTML>
```

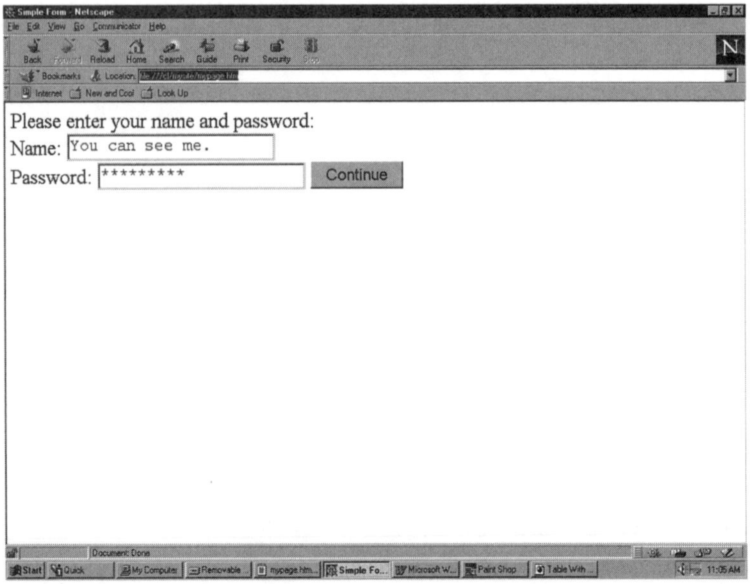

FIGURE 6.5.

A password box.

> ### NOTE
>
> It's important to realize that text entered in a password box, though hidden, is not en-crypted when it's submitted. In theory, this means that someone could steal the text entered into a password box off the wires as it moves across the Internet to your Web site. For most applications, this shouldn't cause great concern. However, you can encrypt the information that's submitted in an HTML form to prevent even this very unlikely event from happening. See the section "Using the Secure Sockets Layer" in Chapter 2, "Installing and Using Internet Information Server."

When the preceding HTML file is displayed in a Web browser, you can enter text into the password box in the same way as you would with a normal text box. However, all of the text entered will be masked (typically with asterisks). You can use both the SIZE and MAXLENGTH attributes with password boxes to control the screen width of the box and the maximum num-ber of characters that can be entered into it.

Check Boxes

Check boxes are useful in two types of situations. In the simplest case, you can use a check box to pose a simple true-or-false question to a user, as in the following example:

```
<HTML>
<HEAD>
<TITLE> Simple Form </TITLE>
</HEAD>
<BODY>
```

```
<FORM ACTION="/somedirectory/mypage.asp" METHOD="POST">
<BR> Do you like this web site?
<BR> <INPUT NAME="Like" TYPE=CHECKBOX VALUE="yes">
<BR> <INPUT TYPE=SUBMIT VALUE="Submit Me!">
</FORM>

</BODY>
</HTML>
```

When this HTML code is displayed in a Web browser, an empty box appears beneath the question Do you like this web site? If the box is checked when the submit button is clicked, the value of the VALUE attribute is also submitted. In this case, the name-and-value pair of Like and yes is submitted.

If the check box isn't checked when the user clicks the submit button, on the other hand, absolutely nothing is submitted. Not even the name of the check box is submitted. You can't specify the "off" value of a check box.

You also can use multiple check boxes with the same name to gather information (see Figure 6.6). For example, suppose you want to find out how the visitors to your Web site discovered the site, and you want to allow for the possibility that some users discovered your site in more than one way. You could use the following HTML code:

```
<HTML>
<HEAD>
<TITLE> Simple Form </TITLE>
</HEAD>
<BODY>

<FORM ACTION="/somedirectory/mypage.asp" METHOD="POST">

<BR> How did you find out about this web site?
<BR> Magazine: <INPUT NAME="discover" TYPE=CHECKBOX VALUE="Magazine">
<BR> Search Engine: <INPUT NAME="discover" TYPE=CHECKBOX VALUE="Search">
<BR> Friend: <INPUT NAME="discover" TYPE=CHECKBOX VALUE="Friend">
<BR> <INPUT TYPE=SUBMIT VALUE="Submit Me!">
</FORM>

</BODY>
</HTML>
```

Notice in this example that all three check boxes have the same name. When a user clicks the submit button, the value of each check box that has been selected will be submitted. In this case, every value will be associated with the name discover.

NOTE

Don't confuse multiple check boxes with radio buttons (described shortly). Unlike radio buttons, more than one check box can be selected at the same time, even if the check boxes have the same name.

Figure 6.6.

Multiple check boxes.

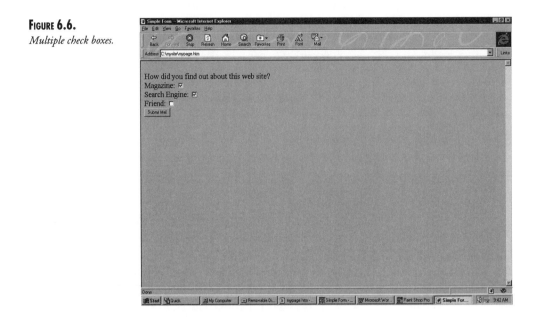

You can have as many check boxes in a form as you want. Whenever you want the values of a group of check boxes to be associated with the same name, just provide every check box in the group with the same name.

By default, check boxes initially appear without a check mark. You can override this default by including the CHECKED attribute. The CHECKED attribute is one of those rare attributes that doesn't take a value. To create a check box that has a default value of CHECKED, you would use this tag:

```
<INPUT NAME="mycheckbox" TYPE=CHECKBOX VALUE="yes" CHECKED>
```

Radio Buttons

Radio buttons have an odd name, but you most likely have encountered them in both Web pages and normal computer applications (see Figure 6.7). Using radio buttons, you can present a choice of multiple values. Unlike when using check boxes, however, the user can select only one radio button at a time.

For example, suppose you want to determine the gender of visitors to your Web site. You could use radio buttons to allow visitors to specify whether they are male or female, since no visitor can be both. Here's an example of how you could do this:

```
<HTML>
<HEAD>
<TITLE> Radio Form </TITLE>
</HEAD>
<BODY>

<FORM ACTION="/somedirectory/mypage.asp" METHOD="POST">

<BR> Please indicate your sex:
<BR> Male: <INPUT NAME="sex" TYPE=RADIO VALUE="male">
```

```
<BR> Female: <INPUT NAME="sex" TYPE=RADIO VALUE="female">
<BR> <INPUT TYPE=SUBMIT VALUE="Submit Me!">
</FORM>

</BODY>
</HTML>
```

FIGURE 6.7.
Radio buttons.

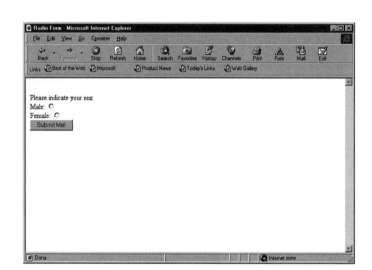

Notice that both radio buttons are given the same name. When the user of this Web page hits the submit button, the value of only one radio button will be sent. The value sent is specified in the VALUE attribute of the radio button.

As in the case of check boxes, you can use the CHECKED attribute to specify the radio button that will be selected when the Web page is first loaded. You can also have as many radio buttons as you like in a form. If you want to have multiple groups of radio buttons, simply give the radio buttons in each group different names.

Creating Drop-Down List Boxes

As an alternative to check boxes and radio buttons, you can create *drop-down list boxes* to display a menu of alternatives (see Figure 6.8). A drop-down list box shows only one selection at a time. To view the other possible selections, you click the arrow attached to the box. One advantage to using a drop-down list box is that it occupies less space on your Web page than either radio buttons or check boxes.

You create a drop-down list box using the <SELECT> and <OPTION> tags, like this (continued on the following page):

```
<HTML>
<HEAD>
<TITLE> Drop-Down List Box </TITLE>
</HEAD>
<BODY>

<FORM ACTION="/somedirectory/mypage.asp" METHOD="POST">
```

```
<BR> Please indicate your sex:
<BR> <SELECT NAME="sex">
<OPTION VALUE="Is Male">Male
<OPTION VALUE="Is Female">Female
</SELECT>
<INPUT TYPE=SUBMIT VALUE="Submit Me!">
</FORM>

</BODY>
</HTML>
```

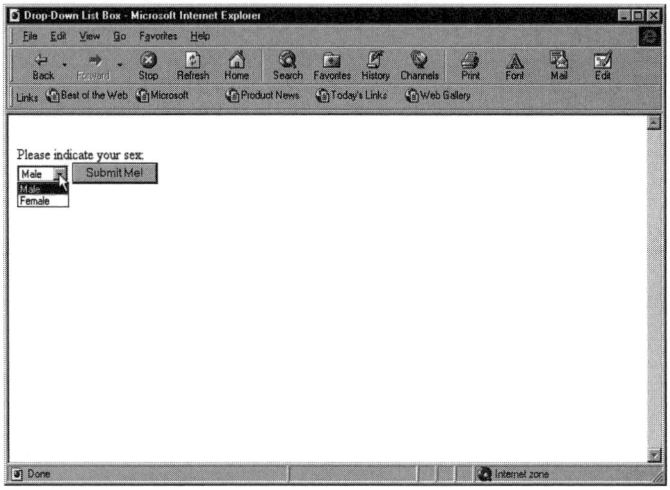

FIGURE 6.8.

A drop-down list box.

In this example, the NAME attribute of the <SELECT> tag provides a name for your drop-down list box. Each of the <OPTION> tags presents a possible selection. The VALUE attribute of the <OPTION> tag specifies the value that will be sent if that option is selected when the form is submitted. Finally, the text that appears after the <OPTION> tag determines how that option appears in the drop-down list box.

The list box in this example has the same function as a group of radio buttons. You are forced to select only one option at a time. For example, if you select Female from the list box, the only value sent when the form is submitted would be Is Female. This value would be associated with the NAME of the list box sex. You can never select more than a single value.

By default, the text following the first <OPTION> tag will appear as the initial value of the drop-down list box. You can override this default by using the SELECTED attribute of the <OPTION> tag. In the following example, Female is selected when the list box appears, even though Male appears before it in the list of options:

```
<HTML>
<HEAD>
<TITLE> Drop Down-List Box </TITLE>
</HEAD>
<BODY>

<FORM ACTION="/somedirectory/mypage.asp" METHOD="POST">
```

```
<BR> Please indicate your sex:
<BR> <SELECT NAME="sex">
<OPTION VALUE="Is Male">Male
<OPTION VALUE="Is Female" SELECTED>Female
</SELECT>
<BR> <INPUT TYPE=SUBMIT VALUE="Submit Me!">
</FORM>

</BODY>
</HTML>
```

One situation when specifying a different default value is useful is when you have an alphabetical list of items, but you want to choose the default value from within the list. For example, suppose you have a list of countries, but you want the default country to be the United States. In that case, you can use the SELECTED attribute to specify that United States is the default value, even though this country name appears near the end of the alphabetical list of country names.

Creating Scrolling List Boxes

Yet another alternative to a group of radio buttons or check boxes is a *scrolling list box* (see Figure 6.9). Using scrolling list boxes, you can create a list of alternatives from which the user can make one or more selections. To create a scrolling list box, you use the same tags used to create a drop-down list box, but with different attributes. Here's an example:

```
<HTML>
<HEAD>
<TITLE> Scrolling List Box </TITLE>
</HEAD>
<BODY>

<FORM ACTION="/somedirectory/mypage.asp" METHOD="POST">
<BR> Please indicate your sex:
<BR> <SELECT NAME="sex" SIZE=2>
<OPTION VALUE="Is Male">Male
<OPTION VALUE="Is Female">Female
</SELECT>
<INPUT TYPE=SUBMIT VALUE="Submit Me!">
</FORM>

</BODY>
</HTML>
```

The SIZE attribute of the <SELECT> tag converts a drop-down list box into a scrolling list box. The SIZE attribute specifies how many options should appear onscreen at a time.

When using scrolling list boxes instead of drop-down list boxes, you lose the advantage of saving screen space. However, scrolling list boxes have one significant advantage: Using a scrolling list box, you can allow for the selection of more than one option. To do this, you use the MULTIPLE attribute of the <SELECT> tag:

```
<HTML>
<HEAD>
<TITLE> Simple Form </TITLE>
</HEAD>
<BODY>
```

```
<FORM ACTION="/somedirectory/mypage.asp" METHOD="POST">
<BR> How did you find out about this web site?
<BR> <SELECT NAME="discover" SIZE=3 MULTIPLE>
<OPTION VALUE="Magazine"> Magazine
<OPTION VALUE="Search"> Search Engine
<OPTION VALUE="Friend"> Friend
</SELECT>
<BR> <INPUT TYPE=SUBMIT VALUE="Submit Me!">
</FORM>

</BODY>
</HTML>
```

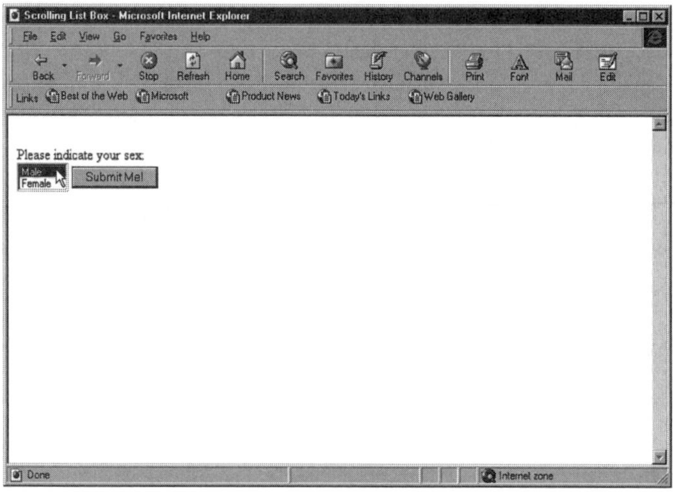

FIGURE 6.9.

A scrolling list box.

When this HTML file is displayed in a browser, a normal scrolling list box appears. However, if you use the Ctrl key on your keyboard while clicking the list box, you can choose more than one alternative. For example, you can select the options Magazine and Friend at the same time. (You can also use the Shift key to select a contiguous group of alternatives.)

> **NOTE**
>
> Often, I feel reluctant to use the MULTIPLE attribute. The fact is that many visitors to a Web site won't know how to make multiple selections. Furthermore, the method for selecting more than one option varies according to the type of computer a person is using. For example, on a Macintosh, you must use the Command key rather than the Ctrl key. Consider using a group of check boxes instead when you want to allow a user to make multiple selections.

Creating Text Areas

With the form elements described so far, the user can't enter more than one line of text. The `<TEXTAREA>` form tag creates a *text area*, where you can give the user more room for freedom of expression (see Figure 6.10). Use this tag whenever you want someone to enter a paragraph of text, as in the following example:

```
<HTML>
<HEAD>
<TITLE> Text Area </TITLE>
</HEAD>
<BODY>

<FORM ACTION="/somedirectory/mypage.asp" METHOD="POST">
<BR> Please enter your comments below:
<BR> <TEXTAREA NAME="comments" COLS=40 ROWS=20></TEXTAREA>
</FORM>

</BODY>
</HTML>
```

FIGURE 6.10.

A text area.

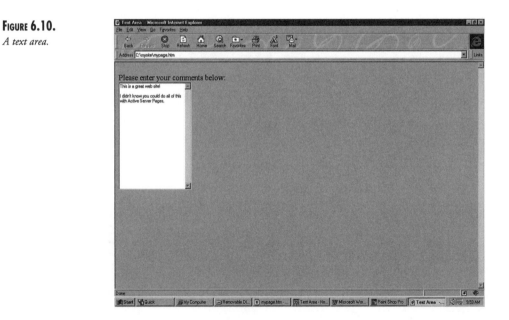

You should notice immediately that, in this example, the `<INPUT>` tag is not used to create the text area. You create text areas using the `<TEXTAREA>` tag. This tag, like all other form elements, must always appear within the `<FORM>` tag.

> **NOTE**
>
> Some browsers allow you to use the following syntax:
>
> `<INPUT TYPE=TextArea COLS=40 ROWS=20>`
>
> Don't do this. There's no advantage to making text areas into attributes of the `<INPUT>` tag. If you want your Web pages to be compatible with the maximum number of Web browsers, use the `<TEXTAREA>` tag and not the `TextArea` attribute.

To specify the width and height of a text area, you use the COLS and ROWS attributes. The COLS attribute specifies the width of the text area in columns; the ROWS attribute specifies the height in rows. Note that both of these attributes are measured in average character widths; because text areas don't use fixed-pitch fonts, you may not get exactly 50 characters in a text area with 50 columns.

You can't provide the COLS and ROWS attributes with a percentage value. This is unfortunate, because it results in text areas looking different on monitors with smaller or larger screen resolutions. This is a shortcoming of HTML.

Also, text areas have no MAXLENGTH attribute. There's no way to prevent someone from entering massive amounts of text into a text area. You have no control over this.

Notice that the `<TEXTAREA>` tag is a container tag. If you want text to appear in the text area when you first load the Web page, place the text within the `<TEXTAREA>` tag, like this:

```
<HTML>
<HEAD>
<TITLE> Text Area </TITLE>
</HEAD>
<BODY>

<FORM ACTION="/somedirectory/mypage.asp" METHOD="POST">
<BR> Please enter your comments below:
<BR> <TEXTAREA NAME="comments" COLS=40 ROWS=20>
I am the default text!
</TEXTAREA>
</FORM>

</BODY>
</HTML>
```

When this HTML file is interpreted by a Web browser, the text `I am the default text!` appears in the text area. Be aware that you can only enter text in text areas (along with the special character codes described in Chapter 5—see the section "Adding Special Characters"). Any HTML tags within a `<TEXTAREA>` tag will simply be ignored.

The official HTML specification is silent on how text should wrap within a text area. When you get to the right edge while typing in a text area with Internet Explorer, the text automatically wraps to a new line. When you do the same thing with Netscape Navigator, on the other hand, the text area keeps scrolling to the right.

If you want to control how the text in a text area wraps to a new line when using Netscape Navigator, use the proprietary Netscape attribute WRAP. This attribute can accept three values: OFF, PHYSICAL, and VIRTUAL. By default, the value of the WRAP attribute is OFF, and text doesn't wrap to a new line. When WRAP=PHYSICAL, on the other hand, text is wrapped to a new line. When the contents of the text area are submitted, carriage returns are added wherever the text wraps. If you want the text in a text area to wrap, but you don't want the extra carriage returns submitted with the form contents, use WRAP=VIRTUAL.

When I create text areas, I almost always include the WRAP=VIRTUAL attribute. When text in a text area doesn't wrap, this confuses the person entering information. By using this attribute, I can guarantee that text will wrap in both the Microsoft and Netscape browsers. Also, typically, I don't want to deal with the extra carriage returns when interpreting the contents of a text area. Using WRAP=VIRTUAL leaves those out.

Creating Hidden Fields

Using *hidden fields*, you can include information in your forms that will never be displayed onscreen. This information will be included, however, when the form is submitted.

Hidden fields are extremely valuable to the Active Server Pages programmer. You'll probably use them quite often to pass hidden information from page to page. For the moment, until you learn how to use Active Server Pages, you'll have to take the usefulness of hidden fields on faith.

You can use hidden fields to create session variables that don't depend on cookies. There are both advantages and disadvantages to doing this. To learn more, read the section "Retaining State Without Cookies" in Chapter 16, "Working with Active Server Pages Sessions."

ASP

Here's an example of a hidden field in a form:

```
<HTML>
<HEAD><TITLE> Hidden Field </TITLE></HEAD>
<BODY>

<FORM ACTION="/somedirectory/mypage.asp" METHOD="POST">
<INPUT NAME="secret" TYPE=HIDDEN VALUE="You cannot see me!">
<INPUT TYPE=SUBMIT VALUE="Submit Me!">
</FORM>

</BODY>
</HTML>
```

When this HTML file is displayed in a Web browser, the only thing you see on the screen is the submit button. The hidden field, named secret, doesn't appear. However, when the form button is clicked, the value You cannot see me! is submitted as part of the contents of the form.

> **CAUTION**
>
> You should never place genuinely private information in hidden fields. A viewer of a Web page can see the value of a hidden field by using the View Source command in a Web browser. Hidden fields are hidden from view, but they aren't hidden from the eyes of a knowledgeable user.

Creating File Upload Buttons

Suppose you want to create a Web site where people can advertise houses for sale. It would be nice if people could upload pictures of their homes. Or suppose you want to create a Web site devoted to short stories. It would nice if people could upload their stories—for example, in Microsoft Word format.

In theory, you can do this with the TYPE=FILE attribute of the <INPUT> tag. Using this attribute, you can create a *file upload button* on a form (see Figure 6.11). When users of your Web site click this button, they can select a file to upload from their local hard drive. Following is an example of how this can be done:

```
<HTML>
<HEAD><TITLE> File Upload </TITLE></HEAD>
<BODY>

<FORM ENCTYPE="multipart/form-data"
ACTION="/somedirectory/mypage.asp" METHOD=POST>
Please choose a picture to upload:
<BR><INPUT NAME="picture" TYPE=FILE ACCEPT="image/*">
<BR><INPUT TYPE=SUBMIT VALUE="Submit Me!">
</FORM>

</BODY>
</HTML>
```

When this HTML file is displayed in Netscape Navigator (version 3 or greater), a normal-looking text box appears next to a Browse button. The user can type the name of the file directly into the text box, or use the Browse button to select a file from a file dialog box. When the form is submitted, the file the user selected is also submitted.

Notice the addition of the ENCTYPE attribute to the <FORM> tag in this example. The ENCTYPE attribute specifies the type of encoding to apply to the form information when it's submitted. Normally, form information is URL-encoded (spaces are replaced with +, and so on). However, this is a bad encoding format to use with information that isn't text. To transfer files such as images efficiently, you should use ENCTYPE="multipart/form-data".

The actual file upload button is created using this tag:

```
<INPUT NAME="picture" TYPE=FILE ACCEPT="image/*">
```

6

INTERMEDIATE
HTML

FIGURE 6.11.
A file upload button.

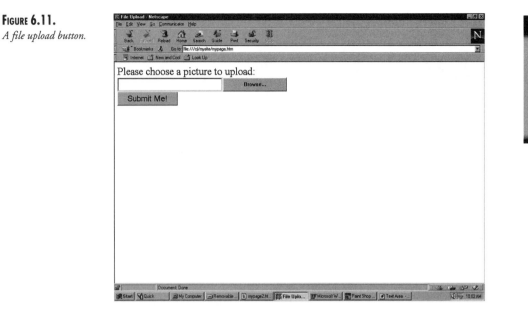

Because the value of the TYPE attribute is FILE, the browser should create a file upload button. The ACCEPT attribute restricts the files that will appear in the file dialog box to a particular file type. In this case, the file type is restricted to image files. You can specify any list of MIME types as the value of the ACCEPT attribute.

NOTE

MIME stands for *multipurpose Internet mail extension*. MIME was originally developed as a means for specifying the file types of e-mail attachments. Browsers use MIME types to associate files with appropriate programs.

Some examples of MIME types are image/gif for GIF images, image/jpeg for JPEG images, application/x-msexcel for Microsoft Excel spreadsheets, and application/msword for Microsoft Word documents.

To view the MIME types that your computer supports, choose View | Options | File Types in Windows Explorer.

Potentially, file upload buttons could be very useful. Regrettably, however, current browsers support file upload buttons only partially—or not at all. This is true even though file upload buttons are part of the official HTML 3.2 specification.

For example, Netscape Navigator (versions 3.0 and 4.0) ignores the ACCEPT attribute. Internet Explorer version 3.0 is even worse. It completely fails to interpret file upload buttons, and displays normal text boxes instead. Internet Explorer version 4.0, however, does recognize the file upload button. Until file upload buttons are supported by more browsers, use them with caution.

Working with Lists

In many situations, you'll want to display a list of information on your Web page. For example, you may want to include a list of links to your favorite Web sites. Alternatively, you might want to have a list of the top 10 reasons for visiting your Web site. Finally, you may be overcome with an intense desire to list your favorite words and their definitions. HTML includes a number of tags created specifically for this purpose.

Creating Unordered Lists

The simplest type of list is an *unordered list*. When you need an easy way to list a number of items, use this type of list (see Figure 6.12). For example, you can create an unordered list of your favorite Web sites, like this:

```
<HTML>
<HEAD><TITLE> Unordered List </TITLE></HEAD>
<BODY>

<UL>
<LI>   <A HREF="http://www.hotwired.com"> HotWired </A>
<LI>   <A HREF="http://www.byte.com"> Byte Magazine </A>
<LI>   <A HREF="http://www.microsoft.com"> Microsoft </A>
</UL>

</BODY>
</HTML>
```

Figure 6.12.

An unordered list.

The <UL> tag contains the list items. Each list item, in turn, is designated by using the <LI> tag. You can list as many items as you like.

When this HTML file is displayed, a bullet appears next to each list item. By default, this bullet is in the shape of a filled disc. However, you can control the shape of the bullet by using the TYPE attribute of the <UL> tag. You can create bullets in the shape of a disc, a square, or a circle. The following file creates three one-item lists, each displaying one of the bullet types:

```
<HTML>
<HEAD><TITLE> Unordered List </TITLE></HEAD>
<BODY>

<UL TYPE="DISC">
<LI>  I have a disc next to me.
</UL>

<UL TYPE="SQUARE">
<LI>  I have a square next to me.
</UL>

<UL TYPE="CIRCLE">
<LI>  I have an empty circle next to me.
</UL>

</BODY>
</HTML>
```

In Netscape Navigator, each list appears with a different type of bullet. Internet Explorer (including version 4.0), on the other hand, ignores this attribute; every bullet always appears in the shape of a filled disc.

You can *nest* one unordered list inside another. This is useful for dividing a list into different sections. For example, you may want to list your favorite Web sites according to type:

```
<BODY>

<UL>
<LI>  Magazine Web Sites
    <UL>
    <LI> <A HREF="http://www.byte.com"> BYTE </A>
    </UL>
<LI>  Company Web Sites
    <UL>
    <LI> <A HREF="http://www.microsoft.com"> Microsoft </A>
    </UL>
</UL>

</BODY>
</HTML>
```

If you display this HTML file in Netscape Navigator, you'd notice that a different type of bullet appears next to each level of nesting. By default, the outermost list appears with a disc, the next level displays a circle, and any additional levels use a square. You can override this behavior by setting the TYPE attribute to particular bullet shapes.

Creating Ordered Lists

If you want a numbered list, use an *ordered list* (see Figure 6.13). For example, suppose you want to list the top reasons for visiting your Web site. An ordered list is perfect for this task:

```
<HTML>
<HEAD><TITLE> Ordered List </TITLE></HEAD>
<BODY>

<OL>
<LI>  This web site uses Active Server Pages.
<LI>  This web site uses advanced HTML tags.
<LI>  This web site contains no <BLINK> blinking </BLINK> text.
</OL>

</BODY>
</HTML>
```

FIGURE 6.13.

An ordered list.

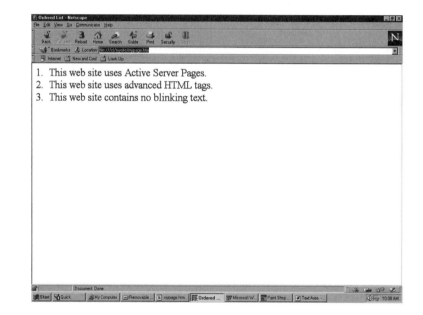

In an ordered list, the <OL> tag contains the list items. Each list item is designated by the <LI> tag. You can list as many items as you want.

By default, the list items are displayed in a browser using Arabic numerals (that is, 1, 2, 3). However, you can change this default with the TYPE attribute of the <OL> tag. You also can list the items using uppercase Roman numerals (I, II, III), lowercase Roman numerals (i, ii, iii), uppercase letters (A, B, C), or lowercase letters (a, b, c). This is useful for, among other things, displaying the table of contents of a book, as in Figure 6.14:

```
<HTML>
<HEAD><TITLE> Ordered List </TITLE></HEAD>
<BODY>
```

```
<OL TYPE=I>
<LI>  Markup and Scripting Languages
    <OL TYPE=i>
    <LI> Basic HTML
    <LI> Intermediate HTML
    <LI> Advanced HTML
    </OL>
</OL>

</BODY>
</HTML>
```

FIGURE 6.14.
Table of contents.

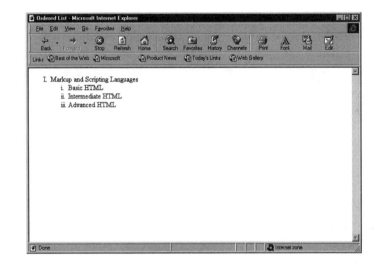

Notice how the TYPE attribute was set in this example. To change how the items are listed, set the TYPE attribute to the first number in the numbering system you want to use. The TYPE attribute can take the values 1, I, i, A, or a.

On occasion, you may need to skip some numbers either at the beginning of your list or somewhere within the list. By using the START attribute of the <OL> tag, you can specify the first number in the list. By using the VALUE attribute of the <LI> tag, you can skip a range of numbers. This example uses both of these attributes:

```
<HTML>
<HEAD><TITLE> Ordered List </TITLE></HEAD>
<BODY>

<OL TYPE=A START=3>
<LI>  I display the letter 'C'.
<LI VALUE=6> I display the letter 'F'.
</OL>

</BODY>
</HTML>
```

In this example, because the START attribute is equal to 3, the list begins with the letter *C* (the third letter in the alphabet). The next item is listed with the letter *F* because the VALUE attribute of this list item is equal to 6 (the sixth letter in the alphabet). Using these two attributes, you have complete control over the sequence of numbers used in your list.

Creating Definition Lists

Suppose you want to share a list of your favorite words and their definitions with the visitors to your Web site. A *definition list* is perfect for this task (see Figure 6.15). Here's an example:

```
<HTML>
<HEAD><TITLE> Definition List </TITLE></HEAD>
<BODY>

<DL>
<DT>  Inveigle
<DD> To entice or lure by artful talk.
<DT>  Frisson
<DD>  A brief moment of emotional excitement:  SHUDDER, THRILL.
</DL>

</BODY>
</HTML>
```

FIGURE 6.15.

A definition list.

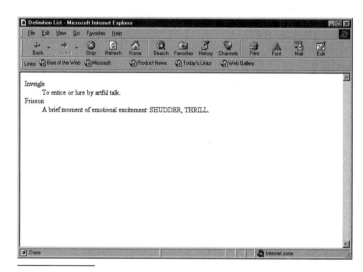

Definitions from *Random House Webster's Dictionary*, 1993, Ballantine Books, and *The Merriam-Webster Collegiate Dictionary, Tenth Edition*, 1993, Merriam-Webster, Incorporated.

Definition lists, unlike other lists, are created using three tags. The <DL> tag contains the definition list. The <DT> tag marks the term to be defined, and the <DD> tag marks the definition of the term.

6

You should feel free to use a definition list for things other than its intended purpose. For example, you can use a definition list to display a list of your favorite Web sites and their descriptions, like this:

```
<HTML>
<HEAD><TITLE> Definition List </TITLE></HEAD>
<BODY>

<DL>
<DT>   <A HREF="http://www.hotwired.com"> HotWired </A>
<DD> A trendy online news source for information on the wired community.
<DT>   <A HREF="http://www.netscape.com"> Netscape </A>
<DD> One of the most visited sites on the Internet.
</DL>

</BODY>
</HTML>
```

By using a definition list instead of an unordered list for this purpose, you can display the Web sites without the bullets.

Formatting with Tables

Tables have both an obvious and a not-so-obvious use. First, the obvious one. Tables can be used to create a table of information. Whenever you need to present information in rows and columns, use a table. For example, you can use a table to display a list of cities and their area codes. You can also use tables to format information retrieved from a database. In general, tables can be used to present in readable form what would otherwise be overwhelming doses of information.

A less obvious but more powerful use of tables is for page formatting. Using tables, you can divide your Web page into different areas. For example, you can use a table to create multiple columns on your Web page, each with a different background color. When you need precise control over the spacing and layout of your Web page, use tables.

Creating a Simple Table of Information

Tables can be extremely complex. Many table tags are available, and each tag has many attributes. Moreover, many of these attributes are either Microsoft- or Netscape-specific. However, a table also can be very simple. Here's an example of a very simple table (see Figure 6.16):

```
<HTML>
<HEAD><TITLE> Table With Border </TITLE></HEAD>
<BODY>

<TABLE BORDER=1>
<TR>
<TD> I am a table and I have a border </TD>
</TR>
</TABLE>

</BODY>
</HTML>
```

FIGURE 6.16.

A simple table with a border.

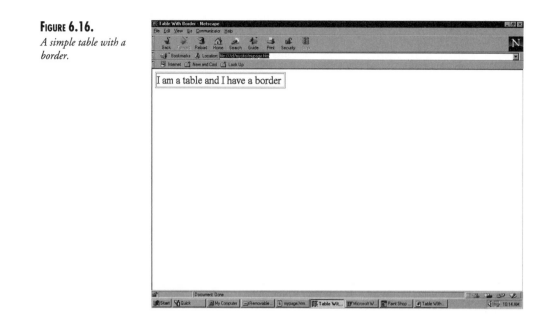

When this HTML file is displayed in a Web browser, the sentence I am a table and I have a border is contained in a table with a three-dimensional border. This effect is created with the help of three tags: <TABLE>, <TR>, and <TD>.

The <TABLE> tag is used to contain all the HTML tags and data associated with a table. Every table begins with the <TABLE> tag and ends with the </TABLE> tag. Generally, the attributes of the <TABLE> tag affect the properties of the table as a whole.

In this example, the BORDER attribute places a border around the outside of the table. You can change the width of this border by providing a different value for the BORDER attribute. As you might expect, a table without a BORDER attribute appears without any border.

The <TR> tag creates a table row. In this example, the table has only one row. However, you can include as many rows in a table as you need.

The <TD> tag is used to contain the actual table data. You can think of the <TD> tag as the table column tag. A table can have as many columns as you need. The <TD> tag can contain any tag that normally appears in the body of an HTML document. For example, this tag can contain images, hypertext links, and forms. It can even contain other tables.

When creating tables, at least conceptually, you should create the rows first and then create the columns within the rows. You can't place the <TR> tag within the <TD> tag; tables have rows and columns, in that order.

The table in the preceding example is extremely simple: It has only one row and one column. Nevertheless, it contains all the tags you would need to display even very large tables of information. To create larger tables, simply add more rows and columns with the <TR> and <TD> tags.

For example, suppose you want to display a table containing a list of cities and their area codes. You could do it like this:

```
<HTML>
<HEAD><TITLE> Area Codes </TITLE></HEAD>
<BODY>

<TABLE BORDER=1>
<TR>
    <TD> Boston     </TD>
    <TD> 617     </TD>
</TR>
<TR>
    <TD> Modesto </TD>
    <TD> 209     </TD>
</TR>
<TR>
    <TD> San Francisco </TD>
    <TD> 415     </TD>
</TR>
</TABLE>

</BODY>
</HTML>
```

In this example, the <TR> tag is used to create three table rows, one row for each city (see Figure 6.17). Each table row contains two <TD> tags, which create the columns containing the city name and the city area code.

FIGURE 6.17.

A simple table with multiple columns and rows.

Creating Table Captions and Headers

The purpose of the table in Figure 6.17 isn't very clear. If a user displays it on a Web page without any accompanying text, he or she wouldn't necessarily understand that the table presents a list of area codes. You can improve this situation by including both a caption and some headers for the table.

A table caption clarifies the purpose of a table as a whole. You can add a caption to a table by using the <CAPTION> tag. Here's an example of how this tag is used:

```
<HTML>
<HEAD><TITLE> Area Codes </TITLE></HEAD>
<BODY>

<TABLE BORDER=1>
<CAPTION>Area Codes</CAPTION>
<TR>
     <TD> Boston      </TD>
     <TD> 617     </TD>
</TR>
<TR>
     <TD> Modesto </TD>
     <TD> 209     </TD>
</TR>
<TR>
     <TD> San Francisco </TD>
     <TD> 415     </TD>
</TR>
</TABLE>

</BODY>
</HTML>
```

Now, when the table is displayed in a browser, the caption Area Codes appears over the top of the table. By default, the caption appears above the table, but you can create a caption that appears underneath a table by adding the ALIGN="bottom" attribute to the <CAPTION> tag.

> **NOTE**
>
> Internet Explorer also recognizes the values "left" and "right" for the ALIGN attribute of the <CAPTION> tag. You might expect that these values would create a caption running down the left or right side of the table, but they merely alter the alignment of the caption over the table, aligning the caption at the left or right edge of the table, respectively.

This table can be made even clearer. Currently, the purpose of each of the columns isn't clear. Some foolish alien from another planet, for example, might believe that the number 415 is the name of a city and the name San Francisco is an area code. To prevent this type of confusion, you should include headers for your columns.

To create a table header, use the <TH> tag. The <TH> tag works very much like the <TD> tag. However, text that appears within this tag is rendered in bold (see Figure 6.18). The table in the following code includes some column headers:

```
<HTML>
<HEAD><TITLE> Area Codes </TITLE></HEAD>
<BODY>

<TABLE BORDER=1>
<CAPTION>Area Codes</CAPTION>
<TR>
    <TH> City     </TH>
    <TH> Area Code    </TH>
</TR>
<TR>
    <TD> Boston    </TD>
    <TD> 617    </TD>
</TR>
<TR>
    <TD> Modesto </TD>
    <TD> 209    </TD>
</TR>
<TR>
    <TD> San Francisco </TD>
    <TD> 415    </TD>
</TR>
</TABLE>

</BODY>
</HTML>
```

FIGURE 6.18.

A table with column headers.

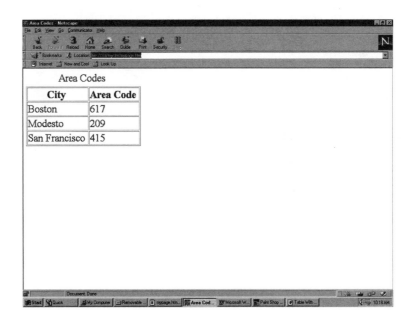

You don't need to use the <TH> tag only for column headers. You also can use it to create row headers by including it at the beginning of a row. In fact, you can place the <TH> tag anywhere in a table where you could place a <TD> tag. In reality, the only difference between these two tags is that the <TH> tag renders text in bold and centers it; by default, the <TD> tag doesn't do either one of these things.

Spanning Columns and Rows

Suppose you want to divide the table of area codes into different regions. For example, you want anyone who looks at your table to know at a glance which cities and area codes are located on the East Coast and which cities and area codes are located on the West Coast.

You could do this by dividing the table into two halves, labeling the left half East Coast and the right half West Coast. The East Coast header would cover the City and Area Code columns for the East Coast. The West Coast header would cover the City and Area Code columns for the West Coast. However, to label more than one column, you need to create a header that spans more than a single column width. You can do this by using the COLSPAN attribute of the <TH> tag (see Figure 6.19). Here's an example of how this attribute is used:

```
<HTML>
<HEAD><TITLE> Area Codes </TITLE></HEAD>
<BODY>

<TABLE BORDER=1>
<CAPTION>Area Codes</CAPTION>
<TR>
    <TH COLSPAN=2> East Coast </TH>
    <TH COLSPAN=2> West Coast </TH>
</TR>
<TR>
    <TH> City     </TH>
    <TH> Area Code     </TH>
    <TH> City     </TH>
    <TH> Area Code     </TH>
</TR>
<TR>
    <TD> Boston     </TD>
    <TD> 617     </TD>
    <TD> Modesto </TD>
    <TD> 209     </TD>
</TR>
<TR>
    <TD></TD>
    <TD></TD>
    <TD> San Francisco </TD>
    <TD> 415     </TD>
</TR>
</TABLE>

</BODY>
</HTML>
```

6

INTERMEDIATE HTML

FIGURE 6.19.

A table with headers spanning multiple columns.

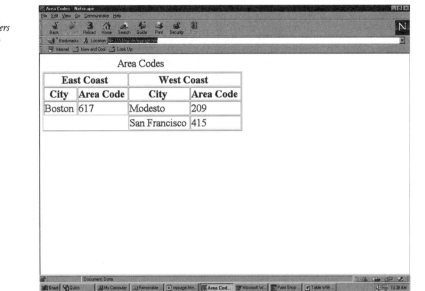

When this HTML file is displayed in a browser, the header East Coast spans the first two columns, and the header West Coast spans the second two. The COLSPAN attribute also can be used with the <TD> tag. Using the COLSPAN attribute, you can force either headers or columns to span two or more columns of normal width.

A corresponding attribute exists for spanning rows. To create a row that spans two or more normal rows, use the ROWSPAN attribute of the <TH> and <TD> tags. You can use this attribute to create labels for multiple rows. This is useful when you want to associate the same label with multiple rows.

Controlling Table and Cell Alignment

By default, tables are aligned at the left side of the browser screen. You can specify the alignment of a table by using the ALIGN attribute of the <TABLE> tag. The ALIGN attribute can be assigned the values "left", "center", and "right". For example, to center a table on the screen, use <TABLE ALIGN=CENTER>.

NOTE

Be careful with the ALIGN attribute of the <TABLE> tag; not all browsers recognize it. If you want to center a table on the screen, it's safer to contain the table within the <CENTER> tag.

You can set the horizontal alignment of all the cells in a table row by using the ALIGN attribute of the <TR> tag. This attribute also can be set equal to the values "left", "center", and "right". To control the vertical alignment of all the cells in a particular row, use the VALIGN attribute of the <TR> tag. Permissible values are "top", "middle", and "bottom" (by default, the value is "middle").

To gain even finer control over the alignment of particular headers or cells in a table, use the ALIGN and VALIGN attributes of the <TH> and <TD> tag. These two attributes take the same values as the <TR> tag. However, the ALIGN and VALIGN attributes of the <TH> and <TD> tag override any alignment specified at the level of a table row.

Controlling Cell Spacing

When a browser displays a table, it normally makes the width of each column equal to the widest cell in that column. The browser also attempts to use the minimum amount of screen room possible by placing table cells very close to each other. You can override these default settings by using the CELLPADDING and CELLSPACING attributes of the <TABLE> tag.

By using the CELLPADDING attribute, you can create more empty space between the contents of a table cell and the cell's border. By using the CELLSPACING attribute, on the other hand, you can create empty space between cell borders. The values of both attributes are specified in pixels. Here's an example of how both of these attributes are used (see Figure 6.20):

```
<HTML>
<HEAD><TITLE> Cell Spacing </TITLE></HEAD>
<BODY>

<TABLE BORDER=1>
<CAPTION> Normal Table  </CAPTION>
<TR>
<TD> First Column </TD>
<TD> Second Column </TD>
</TR>
</TABLE>
<HR>
<TABLE BORDER=1 CELLSPACING=30>
<CAPTION> Table With Cell Spacing </CAPTION>
<TR>
<TD> First Column </TD>
<TD> Second Column </TD>
</TR>
</TABLE>
<HR>
<TABLE BORDER=1 CELLPADDING=30>
<CAPTION> Table With Cell Padding </CAPTION>
<TR>
<TD> First Column </TD>
<TD> Second Column </TD>
</TR>
</TABLE>

</BODY>
</HTML>
```

FIGURE 6.20.

Normal table, spaced table, and padded table.

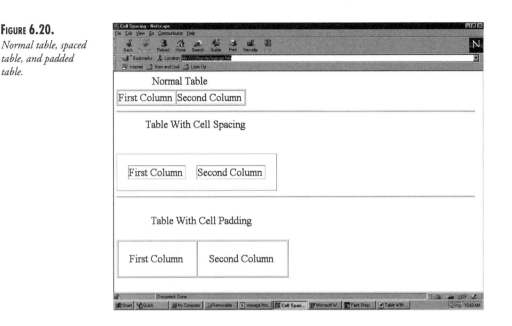

Controlling Table and Cell Size

Sometimes you may want a table to appear wider than normal. You can control the width of a table by using the WIDTH attribute of the <TABLE> tag. You can supply the WIDTH attribute with either an absolute or a relative value.

When the WIDTH attribute is assigned an absolute value, you assign the value in pixels. For example, to create a table at least 100 pixels wide, you would use <TABLE WIDTH=100>. Of course, there's no guarantee that the table will appear with exactly the width assigned. The contents of a table's cells may force the table to be wider than the value specified in its WIDTH attribute.

Alternatively, you can use a relative value to assign a table's width. For example, if you want a table to span the complete width of the browser screen, you can use <TABLE WIDTH="100%">. Again, if you assign too small a percentage of the screen to the WIDTH attribute, the browser may not display the table at that width.

The HEIGHT attribute can be used to assign an overall height to a table. Again, this attribute takes either an absolute or relative value. Be cautious with this attribute. Even though both the Microsoft and Netscape browsers interpret this attribute correctly, it's not part of the official HTML 3.2 specification.

You also can control the size of individual cells by using the WIDTH and HEIGHT attributes of the <TD> and <TH> tags. You must assign these attributes with absolute pixel values. Understand that when you assign these values, at best you're merely providing the browser with suggestions. The browser attempts to follow your wishes, but it may not be able to format a table in exactly the way specified.

Adding Color and Images to Tables

According to the HTML 3.2 specification, tables can't be assigned any color attributes. Happily, however, both Netscape and Microsoft have extended HTML to allow for table background colors. Both browsers recognize the BGCOLOR attribute of the <TABLE> tag.

You can assign the BGCOLOR attribute any color name or RGB code. Here's an example of how this attribute may be used:

```
<HTML>
<HEAD><TITLE> Table Color </TITLE></HEAD>
<BODY BGCOLOR="white">

<CENTER>
<TABLE BGCOLOR="lightblue" CELLPADDING=10>
<TR>
<TD> I have a blue background </TD>
</TR>
</TABLE>
</CENTER>

</BODY>
</HTML>
```

When the text in this example is displayed in a browser, it appears in a light blue box. This is useful for offsetting particular text from the main body of text on your Web page. For instance, you might want to use this trick to offset a quote, a heading, or a brief note from the rest of the page.

You also can use the BGCOLOR attribute with table rows or even individual cells—for example, to display different colors to highlight the data in different table columns.

Perhaps a more exciting use of the BGCOLOR attribute is for formatting the color of your overall Web page. If you make the width of your table the width of the screen, you can create a multiple-column page with a different color for each column. The following example creates a two-column, two-color Web page:

```
<HTML>
<HEAD><TITLE> Two Color Columns </TITLE></HEAD>
<BODY BGCOLOR="white">

<CENTER>
<TABLE WIDTH="100%" HEIGHT="100%">
<TR>
<TD BGCOLOR="Olive" ALIGN="center"> I have an olive background </TD>
<TD BGCOLOR="Aqua" ALIGN="center">I have an aqua background </TD>
</TR>
</TABLE>
</CENTER>

</BODY>
</HTML>
```

Both the Netscape and Microsoft browsers also allow you to specify images for the backgrounds of your tables (see Figure 6.21). You specify an image by using the BACKGROUND attribute of the <TABLE> tag:

```
<HTML>
<HEAD><TITLE> Two Color Columns </TITLE></HEAD>
<BODY BGCOLOR="white">

<CENTER>
<TABLE WIDTH="50%" HEIGHT="100%" BACKGROUND="myimage.gif">
<TR>
<TD ALIGN="center">I have a checkered background </TD>
</TR>
</TABLE>
</CENTER>

</BODY>
</HTML>
```

FIGURE 6.21.

A table with a checkered background.

Netscape 4.0 and Internet Explorer 3.0 and 4.0 also allow you to use the BACKGROUND attribute with table rows and individual cells. By using different images for the backgrounds of different cells, you can create Web pages that have a powerful visual impact.

Advanced Page Layout with Tables

You can create very sophisticated Web page layouts with tables. Tables are very valuable for dividing a Web page into different parts that have different functions. Here's an example (continued on the next page):

```
<HTML>
<HEAD><TITLE> Table Page Layout </TITLE></HEAD>
<BODY BGCOLOR="white">
```

```
<TABLE BGCOLOR="yellow" WIDTH="100%">
<TR>
<TD ALIGN=CENTER VALIGN=CENTER>
<FONT FACE=ARIAL SIZE=+2>Acme Industrial Products</FONT>
</TD>
</TR>
</TABLE>

<TABLE HEIGHT="100%" CELLPADDING=20>
<TR>
<TD ALIGN=CENTER VALIGN=CENTER BGCOLOR="blue">
<FORM METHOD=POST ACTION="/somedirectory/mypage.asp">
<INPUT NAME="Home" TYPE="SUBMIT" VALUE="HOME"><P>
<INPUT NAME="Buy" TYPE="SUBMIT" VALUE="BUY"><P>
<INPUT NAME="Help" TYPE="SUBMIT" VALUE="HELP"><P>
</FORM>
</TD>

<TD ALIGN=CENTER VALIGN=CENTER>
<TABLE HEIGHT="100%" ALIGN=CENTER CELLSPACING=50>
<TR>
<TD>
     
At Acme Industrial, you can buy the latest
manufacturing equipment at the lowest prices.
We have a commitment to quality that has been
unsurpassed for over 50 years.
Browse our store and make up your own mind!
</TD>
</TR>
<TR VALIGN="bottom">
<TD>
<FONT SIZE=-1>&copy; 1997 by Acme Industrial.
Any questions about this web site? Contact the
<A HREF="mailto:webmaster@acme.com">webmaster</A>
</TD>
</TR>
</TABLE>
</TD>

</TR>
</TABLE>

</BODY>
</HTML>
```

This example uses three tables (see Figure 6.22). One table is used to make the title banner
Acme Industrial Products across the top of the screen. The background color of this table is
yellow. The WIDTH attribute is set to "100%" so that the table will span the complete width of the
screen.

The second table is used to provide a button bar down the left side of the screen. This table has
a blue background with three form submit buttons. Notice how easy it is to mix HTML forms
and tables. Also, notice how the CELLPADDING attribute has been used to push the borders of
the table away from the edges of the buttons.

FIGURE 6.22.

Advanced page layout with tables.

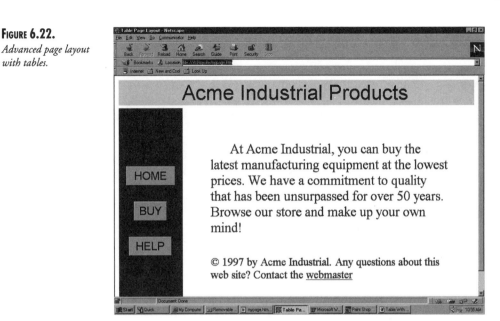

Finally, nested in the previous table, a third table contains the page text that appears on the right side of the screen. This table is nested so that it will appear to the right of the button bar rather than below the button bar. The table is aligned by the values of the cell in which it's contained.

Tables as Sub-Pages

The <TABLE> tag originally was introduced into HTML to format tables of information. However, the attributes of this tag have been greatly expanded over time. Now it's better to think of the <TABLE> tag as a tag for creating sub-pages in a Web page. The tag has been extended with so many additional attributes that it now functions very much like the <BODY> tag. The <TABLE> tag, at least in the case of the Netscape and Microsoft browsers, has many of the same attributes as the <BODY> tag. You can provide a table with its own background color and image. Furthermore, the <TABLE> tag can contain all the HTML tags that can be contained in a <BODY> tag.

However, the <TABLE> tag has a very significant advantage over the <BODY> tag. Every HTML file must contain at least one, but no more than one <BODY> tag. But there's no restriction on the number of <TABLE> tags that an HTML file can include.

When you design your Web pages, don't let the name of the <TABLE> tag fool you. Use the table tag to create sub-pages on your Web page. Whenever you need to divide a single Web page into multiple parts, use the <TABLE> tag.

Summary

This chapter described a number of important HTML tags. For example, you now understand how to create HTML forms that you can use to make your Web site interactive. You also learned a number of useful HTML tags for formatting lists of information. Finally, you discovered how to use tables to format tables of information and, better yet, to create advanced page layouts for your Web site.

The next chapter introduces some of the most advanced tags in HTML. You learn how to work with image maps, frames, and cascading style sheets. After finishing the next chapter, you should be able to create any Web page that you have ever seen—or even imagined.

Advanced HTML

IN THIS CHAPTER

This chapter describes some of the most advanced tags of standard HTML. You learn how to create image maps that you can use to make your Web site easier to navigate. You also learn how to use windows and frames to display multiple Web pages at the same time. Finally, you learn how to gain fine-grain control over the formatting of your Web pages by using cascading style sheets.

Working with Image Maps

The home pages of many Web sites include an image that you can click to navigate to different sections of the Web site (see Figure 7.1). For example, the image might include icons representing a news section, a chat section, and a file download section. If a visitor to the Web site wants to move immediately to the news section from the home page, he or she can simply click the news icon. The image that contains these icons is called an *image map*.

FIGURE 7.1.

An example of an image map.

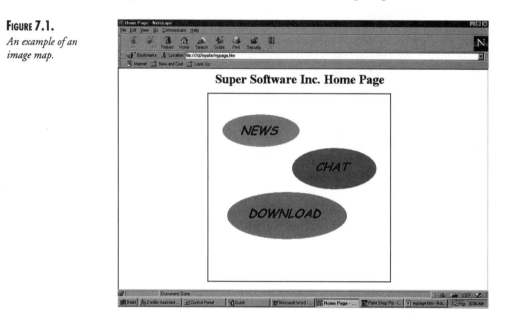

A related use of image maps is for creating *navigation bars* on the top of every page on a Web site. The navigation bar contains a menu of the site's main sections. Again, users can use a navigation bar to quickly and easily navigate to an area of interest. For example, many of the pages on the Netscape Web site include a navigation bar (see Figure 7.2).

These are two of the main uses of image maps. However, there are other, more imaginative ways in which they can be employed. For example, you could use an image map to gather information. Suppose you want to know where in the world the visitors to your Web site are coming from. You could create an image map that has a map of the world. Visitors could indicate their home country by clicking the correct area. Whenever you need to display a choice of options in a single image, use an image map.

FIGURE 7.2.
Netscape Web page with navigation bar.

Navigation bar —

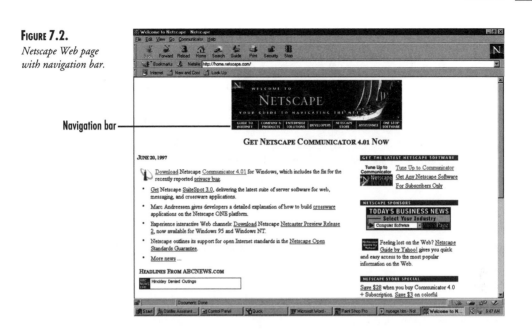

There are two types of image maps: server-side and client-side. When you use a *server-side image map*, the server determines what action to take when a user clicks a region of the image. In a *client-side image map*, the browser determines what action to take. Server-side image maps are compatible with more browsers, but client-side image maps are much faster. Both types of image maps are easy to create. The following sections describe the two types.

Server-Side Image Maps

If you want your image maps to work on the maximum number of browsers, use a *server-side image map*. Server-side image maps are compatible with even the oldest browsers. The only disadvantage of server-side image maps is that they're significantly slower than client-side image maps.

Three steps are involved in creating a server-side image map:

1. Create the image.
2. Include the correct HTML tags in the HTML file.
3. Create a map file.

The following paragraphs provide the details.

You can use any type of image in an image map. Typically, GIF files are used, but you can use JPEG or even PNG images as well. There's nothing special about an image used for an image map. You can create the image using any paint program that supports the standard Web image formats.

When creating your image, make sure that it's large enough that users can easily click different areas with a mouse. If you make your image too small, users struggle to click the correct area. This can be very frustrating. At the same time, don't make your image so large that it takes forever to load into a browser. Too many Web sites on the Internet have huge image maps on their home pages (corporate Web sites are especially guilty of this). Your image may be an artistic masterpiece, but no one will ever see it if it takes many hours to load.

The second step in creating a server-side image map is to include the necessary HTML tags in your HTML file. You specify that an image should be treated as a server-side image map by using the ISMAP attribute of the <IMG> tag. Here's an example:

```
<HTML>
<HEAD><TITLE>Server-Side Image Map </TITLE></HEAD>
<BODY>

<A HREF="/somedirectory/mymap.map"><IMG SRC="myimage.gif" ISMAP></A>

</BODY>
</HTML>
```

This example assumes that you've created a normal GIF image named myimage.gif. This is the image that will be displayed as the image map. The attribute ISMAP warns the browser to interpret the image as an image map rather than as a normal image.

You can use all the usual attributes of the <IMG> tag. For example, you may want to use the BORDER=0 attribute to prevent Netscape Navigator from drawing a border around the outside of your image.

The final step in creating a server-side image map is to create a *map file*. A map file is a normal text file with the file extension .map. You can create map files by using any normal text editor. In the preceding example, notice that the image is contained in the <A> tag. However, the HREF attribute doesn't point to an HTML file as usual. Instead, the HREF attribute points to a file named mymap.map. The file mymap.map is a map file.

A map file associates different areas in an image with different Web addresses (URLs). For example, suppose your image includes an icon of a newspaper and an icon of people talking. If someone clicks the newspaper icon, you want the news page to load in that person's browser. If someone clicks the icon of people talking, you want the chat page to load in that person's browser. To create these associations between areas on the image and Web pages, you must create the map file.

Internet Information Server (the Web server that this book assumes you're using) recognizes map files in both the NCSA and CERN formats. This is an example of an NCSA map file:

```
# WWW NCSA Image Map file for 'myimage.gif'
default /home.htm
rect /news.htm 0,0 100,100
rect /chat.htm 101,0 200,100
```

In this map file, the number (#) character indicates the start of a comment. You can place any text you want after the # character. In this example, the comment includes the name of the image associated with this map file. This is a good practice to follow when you have multiple image maps. By including the name of the image in the map file, you can remember which image to associate with which map file.

The code rect is used to associate a rectangular area of the image with the address of an HTML file. For example, the news.htm file is associated with the rectangle defined by the coordinates 0,0 and 100,100. These coordinates specify an area on the image starting from the upper-left corner and extending 100 pixels across and 100 pixels down. When someone clicks this area of the image, the HTML file news.htm will be loaded into that person's browser.

Finally, the default code specifies the default HTML file that will be loaded when someone clicks the image map, but outside any explicitly defined area. In this example, if someone clicks an area not covered by the areas of the two rectangles, the home.htm HTML file is loaded.

For this map file, the areas are specified by using rectangles. However, you aren't limited to using only rectangles. You can also define areas in the shapes of circles, polygons, and even—if you're feeling especially sadistic—individual points. The following map file uses all four types of areas:

```
# WWW NCSA Image Map file for 'myimage.gif'
default /home.htm
rect /news.htm 0,0 100,100
circle /chat.htm 50,50 20
poly /help.htm 200,0 400,0 400,100 200,100 200,0
point /NeverGetHere.htm 500,6
```

In this map file, the circle code defines a circular area on the image with a center at point 50,50 and a radius of 20 pixels. The poly code defines an area in the shape of a polygon specified by a list of points (in x,y pairs). Finally, the point code specifies an individual point. To cause the NeverGetHere.htm HTML file to load, someone would have to click the single pixel on the image at the coordinates 500,6.

> **NOTE**
>
> Be careful when using polygons to define areas for your image map. Early versions of Internet Information Server couldn't handle polygons defined with more than 100 vertices (this would cause an access violation). The current version can handle polygons that have 160 vertices, but will ignore any larger polygons.

You may have noticed in this map file that the areas defined by the rect and circle codes overlap. In cases where two areas overlap, the first area listed in the map file takes precedence. So, in this example, the rectangle takes precedence over the circle. The news.htm file would be associated with any points that are common between the rectangle and circle.

NOTE

Some paint programs, such as Fractal Design Painter, automatically generate map files for you. Alternatively, a number of shareware and freeware utilities were specifically created for this purpose. See http://www.shareware.com or http://www.tucows.com.

After you have created the image, included the necessary HTML tags, and created the map file, you should have a functioning server-side image map. You can include as many image maps on a page as you want. Also, you can use the same image and map file over and over again on multiple pages. This is useful, for instance, when you need to include the same navigator bar on a number of pages.

Client-Side Image Maps

A *client-side image map* can be used for exactly the same purposes as a server-side image map. However, a client-side image map is much faster. The only disadvantage of a client-side image map is that it won't work on older browsers.

In a client-side image map, the map file is specified with HTML tags. You create the map file by using the <MAP> and <AREA> tags, as in this example:

```
<HTML>
<HEAD><TITLE>Client-Side Image Map </TITLE></HEAD>
<BODY>

<MAP NAME="mymap">
<AREA SHAPE="rect" COORDINATES="0,0,100,100" HREF="/news.htm">
<AREA SHAPE="rect" COORDINATES="101,0,200,100" HREF="/chat.htm">
</MAP>

</BODY>
</HTML>
```

The <MAP> tag is used to contain the <AREA> tags and provides a name for the map. Each <AREA> tag defines an area on an image and associates the area with an address (URL).

In this example, two rectangular areas of the image are specified. The first area begins at the upper-left edge of the image and extends 100 pixels across and 100 pixels down. If someone clicks in this area, the news.htm file is loaded. The second rectangle starts at the x,y coordinates of 101,0 and extends to the coordinates 200,100. This area is associated with the HTML file chat.htm.

NOTE

According to the HTML 3.2 specification, you can use percentages when providing the coordinates of a shape. However, not all browsers support this feature. Therefore, it's best to avoid it.

You also can specify circles and polygons as the values of the SHAPE attribute. Here's an example of a map that uses all three shapes:

```
<HTML>
<HEAD><TITLE>Client-Side Image Map </TITLE></HEAD>
<BODY>

<MAP NAME="mymap">
<AREA SHAPE="rect" COORDINATES="0,0,100,100" HREF="/news.htm">
<AREA SHAPE="circle" COORDINATES="50,50,20" HREF="/chat.htm">
<AREA SHAPE="poly"
COORDINATES="200,0 400,0 400,100 200,100 200,0" HREF="/help.htm">
<AREA SHAPE="rect" COORDINATES="0,0,10,10" NOHREF>
</MAP>

</BODY>
</HTML>
```

In this example, the area of the circle is specified by providing the x,y values of the center of the circle, followed by the radius of the circle. The area of the polygon is given by a string of x,y coordinates that defines the vertices of the polygon.

Notice the NOHREF attribute used in the last <AREA> tag. This attribute is used to specify a dead zone in the image map. If someone clicks this area, no file is loaded. In this example, the last <AREA> tag is used to cut a hole in the rectangle specified in the first <AREA> tag. (This attribute is useful when you're attempting to define complex shapes within an image map.)

Notice that the areas of the first rectangle and the circle overlap. The first <AREA> tag listed takes precedence. So, in this example, the news.htm file is loaded if someone clicks within the area shared by both the rectangle and circle.

In a client-side map, you can't specify a default file to load when someone clicks outside all the defined regions. However, a way exists to get the same effect. If you make your last <AREA> tag cover the whole image, this tag would specify a default file for the image map as a whole.

This HTML file isn't quite complete. You still need to specify an image to use in your image map. You associate an image with a map file by using the USEMAP attribute of the <IMG> tag, like this:

```
<HTML>
<HEAD><TITLE>Client-Side Image Map </TITLE></HEAD>
<BODY>

<MAP NAME="mymap">
<AREA SHAPE="rect" COORDINATES="0,0,100,100" HREF="/news.htm">
<AREA SHAPE="rect" COORDINATES="101,0,200,100" HREF="/chat.htm">
</MAP>

<IMG SRC="myimage.gif" USEMAP="#mymap">

</BODY>
</HTML>
```

7

ADVANCED HTML

In this example, the map `mymap` is associated with the `myimage.gif` image. If you want, you can associate the same map with multiple images on the same page. This could be useful, for example, if you want to include the same navigator bar at both the top and bottom of a page.

Normally, you'll use a GIF image when creating a client-side image map. However, you also can use JPEG and even PNG images. If you want to use a photograph for your image map, a JPEG image may be a better choice (See Chapter 5, "Basic HTML," for a discussion of when to use JPEG rather than GIF images.)

You can use all the usual attributes of the `<IMG>` tag. For example, you should specify the `WIDTH` and `HEIGHT` attributes so the image will load faster. Also, you might want to include the `BORDER=0` attribute of the `<IMG>` tag. If you include this attribute, a border won't appear around the outside of your image.

Be careful when specifying the name of the map file. You must always use the # character before the name of the map when you refer to it in the `<IMG>` tag. Also, the name of a map file is case-sensitive; the map named `Mymap` is not the same as the map named `mymap`.

Working with Windows and Frames

Using windows and frames, you can display multiple HTML documents on the screen at the same time. Using windows, you can create multiple instances of the browser window. Using frames, you can divide a browser window into multiple parts and display a distinct HTML file in each part.

For example, using frames, you could divide your browser window into two halves and display the Netscape home page in the left half and the Microsoft home page in the right half. Pages from the two Web sites could coexist peacefully in the same browser window at the same time by occupying two distinct frames (see Figure 7.3).

Normally, however, frames are used when you want a part of the window to remain the same as users navigate a Web site. The content of one frame remains fixed, while the content of the second frame changes.

Suppose you want to provide the full text of a book on your Web site. In that case, you could display the table of contents of the book in one frame, and display the text of a particular chapter in another. If users want to jump to a particular chapter, they can simply click the name of the chapter in the table of contents frame.

Frames also can be useful for displaying advertisements. If you want to display the same advertisement on the bottom of every page, you can create an advertisement frame. The content of the advertisement frame can remain fixed as users navigate in another frame to different Web pages on your Web site.

Finally, a frame can be used to display a standard corporate logo at the top of each page. By using a standard header frame, you can provide a Web site with a consistent appearance. With every glance to the top of the window, users will be reminded of your company's name.

FIGURE 7.3.

Netscape and Microsoft in the same browser window.

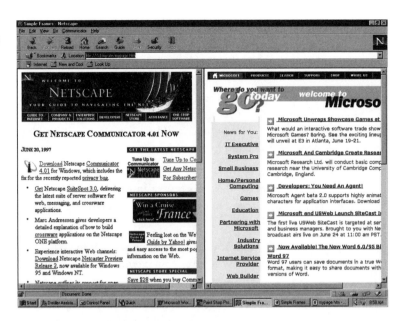

Advantages and Disadvantages of Frames

Before getting into the details of how to create a frame, you should be warned that some people really hate frames. This is not an exaggeration. In order to make sense of this strong emotional reaction to an HTML tag, you need to understand some of the disadvantages of frames:

- **Frames steal.** By default, frames have borders. These borders steal space from the screen that could be used for other purposes, such as content. Especially in the case of people using low-resolution screens, frames can occupy too much space. People resent this.

- **Frames trespass.** A poorly implemented frame can trespass on Web pages at other Web sites. Once a frame appears in the window of a Web browser, it may be difficult to make it go away. The frame may continue to appear even after you leave the Web site that created the frame in the first place. In this respect, a poorly implemented frame can linger longer than even the rudest houseguest.

- **Frames are associated with bad company.** When frames were first introduced, they were mainly used to display banner advertisements. This created an association in the mind of the Web public between frames and banner advertisements. Since people don't normally like advertisements, frames became guilty by association.

- **Frames can be untrustworthy.** Originally, Netscape introduced frames to the world as a Netscape-only extension to HTML. Microsoft soon followed with its own implementation of frames. The attributes of the frame tag are still in contention. This has resulted in frames behaving inconsistently when viewed with different browsers. Moreover, on many browsers, frames fail to work at all.

- **Framed pages can be difficult to identify.** You can't bookmark a Web page that appears in a frame. If you try, you'll end up bookmarking another page (the frameset page). This makes it difficult to navigate to a particular page in a Web site that uses frames.

- **Web sites that use frames can be slow.** All things being equal, two HTML files take longer to load in a browser than one. Because frames allow you to display multiple HTML files in the same browser window, a window with multiple frames may take a long time to display completely.

Therefore, it would seem to follow, the use of frames should be considered criminal. In fact, the designers of a number of Web sites on the Internet should be prosecuted for using frames inappropriately. Frames are often unnecessary. Often, tables can be used instead.

As discussed in Chapter 6, "Intermediate HTML," you can use tables to divide a Web page into sub-pages. Tables have none of the disadvantages of frames; moreover, tables can simulate many of the effects of frames. Whenever you're tempted to use a frame, consider using a table instead.

For example, consider the Web pages displayed in Figures 7.4 and 7.5. These two pages appear to be almost identical. However, the page in Figure 7.4 was created using tables, and the page in Figure 7.5 was created using frames. Because a Web page constructed using a table will typically load faster, you should create this page using tables.

FIGURE 7.4.

Created with tables.

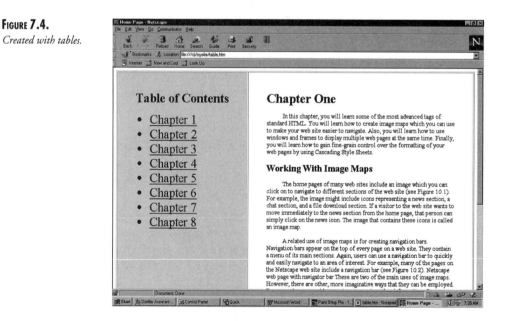

FIGURE 7.5.
Created with frames.

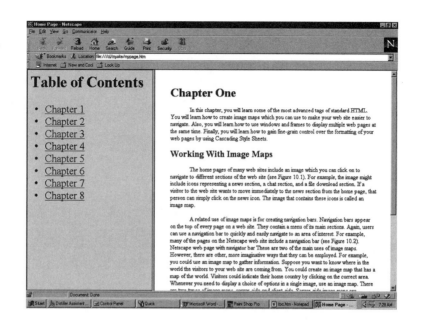

After all these negative points, you may think I'm saying that you should never use frames.

Well, not quite.

Frames do, in fact, have some unique properties. In general, you should use frames instead of tables in three special situations.

First, when you need a scrollbar, you *must* use frames. You can't scroll through the contents of a table without scrolling the whole Web page, but you can scroll through the contents of a frame.

Consider the example of a Web site that contains the text of a book. By using frames, you can display both the table of contents and the text of a particular chapter at the same time (see Figure 7.6). Because you can scroll through the contents of a frame, the table of contents can remain onscreen even as you read through a lengthy chapter. By using frames in this situation, you can display more content in the same amount of screen space than is normally possible.

Second, if you want one part of a window to remain fixed while another part changes, then you need to use frames. For example, suppose you want an advertisement to remain visible at all times in a browser window (see Figure 7.7). You don't want the advertisement to scroll off the screen as someone scrolls down through the contents of the page. To create a portion of the browser window that's always visible, you need to use frames.

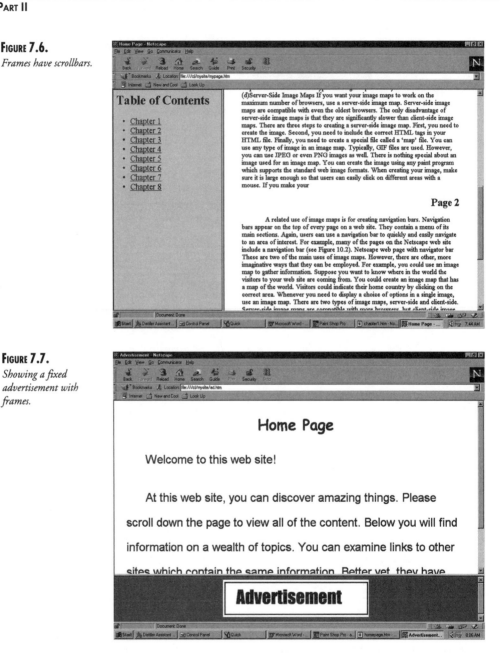

FIGURE 7.7.

Showing a fixed advertisement with frames.

Finally, when you want to display a complete Web page from another Web site, you need to use a frame. Sometimes you want to trespass on other Web sites. Getting more people to a Web site is a full-time obsession for many Webmasters. Once you get someone to visit your Web site, you don't want that person to leave. However, you may want to display hypertext links to other sites. So how can you let people visit other Web sites without leaving your own? Display the Web pages from other Web sites in a window or a frame (see Figure 7.8).

FIGURE 7.8.

Trespassing on other Web sites.

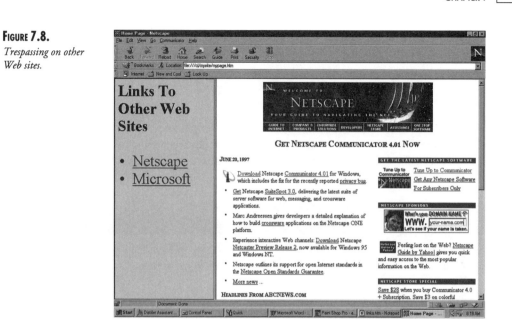

So there are some situations where frames are good or even necessary. However, in deference to the frame haters of the world, you should always provide a frameless version of your Web site. You'll find that this is necessary in any case, because not all browsers support frames.

Creating a New Window

Frames are contained in a browser window. Typically, all HTML content is displayed in the default browser window—the window that appears when you first launch the browser—but you can also create additional windows. By creating multiple browser windows, you can display multiple HTML pages at the same time.

The procedure for creating a new browser window is extremely simple. You use the TARGET attribute, which is an additional attribute of the <A> tag. Here's an example:

```
<HTML>
<HEAD><TITLE> New Window </TITLE></HEAD>
<BODY>

<A HREF="mypage.htm" TARGET="mywindow">Click Me!</A>

</BODY>
</HTML>
```

When this HTML file is displayed in a browser, the hypertext link `Click Me!` appears. If you click this link, a new browser window is displayed on the screen. The new browser window functions in exactly the same way as the default browser window that appears when you start your Web browser.

In the new window, the HTML file `mypage.htm` is loaded. The `<A>` tag works in the usual way, with all the usual attributes. The only difference in the tag's behavior in this example is the creation of a new browser window. The `TARGET` attribute of the `<A>` tag creates the new window. The value of the `TARGET` attribute specifies the window's name. In this example, the name of the new window is `mywindow`.

Whenever the value of the `TARGET` attribute is the name of a window that doesn't already exist, a new window is created. However, if a window by that name exists, the HTML file is loaded into that window. More than one `<A>` tag, in the same document or a different one, can target the very same window by using the `TARGET` attribute.

CAUTION

Don't confuse the name of a window with the title of an HTML document. The name of a window doesn't appear on the top of the browser window. In fact, the name of a window never appears in a Web browser at all. The only reason that a window needs a name is so that HTML tags can refer to it.

You can open as many new windows as you like. However, you should be careful in doing this. The visitor to your Web site probably won't immediately realize that a new window has been created. When a new window opens, normally it overlaps any other open windows. This can be very confusing. Whenever you open a new window, you should warn the user of what you're doing.

NOTE

You now understand how to open a new window, but how can you close it? There's no way of doing this with standard HTML. Normally, only the user of a Web browser can close an open window. However, if you're willing to add a little JavaScript to your page, then it's sometimes possible to close a window when that window isn't the only one open. Here's the JavaScript code:

```
<SCRIPT LANGUAGE="JavaScript">
window.close();
</SCRIPT>
```

This script closes whatever window is currently open. Depending on the browser, a confirmation dialog box may appear.

Dividing a Window into Frames

You should think of frames as the different panes in a window of glass. A *frame* is a particular portion of the browser window. A browser window can be divided into as many separate frames as you feel necessary. An individual frame can even be divided into other frames, resulting in *nested frames*.

To create distinct frames in a browser window, you need to create a special HTML file called a *frameset file.* A frameset file doesn't appear in a Web browser itself. The frameset file specifies how other Web pages should appear in a browser. Following is an example of a simple frameset file:

```
<HTML>
<HEAD>
<TITLE> Simple Frames </TITLE>
</HEAD>

<FRAMESET ROWS="100%" COLS="50%,50%">
  <FRAME SRC="mypage1.htm">
  <FRAME SRC="mypage2.htm">
</FRAMESET>

</HTML>
```

When this frameset file is loaded into a browser, the browser displays the HTML files `mypage1.htm` and `mypage2.htm`. These two files are normal HTML files. The frameset file tells the browser that these files should appear in two separate frames, as shown in Figure 7.9.

FIGURE 7.9.
Two HTML files in two frames.

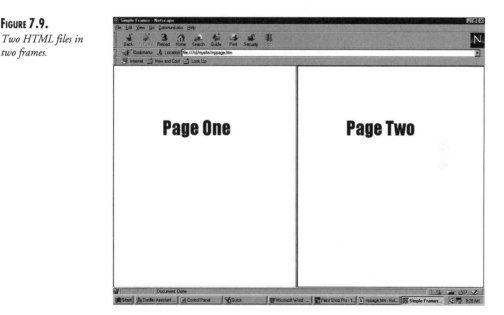

You should notice an odd thing about this frameset file. Unlike a normal HTML file, there's no <BODY> tag. In a frameset file, the <FRAMESET> tag replaces the <BODY> tag. In fact, you should never use a <BODY> tag in the main portion of a frameset file. If you do, the browser will attempt to interpret the frameset file as a normal HTML file.

The <FRAMESET> tag specifies the manner in which the frames should appear in a browser window. The tag divides the browser window into rows and columns. In this example, the browser window is divided into one row and two columns. The attribute ROWS="100%" creates one row that covers the complete height of the browser window. The attribute COLS="50%,50%" creates two columns, each of which covers 50% of the width of the window.

You can divide a window into as many separate COLS and ROWS as you need. Every new division results in a new frame. Remember, however, that too many frames can make a mess of a browser window—especially when viewed on low-resolution monitors (see Figure 7.10).

FIGURE 7.10.

Too many frames.

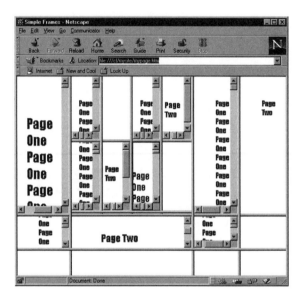

In this example, the <FRAMESET> tag divides a window using percentages of the screen. But you can also specify absolute pixel widths. Here's an example of a frameset file that creates a frame that's 200 pixels wide:

```
<HTML>
<HEAD>
<TITLE> Simple Frames </TITLE>
</HEAD>

<FRAMESET ROWS="100%" COLS="200,*">
  <FRAME SRC="mypage1.htm">
  <FRAME SRC="mypage2.htm">
</FRAMESET>

</HTML>
```

When this frameset file is interpreted in a Web browser, it looks something like Figure 7.11. The left frame should appear 200 pixels wide. Be careful, however, when using absolute values. Remember that your Web page will appear on screens with very different resolutions.

Notice how the asterisk (*) character is used in this example. The attribute COLS="200,*" specifies that the browser window should be divided into two columns. The first value of this attribute specifies that the first frame should be 200 pixels wide. The second value, the asterisk, specifies that the second frame should occupy the remainder of the screen.

FIGURE 7.11.

Frame with absolute pixel width.

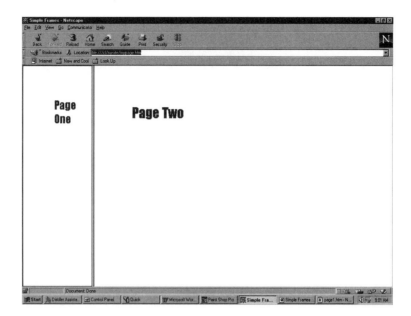

You can use more than one asterisk in the list of values for the ROW or COL attribute. Each additional asterisk divides the screen into another equal amount. Consider how the asterisk is used in the following example:

```
<HTML>
<HEAD>
<TITLE> Simple Frames </TITLE>
</HEAD>

<FRAMESET ROWS="*" COLS="*,*,*">
  <FRAME SRC="mypage1.htm">
  <FRAME SRC="mypage2.htm">
  <FRAME SRC="mypage3.htm">
</FRAMESET>

</HTML>
```

When this frameset file is interpreted by a Web browser, the browser window appears as shown in Figure 7.12. The attribute ROWS="*" tells the browser to make the frames cover the complete height of the screen. The attribute COLS="*,*,*" tells the browser to divide the width of the screen into three frames of equal width.

The <FRAME> tag specifies which HTML pages to load into the separate frames. The SRC attribute points to an HTML file residing on the same Web site or anywhere else on the World Wide Web. Particular HTML files are associated with individual frames according to the order in which they appear. So, in this example, the file mypage1.htm appears in the first column, the file mypage2.htm appears in the second column, and the file mypage3.htm appears in the third column.

FIGURE 7.12.

Frames of equal width.

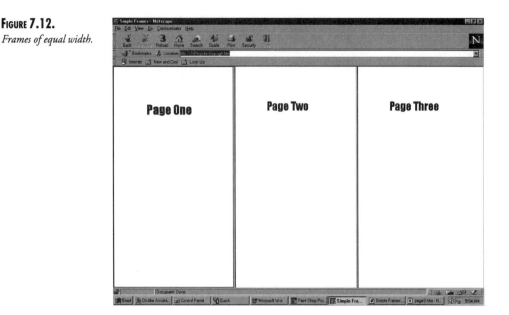

The <FRAME> tag has a number of useful attributes. For example, by default a frame displays a horizontal or vertical scrollbar when the content of the frame warrants it. You can override this behavior by using the attribute SCROLLING="NO". This attribute is useful when you want to preserve screen space by preventing a frame's scrollbars from appearing. Be careful with this attribute, however, as using it may result in page content that's forever hidden from view.

Another useful attribute of the <FRAME> tag is the NORESIZE attribute. By default, the user of a browser can resize the frames on a screen. However, sometimes you don't want anyone to destroy the layout of your carefully positioned frames. By using NORESIZE, you can prevent this from happening. Once again, however, use this attribute with caution. If you prevent people from changing the size of the frames on their browsers, serious frustration might ensue. A small frame with the NORESIZE attribute can make the content of a frame inaccessible.

Use the FRAMEBORDER attribute of the <FRAME> tag to control whether a frame appears with a border. If you use the attribute FRAMEBORDER=0, the border of the individual frame disappears. You also can use this attribute with the <FRAMESET> tag to specify whether all frames in the frameset file should appear with a border.

Finally, you can control the margins of a frame by using the MARGINWIDTH and MARGINHEIGHT attributes. These attributes are useful for creating white space between a frame and its contents. They create margins around the content of a frame.

The following frameset file uses all the attributes just described (see Figure 7.13):

```
<HTML>
<HEAD>
<TITLE> Frames </TITLE>
</HEAD>

<FRAMESET ROWS="*" COLS="*,*,*">
  <FRAME SRC="mypage1.htm" NORESIZE>
  <FRAME SRC="mypage2.htm" FRAMEBORDER=0 SCROLLING="YES"
NORESIZE MARGINWIDTH=50 MARGINHEIGHT=50>
  <FRAME SRC="mypage3.htm" FRAMEBORDER=0 SCROLLING="NO">
</FRAMESET>

</HTML>
```

FIGURE 7.13.
Complicated frames.

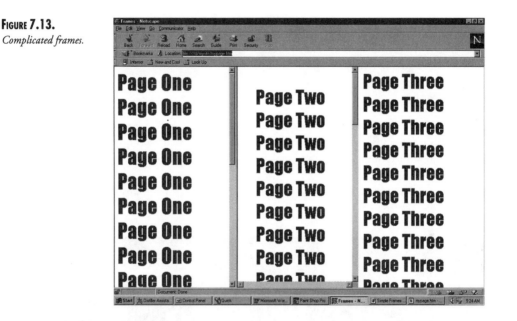

Frames and Older Browsers

Frames were introduced with Netscape Navigator 3.0. Older browsers will fail to interpret any of the frame tags. Normally this wouldn't create a problem. In general, if a browser doesn't recognize a tag or attribute, the browser simply ignores it. However, frames present a special problem in this regard.

The frameset file creates a compatibility problem with older browsers because the frameset file is not a normal HTML file. If you attempt to add normal HTML tags to this file, you get unpredictable results. For example, in the case of the Netscape browser, the frames will no longer function.

This creates a dilemma. You want the frameset file to be compatible with browsers that understand frames and browsers that don't. If you use only the frame tags in a frameset file, this file will be incompatible with older browsers. On the other hand, if you use additional non-frame HTML tags, the file will no longer function as a proper frameset file. So what can you do?

Fortunately, a special tag was introduced to solve this dilemma. By using the `<NOFRAMES>` tag, you can create frameset files that are compatible with both frame-compliant and non-frame-compliant browsers. Here's an example of how this tag works:

```
<HTML>
<HEAD>
<TITLE> Simple Frames </TITLE>
</HEAD>

<FRAMESET ROWS="100%" COLS="50%,50%">
  <FRAME SRC="mypage1.htm">
  <FRAME SRC="mypage2.htm">
</FRAMESET>

<NOFRAMES>
<BODY BGCOLOR="green">

I can only be seen by ancient, pre-frame browsers!

</BODY>
</NOFRAMES>

</HTML>
```

When this frameset file is interpreted by a frame-compliant browser, the browser ignores everything contained in the `<NOFRAMES>` tags (see Figure 7.14). However, if the file somehow gets to an older browser that can't understand frames, the browser ignores everything *except* what's contained in the `<NOFRAMES>` tags (see Figure 7.15). You can place any HTML tags you want within the `<NOFRAMES>` tags.

FIGURE 7.14.

A frame-compliant browser will show frames.

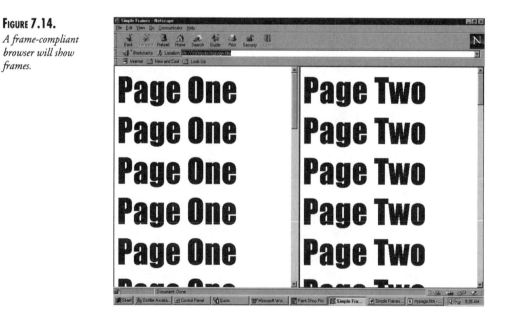

FIGURE 7.15.
A non-frame-compliant browser won't show frames.

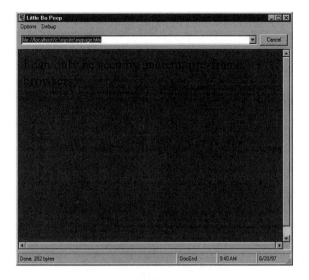

Frames and Links

Suppose you want to create a Web site containing the complete text of a book. You create two frames. In the left frame, you create a list of hypertext links to chapters in the book. In the right frame, you display the actual text for a chapter. You could use the two HTML files in Listings 7.1 and 7.2 to create the frameset file and the table of contents file.

Listing 7.1. The frameset file.

```
<HTML>
<HEAD>
<TITLE> A Great Book On Active Server Pages </TITLE>
</HEAD>

<FRAMESET ROWS="100%" COLS="50%,50%">
  <FRAME SRC="toc.htm">
  <FRAME SRC="chapter1.htm">
</FRAMESET>

</HTML>
```

Listing 7.2. The table of contents file.

```
<HTML>
<HEAD>
<TITLE>Table of Contents </TITLE>
</HEAD>
<BODY>
```

continues

Listing 7.2. continued

```
<UL>
<LI> <A HREF="chapter1.htm">Chapter 1:</A>
Everything You Need To Know About Active Server Pages
<LI> <A HREF="chapter2.htm">Chapter 2:</A>
Even More Information On Active Server Pages
</UL>

</BODY>
</HTML>
```

When the frameset file is displayed in a browser, you see the two pages in Figure 7.16. Everything looks fine. The table of contents and the chapter text appear where they should. However, if you click the link for Chapter 2, you won't get the intended result. The problem is that the page for Chapter 2 loads into the wrong frame (see Figure 7.17).

FIGURE 7.16.

Everything looks fine.

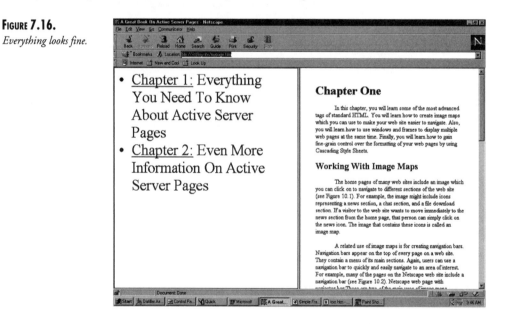

By default, when you click a hypertext link in a frame, the new page loads into the same frame. Sometimes this is what you want to happen. Often, however, you want the page to load into another frame. In the current example, you want the chapter text to load into the right-hand frame rather than the left-hand frame. You can make this happen by targeting particular frames by name.

Just like windows, frames can be given names. You specify the name of a frame, obviously, by using the NAME attribute of the <FRAME> tag. Once you have named a frame, you can target it by using the TARGET attribute of the <A> tag. Listing 7.3 and Listing 7.4 show the two files rewritten to work correctly.

FIGURE 7.17.

The link loads the file into the wrong frame.

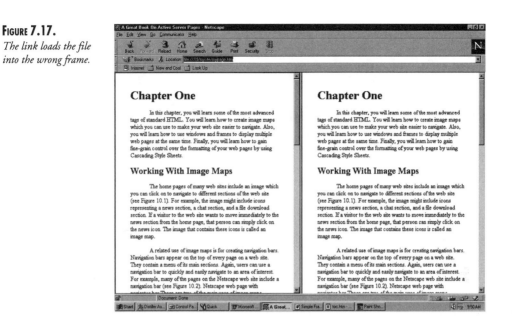

Listing 7.3. The new frameset file.

```
<HTML>
<HEAD>
<TITLE> A Great Book On Active Server Pages </TITLE>
</HEAD>

<FRAMESET ROWS="100%" COLS="50%,50%">
  <FRAME SRC="toc.htm" NAME="TOC">
  <FRAME SRC="chapter1.htm" NAME="CHAPTER">
</FRAMESET>

</HTML>
```

Listing 7.4. The new table of contents file.

```
<HTML>
<HEAD>
<TITLE>Table of Contents </TITLE>
</HEAD>
<BODY>

<UL>
<LI> <A HREF="chapter1.htm" TARGET="CHAPTER">Chapter 1:</A>
Everything You Need To Know About Active Server Pages
<LI> <A HREF="chapter2.htm" TARGET="CHAPTER">Chapter 2:</A>
Even More Information On Active Server Pages
</UL>


</BODY>
</HTML>
```

7

ADVANCED HTML

The NAME and TARGET attributes force the hypertext link and pages to behave correctly. When someone clicks a link in the frame named TOC, the chapter text loads into the frame named CHAPTER. The TARGET attribute of the <A> tags causes the hypertext links to target the correct frame.

Exiting Gracefully from Frames

The unpopularity of frames is a result, in part, of their poor implementation on many Web sites. We have all undergone the distasteful experience of leaving a Web site, only to discover that a frame has not been left behind. This can be very traumatic. However, you can do better: You can learn how to control your frames.

The secret to controlling frames lies in four special values of the TARGET tag. By using the values "_blank", "_parent", "_self", and "_top", you can escape out of different levels of frames.

The most useful of these four values is "_top". This value rids the browser window of all frames. Here's an example of how it's used:

```
<HTML>
<HEAD>
<TITLE>Table of Contents </TITLE>
</HEAD>
<BODY>

<UL>
<LI> <A HREF="home.htm" TARGET="_top">HOME</A>
<LI> <A HREF="chapter1.htm" TARGET="CHAPTER">Chapter 1:</A>
Everything You Need To Know About Active Server Pages
<LI> <A HREF="chapter2.htm" TARGET="CHAPTER">Chapter 2:</A>
Even More Information On Active Server Pages
</UL>

</BODY>
</HTML>
```

This example is the HTML file used to create a table of contents, with one additional hypertext link. The additional hypertext link references the Web site's home page. When you click this link, you don't want the home page to be loaded into the table of contents frame. You also don't want the page to load into the chapter frame. You want all the frames to go away and the home page to appear in their place. In this example, the attribute TARGET="_top" accomplishes this.

Whenever you need to make all the frames in a browser window go away, use the "_top" value. This value is useful for linking to outside Web sites. If you don't want the pages of an outside Web site to appear in a frame, you must use "_top". Finally, if you want to offer a version of your Web site without frames (which is always a nice thing to do), you should use the "_top" value in your link to the version without frames.

Another potentially valuable value of the TARGET attribute is "_parent". You can nest frames by having the SRC attribute of a <FRAME> tag in one frameset file point to another frameset file. You may need to nest frames when creating certain very complicated screen layouts (see Figure 7.18). The "_parent" value enables you to escape one level up to the parent of the current frameset file.

FIGURE 7.18.

Example of nested frames.

7

ADVANCED HTML

> **NOTE**
>
> You may be wondering what happens when you nest a frameset file within itself. For example, the following frameset file named myself.htm references itself in a vicious loop:
>
> ```
> <TITLE> Vicious Frames </TITLE>
> <FRAMESET ROWS="*" COLS="*">
> <TARGET SRC="myself.htm">
> </FRAMESET>
> ```
>
> I'm sorry to report that the computer doesn't begin to melt, catch on fire, and so on. Nothing dramatic happens. A blank page is displayed.

The "_blank" value of the TARGET attribute opens a new, blank window. This value is useful when you want to open a new window, but don't want to bother to give it a name. If you need to link to the same window in the future, however, you should provide the window with a name (see the earlier section "Creating a New Window").

Finally, the "_self" value of the TARGET attribute is this attribute's default value. You should never need to use this value. When you click a link, by default the page referenced by the link loads into the current frame. If the window has no frames, the new page loads into the current window.

Final Thoughts on Frames

Use frames with caution. You always should take into account the strong negative attitudes that many Web surfers have toward frames. When tempted to use frames, consider whether you can use tables instead.

If you use frames, be careful to implement them correctly. Whenever you have a link to the Web outside of your Web site, remember to include the TARGET="_top" attribute to make any frames disappear. Also, you should test your framed pages on low-resolution monitors to make sure that the frames don't obscure any important content.

Finally, if you decide to use frames, consider offering a version of your Web site without frames. You can include a No Frames link on your home page to allow visitors the option of viewing the content of your Web site without frames. You'll most likely need to create versions of your Web pages without frames in any case, because not all browsers support frames.

All of this being said, frames really can improve a Web site in some situations. Certain effects can be achieved only with frames. You risk alienating some users, but Web design is always fraught with risks.

Cascading Style Sheets

Cascading style sheets (*CSS*) have the potential of dramatically altering the appearance of the World Wide Web. Using cascading style sheets, you can gain precise control over the style of each of the elements of your Web page. Style sheets alter the fundamental character of HTML by enabling you to treat HTML more like a traditional page-formatting language.

With style sheets, you can control such elements of traditional page design as precise margins, paragraph indentation, and fonts. Style sheets not only allow you to specify the appearance of an individual Web page, but can also be used to provide a whole Web site with a consistent overall look.

Better yet, you can safely use style sheets without worrying about their effect on older browsers. Style sheets have the important property of graceful degradation. Browsers that don't understand them will simply ignore them.

A cascading style sheets standard has been recommended by the World Wide Web Consortium. Nevertheless, style sheets are still a very new addition to HTML. The first major browser to implement them was Internet Explorer 3.0. They are now supported in Netscape Navigator 4.0 as well.

You should be warned that both browsers currently support the CSS standard haphazardly. To use style sheets effectively, you must invest a considerable amount of time in experimenting. In many cases, the implementation of CSS in both browsers remains extremely quirky.

NOTE

The World Wide Web Consortium endorses the Cascading Style Sheets Level 1 recommendation. For more information, see http://w3.org.

Adding Style to a Web Page

A *style sheet* is a list of rules that determine the appearance of the elements of a Web page. For example, suppose you want to really emphasize all the bold text in a Web page. You want all bold text to appear in the color red. Using a style sheet, you can supply a browser with the rule that all bold text should appear in red, as in the following example:

```
<HTML>
<HEAD>
<TITLE> Simple Style </TITLE>

<STYLE>
B {color: red}
</STYLE>

</HEAD>

<BODY>

<B> I am bold and red </B>

</BODY>
</HTML>
```

When this HTML file is interpreted in a browser that can understand style sheets, the text within the <B> tag appears in red. Notice the new HTML tag <STYLE>. The <STYLE> tag contains the list of rules for the style of the Web page. In this example, there's a single rule:

```
B {color:red}
```

This rule has two parts. The first part of the rule, B, is called the *selector*. A selector is used to select the elements in a Web page that the rule affects. In this example, the B selects all <B> tags that appear in the HTML file. This rule determines the behavior of every <B> tag.

The second part of the rule is called the *declaration*. A declaration contains a property and a value. In this case, the property is color and the value is red. According to this rule, the color property of every <B> tag should be set to the color red.

All rules have this general format. One or more selectors are used to pick out elements in the Web page. The selector is followed by a single space. Next, a property of that element is given a value with a property and value pair. The property and value are separated by a colon and wrapped in braces ({ }).

Notice that no special HTML tags have been added to the body of the document. The style sheet is completely defined within the <HEAD> tags. Nevertheless, the style sheet determines the behavior of every <B> tag that appears in the body of the document.

As mentioned earlier, you can use style sheets without worrying about their effect on older browsers. Older browsers simply ignore the <STYLE> tag itself. However, an older browser might display the list of rules contained within the <STYLE> tag. To prevent this from happening, you should always place HTML comments around the list of rules, like this:

```
<HTML>
<HEAD>
<TITLE> Simple Style </TITLE>

<STYLE>
<!--
B {color: red}
-->
</STYLE>

</HEAD>

<BODY>

<B> I am bold and red </B>

</BODY>
</HTML>
```

Browsers that can understand style sheets are smart enough to look inside the comment tags to get the style rules. Older browsers completely ignore what's between the comment tags and don't display the text of the rules onscreen.

Adding Styles to an HTML Tag

You can apply a style rule to almost any HTML tag. For example, suppose you want all the text in a list to appear in red. You can do this by using the following rule:

```
<HTML>
<HEAD>
<TITLE> Simple Style </TITLE>

<STYLE>
<!--
B {color:red}
OL {color: red}
-->
</STYLE>

</HEAD>

<BODY>

<B> I am bold and red </B>
```

```
<OL>
<LI> I am red.
<LI> So am I.
</OL>

</BODY>
</HTML>
```

In this example, the single rule `OL {color: red}` affects the color of every item listed. If you have more than one list, the items in those lists appear in red as well.

Both of the rules in this style sheet have the same effect on the elements they select. The first rule makes everything contained in every `<B>` tag red; the second rule makes everything contained in every ordered list red. To save typing, you can combine the two rules into one:

```
B,OL {color: red}.
```

Rules can determine the behavior of many properties other than color. For example, you can create a rule that says that all top headings should appear in a 24-point Arial typeface with a yellow background (see Figure 7.19 on the following page):

```
<HTML>
<HEAD>
<TITLE> Simple Style </TITLE>
<STYLE>
<!--
H1 {font-style: italic; font-size: 24pt;
font-family: Arial; background: yellow}
-->
</STYLE>
</HEAD>
<BODY>
<H1> Important Information </H1>
This document contains very important information
</BODY>
</HTML>
```

The single rule in this example creates all the formatting effects on the text contained in the heading. The declaration of this rule contains a number of property and value pairs separated by semicolons. In this way, you can combine as many property and value pairs in a single declaration as you need.

You also can apply style rules to both the `<P>` and `<BODY>` tags. You'll often find this useful when you want to control the formatting of large portions of text. When you apply a rule to the `<BODY>` tag, the rule affects everything contained in the body of the document. When a rule is applied to the `<P>` tag, it affects only what's contained in the tag. Here's an example:

```
<HTML>
<HEAD>
<TITLE> Simple Style </TITLE>
<STYLE>
<!--
BODY {font-size: 24pt}
P {font-style: italic}
-->
```

```
</STYLE>
</HEAD>
<BODY>

This text is above the paragraph.
<P>  This text is inside the paragraph. </P>

</BODY>
</HTML>
```

FIGURE 7.19.

A rule that alters multiple properties.

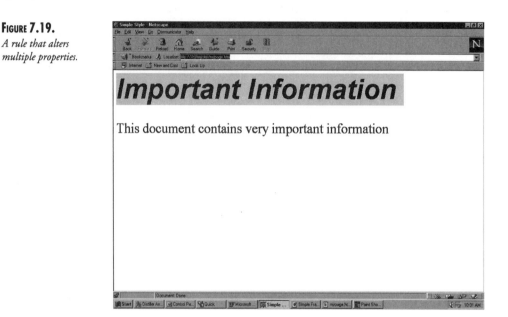

When this HTML file is displayed in a browser, all the text appears in a 24-point font (see Figure 7.20). Even the text within the <P> tag appears in a 24-point font, because the <P> tag is contained within the <BODY> tags. However, only the text that appears in the <P> tag is in italics.

What happens when two style rules conflict? For example, suppose the style rule for the <P> tag in the preceding example specified that the font size should be 10 point. In that case, the style specified in the <P> tag would take precedence. In general, the style of a contained element takes precedence over any style defined in the container of that element.

Adding Styles to a Class of HTML Tags

Suppose you need to apply a rule to certain paragraphs in a Web page, but not to all of them. For example, you may want the first paragraph to appear in 24-point type and the second paragraph to appear in 14-point type. To do this with style sheets, you need a way to distinguish between different instances of the <P> tag.

FIGURE 7.20.

*Rules for the <BODY>
and <P> tags.*

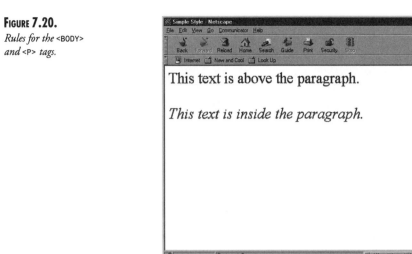

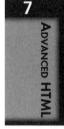

A special attribute was introduced especially for this purpose. Every HTML tag has a CLASS attribute. The CLASS attribute is used to divide tags into different classes. Following is an example of how this attribute is used:

```
<HTML>
<HEAD>
<TITLE> Style </TITLE>
<STYLE>
<!--
P.TheFirstClass {font-size: 24pt}
P.TheSecondClass {font-size: 14pt}
-->
</STYLE>
</HEAD>
<BODY>

<P CLASS="TheFirstClass">
I am the first paragraph and I am formatted with a 24 point font.
</P>
<P CLASS="TheSecondClass">
I am the second paragraph and I am formatted with a 14 point font.
</P>
</BODY>
</HTML>
```

The text contained within the two <P> tags appears with different font sizes (see Figure 7.21). The two paragraphs are distinguished by their respective CLASS attributes. The first paragraph, for example, is associated with the class named TheFirstClass. The second paragraph is associated with the class named TheSecondClass.

FIGURE 7.21.

Using the CLASS
attribute.

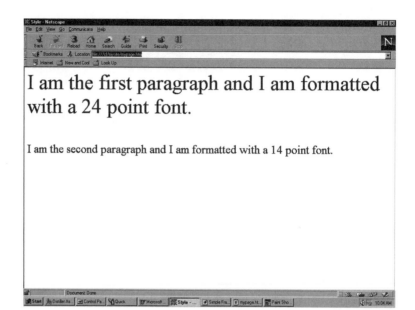

When the rules are specified, they're associated with particular classes as well. For example, the first rule is associated with the class TheFirstClass by using the class selector P.TheFirstClass. A *class selector* can be used to distinguish between different classes of a tag. The formatting of the first paragraph is governed by the first rule, because the rule selects every <P> tag associated with the class TheFirstClass.

More than one <P> tag can be a member of the same class. For example, suppose a third <P> tag is added to the preceding HTML file, with the attribute CLASS="TheFirstClass". The text contained within this new <P> tag is also governed by the first rule. The first rule governs all paragraphs that have the attribute CLASS="TheFirstClass".

Adding Styles to Classes

Up to this point in the chapter, style sheet rules have been associated only with particular types of HTML tags. But you also can associate a rule with a class that isn't associated with any particular tag. Consider the following example:

```
<HTML>
<HEAD>
<TITLE> Style </TITLE>
<STYLE>
<!--
.FreeClass {font-size: 24pt}
-->
</STYLE>
</HEAD>
<BODY>
```

```
<B CLASS="FreeClass">
I am bold and I am formatted with a 24 point font.
</B>
<P CLASS="FreeClass">
I am the second paragraph and I am formatted with a 24 point font.
</P>
</BODY>
</HTML>
```

In this example, both the <B> tag and the <P> tag are associated with the same class. The text contained in both the <B> tag and the <P> tag is formatted with a 24-point font. The rule is not associated with any type of HTML tag. Instead, the rule is associated with the class FreeClass.

NOTE

Don't forget to add the initial period when specifying the class selector in the rule. If you forget the period, the browser thinks you're attempting to select an HTML tag for the rule rather than a class.

Adding Styles to HTML Tags Depending on Context

Suppose you want bold text in a list to appear in the Courier typeface. However, you don't want text to appear in Courier outside the list or when the text is not bold (see Figure 7.22 on the following page). A number of ways are available to do this. Using style sheets, you could create a special class and associate it with only <B> tags that appear in lists. However, a second and more interesting way exists to achieve the same effect. You can specify that a rule should be applied only in certain contexts. For example, you can define a rule that affects text only when the text appears in bold and a list, but not in any other contexts. Here's an example of a rule that uses a *contextual selector*:

```
<HTML>
<HEAD>
<TITLE> Style </TITLE>
<STYLE>
<!--
 UL B {font-family: Courier}
-->
</STYLE>
</HEAD>
<BODY>

<B>I am bold but not in the Courier typeface</B>

<UL>
<LI>  I am plain, but I am <B>bold and use Courier!</B>
<LI>  Yes, but I am <B>bold and use Courier</B> as well!
</UL>

</BODY>
</HTML>
```

FIGURE 7.22.

Using a contextual selector.

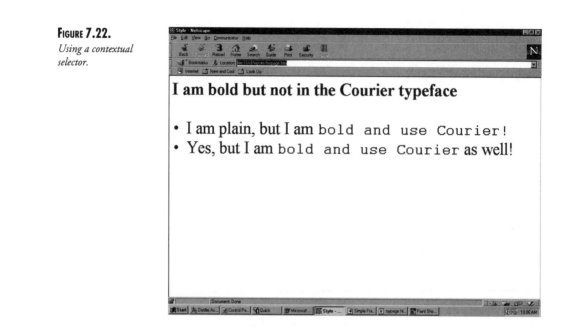

Notice the selector in the rule. The selector contains two HTML tags, but the tags are not separated by commas. The selector is applied only when a <B> tag is contained within a <UL> tag. Text contained within the <B> tag but not appearing in a list isn't governed by this rule.

Adding Styles to a Unique HTML Tag

The CLASS attribute of every HTML tag enables you to associate the same style rule with a group of tags. However, you may want a style rule to govern only a single element and no other. Every HTML tag possesses an attribute that lets you do this; this ID attribute can be used to uniquely identify the tag. Consider the following example:

```
<HTML>
<HEAD>
<TITLE> Style </TITLE>
<STYLE>
<!--
#bigfont {font-size: 24pt}
-->
</STYLE>
</HEAD>
<BODY>

<B ID="bigfont"> I am bold and I am formatted with a 24 point font.</B>
<B> I am bold but I use the default font. </B>

</BODY>
</HTML>
```

Notice the selector used for the rule. It doesn't contain an initial period; therefore, it doesn't select a class. Furthermore, it doesn't refer to any HTML tag. The selector specifies the identity of a unique element in the HTML document.

The ID attribute works very much like the NAME attribute of the <A> tag. To refer to the ID of an HTML tag, you need to prefix the ID with a # character. You should never give the same ID to multiple HTML tags, of course—the whole purpose of the ID attribute is to act as a unique identifier.

Adding Styles with SPAN and DIV

Suppose you want the first half of a paragraph to appear with the Courier typeface, and the second half of the paragraph to appear with the Arial typeface. With the style sheet tags and attributes introduced so far, there's no straightforward way of doing this. The problem is that you don't want to associate a style with the whole paragraph; you want to associate styles with different logical divisions of the paragraph.

Fortunately, a special tag exists that you can use to associate style rules with particular portions of an HTML document. Using the <SPAN> tag, you can associate a style with different divisions within a block of text, as in this example:

```
<HTML>
<HEAD>
<TITLE> Style </TITLE>
<STYLE>
<!--
.CourierPart {font-family: Courier}
.ArialPart {font-family: Arial}
-->
</STYLE>
</HEAD>
<BODY>

<P>
<SPAN CLASS=CourierPart> I am the first part of this paragraph. </SPAN>
<SPAN CLASS=ArialPart>I am the second part of this paragraph.</SPAN>
</P>

</BODY>
</HTML>
```

The <SPAN> tag has the important and admirable property of doing nothing at all. Think of the <SPAN> tag as a convenient hook for the CLASS and ID attributes. The sole purpose of the tag is to surround other elements of your HTML code so you can apply styles to them. In this example, the <SPAN> tag enables you to isolate different portions of a paragraph.

A second tag has a very similar function. The <DIV> tag also functions to create logical divisions in an HTML document. Unlike the <SPAN> tag, however, the <DIV> tag works at the level of blocks of text. The <DIV> tag introduces a line break both before and after the HTML elements it contains.

Formatting with Style Sheets

Now that you have a thorough understanding of how to apply style sheet rules, you must be anxious to learn how these rules can be used to control the formatting of your documents. The following sections present a brief overview of some of the more important properties you can set using style sheet rules. You learn how to format text, work with background images, and precisely position sections of your Web page.

> **NOTE**
>
> For a complete list of every style sheet property, see Appendix D, "Quick HTML Reference," at the back of this book.

Controlling the Typeface of Text

You've already been introduced to the font-family property. This property determines the typeface of a font (see Figure 7.23). Here's an example of how this property can be used:

```
<HTML>
<HEAD>
<TITLE> Style </TITLE>
<STYLE>
<!--
.Courier {font-family: Courier}
.Arial {font-family: Arial}
.Times {font-family: "Times New Roman"}
.Comic {font-family: "Comic Sans MS"}
-->
</STYLE>
</HEAD>
<BODY>

<P CLASS=Courier>I am Courier. </P>
<P CLASS=Arial>I am Arial. </P>
<P CLASS=Times>I am Times New Roman. </P>
<P CLASS=Comic>I am Comic Sans MS. </P>
</BODY>
</HTML>
```

You can't guarantee that a typeface will actually be available on every computer that displays your Web page. Different computers have different sets of fonts installed. Even if the same typeface is installed on a computer, it might have a different name. There are two ways you can attempt to get around this problem.

First, you can list alternative typefaces to use if a particular typeface isn't available. In the declaration of a rule, you can create a comma-separated list of alternative typefaces. For example, you could use the following rule to specify that the Helvetica typeface should be used if Arial isn't available:

```
.MyTypeFace {font-family: Arial, Helvetica}
```

According to the Cascading Style Sheets specification, you also can specify an alternative *generic font family* in this list. A generic font family doesn't specify a particular typeface. Instead, it specifies that a typeface with particular characteristics should be used. You can use any one of the following five generic families: serif, sans serif, cursive, fantasy, and monospace.

FIGURE 7.23.

Examples of different typefaces.

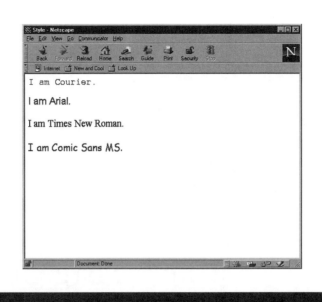

> **NOTE**
>
> When providing a list of alternative typefaces with Internet Explorer, enclose the whole list in quotes.

Remember, however, that different computers have different representatives of these generic font families installed. In other words, using even generic font families may not work if you don't have the proper fonts installed. You should use the name of a generic font family as a final alternative in the list of alternative typefaces.

Controlling the Size of Fonts

You can control the size of your text by using the font-size property. You can specify this property by using either absolute or relative values. Following is an example of how to use this property (see Figure 7.24):

```
<HTML>
<HEAD>
<TITLE> Style </TITLE>
<STYLE>
<!--
.MySmallFont {font-size: small}
.MyMediumFont {font-size: 12pt}
.MyLargeFont {font-size: 150%}
.MyLargerFont {font-size: Larger}
-->
</STYLE>
</HEAD>
<BODY>
```

```
<P CLASS=MySmallFont>I am the small font. </P>
<P CLASS=MyMediumFont>I am the medium font.</P>
<P CLASS=MyLargeFont>I am the large font.</P>
<P CLASS=MyLargerFont>I am the larger font.</P>
</BODY>
</HTML>
```

FIGURE 7.24.

Examples of font sizes.

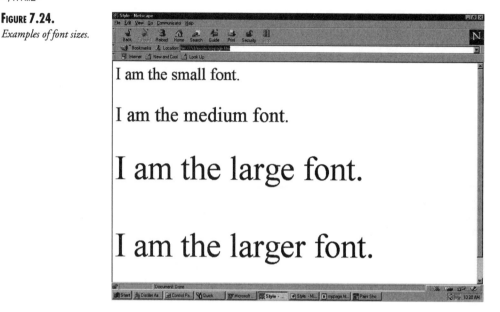

According to the first rule, the font size should be small. You can use the seven keywords xx-small, x-small, small, medium, large, x-large, and xx-large when specifying the font size. This is a way to provide an absolute value for the font-size property.

According to the second rule, the font size should be 12 point. You can use a number of different units of measurements when specifying font sizes. Possible units of measurement include inches (in), points (pt), pixels (px), centimeters (cm), picas (pc), millimeters (mm), and ems (em). When specifying the unit, use the unit's abbreviation.

> **NOTE**
>
> Internet Explorer 3.0 only recognizes centimeters (cm), inches (in), millimeters (mm), picas (pc), points (pt), and pixels (px).

The third rule uses a relative value for the font size. According to this rule, the font should appear half again as large as the default font. A relative size is calculated relative to the current size of the text against which the rule is applied.

Finally, the fourth rule makes the font size one size larger than the current font. This is a second type of relative value. You can use both the keywords `larger` and `smaller` to change the size of a font. In Figure 7.24, the last two fonts are the same size because the keyword `larger` scales the font to 1.5 times its original size.

> **NOTE**
>
> Internet Explorer 3.0 doesn't recognize the `larger` and `smaller` keywords.

Controlling the Spacing of Text

According to the Cascading Style Sheet specification, you should be able to control the line height, the letter spacing, and the word spacing of text. Regrettably, however, current versions of the Netscape and Microsoft browsers support only the line height property. The following HTML file shows these features in use (see Figure 7.25 on the following page):

```
<HTML>
<HEAD>
<TITLE> Style </TITLE>
<STYLE>
<!--
.BigLines {line-height: 200%}
-->
</STYLE>
</HEAD>
<BODY>
<P CLASS=BigLines>
These lines of text have plenty of space between them.
Can you notice the extra space?
These lines of text have plenty of space between them.
Can you notice the extra space?
These lines of text have plenty of space between them.
Can you notice the extra space?
These lines of text have plenty of space between them.
Can you notice the extra space?
</P>
<P>
These lines of text have no space between them.
Do you notice the missing space?
These lines of text have no space between them.
Do you notice the missing space?
These lines of text have no space between them.
Do you notice the missing space?
These lines of text have no space between them.
Do you notice the missing space?
</P>
</BODY>
</HTML>
```

When this file is displayed in a Web browser, the baselines of the text in the first paragraph are separated by 200% (or double the current font size). Instead of using percentages, you can use any of the other units described previously, such as pixels and points.

FIGURE 7.25.

Controlling line height.

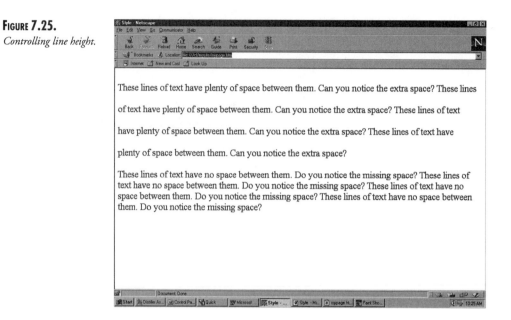

Controlling the Weight, Style, and Variant of a Font

The *weight* of a font determines how bold the font appears. The *style* of a font determines whether a font appears in italics. The *variant property* of a font determines whether the font appears in small caps (SMALL CAPITAL LETTERS).

According to the Cascading Style Sheets recommendation, the weight of a font should determine how bold a font appears. However, current browsers only recognize the absolute values bold and normal. Furthermore, current browsers don't support small caps. Here's an example of both the font-weight and font-style properties (see Figure 7.26):

```
<HTML>
<HEAD>
<TITLE> Style </TITLE>
<STYLE>
<!--
.BoldWeight {font-weight: bold}
.ItalicStyle {font-style: italic}
-->
</STYLE>
</HEAD>
<BODY>
<P CLASS=BoldWeight>
This sentence is bold.
</P>
<P CLASS=ItalicStyle>
This sentence is in italics.
</P>
</BODY>
</HTML>
```

FIGURE 7.26.
Using the weight and style properties of text.

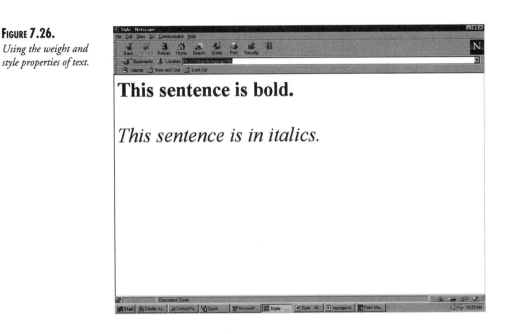

Controlling Multiple Font Properties at the Same Time

By using the font property, you can control a number of properties of text at the same time. This property combines the font-style, font-variant, font-weight, font-size, line-height, and font-family properties into a single property. Following is an example of how this property can be used (see Figure 7.27 on the following page):

```
<HTML>
<HEAD>
<TITLE> Style </TITLE>
<STYLE>
<!--
.FirstFont {font: italic normal bold 14pt/20pt Arial}
.SecondFont {font: 14pt "Comic Sans MS"}
-->
</STYLE>
</HEAD>
<BODY>
<P CLASS=FirstFont>
I am the First Font.
</P>
<P CLASS=SecondFont>
I am the Second Font.
</P>
</BODY>
</HTML>
```

The order in which you list the values for the font property is very important. If you don't list the values in the correct order, the browser won't be able to associate the right property with the right value. Also, notice the forward slash (/) that's used to separate the values of the font size and line height.

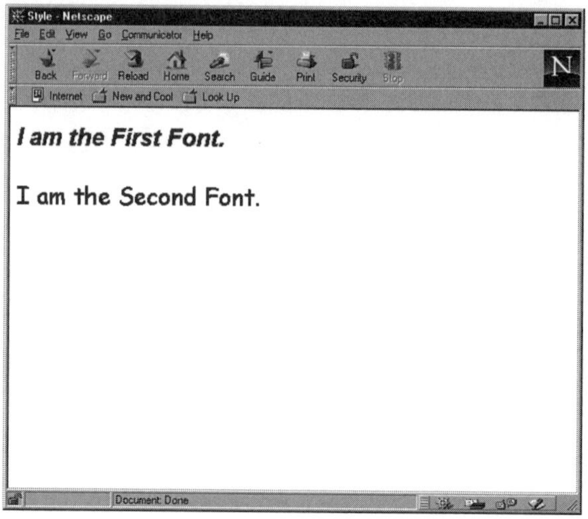

FIGURE 7.27.

Using the font *property.*

The first rule here lists all the values for this property. The second rule leaves out a number of values. This works fine as long as you preserve the correct order.

Controlling the Alignment of Text

You can align text with the text-align property, using the three familiar values left, center, and right. Better yet, with Netscape Navigator 4.0 and Internet Explorer 4.0, you can create fully justified text. Listing 7.5 shows all four values of the text-align property (see Figure 7.28).

Listing 7.5. Alignment examples.

```
<HTML>
<HEAD>
<TITLE> Style </TITLE>
<STYLE>
<!--
.Left {text-align: left}
.Right {text-align: right}
.Center {text-align: center}
.Justify {text-align: justify}
-->
</STYLE>
</HEAD>
<BODY>
<P CLASS=Left>
This text is left aligned.  See how the edges of this paragraph line up.
This text is left aligned.  See how the edges of this paragraph line up.
This text is left aligned.  See how the edges of this paragraph line up.
This text is left aligned.  See how the edges of this paragraph line up.
This text is left aligned.  See how the edges of this paragraph line up.
This text is left aligned.  See how the edges of this paragraph line up.
</P>
<P CLASS=Right>
```

```
This text is right aligned.  See how the edges of this paragraph line up.
This text is right aligned.  See how the edges of this paragraph line up.
This text is right aligned.  See how the edges of this paragraph line up.
This text is right aligned.  See how the edges of this paragraph line up.
This text is right aligned.  See how the edges of this paragraph line up.
This text is right aligned.  See how the edges of this paragraph line up.
</P>
<P CLASS=Center>
This text is centered.  I float in the middle of the screen.
This text is centered.  I float in the middle of the screen.
This text is centered.  I float in the middle of the screen.
This text is centered.  I float in the middle of the screen.
This text is centered.  I float in the middle of the screen.
This text is centered.  I float in the middle of the screen.
</P>
<P CLASS=Justify>
This text is justified.  See how the edges of this paragraph line up.
This text is justified.  See how the edges of this paragraph line up.
This text is justified.  See how the edges of this paragraph line up.
This text is justified.  See how the edges of this paragraph line up.
This text is justified.  See how the edges of this paragraph line up.
This text is justified.  See how the edges of this paragraph line up.
</P>
</BODY>
</HTML>
```

7

ADVANCED HTML

FIGURE 7.28.

Aligning text with style sheets.

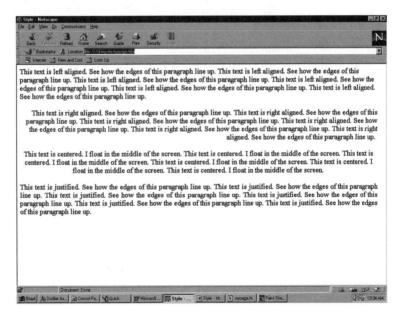

Controlling Paragraph Indentation

A very useful property of style sheets is the text-indent property. Using this property, you can indent text using either percentages or absolute values, as in the next example (see Figure 7.29).

```
<HTML>
<HEAD>
<TITLE> Style </TITLE>
<STYLE>
<!--
.Indented {text-indent: 10%}
-->
</STYLE>
</HEAD>
<BODY>
<P CLASS=Indented>
This paragraph is indented.
This paragraph is indented.
This paragraph is indented.
</P>
<P>
This paragraph is not.
This paragraph is not.
This paragraph is not.
</P>
</BODY>
</HTML>
```

FIGURE 7.29.

Indenting text with style sheets.

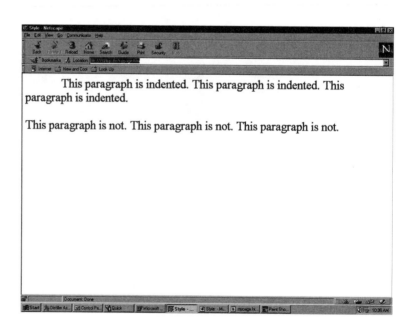

Controlling Background and Foreground Color

You should already be familiar with the color property. You can use this property to specify the foreground color of your text, like this:

```
<HTML>
<HEAD>
<TITLE> Style </TITLE>
```

```
<STYLE>
<!--
.Teal {color: teal}
.Red {color: #FF0000}
.Green {color: #0F0}
.Blue {color: RGB(0,0,255)}
.AlsoBlue {color: RGB(0%,0%,100%)}
-->
</STYLE>
</HEAD>
<BODY>
<P CLASS=Teal> This text is teal. </P>
<P CLASS=Red>  This text is red. </P>
<P CLASS=Green> This text is green. </P>
<P CLASS=Blue> This text is blue. </P>
<P CLASS=AlsoBlue> This text is also blue. </P>
</BODY>
</HTML>
```

In this example, the color of the text is specified in five distinct ways. The first rule uses the color keyword teal in its declaration. The second rule uses a standard six-digit hexadecimal RGB value. The third rule also uses a hexadecimal RGB value, except only one digit is used for each of the three colors. The fourth rule uses a decimal RGB value instead of a hexadecimal value. Finally, the last rule uses percentages.

NOTE

Internet Explorer 3.0 doesn't recognize the last two methods of supplying a color value. This browser can accept only color keywords or six-digit or three-digit hexadecimal color values.

You can use the same methods of specifying colors when providing the value of the background property. The background property can control the background color of your text. In the following listing, for example, the background property makes the background color of the first word in the paragraph green (see Figure 7.30):

```
<HTML>
<HEAD>
<TITLE> Style </TITLE>
<STYLE>
<!--
.Green {background: green}
-->
</STYLE>
</HEAD>
<BODY>
<P> <SPAN CLASS=Green>The</SPAN> first word of this
paragraph has a green background color.
</P>
</BODY>
</HTML>
```

FIGURE 7.30.

Text with background color.

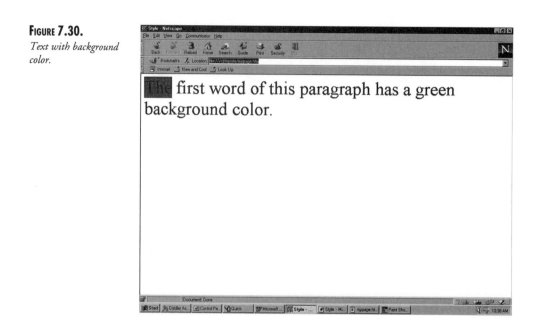

Controlling Images with the background Property

By using style sheets, you can gain much more control over the background images on your Web page. For example, you can specify different background images for different HTML tags (see Figure 7.31). Consider the use of the background property in this listing:

```
<HTML>
<HEAD>
<TITLE> Style </TITLE>
<STYLE>
<!--
Body {background: URL(checker.gif)}
P {background: URL(myimage.gif)}
.SmallImage {background: URL(smallimage.gif)}
-->
</STYLE>
</HEAD>
<BODY>
<P> <SPAN CLASS=SmallImage>This</SPAN>
web page has three distinct background images.
</P>
</BODY>
</HTML>
```

Using standard HTML, you could never place text over an image that's not part of the body's background. Using cascading style sheets, on the other hand, it's very easy. You specify an image by providing the URL of the image, with the syntax URL(myimage.gif). Notice that these are normal parentheses, rather than the curly braces that surround the name of the image file.

FIGURE 7.31.

Web page with multiple background images.

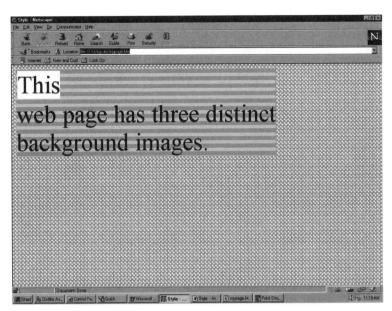

7

ADVANCED HTML

Using the `background` property, you can also achieve precise control over the tiling behavior of a background image. For example, you can specify that an image should tile vertically, but not horizontally, or the other way around (see Figure 7.32 on the next page). In the following example, the rule for the `<BODY>` tag specifies that the background image should only repeat down the y-axis:

```
<HTML>
<HEAD>
<TITLE> Style </TITLE>
<STYLE>
<!--
Body {background: URL(myimage.gif) repeat-y white}
-->
</STYLE>
</HEAD>
<BODY>

The image is only on my left!   The image is only on my left!

</BODY>
</HTML>
```

NOTE

Notice the use of the color keyword white in this example. Even if you use a background image, you should set the background color. While an image is loading, the background color is displayed. Also, if an image doesn't cover a whole area, the background color shows in the remaining area.

FIGURE 7.32.

Tiling background images in one direction.

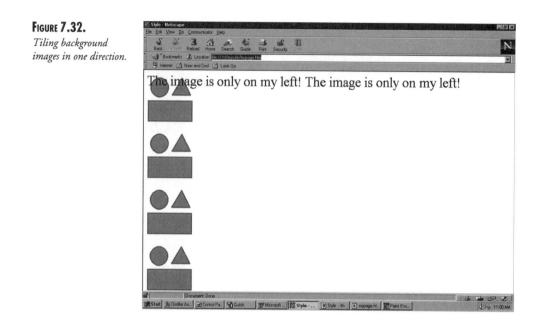

If you use the value repeat-x instead of repeat-y, the image only tiles across the screen and not down it. If you don't want the image to tile at all, you can use the value no-repeat. If you use this value, the image appears only once.

If you want to control the scrolling behavior of an image, you can use the two keywords fixed and scroll. Normally, when you scroll through the content of a Web page, the background image scrolls as well. You can prevent this behavior by using the fixed keyword.

NOTE

No version of Netscape Navigator—including version 4.0—recognizes the fixed keyword. You can't prevent background images from scrolling with this browser. This means that the image-alignment attributes have limited usefulness as well.

NOTE

Internet Explorer version 3.0 gets confused if you use the keyword scroll. The browser interprets this keyword as fixed. You shouldn't need to ever use this keyword, however, because it's the default value.

You can align an image by using the three keywords left, center, and right. You can use these keywords to align an image horizontally. To align an image vertically, use the three keywords top, middle, and bottom. Here's an example (see Figure 7.33):

```
<HTML>
<HEAD>
<TITLE> Style </TITLE>
<STYLE>
<!--
Body {background: URL(myimage.gif) fixed bottom right white}
-->
</STYLE>
</HEAD>
<BODY>

The image is in the bottom right corner of the screen!

</BODY>
</HTML>
```

FIGURE 7.33.

Positioning a background image with style sheets.

Precise Positioning with Margins

Prior to the introduction of cascading style sheets, it was very difficult to control the margins of a Web page. With the four properties margin-left, margin-top, margin-right, and margin-bottom, it's now extremely easy. Listing 7.6 shows an example of how to use these four properties (see Figure 7.34, following the listing).

Listing 7.6. Controlling text margins.

```
<HTML>
<HEAD>
<TITLE> Style </TITLE>
<STYLE>
<!--
.Thin {margin-left: 50pt; margin-right:50pt}
.VeryThin {margin-left: 100pt; margin-right: 100pt}
-->
</STYLE>
</HEAD>
<BODY>
<P CLASS=Thin>
Thin.   Thin.   Thin.   Thin.   Thin.   Thin.   Thin.   Thin.
Thin.   Thin.   Thin.   Thin.   Thin.
Thin.   Thin.   Thin.   Thin.   Thin.   Thin.   Thin.   Thin.
Thin.   Thin.   Thin.   Thin.   Thin.
Thin.   Thin.   Thin.   Thin.   Thin.   Thin.   Thin.   Thin.
Thin.   Thin.   Thin.   Thin.   Thin.
Thin.   Thin.   Thin.   Thin.   Thin.   Thin.   Thin.   Thin.
Thin.   Thin.   Thin.   Thin.   Thin.
Thin.   Thin.   Thin.   Thin.   Thin.   Thin.   Thin.   Thin.
Thin.   Thin.   Thin.   Thin.   Thin.
</P>
<P CLASS=VeryThin>
Very Thin.   Very Thin.   Very Thin.   Very Thin.   Very Thin.
Very Thin.   Very Thin.
Very Thin.   Very Thin.   Very Thin.   Very Thin.   Very Thin.
Very Thin.   Very Thin.
Very Thin.   Very Thin.   Very Thin.   Very Thin.   Very Thin.
Very Thin.   Very Thin.
Very Thin.   Very Thin.   Very Thin.   Very Thin.   Very Thin.
Very Thin.   Very Thin.
Very Thin.   Very Thin.   Very Thin.   Very Thin.   Very Thin.
Very Thin.   Very Thin.
</P>
</BODY>
</HTML>
```

Instead of specifying the margin values one by one, you can use the `margin` property to set all margin values at once. When using the `margin` property, you need to list the values in the order top, right, bottom, left. If you supply only one value, the value is applied to all four sides. If you specify only two or three values, the other values are taken from the opposite sides. Here's a quick example of how this property can be used:

```
<HTML>
<HEAD>
<TITLE> Style </TITLE>
<STYLE>
<!--
.Thin {margin: 50pt}
-->
</STYLE>
</HEAD>
```

```
<BODY>
<P CLASS=Thin>
Thin.  Thin.  Thin.  Thin.  Thin.  Thin.  Thin.  Thin.
Thin.  Thin.  Thin.  Thin.  Thin.
Thin.  Thin.  Thin.  Thin.  Thin.  Thin.  Thin.  Thin.
Thin.  Thin.  Thin.  Thin.  Thin.
Thin.  Thin.  Thin.  Thin.  Thin.  Thin.  Thin.  Thin.
Thin.  Thin.  Thin.  Thin.  Thin.
Thin.  Thin.  Thin.  Thin.  Thin.  Thin.  Thin.  Thin.
Thin.  Thin.  Thin.  Thin.  Thin.
Thin.  Thin.  Thin.  Thin.  Thin.  Thin.  Thin.  Thin.
Thin.  Thin.  Thin.  Thin.  Thin.
</P>
</BODY>
</HTML>
```

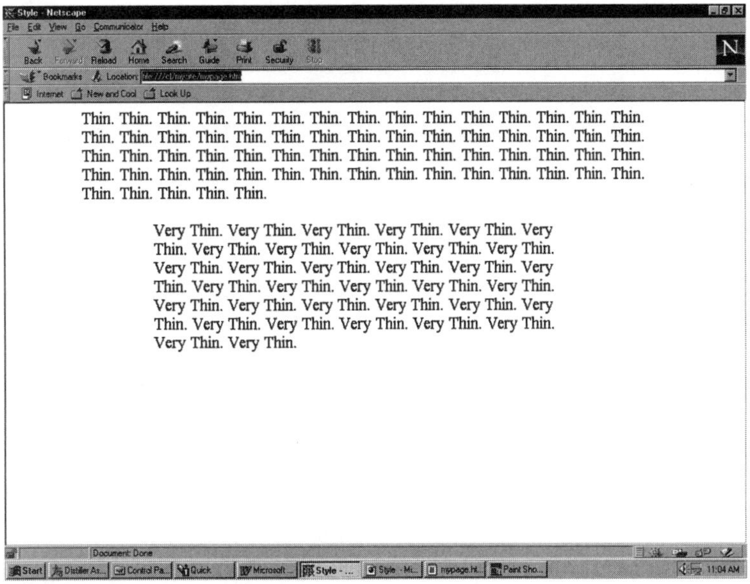

FIGURE 7.34.

Using different margins.

Creating Layers with Cascading Style Sheets

One interesting application of the margin property is in creating layers. By using the margin property, you can layer one paragraph of text over another, as in the next example (see Figure 7.35 on the following page):

```
<HTML>
<HEAD>
<TITLE>STYLE</TITLE>

<STYLE>
BODY {margin: 50px}
.BottomLayer {color: gray; font: 100px "Comic Sans MS"}
.TopLayer {margin-top: -100px; color: yellow; font: italic 40px Verdana}
</STYLE>
</HEAD>
```

```
<BODY>

<P CLASS=BottomLayer>BACKGROUND
<P CLASS=TopLayer>FOREGROUND</P></P>

</BODY>
</HTML>
```

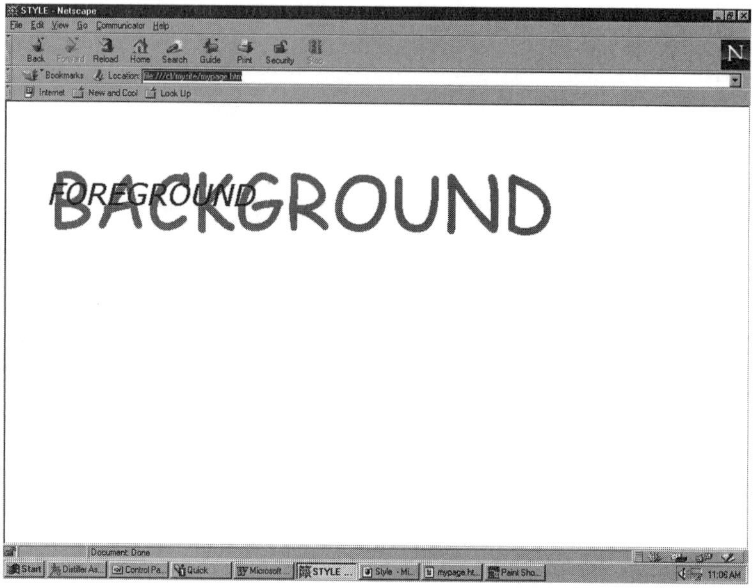

FIGURE 7.35.

Creating overlapping layers of text.

Notice the use of a negative value for the top layer's margin property in this example. The negative value moves the top layer 100 pixels up. You can layer any number of layers in this way.

Notice also that the top layer is contained in the bottom layer. The <P> tag for the top layer is embedded in the <P> tag for the bottom layer. This forces the margins for the top layer to be calculated relative to the bottom layer.

Creating Borders

You can create a number of interesting effects using the border property. The border property enables you to control the visibility, color, width, and style of borders that appear around Web page elements.

> **NOTE**
>
> Internet Explorer 3.0 doesn't recognize border properties.

Following are some examples of how this property is used (see Figure 7.36):

```
<HTML>
<HEAD>
<TITLE>STYLE</TITLE>

<STYLE>
BODY {text-align: center; font: 14pt Verdana}
.BlueBorder {border: solid blue}
.InsetBorder {border: 20px inset}
.OutsetBorder {border: 20px outset}
.DoubleBorder {border: double}
.GrooveBorder {border: 20px groove}
.RidgeBorder {border: 20px ridge}
</STYLE>
</HEAD>
<BODY>

<P CLASS=BlueBorder> I have a blue border </P>
<P CLASS=InsetBorder> I have an inset border </P>
<P CLASS=OutsetBorder> I have an outset border </P>
<P CLASS=DoubleBorder> I have a double border </P>
<P CLASS=GrooveBorder> I have a grooved border </P>
<P CLASS=RidgeBorder> I have a ridged border </P>
</BODY>
</HTML>
```

FIGURE 7.36.
Using the border property.

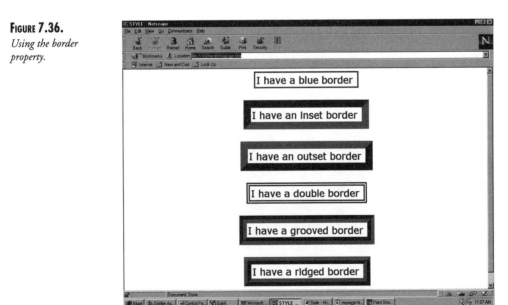

The border property takes three values: the border width, style, and color. To specify a border's width, you can use any of the units of measurement previously discussed. You can also use the keywords thin, medium, and thick.

The style value determines the style of the surrounding border. A number of keywords work with this value: dotted, dashed, solid, double, groove, ridge, inset, and outset. However, the dotted and dashed keywords don't work with Netscape Navigator version 4.0.

Finally, you can specify the color of a border. You can indicate this value by using any of the methods of specifying a color discussed previously.

Using Style Sheets for Multiple Web Pages

You can place your style rules in a separate file and apply the same rules to multiple documents. This is a powerful feature of style sheets. By using the same style rules for multiple Web pages, you can provide your Web site with a consistent overall look.

You create a *style sheet file* by creating a file that contains nothing but style sheet rules. You shouldn't include the <STYLE> tag or any other HTML tags in this file. For example, the following list of rules would constitute a valid style sheet file:

```
H1 {color: green; font-family: Arial}
P {font-family: Impact}
.Title {background: gray; color: yellow; font: bold 14pt "Comic Sans MS"}
```

Create a new file that contains nothing but these three rules. You can save the file with any name. However, you should give it the extension .css. For example, you could save the file as mystyle.css.

To apply the style rules in the file you just created to any other HTML file, you need to include the <LINK> HTML tag in the head of the HTML file, as in this example:

```
<HTML>
<HEAD>
<TITLE>Any Old HTML File </TITLE>
<LINK TYPE="text/css" HREF="mystyle.css" REL=stylesheet TITLE="mystyle">
</HEAD>
<BODY>

<DIV CLASS=TITLE> I am the title of this document</DIV>
<H1>First Section</H1>
<P> I have the Impact typeface because of the linked style sheet. </P>

</BODY>
</HTML>
```

When this HTML file is displayed in a browser, the browser fetches the style sheet rules and formats the Web page accordingly (see Figure 7.37).

The <LINK> tag has four attributes. The first attribute, TYPE, specifies the MIME type of the linked file. Cascading style sheets have the MIME type "text/css". The HREF attribute points to the file containing the style sheet. The REL attribute warns the browser that the linked file is a style sheet. Finally, the TITLE attribute gives the style sheet a title. You can give a style sheet any title you want.

FIGURE 7.37.

Controlling a Web page style with an external style file.

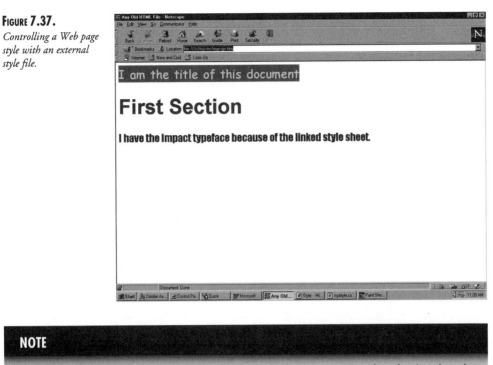

NOTE

Internet Explorer 3.0 doesn't recognize certain style sheet properties when they're placed in a separate file. For example, the background property is ignored.

Summary

This chapter described some of the most advanced tags of HTML. You learned how to create image maps that you can use to make your Web site easier to navigate, and how to display multiple HTML documents at the same time using windows and frames. Finally, with cascading style sheets, you now understand how to apply advanced styles to your Web pages and overall Web site.

VBScript

IN THIS CHAPTER

CHAPTER 8

This chapter shows you how to use Visual Basic Scripting Edition (VBScript), the default scripting language of Active Server Pages. VBScript extends HTML with variables, operators, loops, conditionals, functions, and subroutines. By integrating scripts created with VBScript into your HTML pages, you can make your static HTML pages active. After you read this chapter, you'll understand how to create the Visual Basic scripts that drive Active Server Pages.

An Introduction to VBScript

VBScript is closely related to the BASIC programming language. If you're familiar with BASIC, then you should find VBScript very easy to learn and use. VBScript is a simplified version of Microsoft's Visual Basic and Visual Basic for Applications.

VBScript is a *scripting language*. This means that the language is both easier and harder to use than a full-fledged version of BASIC. A scripting language is typically easier to use when creating simple programs. The syntax of the language itself is simple. However, this simplified syntax can actually make larger applications more difficult to develop.

You can embed scripts created with VBScript directly into your HTML files. This allows you to extend HTML into something more than a page-formatting language. Pages with VBScript can change every time they're loaded into a browser. They can also respond intelligently to user actions.

VBScript is the default language of Active Server Pages. You can use other scripting languages with Active Server Pages, such as JScript (discussed in Chapter 9, "JScript"), Perl, or REXX (a language originally created by Michael Cowlishaw of IBM UK Laboratories). However, all the Active Server Pages programming examples in this book use VBScript.

Client-Side and Server-Side Programming Languages

VBScript acts as both a client-side and server-side programming language. A *client-side programming language* is a language that can be interpreted and executed by a browser. Java and JScript/JavaScript are additional examples of client-side programming languages. When a program written in any of these languages is loaded into a compatible browser, the browser will automatically execute the program.

The advantage of client-side programming languages is that browsers do all the work. This places less of a burden on the server. Client-side programs can also be much faster than server-side programs. A response doesn't have to be fetched over the network whenever the user of a browser performs an action. The client-side program can respond instead.

Currently, however, the only browser that can understand VBScript is Microsoft Internet Explorer. Netscape Navigator, for example, ignores scripts written with VBScript. This means that, at the moment, no compelling reason exists to use VBScript as a client-side language. You shouldn't invest time in developing programs that only a minority of browsers can use.

NOTE

Both Internet Explorer and Netscape Navigator can use client-side JavaScript programs. See the next chapter for more information about this scripting language.

NOTE

You may want to use VBScript as a client-side language if you're developing an intranet. In an intranet, you may have control over the browsers being used.

VBScript is also a server-side programming language. A *server-side programming language* is a language that executes on the server that serves a Web site's files, rather than on the browsers that receive those files. A server-side programming language performs all the work on your Web site's computer; all the burden is on you.

The advantage of using VBScript as a server-side programming language is that the scripts work regardless of the browser being used. The scripts are processed before the pages are sent out across the Internet to browsers. Web browsers receive nothing more than normal HTML files.

When you create Active Server Pages, you'll be using VBScript as a server-side programming language. Therefore, this book focuses exclusively on this use of the language. However, be aware that you can apply much of what you learn in this chapter to using VBScript as a client-side language as well.

Using Visual Basic Scripts with Active Server Pages

In this section, you learn how to create Active Server Pages that can execute Visual Basic scripts. You learn much more about Active Server Pages in Part IV of this book, "Creating Active Server Pages with Objects and Components," which is devoted exclusively to this subject. For the moment, however, you can think of an Active Server Page as nothing more than an HTML file that has the file extension .asp rather than the normal file extension .htm.

To use the examples in this chapter, you need to save all your files with the extension .asp rather than .htm. If you neglect to do this, the scripts won't be interpreted. The actual text of the scripts appear in a browser when the Active Server Pages that contain them are loaded. This probably is not what you want.

To use the examples in this chapter, you must also save the files in a directory of your Web server. For example, you can save the files in the wwwroot directory. For the scripts to execute, the pages must be located in a directory that can be accessed by your Web server.

When you load an Active Server Page, you shouldn't load the file directly from your disk. For example, if you save an Active Server Page as C:\InetPub\wwwroot\mypage.asp, you shouldn't load the file into your browser by typing this file path in the address bar. Request the file by using your Web server instead. For example, if your server is named MyServer and the file is saved in your Web server's root directory, type the address **http://MyServer/mypage.asp** in the address bar of your browser. Again, if you neglect to do this, the scripts in the Active Server Page won't be interpreted.

You must also enable Script or Execute permission on the directory where your Active Server Pages are located. Your Web server won't execute a script unless it has permission to do so. See Chapter 2, "Installing and Using Internet Information Server," for more information on how to do this.

> **NOTE**
>
> When making changes to your Active Server Pages, you may discover that these changes are not reflected in the pages loaded into your Web browser. This may be a result of your Web server's use of a memory cache to increase performance. While developing a Web site, you may want to disable this feature. (See Chapter 2 for more details.)

Integrating Visual Basic Scripts into Active Server Pages

More than one way exists to integrate scripts created with VBScript into your Active Server Pages. (See Chapter 13, "Building Active Server Pages," for a thorough discussion of this topic.) The easiest way is to use the two special characters <% and %>. For example, the following Visual Basic script executes automatically in an Active Server Page:

```
<HTML>
<HEAD>
<TITLE>Simple VBScript</TITLE>
</HEAD>
<BODY>
<% FOR myvar=1 TO 500 %>
<B>Hello World!</B>
<% NEXT %>
</BODY>
</HTML>
```

This script prints the sentence Hello World! 500 times in a row (see Figure 8.1). Notice how the characters <% and %> are used in the example. They indicate where the Visual Basic script begins and where it ends.

FIGURE 8.1.

*Active Server Page
created with VBScript.*

The two characters <% and %> function very much like the two characters < and > in HTML. Whereas the < and > characters are used to indicate HTML tags, the <% and %> characters are used to indicate scripts. Whenever the Web server sees these two special characters, it attempts to interpret what they contain as a script.

For example, the text <% FOR myvar=1 TO 500 %> and the text <% NEXT %> are both examples of Visual Basic scripts. The combination of these two scripts creates a loop that goes through 500 iterations.

Notice also how the Visual Basic scripts are integrated with the HTML tags in the example. You can mix scripts and HTML freely in an Active Server Page. The text <B>Hello World!</B> is not part of the Visual Basic script. The <B> tag is part of HTML and not VBScript. However, the text <B>Hello World!</B> is interpreted and displayed 500 times because it's surrounded by Visual Basic scripts.

You should be aware of an additional expression when you're integrating Visual Basic scripts into Active Server Pages. You can use the delimiters <%= and %> to print the value of a variable or function. Consider the following simple Active Server Page:

```
<HTML>
<HEAD>
<TITLE>Simple VBScript</TITLE>
</HEAD>
<BODY>
<% FOR myvar=1 TO 500 %>
<%=myvar%><B> : Hello World!</B>
<% NEXT %>
</BODY>
</HTML>
```

This example also prints `Hello World!` 500 times. However, a number appears before each `Hello World!` The number is the value of the variable `myvar`.

The expression `<%=myvar%>` prints the value of the variable `myvar`. Whereas the delimiters `<%` and `%>` are used for indicating a script, the delimiters `<%=` and `%>` are used to indicate the value of a variable or function. Whatever follows the `<%=` expression is printed in the browser window.

Here's an example of how to use the `<%=` and `%>` delimiters to print the value of a function. The following Active Server Page prints the current date and time at the top of the page:

```
<HTML>
<HEAD>
<TITLE>Simple VBScript</TITLE>
</HEAD>
<BODY>
This page was created on: <%=NOW%>
<BR>Have a nice day!
</BODY>
</HTML>
```

The VBScript function `NOW` returns the current system date and time. When this file is loaded into a browser, the current date and time appear at the top of the Web page (see Figure 8.2).

FIGURE 8.2.

Active Server Page with date and time.

This page was created on: 7/11/97 12:25:45 AM
Have a nice day!

You should never place VBScript commands that don't return a value within the `<%=` and `%>` delimiters. This will generate an error. For example, don't do this:

```
<%=FOR i=1 to 100%>
```

Never confuse the function of the <% and %> delimiters with that of the <%= and %> delimiters. One set of delimiters is used for indicating scripts; the other is used to display the values of variables and functions.

Declaring Variables

You don't need to explicitly declare a variable before you use it in your Visual Basic scripts. For example, the following Active Server Page works fine:

```
<HTML>
<HEAD>
<TITLE>Simple VBScript</TITLE>
</HEAD>
<BODY>
<% myvar="Hello World!" %>
<%=myvar%>
</BODY>
</HTML>
```

In this example, the variable myvar is never declared. However, it is assigned the value "Hello World!" and the value is outputted to the browser. This works fine and won't result in an error.

However, if you're creating long or complicated programs, you may choose to require variables to be declared. The advantage of doing this is that it makes your scripts easier to debug. If you mistype the name of a variable, an error is generated. This example shows how you can force variables to be explicitly declared:

```
<% OPTION EXPLICIT %>
<HTML>
<HEAD>
<TITLE>Simple VBScript</TITLE>
</HEAD>
<BODY>
<%
DIM myvar
myvar="Hello World!"
%>
<%=myvar%>
</BODY>
</HTML>
```

In this example, the OPTION EXPLICIT statement forces all variables to be explicitly declared. The DIM statement actually declares the variable myvar. If you neglect to declare this variable, you receive the error Variable is undefined: 'myvar'.

You can use the DIM statement to declare more than one variable at a time. Simply separate the names of the variables with commas. In the following example, four variables are declared with one DIM statement:

```
DIM myvar1, myvar2, myvar3, myvar4
```

> **NOTE**
>
> The OPTION EXPLICIT statement is very particular about where it's placed. You must use the OPTION EXPLICIT statement as one of the very first statements in your Active Server Page. It must appear before any HTML or any other VBScript commands. If you don't do this, the Active Server Page acts as if OPTION EXPLICIT is an invalid statement.

Variable Subtypes

When you declare a variable with the DIM statement, you don't provide the variable with a datatype. This is because all variables have the same datatype in VBScript. All variables have the datatype of variant. A *variant* is a special kind of variable that can assume the identity of many other types of variables.

When you need to use a variable that represents a number, you simply assign a number, *without* quotation marks, to the variable. When you need to use a variable that represents a string, you simply assign a string, *with* quotation marks, to the variable. (For numbers you don't use quotes, for strings you do.) A variable of datatype variant automatically adapts to the data it's given.

Normally, you have no reason to worry about exactly how a variable is representing the data you assign to it. However, a special function exists that reveals a variant's subtype. Consider the following example:

```
<%myvar="Hello World!"%><%=TYPENAME(myvar)%>
<%myvar=3%><%=TYPENAME(myvar)%>
```

In this example, the variable myvar is assigned two different types of values. For each type of value, the VBScript function TYPENAME() displays the subtype used by the variable when representing the data. For example, when myvar is assigned the string value "Hello World!", the variant's subtype is string. When myvar is assigned the integer value 3, myvar has a subtype of integer.

The point of this example is to illustrate that variant variables actually do represent values according to internal subtypes. The TYPENAME() function reveals exactly how a variable is representing a value. Most of the time, however, you won't care about exactly how a variable is representing your data (but see the next section).

Variable Data Ranges

The different variable subtypes have different ranges of values that they can represent. Table 8.1 shows a complete list of variable subtypes and their data ranges.

Table 8.1. Variable subtypes and their data ranges.

Subtype	Range
Byte	0 to 255
Boolean	TRUE or FALSE
Integer	-32,768 to 32,767
Long	-2,147,483,648 to 2,147,483,647
Single	-3.402823E38 to -1.401298E-45 for negative values; 1.401298E-45 to 3.402823E38 for positive values
Double	-1.79769313486232E308 to -4.94065645841247E-324 for negative values; 4.94065645841247E-324 to 1.79769313486232E308 for positive values
Currency	-922,337,203,685,477.5808 to 922,337,203,685,477.5807
Date	January 1, 100 to December 31, 9999, inclusive
Object	Any object reference
String	Variable-length strings can range in length from zero to approximately two billion characters

Notice that the string subtype can be of gargantuan proportions. You can store complete Web pages or, for that matter, complete novels in a single string variable. I've often found the ability to store Web pages in strings useful.

Empty Variables versus Null Variables

Before a variable is assigned a value, the variable is empty. You can test whether a variable is empty by using the ISEMPTY() function, as in the following example:

```
<%
myvar="Hello World!"
%>
myvar : <%=ISEMPTY(myvar)%>
myvar2 : <%=ISEMPTY(myvar2)%>
```

In this example, two variables, myvar and myvar2, are tested to see whether they're empty. Since myvar has been assigned a value, the function ISEMPTY() returns FALSE when the variable myvar is supplied as an argument to this function. However, myvar2 has not been assigned a value, so the function ISEMPTY() returns TRUE with this variable as an argument.

An empty variable is not the same as a variable that has been assigned a zero-length string or the value 0. For example, the statements myvar="" and myvar=0 both assign the variable myvar a value. In both cases, the variable is no longer empty. A variable is only empty when it has never been assigned a value.

An empty variable also is not the same as a variable that has the NULL value. Strangely enough, a variable that has been assigned the NULL value is not empty. A special function tests whether a variable has the NULL value. Consider the following example:

```
<%
myvar=NULL
%>
<%=ISEMPTY(myvar)%>
<%=ISNULL(myvar)%>
```

In this example, the first statement returns FALSE and the second statement returns TRUE. A NULL variable is not empty, but has the value NULL. If you want to make a variable empty after it has been assigned a value, you must use the keyword EMPTY, like this:

```
myvar=EMPTY
```

Declaring Constants

VBScript allows you to declare *constants*. A constant is like a variable; however, once you declare a constant, the value of the constant can't be changed. Here's an example:

```
<%
CONST REG_FEE=10.00
%>
You will be charged $<%=REG_FEE%> to register at this web site.
```

In this example, the constant REG_FEE is assigned the value 10.00. Because REG_FEE is a constant, the value of REG_FEE can't be assigned a new value later in the script. If you attempt to change the value of a constant, you get an Illegal Assignment error.

Constants are useful when you have certain values that you don't want altered by a script, but which you may want to alter by hand sometime in the future. For example, you may want the registration fee for your Web site to be a fixed price. However, at some future date, you may hope to raise this fee. You can do this easily by merely changing the value of a single constant.

You can create multiple constants at once by simply separating the constant assignments with commas, like this:

```
<%
CONST REG_FEE=10.00, REG_TERM=20, SITE_NAME="My Web Site"
%>
```

Creating and Altering Arrays

When you need to store a number of related values, you should use an array. An *array* is a variable that can store a list of values. For example, you could create an array that stores a list of all the products you sell at your Web site:

```
<%
DIM Product(10)
Product(0)="Trading Card"
Product(1)="Book on Active Server Pages"
Product(2)="Computer Monitor"
%>
```

In this example, the DIM statement is used to declare an array. Unlike the variables discussed previously, an array must be declared before it's used. This DIM statement declares an array that can store 11 values.

> **NOTE**
>
> Every array in VBScript is zero-based. So every array has one more element than the number used in the array's declaration statement. (Using the Product array just discussed, you can store 11 values.) If you attempt to store an additional value, you get an error.

After declaring an array, you can use an *index* to assign values to its elements. In the preceding example, the array element with an index of 1 is assigned the value "Book on Active Server Pages". If you want to output the value of this element, you can use a statement like this:

```
<%=Product(1)%>
```

The array in the preceding example functions like a list. It has a single index that you can use to refer to all of its elements. However, you can create arrays with more than one index. Consider the following example:

```
<%
DIM Product(10,1)
Product(0,0)="Trading Card"
Product(0,1)="A very valuable trading card."
Product(1,0)="Book on Active Server Pages"
Product(1,1)="A comprehensive book on Active Server Pages"
Product(2,0)="Computer Monitor"
Product(2,1)="This monitor is in excellent shape."
%>
```

The DIM statement in this script creates a *multidimensional array*. This array functions like a table; the first index specifies the row and the second index specifies the column.

This array stores both product names and product descriptions. To refer to a particular product, you use the first index. To specify whether you want the product name or the product description, you use the second index.

You are not limited to 2 dimensions when using arrays. You can declare arrays that have up to 60 dimensions. To create an array with more dimensions, simply add another size number to the array's declaration statement, like this:

```
DIM Product(10,10,10,10)
```

This declaration creates an array with 4 dimensions. Each dimension can hold 11 elements. This means that the array can hold 14,641 distinct values in all ($11 \times 11 \times 11 \times 11 = 14,641$). As you can see, the size of an array expands quickly with more dimensions.

The arrays discussed so far have been *fixed arrays*. Once you have declared a fixed array, you can't change the number of elements it contains. To change the size of a fixed array, you must destroy it and re-create it. However, VBScript includes a second type of array that's dynamic. Here's an example:

```
<%
DIM Product()
REDIM Product(2)
Product(0)="Trading Card"
Product(1)="Book on Active Server Pages"
Product(2)="Computer Monitor"
REDIM PRESERVE Product(3)
Product(3)="Coffee Cup"
%>
```

In this example, the DIM statement declares the Product array as a *dynamic array*. When you declare a dynamic array, you don't specify the array's dimensions. Before you first assign a value to the array, you must specify the array's dimensions by using the REDIM statement.

In this example, the Product array is first created in such a way that it can hold only three elements. Next, the REDIM statement is used once again to increase the size of the array. The array is *redimensioned* to hold four elements. This enables you to store the value "Coffee Cup" in the resized array.

Notice the use of the keyword PRESERVE with the second REDIM statement. This keyword preserves the contents of an array when the array is redimensioned. If you neglect to use this keyword, all the data in the array would be lost.

You can use the REDIM statement both to add dimensions and subtract dimensions. You can also use REDIM to increase or decrease the size of a particular dimension. However, when you remove a dimension or reduce the size of an existing dimension, you lose data.

For example, suppose you use the statement REDIM PRESERVE Product(2) as the final statement in the preceding example. In that case, you would no longer be able to use Product(3). The data "Coffee Cup" would be lost from the Product array.

When using the keyword PRESERVE, you can alter only the last dimension of a multidimensional array. You can make this last dimension bigger without losing any data, or make the dimension smaller and lose some data. However, you can't preserve the data in an array when you add or subtract a dimension.

You can expand and contract an array as many times as you like with the REDIM statement. You'll find this ability useful when you retrieve data from database tables. You learn how to do this in Part V of this book, "The Database Component."

Array Functions

There are three functions that you should know about when using arrays. The UBOUND() function returns the size of an array. More specifically, it returns the size of an array's dimensions.

Here are some examples of this function:

```
<%
DIM Product(10,33)
%>
<%=UBOUND(Product)%>
<%=UBOUND(Product,1)%>
<%=UBOUND(Product,2)%>
```

In this example, the first UBOUND() function returns the value 10. By default, the function returns the upper bound of an array's first dimension.

The second UBOUND() function returns the same value. It returns the upper bound of the Product array's first dimension.

CAUTION

Don't get confused here. While the first *index value* of an array's dimension is always 0, the first *dimension* of an array is always 1.

Finally, the third UBOUND() function returns the value 33. This is the declared size of the Product array's second dimension.

The UBOUND() function is very useful when you need to determine the size of an array and you haven't declared the array. For example, in Chapter 23 of this book, "Working with Recordsets," you learn how to retrieve the records from a database table into an array. If you need to know the size of the array that results from this operation, you can use the UBOUND() function. (Knowing the size of the array enables you to step through and display all of its elements.)

VBScript includes a useful statement that works with both fixed and dynamic arrays. By using the ERASE statement with a static array, you can clear the array. If the array is a string array, the ERASE statement reinitializes all the elements of the array to the value "". If the array is a numeric array, the ERASE statement reinitializes all the elements of the array to the value 0. Here are some examples:

```
<%
DIM Product(2)
Product(1)="Running Shoes"
ERASE Product
%>
<%=Product(1)%>
```

When this script is executed, nothing is outputted. The ERASE statement clears all the values of the Product array, no matter how many elements have been assigned values.

The ERASE statement works differently when used with dynamic arrays. When you erase a dynamic array, the array itself is destroyed. Before you can use the array again, you must reinitialize it, as shown in the following example:

```
<%
Dim Product()
REDIM Product(100)
Product(1)="Running Shoes"
ERASE Product
%>
```

This script creates a dynamic array named Product. The element of the array with an index of 1 is assigned a value. Next, the array is erased with the ERASE statement. If you attempt to access any of the elements of the Product array after it has been erased, you get an error.

When you erase an array, you reclaim memory. In the case of a Web site with heavy traffic, every byte of memory counts. So it's not a bad idea to use the ERASE statement to destroy dynamic arrays when you're no longer using them.

One final useful function for working with arrays is the ISARRAY() function. The ISARRAY() function can be used to test whether a variable expression is an array. Here's an example:

```
<%
DIM Product(10)
DIM somevar
%>
<%=ISARRAY(Product)%>
<%=ISARRAY(somevar)%>
```

In this example, the first ISARRAY() function returns TRUE because Product is, in fact, an array. The second ISARRAY() function returns FALSE because the variable somevar has not been declared as an array.

Commenting Your Visual Basic Scripts

You can use HTML-style comments in your Active Server Pages. However, you can't use these comments within a Visual Basic script. To place comments in a script, you must do it like this:

```
<!-- I am an HTML comment. -->
<%
REM I am a VBScript comment.
' I am also a VBScript comment.
%>
```

In this example, the REM statement is used to create a comment (a REMark). Notice that an apostrophe can be used for the same purpose. The REM statement and the apostrophe perform an equivalent function.

Both types of comments can only be used to comment a single line. A comment created with either the REM statement or apostrophe is terminated at the end of the line. However, you can include a comment on a line that contains other Visual Basic statements:

```
<%
FOR i=1 TO 100 ' The start of a loop
myvar=myvar+1  ' Increments myvar
NEXT           ' The end of a loop
%>
```

One significant difference between HTML-style comments and VBScript comments is that VBScript comments aren't sent to the browser. You can't use the View Source command on a Web browser to view VBScript comments.

Adding Data and Time Functions to Scripts

VBScript includes a number of functions that allow you to retrieve and format dates and times. You have already been introduced to one of these functions. You can use the NOW function to return the current date and time:

```
At the tone, the time will be: <%=NOW>
```

You should be aware that the date and time returned are the date and time according to your Web server's clock. If someone is viewing your Web page from a city in Borneo, the date and time she sees won't be accurate for her region.

The NOW function retrieves both the current date and time. If you want to retrieve only the current date, you can use the DATE function. If you want to retrieve only the current time, you can use the TIME function. Here's a quick example:

```
The date is: <%=DATE%>
The time is: <%=TIME%>
```

Using Dates

You can break a date into smaller parts by using the MONTH(), DAY(), WEEKDAY(), and YEAR() functions. All of these functions take a date expression as an argument. All of these functions return a whole number. Here is an example of how each of these functions is used:

```
The Month is: <%=MONTH(DATE)%>
<BR>
The Day is: <%=DAY(DATE)%>
<BR>
The weekday is: <%=WEEKDAY(DATE)%>
<BR>
The year is: <%=YEAR(DATE)%>
```

Suppose the current date is Wednesday, July 9, 1997. If you include the preceding example in an Active Server Page, the following text is displayed in the browser:

```
The Month is: 7
The Day is: 9
The weekday is: 4
The year is: 1997
```

Notice that the WEEKDAY() function assumes that the first day of the week is Sunday. If you want the first day of the week to be Wednesday, you can use the following statement:

```
The weekday is: <%=WEEKDAY(DATE,vbWednesday)%>
```

8

VBSCRIPT

You can make the first day of the week any day you want. To specify a particular starting day for the week, substitute vbSunday, vbMonday, vbTuesday, vbWednesday, vbThursday, vbFriday, or vbSaturday as the second argument in the WEEKDAY() function.

You can use an argument other than the DATE() function as an argument for these functions. You can provide either a string or a date literal as an argument instead, as in the following examples:

```
The weekday is: <%=WEEKDAY(#12/25/2000#)%>
```

```
The weekday is: <%=WEEKDAY("12-25-2000")%>
```

Both of these functions return the weekday of Christmas in the year 2000. (In case you're curious, the answer is 2, which represents Monday.) The expression #12/25/2000# is a *date literal*. Date literals are always surrounded by the number symbol (#). The expression "12-25-2000" is a *date string*. Either method of supplying a date to these functions will work.

To return a weekday or a month in more human-readable form, you can use the functions WEEKDAYNAME() or MONTHNAME(). These two functions return strings. Here's an example of how they're used:

```
The month is: <%=MONTHNAME(MONTH(DATE))%>
The weekday is: <%=WEEKDAYNAME(WEEKDAY(DATE))%>
```

Suppose it's a Wednesday in July. In that case, the first function returns the string July and the second function returns the string Wednesday. You can supply the MONTHNAME() function with any number between 1 and 12. You can supply the WEEKDAYNAME() function with any number between 1 and 7.

By default, neither function abbreviates the string it returns. The function MONTHNAME() returns July rather than Jul. The function WEEKDAYNAME() returns Wednesday rather than Wed. However, you can force these functions to return an abbreviated name of the month or weekday by supplying a second argument of TRUE (TRUE means abbreviated, FALSE means unabbreviated), like this:

```
The month is: <%=MONTHNAME(MONTH(DATE),TRUE)%>
The weekday is: <%=WEEKDAYNAME(WEEKDAY(DATE),TRUE)%>
```

Using Times

You can also break the time into smaller parts. You can return parts of times by using the HOUR(), MINUTE(), and SECOND() functions. Here are some examples of these functions and some possible values they may return:

```
The hour is: <%=HOUR(TIME)%>
The hour is: 21

The minute is: <%=MINUTE(TIME)%>
The minute is: 39

The second is: <%=SECOND(TIME)%>
The second is: 34
```

The HOUR() function returns a number between 0 and 23 (the 0 hour is the hour after midnight). The MINUTE() function returns a number between 0 and 59. Finally, the SECOND() function returns a number between 0 and 59.

You can supply these functions with an argument other than the TIME function. You can supply either a *time literal* or a *time string*. Both of these examples extract the value 34 for the minute:

```
The minute is: <%=MINUTE(#12:34:19#)%>
The minute is: 34

The minute is: <%=MINUTE("12:34:28")%>
The minute is: 34
```

Comparing Dates and Times

VBScript includes two functions for comparing dates and times. You can use the DATEADD() function to add dates and times and the DATEDIFF() function to calculate the difference between two dates or times. Following are some examples of the DATEADD() function:

```
Your registration will expire on <%=DATEADD("ww",6,DATE)%>

Exactly fifteen seconds from now, at <%=DATEADD("s",15,TIME)%> your computer
will melt.
```

The first example returns the date that's 6 weeks in the future from the current date. The second example returns the second that's 15 seconds in the future.

The DATEADD() function takes three arguments:

- The first argument specifies an interval of time (see Table 8.2).
- The second argument specifies a multiplier for that interval.
- Finally, the third argument is a variant or literal date or time.

Table 8.2. Date and time intervals.

Interval	Description
yyyy	Year
q	Quarter
m	Month
y	Day of year
d	Day
w	Weekday
ww	Week of year
h	Hour
m	Minute
s	Second

You can use the DATEDIFF() function to determine the difference between two dates or times. These examples show how this function is used:

```
You have been a member for <%=DATEDIFF("d","1/1/1988",DATE)%> days.

There are exactly <%=DATEDIFF("s",DATE,"1/1/2000")%> seconds remaining until the
year 2000.
```

The DATEDIFF() function in the first example returns the number of days between 1/1/1988 and the current date. The DATEDIFF() function in the second example returns the number of seconds remaining between the current date and the year 2000.

The DATEDIFF() function takes three arguments:

- The first argument is a date or time interval (refer to Table 8.2).
- The final two arguments are two dates. To avoid a negative number, the first date argument listed should be an earlier date than the second. (If the function returns a negative number, you know that the first date is later than the second.)

Formatting Dates and Times

You can format how a date or time appears. By default, when you display a date from the DATE function, it looks like this:

```
7/9/97
```

However, you can use the FORMATDATETIME() function to display a date according to your computer's regional settings. You can display a date as either a *short date* or a *long date*.

> **NOTE**
>
> You can set the regional settings for your computer by choosing the Regional Settings icon from the Control Panel. You can use Regional Settings to specify the appearance of both long and short dates and times.

Here's how you control the display of long versus short dates:

```
Short Date: <%=FORMATDATETIME(DATE,vbShortDate)%>
Long Date: <%=FORMATDATETIME(DATE,vbLongDate)%>
```

When displayed according to the English (United States) regional settings, the dates appear with the following formatting:

```
Short Date: 7/9/97
Long Date: Wednesday, July 09, 1997
```

Notice that the short date appears exactly the same as a date without any formatting. By default, a date appears in short format.

You can also use the FORMATDATETIME() function to format a time. Again, you can specify that a time should appear with either a long or a short format. When you display a time in short format, it uses a 24-hour clock (military time). Here's how you can use the FORMATDATETIME() function with times:

```
Short Time: <%=FORMATDATETIME(TIME,vbShortTime)%>
Long Time: <%=FORMATDATETIME(TIME,vbLongTime)%>
```

When displayed with the English (United States) regional settings, the times have the following formatting:

```
Short Time: 03:20
Long Time: 3:20:08 AM
```

Formatting Currency Values

To display currency values, you can use the FORMATCURRENCY() function, as in the following example:

```
<%
ad_revenue=30000
%>
<%=FORMATCURRENCY(ad_revenue)%>
```

In this example, the variable ad_revenue is formatted before it's outputted to the browser. The exact way in which the value of the variable will be displayed depends on your regional settings. When using the English (United States) regional settings, the currency value is formatted like this:

```
$30,000.00
```

You can control many aspects of the currency formatting by changing the settings in both the Currency and Number pages of your computer's Regional Settings dialog box. For example, to change the currency symbol, you need to select a new symbol from the Currency page.

You can also alter the formatting by supplying additional arguments to the FORMATCURRENCY() function. You can control such aspects of the formatting as the number of leading digits displayed and whether negative numbers are displayed with parentheses. See Appendix C, "Quick VBScript Reference," for all the possible arguments and their values.

Formatting Numbers

VBScript includes two functions for formatting numbers. With the FORMATNUMBER() function, you can specify such formatting properties as the number of digits to display after the decimal point, whether to display a leading digit, whether to use parentheses for negative numbers, and whether to group the numbers. Following are some examples and the values they would return (continued on the following page):

```
<%=FORMATNUMBER(6665.8999)%>
6,665.90
```

```
<%=FORMATNUMBER("6665.8999")%>
6,665.90

<%=FORMATNUMBER(6665.8999,3)%>
6,655.900

<%=FORMATNUMBER(-6665.8999,3,-1,-1,0)%>
(6665.900)
```

Notice that the second example uses a string rather than a number. You can use a string when the string can be interpreted as a number. If the string can't be interpreted as a number, an error is returned.

The final example uses all the possible arguments of the FORMATNUMBER() function:

- The first argument (-6665.8999) specifies the number to be formatted.
- The second argument (3) specifies the number of digits after the decimal point.
- The third argument (-1) specifies whether a leading digit should be included.
- The fourth argument (-1) specifies whether to use parentheses for negative numbers.
- The fifth and final argument (0) specifies whether the digits should be grouped.

NOTE

A number of VBScript functions use *tristate constants*. The third, fourth, and fifth arguments of the FORMATNUMBER() function accept either tristate contants or their values. The following table shows the three tristate constants.

Constant	Value	Description
TristateTrue	-1	True
TristateFalse	0	False
TristateUseDefault	-2	Use regional settings

You can also indicate that certain of these formatting properties should depend on the regional settings set in the Windows Control Panel of your computer. See Appendix C for more details.

If you need to format percentages, use the FORMATPERCENT() function:

```
<%=FORMATPERCENT(12)%>
1,200.00%
<%=FORMATPERCENT("12")%>
1,200.00%
```

This function multiplies its first argument by 100 and appends a % character to the result. The FORMATPERCENT() function also accepts a number of additional arguments that affect other aspects of the formatting. See Appendix C for more details.

Using Mathematical Operators and Functions

VBScript includes all the mathematical operators that you would expect in a programming language. You can perform such operations as addition, subtraction, multiplication, and division. Here are some examples and the values they would return:

```
Addition: <%=1+1%>
2
Subtraction: <%=45-23%>
22
Multiplication: <%=2*2%>
4
Division: <%=3/2%>
1.5
Integer Division: <%=3\2%>
1
Modulus: <%=3 MOD 2%>
1
Exponentiation: <%=2^8%>
256
```

Integer division returns only whole numbers. In this example, the expression `<%=3\2%>` returns the value 1, and the expression `<%=3/2%>` returns the value 1.5. The *modulus* operator, MOD, returns the remainder of a division. For example, the expression `<%=3 MOD 2%>` returns the value 1.

VBScript also includes a small set of mathematical functions. The functions include the four trigonometric functions: ATN() for the arctangent, COS() for the cosine, SIN() for the sine, and TAN() for the tangent. The mathematical functions also include the LOG() function for natural logarithms, the SQR() function for square roots, and the EXP() function for the antilogarithm.

In addition, VBScript has five rounding functions. The functions are ABS(), INT(), FIX(), ROUND(), and SGN(). Following are some examples of statements and the values that would be returned:

```
<%=ABS(-23.5)%>
23.5
<%=INT(-23.5)%>
-24
<%=FIX(-23.5)%>
-23
<%=ROUND(-23.555,1)%>
-23.6
<%=SGN(-23.5)%>
-1
```

The ABS() function returns an absolute value. The INT() function returns the nearest integer after rounding. The FIX() component also returns the nearest integer, except this function rounds down in the case of negative numbers rather than up. The ROUND() function lets you specify the number of decimal places to round. Finally, the SGN() function returns 1, 0, or -1, depending on whether its argument is positive, zero, or negative.

8

VBSCRIPT

One additional function is useful when working with numbers. The ISNUMERIC() function returns TRUE only if the expression it contains as an argument is, in fact, a number. Here's an example of how this function is used:

```
<%=ISNUMERIC("1")%>
TRUE
<%=ISNUMERIC(1)%>
TRUE
<%=ISNUMERIC(DATE)%>
FALSE
<%=ISNUMERIC("APPLE")%>
FALSE
```

Notice that the first example uses the string "1" as an argument. As long as the argument passed to the function can be interpreted as a number, the function returns TRUE. The argument "three", on the other hand, would return FALSE.

Using Logical Connectives and Operators

VBScript includes a number of comparison operators. These operators can be used to compare both numbers and strings. Look at the following examples and the values they return:

```
<%=1=1%>
TRUE
<%="Apple"="APPLE"%>
FALSE
<%="Apple"="Apple"%>
TRUE
<%=3<>4%>
TRUE
<%=3>4%>
FALSE
<%=3<4%>
TRUE
<%=3<=4%>
TRUE
<%=3>=4%>
FALSE
```

The equal operator (=) tests equality. When used with strings, all the letters of the two strings being compared must be of the same case. The inequality operator (<>) tests for inequality. This operator is also case-sensitive when used with strings. The less-than (<) and greater-than (>) operators compare whether two expressions are greater than or less than each other. The less-than-or-equal operator (<=) returns TRUE only if the expression on the left side of the operator is less than or equal to the expression on the right side of the operator. Finally, the greater-than-or-equal operator (>=) returns TRUE only if the expression on the left side of the operator is greater than or equal to the expression on the right.

VBScript also includes all the truth-functional connectives necessary for propositional logic. You can use the values TRUE, FALSE, and NULL to represent the truth values of statements. You can form statements that include negations (NOT), conjunctions (AND), exclusive disjunctions

(XOR), nonexclusive disjunctions (OR), material implications (IMP), and material equivalencies (EQV).

A *material implication* is true whenever its antecedent is false or its consequent is true. A *material equivalency* (or *biconditional*) is true whenever both of its arguments are false or both are true. Here are some examples and the values they would return:

```
<%=TRUE AND FALSE%>
FALSE
<%=TRUE OR FALSE%>
TRUE
<%=FALSE XOR FALSE%>
FALSE
<%=FALSE IMP TRUE%>
TRUE
<%=TRUE EQV FALSE%>
FALSE
```

The truth-functional connectives are extremely useful when used as part of the conditions of statements such as the IF...THEN, SELECT CASE, WHILE, and DO statements. You learn more about all these statements in the following sections.

Testing for a Single Condition with IF...THEN

One of the most useful VBScript statements is the IF...THEN statement. The following example shows how to use it:

```
<%
IF TIME > #5:00:00PM#   THEN
 Greeting="Good Evening!"
END IF
%>
```

This script assigns the value "Good Evening" to the variable Greeting only if it's after 5:00 p.m. (the # characters are used to delimit a date or time literal). Notice the expression END IF. The END IF expression designates the end of the conditional block of code. You can place more than one statement before the END IF expression, like this:

```
<%
IF TIME > #5:00:00PM#   THEN
 Greeting="Good Evening!"
 Evening_Visitor=Evening_Visitor+1
END IF
%>
```

Both statements in this example execute only if the time is after 5:00 p.m.

You can also use the ELSE expression with a conditional. Statements that follow the ELSE expression execute only if the conditional is false. Check out this example (continued on the next page):

```
<%
IF TIME > #5:00:00PM#   THEN
 Greeting="Good Evening!"
```

```
ELSE
 Greeting="Good some other time!"
END IF
%>
```

You can place multiple statements after the ELSE statement. Because every conditional must be either TRUE or FALSE, you are guaranteed that only the statements following the THEN expression or only the statements following the ELSE expression will execute.

You can also nest conditionals. This is often very useful. Here's an example:

```
<%
IF TIME > #5:00:00PM#    THEN
  IF TIME < #10:00:00PM# THEN
    Greeting="Good Evening!"
  ELSE
   Greeting="Good Late Evening!"
  END IF
ELSE
 Greeting="Good some other time!"
END IF
%>
```

In this example, the greeting is Good Evening! if it's before 10:00 p.m., but Good Late Evening! if it's later. If it's not after 5:00 p.m., the greeting Good some other time! is used instead.

If you only need to execute a single statement with a conditional, then you don't need to use the END IF expression. Here are two examples:

```
<%
IF TIME<#5:00:00PM# THEN Greeting="Good Day!"
%>
```

```
<%
IF TIME<#5:00:00PM# THEN Greeting="Good Day!" ELSE Greeting="Good Evening!"
%>
```

Testing for Multiple Conditions with SELECT CASE

The SELECT CASE statement is closely related to the IF...THEN statement. The IF...THEN statement enables you to test only one condition; the SELECT CASE statement enables you to test multiple conditions at a time, as in this example:

```
<%
SELECT CASE Visitor_Name
CASE "Bill Gates"
 Greeting="Welcome Bill Gates!"
CASE "President Clinton"
 Greeting="Welcome President Clinton!"
CASE ELSE
 Greeting="Welcome Someone!"
END SELECT
%>
```

In this example, the variable Visitor_Name represents the name of a visitor to your Web site. If a match is made with the name, an appropriate greeting is assigned to the Greeting variable. Otherwise, the statement following the CASE ELSE expression is executed.

The CASE ELSE expression is optional. If you omit this expression and none of the CASE conditions is matched, no statement is executed.

Repeating Operations with FOR Loops

When you need to repeat a group of statements a set number of times, you can use a FOR...NEXT loop, as in this example:

```
<%
FOR i=1 to 500
%>
Hello Again!
<%
NEXT
%>
```

In this example, the sentence Hello Again! is printed to the browser screen 500 times. Anything contained between the FOR statement and the NEXT statement is repeated. This is true even if, as in this example, HTML code is contained within the loop.

You can make a FOR...NEXT loop move backwards by using the keyword STEP. Consider the following example:

```
<%
FOR i=500 to 1 STEP -1
%>
Hello Again!
<%
NEXT
%>
```

This example outputs the very same results as the previous example. However, in this example, the FOR...NEXT loop starts with the number 500 and steps backwards to the number 1.

You can step through a loop with different-sized steps. In the following example, the value of the i variable is incremented by 10 at each step:

```
<%
FOR i=1 TO 500 STEP 10
%>
<%=i%><BR>
<%
NEXT
%>
```

You can use the statement EXIT FOR to exit out of a FOR...NEXT loop. Suppose you're hunting through an array to find a match to a certain string expression. You don't need to continue looping through the elements of the array after you've found a match (see the next page):

8

VBScript

```
<%
DIM myarray(10)
myarray(4)="Running Shoes"
FOR i=0 to UBOUND(MyArray)
  IF MyArray(i)="Running Shoes" THEN EXIT FOR
NEXT
%>
```

In this example, if the value of one element of the array matches the expression `"Running Shoes"`, the `FOR...NEXT` loop is immediately exited. The value of the `i` variable equals the index of the matched element in the array.

The `FOR EACH...NEXT` statement is closely related to the `FOR...NEXT` statement. The `FOR EACH...NEXT` statement is particularly appropriate for stepping through the elements of an array or a collection, as in this next example:

```
<%
DIM myarray(10)
myarray(4)="Running Shoes"
FOR EACH i in MyArray
  if i="Running Shoes" THEN EXIT FOR
NEXT
%>
```

The script in this example accomplishes the very same task as the script in the preceding example. The loop is exited when a match is made with the string expression. However, when the script completes, the value of the variable `i` is equal to `"Running Shoes"`.

Unlike in the case of a `FOR...NEXT` loop, the variable `i` here doesn't act as a counter. Instead, the variable `i` assumes the value of each member of the array or collection through which the loop is stepping. If you want to display the values of all the elements of an array, you could do it like this:

```
<%
FOR EACH i in MyArray
%>
<%=i%>
<%
NEXT
%>
```

Looping Conditionally with WHILE and DO

A `FOR...NEXT` loop is useful for executing a group of statements or displaying a hunk of HTML a specified number of times. However, in many situations you won't know the number of iterations a loop should make before it exits. In these situations, you need to use either a `WHILE` loop or a `DO` loop.

A `WHILE` loop continues to loop through a group of statements while a certain condition remains true. Consider the following example (as shown on the following page):

```
<%
TheFuture=DATEADD("s",15,TIME)
WHILE TIME<TheFuture
%>
<%=TIME%> : Waiting For The Future... <BR>
<%
WEND
%>
<B>The Future's Here!</B>
```

In this example, all the statements that are contained within the WHILE and WEND statements are repeated until 15 seconds pass. The WHILE statement checks whether the current time is less than the time stored in the variable TheFuture. As soon as the current time is greater than or equal to TheFuture, the WHILE loop is exited.

A DO loop is closely related to a WHILE loop, but DO loops are more flexible. With a DO loop, you can create a loop that continues to execute while a certain condition remains true, or a loop that executes until a certain condition is true. Here's an example:

```
<%
DO WHILE sentence<>"Hello There!"
sentence="Hello There!"
%>
<%=sentence%>
<%
LOOP
%>
```

In this example, all the statements contained between the DO statement and the LOOP statement are executed while the variable sentence is not equal to the string "Hello There!". Because the variable sentence is assigned the value "Hello There!" within the loop, the WHILE condition remains true for only one iteration. In other words, the statements contained in the DO loop are executed only once, and Hello There! is printed to the screen only once.

In this example, the loop continues to loop while a certain condition remains true. You can also create a DO loop that loops only until a certain condition is true, as in this example:

```
<%
DO UNTIL sentence="Hello There!"
sentence="Hello There!"
%>
<%=sentence%>
<%
LOOP
%>
```

This script accomplishes the same thing as the preceding one. The DO loop executes only once. As soon as the variable sentence is equal to the string "Hello There!", the loop is no longer executed. The loop is executed only once, and the sentence Hello There! is printed only once.

If you prefer, you can shift either the WHILE or UNTIL expression to the bottom of the loop, like this (shown on the following page):

8

VBSCRIPT

```
<%
DO
sentence="Hello There!"
%>
<%=sentence%>
<%
LOOP UNTIL sentence="Hello There!"
%>
```

When using a DO loop, you can use the statement EXIT DO to exit out of the loop. Consider the following loop:

```
<%
DO UNTIL 1<>1
  exclaim=exclaim&"!"
  IF exclaim="!!!!!" THEN EXIT DO
LOOP
%>
<%=exclaim%>
```

In this example, the DO loop continues to loop until 1 is not equal to 1. In other words, it loops forever. However, in each iteration of the DO loop, the variable exclaim grows by one exclamation mark. When the variable exclaim equals the string "!!!!!", the EXIT DO statement forces the loop to be exited.

When creating loops with WHILE or DO, be careful not to create infinite loops. If you accidentally create an infinite loop, don't worry. Be patient and the script will automatically terminate after a set period of time (usually 90 seconds).

> **NOTE**
>
> You can control how long a script executes before it times out by using the ScriptTimeOut property of the Server object. See Chapter 14, "Working with a Single Active Server Page."

Using String Functions

VBScript includes a rich set of functions for working with strings. You'll find these functions very useful when you need to manipulate data pulled from HTML forms or databases. You can use these functions to concatenate strings, extract strings, search strings, and compare strings.

Concatenating Strings

When you need to build a larger string from smaller ones, use the concatenation operator (&). The following script builds a sentence from smaller expressions:

```
<%
exp1="The house "
```

```
exp2="is on a "
exp3="hill."
Sentence=exp1&exp2&exp3
%>
```

You can also use the addition sign (+) to concatenate strings. However, this isn't recommended. Unlike the & operator, the + operator is not guaranteed to return a string. Consider the following example:

```
<%
myvar=1
%>
<%="The value of myvar is:"&myvar%>
<%="The value of myvar is:"+myvar%>
```

When the concatenation operator & is used to output the value of myvar, the statement executes successfully. The operator & automatically converts the value of myvar to a string. However, when the operator + is used, an error is generated, because an attempt is made to actually add the value of myvar to the string expression.

If you have an array of strings, you can use the JOIN() function to join together all the strings in the array. Here's an example:

```
<%
DIM MyArray(2)
MyArray(0)="The house "
MyArray(1)="is on a "
MyArray(2)="hill."
Sentence=JOIN(MyArray)
%>
```

When this script is executed, the variable named Sentence equals all the expressions in the MyArray array joined together. To use this function, MyArray must be a one-dimensional array (a list). You can supply an optional second argument to the function to create a separator other than a space:

```
Sentence=JOIN(MyArray,"/")
```

In this case, the JOIN() function would return the value The house /is on a /hill.

If you need to join a number of spaces, you can use the SPACE() function, like this:

```
Sentence="Over"&SPACE(20)&"There."
```

In this example, the value of the variable Sentence equals the word Over separated by twenty spaces from the word There. You should be aware, however, that because HTML ignores extra spaces, this function won't actually output additional spaces to the browser screen. If you really need to use this function to create additional spaces, you must place the output within the HTML <PRE> tag, like this:

```
<%
Sentence="Over"&SPACE(20)&"There."
%>
<PRE><%=Sentence%></PRE>
```

8

VBScript

The disadvantage of doing this is that HTML displays whatever is contained in the <PRE> tag with a fixed-width font (for the majority of browsers, in the Courier typeface). This usually isn't visually appealing. Instead of using the SPACE() function, consider using a script like this:

```
<%
Sentence="Over"
FOR i=1 to 20
  Sentence=Sentence&" "
NEXT
Sentence=Sentence&"There."
%>
<%=Sentence%>
```

In this example, the special HTML code for a nonbreaking space ( ) is used to make the spaces. This doesn't work on older browsers. However, the   code is the closest thing in HTML to a true space character.

Finally, if you want to repeat any single character any number of times, you can use the STRING() function, as in the following example:

```
<%
Sentence=STRING(500,"!")
%>
<%=Sentence%>
```

This script prints an exclamation mark (!) to the screen 500 times. You can't use this function with any string longer than a single character. If you need to repeat a longer expression, use a loop.

Extracting Strings

VBScript includes a number of functions for extracting one string from another. You can use the RIGHT(), LEFT(), and MID() functions to extract the left part, the right part, and the middle part of a string. Here are some examples and the values they return:

```
<%
Sentence="Once upon a time, there were three bears."
%>
<%=LEFT(Sentence,16)%>
Once upon a time
<%=RIGHT(Sentence,23)%>
there were three bears.
<%=MID(Sentence,13,4)%>
time
```

The LEFT() function returns a certain number of characters, starting with one, counting from the left side of the string. The RIGHT() function returns a certain number of characters, starting with one, counting from the right side of the string. Finally, the MID() function extracts a string that's a certain number of characters from the left side of the string and a certain length; if you omit this third argument to the MID() function, all remaining characters are returned.

When using these functions, it's often useful to know the length of a string. To determine this, you can use the LEN() function. The following script uses the LEN() function to extract the left half of a string:

```
<%
mystring="Once upon a time, there were three bears."
%>
<%=LEFT(mystring,LEN(mystring)\2)%>
```

When interpreting data gathered from HTML forms, you'll often find it necessary to remove extraneous spaces from the data gathered. Three functions enable you to do this. The RTRIM(), LTRIM(), and TRIM() functions trim the spaces from the right, left, or both sides of a string. Here are some examples:

```
<%
Sentence="   I have extra spaces     "
Sentence=LTRIM(Sentence)
Sentence=RTRIM(Sentence)
Sentence=TRIM(Sentence)
%>
```

These functions remove spaces on either edge of a string—no matter how many spaces occur. If you need to remove extra spaces inside a string, use the REPLACE() function (described shortly).

The string function SPLIT() splits a string into multiple parts. The result of this operation is placed in an array. Consider the following script:

```
<%
MyArray=SPLIT(forminput)
FOR z=0 TO UBOUND(MyArray)
  IF MyArray(z)="You" THEN MyArray(z)="I"
NEXT
newoutput=JOIN(MyArray)
%>
<%=newoutput%>
```

This script takes any string stored in the forminput variable and splits it into the array MyArray. (You don't declare this array; the function creates it.) Next, every time the word You appears in the array, the word is replaced with I. Finally, the array is pasted together again by the JOIN() function and outputted to the browser screen.

If a visitor to your Web site enters the sentence **You are a computer** into an HTML form and this value is stored in the variable forminput, the sentence I are a computer is returned to the browser screen. Using the SPLIT() function, you can easily manipulate information entered into HTML forms.

By default, the SPLIT() function divides a string by breaking the string apart at spaces. However, you can supply a second argument to the function to split the string at another character. Also by default, the function splits a string into as many parts as it can. But you can supply a third argument to limit the number of substrings the function returns. This example uses both of these additional arguments:

```
<%
MyArray=SPLIT("Once upon a time, there were three bears.",",",2)
%>
```

In this example, the string is split into two. The substring that occurs to the left of the comma is placed in the first element of the array; the substring that occurs to the right of the comma is stored in the second element of the array.

Finally, the FILTER() function enables you to filter an array. Suppose you want to filter out of a sentence every word that doesn't contain the letter *t*. Using the FILTER() function, you could do this with the following script:

```
<%
MyArray=SPLIT("Once upon a time, there were three bears.")
MyArray=FILTER(MyArray,"t")
%>
<%=JOIN(MyArray)%>
```

When this script is executed, the string `time, there three` is displayed. The FILTER() function filters out any array element that doesn't match the string t.

You can also use the FILTER() function to filter any array element that matches a particular string. The following script, for example, returns the string `Once upon a were bears`.

```
<%
MyArray=SPLIT("Once upon a time, there were three bears.")
MyArray=FILTER(MyArray,"t",FALSE)
%>
<%=JOIN(MyArray)%>
```

Replacing Strings

One of the most useful string functions is the REPLACE() function. You can use the REPLACE() function to replace part of one string with another string. Here's an example:

```
<%
newuser="Edwin C. Orr"
mystring="Thank you, someone, for registering at our web site!"
mystring=REPLACE(mystring,"someone",newuser)
%>
<%=mystring%>
```

In this example, the REPLACE() function is used to replace the expression `"someone"` with the name of a visitor to your Web site. The function returns the value `"Thank you, Edwin C. Orr, for registering at our web site!"`

By default, the REPLACE() function replaces all occurrences of one string in another. For example, the following script removes all the spaces from a string, no matter how many spaces are in the string:

```
<%
mystring=REPLACE(mystring," ","")
%>
```

However, you can limit the number of strings that the REPLACE() function replaces by specifying both a start position and a number that specifies how many times to replace the string. Consider the following example:

```
<%
mystring="Welcome someone, your name is someone."
mystring=REPLACE(mystring,"someone","Edwin C. Orr",17,1)
%>
```

The REPLACE() function in this example returns the string "your name is Edwin C. Orr." The second argument specifies that the string should be replaced starting 17 characters from the left. The third argument specifies that only one occurrence of the string should be replaced. If the expression "someone" appeared again later in the string, the expression would not be replaced.

By default, the REPLACE() function is case-sensitive. In many cases, this won't be what you want. To force the REPLACE() function to match a string regardless of case, you can supply a sixth argument to the function, like this:

```
<%
mystring="Welcome SoMeoNe, your name is SomeOne."
mystring=REPLACE(mystring,"someone","Edwin C. Orr",1,-1,1)
%>
```

In this example, the fourth argument (with the value 1), indicates that the string should be searched starting from its first character, the fifth argument (with the value -1) indicates that every substring should be replaced, and the sixth argument (with the value 1) specifies that the comparison shouldn't be case-sensitive.

In case for some odd reason you want to reverse a string, a special function exists specifically for this purpose. The STRREVERSE() function reverses the order of the characters in a string. Here's an example and the value it would return:

```
<%=STRREVERSE("Once upon a time, there were three bears.")%>
.sraeb eerht erew ereht ,emit a nopu ecnO
```

Finally, if you need to replace a string with an uppercase or lowercase version of the same string, you can use the two functions UCASE() and LCASE(). Consider the following examples:

```
<%=UCASE("Once upon a time")%>
ONCE UPON A TIME
<%=LCASE("Once upon a time")%>
once upon a time
```

Searching Strings

If you need to check whether a string is included in another string, you can use the INSTR() function. The INSTR() function returns the position of one string in another counting from 1. Here are some examples of this function and the values it would return:

```
<%=INSTR("Once upon a time","time")%>
13
<%=INSTR("Once upon a time","TIME")%>
0
```

8

VBSCRIPT

By default, the INSTR() function starts hunting for a match from the very first character of the string supplied. However, you can supply an optional argument that specifies the position in the string to start looking for a match, as in this example:

```
<%=INSTR(2,"Once upon a time", "Once")%>
```

The INSTR() function in this example would return the value 0. Even though the string Once occurs in the target string, it's not a match because the comparison begins with the second character.

Notice that by default the comparison is case-sensitive. In the following example, the string time is not matched because the string is lowercase:

```
<%=INSTR("Once upon a time","TIME")%>
0
```

You can force the INSTR() function to ignore case by using an additional argument like this:

```
<%=INSTR(1,"Once upon a time","TIME",1)%>
```

The fourth argument to this function specifies that a match is valid regardless of the case of the string being matched. When you use this argument, you must also supply all other arguments to the function—including the normally optional start position argument. Otherwise, the function becomes confused.

The INSTR() function returns the first match relative to the left of a string. A second function, INSTRREV(), matches a string starting from the right side of the string. To clarify the distinction between these two functions, here's an example of each and the values returned:

```
<%=INSTR("Once upon a time","n")%>
2
<%=INSTRREV("Once upon a time","n")%>
9
```

Notice that both functions return a value counted from the left side of the string—the INSTRREV() function returns the value 9 rather than 8. However, the INSTR() function matches the first occurrence of a string, searching from the left side, while the INSTRREV() function matches the first occurrence of a string, searching from the right side.

Comparing Strings

You can use the equality operator (=) to compare two strings. However, this operator is case-sensitive. When you don't want the case of the strings to affect the comparison, you have two choices.

First, you can convert both of the strings you want to compare to uppercase or lowercase, using the UCASE() or LCASE() function:

```
<%
user_name="Andrew Jones"
IF UCASE(user_name)="ANDREW JONES" THEN Greeting="Welcome Andrew Jones!"
%>
```

Second, you can use the STRCOMP() function to perform the comparison. The STRCOMP() function compares two strings and returns the value 0 when they're the same. You can use the STRCOMP() function to perform either a case-sensitive comparison or a case-insensitive comparison. Here are some examples of this function and the values returned:

```
<%=STRCOMP("Apple","Apple")%>
0
<%=STRCOMP("Apple","APPLE")%>
1
<%=STRCOMP("Apple","APPLE",1)%>
0
```

In the first two examples, a case-sensitive comparison is performed. In the last example, a case-insensitive comparison is performed. To perform a case-insensitive comparison, you provide a third argument with the value 1.

Creating Subroutines

If you discover that you need to execute the same group of statements in more than one place in a script, consider using a *subroutine*. A subroutine can contain any collection of VBScript statements. You can call the same subroutine as many times as you need. Here's an example:

```
<HTML>
<HEAD><TITLE>Subroutine Example</TITLE></HEAD>
<BODY>
<%
SUB ShowSentence
%>
This sentence was created by a subroutine.
<%
END SUB
ShowSentence
ShowSentence
ShowSentence
%>
</BODY>
</HTML>
```

If this file is displayed in a browser, the sentence This sentence was created by a subroutine would be displayed three times. The subroutine named ShowSentence displays this sentence, and the subroutine is called three times in a row within the main script by using the name of the subroutine.

A subroutine can accept arguments. For example, you can create a subroutine that displays different messages, depending on the value of an argument passed to it. Here's an example (continued on the following page):

```
<%
SUB ShowError(theError)
%>
<TITLE>Login Invalid</TITLE>
<BR>The login information you provided was invalid:
<BR><%=theError%>
```

```
<%
END SUB
IF user_name<>"Andrew Jones" THEN ShowError "Bad user name."
IF user_password<>"secret password" THEN ShowError "Bad password"
%>
```

In this example, different error messages are displayed by the subroutine, depending on the string passed to it. For example, if the value of the variable user_name is not equal to "Andrew Jones", the subroutine is called with the string "Bad user name". If the value of the variable user_password is not equal to "secret password", the string "Bad password" is passed to the subroutine to be displayed.

You can pass more than one argument at a time to a subroutine. To do this, simply separate arguments with a comma, as in the following example:

```
<TITLE>Subroutine Example</TITLE>
<%
Sub MySub(myvar1,myvar2)
mystring=myvar1&myvar2
%>
<%=mystring%>
<%
End Sub
MySub "The house ", "is on a hill."
%>
```

If a variable is declared or first used within a subroutine, the variable exists only within that subroutine. This means that if you assign any values to the variable, you can't read these values outside the subroutine. Consider the following example:

```
<TITLE>Subroutine Example</TITLE>
<%
SUB AssignVar
  myvar="Hello There!"
END SUB
AssignVar
%>
<%=myvar%>
```

In this example, the variable myvar is assigned the value "Hello There!" within the subroutine. Outside the scope of this subroutine, an attempt is made to display the value of this variable. But nothing is displayed.

On the other hand, if a variable is declared or first used outside a subroutine (at the level of the script), the variable can be accessed within the subroutine. Consider the following example:

```
<TITLE>Subroutine Example</TITLE>
<%
SUB ShowVar
%>
<%=myvar%>
<%
END SUB
myvar="Hello There!"
AssignVar
%>
```

In this example, the variable myvar is assigned the value "Hello There!" within the main script. When the subroutine ShowVar is called, the value of this variable is displayed.

Creating Functions

Functions are very similar to subroutines, with one crucial difference: Functions can pass back a result. Here's an example:

```
<TITLE>Function Example</TITLE>
<%
FUNCTION MyFunction(myvar1,myvar2)
  MyFunction=myvar1*myvar2
END FUNCTION
%>
<%=MyFunction(2,2)%>
```

In this example, the function named MyFunction is passed two numeric values. The function multiplies these two values together and assigns the result to MyFunction. The value of MyFunction is displayed to the screen.

Whatever value is assigned to the name of a function within the function is the value returned. In this example, the function named MyFunction is assigned a particular value within the function. It's this value that's returned. A function can return only one value.

In this example, the function returns a numeric value. However, you can use a function to pass back any type of value. Consider the following example:

```
<TITLE>Function Example</TITLE>
<%
FUNCTION MyFunction(myvar)
  MyFunction=STRREVERSE(myvar)
END FUNCTION
mystring="Hello There!"
mystring=MyFunction(MyFunction(mystring))
%>
<%=mystring%>
```

In this example, the function MyFunction reverses any string passed to it by calling the STRREVERSE() function. The variable mystring is assigned the value "Hello There!" Next, the function MyFunction is called twice. This results in the string expression being reversed twice (so the result is "Hello There!"). Finally, the value of the mystring variable is printed to the screen.

Using Random Numbers

A very important function for Web sites is the RND() function. If you want to create a random greeting, a random tip of the day, or even a game, you'll need to use this function.

The RND() function returns a random number greater than or equal to zero and less than one. Here's an example of this function and a possible value it might return:

```
<%=RND()%>
0.7055475
```

8

VBSCRIPT

Typically, you'll be more interested in using this function to return integers that fall in a certain range. To return a number greater than or equal to zero but less than a certain integer, you can use the following statement:

```
<%=INT((upperbound+1)*RND)%>
```

Replace the expression upperbound with the highest random number that you want generated. For example, the following script returns a number between zero and five, including both zero and five:

```
<%=INT((5+1)*RND)%>
```

If you want to generate a random number that falls in a range with a lower bound greater than zero, use the following formula:

```
<%=INT((upperbound - lowerbound + 1) * RND + lowerbound)%>
```

For example, the following script generates random numbers between 50 and 75 (including both 50 and 75):

```
<%=INT((75 - 50 + 1) * RND + 50)%>
```

You may be surprised to learn that the RND() function returns the same random numbers in the same sequence whenever it's used. Consider the following script:

```
<%
Pick_Greeting=INT((2+1)*RND)
SELECT CASE Pick_Greeting
 CASE 0
  Greeting="Welcome!"
 CASE 1
  Greeting="Hello!"
 CASE 2
  Greeting="Happy To See You!"
END SELECT
%>
<%=Greeting%>
```

This script creates and prints a random greeting. However, it probably doesn't work in the way you might think. The same random greeting is printed whenever someone loads a page with this script. If someone returns to this page more than once, he or she gets the same greeting. A random number is generated, but it's the same random number every time.

There's a special statement that can help with this problem. The RANDOMIZE statement is used to force the RND() function to use a new sequence of random numbers. The RANDOMIZE statement provides the RND() function with a new seed value from the computer's system timer. Here's how you could modify the previous example to work correctly:

```
<%
RANDOMIZE
Pick_Greeting=INT((2+1)*RND)
SELECT CASE Pick_Greeting
 CASE 0
```

```
  Greeting="Welcome!"
 CASE 1
  Greeting="Hello!"
 CASE 2
  Greeting="Happy To See You!"
END SELECT
%>
<%=Greeting%>
```

This script works correctly. A new random greeting is generated each time the script is executed. The RANDOMIZE statement forces the RND() function to use a new sequence of random numbers.

Finally, if you're curious about the distribution of the values generated by the RND() function, you could use the following script to determine this:

```
<%
CONST upperbound=9, iterations=100
REDIM DIST(upperbound)
RANDOMIZE
FOR i=1 to iterations
  rnd_num=INT((upperbound+1)*RND)
  DIST(rnd_num)=DIST(rnd_num)&"#"
NEXT
FOR i=0 to upperbound
%>
<%=i&" : "&DIST(i)%> <BR>
<%
NEXT
%>
```

This script generates 100 random numbers between 0 and 9. It keeps track of how many random numbers are generated for each value. Finally, it displays a bar graph representing the results (see Figure 8.3).

FIGURE 8.3.

Distribution of random numbers.

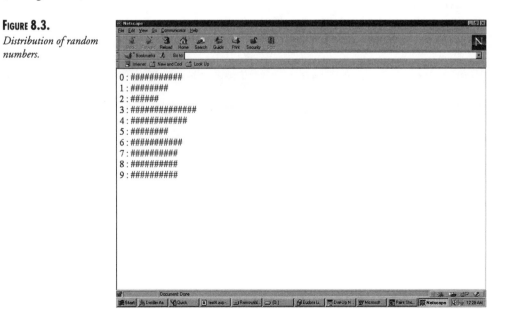

8

VBSCRIPT

Hiding Errors

Bugs in a program are always bad. However, they're particularly bad on a Web site, where potentially thousands of people can gain firsthand knowledge of your programming mistakes. No matter how careful you are, your scripts will contain errors. In this section, you learn how to hide them.

Consider the following script:

```
<%
mystring="Once upon a time"
mystring=UPPERCASE(mystring)
%>
<%=mystring%>
```

This script contains an error. The problem is that there's no such thing as the UPPERCASE() function. There's a UCASE() function, but no UPPERCASE() function. If you attempt to execute this script, an error is generated. The error would appear in a Web page for all the world to see.

Now, consider the following script:

```
<%
ON ERROR RESUME NEXT
mystring="Once upon a time"
mystring=UPPERCASE(mystring)
%>
<%=mystring%>
```

This script is exactly the same as the previous one except for the single statement ON ERROR RESUME NEXT. If you execute this script, the script executes without an error being reported. The ON ERROR RESUME NEXT statement forces the script to continue with the next statement when it encounters an error.

Of course, the statement does nothing about fixing the actual error. The string mystring remains in lowercase. The UPPERCASE() function is simply ignored.

If you need to check whether an error has occurred within a script, you can add the following bit of code:

```
<%
ON ERROR RESUME NEXT
mystring="Once upon a time"
mystring=UPPERCASE(mystring)
IF ERR.NUMBER>0 THEN
%>
<%=ERR.NUMBER%>
<%
ERR.CLEAR
END IF
%>
<%=mystring%>
```

Whenever an error occurs, the error number is recorded in the ERR object. If ERR.NUMBER is greater than zero, you know an error has occurred.

Once an error occurs, you should clear it by using the statement ERR.CLEAR. You need to clear the error so you can record a new one if it happens. An error is automatically cleared whenever the ON ERROR RESUME NEXT statement is executed again. An error is also cleared automatically whenever a procedure or subroutine is exited.

Summary

This chapter provided a comprehensive survey of VBScript. You learned how to use VBScript variables, operators, date functions, and string functions. You also learned how to use conditionals and loops, and how to create functions and procedures of your own. Finally, you learned how to use random numbers and how to handle errors.

After reading this chapter, you should be fully prepared to use VBScript in your Active Server Pages. In the next part of this book, you learn how to use VBScript to access the objects and components of Active Server Pages. This knowledge enables you to create genuinely interactive Web sites.

8

VBSCRIPT

JScript

IN THIS CHAPTER

This chapter describes how to use JScript, the second scripting language included with Active Server Pages. Like VBScript, JScript can be used to extend HTML into something more than a page-formatting language. Using JScript, you can integrate variables, operators, loops, conditionals, and functions into your HTML files. After you read this chapter, you'll understand how to use JScript to create Active Server Pages.

An Introduction to JScript

JScript is Microsoft's implementation of the JavaScript language. If you already understand JavaScript, you'll be very familiar with the material covered in this chapter. Except for a few minor differences, JScript is exactly the same language as JavaScript.

JScript is *not* the same language as Java. Although JScript owes the *J* in its name to the Java programming language, it would take a person with a strong imagination to find significant similarities between the two languages. Whereas Java is a full programming language, JScript is a scripting language.

JScript can be used to perform exactly the same scripting tasks as VBScript. If you plan to use VBScript exclusively in your Active Server Pages, you may want to skim or even skip this chapter. All the scripting examples in the remainder of this book use VBScript instead of JScript.

However, in certain situations, there may be reasons to prefer JScript over VBScript as a scripting language. Even though almost every Active Server Pages script can be written using either VBScript or JScript, certain scripts can be written more easily with one language than the other. There are some significant differences between the features of the two languages, which you'll learn about as you read this chapter.

Furthermore, there's no reason not to mix Active Server Pages created with the two scripting languages on your Web site. You can create certain Active Server Pages with JScript and certain Active Server Pages with VBScript, depending on which language is more appropriate. Moreover, you can even combine scripts written with the two languages within the same Active Server Page (see Chapter 13, "Building Active Server Pages," for more information on this topic).

In short, it doesn't hurt to know JScript when creating Active Server Pages. As your scripts become more complex or specialized, you may feel grateful that Microsoft has provided you with a choice of scripting languages.

Client-Side and Server-Side Programming Languages

JScript can be used as either a client-side or a server-side programming language. A *client-side programming language* is a language that can be interpreted and executed by a browser such as Netscape Navigator or Microsoft Internet Explorer. Another prime example of a client-side programming language is Java. When a program written with one of these languages is loaded into a compatible browser, the browser automatically executes the program.

The advantage of client-side programming languages is that browsers do all the work. This places less of a burden on the server. Client-side programs can also be much faster than server-side programs. A response doesn't need to be fetched over the network whenever the user of a browser performs an action. The client-side program can respond instead.

JScript is a very good language to use as a client-side programming language. Unlike VBScript, JScript creates client-side scripts that the majority of recent browsers can recognize. Both Netscape Navigator and Internet Explorer can interpret and execute HTML files that include JScript.

However, like VBScript, JScript is also a server-side programming language. A *server-side programming language* is a language that executes on the server that serves a Web site's files, rather than on the browsers that receive those files. A server-side programming language performs all of the work on your Web site's computer; all the burden is on you.

The advantage of using JScript as a server-side language is that the scripts work regardless of the browser being used. Your pages are compatible with even the ancient Web browsers that don't recognize JScript as a client-side language. This is true because the scripts are processed before the pages are sent out across the Internet to browsers. Web browsers receive nothing more than normal HTML files.

When you create Active Server Pages, you'll be using JScript as a server-side programming language. Therefore, this book focuses entirely on this use of the language. However, you should realize that the programming skills you acquire while reading this chapter are also valuable for creating client-side programs.

Using JScript with Active Server Pages

In this section, you learn how to create Active Server Pages that can execute scripts created with JScript. You learn much more about Active Server Pages in Part IV of this book, "Creating Active Server Pages with Objects and Components," which is devoted exclusively to this topic. For the moment, however, you can think of an Active Server Page as nothing more than an HTML file that has the file extension .asp rather than the normal file extension .htm.

To use the examples in this chapter, you need to save all your files with the extension .asp rather than .htm. If you neglect to do this, the scripts won't be interpreted. The actual text of the scripts appears in the browser when the Active Server Pages that contain them are loaded. This probably is not what you want.

To use the examples in this chapter, you must also save the files in a directory of your Web server. For example, you can save the files in the wwwroot directory. For the scripts to execute, the pages must be located in a directory that can be accessed by your Web server.

When you load an Active Server Page, you shouldn't load the file directly from your disk. For example, if you save an Active Server Page as C:\InetPub\wwwroot\mypage.asp, you shouldn't load the file into your browser by typing this file path in the address bar. Request the file by using your Web server instead. For example, if your server is named MyServer and the file is saved in your Web server's root directory, type the address **http://MyServer/mypage.asp** in the address bar of your browser. Again, if you neglect to do this, the scripts in the Active Server Page won't be interpreted.

You must also enable Script or Execute permission on the directory where your Active Server Pages are located. Your Web server won't execute a script unless it has permission to do so. See Chapter 2, "Installing and Using Internet Information Server," for more information on how to do this.

NOTE

When making changes to your Active Server Pages, you may discover that these changes are not reflected in the pages loaded into your Web browser. This may be a result of your Web server's use of a memory cache to increase performance. While developing a Web site, you may want to disable this feature. See Chapter 2 for more details.

Integrating JScript into Active Server Pages

JScript is not the default scripting language of Active Server Pages. By default, when a script is encountered in an Active Server Page, the server attempts to interpret it as a script created with VBScript. Before you can use scripts created with JScript in your Active Server Pages, you need to warn the server.

If you plan on using JScript as your primary scripting language, you can make JScript the default language of all the Active Server Pages on your Web site by using the Internet Service Manager (see Chapter 13). Alternatively, you can also indicate that JScript should be the default scripting language for a particular page. To do this, you place the following Active Server Page directive as the very first line in your Active Server Page file:

```
<%@ LANGUAGE=JScript %>
```

This directive indicates that all the scripts contained in the file in which the directive appears should be executed as scripts created with JScript rather than VBScript. When you use this directive, be sure to include a space between the @ character and the keyword LANGUAGE. Furthermore, it's very important that this directive appears as the first line in your Active Server Page file.

NOTE

You can also mix scripts created with JScript and VBScript within the same Active Server Page. To learn how to do this, see Chapter 13.

After you have included the LANGUAGE directive in your Active Server Page, you can create JScript scripts by using the two special characters <% and %>. For example, the following JScript script executes automatically in an Active Server Page:

```
<%@ LANGUAGE=JScript %>
<HTML>
<HEAD>
<TITLE>Simple JScript</TITLE>
</HEAD>
<BODY>
<% for (myvar=0; myvar<500; myvar++) %>
<B>Hello World!</B>
</BODY>
</HTML>
```

This script prints the sentence Hello World! 500 times in a row (see Figure 9.1). Notice how the characters <% and %> are used in this example. They indicate the places where the JScript script begins and ends.

> **NOTE**
>
> Unlike any of the other languages described in this book, JScript is case-sensitive. For example, using the following statement results in an error:
>
> ```
> <% For (myvar=0; myvar<500; myvar++) %>
> ```
>
> The problem with this statement is that the keyword (for) needs to be in lowercase for JScript to recognize it.

FIGURE 9.1.

Active Server Page created with JScript.

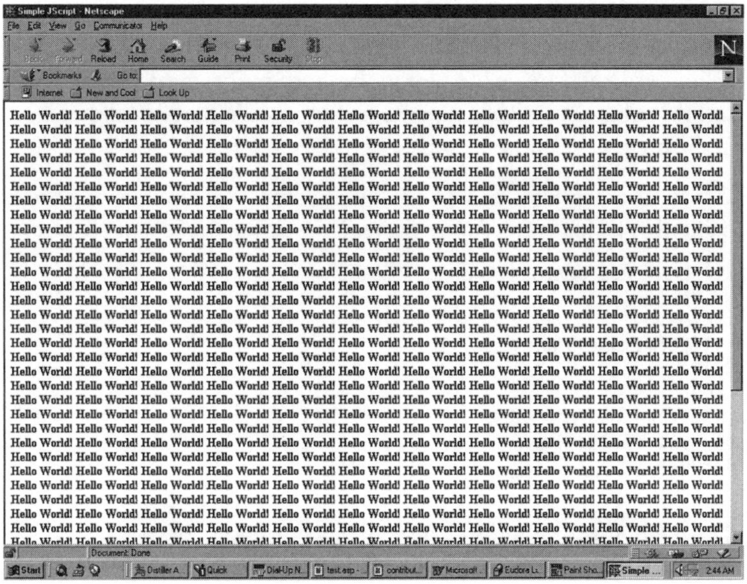

9

JSCRIPT

The two characters <% and %> function very much like the two characters < and > in HTML. Whereas the < and > characters are used to indicate HTML tags, the <% and %> characters are used to indicate scripts. Whenever the Web server sees these two special characters, it attempts to interpret what they contain as a script.

For example, the text <% for (myvar=0; myvar<500; myvar++) %> is an example of a JScript script. This script creates a loop that goes through 500 iterations. The text Hello World! that immediately follows this statement is displayed 500 times.

Notice also how the JScript script is integrated with the HTML tags in the example. You can mix scripts and HTML freely in an Active Server Page. The text <B>Hello World!</B> is not part of the JScript script. The <B> tag is part of HTML and not JScript. However, the text <B>Hello World!</B> is interpreted and displayed 500 times because it's preceded by a JScript script.

You should be aware of an additional expression when you're integrating JScript scripts into Active Server Pages. You can use the delimiters <%= and %> to print the value of a variable, method, or function. Consider the following simple Active Server Page:

```
<%@ LANGUAGE=JScript %>
<HTML>
<HEAD>
<TITLE>Simple JScript</TITLE>
</HEAD>
<BODY>
<% myvar="Hello World!" %>
<%=myvar%>
</BODY>
</HTML>
```

This example prints Hello World! once. The first script assigns the value "Hello World!" to the variable named myvar. The expression <%=myvar%> prints the value of the variable. Whereas the delimiters <% and %> are used for indicating a script, the delimiters <%= and %> are used to indicate the value of a variable, method, or function. Whatever follows the <%= expression is printed in the browser window.

Here's an example of how to use the <%= and %> delimiters to print the value returned by a method. The following Active Server Page prints the text Hello World! in bold:

```
<%@ LANGUAGE=JScript %>
<HTML>
<HEAD>
<TITLE>Simple JScript</TITLE>
</HEAD>
<BODY>
<% myvar="Hello World!" %>
<%=myvar.bold()%>
</BODY>
</HTML>
```

The method bold() returns the contents of the variable myvar in bold. The method does this by surrounding the text with the HTML tags <B> and </B>. The text <B>Hello World!</B> is outputted to the browser.

You should never place JScript commands that don't return a value within the <%= and %> delimiters. This will generate an error. For example, don't do this:

```
<%= for (myvar=0; myvar<500; myvar++) %>
```

Never confuse the function of the <% and %> delimiters with that of the <%= and %> delimiters. One set of delimiters is used for indicating scripts; the other is used to display the values of variables, methods, and functions.

Creating JScript Scripts

When creating scripts with multiple statements, you should terminate each statement with a semicolon. The semicolon marks where one statement ends and another statement begins. Here's an example:

```
<%
myvar="Hello World!";
myvar2="How are you?";
myvar3=myvar+myvar2;
%>
<%=myvar3%>
```

> **NOTE**
>
> In fact, when using Microsoft's JScript, you can neglect to include the semicolons and no error will be generated. JScript detects the end of a statement by detecting a new line instead. However, JavaScript, in contrast to JScript, is much less forgiving of missing semicolons. For this reason, you should develop the habit of always including them.

It's also important to remember that JScript is a case-sensitive language. When using variables, functions, objects, and methods, you must identify them with an expression of the proper case. For example, the following script results in an error:

```
<%
myvar="Hello World!";
%>
<%=MyVar%>
```

When this script is executed, the error `'MyVar' is undefined` is reported. The problem with this script is that MyVar is not the same variable as myvar. Because MyVar has not been assigned a value, the script results in an error.

Commenting Your JScript Scripts

It's always wise to place comments in your code. Time can make any script unreadable. When you return to rewrite or fix a bug in a script that you wrote months ago, you'll thank yourself for your foresight.

There are two ways that you can place comments in your scripts. You can create single-line comments by using the special characters //. Any text after these characters to the end of the line is ignored. This type of comment is useful for explaining what you're trying to accomplish in a particular line of code:

```
<%
myvar="Hello There!" // This is an assignment to a variable
%>
```

When you need to include comments that span more than a single line, you must bracket your comments with the expressions /* and */. This type of comment is useful for explaining whole sections of code or even a whole script, as in this example:

```
<%
/*  This script prints Hello World! 500 times.
    It was initially created on July 5, 1997.
    It was last revised on August 28, 1997.
*/
for (myvar=0; myvar<500; myvar++) %>
<B>Hello World!</B>
```

Another use for comments is to temporarily disable a section of a script. To disable one or more JScript statements, simply mark them as comments. This can be very useful when you're trying to isolate a bug.

Objects, Methods, and Properties

The JScript language, in contrast to VBScript, is very object-oriented. Whereas most of the work in a script created with VBScript is performed by functions, most of the work in a script created with JScript is performed by objects and their methods and properties. This difference between the two languages can be illustrated by considering how the current date and time can be displayed in each language.

To display the current date and time using VBScript, you would call the function NOW, like this:

```
<HTML>
<HEAD>
<TITLE>VBScript Date</TITLE>
</HEAD>
<BODY>
The date and time is: <%=NOW%>
</BODY>
</HTML>
```

To display the current date and time using JScript, on the other hand, you would need to first create a date object, like this:

```
<%@ LANGUAGE=JScript %>
<HTML>
<HEAD>
<TITLE>JScript Date</TITLE>
</HEAD>
```

```
<BODY>
<%mydate=new Date(); %>
The date and time is: <%=mydate%>
</BODY>
</HTML>
```

In this example, the statement `mydate=new Date()` creates a new date object named `mydate` that contains the current date and time. This object must be created before the date can be displayed.

To display the date and time using VBScript, you perform a simple function call. To display the date and time using JScript, you must create a new object. This is the reason that JScript is considered an *object-oriented language.*

What exactly is an object? An *object* is something that has methods and properties. The *methods* of an object are the things that you can do to the object. The *properties* of an object are particular values (or even other objects).

To take an everyday example, a book has certain methods and properties. For example, you can perform certain actions with the book *Huckleberry Finn.* You can read it, press flowers with it, or even, if you are feeling particularly malicious, burn it. These are the methods associated with the book. A book also has certain properties. For instance, the book *Huckleberry Finn* has a certain author and a certain number of pages. These methods and properties of the book determine the ways in which you can interact with it.

In the very same way, a JScript object has certain methods and properties. You can perform particular actions with JScript objects, and you can assign and read an object's properties. An object's methods and properties determine the ways in which you can interact with it.

Now suppose you want to display the current day of the month instead of the current date and time. Using VBScript, you would call another function, the DAY() function, with the DATE function as an argument, like this:

```
<HTML>
<HEAD>
<TITLE>VBScript Day of Month</TITLE>
</HEAD>
<BODY>
The day of the month is: <%=DAY(DATE)%>
</BODY>
</HTML>
```

Using JScript, on the other hand, you would call a method of the Date object. Once you have created a Date object, you can use the object's `getDate()` method to retrieve the current day of the month. Here's an example (continued on the next page):

```
<%@ LANGUAGE=JScript %>
<HTML>
<HEAD>
<TITLE>JScript Date</TITLE>
</HEAD>
<BODY>
```

```
<%mydate=new Date(); %>
The day of the month is: <%=mydate.getDate()%>
</BODY>
</HTML>
```

In this example, the getDate() method of the Date object is called by appending the name of the method (preceded by a single period) to the Date object mydate. As you can see, a method is very much like a function. However, a method is a function that's associated with a particular object.

Declaring Variables

When using JScript, you don't need to explicitly declare a variable before you assign a value to it. For example, the following script works fine:

```
<%
myvar="Hello World!";
%>
<%=myvar%>
```

In this example, the variable myvar is assigned a value, and that value is outputted to the browser window. The text Hello World! is displayed.

However, the following script results in an error:

```
<%
myvar2="Hello World!"+myvar;
%>
<%=myvar2%>
```

The problem with this script is that the variable myvar is used before it has been assigned any value. Unlike in the case of VBScript, a JScript variable must be assigned a value before it can be used in any statements, methods, or functions.

If you want, you can also explicitly declare a variable before you assign a value to it. You do this by using the var statement. Here's an example:

```
<%
var myvar
myvar="Hello World!"
%>
<%=myvar%>
```

In this script, the variable myvar is declared in the first statement. This isn't really necessary because the variable would be implicitly declared in the assignment statement that follows it. However, you can make your scripts more readable and keep better track of your variables by explicitly declaring them at the top of your scripts.

You can also explicitly declare and assign values to more than one variable at a time by using the var statement. All the variable declarations in the following script are valid:

```
<%
var myvar1,myvar2;
var myvar3="Hello There!";
var myvar4="How are you?", myvar5, myvar6="I am fine";
%>
```

> **NOTE**
>
> You must use the var statement when declaring variables that have functional scope. See the later section "Dividing Your Scripts into Functions (the Function Object)."

Working with Dates and Times (the Date Object)

You have already been briefly introduced to the Date object. The Date object has a number of useful methods for manipulating and retrieving dates and times. Here are a few examples of the Date object's methods:

```
<%
mydate=new Date()
%>
<BR>The current date and time is:
<%=mydate%>
<BR>The current month is:
<%=mydate.getMonth()%>
<BR>The current day of the month is:
<%=mydate.getDate()%>
<BR>The current day of the week is:
<%=mydate.getDay()%>
<BR>The current year is:
<%=mydate.getYear()%>
<BR>The current hour is:
<%=mydate.getHours()%>
<BR>The current minute is:
<%=mydate.getMinutes()%>
<BR>The current second is:
<%=mydate.getSeconds()%>
```

Notice that you must create a Date object before you can retrieve any date or time information. In this script, the Date object mydate is created with the first statement in the script. After you create a Date object, each of the methods shown here returns an integer value.

Be aware that many of the values returned by the Date methods are zero-based. For example, the first month of the year, January, is month 0 instead of 1. This can be confusing because the month, by normal conventions, is one greater than the value returned by this method. (See Figure 9.2 for an example of the values returned by these methods.)

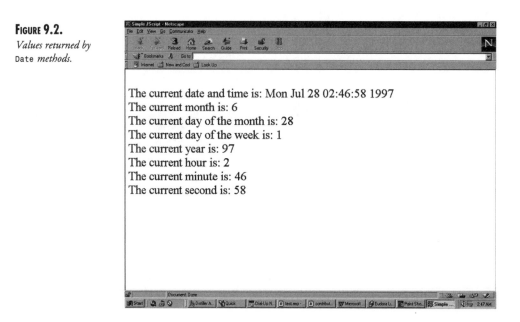

You can also use the Date object to work with dates and times other than the current date and time. To specify another date, simply pass the date to the object when you create it. For example, to create a Date object that represents July 4, 2000, you would use the following script:

```
<%
iday=new Date(2000,6,4,3,27,13)
%>
<%=iday%>
```

The arguments passed to the Date object represent the year, month, day, hour, minute, and second. In this example, the Date object is created to represent the date "July 4, 2000, 3:27:13." If you leave out the hour, minute, or second, they default to zero. You can use any of the Date methods previously described with a Date object created in this way.

You can also create a Date object by passing a string representing a date to the object when you create it. For example, the following script has the same effect as the previous one:

```
<%
iday=new Date("July 4, 2000 3:27:13")
%>
<%=iday%>
```

Again, if you leave out the hours, minutes, or seconds, they default to zero. When this script is executed, the value Tue Jul 04 03:27:13 2000 is outputted to the browser.

The Date object has a number of methods for setting particular parts of dates and times. Using the setMonth(), setDate(), and setYear() methods, you can alter the month, day of month, and year that a Date object represents. Using the setHours(), setMinutes(), and setSeconds() methods, you can change the hour, minute, and second that a Date object represents.

For example, suppose when someone registers at your Web site that you want that person's registration to expire exactly one month from the current date. You could display the expiration date with the following script:

```
<%
currentdate=new Date();
expiredate=new Date();
expiredate.setMonth(currentdate.getMonth()+1);
%>
<%=expiredate%>
```

In this example, two Date objects are created. Both Date objects initially represent the current date and time. Next, the setMonth() method is used to set the month of expiredate to one month past the current date. Finally, the value of expiredate is displayed to the browser.

> **CAUTION**
>
> Contrary to what you might expect, using this script to add a month to a date doesn't add 30 days. The script simply increments the month by 1 while preserving the day of the month. This means that someone who registers in December will get 2 or 3 more days than someone who registers in February. To get around this problem, you can add days instead of months with the setDate() and getDate() methods.

The Date object only tracks dates after midnight, January 1, 1970. The object represents all dates and times relative to this particular moment in history. This is a strange and inconvenient limitation of the object. There's a method that illustrates this property of the Date object. The getTime() method retrieves the number of milliseconds that have passed since midnight, January 1, 1970. The following script returns the number of milliseconds between the stroke of midnight on July 4, 2000, and midnight on January 1, 1970:

```
<%
iday=new Date("July 4, 2000 3:27:14");
%>
<%=iday.getTime()%>
```

The getTime() method in this example retrieves the number of milliseconds between July 4, 2000, and January 1, 1970 (in case you're curious, the answer is 962706434000). All dates and times are actually represented by the Date object in this way.

Finally, the Date object includes two methods that are especially valuable for Web sites that may be browsed by a national or international audience. The getTimezoneOffset() method returns the number of minutes between the time stored in a Date object and Greenwich Mean Time. The toGMTString() method formats a date and time according to the Greenwich Mean Time standard. Following is an example of how both methods are used (continued on the next page):

```
<%
mytime=new Date();
```

```
HoursFromGMT=mytime.getTimezoneOffset()/60;
%>
<BR>The current time is:
<%=mytime%>
<BR>The current Greenwich Mean Time is:
<%=mytime.toGMTString()%>
<BR>These times are separated by the following number of hours:
<%=HoursFromGMT%>
```

Working with Strings (the String Object)

One of the most useful built-in objects included with JScript is the String object. The methods of this object can be used to format and manipulate strings in various ways. For example, you can use the String methods to provide a string with HTML formatting. You can also use the methods to search, compare, and extract substrings from a string.

You can create a new String object by using the new statement. Consider the following script:

```
<%
mystring=new String("I am a string");
%>
<%=mystring%>
```

In this example, the String object named mystring is created. It contains the string "I am a string". When the object is outputted, this text is displayed.

Typically, however, you'll have no reason to explicitly create a String object. Instead, you can create String objects implicitly by using *string literals*. For example, the following script works perfectly well:

```
<%
mystring="I am a string";
%>
<%=mystring%>
```

In this example, the string literal "I am a string" implicitly creates a String object. In most situations, this means that you have no reason to explicitly create a String object. You can simply call the String object's methods on a string literal instead.

> **NOTE**
>
> When must you create a String object explicitly? If you want a group of strings to have certain properties that other strings lack, then you must explicitly create a distinct String object that has these properties. This is true because all strings created implicitly share a common, global String object.

Adding HTML to Strings

A number of the methods of the String object enable you to add various types of HTML formatting to your strings. In the following example, all three strings are outputted in bold:

```
<%
mystring="I am bold!";
mystring2="I am also bold!".bold();
%>
<%=mystring.bold()%>
<%=mystring2%>
<%="I too am bold!".bold()%>
```

The `bold()` method places the HTML tags `<B>` and `</B>` around a string. You could achieve the same effect by doing this explicitly yourself. For example, the two strings outputted by the following script appear the same when displayed in a browser:

```
<%="I am bold!".bold()%>
<%="<B>I am bold!</B>"%>
```

If you use the View Source command on your Web browser, you'll discover that exactly the same string is outputted in each case. The `bold()` method merely makes the HTML formatting of strings more convenient.

The `bold()` method isn't the only `String` method that adds HTML tags to a string. Consider all the methods used in the following script (see Figure 9.3 for the Web browser output):

```
<BR><%="I am big!".big()%>
<BR><%="I am bold!".bold()%>
<BR><%="Blink, blink".blink()%>
<BR><%="I am formatted with a fixed-width font".fixed()%>
<BR><%="I am in italics".italics()%>
<BR><%="I am small".small()%>
<BR><%="I have a line through me".strike()%>
<BR><%="I am in subscript".sub()%>
<BR><%="I am in superscript".sup()%>
<BR><%="I am the color red".fontcolor("red")%>
<BR><%="I am big!".fontsize(4)%>
```

FIGURE 9.3.

Sample output returned by String *methods.*

You can also use `String` methods to create hypertext links and named anchors. For example, the following script creates a list of hypertext links to various Internet sites and a single named anchor:

```
<%="Top Of Page".anchor("top")%>
<H1> My Favorite Links </H1>
<BR><%="Yahoo".link("http://www.yahoo.com")%>
<BR><%="Microsoft".link("http://www.microsoft.com")%>
<BR><%="Collegescape".link("http://www.collegescape.com")%>
<BR><%="CityAuction".link("http://www.cityauction.com")%>
<P>
Back to the top of the page:
<%="TOP".link("#top")%>
```

Again, there's no reason not to add the HTML formatting explicitly. However, your scripts may be more readable (and a tiny bit shorter), if you use these `String` methods instead.

Extracting and Searching for Substrings

The `String` object includes two methods for searching a string for a substring. The `indexOf()` method searches a substring from left to right. The `lastIndexOf()` method searches a string from right to left. Following are some examples of these two methods and the values they would return:

```
<%="The box contained three boxes".indexOf("box")%>
4
<%="The box contained three boxes".lastIndexOf("box")%>
24
<%="The box contained three boxes".indexOf("box",6)%>
24
<%="The box contained three boxes".lastIndexOf("box",22)%>
4
```

In each of these examples, the string `"The box contained three boxes"` is searched for a particular substring. The `indexOf()` method searches this string starting from the left. The `lastIndexOf()` method searches this string starting from the right. When there's no match, each method returns the value -1.

Both methods perform a case-sensitive search. Therefore, a search for the substring `"Box"` would return no matches when used with any of these examples. To perform a case-insensitive search, you need to convert the case of the strings being compared (using one of the two methods described in the next section).

Notice that both methods count from the left side of the string, starting at zero. In the second statement, the value 24 is returned because the string `"box"` is part of the string `"boxes"`.

As you can see from these examples, you can include an integer that specifies where to begin searching in the string. In the third example, the substring is searched starting at the letter x of the first word box. In the fourth example, the string is searched starting at the second character e of three.

If you want to retrieve an individual character from a string, you can use the `charAt()` method of the `String` object. The `charAt()` method returns a character at a particular position in the string. These are some example scripts and the values they would return:

```
<%="The box contained three boxes".charAt(4)%>
b
<%="The box contained three boxes".charAt(10)%>
n
```

Notice once again that the first character in a string is considered to have an index of zero. The character that occupies the fourth position in the string is the letter b. If you specify a character index that's larger than the size of the string, no error is generated, but nothing is returned.

If you need to extract a substring from a string, you can use the `substring()` method. This method accepts two arguments: The first argument specifies where to start extracting the substring, and the second argument specifies where to stop. Here are some examples:

```
<%="The box contained three boxes".substring(4,7)%>
box
<%="The box contained three boxes".substring(24,29)%>
boxes
```

In reality, the order in which you list the start and end indexes for the substring doesn't matter. For positive values, the lower of the two values is automatically considered to be the starting index and the higher value is considered to be the ending index.

When using these methods, it's valuable to know the length of a string. You can determine this by using the `length` property of the `String` object, as in the following examples:

```
<%="The box contained three boxes".length%>
29
<%="box".length%>
3
<%="".length%>
0
```

Changing the Case of a String

Finally, the `String` object contains two methods that enable you to change the case of a string to uppercase or lowercase. The `toUpperCase()` method changes the case of a string to uppercase; the `toLowerCase()` method changes the case of a string to lowercase:

```
<%="The box contained three boxes".toUpperCase()%>
THE BOX CONTAINED THREE BOXES
<%="The BOX contained THREE boxes".toLowerCase()%>
the box contained three boxes
```

These two methods are particularly useful when you need to perform a case-insensitive search for a substring. For example, suppose you want to find the first occurrence of the word box in a string, regardless of case:

```
<%="The box contained three boxes".toUpperCase().indexOf("BOX")%>
```

In this example, the string is first converted to uppercase before the indexOf() method is used to find the substring. By converting the string to uppercase, you can guarantee that a match will be made regardless of the case of the word box.

Performing Mathematical Operations (the Math Object)

JScript includes a valuable built-in object for working with numbers. The methods of the Math object enable you to perform various types of mathematical operations with numbers. The properties of the Math object enable you to work with particular mathematical constants. You don't need to explicitly create a new Math object to use the methods and properties of this object.

General Mathematical Methods

If you need to use trigonometric functions for whatever reasons, the Math object can help. Following are some of the Math object's methods:

- cos() for computing cosine
- sin() for computing sine
- tan() for computing tangent
- acos() for computing arccosine
- asin() for computing arcsine
- atan() for computing arctangent

The Math object also has two methods for comparing two numbers. The min() method returns the smaller of two numbers and the max() method returns the greater of two numbers. Here are examples of both functions and the values they would return:

```
<%=Math.min(290909,899)%>
899
<%=Math.max(290909,899)%>
290909
```

Finally, the Math object includes these additional methods:

- exp() for computing e to a certain power
- log() for computing the natural logarithm
- pow() for computing the power
- sqrt() for computing square roots

Rounding Numbers

The Math object possesses four methods that can be roughly categorized as "rounding" methods: abs(), round(), floor(), and ceil(). Here are some examples of how these methods are used and the values they return:

```
<%=Math.abs(-22)%>
22
<%=Math.round(5.5)%>
6
<%=Math.floor(5.5)%>
5
<%=Math.ceil(5.5)%>
6
```

The abs() method returns the absolute value of the number passed to it. The round() method rounds a number to the nearest integer. It rounds up if the fractional portion is greater than or equal to .5 and rounds down otherwise. The floor() method always rounds down to the nearest integer. The ceil() method always rounds up to the nearest integer.

Generating Random Numbers

One of the most useful methods of the Math object is the random() method. Using the random() method, you can generate random numbers:

```
The random number is: <%=Math.random()%>
```

In this example, a random number between 0 and 1 (inclusive) is generated. You don't need to provide the random() method with a seed in order to generate new random numbers. Unlike in the case of VBScript, the random() method automatically generates a new random number every time a Web page is refreshed. (The random number generator is automatically seeded whenever JScript is loaded.)

Typically, you'll want to generate a random number between zero and some integer value. To return a number that's greater than or equal to zero but less than or equal to a certain integer, you can use the following script:

```
<%=Math.round(upperbound*Math.random())%>
```

Replace the expression upperbound with the highest random number you want returned. For example, if you want to generate a random number between 0 and 10, replace the expression upperbound with 10, like this:

```
<%=Math.round(10*Math.random())%>
```

You may also need to generate random numbers that fall in a certain range of integers. In other words, you may want to generate a random number that has both a lower and an upper bound. To do this, you can use the following script:

```
<%=Math.round((upperbound-lowerbound)*Math.random()+lowerbound)%>
```

For example, the following script generates random numbers between 75 and 100 (inclusive):

```
<%=Math.round( (100-75)*Math.random()+75 )%>
```

Math Constants

If you have a burning need to use pi or Euler's constant (e) in a script for your Web site (and who doesn't occasionally find oneself in this situation?), then you're in luck. The Math object

includes a rich set of mathematical constants. These constants are properties of the Math object. Here are all of the constants and the values they return:

```
The value of e is: <%=Math.E%>
The value of e is: 2.71828182845905
The natural logarithm of 2 is: <%=Math.LN2%>
The natural logarithm of 2 is: 0.693147180559945
The natural logarithm of 10 is: <%=Math.LN10%>
The natural logarithm of 10 is: 2.30258509299405
The base 2 logarithm of e is: <%=Math.LOG2E%>
The base 2 logarithm of e is: 1.44269504088896
The base 10 logarithm of e is: <%=Math.LOG10E%>
The base 10 logarithm of e is: 0.434294481903252
The value of pi is: <%=Math.PI%>
The value of pi is: 3.14159265358979
The square root of .5 is: <%=Math.SQRT1_2%>
The square root of .5 is: 0.707106781186548
The square root of 2 is: <%=Math.SQRT2%>
The square root of 2 is: 1.4142135623731
```

Dividing Your Scripts into Functions (the `Function` Object)

When one of your scripts begins to get long or complex, it's a good idea to divide the script into separate functions. *Functions* are blocks of statements. You can call the same function more than once. You can also pass and retrieve values from functions.

From the object-oriented perspective of JScript, functions are actually objects. Even though JScript functions are objects, they behave very much like VBScript subroutines and functions (there are no subroutines in JScript). You can explicitly create a new function like this:

```
<%
myfunc=new Function("myvar","myvar2","return myvar-myvar2");
%>
```

This script creates a function named `myfunc()`. The function accepts two arguments named `myvar` and `myvar2`, and subtracts the value of one argument from the other. After creating this function, you can output the value of the function like this:

```
<%=myfunc(3,1)%>
```

In this example, the values 3 and 1 are passed to the function and the value 2 is returned.

You don't need to explicitly create `Function` objects in this way, however. You can also create `Function` objects implicitly. This allows you to create functions in the same way as you would for other programming languages, as in this example:

```
<%
function myfunc(myvar,myvar2)
{
return myvar-myvar2;
}
%>
```

This script creates exactly the same function as the one created in the preceding example. The function has two arguments named `myvar` and `myvar2`. The function returns the value of the first argument minus the second argument by using the `return` statement.

Notice the use of curly braces ({ }) to indicate the body of the function. Braces are used in JScript to group statements into blocks. The body of a function can contain multiple statements. Consider the following example:

```
<%
function emphasize(thestring)
{
thestring=thestring.bold();
thestring=thestring.italics();
thestring=thestring.big();
return thestring;
}
%>
<%=emphasize("This is important!")%>
```

In this example, the function `emphasize()` is created. This function accepts a single string argument. The function returns whatever string is passed to it, reformatted in bold, italics, and in a larger size.

You are under no obligation to return a value from a function. A function can also be defined without any arguments. The following script results in the same output as the preceding one:

```
<%
function emphasize()
{
thestring="This is important!";
thestring=thestring.bold();
thestring=thestring.italics();
thestring=thestring.big();
%>
<%=thestring%>
<%
}
%>
<%=emphasize()%>
```

In this example, unlike the preceding script, the value of the string variable is outputted within the body of the function itself. The function is also hardwired to always return the string "This is important!". This function will always perform exactly the same action. One of the main advantages of using arguments and return values is that they make a function more flexible and, therefore, more reusable.

Notice how the string variable named `thestring` is used in the function body in this example. The variable `thestring` is first assigned a value within the function. For this reason, you might think that the variable wouldn't exist outside of the scope of the function. However, in this example, the variable `thestring` actually exists throughout the script.

To create a variable that's local to a particular function, you need to explicitly declare it within the body of the function. You can do this with the var statement. Consider the two variables used in the following script:

```
<%
function greet()
{
myvar="Hello!";
var myvar2="How are you?";
return myvar+myvar2;
}
myvar2="Goodbye!";
%>
<%=greet()%>
<%=myvar2%>
```

When this script is executed, the string "Hello! How are you? Goodbye!" is outputted to the browser. Notice how the variable named myvar2 is assigned different values. There are actually two variables with the same name in this script. The variable myvar2 that is declared within the function only exists within the function. Assigning a value to this variable doesn't affect the value of the variable myvar2 that exists outside the function. This is why the script outputs the value "Goodbye!" in its last output statement rather than "How are you?".

Storing Multiple Values (the Array Object)

When you need to store a number of related values, you should use an array. You can place a list of any type of values within an array. You can even create an array of objects.

After reading this far, you shouldn't be surprised to learn that arrays are objects in JScript. You can create an Array object with the new statement just like any other type of object. Here's an example:

```
<%
myarray=new Array(10);
myarray[0]="Running Shoes";
myarray[2]="Fishing Rod";
myarray[9]="Sailing Boat";
%>
<%=myarray[9]%>
```

In this example, an array named myarray is created with 10 elements. All arrays in JScript are zero-based. So in this case the first element is 0 and the last element is 9.

The three statements that follow the Array creation statement assign values to different elements in the array. The first statement assigns the value "Running Shoes" to the first element.

To retrieve the values from an array, you use the index number of the array element. The final statement in this script outputs the value of the ninth element in the array. The text Sailing Boat is printed to the browser screen.

You can also assign values to an array when you create it. To do this, simply separate values with a comma, like this:

```
<%
myarray=new Array("Running Shoes","Fishing Rod","Sailing Boat");
%>
<%=myarray[2]%>
```

This script creates an array with the very same elements as the preceding one. However, the elements of the array are now indexed in consecutive order. To refer to the value of the third element, for example, you would use its index of 2.

The values stored in an array don't have to be of the same type. For example, you can mix strings and numbers together within the same array, like this:

```
<%
myarray=new Array("Andrew Jones",7,844,"John Pyrovolakis")
%>
```

In this example, the Array object is created with two strings and two numbers. This won't cause an error, and you can refer to the elements in the normal way.

Changing the Size of an Array

After an Array object has been created, you can determine its size by using the length property of the Array object. The value of the length property indicates how many elements can be placed in an array. Here's an example:

```
<%
myarray=new Array("Running Shoes","Fishing Rod","Sailing Boat");
%>
<%=myarray.length%>
```

When this script is executed, the value 3 is returned.

You can change the length property of an Array object. You can make the array either larger or smaller by assigning the length property a different integer value. You change the size of an array like this:

```
<%
myarray=new Array(10);
myarray.length=5;   // makes array smaller
myarray.length=20;  // makes array larger
%>
```

If you make an array larger, the new elements have the value undefined. If you shrink an array, the lost elements disappear forever.

Arrays with More Than One Dimension

You can't create Array objects with more than one dimension using JScript. All Array objects in JScript are basically lists. Sometimes this is inconvenient. Sometimes you need to create lists of lists. How can you do this with JScript?

Suppose you want to create an array that stores user names and their passwords. This is a good example of when a two-dimensional array would be useful. You need to be able to index both types of values. Each user of your Web site has both a name and a password.

Fortunately, nothing prevents you from creating an array of arrays. An element of one `Array` object can have another `Array` object as its value. By creating an array of arrays, you create, in effect, a multidimensional array. Here's an example of how you would do this:

```
<%
myarray=new Array(10);
myarray[0]=new Array(1);
myarray[1]=new Array(1);
myarray[0][0]="Andrew Jones";
myarray[0][1]="Dodgy";
myarray[1][0]="John Pyrovolakis";
myarray[1][1]="Godel";
%>
```

In this example, a simple array of arrays is created. The `Array` object `myarray` is created. Next, two of its elements are assigned to new `Array` objects. Once this two-dimensional array is created out of multiple one-dimensional `Array` objects, you can treat the resulting array as a two-dimensional array. In this example, the array stores the names of two users and their passwords.

Array Methods

A JScript `Array` object has three methods. You can use these methods to manipulate the positions of the elements in an array and to combine the elements of an array into a single string. Following is an example of how the `reverse()` method is used:

```
<<%
myarray=new Array(2);
myarray[0]="I am the first element";
myarray[1]="I am the second element";
myarray.reverse()
%>
<%=myarray[0]%>
<BR>
%=myarray[1]%>
```

In this example, an array is created with two elements. Both elements are assigned string values. Next, the elements of the array are reversed by using the `reverse()` method. The `reverse()` method reverses the index order of the elements in an array. This script has the following output:

```
I am the second element
I am the first element
```

If you want to join all the elements of an array together into a single string, you can use the `join()` method. Without any arguments, this method concatenates all the elements of an array, separating each element with a comma. Here's an example:

```
<%
myarray=new Array("John","Paul","George","Ringo")
mystring=myarray.join()
%>
<%=mystring%>
```

When this script is executed, the value of the variable `mystring` is `"John,Paul,George,Ringo"`. You can also use a separator other than a comma. Simply pass the separator that you want to use to the `join()` method like this:

```
<%
myarray=new Array("John","Paul","George","Ringo")
mystring=myarray.join("*")
%>
<%=mystring%>
```

When this newer version is executed, the variable `mystring` is assigned the value `"John*Paul*George*Ringo"`. The separator need not be only a single character. You can use a string of any length.

The final method of the `Array` object is perhaps the most useful method of the three. Using the `sort()` method, you can sort the elements in an array. Without any arguments, the `sort()` method sorts the elements of an array into alphabetical order. Consider the following example:

```
<%
myarray=new Array("John","Paul","George","Ringo")
myarray=sort()
%>
<BR><%=myarray[0]%>
<BR><%=myarray[1]%>
<BR><%=myarray[2]%>
<BR><%=myarray[3]%>
```

When this script is executed, the following values are outputted:

```
George
John
Paul
Ringo
```

You can also use the `sort()` method to perform more complicated sorting operations. To do this, you pass the method a function that determines how the elements should be sorted, as in this example:

```
<%
function mysort(myvar1,myvar2)
{
var choice=Math.round(Math.random());
if (choice==1) {return -1} else return 1;
}
myarray=new Array("John","Paul","George","Ringo")
myarray.sort(mysort);
%>
<BR><%=myarray[0]%>
<BR><%=myarray[1]%>
<BR><%=myarray[2]%>
<BR><%=myarray[3]%>
```

In this example, the elements of the array are sorted randomly. Every time the script is executed, the names are outputted in a different order. The function `mysort()` performs the actual sorting operation. This function is passed to the `sort()` method of the `myarray` Array object.

9

JSCRIPT

Any sorting function you pass to the sort() method must accept two arguments. These two arguments represent the two array elements to be compared. If the function returns a negative number, the element represented by the first element is sorted above the element represented by the second argument. If the function returns a positive value, the second element is sorted above the first. Finally, if the function returns zero, the order of the two elements is not changed.

Creating Your Own Objects

You are not limited to the built-in objects of JScript discussed in the previous sections. You can extend JScript with your own objects that have their own methods and properties. This is a powerful feature of JScript.

For example, you can create an object named webuser that holds information about the users of your Web site. The object can have properties such as the user's name, password, and registration status. By bringing all these properties together into a single object, you can make your scripts more readable, simple, and elegant.

To create an object, you create a function that defines the object. Here's an example:

```
<%
function webuser(name,password,regstatus)
{
this.name=name;
this.password="unknown";
this.regstatus=0;
}
%>
```

This function can be used to define an object named webuser. Notice how the keyword this is used. The keyword this indicates the current object. It's used in this example to specify default values for the properties of the webuser object.

Once you have specified a creation function for an object, you create instances of an object in the normal way. You use the new statement:

```
<%
Fred=new webuser("Fred");
Mike=new webuser("Mike");
%>
```

In this script, two webuser objects are created named Fred and Mike. The Fred object's name property is set to Fred when the object is created. The other properties assume their default values. For example, the value of the Fred object's password property would be "unknown" when the object is first created. You can set the value of a property in the normal way with the following script:

```
<%
Fred.password="my secret password";
%>
```

When you create an object, you can also provide the object with your own methods. To do this, simply create a function and refer to the function in the creation function for the object. Here's an example:

```
<%
function expirepassword()
{
this.password="no good";
}
function webuser(name,password,regstatus)
{
this.name=name;
this.password="unknown";
this.regstatus=0;
this.expirepassword=expirepassword;
}
Fred=new webuser("Fred");
Fred.expirepassword();
%>
```

In the script, the function expirepassword() is first defined. The function is then added to the creation function for the webuser object. The statement this.expirepassword=expirepassword makes the expirepassword function a method of the webuser object.

When the object Fred is created, the value of Fred's password property is initially "unknown". However, once the expirepassword() method is called, the value of Fred's password is changed to "no good".

As you can see, objects are very easy to create. You should take advantage of your own objects in your scripts. Using objects can force you to think more logically about how to store and manipulate information.

Using JScript Functions

Although JScript is an object-oriented language, it does include a limited number of functions. Three of these functions, in particular, are very useful. You can use the parseInt() and parseFloat() functions to convert a string to an integer and a floating-point number. You can use the isNaN() function to test whether the result is actually a number. Here are some examples and the values they would return:

```
<%=parseInt("3.14")%>
3
<%=parseFloat("3.14")%>
3.14
<%=parseInt("I am not a number")%>
1.#QNAN
<%=isNaN("I am not a number")%>
True
```

Notice that the first function truncates the number 3.14. The parseInt() function only parses integers. The parseFloat() function that follows successfully parses the number. Finally, notice the weird result returned by the third statement in the script. To test whether a string could be successfully parsed into a number, you can use the isNaN() function as in the last statement.

Operators

JScript has a rich set of operators. For a complete list of the operators included with this language, see Appendix B, "Quick JScript Reference," at the back of this book. In this section, you learn about the most useful operators.

All the standard arithmetic operators are included. You can perform addition (+), subtraction (-), multiplication (*), division (/), and determine the modulus (%). To compare whether one value is greater than another, you can use the greater-than operator (>). To compare whether one value is less than another, you can use the less-than operator (<).

To determine whether two values are unequal, you use the inequality comparison operator (!=). To determine whether two values are equal, use the equality operator (==).

It's easy to confuse the assignment operator (=) with the equality operator (==). One operator is used to assign values to variables, the other is used to test whether two expressions are equal. Here are some examples of how the assignment operator is used:

```
<%
myvar="Hello!";
myvar2=myvar3=myvar;
myvar4=myvar5=1;
%>
```

The first assignment in this script should be familiar. The string "Hello!" is assigned to the variable named myvar. The second assignment statement assigns the value of myvar to both the variables myvar2 and myvar3. It's perfectly legal to chain assignment statements in this way when using JScript. Finally, the last assignment statement assigns the value 1 to both the variables myvar4 and myvar5.

In VBScript, the equal sign (=) is used to represent both the assignment and equality operators. In JScript, on the other hand, you use the (==) operator to test for equality. Consider the following scripts and the values they return:

```
<%=(1==1)%>
True

<%=("Apple"=="Apple")%>
True

<%=("Apple"=="apple")%>
False

<%=("Apple"==1)%>
False
```

Because one is in fact equal to one, the first equality test returns True. Because the two strings "Apple" are identical, the second equality statement returns True as well. However, because the equality operator is case-sensitive, the third statement returns False. Finally, the last statement returns False because under no situation is the string "Apple" equal to the number 1.

The addition operator (+) can be used to perform addition. However, the operator is also used to concatenate strings. Consider the following examples and the values they would return:

```
<%="Hello"+" "+"World!"%>
Hello World!

<%="Hello"+12%>
Hello12

<%=1+1%>
2
```

You can combine the functions of the assignment operator and the addition operator into a single operator. The compound assignment operator += increments the value of a variable by a certain amount or concatenates a new string to itself. Here are some examples of how the compound assignment operator is used:

```
<%
myvar=1;
myvar+=2;
%>
<%=myvar%>
3

<%
myvar="Hello ";
myvar+="World!";
%>
<%=myvar%>
Hello World!
```

The statement myvar+=myvar2 is equivalent in every way to the statement myvar=myvar+myvar2. The compound addition operator simply saves you from some tedious typing.

The compound addition operator isn't the only compound operator. You can also use -= to decrement the value of a variable by a certain amount, *= to multiply the value of a variable by a certain amount, and /= to divide the value of a variable by a certain amount.

If you merely need to increment a variable by one, you can use the increment operator ++. If you need to decrement a variable by one, you can use the decrement operator --. Here are some examples:

```
<%
myfirstvar=2;
mysecondvar=++myfirstvar;
%>

<%
myfirstvar=2;
mysecondvar=myfirstvar++;
%>
```

After the first script executes, the value of the variable named `mysecondvar` is 3. The increment operator increments the value of `myfirstvar` by one. However, in the second script, the value assigned to the variable `mysecondvar` is 2. What explains this difference?

When the increment operator appears on the left side of a variable, the value of the variable is incremented before it's assigned. When the increment expression appears on the right side of a variable, the value of the variable is incremented after the assignment. The decrement operator works in the same way except, of course, it decrements:

```
<%
myfirstvar=2;
mysecondvar=--myfirstvar;
%>

<%
myfirstvar=2;
mysecondvar=myfirstvar--;
%>
```

The variable `mysecondvar` is assigned the value 1 when the first script is executed. In the second script, on the other hand, the variable `mysecondvar` is assigned the value 2.

JScript also includes the Boolean operators. To form the logical conjunction of two expressions, you use the logical AND operator (`&&`). To form a logical disjunction of two expressions, you use the OR operator (`¦¦`). To form the logical negation of an expression, you use the NOT operator (`!`).

The Boolean operators are especially useful when you need to form conditions for `if...else` statements and loops. You learn how to use these statements in the next section.

Using Conditional Statements (if...then...else)

If you need to execute a single statement or block of statements depending on whether some condition is true or false, then you need to use a conditional. A *conditional* accepts any expression as its condition that returns a Boolean value. Here's an example:

```
<%
greeting="Happy Weekday!"
mydate=new Date();
if (mydate.getDay()==0) greeting="Happy Sunday!";
if (mydate.getDay()==6) greeting="Happy Saturday!";
%>
<%=greeting%>
```

If the day of the week is Saturday or Sunday, this script returns the appropriate greeting. Otherwise, the script outputs the greeting `Happy Weekday!`

Notice how the two conditionals are formed in this script. The `if` statement is followed by an expression in parentheses. The expression in parentheses must return a Boolean value (`True` or

False). For both of these conditionals, the expression in the parentheses performs a comparison to the current day of the week.

Notice also that the word then is not used in a JScript conditional. If the conditional is true, the statement or block of statements following the parentheses is executed. Here's an example of a conditional that executes a block of code:

```
<%
greeting="Happy other day!";
mydate=new Date();
if (mydate.getDay()==0)
{
greeting="Happy Sunday!";
greeting=greeting.bold();
greeting=greeting.italics()
}
%>
<%=greeting%>
```

In this example, the three statements contained within the curly braces ({ }) are not executed on any day except Sunday. The braces indicate the start and end of the consequence of the conditional.

Finally, you can use the keyword else with a conditional to specify a statement or block of statements that will execute if the condition is false. Here's an example:

```
<%
mydate=new Date();
if (mydate.getDay()==0) greeting="Happy Sunday!"
else greeting="Happy other day!";
%>
<%=greeting%>
```

In this example, the variable greeting is guaranteed to have one of two values. If it's Sunday, the variable greeting will have the value "Happy Sunday!"; otherwise, the variable will have the value "Happy other day!"

Repeating Statements with Loops (for...next)

If you need to repeat a single statement or block of statements a particular number of times, you can use a for...next loop. The following for...next prints Hello World! exactly 10 times:

```
<%
for (myvar=0;myvar<10;myvar++)
%>
Hello World!
```

The for statement has three parts. The first part initializes a variable. In this example, the new variable myvar is initialized to the value 0. The second part tests whether some condition is true. This loop keeps executing while the value of myvar is less than 10. Finally, the last part of the for statement increments the myvar variable.

Typically, you'll have a block of code that's executed by the for...next loop. To specify a block of statements to execute, you contain the statements within curly braces ({ }), as in the following example:

```
<%
for (myvar=0;myvar<10;myvar++)
{
%>
<BR>Hello World!
<BR>How are you today?
<%
}
%>
```

In this example, the block of HTML is displayed to the browser 10 times. Notice the single curly brace that ends the for...next loop at the bottom of the script.

A statement that's closely related to the for...next statement is the for...in statement. You can use the for...in statement to step through each of the elements of an array or object. Here's an example of how this statement is used:

```
<%
myarray=new Array("John","Paul","George","Ringo");
for (myvar in myarray)
{
%>
<%=myarray[myvar]%>
<%
}
%>
```

This script outputs the values of all the members of the array named myarray. For each element in myarray, the statement executes the block of code.

Using while Loops

If you need to execute a single statement or a block of code while a certain condition is true, then you can use a while loop. A while loop executes only while a condition is true. Consider the following script:

```
<%
function ThePresent()
{
var ThePresentTime=new Date();
return ThePresentTime.getTime();
}
TheFutureTime=new Date();
TheFutureTime.setSeconds(TheFutureTime.getSeconds()+15);
TheFuture=TheFutureTime.getTime();
while (ThePresent()<TheFuture)
{
%>
<BR> Waiting for the future...
<%
}
%>
```

This script outputs the text `Waiting for the future...` over and over for 15 seconds (see Figure 9.4). The block of code following the `while` statement continues to execute while the condition specified within the parentheses continues to be true. In this case, the `while` loop continues to iterate while the current time is less than 15 seconds later than the time when the script started to execute (the function is used to continuously update the current time).

FIGURE 9.4.

Waiting for the future.

If the condition for a `while` statement is false before the `while` statement is encountered in a script, the block of code contained by the `while` statement never executes. On the other hand, if the condition for a `while` statement never stops being true, the `while` statement attempts to execute forever.

You should be cautious of getting yourself into infinite loops when using the `while` statement. If you accidentally create an infinite loop, don't worry. Be patient and the script will automatically terminate after a set period of time (usually 90 seconds).

NOTE

You can control how long a script executes before it times out by using the `ScriptTimeOut` property of the `Server` object. You learn how to do this in Chapter 14, "Working with a Single Active Server Page."

9

JSCRIPT

Specifying a Default Object (`with`)

The object-oriented nature of JScript can result in a lot of extra typing. Whenever you call a method, you must also specify the method's object. If you have to call a number of methods of a particular object, typing the name of the object over and over can become tedious.

Fortunately, there's a JScript statement that can help. Using the `with` statement, you can specify a default object for a block of statements. Within the block, you don't have to designate the object whenever you use one of the object's methods.

For example, suppose you want to create three random numbers. Normally, you would have to do this with the following script:

```
<%
myrandom1=Math.random();
myrandom2=Math.random();
myrandom3=Math.random();
%>
```

If you make the `Math` object the default object, however, you don't have to type the name of the object repeatedly. Here's how you could rewrite the script using the `with` statement:

```
<%
with (Math)
{
myrandom1=random();
myrandom2=random();
myrandom3=random();
}
%>
```

By using the `with` statement in this situation, you have saved exactly two keystrokes. After being huddled over a keyboard many hours straight, every keystroke counts.

Summary

This chapter has provided you with a comprehensive survey of JScript. You learned how to use the methods and properties of the most important JScript objects, including the `Date`, `Math`, `String`, and `Array` objects. You also learned how to create objects of your own. Finally, you learned how to use JScript statements to control the flow of your scripts.

After reading this chapter, you should be fully prepared to use JScript in your Active Server Pages. In Part IV of this book, you learn how to access the objects and components of Active Server Pages. Your knowledge of JScript will provide you with greater flexibility in creating genuinely dynamic Web sites.

III

PART

Working with Data: SQL

Basic SQL

IN THIS CHAPTER

To create a genuinely interactive Web site, you need to use a database to store information collected from the visitors to your Web site. If you're creating a career services Web site, for example, you need to store such information as résumés and job interests. A database is also useful for creating dynamically generated Web pages. If you want to display the perfect job match for a visitor to your Web site, you need to retrieve this job description from a database. You'll discover that you need to use a database for a surprising number of different tasks.

In this chapter, you learn how to communicate with a database by using *Structured Query Language (SQL)*. SQL is the standard language of databases. Whenever you need to access a database in your Active Server Pages, you'll be using the SQL language; therefore, a good grasp of SQL is very important for Active Server Pages programming.

> **NOTE**
>
> You can pronounce SQL like *sequel* as in "Indiana Jones and the Temple of Doom." Alternatively, you can pronounce the individual letters S-Q-L. Either pronunciation is correct, even though each pronunciation has strong and vocal adherents. In this book, consider SQL to be pronounced *sequel*.

After you read this chapter, you'll understand how to use SQL to construct database queries. You'll learn how to use these queries to retrieve information from a database table. Finally, you'll understand how to design and create database tables of your own.

> **NOTE**
>
> By reading the introductory material on SQL in the next few chapters, you'll gain a sufficient understanding of the language to use Active Server Pages effectively. However, SQL is a complicated language and this book can't cover all of its nuances. To learn everything you'd ever need to know about using SQL with Microsoft SQL Server, rush to your local bookstore and buy *Microsoft SQL Server 6.5 Unleashed, Second Edition* by David Solomon, Ray Rankins, et al. (1996, Sams Publishing, ISBN 0-672-30956-4.)

An Introduction to SQL

This book assumes that you will be using SQL with the Microsoft SQL Server database. However, you can use SQL with many other databases. SQL is a standard language for working with databases. (Indeed, there's an ANSI standard for SQL.)

NOTE

Don't be tempted to use Microsoft Access instead of Microsoft SQL Server as the database for your Web site. SQL Server can handle many more concurrent users. If you plan to have much traffic on your Web site, Microsoft Access won't be able to handle the work.

Before getting into the details of this language, you need to understand two of its general features. One feature is easy to grasp; the other is a little more difficult.

The first feature is that all data stored in a SQL database is stored in tables. A table consists of columns and rows—very much like a standard spreadsheet. For example, you might have a simple table that contains names and e-mail addresses like this:

```
Name                Email Address
----------------    ----------------------
Bill Gates          billg@microsoft.com
President Clinton   president@whitehouse.com
Stephen Walther     swalther@somewhere.com
```

This table has two columns: `Name` and `Email Address`. The table also contains three rows. Each row contains particular pieces of data. The combination of columns in a row is called a *record*.

Whenever you add new data to a table, you add a new record. A database table may contain dozens, thousands, or even billions of records. While you may never need to store a billion e-mail addresses, it's good to know that you could if you ever found the need.

Your database will most likely contain dozens of tables. All the information stored in your database will be stored in these tables. When you consider how to store information in a database, you should consider how you can store that information in tabular form.

The second feature of SQL is a little more difficult to grasp. The language wasn't designed to allow you to retrieve rows according to a certain order. Doing so would undermine SQL Server's ability to retrieve the rows efficiently. Using SQL, you retrieve rows based on criteria instead.

When thinking of how to retrieve rows from a table, it's only natural to think of retrieving the rows according to their positions. For example, it's tempting to think of programming a loop that goes through each row one by one to select certain rows. You must train yourself not to think in this way when using SQL.

Suppose you want to retrieve any table row that has the e-mail address for Bill Gates. Using a traditional programming language, you might construct a loop that moves through each row in the table and tests to see whether the `Name` column is equal to `"Bill Gates"`.

10

BASIC SQL

This method of retrieving rows would work, but it wouldn't be very efficient. Using SQL, you simply say, "Retrieve any row where the Name column equals Bill Gates," and the language complies by handing you any row that fits the criteria. SQL Server determines the best method of doing this.

Suppose you want to retrieve the first ten rows from a table. Using a traditional programming language, you would loop through the first ten rows and then stop. Using a standard SQL query, however, this just isn't possible. From the perspective of SQL, there's no such thing as the first ten rows in a table.

At first, you may experience severe frustration when you realize that you simply can't do certain things with SQL that you feel you really ought to be able to do. You'll pound your head against the nearest wall and think dark thoughts about writing nasty letters to the designers of SQL. After a while, however, you'll realize that this feature of the language isn't a limitation, but one of its greatest strengths. Because SQL doesn't retrieve rows based on their positions, it can retrieve rows much faster.

So SQL has two general features: All data is stored in tables, and, from the perspective of SQL, the rows in a table have no inherent order. In the next section, you learn how to use SQL to retrieve particular records from a table.

Using SELECT to Retrieve Records from a Table

One of the main functions of SQL is to construct database queries. If you're familiar with Internet search engines such as Yahoo! or Alta Vista, then you're already familiar with queries. You use a query to retrieve information based on particular criteria.

For example, if you want to find every Web site that has information on Active Server Pages, you could surf to the Yahoo! Web site and perform a search on "Active Server Pages". After you enter this query, you'll receive a list of all the listed Web sites that have this search expression in their descriptions.

Most Internet search engines allow you to perform *Boolean queries*. In a Boolean query, you can include special operators such as AND, OR, and NOT. You use these operators to select only certain records to be retrieved. For example, you can use AND to restrict your search results. If you perform a search on "Active Server Pages" AND "SQL" you'll retrieve only those records that include both the expressions "Active Server Pages" and "SQL" in their descriptions. When you need to limit the results of a query, you can use AND.

If you need to expand the results of a search, you can use the Boolean operator OR. For example, if you perform a search for all Web sites that contain "Active Server Pages" OR "SQL" in their descriptions, you'll receive a list of Web sites that contain either or both search expressions in their descriptions.

If you need to exclude certain Web sites from your search results, you can use NOT. For example, the query "Active Server Pages" AND NOT "SQL" will retrieve a list of every Web site that contains "Active Server Pages" in its description but not the expression "SQL". When you need to exclude particular records from your database, you can use NOT.

Queries performed using the SQL language are very similar to those performed using Internet search engines. When you perform a SQL query, you can retrieve a list of records by using selection criteria that include Boolean operators. However, when you perform a SQL query, the query selects its results from one or more tables.

The syntax for a SQL query is very simple. Suppose you have a table named email_table that contains names and e-mail addresses, and you want to retrieve the e-mail address for Bill Gates. You could retrieve his e-mail address by using the following SQL query:

```
SELECT email from email_table WHERE name="Bill Gates"
```

When this query is executed, the e-mail address for Bill Gates is retrieved from the table named email_table. This simple SELECT statement has three parts:

- The first part of the SELECT statement specifies the columns to be retrieved. In this example, only the email column is retrieved. When the query executes, only the value of the email column, billg@microsoft.com, is displayed.

- The second part of the SELECT statement names the table(s) from which the query results are pulled. In this example, the query is executed against the table named email_table.

- Finally, the WHERE clause of the SELECT statement specifies the criteria to use when retrieving the records. In this example, the selection criteria specifies that only the records where the value of the name column is equal to "Bill Gates" should be retrieved.

Most likely, Bill Gates has more than one e-mail address. If the table contains multiple e-mail addresses for Bill Gates, all his e-mail addresses would be retrieved using the SELECT statement just shown. The SELECT statement retrieves every e-mail address FROM the table email_table WHERE the value of the name column is equal to "Bill Gates".

As mentioned earlier, a SQL query can contain Boolean operators in its selection criteria. Suppose you want to retrieve every e-mail address for either Bill Gates or President Clinton. In that case, you could use the following SQL SELECT statement:

```
SELECT email FROM email_table WHERE name="Bill Gates"
➥OR name="President Clinton"
```

The selection criterion in this example is a little more complicated than the one used previously. This SELECT statement retrieves every record from the table email_table where the value of the name column equals "Bill Gates" or "President Clinton". If email_table contains more than one e-mail address for Bill Gates or President Clinton, all those e-mail addresses are retrieved as well.

The structure of a SQL SELECT statement should seem very intuitive. If you were to ask a friend to select a group of records from a table, you might phrase the request in a very similar way. In a SQL SELECT statement, you SELECT certain columns FROM a table WHERE the columns of a row meet a certain criterion.

The next section explains how to execute actual SQL queries and retrieve records. This should help you become familiar with the various ways in which you can use the SELECT statement to pull data from database tables.

Using ISQL to Execute SELECT Queries

When you installed SQL Server, you also installed a useful utility program called ISQL/w. The program ISQL/w allows you to perform interactive SQL queries. It's very useful for testing queries before you include them in your Active Server Pages.

> **NOTE**
>
> In the first part of this book, you learned how to install and configure Microsoft SQL Server. If SQL Server is not installed or the SQL service currently isn't running, see Chapter 3, "Installing and Using SQL Server."

Start this program now by selecting ISQL_w from the SQL Server program group on the Start menu. When the program starts, a dialog box appears demanding server and login information (see Figure 10.1). In the Server box, enter the name of your SQL server. If the SQL server is running on your local machine, the server name will be the same as your machine name. Complete the login information by providing a login ID and password or by using a trusted connection, and click the Connect button.

FIGURE 10.1.

Server and login information.

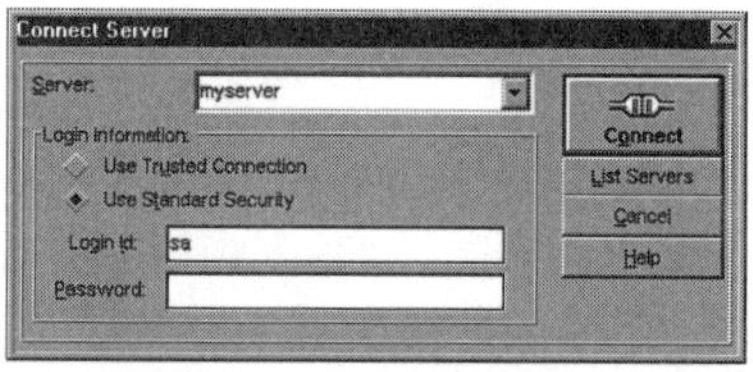

> **NOTE**
>
> If you configured SQL Server to use either integrated or mixed security, you can use a trusted connection. If you're using standard security, however, you need to supply a user ID and password. For more information, see Chapter 3.

If all goes well, after you click the Connect button a query window will appear, as shown in Figure 10.2. (If all doesn't go well, refer to Chapter 3.)

FIGURE 10.2.

The ISQL/w query window.

The Execute Query button

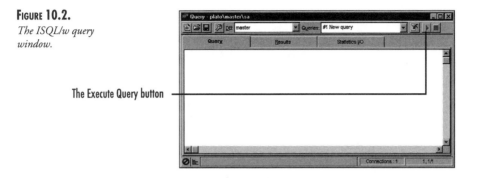

Before you execute a query, you need to choose a database. When you installed SQL Server, you created a database of your own. However, SQL Server also has a number of system databases, such as the `master`, `model`, `msdb`, and `tempdb` databases.

Conveniently, SQL Server also includes a special sample database called the `pubs` database. The `pubs` database includes tables used by a fictional book publisher. All the SQL programming examples in the SQL documentation refer to this database. Many of the examples in this book also make use of the `pubs` database.

Choose the `pubs` database in ISQL/w by selecting `pubs` from the drop-down DB list at the top of the query window. Now that you've selected the `pubs` database, all your queries will be executed against tables in this database. You're now ready to execute your first SQL query. This is exciting!

You'll be executing your first query against a table named `authors` that includes data about all the authors who work for a fictional publisher. Click the query window and enter the following `SELECT` statement:

```
SELECT phone FROM authors WHERE au_lname="Ringer"
```

After entering the `SELECT` statement, click the Execute Query button (it looks like a VCR Play button—a green triangle). When you click this button, any SQL statement that appears in the query window is executed. The query window should automatically switch to the results window, and you should see the results of your query (see Figure 10.3).

The results of your query may differ from those shown in Figure 10.3; depending on the version of SQL Server you're using, the data in the `pubs` database might differ. For SQL Server 6.5, two rows should be retrieved. The results window should display the following:

```
phone
-----------
801 826-0752
801 826-0752
(2 row(s) affected)
```

10

BASIC SQL

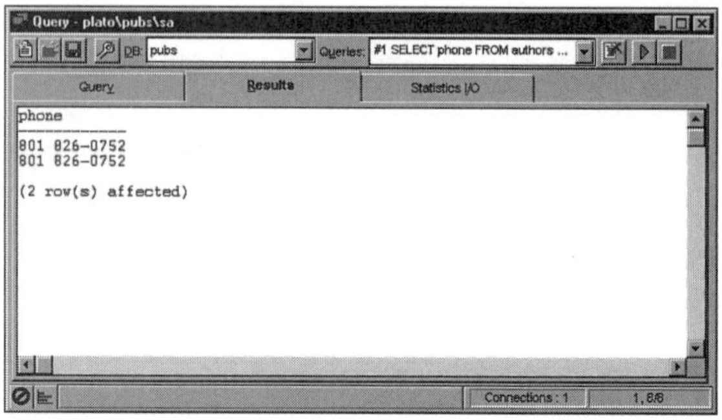

FIGURE 10.3.

The results of your first SQL query.

The SELECT statement you executed retrieved every phone number FROM the authors table WHERE the author's last name is Ringer. You restricted the results of your query by using a particular selection criteria in your WHERE clause. However, you can omit the selection criteria and retrieve the phone number of every author from the authors table. To do this, click the Query tab to return to the query window, and enter the following SELECT statement:

```
SELECT phone FROM authors
```

When this query is executed, every phone number in the authors table is retrieved (in no particular order). If the authors table contained one hundred phone numbers, one hundred rows would be retrieved. If the authors table contained one billion phone numbers, all one billion rows would be retrieved. (Depending on your computer system, this might take some time.)

The authors table includes columns for first names, last names, phone numbers, addresses, cities, states, and ZIP codes. You can retrieve any of these columns by referring to them in the first part of a SELECT statement. You can also retrieve multiple columns at once in a single SELECT statement, like this:

```
SELECT au_fname, au_lname, phone FROM authors
```

When this SELECT statement is executed, the values of all three columns are retrieved. Following is an example of the results from this query. (To save page space, only part of the results are shown, and the remaining rows are indicated with an ellipsis.)

```
au_fname              au_lname                          phone
-------------------- --------------------------------- -----------
Johnson              White                             408 496-7223
Marjorie             Green                             415 986-7020
Cheryl               Carson                            415 548-7723
Michael              O'Leary                           408 286-2428
...
(23 row(s) affected)
```

In your SELECT statement, you can list as many columns from a table as you need. Always remember to separate the column names with commas. You can also use the asterisk (*) character to retrieve every column from a table. Here's an example of how you use the asterisk:

```
SELECT * FROM authors
```

When this SELECT statement is executed, the value of every column is retrieved from the authors table. You'll find yourself using the asterisk in your SQL queries quite often.

> **TIP**
>
> You can also use the asterisk as a way to discover the names of all of the columns in a table. To do this, just look at the column headings when the rows are retrieved after executing the SELECT statement.

Working with Multiple Tables

Up to this point, you have retrieved data from only one table with a SQL query. But you can use a SELECT statement to retrieve data from multiple tables at the same time. Simply list additional table names in the FROM clause of your SELECT statement:

```
SELECT au_lname, title FROM authors, titles
```

When this SELECT statement is executed, data is pulled from both the authors and titles tables. All the authors' last names are retrieved from the authors table and all the book titles are retrieved from the titles table. Execute this query in the ISQL/w program, and take a look at the results. When you examine the results from this query, you'll notice something odd and unexpected: The last names of the authors are not associated with the titles of their books. Instead, the authors' last names and the book titles appear in every possible combination. This probably is not what you wanted.

What went wrong? The problem is that you haven't specified the relationship between the two tables. You haven't told SQL how to join together the authors and titles tables in any meaningful way. Without knowing how to join the two tables, the server simply spits back every possible combination of the rows selected from the two tables.

To select records from two tables in a meaningful way, you need to join the two tables by establishing a relationship between a column from each of the tables. One way to do this is to create a third table that explicitly states the relationship between the columns of the other two.

The authors table includes a column called au_id that contains a unique ID for each author. The titles table contains a column called title_id that has a unique ID for each book title. If you could forge a relationship between the au_id column and the title_id column, you could join the two tables. A third table in the pubs database, called titleauthor, does exactly that. Each row in the titleauthor table contains both an au_id column and a title_id column. The titleauthor table joins the titles and authors tables. Here's a SELECT statement that uses all three tables to retrieve the proper results:

```
SELECT au_lname, title FROM authors, titles, titleauthor
➥WHERE authors.au_id=titleauthor.au_id
➥AND titles.title_id=titleauthor.title_id
```

10

BASIC SQL

When this SELECT statement is executed, each author is associated with the correct title. The titleauthor table specifies the relationship between the authors and titles tables. It does this by including a column from each table. The sole purpose of this third table is to create a correspondence between the columns of the other two. The third table doesn't contain any additional data.

Notice how the names of the columns are written in this example. To differentiate between the column named au_id in the authors table and the column by the same name in the titleauthor table, the name of each column is prefixed with the table name and a period. The column named author.au_id is unambiguously part of the author table and the column titleauthor.au_id is unambiguously part of the titleauthor table.

By using a third table, you can specify many types of relationships between the columns of two tables. For example, one author may write many different books, or a single book may be written by many different authors. When you have this type of many-to-many relationship between the columns of two tables, you need to use a third table to represent the relationship.

In many cases, however, the relationship between two tables is less complex. Suppose you need to specify the relationship between the titles table and a table of publishers. Because no title will be associated with more than one publisher, you don't need to indicate the relationship between the two tables with a third table. To specify the relationship between the titles table and the publishers table, you need nothing more than a common column shared between the two tables. In the pubs database, the titles table and publishers table both have a column named pub_id. If you want to retrieve a list of book titles and their publishers, you can use the following SELECT statement:

```
SELECT title, pub_name FROM titles, publishers
➥WHERE titles.pub_id=publishers.pub_id
```

If a book title was ever jointly published by two publishers, of course, you would need a third table to represent that relationship.

In general, when you foresee the possibility of a many-to-many relationship between the columns of two tables, use a third table to join the two tables. On the other hand, if the columns of two tables are related in a one-to-one or one-to-many relationship, you can use a common column to join the tables.

Working with Table Columns

Normally, when you retrieve column values from a table, the values are associated with the column name assigned when the table was created. So if you selected all the author last names from the authors table, all those values would be associated with the au_lname column. In some situations, however, you need to manipulate the column name. You can alter a default column name by placing a new name immediately after it in the SELECT statement. In the case of the following SELECT statement, for example, the column name au_lname is given the more readable name Author Last Name:

```
SELECT au_lname "Author Last Name" from authors
```

When this SELECT statement is executed, the values from the au_lname column will be assigned to Author Last Name. The results of this query would look like this:

```
Author Last Name
----------------------------------------
White
Green
Carson
O'Leary
Straight
...
(23 row(s) affected)
```

Notice that the column heading no longer reads au_lname as usual. Instead, the column heading is replaced by Author Last Name.

You can also manipulate the value returned by a column, by performing operations on the column. For example, suppose you want to double the price of every book in the titles table. You could do this with the following SELECT statement:

```
SELECT price*2 from titles
```

When this query is executed, the price of every book is doubled as it's retrieved from the table. However, manipulating a column in this way doesn't change the price of the books in the table itself. Operations on columns affect only the output of a SELECT statement and not the underlying table data. To display both the original price of the books and the new, highly inflated price, you could use the following query:

```
SELECT price "original price", price*2 "new price" FROM titles
```

When the data is retrieved from the titles table, the original price is displayed under the heading original price and the doubled price appears under the heading new price. The results would look like this:

```
original price            new price
------------------------- -------------------------
19.99                     39.98
11.95                     23.90
2.99                      5.98
19.99                     39.98
19.99                     39.98
...
(18 row(s) affected)
```

You can manipulate the values of columns by using most of the standard arithmetic operators, such as addition (+), subtraction (-), multiplication (*), and division (/). You can also perform operations on more than one column at a time, like this:

```
SELECT price*ytd_sales "total revenue" from titles
```

10

BASIC SQL

In this example, the total revenue from a book is calculated by multiplying the price by the year-to-date sales. The results of this SELECT statement would look like this:

```
total revenue
- - - - - - - - - - - - - - - - - - - - - - - - -
81,859.05
46,318.20
55,978.78
81,859.05
40,619.68
...
(18 row(s) affected)
```

Finally, you can also concatenate the values of two string columns by using the *concatenation operator* (which looks suspiciously like an addition sign):

```
SELECT au_fname+" "+au_lname "author names" FROM authors
```

In this example, you paste the au_fname and au_lname columns together with a separating space, and provide the result with the column heading author names. This is how the results of this SELECT statement would look:

```
author names
- - - - - - - - - - - - - - - - - - - - - - - - - - - - - - - - - - - - - - - - - - - - - - - - - - - -
Johnson White
Marjorie Green
Cheryl Carson
Michael O'Leary
Dean Straight
...
(23 row(s) affected)
```

As you can see, SQL provides you with a great deal of control over the results of your queries. You should take advantage of these features of SQL in your Active Server Pages programming. It's almost always more efficient to manipulate the results of your queries with SQL than to use scripts for the same purpose.

Ordering Results

The introduction to this chapter emphasized that SQL tables have no inherent order. For example, it makes no sense to retrieve the second row from a table by using SQL. From the point of view of SQL, no row appears before any other.

Nevertheless, you can manipulate the order of the results of a SQL query. By default, when rows are retrieved from a table, the rows appear in no particular order. For example, when the au_lname column is retrieved from the authors table, the results of the query appear like this:

```
au_lname
- - - - - - - - - - - - - - - - - - - - - - - - - - - - - - - - - - - -
White
Green
Carson
```

```
O'Leary
Straight
...
(23 row(s) affected)
```

Viewing a list of names in no particular order is not very convenient. The list would be much easier to read if the list of names appeared alphabetically. You can force the results of a query to appear in ascending order by using an ORDER BY clause, like this:

```
SELECT au_lname FROM authors ORDER BY au_lname
```

When this SELECT statement is executed, the names of the authors appear in alphabetical order. The ORDER BY clause orders the authors' names in ascending order.

You can also use the ORDER BY clause with multiple columns at the same time. For example, if you want to display the values from both the au_lname and au_fname columns in ascending order, you need to order the results by both columns:

```
SELECT au_lname, au_fname FROM authors ORDER BY au_lname, au_fname
```

This query orders the results first by the au_lname column and then by the au_fname column. The rows are retrieved in the following order:

```
au_lname                                     au_fname
-------------------------------------------- --------------------
Bennet                                       Abraham
Ringer                                       Albert
Ringer                                       Anne
Smith                                        Meander
...
(23 row(s) affected)
```

Notice that two authors share the last name Ringer. The author named Albert Ringer appears before Anne Ringer because the first name Albert precedes the first name Anne alphabetically.

If you want to reverse the order of the results of a query, you can use the keyword DESC. The DESC keyword orders the results of a query in descending order, as in this example:

```
SELECT au_lname, au_fname FROM authors
➥WHERE au_lname="Ringer" ORDER BY au_lname, au_fname DESC
```

This query retrieves every author from the authors table where the author's last name is equal to "Ringer". The ORDER BY clause orders the results in descending order, based on the columns for the authors' last and first names. The results look like this:

```
au_lname                                     au_fname
-------------------------------------------- --------------------
Ringer                                       Anne
Ringer                                       Albert

(2 row(s) affected)
```

Notice that the first name Anne now appears before the first name Albert in this list of names. The authors' names are listed in descending order.

You can also order the results of a query on a column with numeric values. For example, if you want to retrieve all the book prices in descending order, you could use the following SQL query:

```
SELECT price FROM titles ORDER BY price DESC
```

This SELECT statement retrieves all the book prices from the titles table. When the prices are displayed, the highest priced books are displayed first and the lowest priced books are displayed last.

> **CAUTION**
>
> Don't order the results of your queries when you don't have a pressing need. The server must work harder to do this. This means that a SELECT statement with an ORDER BY clause may take longer to process than a normal SELECT statement.

Retrieving Distinct Rows

A table may contain duplicate values in the same column. For example, the authors table in the Pubs database has two authors with the last name Ringer. If you select all the last names from this table, the last name Ringer will be displayed twice.

In certain circumstances, you may only be interested in retrieving distinct values from a table. If a column has duplicate values, you may want each unique value to be retrieved only once. You force this to happen by using the DISTINCT keyword:

```
SELECT DISTINCT au_lname FROM authors WHERE au_lname="Ringer"
```

When this SELECT statement is executed, only one row is returned. By including the DISTINCT keyword in a SELECT statement, you eliminate all duplicate values. For example, suppose you have a table that contains newsgroup postings, and you want to retrieve a list of names of everyone who has posted to the newsgroup. You can use the DISTINCT keyword to retrieve every user name only once—even if the user has posted multiple messages.

> **CAUTION**
>
> As in the case of the ORDER BY clause, forcing the server to return only distinct values results in a performance cost. The server has to work harder to do this. Use the DISTINCT keyword only when you have a pressing need.

Creating New Tables

As mentioned earlier, all the data in a database is held in tables, and a database table, like a spreadsheet, has both columns and rows. The columns determine the type of data the table contains. The rows contain the actual data.

For example, the authors table in the pubs database has nine columns. One of these columns is named au_lname. This column is used to hold information about the last names of authors. Every time you add a new author to this table, the name of the author is added to this column and a new row is created.

You create a new table by specifying its columns. Each column has a certain name and a certain datatype. (Datatypes are explained in the later section "Column Datatypes.") The au_lname column, for example, holds character data. However, a table column can hold other types of data as well.

A number of ways exist to create a new table using Microsoft SQL Server. You can create a new table by executing a SQL statement or by using the SQL Enterprise Manager. In the next section, you learn how to create a new table with a SQL statement.

Creating New Tables with SQL

> **NOTE**
>
> If you haven't already created a database of your own, jump back to Chapter 3 and create this database now. You should never add tables to master, tempdb, or any of the other system databases.

Start the program ISQL/w from the SQL Server program group (from the Start menu). After you have arrived at the query window, select the database you created in Chapter 3 from the drop-down list at the top of the window. Next, type the following SQL statement in the query window and execute it by clicking the Execute Query button:

```
CREATE TABLE guestbook (visitor VARCHAR(40), comments TEXT, entrydate DATETIME)
```

If all goes well, you should see the following text in the results window (if all does not go well, refer to Chapter 3):

```
This command did not return data, and it did not return any rows
```

Congratulations, you've created your first table!

The table you created is named guestbook. You could use this table to store information gathered from guests to your Web site. You created the table by using the CREATE TABLE statement. This statement has two parts: The first part specifies the table's name; the second part contains a list of column names and properties separated by commas and enclosed in parentheses.

The guestbook table has three columns: visitor, comments, and entrydate. The visitor column stores the names of the visitors to your Web site. The comments column stores comments your guests may have about your Web site. Finally, the entrydate column stores both the date and time when a guest visited your Web site.

10

BASIC SQL

Notice that each column name is followed by a special expression. For example, the comments column name is followed by the expression TEXT. This expression specifies the datatype of the column. The datatype determines the type of data a column can contain. Because comments holds textual information, this column has a datatype of TEXT.

Columns can have a number of different datatypes. The next section describes the important column datatypes that SQL recognizes.

Column Datatypes

Different column datatypes are used for holding different types of data. There are five general kinds of column datatypes that you should understand when creating and using tables: characters, text, numbers, Boolean values, and dates/times.

Character Data

The *character datatypes* are very useful. You should use these datatypes whenever you need to store short strings of information. For example, you can store the information you gather in the text boxes of HTML forms in character columns.

To create a column that holds variable-length character information, you use the expression VARCHAR. Consider the guestbook table you created earlier:

```
CREATE TABLE guestbook (visitor VARCHAR(40), comments TEXT, entrydate DATETIME)
```

The visitor column in this example has a VARCHAR datatype. Notice the number that follows the datatype in parentheses. This number indicates the maximum number of characters that the column is allowed to contain. In this example, the visitor column can hold a maximum of 40 characters. If the name is longer, it will be cut off at the 40-character limit.

The VARCHAR datatype can store up to 255 characters. To hold longer strings of data, use the TEXT datatype instead (described in the next section).

A second kind of character datatype is used to store fixed-length character data. Here's an example of how this datatype is used:

```
CREATE TABLE guestbook (visitor CHAR(40), comments TEXT, entrydate DATETIME)
```

In this example, the column named visitor is used to store character data that has a fixed length of 40 characters. The expression CHAR specifies that the column should be a fixed character length.

The distinction between the VARCHAR and CHAR datatypes is subtle but important. Suppose you enter the data **Bill Gates** into a VARCHAR column that has a length of 40 characters. When you later retrieve this data from the column, the data you retrieve will be 10 characters long—the length of the Bill Gates string.

Now suppose you enter the character string **Bill Gates** into a CHAR column with a length of 40 characters. When you retrieve data from this column, the data retrieved will always be 40 characters long. Extra spaces will be appended to the end of the string Bill Gates.

When you create your Web site, you'll find it more convenient to use VARCHAR columns than CHAR columns. When you use VARCHAR columns, you don't have to worry about trimming away extra spaces from your data.

Another significant advantage of VARCHAR columns is that they can occupy less memory and hard drive space than CHAR columns. When your database tables grow large, this savings in memory and disk space becomes extremely important.

Text Data

The character datatypes limit you to string data that's no longer than 255 characters. Using the TEXT datatype, on the other hand, you can store more than two billion characters. When you need to store big chunks of string data, use this datatype.

Here's an example of how this datatype is used:

```
CREATE TABLE guestbook (visitor VARCHAR(40), comments TEXT, entrydate DATETIME)
```

In this example, the comments column is used to hold comments from the visitors to your Web site. Notice that the TEXT datatype has no length, as is the case for the character datatypes described in the preceding section. The length of the data in a TEXT column is always either empty or huge.

When you collect information from a TEXTAREA in an HTML form, you should store the information in a TEXT column. However, you should avoid using TEXT columns whenever you can. TEXT columns, like pre-"Jurassic Park" dinosaurs, are slow and big. Using TEXT columns indiscriminately can result in slow server performance. They also eat up quite a bit of hard drive space.

CAUTION

As soon as you enter any data into a TEXT column (even a NULL value), a 2KB data page is automatically allocated. Once this storage space is created, you can't reclaim it without deleting the row.

Numeric Data

SQL Server recognizes a number of different *numeric datatypes*. You can store integers, fractions, and, best of all, money.

Normally, you'll use the INT datatype when you need to store numbers in your tables. The INT datatype can hold integers ranging from -2,147,483,647 through 2,147,483,647, inclusive. Following is an example of how the INT datatype is used:

```
CREATE TABLE visitlog (visitor VARCHAR(40), numvisits INT)
```

This table can be used to keep track of the number of visits made by the visitors to your Web site. As long as no individual visits your Web site more than 2,147,483,647 times, the numvisits column can accurately store the number of visits.

To save memory, you can use the SMALLINT datatype. The SMALLINT datatype can range from -32,768 through 32,768, inclusive. This datatype is used in exactly the same way as the INT datatype.

Finally, if you really need to save memory, you can use the TINYINT datatype. Again, this datatype is used exactly like the INT datatype, except a column of this datatype can only store numbers from 0 through 255, inclusive. A TINYINT column can't be used to store negative numbers.

In general, you should use the smallest integer datatype possible, in order to save memory. A TINYINT datatype occupies only a single byte; an INT datatype occupies four bytes. This difference may seem minor, but in large tables the bytes add up quickly. On the other hand, it's very difficult to alter a table column once you have created it. Therefore, to be safe, you should imagine the highest possible value that a column may need to store, and then imagine it a little larger to pick the appropriate datatype.

To gain more control over the numbers that a column can store, you can use the NUMERIC datatype to specify both the integer and fractional components of a number. The NUMERIC datatype enables you to specify very large numbers—numbers much larger than the INT datatype can store. A NUMERIC column can store numbers that range from -10^{38} through 10^{38}. The NUMERIC datatype also enables you to specify numbers with fractional components. For example, you can store the number 3.14 in a NUMERIC column.

When specifying a NUMERIC datatype, you include both the size of the integer component and the size of the fractional component. Here's an example of how this datatype is used:

```
CREATE TABLE numeric_data (bignumber NUMERIC(28,0), fraction NUMERIC(5,4))
```

When this SQL statement is executed, a table named numeric_data is created with two columns. The bignumber column can hold integer values with up to 28 digits. The fraction column can hold fractions with up to 5 integer digits and up to 4 fractional digits.

The maximum value of the integer component of a NUMERIC datatype is 28 digits. The fractional component must always be the same as or less than the integer component. The fractional component may not contain any digits—in other words, may actually be zero.

You could use INT or NUMERIC columns to store money values, but two datatypes are available especially for this purpose. If you anticipate that your Web site will make a lot of money, you can use the MONEY datatype. If you have humbler ambitions, you can use the SMALLMONEY datatype.

The MONEY datatype can hold values in the range of $-922,337,203,685,477.5808 through $+922,337,203,685,477.5807. If you need to store monetary values even larger than this, you can use the NUMERIC datatype.

The SMALLMONEY datatype is limited to a range of values between $-214,748.3648 through $+214,748.3647. As usual, if you can, use the SMALLMONEY datatype instead of the MONEY datatype to save memory. The following example shows how both monetary datatypes are used:

```
CREATE TABLE products (product VARCHAR(40), price MONEY,
➥discount_price SMALLMONEY)
```

This table can be used to hold data on the discount and normal prices for products. The price column has a datatype of MONEY and the discount_price column has a datatype of SMALLMONEY.

Storing Boolean Values

If you're using a Web form to collect information with check boxes, you can store this information in BIT columns. A BIT column can take only two values: 0 or 1. Here's an example of how this datatype is used:

```
CREATE TABLE opinion (visitor VARCHAR(40), good BIT)
```

This table could be used to hold information gathered from an opinion poll on the quality of your Web site. Visitors can vote on whether or not they like your Web site. If they vote yes, 1 is stored in the BIT column. On the other hand, if they vote no, the value 0 is stored in the BIT column (in the next chapter, you learn a method to tally the votes).

Be warned that you can't add a BIT column to a table after you create the table. If you're going to include BIT columns in a table, you need to include them when you first create it.

Storing Dates and Times

When you create a Web site, you may quickly become obsessed with tracking the number of visitors it receives in any given interval of time. To be able to store date and time values, you need to use the DATETIME datatype, as in the next example:

```
CREATE TABLE visitorlog (visitor VARCHAR(40),
➥arrivaltime DATETIME, departuretime DATETIME)
```

This table could be used to track the dates and times when visitors to your Web site arrive and depart. A column with the DATETIME datatype can store dates between the first millisecond on January 1, 1753 and the last millisecond on December 31, 9999.

If you don't need to cover this wide range of dates and times, you can use the SMALLDATETIME datatype. It works like the DATETIME datatype, except it ranges over a smaller interval of dates and isn't quite as precise. A column with a SMALLDATETIME datatype can store dates between January 1, 1900 and June 6, 2079. Unlike DATETIME, SMALLDATETIME is accurate only to the second.

It's important to realize that DATETIME columns don't actually hold a date or a time until you put one there. In the next chapter, you learn how to use a number of SQL functions to retrieve and manipulate dates and times (also, see the section "Default Values" at the bottom of this page). However, you *can* use the date and time functions in VBScript and JScript to store a date and time in a DATETIME column.

Column Properties

The preceding section explained how to create tables with columns of different datatypes. In this section, you learn how to use three special properties of columns. These properties allow you to control NULL values, default values, and identity values.

Allowing and Preventing NULL Values

Most columns can accept NULL values. When a column accepts NULL values, the column will have this value when you haven't explicitly given it any other value. The value NULL is not the same as zero. Strictly speaking, a NULL value is the absence of any value at all.

To allow a column to accept NULL values, you use the special expression NULL after the column definition. The following table, for example, allows NULL values for both of its columns:

```
CREATE TABLE empty (empty1 CHAR(40) NULL, empty2 INT NULL)
```

> **NOTE**
>
> The BIT datatype can't take NULL values. A column of this datatype must always contain either 0 or 1.

You may want to forbid NULL values in a column. For example, suppose you have a table that contains credit card numbers and credit card expiration dates. You would never want someone to enter a credit card number without an expiration date. To force both columns to always contain a value, you create the table in the following way:

```
CREATE TABLE creditcards (creditcard_number CHAR(20) NOT NULL,
➥creditcard_expire DATETIME NOT NULL)
```

Notice the words NOT NULL following the column definitions. By including the expression NOT NULL, you prevent anyone from inserting data in one column but not the other.

You'll find that this ability to prevent NULL values is extremely useful during the development phase of your Web site. If you specify that a column shouldn't receive NULL values, an error will be reported when you attempt to enter a NULL value. These errors can provide clues that are valuable for debugging.

Default Values

Suppose you have a table that stores address information. The table includes columns for a street address, a city, a state, a postal code, and a country. If you anticipate that the majority of the addresses will be located in the U.S., you might want to give the country column this default value.

To add a default value to a column during table creation, you can use the special expression DEFAULT. Look at this example of how to use default values in a table creation statement:

```
CREATE TABLE addresses (street VARCHAR(60) NULL,
➥city VARCHAR(40) NULL,
➥state VARCHAR(30) NULL,
➥zip VARCHAR(20) NULL,
➥country VARCHAR(30) DEFAULT 'USA')
```

In this example, the country column is given the default value 'USA'. Notice the use of single quotes. The quotes indicate that the value is character data. To specify the default value for non-character columns, you don't place the value in quotes:

```
CREATE TABLE orders (price MONEY DEFAULT $38.00,
➥quantity INT DEFAULT 50,
➥entrydate DATETIME DEFAULT GETDATE())
```

In this CREATE TABLE statement, each column is given a default value. Notice the value given to the DATETIME column entrydate. The default value is the value returned by the function GETDATE(), which returns the current date and time.

Identity Columns

Each table can have one and only one identity column. An *identity column* is a special column that uniquely identifies every row in a table. For example, the jobs table in the pubs database includes an identity column that uniquely identifies every job:

```
job_id job_desc
------ --------------------------------------------------
1      New Hire - Job not specified
2      Chief Executive Officer
3      Business Operations Manager
4      Chief Financial Officier
5      Publisher
```

The job_id column provides a unique number for every job description. If you decide to add a new job description, the job_id column for the new row would be given a new unique value automatically.

To create an identity column, you need only add the expression IDENTITY after the column definition. You should create identity columns only for NUMERIC and INT columns. Here's an example:

```
CREATE TABLE visitorID (theID NUMERIC(18) IDENTITY, name VARCHAR(40))
```

The table created with this statement includes an identity column named theID. This column is given a new value automatically whenever a new visitor name is added to the table. You could use this table to provide all users of your Web site with a unique identifier.

> **TIP**
>
> When creating an identity column, be careful to use a large enough datatype. If you use a TINYINT datatype, for example, you can add only 255 rows to a table. If you anticipate that a table will grow very large, use a NUMERIC datatype.

The existence of identity columns may tempt you into attempting a number of impossible things. For example, you may want to use the identity column to perform operations on rows based on their position in a table. Resist this temptation. The value in each instance of an identity column is guaranteed to be unique. However, this doesn't prevent the existence of gaps between the identifying numbers in an identity column. For example, you should never attempt to retrieve the first 10 rows by using a table's identity column. This course of action can lead to failure, for example, if rows 6 and 7 don't exist.

Creating a New Table with the SQL Enterprise Manager

You can create tables by using the methods described in the previous sections. However, it's much easier to create a new table by using the SQL Enterprise Manager. This section describes how you to use this program to create a table.

Start the SQL Enterprise Manager by selecting it from the Microsoft SQL Server program group on the Start menu. You should see a screen like the one shown in Figure 10.4. Select the folder named Databases by navigating through the tree in the Server Manager pane. After opening the Databases folder, select the name of the database that you created in Chapter 3.

> **NOTE**
>
> If you haven't already created a database of your own, return to Chapter 3 and create this database now. You should never add tables to master, tempdb, or any of the other system databases.

After selecting your database, you should see a folder named Group/Users and a folder named Objects. Open the Objects folder; you should see a number of folders, including one called Tables. Right-click the Tables folder and select New Table. The screen in Figure 10.5 should appear.

You can use the Manage Tables window to create a new table. The Manage Tables window has seven columns named Key, Identity, Column Name, Datatype, Size, Nulls, and Default. Each row in the Manage Tables window specifies the information for a table column.

FIGURE 10.4.

SQL Enterprise Manager.

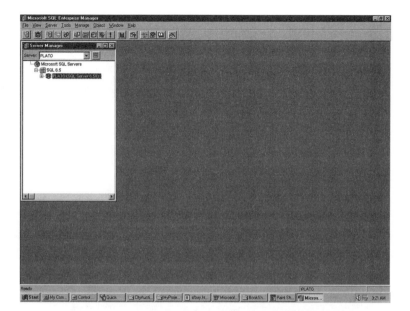

FIGURE 10.5.

The Manage Tables window.

To create a new table, you need to enter at least one row of information. Under the column named Column Name, type **mycolumn**. Next, select the column named Datatype and choose CHAR from the drop-down list. When you enter the information in both columns, your screen should look like Figure 10.6 (shown on the following page).

You have created a simple one-column table. To save your new table, click the Save button (the icon of a disk). When you're asked for a new table name, enter **MyTable** and click OK. Your table has now been saved in your database.

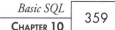

10

BASIC SQL

Figure 10.6.

A completed row in the Manage Tables window.

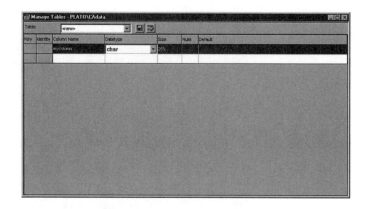

If you open the TABLES folder in the Server Manager window, you should see your new table listed. You can edit your table by double-clicking its icon. The Manage Tables window should reappear, and you can add new columns and save your table again.

Everything you can do with the SQL Enterprise Manager, you can do with SQL statements. However, the SQL Enterprise Manager makes the process of table creation much easier.

Populating a Table with Data

The next chapter discusses how to use SQL to insert new data into a table. However, if you need to add many rows of data to a table, using SQL statements to enter data is very inconvenient. Fortunately, Microsoft SQL Server includes a client utility called *Microsoft Query* that makes the process of adding table data easy.

Start the program named MS Query, located in the Microsoft SQL Server program group on the Start menu. After the program loads, choose File | New Query from the menu at the top of the screen. A dialog box named Select Data Source should be displayed (see Figure 10.7). Select the name of your data source and click Use.

Figure 10.7.

The Select Data Source dialog box.

After entering your login ID and password, you're asked to select a table and a database. Select the table you created in the preceding section (MyTable), click the Add button, and click the Close button to close the dialog box.

In the upper-left corner of the screen, a dialog box appears with a list of columns from the table `MyTable`. You can double-click any of these columns to add the column to the main window. If you double-click the asterisk (*) character, all of the columns are added.

If your table contained any records, they would now appear under the column headings in the main window. However, because you just created the table, the table is empty. To add new records, choose Records | Allow Editing. A new row should appear in the main window. You can enter a new row of data into your table by completing this row (see Figure 10.8).

FIGURE 10.8.

Editing table data with Microsoft Query.

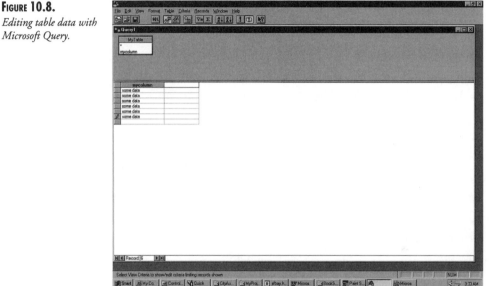

Whenever you move to a new row, the data you entered into the previous row is automatically saved. You can use Microsoft Query to enter hundreds of rows of table data, if you have the need.

Destroying and Altering Tables

You should plan your tables carefully before you create them, because you're very limited on the changes you can make to an existing table. For example, you can't remove table columns once you've added them, or change the datatypes of existing columns. Your only option in these cases is to destroy the table and start over (but see the section "Creating Records and Tables with SELECT" in Chapter 11, "Intermediate SQL").

To destroy a table, you can use the SQL statement DROP TABLE. For example, to permanently remove the table `MyTable` from the database, you would use the following statement:

```
DROP TABLE MyTable
```

10

BASIC SQL

CAUTION

Be careful with the DROP TABLE command; you can't retrieve a table once it has been dropped.

While you're developing a Web site, you'll probably need to enter test data into your database tables. Once you're ready to present your Web site to the world, however, you'll want to empty your tables of this test information. If you want to remove all the data from a table without destroying the table itself, you can use the TRUNCATE TABLE statement. For example, the following SQL statement deletes all the data in the MyTable database table:

```
TRUNCATE TABLE MyTable
```

While you can't remove or alter existing columns, you *can* add new ones. The easiest way to do this is to use the Manage Tables window in the SQL Enterprise Manager. However, you can also use the SQL statement ALTER TABLE. Here's an example of how this statement is used:

```
ALTER TABLE MyTable ADD mynewcolumn INT NULL
```

This statement adds a new column named mynewcolumn to the table MyTable. When you add a new column, you must allow the new column to accept NULL values. This only makes sense, because the column may be added to a table that already has a number of rows.

Summary

This chapter introduced you to SQL. Using SQL, you can communicate with the Microsoft SQL Server database. You learned how to use the SELECT statement to retrieve data from a database. You also learned how to create new tables by using the CREATE TABLE statement and the SQL Enterprise Manager. Finally, you learned how to specify a number of important column properties.

The next chapter shows you how to use indexes to improve the performance of your SQL queries. You also broaden your knowledge of Structured Query Language by learning how to use a number of additional SQL statements and functions.

Intermediate SQL

IN THIS CHAPTER

Chapter 10, "Basic SQL," introduced you to SQL. You learned how to create SQL queries using the SELECT statement. You also learned how to create tables of your own. In this chapter, you deepen your knowledge of SQL. You learn how to create table indexes that make your queries faster. You also learn how to use a number of additional SQL statements and functions to manipulate the data in your tables.

Creating Indexes

Suppose you wanted to find a particular sentence in this book. You could search the book page by page, but that could take days. By using the index of this book, you can find the subject of your search must faster.

A *table index* is very similar to the index at the back of a book. It can dramatically improve the speed of your SQL queries. On a large table, a query that would once take hours could take just minutes with the addition of an index. There's no reason not to add an index to every table that you plan to query frequently.

> **NOTE**
>
> One situation in which you may not want to place an index on a table is when you're short on either memory or hard drive space. SQL Server needs a considerable amount of extra space in a database to contain an index. To create a clustered index, for example, SQL Server requires space equal to approximately 1.2 times the size of the table data. To view the amount of database space that an index on a table occupies, you can use the sp_spaceused system stored procedure with the name of the table.

Clustered and Non-Clustered Indexes

Imagine that you've used the index of this book to find the page number of a particular sentence. Once you know the page number, you'd probably flip somewhat haphazardly through the book until you arrived at the page with the correct number. By randomly flipping through the pages of this book, you would find the right page eventually. There is, however, a more efficient way to find the page.

First, open the book at about its halfway point. If the page number is less than the page number at the halfway point, open the book at its quarter-way point. Otherwise, open the book at its three-quarter mark. You can continue to divide the book into ever smaller halves in this way until you arrive near the correct page. This is a very efficient method of finding the page.

A SQL Server table index works in a similar fashion. A table index is composed of a group of pages that form a branching tree structure. The root page logically divides the rows of a table into two halves by pointing to two other pages. Each of these two pages, in turn, divides the rows of the table into smaller halves. Each page divides the rows into smaller halves until the *leaf pages* are reached.

There are two types of indexes: clustered and non-clustered. In a *clustered index*, the leaf pages of the index tree consist of the actual table rows; the rows are sorted in the same physical order as the index. In a *non-clustered index*, the leaf pages point to the table rows; the physical order of the rows doesn't necessarily have any relationship to their index order.

A clustered index is very much like a table of contents. The order of the entries in the table of contents corresponds to the order of the pages in a book. A non-clustered index is more like a standard book index. The order of the entries in a book's index doesn't usually correspond to the order of the pages. Also, a book may have multiple indexes. For example, it may have both a subject and an author index. In the same way, a table may have multiple non-clustered indexes.

Normally you'll use clustered indexes, but you should understand the advantages and disadvantages of both types.

Each table can have only one clustered index, because the rows in a table can be physically sorted in only one way. Typically you'll use a clustered index with the identity column of a table. However, you can also create a clustered index on other types of columns, such as character, numeric, and date and time columns.

You can retrieve data faster from a table with a clustered index than from a table with a non-clustered index. A clustered index is also good when you need to pull data that falls into a certain range. For example, suppose you have a table that logs the activity at your Web site. If you want to retrieve log entries that occur between certain dates, you should index the DATETIME column of this table with a clustered index.

The primary limitation of a clustered index is that each table can have only one. However, a table can have more than one non-clustered index. In fact, you can create as many as 249 non-clustered indexes on an individual table. You can also create tables that have both clustered and non-clustered indexes at the same time.

Suppose you anticipate retrieving data from your Web site's activity log not only by date, but also by user name. In this case, indexing the table with both a clustered and non-clustered index would make sense. You would place a clustered index on the date and time column and a non-clustered index on the user name column. If you discover that you need to index this table in even more ways, you can add more non-clustered indexes.

A non-clustered index requires a lot of hard drive space and memory. Furthermore, although a non-clustered index can speed data retrieval from a table, the index will actually slow inserting and updating data in a table. Every time you change data in a table with non-clustered indexes, the indexes must be updated as well. So you shouldn't add non-clustered indexes to a table without careful consideration. If you anticipate that a table will need to be updated very frequently, don't add too many non-clustered indexes to it. Also, if memory and hard drive space are issues, limit the number of non-clustered indexes you use.

Index Properties

Both types of indexes have two important properties: You can use either type of index to create an index on multiple columns (a *composite index*), and either type of index can be specified as unique.

You can create a single composite index that indexes multiple columns, even with a clustered index. Suppose you have a table that contains both the first and last names of the visitors to your Web site. If you anticipate retrieving records from this table by using full names, you should create a single index that indexes both the first name and last name columns. This isn't the same as creating two separate indexes, one for each column. You should create a single index on multiple columns when you anticipate using queries that refer to more than one column at the same time. If you anticipate using many queries on the columns separately, create separate indexes.

Either type of index can be specified as a unique index. If a table column has a unique index, you won't be able to insert duplicate values into the column. An identity column is automatically a unique column, but you can create a unique index on other types of columns as well. Suppose you have a table that holds user passwords for your Web site. You wouldn't want two individuals to have the same password. You could prevent this from happening by forcing a column to be unique.

Creating Indexes with SQL

To create an index for a table, start the program ISQL/w from the SQL Server program group on the Start menu. When you arrive at the query window, enter the following SQL statement:

```
CREATE INDEX mycolumn_index ON MyTable (mycolumn)
```

This statement creates an index named `mycolumn_index`. You can name an index anything you want, but you should include the name of the index column in the index name. This will help you keep track of the purpose of the index in the future.

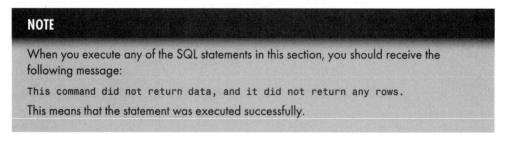

NOTE

When you execute any of the SQL statements in this section, you should receive the following message:

```
This command did not return data, and it did not return any rows.
```

This means that the statement was executed successfully.

The index `mycolumn_index` is created on the column `mycolumn` in the table `MyTable`. This index is both non-clustered and non-unique. (These are the default properties of any index.)

If you need to change the type of index used on a column, you must drop the previous index and create a new one. After you create an index, you can destroy it by using the following SQL statement:

```
DROP INDEX MyTable.mycolumn_index
```

Notice that you need to include the name of the table in the DROP INDEX statement. In this example, you're dropping the index named mycolumn_index, which is the index for the table MyTable.

To create a clustered index, use the keyword CLUSTERED. (Remember that every table can have only one clustered index.) Here's an example of how you can add a clustered index to a table:

```
CREATE CLUSTERED INDEX mycolumn_clust_index ON MyTable (mycolumn)
```

If your table has duplicate rows, you may receive an error when you try to create a table with this statement. But a table with duplicate rows *can* have an index; you merely need to warn SQL server of this by using the keyword ALLOW_DUP_ROW:

```
CREATE CLUSTERED INDEX mycolumn_cindex ON MyTable (mycolumn) WITH ALLOW_DUP_ROW
```

This statement creates an clustered index that allows duplicate rows. You should try to avoid having a table with duplicate rows, but, if it happens, you can use this option.

To create a unique index on a table, use the keyword UNIQUE. You can use this keyword with either clustered or non-clustered indexes. Here's an example with a clustered index:

```
CREATE UNIQUE CLUSTERED INDEX mycolumn_cindex ON MyTable (mycolumn)
```

This is the index creation statement that you'll use most often. Whenever you can, include a unique clustered index on a table to improve query performance.

Finally, to create an index that indexes more than one column—a composite index—include the names of both columns in the index creation statement. The following example uses columns named firstname and lastname:

```
CREATE INDEX names_index ON usernames (firstname, lastname)
```

This example creates a single index that indexes both columns. You can use as many as 16 columns at the same time when creating a composite index.

Creating Indexes with the Enterprise Manager

Creating indexes is much easier with the Enterprise Manager than with SQL statements. Using the Enterprise Manager, you can see a list of the indexes that you have already created, and pick-and-choose index options directly from a graphical interface.

You can use the Enterprise Manager to create an index in two ways: by using the Manage Tables window or by using the Manage Indexes window.

To create a new index with the Manage Tables window, click the Advanced Options button (it looks like a table with a plus sign in front of it). Doing this opens the Advanced Options dialog box. One section of this window is labeled Primary Key (see Figure 11.1).

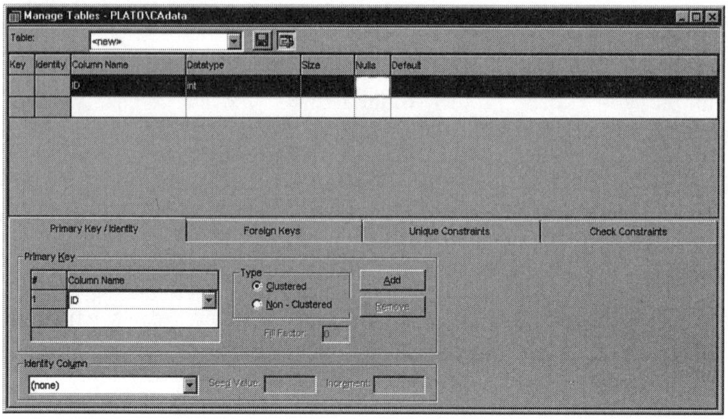

FIGURE 11.1.

Creating an index with the Manage Tables window.

To create a new index, select the column name you want to index, using the drop-down list box. You can select more than one column name if you want to create an index on multiple columns. You can also choose whether the index should be clustered or non-clustered. After you save your table information, the index is automatically created for you. Next to the column name in the Manage Tables window, a key should appear.

Technically, you have created a *primary key* for your table. A primary key must be created on a column that doesn't have NULL values. Also, a primary key enforces uniqueness on a column.

To create indexes without these constraints, you need to use the Manage Indexes window. To open the Manage Indexes window, choose Manage | Indexes from the menu. In the Manage Indexes window, you can select both tables and particular indexes by using the drop-down list boxes (see Figure 11.2). To create a new index, select new index from the Index drop-down list box. You will then be given the opportunity to select the columns you want to include in the index. Simply click Add to include an additional column in your index.

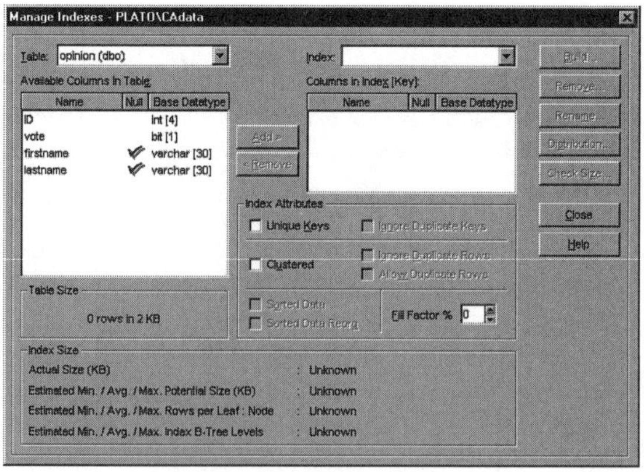

FIGURE 11.2.

Creating an index with the Manage Indexes window.

You can select a number of different options for your index. For example, you can choose whether the index should be clustered or non-clustered. You can also specify that the index should be unique. When you are finished designing your index, click the Build button to create the index.

Core SQL Statements

In Chapter 10, you learned how to use the SQL SELECT statement to retrieve records from a database table. Up to this point, however, no method of adding, changing, or deleting the data stored in tables has been discussed. In this section, you learn how to make these changes.

Inserting Data

To add a new record to a table, you use the SQL INSERT statement. Here's an example of how this statement is used:

```
INSERT MyTable (mycolumn) VALUES ('some data')
```

This statement inserts the character string 'some data' into the column mycolumn in the table named MyTable. The name of the column in which the data will be inserted is specified in the first set of parentheses. The actual data is given in the second set of parentheses.

Here's the complete syntax for the INSERT statement:

```
INSERT [INTO]    {table_name ¦ view_name} [(column_list)]{DEFAULT VALUES ¦
  values_list ¦ select_statement}
```

If a table has multiple columns, you can insert data into all of the columns by separating the column names and the column values with commas. Suppose the table MyTable has three columns named first_column, second_column, and third_column. The following INSERT statement adds a new record with values for all three columns:

```
INSERT MyTable (first_column, second_column, third_column)
  VALUES ('some data', 'some more data', 'yet more data')
```

When this statement is executed, a new row is added to the table, with the specified column values.

NOTE

You can use the INSERT statement to insert data into a TEXT column. However, if you need to enter very long character strings, the WRITETEXT statement should be used instead. This topic is too advanced to be covered in this book. For more information, consult your Microsoft SQL Server documentation.

What if you specified only two columns and values in the INSERT statement? In other words, suppose you insert a new record into a table and *don't* provide a value for a column. In that case, one of four things will happen:

■ If the column has a default value, that value will be used. For example, suppose you neglect to give the column named third_column a value when you insert a new record, and the column has a default value of 'some value'. In that case, the default value 'some value' will be inserted when the new record is created.

■ If the column accepts NULL values, and doesn't have a default value, the value NULL will be inserted. This only makes sense. A NULL value means the absence of any value.

■ If the column doesn't accept NULL values, and doesn't have a default value, an error will occur. You'll receive the error message The column third_column in table MyTable may not be null. Further, no new record will be inserted.

■ Finally, if the column is an identity column, a new value for the column will be generated automatically. You should never explicitly insert a value into an identity column. When you insert a new record into a table with an identity column, just ignore it, and the identity column will give itself a new value.

NOTE

After you insert a new row into a table with an identity column, you can use the SQL variable @@identity to access the value of the identity column in the new row. Consider the following SQL statements:

```
Insert MyTable (first_column)
  VALUES ('some value')

Insert AnotherTable (another_first, another_second)
  VALUES (@@identity,'some value')
```

If the table MyTable has an identity column, the value of that column is inserted into the another_first column of AnotherTable. This happens because the variable @@identity always holds the value inserted in the last identity column.

The column another_first should be of the same datatype as the column first_column. However, another_first should not be an identity column itself. The another_first column is used to hold the value from the column first_column.

Deleting Records

To delete one or more records from a table, use the SQL DELETE statement. You can provide the DELETE statement with a WHERE clause. This clause is used to select the rows to delete. For example, the following DELETE statement removes only the rows in which first_column is equal to 'Delete Me':

```
DELETE MyTable WHERE first_column='Delete Me'
```

Here's the complete syntax for the DELETE statement:

```
DELETE [FROM] {table_name ¦ view_name}     [WHERE clause]
```

You can provide any criteria in the WHERE clause of a DELETE statement that you can use with a SQL SELECT statement. For example, the following DELETE statement deletes only those records in which first_column equals 'goodbye' or second_column equals 'so long':

```
DELETE MyTable WHERE first_column='goodbye' or second_column='so long'
```

If you neglect to provide the DELETE statement with a WHERE clause, every row in the table will be deleted. You shouldn't do this on purpose. If you want to delete every record in a table, use the TRUNCATE TABLE statement described in Chapter 10 instead.

> **NOTE**
>
> Why should you use TRUNCATE TABLE instead of DELETE? When you use TRUNCATE TABLE, the row deletions are not logged. Among other things, this means that TRUNCATE TABLE is much faster than DELETE.

Updating Records

To alter one or more records that already exist in a table, use the SQL UPDATE statement. Like the DELETE statement, the UPDATE statement can use a WHERE clause to select only certain records to update. Look at this example:

```
UPDATE MyTable SET first_column='Updated!' WHERE second_column='Update Me!'
```

This UPDATE statement updates every row in which second_column equals 'Update Me!'. For every row selected, the value of first_column is set equal to 'Updated!'.

Here's the complete syntax for the UPDATE statement:

```
UPDATE {table_name ¦ view_name} SET [{table_name ¦ view_name}]
  {column_list ¦ variable_list ¦ variable_and_column_list}
  [, {column_list2 ¦ variable_list2 ¦ variable_and_column_list2}...
  [, {column_listN ¦ variable_listN ¦ variable_and_column_listN}]][WHERE clause]
```

> **NOTE**
>
> You can use the UPDATE statement with a TEXT column. If you need to update very large character strings, however, use the UPDATETEXT statement instead. This topic is too advanced to be covered in this book. For more information, consult your Microsoft SQL Server documentation.

If you neglect to include the WHERE clause, every row in a table will be updated. Sometimes this is useful. For example, if you want to double the price of every book in the titles table, you could use the following UPDATE statement:

```
UPDATE titles SET price=price*2
```

You can also update multiple columns at the same time. For example, the following UPDATE statement updates the columns named first_column, second_column, and third_column:

```
UPDATE MyTable
SET first_column='Updated!',
  second_column='Updated!',
  third_column='Updated!'
WHERE first_column='Update Me!'
```

> **TIP**
>
> SQL ignores extra spaces in your statements. Feel free to format your statements in whatever way is easiest for you to read.

Creating Records and Tables with SELECT

You may have noticed that the INSERT statement is a little different from the DELETE and UPDATE statements in that it affects only one record at a time. A method exists, however, to cause the INSERT statement to add multiple records at once. To do this, you need to combine the INSERT statement with the SELECT statement like this:

```
INSERT MyTable (first_column, second_column)
SELECT another_first, another_second
FROM AnotherTable
WHERE another_first='Copy Me!'
```

This statement copies rows from AnotherTable to MyTable. The only rows that are copied are those in AnotherTable in which the column named another_first is equal to 'Copy Me!'.

This type of INSERT statement is very useful for creating an archive of the records in a table. Before you delete records in a table, you can first copy them to another table by using this method.

If you need to copy a whole table, you can use the SELECT INTO statement. For example, the following statement creates a new table called NewTable that contains all of the data of MyTable:

```
SELECT * INTO NewTable FROM MyTable
```

You can also specify that only certain columns be used in creating the new table. To do this, simply specify the columns that you want copied in the column list. Also, you can restrict the records copied into the new table by using the WHERE clause. Here's an example that copies only the column named first_column from the rows in which second_column is equal to 'Copy Me!':

```
SELECT first_column INTO NewTable
FROM MyTABLE
WHERE second_column='Copy Me!'
```

Altering tables after they're created is very difficult with SQL. For example, if you accidentally add a column to a table, there's no easy way to get rid of it. Also, if you inadvertently create a column of the wrong datatype, there's no way to change it. However, using the SQL statements described in this section, you can get around these two problems.

For example, suppose you want to remove a column from a table. Using the SELECT INTO statement, you can create a duplicate of your table without the offending column. Doing this allows you to save the data in the table.

If you want to change the datatype of a column, you can create a new table with a column of the correct datatype. After the table is created, you can then copy all the data from the original table into the new one by using the UPDATE statement in combination with the SELECT statement. Again, this will preserve your data while allowing you to alter the structure of your table.

The Aggregate Functions

Up to this point, you've learned how to pull one or more records from a table based on certain criteria. However, suppose you want summary data on the records in a table. For example, suppose you want to tally the votes in a table that holds the data for an opinion poll. Or suppose you want to know the average amount of time a visitor spends at your Web site. To gather either type of data from a table, you need to use *aggregate functions*.

Microsoft SQL recognizes five types of aggregate functions. You can retrieve a count, an average, a minimum value, a maximum value, or a sum of values. When you use an aggregate function, only a single number is returned, representing one of these aggregate values.

NOTE

To use a value retrieved from an aggregate function in your Active Server Pages, you need to provide the value with a name. You can do this by supplying a column name immediately following the aggregate function in the SELECT statement, as in this example:

```
SELECT AVG(vote) 'the_average' FROM opinion
```

In this example, the value of the average of votes is given the name the_average. You can now refer to this name in the database methods of your Active Server Page.

Retrieving a Count of Column Values

Perhaps the most useful aggregate function is the COUNT() function. You can use this function to discover how many records exist in a table. Here's an example:

```
SELECT COUNT(au_lname) FROM authors
```

This example counts the number of last names that exist in the authors table. A single number representing this count is returned. If the same last name appears more than once, the last name is counted more than once. If you want to know the number of authors with a particular last name, you can use a WHERE clause like this:

```
SELECT COUNT(au_lname) FROM authors WHERE au_lname='Ringer'
```

This example returns the number of authors who have the last name Ringer. If this last name occurs twice in the authors table, the number returned by this function is 2.

Suppose you want to know the number of people who have distinct last names. By using the keyword DISTINCT, you can retrieve the number, like this:

```
SELECT COUNT(DISTINCT au_lname) FROM authors
```

If the last name Ringer occurs more than once, for example, this last name will be counted only once. The DISTINCT keyword forces only unique values to be counted.

Normally, when you use COUNT(), the NULL values in a column are ignored. Usually this is what you want. However, if you simply want to know the number of rows that exist in a table, you need to count every row—regardless of whether it contains a NULL value. Following is an example of how you can do this:

```
SELECT COUNT(*) FROM authors
```

Notice that no column is contained in the COUNT() function. This SELECT statement counts all the rows in a table, including the ones with NULL values. Therefore, you don't need to include a specific column to be counted.

The COUNT() function is useful in a number of very different situations. For example, suppose you have a table that holds the results of an opinion poll on the quality of your Web site. Imagine that this table has a column named vote that holds either 0, which represents a negative vote, or 1, which represents a positive vote. To determine the number of positive votes, you can use the following SELECT statement:

```
SELECT COUNT(vote) FROM opinion_table WHERE vote=1
```

Retrieving an Average of Column Values

Using the COUNT() function, you can retrieve the number of values in a column. But suppose you need to retrieve the average of these values. Using the AVG() function, you can retrieve a number that is the result of averaging all the values in a column together.

Imagine you have a more complicated opinion poll on the quality of your Web site. People can offer a vote of between 1 and 10 to indicate how much they like your site. You store the votes in a column of datatype INT named vote. To determine the average vote of the users of your Web site, you need to use the AVG() function like this:

```
SELECT AVG(vote) FROM opinion
```

The result returned from this SELECT statement represents the average opinion of your Web site. This function can be used only with columns that have a numeric datatype. The function also ignores NULL values when calculating an average.

Retrieving a Sum of Column Values

Imagine that your Web site, devoted to selling trading cards, has been up and running for a couple of months, and the time has come to determine how much money the site has made. Suppose you have a table named orders that holds information on all the orders placed by the visitors to your Web site. To determine the grand sum of all trading card purchases, you can use the SUM() function like this:

```
SELECT SUM(purchase_amount) FROM orders
```

The number returned by the SUM() function represents the sum of all the values in the purchase_amount column. The purchase_amount column may be of datatype MONEY, but you can use the SUM() function with other numeric datatypes as well.

Retrieving a Maximum or Minimum Value

Once again, suppose you have a table that holds the results from an opinion poll on your Web site. Visitors can rank their experience of your Web site by choosing a value between 1 and 10. If you want to determine the highest ranking given to your Web site by any visitor, you could use the following statement:

```
SELECT MAX(vote) FROM opinion
```

You would hope that someone has given your Web site a very positive vote. With the MAX() function, you can determine the maximum value of all the values in a numeric column. If anyone has endorsed your Web site with a vote of 10, this value will be returned.

On the other hand, suppose you want to know the lowest vote given to your Web site by any-one. To retrieve this value, you use the MIN() function, as in this example:

```
SELECT MIN(vote) FROM opinion
```

The MIN() function returns the lowest of all the values in a column. If the column is empty, the NULL value is returned.

Other Useful SQL Expressions, Functions, and Procedures

This section covers a number of additional valuable SQL techniques. You learn how to retrieve data from a table when a column matches a particular range of values, how to convert column values from one datatype to another, and how to manipulate string or date-and-time data. Finally, you learn a simple way to send mail from your database.

Retrieving Data by Matching a Range of Values

Suppose you have a table that contains the results from an opinion poll on the quality of your Web site. Now imagine that you want to send a written thank you note to everyone who gave your Web site a ranking between the values of 7 and 10. To retrieve the names of these people, you could use a SELECT statement like the following:

```
SELECT username FROM opinion WHERE vote>6 and vote<11
```

This SELECT statement would work fine. However, you can also use the following SELECT statement to retrieve the same results:

```
SELECT username FROM opinion WHERE vote BETWEEN 7 AND 10
```

This SELECT statement is equivalent to the preceding one. The choice of which SELECT statement to use is a matter of programming style, but you may find that SELECT statements using the expression BETWEEN are more readable.

Now suppose you want to retrieve only the names of visitors who gave your Web site a ranking of 1 or 10. To pull these names from the opinion table, you could use a SELECT statement like the following:

```
SELECT username FROM opinion WHERE vote=1 or vote=10
```

This SELECT statement would retrieve the correct results, and there's no reason not to use it. However, there is an alternative. You can retrieve the same records by using the following SELECT statement:

```
SELECT username FROM opinion WHERE vote IN (1,10)
```

Notice the use of the expression IN. This SELECT statement pulls only the records where the vote equals one of the members of the set contained in the parentheses.

You can also use IN for matching character data. For example, suppose you want to retrieve only the votes made by either Bill Gates or President Clinton. You could use the following SQL statement:

```
SELECT vote FROM opinion
WHERE username IN ('Bill Gates','President Clinton')
```

Finally, you can use the expression NOT with both the expressions BETWEEN and IN. For example, to retrieve the names of only those voters who didn't cast a vote between 7 and 10, you could use the following statement:

```
SELECT username FROM opinion WHERE vote NOT BETWEEN 7 and 10
```

To select only those records where a column value is not in a set of values, you can use NOT with IN, as in the following statement:

```
SELECT vote FROM opinion
WHERE username NOT IN ("Bill Gates", "President Clinton")
```

You are under no obligation to use BETWEEN or IN when creating SQL statements. However, to phrase your queries in a way that's closer to natural language, these two expressions may prove helpful.

Converting Values

SQL Server is smart enough to convert most numeric values from one datatype to another when necessary. For example, to compare a SMALLINT datatype with an INT datatype, you don't need to perform any explicit conversion. SQL Server will do this for you. However, when you want to convert between most datatypes and character values, you do need to perform an explicit conversion. For example, suppose you want to retrieve all the values from a MONEY column and add the string "US Dollars" to the result. You need to use the CONVERT() function, like this:

```
SELECT CONVERT(CHAR(8),price)+'US Dollars' FROM orders
```

The CONVERT() function takes two variables. The first variable specifies a datatype and length. The second variable contains the column being converted. In this example, the price column is converted to a CHAR column that can hold eight characters. The price column needs to be converted to a character column to allow the string 'US Dollars' to be concatenated to it.

You need to perform the same type of conversion when adding a string to a BIT, DATETIME, INT, or NUMERIC column. For example, the following statement adds the string 'The vote is ' to the results of a SELECT statement that retrieves all the values from a BIT column:

```
SELECT 'The vote is '+convert(char(1),vote) FROM opinion
```

Here's a sample result from this query:

```
- - - - - - - - - - - -
The vote is 1
The vote is 1
The vote is 0
(3 row(s) affected)
```

If you don't perform an explicit conversion in this case, you'll get the following error:

```
Implicit conversion from datatype 'varchar' to 'bit' is not allowed.
Use the CONVERT function to run this query.
```

Working with String Data

SQL Server has a number of functions and expressions that enable you to perform interesting tasks with strings, including various types of pattern matching and character conversions. In this section, you learn how to use the most important string functions and expressions.

Matching Wildcards

Imagine that you want to create an Internet directory that functions like Yahoo!. You can create a table that holds a list of Web site names, URLs, descriptions, and categories, and allow visitors to your Web site to search this table by entering a keyword in an HTML form.

Suppose a visitor wants to retrieve a list of every Web site from this directory that has the keyword `trading card` in its description. To retrieve the proper list of Web sites, you might be tempted to use a query like this:

```
SELECT site_name FROM site_directory
WHERE site_desc='trading card'
```

This query would work. However, it would retrieve only those Web sites that have nothing more than the expression `trading card` in the description. For example, a Web site with the description `We have the greatest collection of trading cards in the world!` would not be retrieved.

To match one string with part of another string, you need to use wildcards. You use wildcards with the LIKE keyword to perform pattern matching. In the following statement, the preceding query has been rewritten with wildcards and the LIKE keyword to retrieve the names of all of the correct Web sites:

```
SELECT site_name FROM site_directory
WHERE site_desc LIKE '%trading card%'
```

In this example, every Web site containing the expression `trading card` anywhere in its description is retrieved. The site with the description `We have the greatest collection of trading cards in the world!` would also be retrieved. Of course, if a Web site's description contains `I am trading cardboard boxes online`, the name of this Web site is retrieved as well.

Notice the use of the percent (%) character in this example. The % character is an example of a wildcard. It stands for zero or more characters. By surrounding the expression `trading card` with % characters, any string that has `trading card` embedded in it is matched.

Now, suppose your directory of Web sites becomes too large to display on a single page. You decide to divide the directory in half. On one page, you'll display all the Web sites whose names begin with the letters *A* through *M*. On the second page, you'll list all the Web sites whose names begin with the letters *N* through *Z*. To retrieve the list of Web site names for the first page, you could use the following SQL query:

```
SELECT site_name FROM site_directory
WHERE site_name LIKE '[A-M]%'
```

In this example, the expression [A-M] is used to retrieve only those Web sites that have a name starting with the letters *A* through *M*. The brackets ([ ]) are used as a wildcard for any single character that falls in the range specified. To retrieve all the names for the second page, you would use this statement:

```
SELECT site_name FROM site_directory
WHERE site_name LIKE '[N-Z]%'
```

In this example, the bracketed expression stands for any single character that falls between the letters *N* and *Z*. All the Web sites from the second half of the alphabet are pulled from the `site_directory` table.

Suppose your directory of Web sites grows even larger. You now need to divide your directory into even more pages. If you want to display only those Web sites that begin with the letters *A*, *B*, or *C*, you could retrieve these Web sites with the following query:

```
SELECT site_name FROM site_directory WHERE site_name LIKE '[ABC]%'
```

In this example, the bracketed expression no longer specifies a range. Instead, a set of letters is provided. Any Web site whose name begins with any one of the letters from this set is retrieved.

You can combine both of these methods by including both a range and a set of characters in the bracketed expression. For example, you can use the following query to retrieve only those Web sites whose names begin with the letters *C* through *F*, or those that begin with the letter *Y*:

```
SELECT site_name FROM site_directory WHERE site_name LIKE '[C-FY]%'
```

In this example, Web sites named *Collegescape* and *Yahoo!* would be retrieved. However, the Web site named *Microsoft* would not be.

You can also use the caret (^) character to exclude certain letters. For example, to retrieve only those Web site names that *don't* start with the letter *Y*, you could use the following query:

```
SELECT site_name FROM site_directory WHERE site_name LIKE '[^Y]%'
```

You can use the ^ character with sets of letters and ranges of letters as well.

Finally, by using the underscore character (_) , you can create a wildcard that stands for any single character. For example, the following query retrieves every Web site name that has any letter in the name's second position:

```
SELECT site_name FROM site_directory WHERE site_name LIKE 'M_crosoft'
```

This example would retrieve both the Web site named *Microsoft* and the Web site named *Macrosoft*. However, it would not retrieve a Web site named *Moocrosoft*. The underscore (_) wildcard, unlike the % wildcard, stands for a single character position.

NOTE

If you want to match the percent (%) or underscore (_) characters themselves, you need to surround them in brackets. If you want to match the hyphen (-) character, use it as the first character in brackets. If you want to match the bracket ([ ]) characters, use them by themselves. For example, the following SELECT statement pulls every Web site name that has the character % in its description.

```
SELECT site_name FROM site_directory WHERE site_desc LIKE '%[%]%'
```

Matching Sounds

Microsoft SQL includes two functions that allow you to match string expressions phonetically. The SOUNDEX() function assigns a phonetic code to a character string. The DIFFERENCE()

function compares two strings phonetically. These functions can be useful for retrieving records when you know more or less how a name sounds, but not exactly how the name is spelled.

For example, if you create an Internet directory, you may want to add the option to search the names of Web sites by sound rather than by name. Consider the following statement:

```
SELECT site_name FROM site_directory
WHERE DIFFERENCE(site_name,'Microsoft')>3
```

This SELECT statement uses the DIFFERENCE() function to retrieve only the site names that sound very similar to *Microsoft*. The DIFFERENCE() function returns a number between 0 and 4. If the DIFFERENCE() function returns a value of 4, that means a close match in sound was made. If the DIFFERENCE() function returns 0, that means that the two string expressions are not very similar in sound.

For example, the preceding statement would return Web sites named *Macrosoft* and *Microshoft*. Both of these names sound very similar to *Microsoft*. If you changed the statement to return any Web site name with a difference greater than 2, the Web sites named *Zicrosoft* and *Megasoft* would also be returned. Finally, if you required only a difference greater than 1, the Web sites named *Picosoft* and *Minisoft* would be included.

To gain more insight into how the DIFFERENCE() function works, you can use the SOUNDEX() function to return the phonetic code that the DIFFERENCE() function uses. Here's an example of how this function is used:

```
SELECT site_name 'site name', SOUNDEX(site_name) 'sounds like'
FROM site_directory
```

This statement selects every value from the site_name column and all of the soundex values of the column. Following are the results from this query:

```
site name                                 sounds like
----------------------------------------  ----------
Yahoo                                     Y000
Mahoo                                     M000
Microsoft                                 M262
Macrosoft                                 M262
Minisoft                                  M521
Microshoft                                M262
Zicrosoft                                 Z262
Zaposoft                                  Z121
Millisoft                                 M421
Nanosoft                                  N521
Megasoft                                  M221
Picosoft                                  P221
(12 row(s) affected)
```

If you look closely at the soundex codes, you'll notice that the first letter of the code corresponds to the first letter of the column value. For example, the soundex codes for *Yahoo* and *Mahoo* are the same except for the first letter. You should also notice that *Microsoft* and *Macrosoft* are given exactly the same soundex code.

The SOUNDEX() function compares the first letters of two strings, and all of their consonants. The function ignores any vowels (including *y*) unless a vowel occurs as the first character in a string.

Sadly, there's a drawback to using both the SOUNDEX() and DIFFERENCE() functions. Queries that contain these functions in their WHERE clauses perform very poorly. Therefore, you should use these functions with caution.

Ridding Strings of Spaces

Two functions, RTRIM() and LTRIM(), are useful for removing spaces from strings. The LTRIM() function removes all the spaces at the beginning of a string; the RTRIM() function removes all the spaces at the end of a string. Here's an example of how the RTRIM() function is used:

```
SELECT RTRIM(site_name) FROM site_directory
```

In this example, if any of the site names have extraneous spaces, those spaces are removed from the query results.

You can nest these two functions to strip away both leading and trailing spaces at the same time:

```
SELECT LTRIM(RTRIM(site_name)) FROM site_directory
```

You'll find these functions useful when trimming blank spaces from columns of datatype CHAR. Remember, if you store a string in a CHAR column, the string is padded with extra blank spaces to match the column size. With these two functions, however, you can take care of this problem by stripping away the unneeded spaces.

Working with Dates and Times

The date and time functions are very useful to the builder of a Web site. Webmasters are often very curious about exactly when data in a table has been modified. With the date and time functions, you can track changes in a table down to the millisecond.

Retrieving the Current Date and Time

With the GETDATE() function, you can retrieve the current date and time. For example, the statement SELECT GETDATE() returns the following results:

```
--------------------------
Nov 30 1997  3:29AM
(1 row(s) affected)
```

Obviously, if you were to use this function, you would retrieve a later date, and perhaps an earlier time.

The GETDATE() function can be used as the default value for a DATETIME column. This is very useful for marking a record with the date and time it was inserted. For example, suppose you have a table that holds a log of activity for your Web site. Every time a visitor arrives at your Web site, an entry is made in the table, recording the visitor's name, activity, and the date and time the visit was made. To create a table that stamps the table rows with the current date and time, add a DATETIME column with the default value of GETDATE(), like this:

```
CREATE TABLE site_log (
  username VARCHAR(40),
  useractivity VARCHAR(100),
  entrydate DATETIME DEFAULT GETDATE())
```

Converting Dates and Times

You may have noticed that the value returned by the GETDATE() function in the example in the preceding section shows the time only to the minute. Actually, SQL Server can internally represent time to the millisecond (with an accuracy of 3.33 milliseconds, to be precise).

To retrieve dates and times in different formats, you need to use the CONVERT() function. For example, when the following statement is executed, the time shown includes the millisecond:

```
SELECT CONVERT(VARCHAR(30),GETDATE(),9)
```

Notice the number 9 used in this example. This number specifies which date and time format to use when displaying the date and time. When this statement is executed, the following date and time are shown:

```
----------------------------
Nov 30 1997  3:29:55:170AM
(1 row(s) affected)
```

You can use a number of different date and time styles with the CONVERT() function. Table 11.1 shows all the possible formats.

Table 11.1. Style codes for dates and times.

Style Code	Standard	Output
0	Default	mon dd yyyy hh:miAM
1	USA	mm/dd/yy
2	ANSI	yy.mm.dd
3	British/French	dd/mm/yy
4	German	dd.mm.yy
5	Italian	dd-mm-yy
6	–	dd mon yy
7	–	mon dd, yy
8	–	hh:mi:ss
9		Default + milliseconds—mon dd yyyy hh:mi:ss:mmmAM (or PM)
10	USA	mm-dd-yy

Style Code	Standard	Output
11	JAPAN	yy/mm/dd
12	ISO	yymmdd
13	Europe	Default + milliseconds—dd mon yyyy hh:mi:ss:mmm(24h)
14	–	hh:mi:ss:mmm(24h)

Styles 0, 9, and 13 always return the century (yyyy). To show the century for other styles, add 100 to the style code. Styles 13 and 14 return the time using a 24-hour clock. Styles 0, 7, and 13 return the month in three-character format (Nov instead of November).

For any of the styles listed in Table 11.1, you can add 100 to the style code to show the complete century rather than an abbreviated century (for example, the year 2000 instead of the year 00). For example, to show the date according to the Japanese standard, including the full century, you would use the following statement:

```
SELECT CONVERT(VARCHAR(30),GETDATE(),111)
```

This CONVERT() function converts the date style to show the date as 1997/11/30.

Extracting Date and Time Parts

In a number of situations, you may be interested in retrieving part of a date and time rather than a whole date and time. For example, suppose you want to list the month on which each entry in your directory of Web sites was posted. You don't want to clutter a Web page with exact dates and times; to extract a particular part of a date, you can use the DATEPART() function, like this:

```
SELECT site_name 'Site Name',
DATEPART(mm,site_entrydate) 'Month Posted' FROM site_directory
```

The DATEPART() function takes two variables. The first variable specifies which date part to extract; the second variable holds the actual date. In this example, the DATEPART() function extracts the month, because the code mm stands for the month. Here's the output from this SELECT statement:

```
Site Name                                    Month Posted
-------------------------------------------- ------------
Yahoo                                        2
Microsoft                                    5
Netscape                                     5
(3 row(s) affected)
```

The Month Posted column lists the month in which each Web site was posted. The DATEPART() function returns an integer as its value. You can use this function to extract a number of different date parts, as shown in Table 11.2.

Table 11.2. Date parts and their abbreviations.

Date Part	Abbreviation	Values
year	yy	1753–9999
quarter	qq	1–4
month	mm	1–12
day of year	dy	1–366
day	dd	1–31
week	wk	1–53
weekday	dw	1–7 (Sunday–Saturday)
hour	hh	0–23
minute	mi	0–59
second	ss	0–59
millisecond	ms	0–999

Retrieving integer values using the DATEPART() function is useful when you need to perform date and time comparisons. However, the results retrieved in the earlier example (2, 5) are not very readable. To retrieve a partial date and time in a more readable format, you can use the DATENAME() function, as in the following example:

```
SELECT site_name 'Site Name',
DATENAME(mm,site_entrydate) 'Month Posted'
FROM site_directory
```

The DATENAME() function accepts exactly the same variables as the DATEPART() function. However, the value it returns is a string rather than an integer. These are the results from the preceding statement:

```
Site Name                                 Month Posted
---------------------------------------- ------------------
Yahoo                                     February
Microsoft                                 June
Netscape                                  June
(3 row(s) affected)
```

You can also use the DATENAME() function to extract a particular day of the week. This example extracts both the day of the week and the month from a date:

```
SELECT site_name 'Site Name',
DATENAME(dw,site_entrydate)+' - ' +DATENAME(mm,site_entrydate)
  'Day and Month Posted' FROM site_directory
```

When this statement is executed, the following results are retrieved:

```
Site Name                                    Day and Month Posted
----------------------------------------     --------------------
Yahoo                                        Friday - February
Microsoft                                    Tuesday - June
Netscape                                     Monday - June
(3 row(s) affected)
```

Retrieving Date and Time Ranges

When you want to analyze the data in a table, you may want to retrieve data that falls on a certain date or time. You may be interested in all the activity on your Web site for a certain day, say December 25, 2000. To retrieve this type of data, you might be tempted to use a SELECT statement like this:

```
SELECT * FROM weblog WHERE entrydate="12/25/2000"
```

Don't do this. This SELECT statement won't retrieve the proper records—it will retrieve only the table entries that have a date and time of 12/25/2000 12:00:00:000AM. In other words, only records that were entered on the very stroke of midnight will be retrieved.

> **NOTE**
>
> The discussion in this section assumes that the ENTRYDATE column is a DATETIME column rather than a SMALLDATETIME column. The same points apply to SMALLDATETIME columns, but SMALLDATETIME columns are accurate only to the minute.

The problem is that SQL Server replaces a partial date with a full date. Whenever you neglect to include a time in a date, for example, SQL Server adds the default time "12:00:00:000AM". When you neglect to include the date with a time, SQL Server adds the default date "Jan 1 1900".

To retrieve the correct records, you need to use a date and time range, but there's more than one way to do this. The following SELECT statement, for example, retrieves all the correct records:

```
SELECT * FROM weblog
WHERE entrydate>="12/25/2000" AND entrydate<"12/26/2000"
```

This statement works because it retrieves every entry in the table with a date and time greater than or equal to 12/25/2000 12:00:00:000AM and less than 12/26/2000 12:00:00:000AM. In other words, it will correctly retrieve every record that was entered on Christmas Day in the year 2000.

Alternatively, you can use LIKE to retrieve the correct records. By including the wildcard character % in the date expression, you can match every time that occurs on a certain date. Here's an example:

```
SELECT * FROM weblog WHERE entrydate LIKE 'Dec 25 2000%'
```

This statement matches the correct records because the wildcard % matches any time string.

Using these two methods of matching date and time ranges, you can select records that were entered on a certain month, a certain day, a certain year, a certain hour, a certain minute, a certain second, or even a certain millisecond. However, if you need to match seconds or milliseconds using LIKE, you first need to convert the date and time to a more precise format, using the CONVERT() function (see the earlier section "Converting Dates and Times").

Comparing Dates and Times

Two final date and time functions may prove useful when retrieving records by dates and times. Using the DATEADD() and the DATEDIFF() functions, you can compare later and earlier dates. For example, the following SELECT statement displays the number of hours that have passed since each record in a table was entered:

```
SELECT entrydate 'Time Entered',
DATEDIFF(hh,entrydate,GETDATE()) 'Hours Ago' FROM weblog
```

If the current date is December 30, 2000 and the time is 6:15 p.m., the following results would be retrieved:

```
Time Entered              Hours Ago
------------------------- ---------
Dec 30 2000   4:09PM         2
Dec 30 2000   4:13PM         2
Dec 1 2000   4:09PM          698
(3 row(s) affected)
```

The DATEDIFF() function accepts three variables. The first variable contains a code for the date part. In this example, the dates are compared by hour. (To see a complete list of date part codes, refer to Table 11.2.) There are 698 hours between the two dates, December 1, 2000, and December 30, 2000, at the specified times. The next two variables hold the dates to be compared. To return a positive integer, the earlier date should be listed first.

The DATEADD() function adds one date to another. This function can be useful when you need to report such things as expiration dates. For example, suppose the visitors to your Web site must register to use it. Once they register, they can use the Web site for one month without paying. To determine when their time will be up, you can use a SELECT statement like the following:

```
SELECT username 'User Name',
DATEADD(mm,1,firstvisit_date) 'Registration Expires'
FROM registration_table
```

The DATEADD() function accepts three variables. The first variable is a date part code (refer to Table 11.2). This example uses the month code, mm. The second variable specifies an interval of time—in this case, one month. The last variable holds a date. In this example, the date is retrieved from the DATETIME column `firstvisit_date`. Assuming that the current date is June 30, 2000, this statement would retrieve the following results:

```
User Name                                   Registration Expires
-------------------------------------------- --------------------
Bill Gates                                  Jul 30 2000  4:09PM
President Clinton                           Jul 30 2000  4:13PM
William Shakespeare                         Jul 1 2000  4:09PM
(3 row(s) affected)
```

NOTE

Contrary to what you might expect, using the DATEADD( ) function to add a month to a date doesn't add 30 days. The function simply increments the month by 1 while preserving the day of the month. This means that someone who registers in December will receive 2 or 3 more days than someone who registers in February. To get around this problem, you can add days instead of months with the DATEADD( ) function.

Sending Mail

You can use SQL Server to send simple e-mail messages. To do this, you need to have a mail server such as Microsoft Exchange Server installed on your system. (See Chapter 4, "Exchange Active Server, Index Server, and NetShow.") You also need to configure SQL Server to recognize your mail server.

To allow SQL Server to recognize your mail server, start the Enterprise Manager and choose Server | SQL Mail | Configure from the menu. A dialog box like the one in Figure 11.3 should appear. Enter the name and password you use for your mail server and click OK.

NOTE

If you're using Microsoft Exchange Server, the procedure for configuring SQL Mail is significantly different. You need to run the MSSQLServer service and Exchange Server under the same (domain) user account. You also need to install the Exchange Client on the same machine as SQL Server and create a profile for this account. After you've done this, you can enter the profile name in the SQL Mail Configuration dialog box.

Figure 11.3.

*SQL Mail Con-
figuration.*

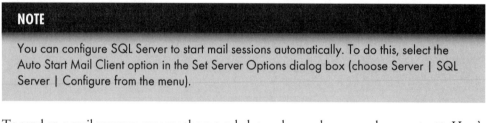

You need to start SQL Mail before you can send any messages. Choose Server | SQL Mail | Start from the menu. If your mail server is configured correctly and you have entered the correct name and password, SQL Mail should start.

> **NOTE**
>
> You can configure SQL Server to start mail sessions automatically. To do this, select the Auto Start Mail Client option in the Set Server Options dialog box (choose Server | SQL Server | Configure from the menu).

To send an e-mail message, you use the extended stored procedure named xp_sendmail. Here's an example of how this procedure is used:

```
master..xp_sendmail "president@whitehouse.gov", "Hello Mr. President"
```

This procedure sends the short e-mail message Hello Mr. President to the e-mail address president@whitehouse.gov. You can substitute any other e-mail address and message you want, but your message can be no longer than 255 characters.

The xp_sendmail procedure is useful when you want to be constantly updated on the status of your Web site's database. For example, you can send e-mail messages to a pager. If there's trouble at your Web site, you can know instantly. The next chapter provides more details about using procedures like this one.

Summary

This chapter deepened your knowledge of SQL. You learned how to create indexes that allow your database queries to retrieve data much faster. You learned how to insert, delete, and update data in a database table, and how to use aggregate functions to retrieve summary information from the data stored in a table. Finally, you learned a number of valuable expressions, functions, and procedures for manipulating strings, dates and times, and mail.

The following chapter further extends your knowledge of Microsoft SQL Server. You learn how to treat SQL as if it were a full programming language, and how to create stored procedures, triggers, and scheduled tasks. Even more exciting, you learn a simple way to cause SQL Server to create Web pages automatically.

Advanced SQL

IN THIS CHAPTER

In Chapters 10, "Basic SQL," and 11, "Intermediate SQL," you learned how to execute SQL statements one at a time. In this chapter, you learn how to execute a group of SQL statements at once. This enables you to treat SQL more like a traditional programming language. You learn how to create stored procedures, triggers, and scheduled tasks.

First, however, you learn about the SQL Server Web Assistant. This program enables you to create static Web pages automatically from the information stored in database tables.

Using the SQL Server Web Assistant

In the next part of this book, you learn how to use Active Server Pages to create Web pages that are generated dynamically from a database. When you need to display database information that changes rapidly, you should use ASP scripts to retrieve this information. However, in certain circumstances, using ASP scripts to display database information proves inefficient.

For example, suppose your Web site includes a directory of other Web sites. One page displays a list of links to your favorite Web sites, such as Yahoo! and Microsoft. Now suppose this page doesn't change very often—at most, you add new links to this page once a week or so. You could create this Web page dynamically whenever a visitor accesses it, using ASP scripts to pull the list of links from a database table. This strategy would ensure that the Web page always displays the latest information. Considering how rarely the information displayed on this page changes, however, this plan would be overkill.

Active Server Pages have costs in terms of computational resources. Using an ASP script to open a database connection and execute a query takes time and places a burden on the database server. Furthermore, your processor has to work to execute the scripts. Because the data on this page doesn't change often, these burdens on your server are unnecessary. A much more efficient scheme would be to generate the page only when the data in the underlying database table changes, or when some interval of time passes. The page doesn't need to be updated every time a visitor views it. What you really need is a static Web page that's recreated automatically every so often.

Using the SQL Server Web Assistant, you can generate Web pages automatically from database tables. You can create a Web page from a table once, on a scheduled basis, or whenever the data in the table changes. The next section describes how to do this.

Creating Web Pages with the SQL Server Web Assistant

This section provides a step-by-step guide to using the SQL Server Web Assistant. You learn how to create a Web page that displays links to your favorite Web sites. This Web page will be updated automatically whenever the data in a table changes.

Before doing anything else, you need to create the table that holds the information about your favorite Web sites. Create this table by executing the following SQL statement in ISQL/w:

```
CREATE TABLE site_directory (site_name VARCHAR(30),
➥site_URL VARCHAR(30), site_desc VARCHAR(100))
```

This statement creates a table named `site_directory` with three columns named `site_name`, `site_url`, and `site_desc`. These columns contain a list of Web site names, URLs, and brief descriptions. To automatically generate a Web page that displays your favorite links from this table, follow these five steps:

1. Start the SQL Server Web Assistant from the SQL Server program group. When the program starts, you're asked for login information. Enter the name of your SQL Server, your user ID, and your password. (If you're using integrated or mixed security, you can log in by using a trusted connection instead.) Click the Next button to move to the next step.

2. The dialog box prompts you to specify how to select data for the Web page. Select the option Enter a Query as Free-Form Text. A blank text window should appear below the radio buttons (see Figure 12.1). Select the database where the table `site_directory` is located and then type the following SQL query in the text box:

```
SELECT * FROM site_directory ORDER BY site_name
```

This query will pull all the records from the `site_directory` table and will order the results alphabetically. Click Next.

FIGURE 12.1.
The SQL Server Web Assistant - Query dialog box.

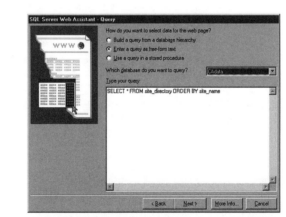

3. Next, you're asked for scheduling options. You can choose to have your Web page generated automatically now, at some later time, when the data changes, on certain days of the week, or on a regular basis. From the drop-down list box, select When Data Changes. After you do this, a list of tables will appear. Select the `site_directory` table. This will cause a new page to be generated only when data in the `site_directory` table changes. Click Next.

4. In this step, you're asked for file options (see Figure 12.2). For the filename of your Web page, use the name **Favorites.htm**. You should include the directory path of the Web directory with the filename; typically, this would be the directory path `c:\InetPub\wwwroot\Favorites.htm`. To format the page, select the option The Following Information, and enter the title **Favorite Web Sites** for the title of your

Web page. Enter the heading **Web Site List** for the title of your query results. Select No to indicate that you don't want to include URL links and reference text. (This is the default selection.) Click Next.

FIGURE 12.2.

Specifying the file options.

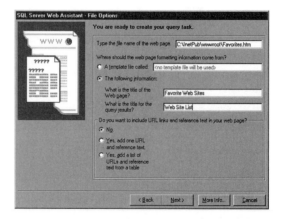

5. The final step lets you control how the Web page will be formatted when it's generated. You can choose different size column headings, and formatting options for the query results. Finally, you can specify such options as whether the page should include the date and time it was last generated, the column headings, or a limited number of query results. Leave all the settings at their default values, and click Finish.

The HTML file `Favorites.htm` will now be regenerated whenever the data in the table `site_directory` changes. Initially, the file doesn't exist, because you need to alter the table at least once for the file to be generated. Do this now by executing the following SQL statement:

```
INSERT site_directory (site_name, site_URL, site_desc)
➥VALUES ('Microsoft', 'www.microsoft.com',
➥'The creators of Active Server Pages')
```

This statement inserts one record into the `site_directory` table. If you look in your Web directory, you should be able to find the file `Favorites.htm`. If you load this file into a Web browser, it will appear as shown in Figure 12.3.

How the SQL Server Web Assistant Works

You may be wondering how the SQL Server Web Assistant works. You can choose to have the program generate Web pages on a scheduled basis or when data in a table changes. How is this program able to do this?

The SQL Server Web Assistant uses stored procedures, triggers, and scheduled tasks. To create Web pages, the program uses three *stored procedures* named sp_makewebtask, sp_runwebtask, and sp_dropwebtask. These stored procedures actually create the Web pages.

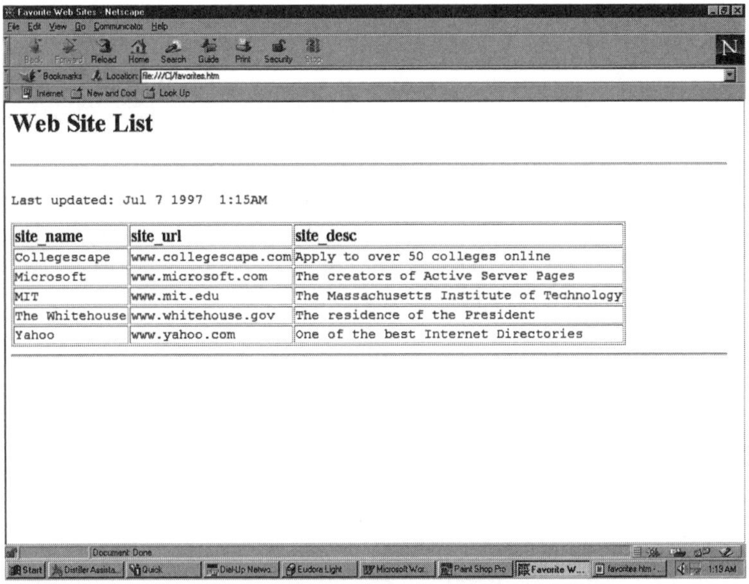

FIGURE 12.3.
The automatically generated Favorites page.

NOTE

The three stored procedures—`sp_makewebtask`, `sp_runwebtask`, and `sp_dropwebtask`—can be executed directly from ISQL/w rather than through the SQL Server Web Assistant.

To detect when the data in a table changes, the SQL Server Web Assistant uses *triggers.* A trigger is a collection of SQL statements executed whenever data in a table is updated, deleted, or inserted. For example, when you insert data into the `site_directory` table, a trigger is executed that regenerates the `Favorites.htm` Web page.

Finally, in order to generate a Web page on a scheduled basis, the SQL Server Web Assistant uses *scheduled tasks.* For example, by using the Web Assistant, you could schedule the Favorites page to be regenerated once a week. To do this, the Web Assistant would create a scheduled task that's timed to execute once a week.

The remainder of this chapter explains how to create your own procedures, triggers, and scheduled tasks, which will enable you to perform very sophisticated operations on your tables in response to user actions or timed events. To be able to do this, you first need to extend your knowledge of SQL, to allow you to treat the language more like a traditional programming language.

Programming with Transact-SQL

Many of the statements in the following sections are not part of the SQL standard, but are part of an extension of SQL called *Transact-SQL* (*T-SQL*). T-SQL extends SQL by adding, among other things, such traditional programming elements as variables, conditionals, and loops.

The only reason you might care about this distinction is if you plan to ever use a database server other than Microsoft SQL Server. The statements and techniques described in the following sections may not all be transferable. However, if you want to exploit the full capabilities of Microsoft SQL Server, you need to use T-SQL.

Executing Multiple Statements in Batches

To execute multiple SQL statements at once, you can place them together in a *batch*. A batch, as the name implies, is simply one or more SQL statements executed as a group. For example, if you enter the following two statements into ISQL/w, they would be executed together as a batch:

```
SELECT pub_name FROM publishers
SELECT pub_name FROM publishers
```

When you execute this simple batch, the same records are pulled from the table twice—once for each SELECT statement. Now suppose you mistype the name of the second table, and attempt to execute the following batch:

```
SELECT pub_name FROM publishers
SELECT ub_name FROM publishers
```

You might expect that the first statement would execute successfully, and the second statement would fail. Actually, this wouldn't happen. In most cases, if any statement in a batch fails to execute successfully, none of the statements will execute (but see the following note). SQL Server treats the statements in a batch as a group.

> **NOTE**
>
> In some circumstances, one statement will fail but the other statements in a batch will execute. All the statements in a batch will fail if the server detects an error while in the process of parsing and compiling a batch. If the batch survives compilation but still contains an error, only some of the statements will be executed.

You can divide a group of statements into separate batches. To do this with ISQL/w, you use the command GO. Consider the following example:

```
SELECT pub_name FROM publishers
GO
SELECT ub_name FROM publishers
```

If you execute these statements in ISQL/w, the first statement would return a result set successfully. This is true even though an error remains in the second SELECT statement. The GO command forces SQL Server to treat the two statements as separate batches.

Assigning Values to Variables

SQL Server recognizes two types of variables: global variables and local variables. *Global variables* are read-only; you can't modify them. However, you can access the values of global variables in multiple batches. *Local variables*, on the other hand, are local to a particular batch. The advantage of local variables is that you can both read and modify their values. In this section, you learn how to use both types of variables.

Global Variables

The number of global variables is limited, and you can't make more of them yourself. The two most important global variables are @@IDENTITY and @@ROWCOUNT. The @@IDENTITY variable holds the value from the last INSERT into an identity column. Consider the following example:

```
INSERT Authors (author_name)
  VALUES ('James Joyce')
INSERT Books (book_id,book_title)
  VALUES (@@IDENTITY,'Portrait of the Artist as a Young Man')
```

Assume that the table Authors has two columns. The first column is named author_id and is an IDENTITY column. It's used to give each author in the Authors table a unique identifier. The second column is named author_name and is used to hold the names of the authors. Assume that the table Books also has two columns. The first column is named book_id and is an INT column. The second column is named book_title and is a VARCHAR column.

When this batch is executed, the value of the identity column from Authors is inserted into the integer column of Books. This allows you to join the two tables together for queries. For example, suppose you want to retrieve a list of authors' names and their books from these two tables. You could do this with the following SELECT statement:

```
SELECT author_name, book_title FROM Authors, Books
  WHERE author_id=book_id
```

It's important to understand that the @@IDENTITY variable is assigned the value NULL immediately after a record is inserted into a table without an identity column. For example, consider the following batch:

```
INSERT Authors (author_name) VALUES ('James Joyce')
SELECT @@IDENTITY
SELECT @@IDENTITY
INSERT Books (book_id,book_title)
  VALUES (@@IDENTITY,'Portrait of the Artist as a Young Man')
SELECT @@IDENTITY
```

When this batch is executed, the first and second SELECT statements both report the value of the identity column from the Authors table. However, the third and final SELECT statement returns NULL because another INSERT statement occurs before it.

NOTE

When retrieving the values of global variables in your Active Server Pages, you should provide the variable with a column name. For example, to retrieve the value of the global variable @@IDENTITY in your ASP scripts, use a statement like the following:

```
SELECT @@IDENTITY 'myidentity'
```

The second important global variable is @@ROWCOUNT. The @@ROWCOUNT variable records the number of rows affected by the last statement executed. To get a better idea of how this variable works, consider the following batch:

```
UPDATE Authors SET author_name="Samuel Clemens"
  WHERE author_name="Mark Twain"
SELECT @@ROWCOUNT
SELECT * FROM Authors WHERE 1=2
SELECT @@ROWCOUNT
```

After the UPDATE statement is executed, the variable @@ROWCOUNT is set equal to the number of authors whose name is Samuel Clemens. When the final SELECT statement is executed, it returns no records, and the @@ROWCOUNT variable is set to zero. (The clause WHERE 1=2 guarantees that no records will be returned, because no record could match this condition.)

You can't create your own global variables. You also can't assign a value to an existing global variable. This means that you can't use a variable to pass information between multiple batches.

If you need to store information that's accessible to multiple batches, you should store that information in a table. You're under no obligation to make all of your tables large; you can create very small tables that contain few rows. The rows in these tables would function very much like the global variables of a traditional programming language.

NOTE

You can also use temporary tables to mimic the functionality of traditional global variables. Temporary tables are a special kind of table that doesn't permanently exist in a database. For more information, consult your SQL Server documentation.

Local Variables

Local variables in SQL are very similar to the variables in a traditional programming language. You can declare your own local variables and assign values to them. The primary limitation of a local variable is that it only survives in the batch where it's declared. Here's an example of a batch that uses a local variable:

```
DECLARE @myvariable INT
SELECT @myvariable=2+2
SELECT @myvariable
```

The names of all local variables begin with a single @ character. In this example, the local variable @myvariable is declared to be of datatype INT. Next, the variable is assigned the value 2+2 with a SELECT statement. The final SELECT statement returns the value of the variable.

Before you use a variable in a batch, you need to *declare* it. You declare a variable by providing a name and specifying a datatype. You can declare multiple variables with a single declaration, like this:

```
DECLARE @firstname VARCHAR(20),@secondname VARCHAR(20)
SELECT @firstname="Mark Twain"
SELECT @secondname="Samuel Clemens"
SELECT @firstname=@secondname
```

In this batch, two variables are created, named @firstname and @secondname. Both variables are declared to be of datatype VARCHAR. Next, the variables are assigned various values by using the SELECT statement. The last SELECT statement, for example, assigns the value of one variable to the other.

You can also assign a local variable to the results of a query. This is very useful. Consider the following batch:

```
DECLARE @queryresults VARCHAR(30)
SELECT @queryresults=author_name FROM Authors WHERE author_id=1
SELECT @queryresults
```

In this example, the variable @queryresults is assigned the results of a query from the Authors table. For example, if the author with an author_id of 1 is named James Joyce, the value of the @queryresults variable would be James Joyce.

The identity column from the Authors table is used here to ensure that at most one value is assigned to the variable. This raises two questions. What happens when you assign a variable to a query that returns no values? And what happens when you assign a variable to a query that returns more than one value?

If a query returns no values, the variable retains its previous value. When a variable is first declared, the variable has a value of NULL. So, in the previous example, if no author has an author_id of 1, the variable would retain the value NULL. However, consider the following example:

```
DECLARE @queryresults INT
SELECT @queryresults=12
SELECT @queryresults=author_id FROM Authors WHERE 1=2
SELECT @queryresults
```

In this example, the query is guaranteed to return no results because 1 is not equal to 2. Because no results are returned, the @queryresults variable retains its previous assignment of 12.

If you assign a variable to a query that returns more than one value, the variable is assigned the last value returned. For example, suppose the Authors table contains five authors. If there are no gaps in the identity column, the variable @queryresults would be assigned the value 5 at the end of the following batch (shown on the next page):

```
DECLARE @queryresults INT
SELECT @queryresults=author_id FROM Authors
SELECT @queryresults
```

When your batches grow in size, you'll find yourself using local variables quite often. Local variables are especially useful when you need to compare data in multiple tables. You can retrieve a value stored in one table into a local variable and then compare this value with data in another table. Here's a simple example:

```
DECLARE @queryresults INT
SELECT @queryresults=author_id FROM Authors
➥WHERE author_name="James Joyce"
SELECT book_title FROM Books WHERE author_id=@queryresults
```

In this example, the first SELECT statement is used to retrieve the author_id of James Joyce. This unique identifier for James Joyce is stored in the local variable @queryresults. The local variable is then used in the WHERE clause of the second SELECT statement. This SELECT statement uses the variable to return only the books written by James Joyce from the Books table.

Printing Data to the Screen

Typically, you'll have no reason to print anything to the screen when you're executing a batch. However, the PRINT statement can be useful while you are debugging a group of SQL statements. Here's a quick example of the PRINT statement:

```
DECLARE @myvariable VARCHAR(30)
SELECT @myvariable="Hello There!"
PRINT @myvariable
```

You can't use the PRINT statement to print any datatypes other than the character datatypes. If you need to print other datatypes, you must first convert them by using the CONVERT() function, like this:

```
DECLARE @myvariable VARCHAR(10), @mynumber INT
SELECT @mynumber=12
SELECT @myvariable=CONVERT(VARCHAR(10),@mynumber)
PRINT @myvariable
```

In this example, the variable @mynumber is assigned the value 12. You can't print this variable directly, however, because the value of this variable is not a character datatype. The CONVERT() function is used to convert the value to the VARCHAR datatype so it can be printed.

TIP

If you just want to view the value of a variable for debugging purposes, you can use SELECT rather than PRINT. With the SELECT statement, you don't need to worry about converting the variable to a character datatype.

Commenting Your SQL Statements

When your collection of SQL statements grows large enough to be complex, you'll need to comment your statements. You can add comments to your statements in one of two ways. If you need to add a single-line comment, you can use two hyphens in a row, as in this example:

```
DECLARE @myvariable DATETIME
SELECT @myvariable=GETDATE()  -- Gets The Current Date
SELECT DATENAME(dw,@myvariable) -- Gets The Day Of The Week
```

When you use the double hyphens, the comment extends from the hyphens to the end of the line. To create multiple-line comments, you need to enclose the comments in the characters /* and */ like this:

```
DECLARE @myvariable DATETIME
/*
The following statements retrieve the current
date and time and extract the day of the
week from the results.
*/
SELECT @myvariable=GETDATE()
SELECT DATENAME(dw,@myvariable)
```

Comments aren't only useful for documenting code; they're also useful for debugging code. If you want to disable a section of SQL statements temporarily, you can simply surround them with the comment characters. When you're ready to include the statements again, you need only delete the comment characters.

Controlling Statement Execution with Conditionals

When you want a single statement or a block of statements to execute (or not) depending on some condition, you need to use a *conditional*. Look at the following example:

```
IF (SELECT COUNT(*) FROM Authors)>10 PRINT "More than 10 Authors!"
```

If more than 10 authors exist in the Authors table, this statement will print More than 10 Authors! as the result.

> **NOTE**
>
> Look closely at the structure of the conditional. Notice something missing? There's no THEN. If you include a THEN in your conditional, you'll get an error.

You can create a conditional that executes a block of statements. To do this, enclose the block of statements with the keywords BEGIN and END:

```
IF DATENAME(mm,GETDATE())="July"
BEGIN
  PRINT "It is July!"
  PRINT "Happy July!"
END
```

If it happens to be the month of July when you execute this batch, the two statements enclosed in the BEGIN and END block will be executed.

You can nest IF statements, if necessary, as in this example:

```
IF DATENAME(mm,GETDATE())="July"
BEGIN
  PRINT "It is July!"
  PRINT "Happy July!"
  IF DATEPART(dd,GETDATE())=4
    BEGIN
      PRINT "And it is the 4th!"
      PRINT "Happy 4th of July!"
    END
END
```

If it happens to be the fourth of July when you execute this batch, the statements in the inner block will be executed. Here are the results from this batch (executed on the fourth of July):

```
It is July!
Happy July!
And it is the 4th!
Happy 4th of July!
```

You can use the keyword ELSE with the IF statement to create logically contrary blocks of code. The next example prints It is Friday only if it's Friday, and prints Some other day otherwise:

```
If DATENAME(dw,GETDATE())="Friday"
PRINT "It is Friday"
ELSE
PRINT "Some other day"
```

Finally, you can use the keyword EXISTS in a conditional to test whether a result is returned from a query. The following example uses EXISTS to test whether the author James Joyce is in the Authors table:

```
IF EXISTS(SELECT author_name FROM authors WHERE author_name="James Joyce")
PRINT "James Joyce is an author"
ELSE
PRINT "James Joyce is not an author"
```

Controlling Statement Execution with CASE

Suppose you want to display a list of names, URLs, and brief descriptions of your favorite Web sites on a Web page. Furthermore, you want to indicate the type of each Web site next to its name when you list the sites. For example, next to government Web sites, you want to display the word Government; next to commercial Web sites, you want to display the word Commercial. To do this, you could create a table that has four columns. It would have a column for the names, a column for the URLs, and a column for the brief descriptions. In addition, the table would have a column that contains the type of each Web site.

But wait. You shouldn't do this—there's a better way to achieve the same results.

The problem is that your table would contain redundant information. The URL column already contains information on the type of each Web site. By looking at the last three characters of each URL, you can determine whether a Web site is commercial, governmental, educational, and so on. You shouldn't repeat the same information in your table by adding an additional column. But how can you extract this information from the URL column when you retrieve records from the table? You can do this by using the CASE expression. Here's an example:

```
SELECT
(
CASE
WHEN site_url LIKE "%edu" THEN "Educational"
WHEN site_url LIKE "%gov" THEN "Government"
WHEN site_url LIKE "%com" THEN "Commercial"
ELSE "Other"
END
) "Type",
site_name "Name",
site_URL "URL",
site_desc "Description"
FROM site_directory
```

> **NOTE**
>
> The letters .edu, .gov, and .com are all common examples of top-level domain names. There are many other top-level domain names in use. For example, if the domain name of a Web site ends with .jp, that indicates the site is located in Japan.

When this SELECT statement is executed, you retrieve the correct results. The CASE expression tests the site_url column in order to return the correct values. When the value of the site_url column ends with the three characters edu, for example, the value Educational is returned. Here's an example of the results from this query:

```
Type          Name          URL                   Description
-----------   -----------   -------------------   ----------------------------
Commercial    Microsoft     www.microsoft.com     The creators of Active Server Pages
Commercial    Yahoo         www.yahoo.com         One of the best Internet Directories
Commercial    Collegescape  www.collegescape.com  Apply to over 50 colleges online
Educational   MIT           www.mit.edu           The Massachusetts Institute of Technology
Government    The Whitehouse www.whitehouse.gov    The residence of the President
(5 row(s) affected)
```

Using the CASE statement, you can test multiple conditions and return a value based on the results. For each test, you include a WHEN clause. In this example, whenever the statement that follows the WHEN clause is true, the value that follows the THEN clause is returned. If none of the statements is true, the value following the ELSE clause is returned instead.

All the WHEN clauses and an optional single ELSE clause must appear between the expressions CASE and END. The keyword CASE identifies the beginning of a CASE statement. The keyword END identifies the end of the CASE statement.

The CASE statement has a second format that's slightly different. Consider how the CASE statement is used in the following example:

```
SELECT
(
CASE
site_name
WHEN "Yahoo" THEN "Internet Directory"
WHEN "Microsoft" THEN "Software Giant"
ELSE "Other"
END
) "Type",
site_name "Name",
site_URL "URL",
site_desc "Description"
FROM site_directory
```

This example also displays a list of Web site types, names, URLs, and brief descriptions. However, in this example, the type of each Web site is determined by the name of the Web site rather than its URL. These are the results from this batch:

```
Type                Name           URL                     Description
------------------  -------------  ----------------------  ----------------------
Software Giant      Microsoft      www.microsoft.com       The creators of Active Server Pages
Internet Directory  Yahoo          www.yahoo.com           One of the best Internet Directories
Other               Collegescape   www.collegescape.com    Apply to over 50 colleges online
Other               MIT            www.mit.edu             The Massachusetts Institute of Technology
Other               The Whitehouse www.whitehouse.gov      The residence of the President
(5 row(s) affected)
```

Notice how the CASE statement is written in this example. In this CASE statement, a statement doesn't follow each WHEN clause. Instead, the value following each WHEN clause is compared to the value of the site_name column.

When you have multiple conditions, each of which can be true or false, you should use the first form of the CASE statement. If you need to compare a single value to multiple values, use the second form of the CASE statement.

Exiting from a Batch with RETURN

To exit from a batch, you can use the RETURN statement. Consider the following example:

```
IF DATENAME(dw,GETDATE())="Saturday"
BEGIN
 PRINT "It is Saturday!"
 RETURN
END
PRINT "It is some other day."
```

When this batch is executed on Saturday, the statement block after the conditional is executed. When the RETURN statement is encountered, the batch is immediately exited. This means that the following text will only appear on days other than Saturday:

```
It is some other day.
```

Grouping Statements into Transactions

Suppose you want to sell trading cards at your Web site. To do this, you create two tables. One table holds a list of credit card accounts to be debited. The other table holds a list of product orders. Whenever a visitor to your Web site orders a trading card, data needs to be inserted into both tables.

Now suppose a visitor to your Web site orders a trading card. The person's credit card number is entered into the credit card table. However, at that very moment, your Web server's hard drive crashes. The person's order is never placed in the product order table. This would be bad. The visitor's credit card would be charged, but the product ordered would never be sent. The person who placed the order would be justifiably angry. How can you prevent this from happening?

Three statements, BEGIN TRANSACTION, COMMIT TRANSACTION, and ROLLBACK TRANSACTION, can help. A *transaction* is a group of statements that either run as a group or not at all. Here's a simple example of how these statements are used:

```
BEGIN TRANSACTION
INSERT credit_cards (username, ccnumber)
  VALUES ('Andrew Jones', '5555-55-555-55-5555')
INSERT orders (username) VALUES ('Andrew Jones')
COMMIT TRANSACTION
```

In this example, a transaction block is defined by using the BEGIN TRANSACTION and COMMIT TRANSACTION statements. The statements that appear within this block don't take effect until the COMMIT TRANSACTION statement is executed. If something goes wrong at any point before this statement is reached, all the statements in the transaction are rolled back. If your server's hard drive crashes after the first INSERT statement but before the second, the data won't be inserted into either table. The first INSERT statement will be rolled back and won't take effect.

You can explicitly roll back a transaction by using the ROLLBACK TRANSACTION statement like this:

```
BEGIN TRANSACTION
INSERT credit_cards (username, ccnumber)
  VALUES ('Andrew Jones', '5555-55-555-55-5555')
INSERT orders (username) VALUES ('Andrew Jones')
IF DATENAME(dw,GETDATE())="Tuesday"
ROLLBACK TRANSACTION
ELSE
COMMIT TRANSACTION
```

In this example, the transaction is committed on every day except Tuesday. If the day of the week happens to be Tuesday, the transaction is rolled back and never takes effect. In other words, no new orders will be accepted on Tuesdays.

NOTE

The ROLLBACK TRANSACTION command is especially valuable when used with triggers. See the later section "Combining Triggers and Transactions."

Using Stored Procedures

This section describes how to create and use your own *stored procedures*. Stored procedures are the closest thing in SQL Server to traditional computer applications, and offer a number of benefits:

■ If you have a complicated set of SQL statements that you need to execute on multiple Active Server Pages, you can place them in a stored procedure and execute the procedure instead. This reduces the size of your Active Server Pages, and ensures that the same SQL statements are executed on each page.

■ When you execute a batch of SQL statements, the server must first compile the statements in the batch. This takes time and server resources. By contrast, after a stored procedure is first executed, it doesn't need to be recompiled. By using a stored procedure, you can bypass the compilation step and execute collections of SQL statements faster. Executing a stored procedure from an Active Server Page is more efficient than executing a collection of SQL statements.

■ You can pass values both to and from a stored procedure. This means that stored procedures can be very flexible. The same stored procedure can return very different information, depending on the data passed to it.

■ When you pass a collection of SQL statements to the database server, each of the individual statements must be passed. When you execute a stored procedure, on the other hand, only a single statement is passed. By using stored procedures, you can reduce the strain on your network.

■ You can configure a table's permissions in such a way that users can modify a table only by using a stored procedure. This can improve the security of the data in your database tables.

■ You can execute a stored procedure from within another stored procedure. This strategy enables you to build very complex stored procedures from smaller ones. This also means that you can reuse the same stored procedure for many different programming tasks.

Whenever you add SQL statements to your Active Server Pages, you should carefully consider whether you can place these statements in a stored procedure instead. The benefits listed here are substantial. Stored procedures are also very easy to create, as described in the next section.

Creating Stored Procedures with CREATE PROCEDURE

To create a stored procedure, you use the CREATE PROCEDURE statement. Here's an example of a very simple stored procedure:

```
CREATE PROCEDURE retrieve_authors AS SELECT * FROM Authors
```

When you create a stored procedure, you provide it with a name. In this example, the name of the stored procedure is retrieve_authors. You can give a stored procedure any name you want, but you should try to make the name descriptive of the stored procedure's function.

Every stored procedure contains one or more SQL statements. To specify the SQL statements that are part of the stored procedure, you simply include them after the keyword AS. The stored procedure in the preceding example contains a single SQL statement. Whenever this stored procedure is executed, it retrieves all the records from the Authors table.

You can execute a stored procedure by using the EXECUTE statement. For example, to execute the retrieve_authors stored procedure, you would use the following statement:

```
EXECUTE retrieve_authors
```

When you execute a stored procedure, all the SQL statements contained in the stored procedure are executed. In this example, all the records from the Authors table are returned.

When a call to a stored procedure is the first statement in a batch, you don't need to use the EXECUTE statement. You can execute the stored procedure simply by providing the stored procedure's name. For example, you can execute the retrieve_authors stored procedure in ISQL/w like this:

```
retrieve_authors
```

This would work. The stored procedure would execute and results would be returned. However, if any statements precede this stored procedure call, you would receive an error (typically, a syntax error).

When you create or execute a stored procedure, this is done within the context of a database. Suppose you create the stored procedure retrieve_authors while in the database MyDatabase. You can't access that procedure while in another database, such as MyDatabase2, without qualifying the procedure call. If you need to execute the procedure retrieve_authors while in MyDatabase2, you should use the following statement (notice the two consecutive periods):

```
EXECUTE MyDatabase..retrieve_authors
```

Once a stored procedure has been created, you can view the statements that are included in the stored procedure by using the system stored procedure sp_helptext. For example, if you issue the command **sp_helptext retrieve_authors**, the following results would be returned:

```
text
- - - - - - - - - - - - - - - - - - - - - - - - - - - - - - - - - - - - - - - - - - - - -
CREATE PROCEDURE retrieve_authors AS SELECT * FROM Authors
```

> **NOTE**
>
> In case you're curious, the `sp_helptext` system procedure is itself a type of stored procedure. It is a *system stored procedure*. (System stored procedures are stored in the Master database and are accessible from all databases.) For amusement value, you could type **sp_helptext sp_helptext** to view the SQL statements that constitute sp_helptext itself.

You can't modify a stored procedure after you create it. If you need to change a stored procedure, you must destroy it and create it again. To destroy a stored procedure, you use the DROP PROCEDURE statement. For example, the following statement drops the `retrieve_authors` stored procedure:

```
DROP PROCEDURE retrieve_authors
```

> **NOTE**
>
> To view a list of all of the stored procedures contained in the current database, you can use the system stored procedure `sp_help`. If you execute `sp_help` without any modifiers, the procedure will display all the procedures, triggers, and tables in the current database. If `sp_help` is followed by the name of a specific procedure, `sp_help` will display information on only that procedure.

Creating Stored Procedures with the SQL Enterprise Manager

If you need to create a complicated stored procedure, it's easier to do it with the SQL Enterprise Manager than with ISQL/w. The program allows you to modify a stored procedure easily, by automatically dropping and re-creating it for you.

To create a stored procedure with the SQL Enterprise Manager, start the program and select the database that you're using to store your tables. Next, choose Manage | Manage Stored Procedures from the menu. The dialog box shown in Figure 12.4 should appear.

FIGURE 12.4.

The Manage Stored Procedures dialog box.

The Save Object button ──

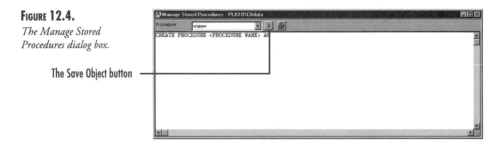

When you first open the Manage Stored Procedures dialog box, the text CREATE PROCEDURE <PROCEDURE NAME> AS appears automatically. This text should be familiar from the preceding section; it's the CREATE PROCEDURE statement. Replace the expression <PROCEDURE NAME> with a name of your choosing.

Below the keyword AS, you can enter the statements that make up your stored procedure. For example, suppose you have a table named Philosophers in your database, containing a list of philosophers. The following stored procedure will print Plato is a philosopher if Plato exists in the database and Plato is not a philosopher otherwise:

```
CREATE PROCEDURE check_philosophers AS
IF EXISTS(SELECT name FROM Philosophers WHERE name="Plato")
PRINT "Plato is a philosopher"
ELSE
PRINT "Plato is not a philosopher"
```

When you've finished entering your stored procedure, you can click the Save Object button to save it (it looks like a green triangle).

To view the text of a procedure after you first save it, you need to select the procedure again from the Procedure drop-down list box. SQL Server will automatically insert additional statements into your text. For example, after saving the check_philosophers procedure, the following text will appear:

```
if exists (select * from sysobjects
   where id = object_id('dbo.check_philosophers') and sysstat & 0xf = 4)
drop procedure dbo.check_philosophers
GO
CREATE PROCEDURE check_philosophers AS
IF EXISTS(SELECT name FROM Philosophers WHERE name="Plato")
PRINT "Plato is a philosopher"
ELSE
PRINT "Plato is not a philosopher"
GO
```

Why does SQL Server insert these additional statements? What do they do? The additional statements aren't included in the stored procedure itself; they are added to make the process of modifying `BCtored procedure easier.

When the first statement in the procedure is executed, it checks whether the stored procedure check_philosophers already exists in the database. If it does exist, the statement will drop it. If you were to modify your stored procedure and click the Save Object button, this statement would ensure that your procedure is first dropped before it's created once again with the modifications.

CAUTION

When modifying your stored procedures, be careful not to remove these additional statements. If you remove the first statement, for example, you won't be able to save your stored procedure. Instead, you'll get an error reporting that your stored procedure already exists in the database. (If you ever find yourself in this situation, just drop the previous version by using the DROP PROCEDURE statement.)

The primary advantage of using the SQL Enterprise Manager over ISQL/w to create your procedures is that you can use the Enterprise Manager to easily change your stored procedures in the future. After a procedure is saved, you can use the Manage Stored Procedures dialog box to both select and modify it. Modifying a stored procedure after it's created is very difficult to do with ISQL/w.

Passing Values to a Stored Procedure

When you call a stored procedure, you can pass values to it by using parameters, making your stored procedures flexible. For example, suppose you want to modify the check_philosophers procedure to check whether a particular philosopher exists. You could create the modification like this:

```
CREATE PROCEDURE check_philosophers
(@philosopher VARCHAR(30))
AS
IF EXISTS(SELECT name FROM Philosophers WHERE name=@philosopher)
PRINT "A philosopher"
ELSE
PRINT "Not a philosopher"
```

When this procedure is executed, it checks whether or not the name passed to the variable @philosopher is contained in the Philosophers table. If the value of @philosopher is included in the table, the text A philosopher is printed. Otherwise, the text Not a philosopher is printed.

When you include parameters in a stored procedure, you list them in parentheses after the CREATE PROCEDURE statement, but before the AS keyword. For each parameter, you need to specify the datatype. You can include as many as 255 parameters in a single procedure. For example, the following procedure checks whether at least one of the names passed is the name of a philosopher:

```
CREATE PROCEDURE check_philosophers
(@firstname VARCHAR(30),@secondname VARCHAR(30))
AS
IF EXISTS(SELECT name FROM Philosophers
  WHERE name=@firstname OR name=@secondname)
PRINT "At least one of them is a philosopher"
ELSE
PRINT "Neither one of them is a philosopher"
```

To execute a procedure that has one or more parameters, you can simply list the values of the parameter after the procedure name. For example, the following statement checks whether either Plato or Aristotle is a philosopher:

```
EXECUTE check_philosophers "Plato", "Aristotle"
```

If a procedure has multiple parameters, you need to pass the values in the correct order. Sometimes this is inconvenient. Instead, you can pass the parameters by name, like this:

```
EXECUTE check_philosophers @firstname="Plato", @secondname="Aristotle"
```

This statement accomplishes exactly the same thing as the previous one. However, by using parameter names, you can pass the parameter values in any order you choose.

Passing Values from a Stored Procedure

You can retrieve values from a stored procedure. These values can be accessed directly in your Active Server Pages (see Chapter 24, "Working with Commands"). You can also access these values in another stored procedure. If one stored procedure calls a second, the first procedure can retrieve the values of the parameters set by the second procedure.

For example, the following stored procedure outputs the value of the variable @conclusion:

```
CREATE PROCEDURE check_philosophers
(@philosopher VARCHAR(30),@conclusion VARCHAR(30) OUTPUT)
AS
IF EXISTS(SELECT name FROM Philosophers WHERE name=@philosopher)
SELECT @conclusion="A philosopher"
ELSE
SELECT @conclusion="Not a philosopher"
```

Notice the use of the keyword OUTPUT in this example. The keyword follows the declaration of the parameter @conclusion. This indicates that the parameter will be used to output information from the procedure. In this specific example, the value of the parameter will be either A philosopher or Not a philosopher, depending on the value of the @philosopher variable.

To execute a procedure with an output parameter, you need to use the keyword OUTPUT with the EXECUTE statement. If you're executing the procedure within a batch or another stored procedure, you must also declare a variable to store the value passed out of the procedure, as in this example:

```
DECLARE @proc_results VARCHAR(30)
EXECUTE check_philosophers "Plato", @proc_results OUTPUT
PRINT @proc_results
```

The first statement in this example declares a variable that will be used to store the parameter passed out of the procedure check_philosophers. This variable should be of the same datatype as the output parameter. The second statement executes the stored procedure. Notice that the @proc_results variable must be followed by the keyword OUTPUT. Finally, the variable @proc_results is printed to the screen.

You can also retrieve the value of an output parameter by name. Here's an example:

```
DECLARE @proc_results VARCHAR(30)
EXECUTE check_philosophers @philosopher="Plato",
➥@conclusion=@proc_results OUTPUT
PRINT @proc_results
```

Notice that the name of the parameter is always listed first in the EXECUTE statement. You use @conclusion=@proc_results to retrieve the value of the @conclusion parameter, rather than @proc_results=@conclusion, as you might expect.

Using RETURN with Stored Procedures

You've already been introduced to the RETURN statement. You can use this statement in procedures in the same way as you use it with batches. The RETURN statement causes the procedure to be exited immediately. Check out this example:

```
CREATE PROCEDURE check_tables
(@who VARCHAR(30))
AS
IF EXISTS(SELECT name FROM Philosophers WHERE name=@who)
BEGIN
  PRINT "In the Philosophers Table"
  RETURN
END
IF EXISTS(SELECT author_name FROM Authors WHERE author_name=@who)
BEGIN
  PRINT "In the Authors Table"
  RETURN
END
PRINT "Not in any tables!"
RETURN
```

This procedure checks two tables to determine whether a person is a philosopher or an author. If the name supplied is not the name of either a philosopher or author, the text Not in any tables! is printed. The RETURN statement causes the procedure to exit as soon as a match is made.

For example, suppose you execute this procedure with the parameter "Plato". First, the table Philosophers is checked for the existence of "Plato". Because this name is contained in the table, the procedure prints In the Philosophers Table. The procedure then exits when the RETURN statement is reached.

> **NOTE**
>
> You can end any procedure with the RETURN statement. This doesn't actually accomplish anything, however, because the procedure exits in any case.

When you use the RETURN statement with procedures but not with batches, you can return a single integer value. This integer value represents a status code. Here is the preceding procedure, rewritten to return particular integer values:

```
CREATE PROCEDURE check_tables
(@who VARCHAR(30))
AS
IF EXISTS(SELECT name FROM Philosophers WHERE name=@who)
BEGIN
  RETURN(1)
END
IF EXISTS(SELECT author_name FROM Authors WHERE author_name=@who)
BEGIN
  RETURN(2)
END
RETURN(3)
```

This procedure accomplishes the same purpose as the preceding one. However, when a name is found in a table, a message isn't printed. Instead, the procedure uses the RETURN statement to indicate the table where the name is found. For example, if you execute the procedure with the parameter "James Joyce", the procedure would return the value 2 because James Joyce is in the Authors table but not the Philosophers table. You could use this status value in either your Active Server Page or another procedure to determine the table where a name is located.

When using status values, you should always use values greater than 1 or less than -99. SQL Server uses the value 0 to report the successful completion of a stored procedure. It also uses values less than 0 but greater than -100 to report errors. (See Table 12.1 for a complete list of the status values used by SQL Server.)

Table 12.1. Procedure status values (from Transact-SQL Help).

Value	Meaning
0	Procedure was executed successfully.
-1	Object is missing.
-2	Datatype error occurred.
-3	Process was chosen as deadlock victim.
-4	Permission error occurred.
-5	Syntax error occurred.
-6	Miscellaneous user error occurred.
-7	Resource error, such as out of space, occurred.
-8	Nonfatal internal problem was encountered.
-9	System limit was reached.
-10	Fatal internal inconsistency occurred.
-11	Fatal internal inconsistency occurred.
-12	Table or index is corrupt.
-13	Database is corrupt.
-14	Hardware error occurred.

Values between -15 and -99, inclusive, are reserved for future use.

> **CAUTION**
>
> When you use the RETURN statement to return a status value, be careful never to return a NULL value. This will result in an error.

To access the status value returned by the procedure in the preceding example, you can use the following statements:

```
DECLARE @conclusion INT
EXECUTE @conclusion=check_tables "James Joyce"
SELECT @conclusion
```

The variable @conclusion is used to hold the status value. It must be declared as an INT datatype. When you execute the stored procedure check_tables, the status value returned is assigned to this variable by using the following statement:

```
EXECUTE @conclusion=check_tables "James Joyce"
```

Using Triggers

A *trigger* is a collection of SQL statements executed when the data in a table is modified. You can create triggers that fire when the data in a table is inserted, updated, or deleted. In this section, you learn how to create and use triggers.

Creating Triggers with CREATE TRIGGER

To create a trigger, you use the statement CREATE TRIGGER. Unlike a stored procedure, every trigger must be associated with a particular table, and every trigger must be associated with one or more actions performed on a table. Here's an example of the CREATE TRIGGER statement:

```
CREATE TRIGGER tr_webusers_insert ON webusers FOR INSERT AS
EXECUTE master..xp_sendmail "administrator", "New user registered!"
```

This trigger is named tr_webusers_insert. You can name a trigger anything you want, but every trigger must have a unique name. It's a good idea to include both the table and action associated with the trigger as part of the trigger's name.

The ON clause of the CREATE TRIGGER statement specifies the table associated with the trigger. The trigger in this example is associated with the table webusers. It will be fired whenever the data in this table is modified.

The FOR clause specifies the action that will fire the trigger. In the example, the trigger will be fired whenever new data is inserted into the table. You can also create a trigger that fires whenever data is updated or deleted from a table. To do this, use the keyword UPDATE or DELETE.

Following the AS clause, you can list one or more SQL statements. In this example, the trigger includes a single statement. Whenever a new record is inserted into the table, the administrator is automatically sent the e-mail message New user registered!

Keep the following important points about triggers in mind:

■ Triggers are associated with particular tables. If the table is dropped, any triggers associated with the table will also be dropped. For example, if the webusers table is dropped, the tr_webusers_insert trigger will be dropped as well.

■ Each action on a table can have only one trigger associated with it. For example, you can't create a second trigger on the webusers table that's fired when the data in the table is updated.

■ At most, you can have three triggers on a single table: one INSERT trigger, one DELETE trigger, and one UPDATE trigger.

■ If you attempt to add a second trigger that's fired by the same action, the first trigger will be dropped without warning. This can be very irritating. Keep careful track of your triggers to prevent this from happening.

> **NOTE**
>
> To view a list of all of the triggers contained in the current database, you can use the system stored procedure sp_help. If you execute sp_help without any modifiers, the procedure will display all of the procedures, triggers, and tables in the current database. If sp_help is followed by a name of a specific trigger (for example, sp_help tr_webusers), sp_help will display information on only that trigger.

You can associate a trigger with more than one action on a single table. For example, you could modify the trigger in the preceding example to be fired whenever data in the table is inserted *or* updated. Here's how you'd do it:

```
CREATE TRIGGER tr_webusers ON webusers FOR INSERT, UPDATE AS
EXECUTE master..xp_sendmail "administrator", "User registered or modified!"
```

After you create a trigger, you can view the statements it includes by using the system stored procedure sp_helptext. This procedure displays the text of a trigger. The command **sp_helptext tr_webusers**, for example, would display the following results:

```
text
-----------------------------------------------------------------
CREATE TRIGGER tr_webusers ON webusers FOR INSERT, UPDATE AS
EXECUTE master..xp_sendmail "administrator",
"User registered or modified!"
```

A trigger is fired only when the action specified in its FOR clause takes place. You can never execute a trigger directly. If you attempt to execute the tr_webusers trigger, for example, you receive the following error:

```
The request for procedure 'tr_webusers' failed because 'tr_webusers'
is a trigger object
```

12

ADVANCED SQL

There are three ways to destroy a trigger. You can use the statement `DROP TRIGGER` followed by the trigger's name to explicitly drop a trigger. For example, the following statement drops the trigger `tr_webusers`:

```
DROP TRIGGER tr_webusers
```

A trigger is dropped automatically when the table associated with it is dropped. For example, if the table `webusers` is dropped, the trigger `tr_webusers` is also dropped.

Finally, a trigger is dropped automatically whenever a new trigger that performs the same action on the same table is created. For example, when the trigger `tr_webusers` is created, the trigger `tr_webusers_insert` is automatically dropped. This happens because both triggers are fired by an insert performed on the same table.

> **NOTE**
>
> If the trigger `tr_webusers` was created before the trigger `tr_webusers_insert`, the `tr_webusers` trigger would only be partially dropped. This is true because the `tr_webusers` trigger is fired by both inserts and updates. The `tr_webusers` trigger would continue to fire when there are updates. However, the trigger would no longer fire when data is inserted. The newer trigger `tr_webusers_insert` would take over that action.

Creating Triggers with the SQL Enterprise Manager

Creating a trigger with the SQL Enterprise Manager is easier than with ISQL/w. The primary advantage of using the SQL Enterprise Manager is that it preserves the text of a trigger so you can return and modify it at a later date. By using this program, you can also easily keep track of the triggers that you've created.

To create a trigger with the SQL Enterprise Manager, start the program and select the database where your tables are stored. Choose Manage | Triggers from the menu. The Manage Triggers dialog box should appear (see Figure 12.5).

At the top of the dialog box are two drop-down list boxes. From the Table list, you can select a table. Every trigger must be associated with one table and can only be associated with one table. The Triggers drop-down list box contains three icons next to the word <new>. The three icons represent INSERT, UPDATE, and DELETE. You can use this list box to choose between the triggers that are fired by these actions. The word <new> will be replaced with the name of your trigger after you save it.

In the text area of the dialog box, the following default text for your trigger is provided:

```
CREATE TRIGGER <TRIGGER NAME> ON dbo.webusers
FOR INSERT,UPDATE,DELETE
AS
```

INSERT   UPDATE   DELETE

FIGURE 12.5.
The Manage Triggers dialog box.

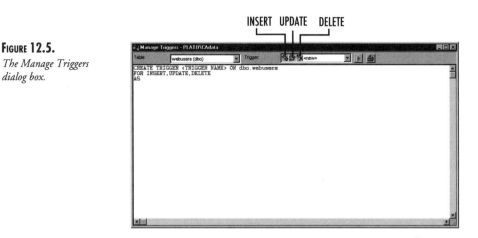

This statement should be familiar from the preceding section; it's the creation statement for a trigger. Replace the expression <TRIGGER NAME> with a name for your trigger.

This automatic creation statement creates a trigger that's fired for INSERT, UPDATE, and DELETE actions. To create separate triggers for these actions, or to create a trigger that fires for only a specific action, you need to change this default statement. Simply erase the actions that you don't want to use.

Below the keyword AS, you can enter the statements for your trigger. For example, the following trigger inserts an entry into a table named weblog whenever a new user is inserted into the webusers table:

```
CREATE TRIGGER tr_webusers_update ON dbo.webusers
FOR INSERT
AS
INSERT weblog (activity) VALUES ("New User Added")
```

You save a trigger in the Manage Triggers dialog box by clicking the Save Object button (the green triangle). When a trigger is first saved, the text of the trigger disappears from the screen. You need to select the trigger once again from the Trigger drop-down list box.

After a trigger is first saved, SQL Server automatically inserts additional statements among the statements for your trigger. For example, after the trigger tr_webusers_update is saved, the following text appears:

```
if exists (select * from sysobjects
➥where id = object_id('dbo.tr_webusers_update') and sysstat & 0xf = 8)
➥drop trigger dbo.tr_webusers_update
GO
CREATE TRIGGER tr_webusers_update ON dbo.webusers
FOR INSERT
AS
INSERT weblog (activity) VALUES ("New User Added")
GO
```

12

ADVANCED SQL

What do these additional statements do? Why does SQL Server modify your code in this way? These additional statements are inserted into your text so that your trigger will be dropped automatically before it's created. The first statement checks whether the trigger already exists. If the trigger does exist, the statement drops it.

You can use the SQL Enterprise Manager to create up to three triggers for each table. After you've saved a trigger, you can use the Manage Triggers dialog box to perform modifications on it in the future. This isn't easy to do outside of the SQL Enterprise Manager.

Using the Inserted and Deleted Tables

There are two special tables named Inserted and Deleted, which exist only while a trigger is running. You can use these two tables to determine the exact changes made by the action that fired a trigger. For example, by checking the Deleted table, you can determine exactly which records were deleted by an action. Consider the following example:

```
CREATE TRIGGER tr_webusers_delete ON webusers
FOR DELETE
AS
INSERT weblog (activity) SELECT user_name FROM Deleted
```

This trigger automatically creates an archive of the webusers table. Whenever a user name is deleted from the webusers table, the trigger automatically inserts that name into the weblog table. Suppose you accidentally execute the following statement:

```
DELETE webusers
```

This statement deletes every record in the webusers table. Normally, these records would be lost forever. However, the preceding trigger is automatically fired when records from the webusers table are deleted. The trigger examines the table Deleted to determine the particular records that have been deleted, and copies all the deleted records into the weblog table.

To recover the accidentally deleted records, you can use the INSERT and SELECT statements to copy them from the weblog table to the webusers table again. You should use this method of creating a backup of table data when you can't afford to lose even a single record accidentally.

The Deleted table has the same column structure as the table from which the records have been deleted. In the preceding example, the Deleted table has the same columns as the webusers table.

Now suppose you want to track all the records that are inserted into a particular table. For example, you want every record that's inserted into the webusers table to be copied to the weblog table. You can do this with the following trigger:

```
CREATE TRIGGER tr_webusers_insert ON webusers
FOR INSERT
AS
INSERT weblog (activity) SELECT user_name FROM Inserted
```

This trigger is the same as the previous one, except for two changes:

- This trigger is fired whenever a record is *inserted into* the webusers table; the trigger is created FOR INSERT.
- The trigger *copies* records from the Inserted table to the weblog table.

The Inserted table contains all the new records that have been inserted into a table. If the name of a new user is inserted into the webusers table, the trigger will automatically copy that new name from the Inserted table to the weblog table.

This method of duplicating data is useful when you want a single table to record the activity that takes place in other crucial tables in your database. You can use this table to gain an overview of the activity in your database and to track and diagnose problems that may occur.

You can also use the Inserted and Deleted tables to track changes made to a trigger's table by an UPDATE. When a table with a trigger is updated, the Deleted table contains the values of all the columns before they're updated, and the Inserted table contains the values of all the columns after they're updated. Look at Table 12.2 to see how each action affects the Inserted and Deleted tables.

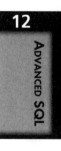

Table 12.2. Contents of the Inserted and Deleted tables.

Table	INSERT	DELETE	UPDATE
Inserted	Inserted rows	Empty	Rows before update
Deleted	Empty	Deleted	Rows after update

It's important to understand that the Inserted and Deleted tables exist only while a trigger is executing. They exist relative to a particular trigger at a particular time. Once a trigger finishes executing, the data in both tables is lost. If you want to create a permanent copy of the data in either of these tables, you need to copy the data into a permanent table within the trigger.

Combining Triggers and Transactions

Triggers and transactions are a powerful combination. You can use the statement ROLLBACK TRANSACTION to reverse the action that fires a trigger. Consider the following trigger:

```
CREATE TRIGGER tr_webusers ON webusers FOR INSERT,UPDATE,DELETE AS
If DATENAME(dw,GETDATE())="Tuesday"
ROLLBACK TRANSACTION
```

This trigger prevents anyone from entering new records into the webusers table on Tuesdays. If you attempt to insert a new record on a Tuesday, the action is rolled back by the ROLLBACK TRANSACTION statement.

Suppose you become obsessed with preventing a particular individual from using your Web site. You never want this person to be able to register. To prevent this from happening, you can place a trigger on the webusers table that checks for this person's name, like this:

```
CREATE TRIGGER tr_webusers ON webusers FOR INSERT,UPDATE AS
If EXISTS(SELECT user_name FROM Inserted WHERE user_name="Andrew Jones")
ROLLBACK TRANSACTION
```

This trigger prevents the name Andrew Jones from ever being inserted into the webusers table. Whenever the name Andrew Jones is included in an INSERT or UPDATE statement, the action is rolled back with the ROLLBACK TRANSACTION statement.

Using Scheduled Tasks

Many tasks need to be performed at timed intervals. For example, you may want to receive summary information on the data in a table by e-mail, on an hourly basis. Or you may want to prune a table of old data on a particular day every week. To execute procedures at particular intervals of time, you use *scheduled tasks*.

This section provides a step-by-step guide to creating and scheduling a particular task. You learn how to create a task that automatically e-mails summary information on the data contained in the log of your Web server.

> **NOTE**
>
> To use the scheduled task described in this section, you need a functioning mail server such as Microsoft Exchange Server (see Chapter 4, "Exchange Active Server, Index Server, and NetShow"). You also need to configure Internet Information Server (IIS) to store its log in SQL Server rather than a text file. To do this, choose ODBC logging as the active log format with the Internet Service Manager (see the Internet Service Manager online help for more information on how to configure ODBC logging).

The first step in creating a scheduled task is to create the stored procedure you want to schedule. The stored procedure in this example retrieves the number of distinct IP addresses that occur in your server log. This number provides a rough estimate of the number of visitors your Web site has received.

The stored procedure also retrieves the number of times the home page of your Web site has been requested. The home page of your Web site is assumed to be the file default.html, located in your Web's root directory. If your home page is another file, substitute the name of the correct file in the following procedure.

This procedure also assumes that the table where the log of your Web server is stored is named weblog. If you configured IIS to log to a table with a different name, substitute the name of the correct table in the procedure.

Finally, your e-mail account name is assumed to be configured to be Administrator. You can replace this name with any valid e-mail address (for example, someone@somewhere.com). You can even have the e-mail sent to a pager if your paging service accepts e-mail.

Here's the stored procedure:

```
CREATE PROCEDURE get_stats AS
DECLARE @IPCount INT, @HomePageCount INT,
➥@LogSum VARCHAR(100),@Subj VARCHAR(100)

SELECT @IPCount=COUNT(DISTINCT ClientHost)
➥FROM weblog WHERE DATEDIFF(hh,LogTime,GETDATE())<1

SELECT @HomePageCount=COUNT(target)
➥FROM weblog WHERE target='/default.html'
➥AND DATEDIFF(hh,LogTime,GETDATE())<1

SELECT @LogSum='Number of visitors:'+CONVERT(VARCHAR(4),@IPCount)

SELECT @LogSum=@LogSum+' --- Number of times home
➥page accessed: '+CONVERT(VARCHAR(4),@HomePageCount)

SELECT @Subj='Hourly Site Stats '+CONVERT(VARCHAR(20),GETDATE())

EXECUTE master..xp_sendmail
@@recipients='administrator',
@@subject=@Subj,
@@message=@LogSum
RETURN
```

All the statements in this procedure should be familiar. The first two SELECT statements use aggregate functions to retrieve a count of the number of distinct IP addresses and the number of times the home page was requested. The information retrieved covers a single hour. The next two SELECT statements format the values retrieved in readable form. Finally, the xp_sendmail system stored procedure e-mails the results of the queries.

You should create this stored procedure in the normal way by using either ISQL/w or the Manage Stored Procedures dialog box in the SQL Enterprise Manager. Before continuing, test the procedure by executing it in ISQL/w. If everything on your database, mail, and Internet server is configured correctly, you should receive an e-mail.

The stored procedure retrieves statistics on your Web server's log for the previous hour. If you schedule the procedure to execute every hour automatically, you can constantly keep track of the activity on your Web site.

To schedule the stored procedure, start the SQL Enterprise Manager. Select your database and choose Server | Scheduled Tasks from the menu. The Manage Scheduled Tasks dialog box should appear (see Figure 12.6).

FIGURE 12.6.
The Manage Scheduled Tasks dialog box.

New Task button ——

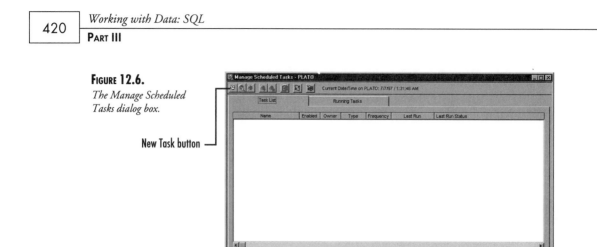

Click the New Task button (it looks like a clock with a shiny new gleam). The New Task dialog box should appear (see Figure 12.7).

FIGURE 12.7.
The New Task dialog box.

Follow these steps to complete the information in the New Task dialog box:

1. In the Name text box, provide a name for your scheduled task. For example, you can name this scheduled task **send_stats**.

2. In the Type drop-down list box, select TSQL. This indicates that you will be using a T-SQL statement.

3. In the Database drop-down list box, select the name of the database where your scheduled task is stored.

4. In the Command text box, enter the statement **EXECUTE get_stats** to execute the procedure that you just created.

5. In the Schedule section of the dialog box, select the Recurring option. This will cause your procedure to be executed on scheduled time intervals.

After you've entered all the specified information, click the Change button. This will allow you to change the schedule for your task. When you click Change, the Task Schedule dialog box should appear (see Figure 12.8).

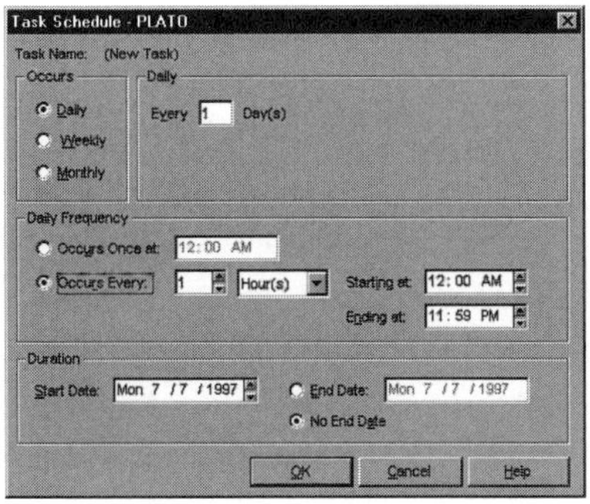

FIGURE 12.8.

The Task Schedule dialog box.

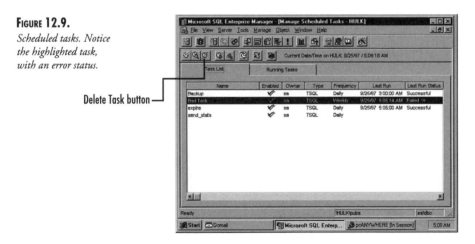

In the Task Schedule dialog box, schedule your task to execute every hour. In the Occurs section, select the Daily option. In the Daily Frequency section, select Occurs Every and specify 1 Hour(s). Click OK to close the Task Schedule dialog box.

Finally, in the Manage Scheduled Tasks dialog box, click the Add button to add your scheduled task. The name of your scheduled task should appear on the Task List page of the dialog box. You can return here at any time in the future to check on the status of the scheduled task, view the last time the scheduled task was run, or check to see whether the task encountered any errors (see Figure 12.9).

FIGURE 12.9.

Scheduled tasks. Notice the highlighted task, with an error status.

Delete Task button ─

The Manage Scheduled Tasks dialog box can also be used to delete a task after you have added it. To delete a task, click the Delete Task button (it depicts a clock with a red diagonal stripe).

You can also use the Manage Scheduled Tasks dialog box to view a history of your scheduled task. The history of a scheduled task provides detailed information on the past activity of your scheduled task. Click the Task History button to view this information.

Summary

This chapter explored some very powerful features of Microsoft SQL Server. You learned how to use the SQL Server Web Assistant to generate Web pages automatically from a database table. You also learned how to create stored procedures, triggers, and scheduled tasks.

At this point in the book, you have learned how to use markup, scripting, and query languages to create HTML pages, server-side scripts, and database queries. In the next part of this book, you put this knowledge to good use by learning how to integrate these languages into Active Server Pages. This will allow you to create very advanced Web sites.

IV
PART

Creating Active Server Pages with Objects and Components

Building Active
Server Pages

CHAPTER 13

IN THIS CHAPTER

This chapter formally introduces you to Active Server Pages, the subject of this book. You learn what Active Server Pages are, what you can do with them, and how they work. The chapter provides a thorough explanation of how to integrate Active Server Pages scripts into an HTML page, and includes an overview of the objects and components of Active Server Pages. Finally, you learn how to configure your Web server to use Active Server Pages and troubleshoot any problems that might arise.

What Are Active Server Pages?

An Active Server Page is a standard HTML file that has been extended with additional features. Like a standard HTML file, an Active Server Page can contain HTML tags that will be interpreted and displayed by a Web browser. Anything you could normally place in an HTML file—Java applets, blinking text, client-side scripts, client-side ActiveX controls—you can place in an Active Server Page. However, an Active Server Page has four important features that make it unique:

- An Active Server Page can contain server-side scripts. In the second part of this book, you learned how to create Active Server Pages scripts with VBScript and JScript. By including server-side scripts in an Active Server Page, you can create Web pages with dynamic content. To take an extremely simple example, you could create a Web page that displays different messages at different times of the day.

- An Active Server Page provides a number of built-in objects. By using the built-in objects accessible in an Active Server Page, you can make your scripts much more powerful. Among other things, these objects allow you to both retrieve information from and send information to browsers. For example, by using the Request object, you can retrieve the information that a user has posted in an HTML form and respond to that information within a script.

- An Active Server Page can be extended with additional components. Active Server Pages comes bundled with a number of standard server-side ActiveX components. These components allow you to do such things as determine the capabilities of different Web browsers or include a page counter on a Web page.

  These standard ActiveX components are very useful. However, you're not limited to only these components. You can create additional ActiveX components of your own. This means that there's no limit to how you can extend Active Server Pages. (See Chapter 28, "Extending Active Server Pages," to learn how to do this.)

- An Active Server Page can interact with a database such as Microsoft SQL Server. In the third part of this book, you learned how to use the SQL language with Microsoft SQL Server. By using a special collection of objects, the ActiveX Data Objects (ADO), you can use SQL within your Active Server Pages.

  Again, this is a very powerful feature of Active Server Pages. By creating Active Server Pages that can interact with a database, you can create very advanced Web sites. For example, in the final part of this book, you learn how to use the ActiveX Data Objects to create an online career Web site.

These four features define an Active Server Page. An Active Server Page is a standard HTML page that has been extended with server-side scripts, objects, and components. By using Active Server Pages, you can create Web sites with dynamic content.

The discussion of Active Server Pages in this book assumes that you'll be using Active Server Pages with Microsoft's Internet Information Server. However, you can use Active Server Pages with many other Web servers as well. Active Server Pages can be used with Microsoft's Personal Web Server for Windows 95 and the Peer Web Server for Windows NT.

You aren't even limited to using Active Server Pages with Microsoft Web servers. By using Chili!Soft's Chili!ASP, you can use Active Server Pages with the Netscape Enterprise and FastTrack servers, the Lotus Domino and Go servers, O'Reilly's WebSite, and many other Web servers (for more information, visit the Chili!Soft Web site at www.chilisoft.net).

What Can You Do with Active Server Pages?

There's no limit to what you can accomplish with Active Server Pages. Just about any Web site that exists on the Internet today could have been created with Active Server Pages. The following list shows some simple examples of what you can do:

13
BUILDING ACTIVE
SERVER PAGES

- Include rotating banner advertisements on the Web pages of your Web site.
- Retrieve information entered into an HTML form and store that information in a database.
- Create personalized Web pages that display different content to different users.
- Add hit counters to one or more pages of your Web site.
- Display different Web pages, depending on the capability of a user's browser.
- Link together multiple Web pages in such a way that they can be navigated easily.
- Track information about user activity at your Web site and save that information in a custom log file.

Again, these are very simple examples. As you read through the following chapters, you'll gain a fuller appreciation of what you can accomplish with Active Server Pages. Whatever your Web project may be, you'll learn how to complete it using Active Server Pages.

How Do Active Server Pages Work?

The best way to understand how Active Server Pages work is by contrasting a Web server that supports Active Server Pages with a Web server that doesn't. Microsoft introduced Active Server Pages with the third release of Internet Information Server (IIS). The introduction of Active Server Pages transformed IIS from being a mere server of static content to being a server of dynamic content. What does this mean?

Prior to the introduction of Active Server Pages, the main function of IIS was to serve static HTML pages. When someone requested a Web page from a Web site using IIS, the server would fetch a static HTML file from disk or memory and send it out to the person's browser. The primary responsibility of IIS was to act as an efficient interface between browsers and a bunch of files sitting on the Web server's hard drive.

> **NOTE**
>
> Earlier versions of IIS included something called the *Internet Database Connector* (*IDC*). The IDC could be used to retrieve and store data in a database. You can still use the IDC for this purpose, but Active Server Pages does this much better.

IIS was no different from other Web servers in this respect. The main function of any Web server is to serve HTML files. It's important to understand how this process of serving an HTML file is carried out, so here are the steps:

1. A user enters the Internet address of an HTML file into the address bar of a Web browser and presses Enter to request a Web page (for example, `http://www.aspsite.com/hello.htm`).

2. The browser sends a request for the Web page to a Web server such as IIS.

3. The Web server receives the request and recognizes that the request is for an HTML file because the requested file has the extension `.htm` or `.html`.

4. The Web server retrieves the proper HTML file from disk or memory and sends the file back to the browser.

5. The HTML file is interpreted by the person's Web browser and the results are displayed in the browser window.

Of course, this process is often more complicated (for example, the contents of forms are posted and query strings are passed). But, in broad strokes, these steps outline the moment-to-moment activity of a typical Web server. A server receives requests for particular files and responds by sending the correct file, by retrieving it from the hard drive or memory.

Active Server Pages changed all of this. While IIS can still be used to serve static HTML pages, Active Server Pages allows IIS to serve dynamic content as well. Using Active Server Pages, pages with new content can be created in response to user requests. The Web server itself becomes active in the process of creating the Web page.

It's important to understand how this process of serving an Active Server Page contrasts with the normal process of serving an HTML page, so we'll break it into steps:

1. A user enters the Internet address of an Active Server Page file into the address bar of a Web browser and presses Enter to request an Active Server Page (for example, `http://www.aspsite.com/hello.asp`).

2. The browser sends a request for the Active Server Page to IIS.

3. The Web server receives the request and recognizes that the request is for an Active Server Page file because the requested file has the extension `.asp`.

4. The Web server retrieves the proper Active Server Page file from disk or memory.

5. The Web server sends the file to a special program named `ASP.dll`.

6. The Active Server Page file is processed from top to bottom and any encountered commands are executed. The result of this process is a standard HTML file.

7. The HTML file is sent back to the browser.

8. The HTML file is interpreted by the person's Web browser and the results are displayed in the browser window.

> **NOTE**
>
> For clarity's sake, the steps presented here have been slightly simplified. An Active Server Page doesn't need to be recompiled every time it's requested. If an Active Server Page has previously been requested and hasn't been altered, the Active Server Page will be retrieved from the cache instead of being processed again.

From the perspective of the Web server, an Active Server Page is very different from a normal HTML page. A normal HTML file is sent without processing to the browser. All the commands in an Active Server Page, on the other hand, must first be executed to create an HTML page. This allows an Active Server Page to contain dynamic content.

From the perspective of the browser, on the other hand, an Active Server Page is almost exactly the same as a normal HTML page. The only difference is that an Active Server Page typically must end with the extension `.asp` rather than `.htm` or `.html`. When a request is made for an Active Server Page, the browser receives a normal HTML page. This allows an Active Server Page to be compatible with all browsers.

Integrating Scripts into Active Server Pages

An Active Server Page is primarily a scripting environment. As you learned in the second part of this book, you can integrate scripts created with both JScript and VBScript into your Active Server Pages. You can use other scripting languages with Active Server Pages as well. Any scripting language that has a scripting engine compatible with the ActiveX scripting standard can be used in an Active Server Page.

13

BUILDING ACTIVE
SERVER PAGES

> **NOTE**
>
> If you're familiar with Perl, you'll be happy to know that an implementation of Perl is compatible with Active Server Pages. For more information, see http://www.hip. activeware.com or visit the companion Web site to this book at http://www.aspsite.com.

In the chapters on VBScript and JScript (Chapters 8 and 9, respectively), you learned the basics of how to integrate scripts into an Active Server Page. This section presents a more detailed explanation and some alternative ways to integrate scripts into an Active Server Page.

The easiest way to add a script to an Active Server Page is by using the script delimiters <% and %>. Any text enclosed within these delimiters will be processed as a script. Here's an example:

```
<HTML>
<HEAD><TITLE>ASP Script</TITLE></HEAD>
<BODY>
This is a
<% FOR i=1 TO 10 %>
very,
<% NEXT %>
very long sentence.
</BODY>
</HTML>
```

When this Active Server Page is displayed by a Web browser, the following sentence is displayed:

```
This is a very, very, very, very, very, very, very, very, very, very,
very long sentence.
```

The script creates 11 copies of the word very by using a VBScript FOR...NEXT loop.

By default, an Active Server Page assumes you'll be using VBScript as your primary scripting language. This means that you don't need to do anything beyond using the <% and %> script delimiters to use this language. However, there are three ways to explicitly specify a language to use in an Active Server Page.

First, you can use the Internet Service Manager to specify a particular scripting language as the default language for all your Active Server Pages. To do this, perform the following steps:

1. Launch the Internet Service Manager from the Microsoft Internet Information Server program group on the Start menu.
2. Right-click the name of your Web site. If you haven't changed the default configuration, the name of this Web site will be Default Web Site.
3. Choose Properties.
4. Click the Home Directory tab.
5. Click the Configuration button. (To do this, you must have an existing application. If you don't, create one now by clicking Create.)

6. In the Application Configuration dialog box, click the App Options tab.

7. In the Default ASP Language text box, enter the name of the scripting language that you want to use as your primary scripting language; for example, enter **vbscript** or **jscript** (see Figure 13.1).

FIGURE 13.1.

Using the Internet Service Manager to specify a default scripting language.

After you have specified a particular scripting language as the default scripting language, you can use it in your Active Server Pages simply by using the delimiters <% and %>. If you plan to use JScript for the majority of your Active Server Pages, for example, you should configure this language as your default language.

You can also specify the primary scripting language for a particular page. To do this, place the LANGUAGE directive as the very first line in your Active Server Page file, like this:

```
<%@ LANGUAGE=JScript %>
<HTML>
<HEAD><TITLE>ASP Script</TITLE></HEAD>
<BODY>
This is a
<% for(i=1;i<11;i++){ %>
very,
<% } %>
very long sentence.
</BODY>
</HTML>
```

The directive in the first line of this script indicates that all the scripts contained in the file should be executed as scripts created with JScript rather than some other scripting language. When you use this directive, be sure to include a space between the @ character and the keyword LANGUAGE. Furthermore, it's very important that this directive appear before any other commands in your Active Server Page file (otherwise you'll get an error).

Yet a third alternative exists for including scripts in your Active Server Pages. You can use Microsoft's extended <SCRIPT> HTML tag, as in this example (continued on the next page):

```
<HTML>
<HEAD><TITLE>ASP Script</TITLE></HEAD>
```

13

BUILDING ACTIVE
SERVER PAGES

```
<BODY>
<SCRIPT LANGUAGE="JScript" RUNAT="server">
function sayhello()
{
response.write("Hello!")
}
</SCRIPT>
<%
sayhello()
%>
</BODY>
</HTML>
```

Here, the <SCRIPT> tags contain a JScript function. The LANGUAGE attribute of the <SCRIPT> tag specifies which scripting language to use. The RUNAT attribute indicates that the script should be executed on the server rather than the client (the browser).

The function named sayhello() is defined in the first script. The second script, marked with the usual <% and %> tags, is where the JScript function is actually called. This Active Server Page prints the text Hello! to the screen.

> **NOTE**
>
> The response.write() statement in the preceding script outputs text to the screen. You learn more about this method later in this section.

If you have created client-side JScript or VBScript scripts, you should be familiar with the <SCRIPT> tag. Microsoft's extended <SCRIPT> tag can be used to specify either client-side or server-side scripts. If you neglected to include the RUNAT="server" attribute in the preceding example, the script would be treated as a client-side script. In this case, the server would ignore the script and the browser would attempt to execute the script (and it would fail miserably, because the script isn't a valid client-side script).

Why would you ever want to use the <SCRIPT> tag rather than the <% and %> script delimiters? Normally, you wouldn't use the <SCRIPT> tag. However, there are two significant differences between these two ways of specifying a script.

First, scripts that are contained in the <SCRIPT> tag are executed immediately, no matter where they appear in an Active Server Page. For example, consider the following page:

```
<HTML>
<HEAD><TITLE>ASP Script</TITLE></HEAD>
<BODY>
This is the first sentence.
<SCRIPT LANGUAGE="JScript" RUNAT="server">
response.write("This is the second sentence.")
</SCRIPT>
</BODY>
</HTML>
```

From looking at the script, you might be tempted to believe that the sentence `"This is the first sentence."` and the sentence `"This is the second sentence."` are printed to the screen in that order. However, when the Active Server Page is displayed in a browser, the order of the two sentences is actually reversed (or worse, nothing is displayed, because an invalid HTML page is generated).

Why does this happen? Whatever is contained in the `<SCRIPT>` tag is executed before anything else in a page. If you use the `VIEW SOURCE` command on your Web browser, you'll see the following results from the preceding Active Server Page:

```
This is the second sentence.<HTML>
<HEAD><TITLE>ASP Script</TITLE></HEAD>
<BODY>
This is the first sentence.
</BODY>
</HTML>
```

This behavior of the `<SCRIPT>` tag has two implications. First, you can place scripts contained in a `<SCRIPT>` tag anywhere you want in an Active Server Page. Second, the `<SCRIPT>` tag, for most purposes, is restricted to containing functions or procedures. The output of any script that's not contained in a function or procedure is displayed immediately and results in an invalid HTML page.

The `<SCRIPT>` tag has one main advantage over the `<%` and `%>` script delimiters. Using the `<SCRIPT>` tag, you can mix multiple scripting languages within a single Active Server Page. Consider the following example:

```
<%@ LANGUAGE="VBScript" %>
<HTML>
<HEAD><TITLE>ASP Script</TITLE></HEAD>
<BODY>
<SCRIPT LANGUAGE="JScript" RUNAT="server">
function sayhello()
{
response.write("Hello!")
}
</SCRIPT>
<%
FOR i=1 to 10
sayhello()
NEXT
%>
</BODY>
</HTML>
```

This script prints `Hello!` 10 times in a row. But notice how it does this. The script contained in the `<%` and `%>` delimiters is a Visual Basic script. However, this script calls a JScript function. The JScript function is defined within the `<SCRIPT>` tag. When you want to use one scripting language as your primary scripting language, but need to call a function from another language, you can use this method. This is useful when one language has particular functions or methods that another language lacks.

To summarize, there are three methods of including a script in an Active Server Page:

- Specify a scripting language for all of your Active Server Pages by using the Internet Service Manager to specify a default language.
- Specify a scripting language for a single page by using the Active Server Page directive `<%@ LANGUAGE="scripting language" %>`.
- Mix multiple scripting languages in a single Active Server Page by using the extended `<SCRIPT>` tag.

Before ending this section, one final Active Server Pages directive should be discussed. By using the Active Server Pages output directive, you can display the value of an expression. Here's an example:

```
<HTML>
<HEAD><TITLE>ASP Example</TITLE></HEAD>
<BODY>
At the tone, the time will be: <%=TIME%>
</BODY>
</HTML>
```

You use the delimiters `<%=` and `%>` to print the value of a variable, method, or function. In the preceding example, the output directive is used to output the value of the VBScript TIME function.

There's another way to accomplish the same thing. Consider the following example:

```
<HTML>
<HEAD><TITLE>ASP Example</TITLE></HEAD>
<BODY>
At the tone, the time will be: <% Response.Write(TIME) %>
</BODY>
</HTML>
```

In this example, the value of the VBScript TIME function is outputted by using the Active Server Pages Response object. The Write() method of the Response object outputs the value of expressions to the screen. (In the next section, you learn more about using objects.)

When should you use the Response.Write() method rather than the `<%=` and `%>` output directive? It really doesn't matter. Active Server Pages internally represents the output directive as a Response.Write() method call in any case. The two methods of outputting the values of expressions are completely interchangeable.

> **NOTE**
>
> When you receive an error using the `<%=` and `%>` output directive, the error will refer to a line of code that uses the Response.Write() method. This can be confusing because this line of code actually doesn't exist in your Active Server Page. However, it illustrates that Active Server Pages represents the two methods of outputting the values of expressions in the same way.

Nevertheless, there are situations where one way of outputting the values of expressions is more convenient than the other. For example, when you need to output the value of an expression within a script, the `Response.Write()` method is often easier to use. On the other hand, when you want to output the value of an expression within a section of HTML code, the `<%=` and `%>` directive is often easier to use. The following page illustrates both approaches:

```
<HTML>
<HEAD><TITLE>ASP Example</TITLE></HEAD>
<BODY>
<%
FOR i=1 TO 10
myvar=myvar&"very,"
Response.Write(i&":"&myvar&"<BR>")
NEXT
%>
<HR>
This is a <%=myvar%> long sentence.
</BODY>
</HTML>
```

In this example, the `Response.Write()` method is used within the loop to display the value of the variable named `myvar` as it increases in size. The `<%=` and `%>` output directive is embedded within normal HTML code. The output directive is used to display the value of `myvar` (see Figure 13.2).

13

BUILDING ACTIVE
SERVER PAGES

FIGURE 13.2.

Two methods of outputting expressions.

Integrating Objects and Components into Active Server Pages

Active Server Pages includes a number of built-in objects and installable ActiveX components. These objects and components can be used to extend the power of your Active Server Pages scripts. But what exactly are objects and components?

An *object* is something that typically has methods, properties, or collections. An object's *methods* determine the things you can do with the object. An object's *properties* can be read or set to specify the state of the object. An object's *collections* constitute different sets of key and value pairs related to the object.

To take an everyday example, the book *Tom Sawyer* is an example of an object. The object has certain methods that determine the things you can do with it. For example, you can read the book, use it as a doorstop, or even, if you're feeling particularly malicious, tear it into shreds. The object has certain properties. For example, it has a certain number of pages and a particular author. Finally, it has a collection of key and value pairs. Each page number (the key), has a corresponding page of text (the value).

An ActiveX *component* is very similar to an Active Server Page built-in object. However, when using Active Server Pages, there are two important differences between a component and an object. First, a component may contain more than one object. Second, an instance of a component must be explicitly created before it can be used.

Both the VBScript and JScript languages include a small number of objects. For example, using either VBScript or JScript, you can access and manipulate the Dictionary object. The Dictionary object is not officially part of Active Server Pages, but you can access it within your Active Server Pages scripts. Here's an example using VBScript:

```
<%
Set MyDict=Server.CreateObject("Scripting.Dictionary")
MyDict.add "CA", "California"
MyDict.add "MA", "Massachusetts"
MyDict.add "MI", "Missouri"
%>
My dictionary has <%=MyDict.Count %> entries.
<BR>
The first entry in my dictionary is <%=MyDict.item("CA")%>.
```

When this script is executed, an instance of the Dictionary object is created. Next, three key and value pairs are added to the dictionary. Finally, two properties of the dictionary are displayed (see Figure 13.3).

The first statement in this example illustrates the general method of creating a new instance of an ActiveX object by using Active Server Pages. The method Server.CreateObject creates an instance of an object. In this example, the variable named MyDict is assigned to an instance of the Dictionary object.

FIGURE 13.3.

An example of the Dictionary *object.*

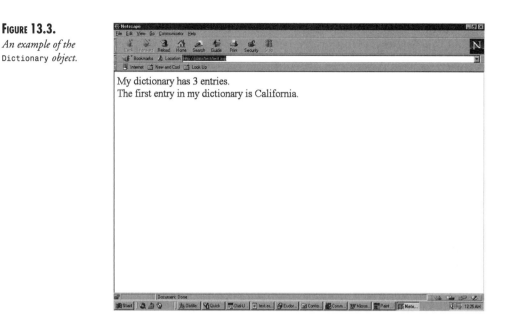

Once an instance of an object has been created, its methods can be called. In this example, the Add method of the Dictionary object is called to add entries to the dictionary. The first Add method call is used to add the key and value pair "CA" and "California".

After an instance of an object has been created, you can also access its properties. In this example, the Count property of the Dictionary object is read to determine the number of entries in the dictionary. The Item property is also read to return the value of a particular key.

Finally, when you're done using an instance of an object, you can destroy it. An object created by the preceding method will automatically be destroyed after the server finishes processing the Active Server Page. Therefore, there's usually no reason to explicitly destroy an object. However, you can destroy the MyDict object explicitly by assigning MyDict to a new value or by setting the variable to the value Nothing like this:

```
<% Set MyDict=Nothing %>
```

Although the Dictionary object is not officially part of Active Server Pages, the example above illustrates how you can use Active Server Pages objects. You create an instance of an object by calling the Server.CreateObject() method. After you create a new object, you can call its methods and read and set its properties.

Active Server Pages Objects

Active Server Pages includes a number of built-in objects. These objects allow you to extend the power of your scripts. By using these objects, you can gain access to browser requests and control how the server responds to these requests. The built-in objects also provide you with control over user sessions and Web server applications.

13

BUILDING ACTIVE
SERVER PAGES

You have already been introduced to one example of a built-in object—the `Response` object. You can use the `Response` object to send output to a browser. However, the `Response` object also has a number of other important properties, collections, and methods.

The following chapters explain in detail how to use each of the built-in objects. The following list provides a quick overview of each of the built-in objects:

- The `Application` object. The `Application` object is used to store and retrieve information that can be shared among all users of an application. For example, you can use the `Application` object to pass information between users of your Web site.

- The `Request` object. The `Request` object can be used to access all information sent in a request from a browser to your server. You can use the `Request` object to retrieve the information that a user has entered into an HTML form.

- The `Response` object. The `Response` object is used to send information back to a browser. You can use the `Response` object to send output from your scripts to a browser.

- The `Server` object. The `Server` object allows you to use various utility functions on the server. For example, you can use the `Server` object to control the length of time a script executes before it times out. You can also use the `Server` object to create instances of other objects.

- The `Session` object. The `Session` object can be used to store and retrieve information about particular user sessions. You can use the `Session` object to store information that persists over the course of a visit by a user to your Web site.

- The `ObjectContext` object. The `ObjectContext` object is used to control Active Server Pages transactions. The transactions are managed by the Microsoft Transaction Server (MTS).

The built-in objects differ from normal objects. You don't need to create an instance of a built-in object before you can use it in a script. The methods, collections, and properties of a built-in object are automatically accessible throughout a Web site application.

> **NOTE**
>
> See Appendix A, "Quick ASP Object and Component Reference," for a complete list of all of the methods, properties, and collections of the built-in objects.

Active Server Pages Components

Like the built-in objects discussed in the preceding section, Active Server Pages components can be used to extend the power of your scripts. Components differ from the built-in objects because they're typically used for more specialized tasks. The following list provides a brief overview of some of the components bundled with Active Server Pages:

- **The Ad Rotator component.** The Ad Rotator component is used to display banner advertisements on the Web pages of a Web site. You can use this component to specify how frequently different banner advertisements should be displayed.

- **The Browser Capabilities component.** The Browser Capabilities component can be used to display different HTML content, according to the capabilities of different browsers. For example, you can use this component to display Web pages with frames only to frames-compliant browsers.

- **The Content Linking component.** Using the Content Linking component, you can link together a number of HTML pages so that they can be navigated easily. For example, you can use this component to display the pages of an online book.

- **The Counters component.** The Counters component can be used to keep track of the number of visitors to your Web site. You can use the Counters component to add a hit counter to a Web page.

- **The Content Rotator component.** The Content Rotator component enables you to rotate through HTML content on a page. For example, you can use the component to randomly display different announcements on the home page of your Web site.

- **The Page Counter component.** Exactly like the Counters component, the Page Counter component can be used to track the number of visitors to a Web page. You can use this component to add a hit counter to a particular Web page.

- **The Permission Checker component.** The Permission Checker component can be used to display links to Web pages only if a user has permission to see them. You can use this component to create Web pages that can be viewed only by the administrators of a Web site.

- **The ActiveX Data Objects.** The ActiveX Data Objects (ADO) enable you to retrieve and store data in a database such as Microsoft SQL Server. These objects are extremely important. For this reason, they are covered in a separate section, where each of the objects in this group is thoroughly discussed.

The following chapters describe in detail how to use each of these components. Chapter 28 also explains how to create new components of your own.

13

BUILDING ACTIVE SERVER PAGES

NOTE

See Appendix A for a complete list of all of the methods, properties, and collections of the components.

Configuring and Troubleshooting Active Server Pages

Before you can use Active Server Pages, you need to make sure that Active Server Pages are installed on your system. If you installed Internet Information Server while installing Windows NT Server, Active Server Pages may not be installed. Active Server Pages are included with IIS versions 3.0 and above (the current version is version 4.0). To download the latest version of Active Server Pages, visit the Internet Information Server section of the Microsoft Web site at `http://www.microsoft.com/iis`.

After Active Server Pages are installed, you still need to configure IIS to use Active Server Pages. You need to configure at least one directory in your Web site with permissions to execute an Active Server Pages file. Follow these steps:

1. Launch the Internet Service Manager from the Microsoft Internet Information Server program group on the Start menu.

2. In the left pane of the Internet Service Manager, navigate to your default Web site. (If you haven't changed anything, the Web site will be named Default Web Site.)

3. Choose the directory in your Web site where you want to store your Active Server Pages files by navigating to it in the Internet Service Manager.

4. Right-click the name of this directory and choose Properties.

5. Click the tab labeled Directory or Virtual Directory (depending on the type of directory).

6. In the Permissions section, choose either Script or Execute (see Figure 13.4).

FIGURE 13.4.

Setting directory permissions.

Now that you have created a directory with permissions to execute your Active Server Pages, you need to store all your Active Server Pages in this directory in order to use them. If the directory is a physical directory, you can simply store your pages in the directory with this name. If the directory is a virtual directory, you need to determine the local path to this directory on your hard drive. You can determine the local path of a virtual directory by looking at the same tabbed dialog box where you just configured the permissions.

> **CAUTION**
>
> If you're using a browser on the same machine as IIS, be careful how you retrieve an Active Server Page with your browser. When you load an Active Server Page into your Web browser, don't load the page by using your browser's Open command. Using the Open command bypasses IIS and the Active Server Page won't be processed. You'll see the text of your Active Server Pages scripts instead of the page that these scripts produce. This probably isn't what you want.

To load an Active Server Page into a browser that's located on the same machine as IIS, use the address bar of your Web browser. For example, if your machine is named mymachine, and the Active Server Page is located in the root directory of your Web site, you can load the page by typing **http://mymachine/mypage.asp** into the address bar of your Web browser. This will load the Active Server Page named mypage.asp.

Testing Your Configuration

You can test whether Active Server Pages are configured properly on your system by creating a simple Active Server Page. If you can display this page successfully in your Web browser, you'll know that everything is set up properly.

To create an Active Server Page, you can use any text editor. For example, you can use Notepad, which is included as an accessory with Windows NT Server. Start Notepad (or your favorite text editor) and enter the following text:

```
<HTML>
<HEAD><TITLE>ASP Page</TITLE></HEAD>
<BODY>
<%
Response.Write("Hello World!")
%>
</BODY>
</HTML>
```

Save the Active Server Pages file as **test.asp**. Make sure that your text editor doesn't append an extra .txt extension to the filename. Also, make sure that you save the file in a directory with Execute or Script permission (see the preceding section).

Now, launch your favorite Web browser in order to display your new Active Server Page. If you saved your Active Server Page in the root directory of your Web site, you can load the page by typing **http://mymachine/test.asp**. If you saved the Active Server Page in a subdirectory of this root directory, include the full path by entering an address such as **http://mymachine/mysubdir/test.asp**. If you saved the page in a virtual directory, include the name of the virtual directory in the address. For example, if your virtual directory is named myvirtualdir, you should type **http://mymachine/myvirtualdir/test.asp**.

If everything works, the Active Server Page should be displayed. The text Hello World! should appear in your Web browser's window (see Figure 13.5). If everything doesn't work, see the next section.

FIGURE 13.5.

An Active Server Page.

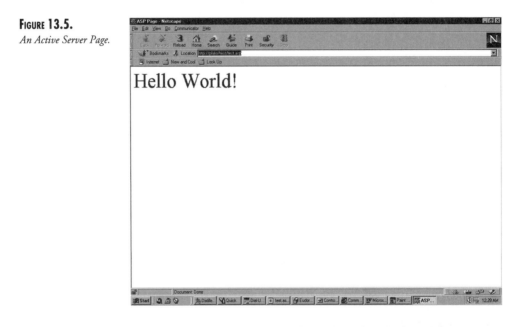

NOTE

The appearance of the Active Server Page may vary slightly, depending on your browser and its current settings. For example, the size of the text may be larger or smaller than that shown in Figure 13.5.

Troubleshooting Your Active Server Pages Configuration

I sincerely hope that you never need to read this section. However, if you encounter problems displaying an Active Server Page, this section should help. Following are listed both symptoms and possible causes for a number of common problems that you may encounter while attempting to access an Active Server Page.

- **Symptom:** When attempting to load an Active Server Page, you receive a message complaining that the browser couldn't connect to the server. For example, using Netscape Navigator, you receive this message:

  ```
  There was no response. The server could be down or is not responding.
  ```

  Or, using Internet Explorer, you receive this message:

  ```
  Internet Explorer cannot open the Internet site http://mymachine/test.asp.
  A connection with the server could not be established.
  ```

  Cause: If you're not attempting to connect to your server over the Internet, this problem is almost certainly the result of your Web server being turned off. Make sure that your Web server is running. To do this, launch the Internet Service Manager from the Microsoft Internet Information Server program group on the Start menu. Select the name of your default Web site and check the "VCR controls" at the top of the window. If IIS isn't running, the Run button will be inactive. Click this button to start the service.

  Cause: If you're attempting to connect to your server over the Internet, the error message may result from heavy Internet traffic. Wait a while and try again. If you still can't connect to your server, contact your Internet service provider.

- **Symptom:** When attempting to load an Active Server Page, you receive the message `HTTP/1.0 404 Object Not Found`.

  Cause: You entered the wrong address for the Active Server Page in your Web browser. If you saved your Active Server Page in the root directory of your Web site, you can load the page by entering **http://mymachine/test.asp**. If you saved the Active Server Page in a subdirectory of this root directory, include the full path by entering an address such as **http://mymachine/mysubdir/test.asp**. If you saved the page in a virtual directory, include the name of the virtual directory in the address. For example, if your virtual directory is named myvirtualdir, you should type **http://mymachine/myvirtualdir/test.asp**.

  Cause: Your text editor has appended an extra extension to the end of your Active Server Pages file. Notepad, for example, appends .txt on the end of the name of a file when you save it as a text file. If you save a file as type All Files, however, Notepad won't do this.

- **Symptom:** When attempting to load an Active Server Page, you receive the message `HTTP/1.1 403 Access Forbidden. Execute Access Denied.`

  Cause: The permissions are improperly configured for the directory or virtual directory where the Active Server Page is stored. See the earlier discussion of configuring permissions.

- **Symptom:** When the Active Server Page loads, you see the text of your scripts rather than the results of the scripts.

Cause: You saved the Active Server Page file with the extension `.htm` or `.html` instead of `.asp`. For the Web server to process an Active Server Page, the Active Server Page file must end with the extension `.asp`.

Cause: When loading the Active Server Page, you used the Open command on your Web browser. For the Web server to process an Active Server Page, you must load the page using the address bar of your Web browser.

Summary

This chapter introduced you to using Active Server Pages. You learned all the alternative methods for integrating scripts into your Active Server Pages. The chapter also provided an overview of the built-in objects and ActiveX components included with Active Server Pages. Finally, you learned how to configure Active Server Pages and troubleshoot any problems that might arise.

The following chapters explore in detail how to use all the objects and components of Active Server Pages. Whatever your Web project might be, the following chapters will help you accomplish it.

CHAPTER 14

Working with a Single Active Server Page

IN THIS CHAPTER

This chapter details how to work with a single Active Server Page. The first section provides an overview of the Request and Response objects. In the second section, you learn how to buffer the output of your Active Server Pages. The third section describes some methods for working with long-running scripts and very large HTML pages. Finally, in the fourth section, you learn how to work with HTTP headers and server variables.

The Request and Response Objects

This section introduces the Request and Response objects. These two objects are the ones that you'll use most often in your Active Server Pages scripts. To understand how to use these objects, however, you first need some background on the HTTP protocol, which is provided in the following section.

The HTTP Protocol

How does the World Wide Web really work? When you type the address of a Web page in your Web browser, if all goes smoothly, the Web page appears. For example, if you type the Internet address of HotWired into your Web browser, the home page of the HotWired Web site appears in your browser window. What goes on in the background to make this happen?

When you use a browser to retrieve an HTML page from a Web site, you're using the *Hypertext Transfer Protocol* (*HTTP*). The HTTP protocol specifies how messages can be transported over the Internet. In particular, the protocol specifies the ways in which a browser and a Web server can interact.

> **NOTE**
>
> As I write this, most browsers and servers support the HTTP 1.0 protocol. However, Internet Information Server also supports HTTP 1.1. The HTTP 1.1 protocol is much faster than HTTP 1.0 because it supports persistent connections and pipelining. To learn more, visit the World Wide Web Consortium at http://w3.org.

When you retrieve a page from a Web site, your browser opens a connection to a Web server at the Web site and issues a request. The Web server receives the request and issues a response. For this reason, the HTTP protocol is called a *request and response protocol.*

All communication between a browser and a Web server takes place in discrete request and response pairs. The browser must always initiate the communication, by issuing a request. The Web server's role is completely passive; it must be nudged into action by the request.

A browser request has a certain structure. A request message contains a request line, header fields, and possibly a message body. The most common type of request is a simple request for a Web page, as in the following example:

```
GET /hello.htm HTTP/1.1
Host: www.aspsite.com
```

This request message is a request for the Web page `hello.htm` at the Web site `www.aspsite.com`. The first line is the request line. The request line specifies the method of the request, the resource being requested, and the version of the HTTP protocol being used.

In this example, the *method* of the request is the `GET` method. The `GET` method retrieves a particular *resource*. In this case, the `GET` method is being used to retrieve the Web page `hello.htm`.

Other types of request methods include `POST`, `HEAD`, `OPTIONS`, `DELETE`, `TRACE`, and `PUT`. Only `GET` and `POST` are commonly used. The `POST` method is used to submit the contents of an HTML form.

The second line in this example is a *header*. The `Host` header specifies the Internet address of the Web site where the `hello.htm` file is located. In this case, the host is `www.aspsite.com`.

Typically, a request will include many headers. Headers provide additional information about the content of a message or about the originator of the request. Some of these headers are standard; others are browser-specific. The later section "Working with Headers" covers these specific topics.

A request may also contain a *message body*. For example, if the request uses the `POST` method rather than the `GET` method, the message body may contain the contents of an HTML form. When you click the submit button on an HTML form, and the form uses the `ACTION="POST"` attribute, any data you entered into the form is posted to the server. The form contents are sent within the message body of the request, using the `POST` method.

When a Web server receives a request, it returns a *response*. A response also has a certain structure. Every response begins with a status line, contains a number of headers, and optionally may contain a message body.

You're probably already familiar with the status line. If you have ever requested a Web page and mistyped the address, you've seen an example of a status line (see Figure 14.1 on the following page). A status line indicates the protocol being used, a status code, and a text message (the *reason phrase*). For example, if a Web server has problems with a request, it returns an error and a description of the error in the status line. If a server can successfully respond to a request for a Web page, it returns a status line that contains `200 OK`.

> **NOTE**
>
> The status line is not the same thing as the status bar that typically appears at the bottom of a Web browser. You normally never see the status line. A browser only shows the status line in the main browser window when something has gone wrong with a request.

FIGURE 14.1.

*An example of a status
line.*

Response headers contain information about the content of the response or information about
the server providing the response. Some of these headers are standard; others depend on the
Web server. For more about headers, see the later section "Working with Headers."

Finally, the message body of a response typically contains the contents of a Web page. For
example, if the request was for the Web page hello.htm, the message body of the response would
contain hello.htm. However, a message body can contain other types of content as well (text
documents, Microsoft Word documents, and so on).

The Request and Response Objects

Active Server Pages includes two built-in objects that correspond to the request message and
response message of the Hypertext Transfer Protocol. The Active Server Pages Request object
corresponds to an HTTP request. The Active Server Pages Response object corresponds to an
HTTP response.

Like most Active Server Pages objects, the Request and Response objects have collections, properties, and methods. By using the collections, properties, and methods of the Request object,
you can retrieve information on all aspects of a browser request to your Web server. By using
the collections, properties, and methods of the Response object, you can control almost all aspects of the response of your Web server.

For example, the Request object has a collection that contains all the HTTP headers in a request. The Response object includes a number of methods for modifying response headers. The
following sections provide more details about how to use these two objects.

Buffering Output

Normally, when an Active Server Page is processed on the server, the output from the page is sent to the browser immediately after each command in the page is executed. For example, consider the following Active Server Page:

```
<HTML>
<HEAD><TITLE>Buffer Example</TITLE></HEAD>
<BODY>
<%
FOR i=1 TO 500
  Response.Write(i&"<BR>")
NEXT
%>
</BODY>
</HTML>
```

> **NOTE**
>
> You can view a number of the examples in this book by visiting the companion Web site to this book at http://www.aspsite.com.

This script displays the numbers 1 through 500 down the browser screen. The output from the page is sent immediately to the browser after each command in the page is executed. You can watch the numbers appear down the screen in real time.

In some situations, you may want to buffer the output of an Active Server Page. When you buffer the output of an Active Server Page, none of the page is sent to the browser until the server has finished processing all of the page. Here's a modified version of the preceding script:

```
<% Response.Buffer=True %>
<HTML>
<HEAD><TITLE>Buffer Example</TITLE></HEAD>
<BODY>
<%
FOR i=1 TO 500
  Response.Write(i&"<BR>")
NEXT
%>
</BODY>
</HTML>
```

14

Only one difference exists between this script and the previous one: In the first line of this script, the Buffer property of the Response object is set to True. When this page is displayed in a Web browser, all the contents of the page are sent to the browser at the same time. The page is *buffered* until the script finishes processing.

> **NOTE**
>
> You can use the Internet Service Manager to change the default value of the `Buffer` property to `True`. On the App Options page of the Application Configuration dialog box, select the option `Enable Buffering`.

Any statement that modifies the `Buffer` property must occur before any HTML or script output. If you attempt to modify the `Buffer` property after any HTML or script output, you'll get an error.

By buffering a page, you can display two different Web pages, depending on some condition. For example, the following Active Server Page randomly outputs two different HTML pages:

```
<% Response.Buffer=True %>
<HTML>
<HEAD><TITLE> First Page </TITLE></HEAD>
<BODY>
This is the first page.
</BODY>
</HTML>
<%
Randomize
If INT(2*RND)=1 THEN Response.End
Response.Clear
%>
<HTML>
<HEAD><TITLE> Second Page </TITLE></HEAD>
<BODY>
This is the second page.
</BODY>
</HTML>
```

In this example, two new methods of the `Response` object are used: the `End` method and the `Clear` method. The `End` method immediately stops the processing of an Active Server Page and outputs the results. You can use the `End` method regardless of whether or not you're buffering the output of a page. In this example, the `End` method is used to prevent the second page from being displayed when the first page is displayed.

The `Clear` method empties the current page buffer without outputting the contents of the buffer. You can use the `Clear` method only when buffering the output of an Active Server Page. In this example, the `Clear` method is used to prevent the first page from being displayed when the second page is displayed. It clears the first page from the buffer.

One other method of the `Response` object is used when buffering an Active Server Page. The `Flush` method immediately outputs the contents of the page buffer. As with the `Clear` method, an error occurs if you attempt to use this method with a page that isn't buffered. Unlike the `End` method, after the `Flush` method is called, the page continues to be processed.

Typically, you won't need to buffer the output of an Active Server Page. It's usually a bad idea. In the case of large HTML pages or long-running scripts, buffering a page delays the appearance of the Web page, which may confuse the user.

If you want to display two different HTML pages conditionally, you can simply use a VBScript conditional. For example, here's the preceding example, rewritten without using buffering:

```
<%
Randomize
If INT(2*RND)=1 THEN
%>
<HTML>
<HEAD><TITLE> First Page </TITLE></HEAD>
<BODY>
This is the first page.
</BODY>
</HTML>
<% ELSE %>
<HTML>
<HEAD><TITLE> Second Page </TITLE></HEAD>
<BODY>
This is the second page.
</BODY>
</HTML>
<% END IF %>
```

The one situation where buffering is necessary is when you need to change the headers for a page within the body of the page. If you want to change the headers in a page after you have already outputted content to a browser, you need to set the Buffer property to True. For example, later in this chapter you learn how to use headers to control how a page is cached and to specify the content rating of a page (see "Working with Headers"). If you modify either of these headers after you have already outputted content to a browser, then you need to buffer the page. Otherwise, you get an error.

Working with Long-Running Scripts and Large Pages

By default, the maximum amount of time an Active Server Pages script will execute is 90 seconds. This prevents scripts that become caught in infinite loops from running forever. It's a useful safeguard.

Nevertheless, on occasion you may need to allow a script to execute for longer than 90 seconds. For example, if you're using a script to output a very large HTML page, you wouldn't want the script to time out when only part of the page is displayed. You can control the maximum amount of time for which a script is allowed to execute by using the ScriptTimeout property of the Server object, as in this example (continued on the next page):

```
<% Server.ScriptTimeout=150 %>
<HTML>
<HEAD><TITLE>Falling Star</TITLE></HEAD>
```

```
<BODY>
<%
RANDOMIZE
starx=60
FOR k=1 to 10
 nextsecond=DATEADD("s",10,time)
 DO WHILE TIME<nextsecond
 LOOP
starx=starx+3*RND()-1
FOR i=1 TO starx
  Response.Write(" ")
NEXT
  Response.Write("*<P>")
NEXT
%>
</BODY>
</HTML>
```

This script creates a falling star that falls very slowly. The star (an asterisk) is printed to the browser window in 10-second intervals (see Figure 14.2).

Figure 14.2.

A falling star.

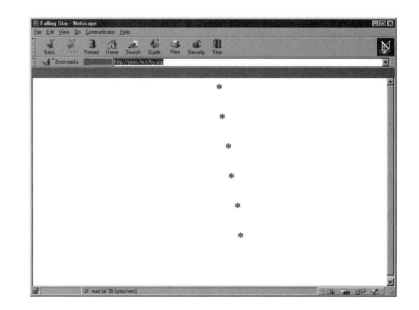

Normally, the script would time out before the star finishes falling. However, the first line in this page prevents this from happening, because the ScriptTimeout property of the Server object has been set to 150 seconds.

You can't use the Server.ScriptTimeout property to reduce the maximum amount of time for which a script will execute to less than 90 seconds. To force your scripts to finish executing before 90 seconds elapses, you need to change the ScriptTimeout property by using the Internet Service Manager. This property is located on the App Options page of the Application Configuration dialog box. If you set the ScriptTimeout property to -1, your scripts will never time out.

Allowing scripts to run for long periods of time could create a significant drain on the resources of your Web server. In fact, a script in an Active Server Page may continue to execute even after the person who requested the Active Server Page has gone away. In this case, if the script continues to execute, it benefits no one. Fortunately, a property of the Response object can help. The IsClientConnected property can be used to check whether a connection is still open between a browser and the server. You can use this property to end further script processing if a user has abandoned a page. For example, the following script continues to execute until the script times out or the browser becomes disconnected from the server:

```
<HTML>
<HEAD><TITLE>Obnoxious Page</TITLE></HEAD>
<BODY>
<%
WHILE 1=1
  Response.Write("Hello.  How are you?")
  IF NOT Response.IsClientConnected THEN Response.End
WEND
%>
</BODY>
</HTML>
```

Note that the IsClientConnected property only reflects whether a browser is still connected since the last Response.Write method call. If you have a long-running script that doesn't output anything to a browser, this property won't be useful.

Working with Headers

Both browser requests and server responses include headers. Headers provide additional information about the content of a request or a response. They can also contain information about the browser making the request or the server providing the response.

Active Server Pages includes a number of collections and methods that can help you manipulate headers. Some of these methods are targeted at a particular task, such as providing a Web page with a content rating or providing an expiration date for the Web page. Other methods and collections allow you to manipulate headers in general. The following sections explain how to use the methods and collections that affect headers.

Retrieving Headers

When a browser requests a Web page from a server, the request includes a number of headers. You can retrieve these headers by using the ServerVariables collection of the Request object. The ServerVariables collection contains both headers and additional items of information about the server. The following Active Server Page dumps all the contents of the ServerVariables collection to the browser window (see Figure 14.3):

```
<HTML>
<HEAD><TITLE>Server Variables</TITLE></HEAD>
<BODY>
```

```
<%
FOR EACH name IN Request.ServerVariables
Response.write("<P><B>"&name&"</B>:")
Response.write(Request.ServerVariables(name))
NEXT
%>
</BODY>
</HTML>
```

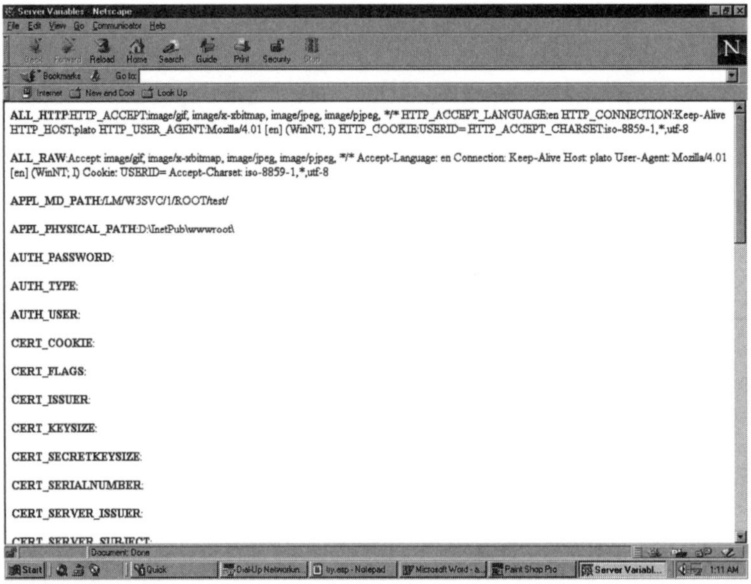

FIGURE 14.3.

The ServerVariables *collection.*

The headers (and server variables) in the ServerVariables collection hold a wide assortment of different types of information. Appendix A, "Quick ASP Object and Component Reference," contains a list of the standard headers and server variables in this collection. The following list explains the more useful ones:

- HTTP_REFERER. When someone has arrived at the current page by clicking a hyperlink, this header contains the Internet address of the referring page. The HTTP_REFERER header is extremely valuable for determining how the visitors to your Web site arrived there. For example, if you want to know the number of people who arrived at your Web site by using Yahoo!, you could use the HTTP_REFERER header to determine this information.

- HTTP_USER_AGENT. This header indicates the type of Web browser a visitor to your Web site is using. This information is valuable when you need to determine the Web browser used most often by the target audience of your Web site.

- REMOTE_ADDR. This header contains the IP address of a visitor to your Web site. The IP address can be interpreted to provide information about the origins of the visitors to your Web site. For example, you can use this header to determine how many people are visiting your Web site from MIT or America Online.

- **QUERY_STRING.** The QUERY_STRING server variable contains the portion of the URL after the question mark. This variable contains the complete query string. Chapter 15, "Working with More Than One Active Server Page," details methods for use with query strings.

- **SCRIPT_NAME.** This server variable contains the virtual path of the current Active Server Page. You can use this variable for self-referencing pages.

- **SERVER_NAME.** This server variable contains the Internet address of the server.

- **PATH_TRANSLATED.** This server variable contains the physical path of the current Active Server Page.

Certain versions of Internet Explorer (such as versions 3.0 and 4.0 in Windows 95) contain additional headers in their requests:

- **HTTP_UA_COLOR.** This header indicates the number of colors that the browser can display.

- **HTTP_UA_CPU.** This header indicates the type of machine being used to execute the browser.

- **HTTP_UA_OS.** This header indicates the operating system of the computer executing the browser.

- **HTTP_UA_PIXELS.** This header indicates the screen resolution being used on the computer executing the browser.

CAUTION

You shouldn't rely on these headers; they're supported only by the Windows 95 versions of Internet Explorer.

You can retrieve the contents of a particular header or server variable by passing its name to the ServerVariables collection. For example, the following script (continued on the next page) allows a user to access the page only if he or she arrived from the Active Server Page named origin.asp:

```
<HTML>
<HEAD><TITLE>Server Variables</TITLE></HEAD>
<BODY>
<%
WhereFrom=request.ServerVariables("HTTP_REFERER")
If WhereFrom="http://www.mysite.com/origin.asp" THEN
%>
Welcome to this page!
<%
ELSE
%>
```

14

WORKING WITH A
SINGLE ACTIVE
SERVER PAGE

```
You are not authorized to view this page!
<%
END IF
%>
</BODY>
</HTML>
```

In this script, the HTTP_REFERER header determines the page the visitor used to link to the current page. If the user didn't arrive from the page located at http://mysite/origin.asp, he or she isn't allowed to view the contents of the page.

> **CAUTION**
>
> Be aware that using headers in this way can be risky. Not all browsers support all headers properly. In particular, older browsers don't support the HTTP_REFERER header.

Using Headers to Control How a Page Is Cached

Proxy servers are used to reduce the amount of time needed to retrieve a Web page over the Internet. Proxy servers keep local copies of Web pages in a cache; when someone requests a Web page, it can be retrieved from the proxy rather than from the original server.

From the point of view of Active Server Pages, however, proxy servers are an evil nuisance. The whole point of an Active Server Page is to display dynamic content. In other words, an Active Server Page can display content that changes every time it's viewed. You don't want a proxy server to respond with stale copies of your Active Server Pages.

By default, proxy servers should not cache your Active Server Pages. The ASP CACHE-CONTROL General header provides directives for how proxy servers should cache Web pages. When you use Active Server Pages, by default, this header directs proxy servers not to cache your pages. However, you can override this default behavior. If for some odd reason you want proxy servers to cache your Active Server Pages, you can modify the CacheControl property of the Response object. Add the following line to the top of an Active Server Page to allow the page to be cached by proxy servers:

```
<% Response.CacheControl="Public" %>
```

You can also indicate how you want Web browsers to cache your Active Server Pages. Browsers commonly have memory and disk caches. Two properties of the Response object control how browsers cache your Web pages. By using the Expires property of the Response object, you can specify the amount of time in minutes that a browser should use a cached copy of a Web page. If you set this property to 0, the browser won't cache the Active Server Page at all. Here's an example:

```
<% Response.Expires=0 %>
```

You can also specify an absolute date and time when a cached copy of an Active Server Page should expire. When you do this, the Web browser will continue to use a cached copy of the Active Server Page until this date and time arrives. The following example directs browsers to cache a page until the year 1998:

```
<% Response.ExpiresAbsolute=#Jan 1,1998 00:00:00# %>
```

> **NOTE**
>
> According to the HTTP 1.1 specification, you shouldn't set the `ExpiresAbsolute` property to more than one year in the future. For more information, visit `http://w3.org`.

> **NOTE**
>
> You can also specify expiration options for your Web pages by using the Internet Service Manager. Select the HTTP Headers page to view these options.

Using Headers to Specify Content Rating

The *Platform for Internet Content Selection* (*PICS*) provides a standard way to label the content of a Web page or a whole Web site. For example, you can use PICS labels to indicate the level of violence or sexual explicitness of the content of a Web site.

PICS itself is not a rating service. PICS is a specification for the format of content labels. The PICS standard is intended to be compatible with the decentralized culture of the Web. The idea is that many different rating services can use PICS to label Web sites according to their own standards. For example, the Parent-Teacher Association might use PICS to label Web sites in a very different way than an organization such as a Beavis and Butt-Head fan club.

The decision of which rating service to use is left in the hands of the individual. In theory, an individual could select the rating service that reflects his or her personal tastes. This is the vision, anyway. Currently, only one rating service is widely supported. Internet Explorer versions 3.0 and above support the PICS standard. However, by default, the only rating service it uses is the one provided by the *Recreational Software Advisory Council* (*RSAC*). This is the same organization that places ratings on computer games. RSAC uses a rating system that has four categories. You can rate your site according to its level of violence, nudity, sex, and language. For each category, you can specify a level between 1 and 5.

The user can configure Internet Explorer to block Web sites that don't meet particular content preferences. For example, someone can indicate that he or she wants all sites blocked that use stronger language than mild expletives. The browser can also be configured to block all sites

that haven't been given a content rating. (Of course, at this time, this would also block the vast majority of sites on the Internet.)

To receive an RSAC rating for your Web site, register the site with RSAC. (Currently there's no fee for this service.) The RSAC Web site is located at `http://www.rsac.org`. Once there, answer a series of questions about the content of your Web site (see Figure 14.4 for an example).

FIGURE 14.4.

Questions from the RSAC Web site.

At the end of the process, you're supplied with a PICS label. For example, the ASPSite Web site (the companion Web site for this book) received the following PICS label:

```
(PICS-1.1 "http://www.rsac.org/ratingsv01.html" l gen true
➥comment "RSACi North America Server"
➥by "walther@aspsite.com"
➥for "http://www.aspsite.com"
➥on "1997.08.10T02:04-0800" r (n 0 s 0 v 0 l 0))
```

After you have a PICS label for the Web site, you need to include the label in the `pics-label` header of your home page. There's a special property of the `Response` object for this particular purpose. You can use the `PICS` property to add a PICS label to the correct header. Here's an example:

```
<% Response.PICS("(PICS-1.1"&CHR(34)
➥&"http://www.rsac.org/ratingsv01.html"&CHR(34)
➥&" l gen true comment "&CHR(34)
➥&"RSACi North America Server"&CHR(34)
➥&" by "&CHR(34)&"walther@aspsite.com"
➥&CHR(34)&" for "&CHR(34)
➥&"http://www.aspsite.com"&CHR(34)&" on "&CHR(34)
➥&"1997.08.10T02:04-0800"&CHR(34)
➥&" r (n 0 s 0 v 0 l 0))") %>
```

This method of adding a PICS label is extremely cumbersome. You must include the whole PICS label in one unbroken line. Furthermore, you must specify all quotation marks by using CHR(34). Fortunately, an easier way to add a PICS label is available. You can simply include the following HTML tag in the head of your HTML document:

```
<META http-equiv="PICS-Label"
 content='(PICS-1.1 "http://www.rsac.org/ratingsv01.html" l gen true
 comment "RSACi North America Server" by "walther2@ix.netcom.com"
 for "http://www.aspsite.com"
 on "1997.08.10T02:04-0800" r (n 0 s 0 v 0 l 0))'>
```

The META http-equiv HTML tag is used to specify a response header within an HTML document. This method of specifying the PICS label accomplishes the same thing as the previous example. However, when using the META tag, you don't have to worry about placing everything on a single line or not using quotation marks.

> **NOTE**
>
> You can also use the Internet Service Manager to specify content ratings. On the HTTP Headers page, choose Edit Ratings.

Authorization Headers

When a Web page is password-protected, four headers are useful for retrieving information about the user accessing the page. The AUTH_TYPE header indicates the authentication method used to access the page. The AUTH_USER and LOGON_USER headers contain the name of the Windows NT account of the user. Finally, when Basic authentication is used, the AUTH_PASSWORD header contains the password that was used to access the page.

> **NOTE**
>
> You can password-protect Web pages by using the Internet Service Manager. To easily password-protect a file, right-click the name of the file, choose Properties, and select the File Security tab. To password-protect a whole Web site or directory, right-click the name of the Web site or directory, choose Properties, and select the Directory Security tab.
>
> You have the option of choosing either Basic authentication or NT Challenge and Response. NT Challenge and Response is more secure because, when using this method, passwords are not sent as plain text over the Internet. However, only Internet Explorer can use this form of authentication. On the other hand, almost every browser can use Basic authentication.

14

WORKING WITH A
SINGLE ACTIVE
SERVER PAGE

For example, the following Active Server Page checks whether the user has used Basic authentication to access the page (see Figure 14.5). This is accomplished by using the AUTH_TYPE header.

This header can have only two possible values: Basic for Basic authentication, or NTLM for NT Challenge and Response. (The *LM* stands for *LAN Manager*—Microsoft's pre-Windows NT network operating system.) Next, the Windows NT account of the user is displayed:

```
<HTML>
<HEAD><TITLE>Password Protected</TITLE></HEAD>
<BODY>
<%
IF Request.ServerVariables("AUTH_TYPE")="Basic" THEN
%>
You are logged in using Basic Authentication.
Your account is <%=Request.ServerVariables("LOGON_USER")%>.
<% ELSE %>
You are logged in using NT Challenge and Response.
Your account is <%=Request.ServerVariables("LOGON_USER")%>.
<% END IF %>
<BODY>
</HTML>
```

FIGURE 14.5.

A password-protected page.

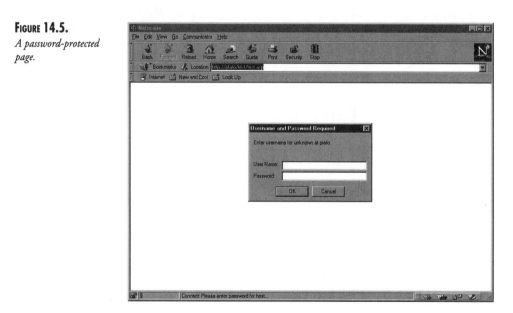

Modifying the Content-Type Header

The Content-Type header indicates the media type of the body of the response (the MIME type). Common examples are "text/HTML", "image/gif", "application/msword", or "text/rtf". You can use the ContentType property of the Response object to set this header.

One common use of the ContentType property is to display the source of an HTML document. If you set the ContentType property to "text/plain", the body of the response is sent as normal text rather than HTML. Consider the following example:

```
<%
Response.ContentType="text/plain"
```

```
%>
<HTML>
<HEAD><TITLE>HTML Document</TITLE></HEAD>
<BODY>
<H1>This is an HTML document!</H1>
</BODY>
</HTML>
```

When this file is displayed in a Web browser, all the text below the script appears exactly as shown here. By setting the ContentType property to "text/plain", you can prevent a Web browser from interpreting the contents of an HTML page.

The Status Code

For the sake of completeness, the Status property of the Response object is discussed here. However, this property doesn't modify a header; the Status property is used to specify the status code returned in an HTTP response.

Whenever a server responds to a request, the first line it sends is the status line. The status line includes a three-digit status code and a description of the status code (called a *reason phrase*). The following list describes the five classes of status codes:

- **1*xx* Informational.** The status codes in this class are mainly experimental.
- **2*xx* Success.** The status codes in this class are used to indicate that a request was fulfilled successfully. For example, status code 200 can indicate that the Web page requested was retrieved successfully.
- **3*xx* Redirection.** The status codes in this class are used to indicate that some further action must be taken before the request can be fulfilled. For example, status code 301 can indicate that a Web page has been moved permanently to another address. In this case, the browser may be redirected automatically to the new address.
- **4*xx* Client Error.** This status code is returned when the browser has made a request that can't be fulfilled. For example, status code 404 indicates that the requested Web page doesn't exist.
- **5*xx* Server Error.** The status codes in this class indicate a problem with the server. For example, status code 503 can indicate the server is currently overwhelmed.

14

WORKING WITH A
SINGLE ACTIVE
SERVER PAGE

NOTE

For a complete list of status codes and their meanings, see the HTTP 1.1 specification at http://w3.org.

You can use the Status property of the Response object to specify the status code that should be returned in a response. For example, if someone attempts to retrieve the following Active Server Page on a Wednesday, the status code 401 Not Authorized is returned (this results in a password dialog box appearing):

```
<%
IF WEEKDAYNAME(WEEKDAY(DATE))="Wednesday" THEN
Response.Status="401 Not Authorized"
Response.End
ELSE
%>
<HTML>
<HEAD><TITLE> Not Wednesday </TITLE></HEAD>
<BODY>
Welcome!   Today is not Wednesday.
</BODY>
</HTML>
<% END IF %>
```

Summary

This chapter introduced you to the Request and Response objects, the two most important objects provided with Active Server Pages. You learned how to use the Response object to buffer the output of your Active Server Pages. You also learned a number of methods for working with long-running scripts and large HTML pages. Finally, the chapter provided a survey of the most important headers and server variables.

In this chapter, you learned the methods, properties, and collections that apply to a single Active Server Page. In the next chapter, you learn a number of valuable techniques for working with multiple Active Server Pages. In particular, you learn how to work with query strings and retrieve the contents of HTML forms.

Working with More Than One Active Server Page

IN THIS CHAPTER

In this chapter, you learn how to work with multiple Active Server Pages. In the first section, you learn how to retrieve information entered into HTML forms. In the second section, some methods for retrieving query strings are discussed. In the third section, you learn how to redirect a user to a new page. Finally, in the fourth section, you learn how to include one Active Server Page in another.

Retrieving the Contents of an HTML Form

You should think of HTML forms as the primary interface to your Active Server Pages applications. The only reliable way to gather information from the visitors to your Web site is through an HTML form.

> **NOTE**
>
> If you need to review the methods of creating an HTML form, see the section on this topic in Chapter 6, "Intermediate HTML."

> **NOTE**
>
> HTML forms are the only reliable way to gather information from visitors to your Web site because HTML forms are the only type of forms that work with all browsers. However, you could also use Java applets, ActiveX controls, or even Adobe Acrobat documents to create fancier forms.

Suppose you want visitors to your Web site to register before they can use it. To gather registration information, you should use an HTML form. Here's an example:

```
<HTML>
<HEAD><TITLE> Register </TITLE></HEAD>
<BODY>
<H4>Registration:</H4>
<FORM METHOD="POST" ACTION="/regresults.asp">
<P>Please Enter Your First Name:
<BR><INPUT NAME="FirstName" TYPE="TEXT">
<P>Please Enter Your Last Name:
<BR><INPUT NAME="LastName" TYPE="TEXT">
<INPUT TYPE="SUBMIT" VALUE="Continue">
</FORM>
</BODY>
</HTML>
```

This form simply asks for the first and last name of the visitor. Once the information is entered, the Continue button can be clicked to move to the next page (see Figure 15.1).

FIGURE 15.1.

A simple registration form.

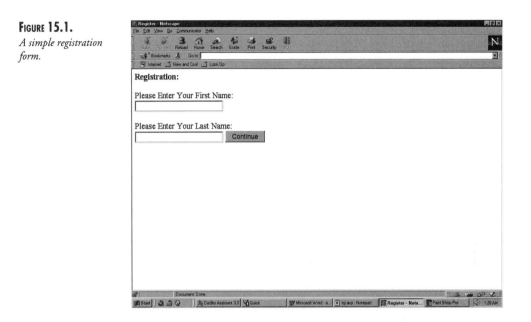

Once a user has entered information into an HTML form, you need a method of retrieving that information. When an HTML form is submitted, it's submitted as part of an HTTP request. In the preceding example, the form would be submitted by using the request method POST. The form is posted to the server.

Because an HTML form is submitted as part of an HTTP request, you can retrieve the contents of the form by using the Active Server Pages Request object. The Request object has a particular collection for this purpose. The Form collection contains all the information entered into an HTML form.

Each key in the Form collection corresponds to an input element in an HTML form. For example, if a user completed and submitted the form in the preceding example, the Form collection would contain two keys. The value of the first key would be the user's first name and the value of the second key would be the user's last name. Consider the following script:

```
<HTML>
<HEAD><TITLE> Registration Results </TITLE></HEAD>
<BODY>
Thank you <%=Request.Form("FirstName")%> for registering!
</BODY>
</HTML>
```

When this page is displayed in a Web browser, the first name the user entered into the HTML form is displayed. For this example to work, the ACTION attribute of the HTML form in the previous example must point to this page.

It's important to understand that you can't access the contents of an HTML form within the same page where the HTML form appears. The HTML form must first be submitted before you can retrieve the values of the elements of the form. In some situations, this is a significant limitation. Whenever you have a page that has an HTML form, you must have an additional page that processes the contents of the form.

This extra page requirement explains why there are so many polite Web sites on the Internet. Typically, when you register at a Web site, an extra page at the end of the registration process thanks you for registering. This extra page is actually required. The final page is needed to process the information entered into the HTML form on the previous page.

Dumping the Contents of the Form Collection

A number of ways exist to retrieve all the contents of the Form collection. If you want to loop through the contents of the collection and display each value, you could use the following script:

```
<%
FOR EACH name IN Request.Form
  Response.Write("<BR>"&name&"=")
  Response.Write(Request.Form(name))
NEXT
%>
```

This script displays each key-and-value pair in the Form collection. If Bill Gates were to visit your Web site and use the registration form discussed in the previous example, the output of this script would look like this:

```
LASTNAME=Gates
FIRSTNAME=Bill
```

Notice how each of the key names has been converted to uppercase. When you refer to an item in the Form collection, you don't have to worry about using the proper case. For example, both FirstName and FiRsTnAme will retrieve the proper value.

Instead of using a FOR...EACH loop, you can use a FOR...NEXT loop to dump the Form collection. The following script outputs the value of each key (but not the key name):

```
<%
FOR i=1 TO Request.Form.Count
  Response.Write("<BR>"&Request.Form(i))
NEXT
%>
```

In this script, the Count property of the Form collection is used to determine the number of items in the collection. You can also use the Count property to discover exactly how many of the HTML form fields were completed when the form was submitted.

Finally, if you simply want to return the items in the Form collection in a single URL-encoded string, you can use the following script:

```
<%=Request.Form%>
```

This single-line script returns the form data in unparsed form. Following is an example of the output from the script:

```
FirstName=Bill&LastName=Gates
```

Notice that the case of the form field names is preserved. This method of returning the items in the Form collection returns the body of the HTTP POST request in unparsed form.

Form Elements with Multiple Values

Certain HTML form elements can have more than one value. For example, both check boxes and list boxes can have multiple values. Consider the following HTML form:

```
<FORM METHOD="POST" ACTION="/regresults.asp">
How did you hear about our web site?
<BR><INPUT NAME="HowHear" TYPE="CheckBox" VALUE="A Newspaper Article">
A Newspaper Article
<BR><INPUT NAME="HowHear" TYPE="CheckBox" VALUE="A Search Engine">
A Search Engine
<BR><INPUT NAME="HowHear" TYPE="CheckBox" VALUE="A Friend">
A Friend
<BR><INPUT NAME="HowHear" TYPE="CheckBox" VALUE="Stumbled Into It">
Stumbled Into It
<P><INPUT TYPE="SUBMIT" VALUE="Continue">
</FORM>
```

This form can be used to determine how visitors to your Web site discovered it. But someone may have found out about your Web site in more than one way. For example, someone may have heard about your Web site both from a friend and from a newspaper article. This form allows the user to select more than one value at a time (see Figure 15.2).

FIGURE 15.2.

A form with multiple values.

How can you retrieve the value of a form element when it can have more than one value? You can use an additional parameter of the Form collection. Look at this example:

```
<HTML>
<HEAD><TITLE> Your Response </TITLE></HEAD>
<BODY>
According to your response, you heard about this web site in
<%=Request.Form("HowHear").Count%> ways.
<P>You heard about this site from:
<%
FOR EACH way IN Request.Form("HowHear")
  Response.Write("<P>"&way)
NEXT
%>
</BODY>
</HTML>
```

In this script, the Count property is used to return the number of check boxes selected. In this example, the Count property doesn't return the total number of items in the Form collection. Instead, it only returns the total number of values of the form element named HowHear.

The FOR...EACH loop iterates through each value. For example, if someone selects both A Friend and A Newspaper Article, both of these values are displayed.

Text Areas and the Form Collection

You can retrieve the text entered into a text area in the same way as any other form element. Remember that VBScript string variables can be quite long. There is no 255-character limitation on the string length, as in many other computer languages.

This is an example of an HTML form with a text area:

```
<FORM METHOD="Post" ACTION="/Response.asp">
Please enter any feedback on this web site below:
<P>
<TEXTAREA NAME="feedback" COLS=30 ROWS=10></TEXTAREA>
<P><INPUT TYPE="SUBMIT" VALUE="Submit Feedback">
</FORM>
```

This HTML form displays a text area that can be used for user feedback on a Web site. When the user clicks the button labeled Submit Feedback, he or she is brought to the Response.asp page. If you want to display the text entered into the feedback text area in the Response.asp page, you can do it like this:

```
<HTML>
<HEAD><TITLE> Feedback Response </TITLE></HEAD>
<BODY>
Thank you for submitting feedback.  You wrote:
<P>
<%=Request.Form("Feedback")%>
</BODY>
</HTML>
```

HTML Tags and Forms

A user can enter any text into either a single-line HTML text field or a multi-line HTML text area. In particular, nothing prevents a user from entering HTML tags. This can be both good and bad.

In some situations, you want a user to be able to format the text entered into a form by using HTML tags. For example, imagine that you have created a bulletin board for your Web site using Active Server Pages and HTML forms. The postings on the bulletin board may be more interesting if the text is displayed using different colors and different fonts. To format the text in a posting, someone posting to the bulletin board can simply use HTML tags. You don't have to do anything special to allow this to happen.

In other situations, you may not want HTML formatting to be applied. For example, suppose you're building a Web site that explains how to program using Active Server Pages. (You might call this Web site the ASP site and locate it at `http://www.aspsite.com`.) If someone posts a code example using HTML, you want the actual HTML tags to be displayed and not interpreted. How can you do this?

Fortunately, Active Server Pages includes a special method for this particular purpose. The `Server.HTMLEncode()` method translates HTML tags into HTML character codes. Check out this example of how this method is used:

```
<%=Server.HTMLEncode("<B>This is bold</B>")%>
```

Normally, if the string `"<B>This is bold</B>"` is outputted to a browser, the text would appear as bold. However, once the text has been HTML-encoded, the actual string is outputted instead.

> **NOTE**
>
> For a complete list of HTML character codes, see Appendix D, "Quick HTML Reference," at the back of this book.

Testing for the Existence of Form Elements

You'll often need to check whether a person has actually completed all the information in a form. For example, a normal registration form has a number of required fields. You don't want to allow a visitor to your Web site to gain access by submitting a blank registration form.

You can check whether information has been entered into a particular form field by using a script like the following (continued on the next page):

```
<%
IF Request.Form("FirstName")="" THEN
  Response.Write("You must enter your first name.")
ELSE
```

```
   Response.Write("Thank you for registering")
END IF
%>
```

This script tests whether the form field named FirstName has a value. The item FirstName is compared to a zero-length string. If the user has neglected to enter a first name, he or she is informed of this fact.

When someone enters incomplete form information, you should redirect the user to the form once again, so the information can be entered. You could do this by supplying a hypertext link back to the proper page. However, it would be much better for the user to be returned to the proper page automatically. You'll learn some methods of doing this later in this chapter. (See "Redirecting a User to Another Page" and "Including Files.")

Retrieving a Query String

A *query string* is the extra portion of the URL that appears after the question mark. If you've ever used Internet search engines such as Alta Vista, you'll be familiar with query strings. Those extra characters that clutter up the address bar of your browser when you use a search engine are an example of a query string.

You can use a query string with a hyperlink to pass information from one page to another. For instance, consider the following HTML page:

```
<HTML>
<HEAD><TITLE> Query String Example </TITLE></HEAD>
<BODY>
<A HREF="http://www.aspsite.com/newpage.asp?Click=YES"> Click Me! </A>
</BODY>
</HTML>
```

In this example, the hyperlink links to the page named newpage.asp. However, the hyperlink also includes a query string. When someone clicks the words Click Me!, the query string "Click=Yes" is passed in the request for the new page.

You can also pass a query string directly by typing it into the address bar of your browser. The server won't know the difference. For example, typing the following string into the address bar of your Web browser would have the same effect as clicking the hyperlink in the preceding example:

```
http://www.aspsite.com/newpage.asp?Click=Yes
```

Query strings are useful when you need to present a menu of choices. If you have a number of hyperlinks that link to the same page, you can use a query string to determine the particular hyperlink that was clicked. Consider the following example:

```
<HTML>
<HEAD><TITLE> Product List </TITLE></HEAD>
<BODY>
<H3> Welcome To Our Store! </H3>
```

```
Please select the item you want to purchase from the list below:
<P><A HREF="/purchase.asp?ITEM=1"> Used Book </A>
<P><A HREF="/purchase.asp?ITEM=2"> Broken Typewriter </A>
<P><A HREF="/purchase.asp?ITEM=3"> Horseshoe </A>
</BODY>
</HTML>
```

This page presents a number of items from which a visitor can select to buy (see Figure 15.3). Each item description is a hyperlink. When the user clicks any of the items, he or she is linked to the purchase.asp page.

FIGURE 15.3.

A page with a list of items for sale.

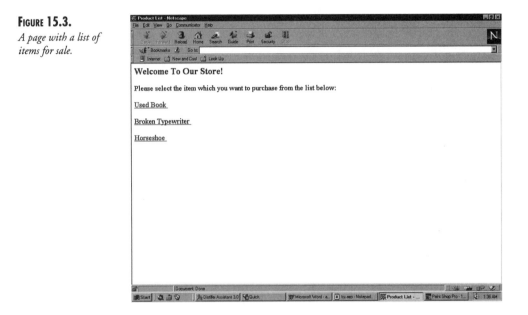

To detect the selection of the buyer, you need to determine which hypertext link was clicked. You need to determine this within the purchase.asp page. Each hypertext link is uniquely identified by a query string. How do you retrieve this information?

Query strings are passed in an HTTP request. Therefore, you shouldn't be surprised to learn that the Active Server Pages Request object has a collection for query strings. Query strings are contained in the QueryString collection of the Request object.

You can retrieve the items in the QueryString collection in the same way that you retrieve the items in the Form collection. To retrieve a particular query string, you simply pass the name of that query string. Here's an example (continued on the following page):

```
<HTML>
<HEAD><TITLE> Purchase </TITLE></HEAD>
<BODY>
<%
SELECT CASE Request.QueryString("item")
```

```
    CASE "1"
      Response.Write("Thank you for purchasing a used book.")
    CASE "2"
      Response.Write("Thank you for purchasing a broken typewriter.")
    CASE "3"
      Response.Write("Thank you for purchasing a horseshoe.")
END SELECT
%>
</BODY>
</HTML>
```

The QueryString collection is used in this example to determine which hyperlink was clicked. The SELECT CASE statement returns an appropriate response, depending on the query string. For example, if someone selected to buy a horseshoe, the user is thanked for purchasing that particular item.

Encoding a Query String

A query string must be URL-encoded before it can be passed from one page to another. For example, all spaces must be converted to addition signs. If you neglect to URL-encode a query string, you may get strange results.

> **NOTE**
>
> You can get away with not URL-encoding a query string when the query string doesn't have any special characters such as spaces or punctuation marks. The previous example works fine because the query string doesn't include any special characters.

Fortunately, it's very easy to URL-encode a query string using Active Server Pages. There's a method for this particular purpose. The Server.URLEncode() method converts any string to URL-encoded form. Look at this example:

```
<A HREF="/response.asp?Message=<%=Server.URLEncode("This query
  string has been URL encoded.")%>"> Click Here </A>
```

Notice that you don't URL-encode the name of the query string or the equal sign. Doing this would create problems. You only URL-encode the value of a query string.

Once the query string in the previous example has been URL-encoded, it looks like this:

```
Message=This+query+string+has+been+URL+encoded%2E
```

You don't need to worry about decoding a string that has been URL-encoded. Active Server Pages will do this for you automatically. For example, suppose the response.asp page included the following line of code:

```
<%=Request.QueryString("message")%>
```

The message wouldn't be outputted in URL-encoded form. It would look like this:

```
This query string has been URL encoded.
```

Query Strings with Multiple Parameters and Multiple Values

You can pass more than one name and value pair in a query string. In other words, you can create a query string with multiple parameters. To pass multiple parameters, simply join them together using the ampersand (&) character. The following query string passes two parameters:

```
<A HREF="/response.asp?FirstParam=<%=Server.URLEncode("This is the
   first parameter.")%>&SecondParam=<%=Server.URLEncode("This is
   the second parameter.")%>"> Click Here </A>
```

This query string includes two parameters named FirstParam and SecondParam. FirstParam has the value "This is the first parameter." SecondParam has the value "This is the second parameter." The Server.URLEncode() method is used to convert the values of the parameters so they can be properly passed.

In the response.asp page, you can output the values of the two parameters like this:

```
<P><%=Request.QueryString("FirstParam")%>
<P><%=Request.QueryString("SecondParam")%>
```

By passing the name of a query string parameter to the QueryString collection, you retrieve the value of the parameter. The output from the previous two statements would appear like this:

```
This is the first parameter.

This is the second parameter.
```

You can also assign a single parameter more than one value. To do this, simply use the name of the parameter twice in the query string. Following is an example:

```
<A HREF="/response.asp?OnlyParam=<%=Server.URLEncode("I am the first
   value of the only parameter.")%>&OnlyParam=<%=Server.URLEncode("I
   am the second value of the only parameter.")%>"> Click Here </A>
```

In this example, the parameter named OnlyParam is assigned a value twice. First the parameter is assigned the value "I am the first value of the only parameter." Next, the parameter is assigned the value "I am the second value of the only parameter."

Once you have assigned a single parameter with more than one value, you can use the Count property to determine the number of values of the parameter. The following example displays a count of the number of values of the OnlyParam parameter and then displays each value:

```
The OnlyParam parameter has
<%=Request.QueryString("OnlyParam").Count%> values.
<P>They are:
<%
FOR EACH pvalue IN Request.QueryString("OnlyParam")
  Response.Write("<BR>"&pvalue)
NEXT
%>
```

The FOR...EACH loop iterates through each value of the OnlyParam parameter. If the OnlyParam parameter has zero values, the Count property would return 0 and no values would be displayed.

Dumping the QueryString Collection

If you want to retrieve all the parameters in the QueryString collection, you can iterate through the collection using a FOR...EACH loop. For example, the following script dumps the contents of the QueryString collection to the screen:

```
<%
FOR EACH QSParam IN Request.QueryString
  Response.Write("<BR>"&QSParam&"=")
  Response.Write(Request.QueryString(QSParam)
NEXT
%>
```

Instead of using a FOR...EACH loop, you can also use a FOR...NEXT loop to dump the QueryString collection. To do this, you need to determine the number of items in the QueryString collection. You can use the Count property to recover this information. Here's an example:

```
<%
FOR i=1 TO Request.QueryString.Count
  Response.Write("<BR>"&Request.QueryString(i))
NEXT
%>
```

Finally, if you simply prefer to retrieve an unparsed query string, you can call the Request.QueryString collection with no parameters. The following example displays the contents of the QueryString collection without any parsing (see Figure 15.4):

```
<%=Request.QueryString %>
```

FIGURE 15.4.

An unparsed query string.

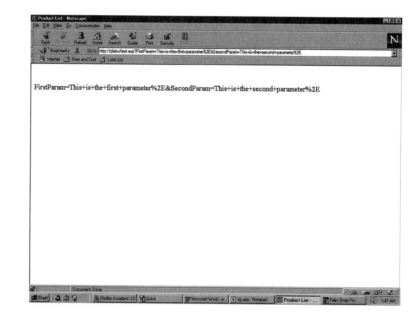

NOTE

You can also retrieve an unparsed query string by using the QUERY_STRING server variable. See the section "Working with Headers" in Chapter 14, "Working with a Single Active Server Page."

When Not to Use Query Strings

Query strings are useful when you need to pass small bits of information from one page to another, but there are two situations in which you definitely shouldn't use a query string: when you're passing hidden information, and when you're passing large chunks of data.

A query string isn't hidden from view in any way. The query string will always appear in the address bar of a browser. This means that passing the password of a user from page to page with a query string is a very bad idea. Anyone looking over the user's shoulder will immediately know the password.

Query strings are also not a good choice for passing large chunks of data. The exact number of characters that a query string can contain depends on a number of factors. One of the main factors is the browser being used. Different browsers have different limitations on query string size. For example, Microsoft Internet Explorer 4.0 can't handle a query string that's larger than about 2,000 characters. A hyperlink with a query string of this size will simply fail to work as a hyperlink with this browser.

You shouldn't conclude from this fact that you can use query strings up to 2,000 characters long. First, the true maximum depends on the length of the URL as well. The combination of the URL and query string—everything in the address bar of the browser—determines the maximum size.

Second, when you URL-encode a query string, this often makes the string considerably longer. For example, periods are converted into three characters (%2E) instead of one. The maximum size of a query string depends on the URL-encoded form of the string.

Third, browsers other than Internet Explorer 4.0 can often handle far fewer than 2,000 characters. Once a query string hits a length of 1,000 characters or so, you risk losing compatibility with a number of browsers.

In brief, it's a good idea to keep your query strings short. Query strings aren't an efficient method of passing large amounts of data. Even worse, a page with a large query string may completely fail to function on certain browsers. If you need to pass a large amount of data from one page to another, use a hidden form field. None of the limitations discussed here applies to form fields. The HTTP protocol passes form fields in a much more efficient way than query strings.

15

WORKING WITH
MORE THAN ONE
ASP PAGE

Redirecting a User to Another Page

In a number of situations, you need to redirect a user to another page. For example, if a user attempts to access a page that requires registration, the user should automatically be redirected to a registration page. Or if the user has entered incomplete form information, he or she should automatically be redirected to the page with the form so that it can be completed.

It's very easy to redirect a user to a new page using Active Server Pages. The Redirect method of the Response object allows you to redirect a user to a new page. Look at this example:

```
<%
IF Request.Form("FirstName")="" THEN Response.Redirect "/register.asp"
%>
<HTML>
<HEAD><TITLE> Registration Results </TITLE></HEAD>
<BODY>
Thank you <%=Request.Form("FirstName")%> for registering!
</BODY>
</HTML>
```

Imagine that a user has just completed a registration form and this page is returned. The Response.Redirect method, in this example, is used to redirect the user back to the page with the registration form if the user hasn't entered a first name.

You must use the Response.Redirect method before any text is outputted to the browser. Therefore, it's a good idea to place this method in a script that appears above the <HTML> tag. The only way around this requirement is to buffer the output of your Active Server Page (see the section "Buffering Output" in Chapter 14 to learn how to do this).

You can use the Response.Redirect method to redirect a user to any valid URL. This could be another page on your Web site or even a page located at another Web site on the Internet. The Response.Redirect method is potentially a very useful method. Microsoft uses this method extensively in its demonstration applications for Active Server Pages. Sadly, however, there are problems with it. The Response.Redirect method works by returning a particular status code. (See Chapter 14 for details on status codes.) Whenever a server responds to a request, the server returns a status code in the first line of its response. When the Response.Redirect method is called, the status code 302 Object Moved is returned. A location header is also added to the response to give the new location of the page. The status code and location header should automatically redirect the browser to the new page.

NOTE

The Response.Redirect method is completely equivalent to the following two lines of code:

```
<%
Response.Status="302 Object Moved"
Response.AddHeader "Location", "URL"
%>
```

> For more information on the AddHeader method, see Appendix A, "Quick ASP Object and Component Reference," at the back of this book.

In reality, however, this doesn't always happen. Older browsers in particular have problems with redirection. Worse yet, even very recent browsers such as Netscape Navigator 4.0 can have difficulties automatically responding to the redirection status code. When a browser can't respond automatically to a status code, you receive a message like that in Figure 15.5.

FIGURE 15.5.

Results of a server redirect.

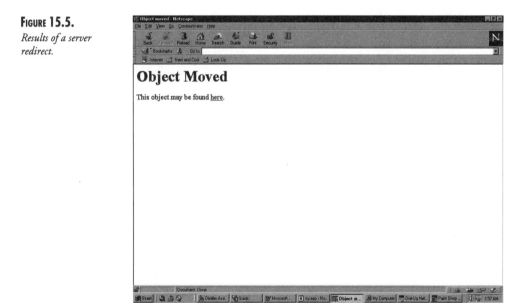

This message isn't pretty, and can lead to confusion. For this reason, you should try to avoid using the Response.Redirect method. Use the simulated redirect method discussed in the next section instead.

Including Files

You can easily include one file in another Active Server Page by using a server-side INCLUDE directive. A server-side INCLUDE directive shouldn't appear within a script; use it outside a script as part of the HTML code:

```
<HTML>
<HEAD><TITLE> Welcome </TITLE></HEAD>
<BODY>
<!-- #INCLUDE VIRTUAL="mybanner.inc" -->
Welcome To Our Web Site!
</BODY>
</HTML>
```

In this example, the file mybanner.inc is inserted into the Active Server Page below the <BODY> tag. When this Active Server Page is processed, any scripts or HTML code in the file mybanner.inc are included in the Active Server Page above.

You can include one file in another in two ways: by providing a virtual path to the file as in the preceding example, or by providing a physical path to the file. Following is an example of the latter method:

```
<HTML>
<HEAD><TITLE> Welcome </TITLE></HEAD>
<BODY>
<!-- #INCLUDE FILE="mybanner.inc" -->
Welcome To Our Web Site!
</BODY>
</HTML>
```

If you supply a physical path to the included file by using the FILE attribute, the file must be located in the current directory or a subdirectory of that directory. The path of the file is relative to the current directory. This is a significant limitation; therefore, you will almost always use the VIRTUAL attribute instead.

The included file can have any name and any extension. By convention, included files usually end with the extension .inc, but you can use .asp, .htm, .html, or any other extension you prefer.

NOTE

When you change a file that's included in another, the change won't always take effect. The problem is that IIS is caching the files. IIS does an even worse job of recognizing changes in included files than it does recognizing changes in normal files.

You have two choices in this situation. You can turn the Web server on and off using the Internet Service Manager (a little drastic). On the other hand, you can load each file that includes the changed file, make a meaningless change, and save it again. For instance, you can add an extra space. The downside of this procedure is that it's boring and time-consuming.

Including one file in another is useful in two situations. The first and most obvious situation is when you want to display the same content or execute the same script page after page. For example, it's not uncommon for every page at a Web site to have the same banner and footer. Instead of repeating the same HTML code over and over, you can simply include a banner and footer file as part of every page.

You can also include the same Active Server Page script on multiple pages by using the INCLUDE directive. However, because the INCLUDE directive must occur outside a script, the script you include must be completely contained in script delimiters. You can't include a fragment of a script.

The second situation in which including one file in another is useful is when you want to simulate server redirection. To do this, you include one whole Active Server Page in a second Active Server Page. Consider the following example:

```
<%
IF Request.Form("FirstName")="" THEN
%>
<!-- #INCLUDE VIRTUAL="register.asp" -->
<%
Response.End
END IF
%>
<HTML>
<HEAD><TITLE> Registration Results </TITLE></HEAD>
<BODY>
Thank you <%=Request.Form("FirstName")%> for registering!
</BODY>
</HTML>
```

This example has exactly the same effect as using the Response.Redirect method. If a user has neglected to enter information into the FirstName field of the registration form, he or she is returned to the registration page. However, because including a file takes place completely on the server, this simulated redirection is more reliable than actual redirection.

Notice the use of the Response.End method in this example. The Response.End method is included to prevent the remainder of the Active Server Page from being displayed if the registration page is displayed.

It's important to realize that IIS processes any INCLUDE directives before it processes scripts. This means that you can't use a script command to dynamically include one file in another. For example, the following script won't work:

```
<%
IF Request.Form("FirstName")="" THEN
  MyInclude="register.asp"
ELSE
  MyInclude="HomePage.asp"
END IF
%>
<!-- #INCLUDE VIRTUAL="<%=MyInclude%>" -->
```

This script won't work because the server will attempt to include any files before the script is executed. This means that the server will attempt to include the file "<%=MyInclude%>", which, of course, doesn't exist.

Summary

In this chapter, you learned how to work with multiple Active Server Pages. First you learned how to retrieve the contents of an HTML form. You learned how to retrieve the values of individual form elements and how to dump the complete contents of the Form collection. In the second section, you learned how to work with query strings, how to use the QueryString collection, and when not to use a query string. The third section described the Response.Redirect method. Finally, you discovered how to include a file in an Active Server Page.

Working with Active Server Pages Sessions

IN THIS CHAPTER

In this chapter, you learn how to work with sessions. You learn how to use session collections, properties, methods, and events. You also learn how to read and create cookies. Finally, some methods are discussed for retaining state without cookies.

An Introduction to Sessions

What are sessions? A *session* is something that starts the moment a user requests a page from your Web site and ends soon after the user leaves. Each visitor to your Web site is given an individual session.

Sessions can be used to store a visitor's preferences. For example, does the visitor prefer that Web pages have a green background or a blue background? Does the visitor have a strong hostility toward frames? Does the visitor prefer to view a text-only version of your Web site? These preferences can be tracked by using sessions.

Sessions can also be used to create virtual shopping carts. Whenever a visitor selects an item to buy at your Web site, the item can be added to a shopping cart. When the user is ready to leave, he or she can purchase everything in the shopping cart at once. All the information about the items in the shopping cart can be stored in a session.

Finally, sessions can be used to keep track of the habits of your visitors. In the same way in which environmentalists use tracking devices to record the roaming habits of the great white shark, you can use sessions to track the movements of your visitors as they roam from page to page. This information can be used for advertising purposes, to improve the design of your Web site, or simply to satisfy your curiosity.

The Stateliness of Sessions

Sessions were invented to address a limitation of the HTTP protocol. Remember how the HTTP protocol works—whenever a user makes a request, the server supplies a response. All interaction between a browser and a Web server takes place in discrete request and response pairs.

Nothing in the HTTP protocol allows a server to keep track of the users making the requests. After a server has finished responding to a request, the server can't continue to identify the browser that made it. From the perspective of a Web server, each new request is made by a new individual. For this reason, the HTTP protocol is called a *stateless protocol*. The HTTP protocol can't be used to retain the state of a user. This is a very serious limitation because it means that you can't identify a user over multiple Web pages.

Sessions were introduced to fix this problem. By using sessions, you can store information about a user over multiple Web pages. Sessions allow you to do many things that would otherwise be very difficult or completely impossible.

NOTE

Be warned that Active Server Pages sessions use cookies, and not all browsers support cookies. For details, see the later section "How Sessions Really Work."

Storing Session Information

Active Server Pages sessions are very easy to use. You can control all aspects of a session by using the Active Server Pages Session object. If you need to store data that will persist throughout a user session, you simply store that data in a collection of the Session object. Here's an example:

```
<HTML>
<HEAD><TITLE> Session Example </TITLE></HEAD>
<BODY>
<%
Session("Greeting")="Welcome!"
Response.Write(Session("Greeting"))
%>
</BODY>
</HTML>
```

When this Active Server Page is displayed in a browser, the greeting Welcome! is displayed. The first line in this script assigns the text "Welcome!" to a session variable named Greeting. The next line in the script outputs the greeting to the screen.

So far, this isn't particularly exciting. You can do the same thing by using a normal VBScript variable. However, imagine that the same user requests another page. For example, imagine that the user requests the following page:

```
<HTML>
<HEAD><TITLE> Another Page </TITLE></HEAD>
<BODY>
<%=Session("Greeting")%>
</BODY>
</HTML>
```

When the user views this page, the same Welcome! greeting is displayed once again. However, the session variable wasn't assigned a value on this page. The session variable Greeting has retained the value it was assigned on the previous page.

You couldn't do this with a normal script variable. The lifetime of a normal variable extends only throughout a single page. A session variable, on the other hand, persists until the user leaves the Web site.

It's important to understand that session variables exist only in relation to a particular user. The values assigned to session variables in one user session don't affect the values of the session variables in another user session. In other words, the data stored in session variables isn't shared among different users. For example, suppose the following script appeared in an Active Server Page:

```
<%
Randomize
If INT(2*RND)=1 THEN
  Session("FavoriteColor")="Blue"
ELSE
  Session("FavoriteColor")="Red"
END IF
%>
```

This script randomly assigns the session variable FavoriteColor with either the value "Blue" or the value "Red". This variable may have a different value in the case of different users. The value of the variable FavoriteColor is relative to a particular user session.

The Contents of a Session

Most session variables are actually stored in a collection of the Session object named Contents. For example, the following two statements are equivalent:

```
<% Session("MyVar")="Some data" %>
```

```
<% Session.Contents("MyVar")="Some data" %>
```

As in the collections discussed previously, you can use the Count property to determine the number of items in the Contents collection. You can also display all the items contained in the Contents collection by using either a FOR...EACH or a FOR...NEXT loop. This example uses both methods:

```
<%
Session("FavoriteColor")="blue"
Session("FavoriteFont")="Comic Sans MS"
%>
There are
<%=Session.Contents.Count %>
items in the Session Contents collection.
<HR>
<%
FOR EACH thing IN Session.Contents
  Response.Write( "<BR>"&thing&"="&Session.Contents(thing))
NEXT
Response.Write("<HR>")
FOR i=1 TO Session.Contents.Count
  Response.Write("<BR>"&Session.Contents(i))
NEXT
%>
```

In this script, two session variables named FavoriteColor and FavoriteFont are created. Next, a count of the number of items in the Contents collection is retrieved. Finally, all of the items in the Contents collection are displayed by using both a FOR...EACH and a FOR...NEXT loop (see Figure 16.1).

Working with Active Server Pages Sessions

CHAPTER 16

485

16

WORKING WITH
ACTIVE SERVER
PAGES SESSIONS

FIGURE 16.1.
The contents of the
Contents *collection.*

Identifying a Session

Active Server Pages assigns each user session a unique identifier. This session ID is created when the user session is first created and persists throughout the time the user remains at your Web site. To retrieve the session ID, you use the SessionID property of the Session object, as in this example:

```
<HTML>
<HEAD><TITLE> Session ID </TITLE></HEAD>
<BODY>
Your session ID is: <%=Session.SessionID %>
</BODY>
</HTML>
```

The Active Server Page here simply outputs the value of the SessionID property (see Figure 16.2). When different users retrieve the page, a different session ID will be displayed for each. However, if the same user retrieves the page multiple times, the same session ID should be displayed.

One use for the SessionID property is to track the movements of your visitors. For example, you can record the pages that a user visits in the log file of your Web site. Simply create the following file and include it in every page:

```
<%
Who=Session.SessionID
CurrentPage=Request.ServerVariables("SCRIPT_NAME")
Response.AppendToLog Who&":"&CurrentPage
%>
```

This script uses the `AppendToLog` method of the `Response` object to append an entry in the server log file. In this example, the string added to the log file contains the session ID that was retrieved from the `SessionID` property. The string also contains the path to the current page, which was retrieved from the `SCRIPT_NAME` server variable.

Figure 16.2.

The value of
`SessionID`.

> **NOTE**
>
> You can use the `AppendToLog` method of the `Response` object to append any string under 80 characters to your Web server's log file. Because commas are used to separate fields in the log file, you shouldn't use commas in the string.
>
> The Internet Information Server log file is a text file that contains a log of the activity of your Web server. You can open it by using any standard text editor. By default, it's located in the `Winnt/system32/LogFiles` directory.

Controlling When Sessions End

How does the server know when a session ends? In other words, how does the server know whether a user has left your Web site for another one or has turned off his or her computer and gone to see a movie?

The server assumes that if someone hasn't requested or refreshed a page for a period of more than 20 minutes, that person has left, and times out that user's session. This strategy allows the server to recover resources that it has been using to track the user's session.

For certain Web site applications, this timeout period of 20 minutes is too short. For example, suppose you have a game site that includes a number of complicated puzzles, which the user must solve with pen and paper. You might expect the user to be inactive, from the Web server's perspective, for long periods of time.

For other Web site applications, the session timeout period of 20 minutes is too long. If you have a very high volume Web site, and you want to ease the burden on your server as much as possible, you may want a shorter session timeout period.

Fortunately, you can control the maximum amount of time for which a user is allowed to be inactive before a session times out. The Session object has a property for this purpose. You can set the amount of time before a session times out by using the Timeout property of the Session object. For example, the following script sets the Timeout property to 60 minutes:

```
<% Session.Timeout=60 %>
```

> **NOTE**
>
> You can also specify the session timeout by using the Internet Service Manager. From the Application Configuration dialog box, click the Active Server Pages tab and specify the number of minutes for the session timeout.

When a user session times out and the user makes a new request, the server treats the user as a new user. The server creates a new session, and all the old session information is lost. You can force this to happen manually by using the Abandon method of the Session object. Consider the following example:

```
<HTML>
<HEAD><TITLE> Abandon Session </TITLE></HEAD>
<BODY>
<BR>The user is <%=Session.SessionID %>.
<% Session.Abandon %>
<BR>The user is <%=Session.SessionID %>.
</BODY>
</HTML>
```

In this example, the session ID of the user is outputted to the screen. Next, the Session.Abandon method is called. When the user ID is outputted once again, the ID is a different number. After the Abandon method is called, the server treats the user as a new user (see Figure 16.3).

FIGURE 16.3.

Abandoning a session.

Session Events

Unlike any of the other objects discussed to this point, the Session object has events. Two of them, in fact: the Session_OnStart event, which is triggered when a session begins, and the Session_OnEnd event, which is triggered when a session ends. You can associate one and only one script with each of these two events.

The statements in the script are executed when the event is triggered. Both of these scripts must be located in a special file named Global.asa. Every Web site application can have only one Global.asa file. The file is located in the root directory of your Web site application. It contains information that's global to your Web site application. The Global.asa file has the following structure:

```
<SCRIPT LANGUAGE=VBScript RUNAT=Server>
SUB Application_OnStart
END SUB
</SCRIPT>

<SCRIPT LANGUAGE=VBScript RUNAT=Server>
SUB Application_OnEnd
END SUB
</SCRIPT>

<SCRIPT LANGUAGE=VBScript RUNAT=Server>
SUB Session_OnStart
END SUB
</SCRIPT>
```

Working with Active Server Pages Sessions

CHAPTER 16

489

16

WORKING WITH
ACTIVE SERVER
PAGES SESSIONS

```
<SCRIPT LANGUAGE=VBScript RUNAT=Server>
 SUB Session_OnEnd
 END SUB
</SCRIPT>
```

> **NOTE**
>
> The next chapter provides more details about the Global.asa file.

The Global.asa file can contain four scripts. One of these scripts is triggered by the Session_OnStart event and one is triggered by the Session_OnEnd event. (The next chapter covers the two remaining scripts.)

Notice that Global.asa uses the Microsoft extended HTML <SCRIPT> tag syntax to specify the scripts. You must use this method of indicating a script within the Global.asa file instead of using the normal script delimiters <% and %>. The Global.asa file in the preceding example uses VBScript as the scripting language, but you can use other scripting languages as well.

You can't include any output within the Global.asa file. In particular, you can't use any HTML tags or the Response.Write() method. The Global.asa file itself is never displayed. The file is used only to contain scripts and objects.

To create a script that executes whenever a new session is started, you simply add the script to the Session_OnStart section of the Global.asa file, as in this example:

```
<SCRIPT LANGUAGE=VBScript RUNAT=Server>
SUB Session_OnStart
  Session("UserName")="Unknown"
  Session("UserPassword")="Unknown"
END SUB
</SCRIPT>
```

This script assigns the value "Unknown" to two session variables named Username and UserPassword. This example illustrates one of the main functions of the Session_OnStart script—initializing session variables.

The Session_OnStart script can be used for other purposes as well. For example, one interesting application of the Session_OnStart script is for redirecting visitors to a new page. Suppose you don't want any visitors of your Web site to go directly to any page other than the home page when they first arrive. You can redirect the first page request to the home page by using the Response.Redirect method. Here's an example:

```
<SCRIPT LANGUAGE=VBScript RUNAT=Server>
SUB Session_OnStart
  MyHomePage="/homepage.asp"
  RequestPage=Request.ServerVariables("SCRIPT_NAME")
IF NOT (STRCOMP(MyHomePage,RequestPage,vbTextCompare)=0)THEN
  Response.Redirect MyHomePage
END IF
END SUB
</SCRIPT>
```

> **NOTE**
>
> Microsoft uses this method of automatically redirecting users to a start page in their Adventure Works sample application.

In this script, the path of the page that the user requests is compared to the path of the home page. If they're not the same, the user is automatically redirected to the home page.

This final example uses both the `Session_OnStart` and `Session_OnEnd` events:

```
<SCRIPT LANGUAGE=VBScript RUNAT=Server>
SUB Session_OnStart
 Response.AppendToLog Session.SessionID&" starting"
END SUB
</SCRIPT>
<SCRIPT LANGUAGE=VBScript RUNAT=Server>
SUB Session_OnEnd
  Response.AppendToLog Session.SessionID&" ending"
END SUB
</SCRIPT>
```

The `Session_OnStart` and `Session_OnEnd` scripts here record the session ID of the user in the log file. Because the `Session_OnStart` script executes when a user first arrives, this `Session_OnStart` script records when the user starts a new session. The `Session_OnEnd` script records when the user leaves. You can use this information to determine the pages that are most often used to enter and exit your Web site.

How Sessions Really Work

Sessions use cookies (see the following section for details on cookies). When a user first requests a page from your Web site, the server creates a single cookie in the user's browser to track the session. When the session ends, the cookie expires as well.

The cookie created for each user is named `ASPSESSIONID`. The only purpose of this cookie is to provide a unique identifier for each user.

> **NOTE**
>
> If you are curious about the value of the `ASPSESSIONID` cookie, one way to view it is by retrieving the `COOKIE` header from the `ServerVariables` collection (the `COOKIE` header contains all the cookies a browser sends). Place the following script in an Active Server Page to display the `COOKIE` header:
>
> `<%=Request.ServerVariables ("HTTP COOKIE") %>`
>
> You may have to refresh or reload the Active Server Page at least once to display the cookies. To learn more about using the `ServerVariables` collection, see Chapter 14, "Working with a Single Active Server Page."

Working with Active Server Pages Sessions

CHAPTER 16

491

16

WORKING WITH
ACTIVE SERVER
PAGES SESSIONS

The session variables themselves are not stored on the user's browser. However, the ASPSESSIONID cookie is needed to use session variables. The server uses the ASPSESSIONID cookie to associate the proper session variables with the proper user. Without the cookie, the server would have no way to identify the same user as he or she moved from page to page on a Web site.

The session ID stored in the ASPSESSIONID cookie is not the same as the SessionID property. Microsoft uses a complicated algorithm to generate the value of the ASPSESSIONID cookie. Microsoft does this in order to prevent hackers from guessing the session ID and pretending to be someone they're not.

> **NOTE**
>
> You can disable sessions in two ways—disable sessions for your entire Web site application, or prevent sessions from being used on a particular page.
>
> To prevent the Web server from creating user sessions entirely, you use the Internet Service Manager. From the Application Configuration dialog box, click the Active Server Pages tab and uncheck the Enable Session State option.
>
> You can also specify that a particular Active Server Page should be sessionless by using the following Active Server Page directive at the top of the file:
>
> ```
> <%@ EnableSessionState=False %>
> ```

Because the Session object uses cookies, the object may be incompatible with both old and very recent browsers. Older browsers simply can't use cookies. What's even worse, many very recent browsers, such as Netscape 4.0, provide the option of disabling cookies altogether.

This presents a problem. Because cookies aren't compatible with all browsers, you should be cautious in using the Session object when building your Web site. Although there are certain things that you simply can't do without using sessions, certain properties of a session can be simulated by other means. Some alternatives to using cookies and the Session object are discussed in the later section "Retaining State Without Cookies."

> **NOTE**
>
> Certain browsers, such as Netscape Navigator, use case-sensitive URLs to determine when to send a cookie. This can create problems with sessions. For this reason, Microsoft recommends that you always use the same case when specifying URLs in Active Server Pages. For example, don't use /WWW/mypage.asp and /www/mypage.asp, as this may confuse the Netscape browser.

Cookies

Few Internet technologies create greater agitation among Web users than *cookies*. Cookies have an innocent-sounding name, but many users assume that they have an evil purpose.

Netscape introduced cookies into the world with the first version of its browser. Since then, the World Wide Web Consortium has endorsed a cookie standard. Most browsers now have the ability to use cookies.

What are cookies? Browsers that support cookies maintain one or more special files. These files, called *cookie files* on Windows machines and *magic cookie files* on the Macintosh, are used to store data from Web sites. A Web server can insert pieces of information into these cookie files. This explains the strong negative reaction some Web users have toward cookies. Some people consider a cookie an invasion of privacy. Even worse, some people consider cookies an invasion of their personal space.

Certain cookies are temporary; others are persistent. For example, the cookies used by Active Server Pages to track user sessions expire after a visitor leaves the Web site. Other cookies can remain in the cookie files to be read by the server when a user returns.

It's the cookies that remain in the cookie files that generate the most concern. The fear is that these cookies can be used to track an individual's Web surfing habits. The worry is that if this information falls into the wrong hands, the individual could become the target of multiple bulk-mail advertising campaigns (a fate worse than death). However, this fear is completely unfounded. One Web server can't read another Web server's cookies. Cookies are implemented in such a way that this is impossible. Nevertheless, this misperception is so widespread that browser manufacturers have had no choice but to respond to it.

> **NOTE**
>
> One indication of the hysteria that currently surrounds cookies is the inflated privacy concerns even expert Webmasters have been known to have about them. Jon Udell, who writes the Web Project column for *BYTE*, suggested in his column that one Web server could steal and inspect another server's cookies. He reported that he was wrong about this in a following issue (see the March and May 1997 issues of *BYTE Magazine*).

Recent versions of both Microsoft Internet Explorer and Netscape Navigator have additional options that allow greater control over cookies. You can configure either browser to warn you before accepting a cookie. Additionally, Netscape Navigator includes the option of disabling cookies entirely. (Early beta versions of Internet Explorer 3.0 also had this option, but then Microsoft came out with Active Server Pages and this feature disappeared before the final release.)

Moreover, various ingenious techniques have been developed to disable cookies even on the browsers that don't provide these options. For example, you can disable cookies on a browser by making the cookie files read-only (see `http://www.cookiecentral.com`).

Unfortunately, the current state of affairs means that you can't depend on cookies when building your Web site. Cookies work on the majority of browsers, but fail completely when used with certain browsers, and this means that sessions will fail as well.

> **NOTE**
>
> A number of Web sites have valuable information on cookies. To view the Netscape specification for cookies, see this site:
>
> `http://search.netscape.com/newsref/std/cookie_spec.html`
>
> To view the World Wide Web Consortium's Reference specification on cookies, visit `http://w3.org`. Finally, for general information on cookies, go to `http://www.cookiecentral.com`.

How Cookies Work

Cookies are passed back and forth between a browser and server through HTTP headers. The server first creates a cookie by using the `Set-Cookie` header in a response. Subsequent requests from the browser will return this cookie in the `Cookie` header.

Suppose you want to create a cookie named `UserName` that contains the name of the visitor to your Web site. To create this cookie, the server would send a header like this:

```
Set-Cookie: UserName=BILL+Gates; path=/; domain=aspsite.com;
 expires=Tuesday, 01-Jan-99 00:00:01 GMT
```

This header instructs the browser to add an entry to its cookie file. The browser adds the cookie named `UserName` with the value `Bill Gates`. Notice that the value of the cookie is URL-encoded.

Furthermore, the header informs the browser that this cookie should be returned to the server regardless of the path used in the request. If the path attribute were set to another value such as `/private`, the cookie would only be returned in requests to this path. For example, the request for the file `/private/mypage.htm` would include the `Cookie` header but not the request `/mypage.htm`.

The `domain` attribute further restricts where the cookie can be sent by the browser. In this example, the cookie can be sent only to the `www.aspsite.com` Web site. The cookie will never be sent to `www.yahoo.com` or any other Web site on the Internet.

> **NOTE**
>
> Certain browsers, such as Netscape Navigator, use case-sensitive URLs. This means that these browsers won't return a cookie to the path /private when requesting the page /PRIVATE/page.htm.

Finally, the Expires attribute specifies when the cookie should expire. The header in the example tells the browser to store the cookie until the first second of January 1, 1999. Actually, the cookie will probably expire much earlier than that. When a cookie file becomes too large, the browser automatically starts removing cookies.

Once the browser has created a cookie, the browser returns the cookie in every request it makes to the Web site—that is, every request that satisfies the path requirement. However, the browser won't send the cookie in requests to a Web site with a different domain name. The browser continues to send the cookie until the cookie expires. The Cookie header looks like this:

```
Cookie: UserName: Bill+Gates
```

Creating and Reading Cookies with Active Server Pages

To create a cookie with Active Server Pages, you use the Cookies collection of the Response object. You can create two types of cookies: a cookie with a single value, or a *cookie dictionary*, which contains multiple name and value pairs.

To create a cookie with a single value, you can use a script like this:

```
<%
Response.Cookies("UserName")="Bill Gates"
Response.Cookies("UserName").Expires="Jan 1, 1999"
%>
```

This script creates a cookie named UserName with the value "Bill Gates". This cookie will be returned by a user's browser until January 1, 1999 or until the browser erases it. If you don't specify an expiration date for the cookie, the cookie expires when the user leaves your Web site.

Because the example script actually creates a header, you must place the script before any output statements in your Active Server Pages file. Alternatively, you can buffer the page (see the section "Buffering Output" in Chapter 14).

The preceding script is a simple example of how you can create a cookie. The example uses only the Expires attribute of the Cookies collection. However, the Cookies collection has a number of additional attributes. Here's a more complicated example:

```
<%
Response.Cookies("UserName")="Steve Jobs"
Response.Cookies("UserName").Expires="Jan 1, 1999"
Response.Cookies("UserName").Path="/examples"
Response.Cookies("UserName").Domain="aspsite.com"
```

```
Response.Cookies("UserName").Secure=True
%>
```

This script also creates a cookie named UserName. However, this cookie has three additional attributes:

- The Path attribute is used to specify more exactly when the browser should send the cookie. In this example, the cookie will be sent only when the path of a requested page begins with /examples. For instance, the cookie will be sent with a request for "/examples/hello.asp" or "/examples/chapter16/cookies.asp", but not "/hello.asp". By default, the application path is used.

- The Domain attribute also specifies when the cookie should be sent. In the preceding example, the cookie will be sent only with requests to the aspsite.com domain. This means that the cookie will be sent to www.aspsite.com, beetle.aspsite.com, or cricket.aspsite.com. If this attribute is not specified, the domain of the Web server is used.

- Finally, the Secure attribute specifies that the cookie should only be sent in an encrypted transmission. You can use this attribute if you're using the Secure Sockets Layer (see Chapter 2, "Installing and Using Internet Information Server").

To read a cookie within an Active Server Page, you use the Cookies collection of the Request object. For example, to output the value of a cookie, you can use the following script:

```
<%=Request.Cookies("UserName") %>
```

This script outputs the value of the cookie named UserName. As in all the collections discussed previously, you can use the Count attribute to determine the number of items in the Cookies collection. You can also use either a FOR...EACH or a FOR...NEXT loop to iterate through the items in the Cookies collection. This example uses a FOR...EACH loop:

```
<%
FOR EACH thing IN Request.Cookies
  Response.write("<BR>"&thing&"="&Request.Cookies(thing))
NEXT
%>
```

Creating More Than One Cookie

You can create more than one cookie, by simply creating multiple cookies with the Response.Cookies collection as in the previous examples. However, many browsers only support three or four cookies from a particular Web site.

An alternative method is available for creating multiple cookies. You can create a *cookie dictionary*. A cookie dictionary is actually a single cookie with multiple name-and-value pairs. Following is an example of how you can create a cookie dictionary:

```
<%
Response.Cookies("User")("Name")="Bill Gates"
Response.Cookies("User")("Password")="billions"
%>
```

This script creates a cookie dictionary with the name User and the keys Name and Password. When a cookie dictionary is created, a header like the following is sent to the browser:

```
Set-Cookie:User=Name=Bill+Gates&Password=billions
```

A cookie named User is created. However, the value of User is actually two name-and-value pairs. The names and values of each key of the cookie dictionary are joined together into one large cookie.

To retrieve a cookie dictionary, you can use the Request.Cookies collection as in the preceding example. If you simply provide the name of the cookie dictionary, the cookie dictionary is returned in unparsed form. To retrieve particular keys of the cookie dictionary, you pass the name of the key to the collection. Here's an example:

```
<%=Request.Cookies("User")%>
<%=Request.Cookies("User")("Name")%>
<%=Request.Cookies("User")("Password")%>
```

> **NOTE**
>
> You should be cautious with storing sensitive information such as passwords in a cookie. By default, a cookie is not encrypted when it's sent back and forth between a browser and Web server. If you're using the Secure Sockets Layer (see Chapter 2 for details), you can use the SECURE attribute to transmit only encrypted cookies. However, the cookie still will be stored in an ordinary text file on a browser.

To determine whether a cookie is a cookie dictionary, use the HasKeys attribute. For example, the following script returns True if the cookie is a cookie dictionary and False otherwise:

```
<%=Request.Cookies("User").HasKeys %>
```

Retaining State Without Cookies

Using either sessions or cookies is risky because not all browsers support them. The moment you use a cookie at your Web site, you'll receive complaints from countless individuals with obscure browsers who can't use cookies.

In this section, you learn some methods to retain state without cookies. In other words, you learn how to retain information about a user from page to page. Three methods are compared.

Retaining State with Query Strings

Chapter 15, "Working with More Than One Active Server Page," explains how to work with query strings. You can add a query string to any hyperlink in your Active Server Pages. By using query strings, you can pass information from page to page, as in this example:

```
<HTML>
<HEAD><TITLE> Query State </TITLE></HEAD>
<BODY>
<%
UserName=Server.URLEncode("Bill Gates")
%>
<A HREF="/nextpage.asp?<%=UserName%>">Click Here</A>
</BODY>
</HTML>
```

This script assigns the name Bill Gates to the variable named UserName. The value of this variable is passed to the page nextpage.asp in the query string when the user clicks the hyperlink.

You can continue to pass the UserName from page to page by retrieving UserName from the QueryString collection. For example, the page nextpage.asp might look like this:

```
<HTML>
<HEAD><TITLE> Next Page </TITLE></HEAD>
<BODY>
<%
UserName=Server.URLEncode(Request.QueryString("Username"))
%>
<A HREF="/nextpage.asp?<%=UserName%>">Click Here</A>
</BODY>
</HTML>
```

The advantage of this method of retaining state is that it works with all browsers. Admittedly, however, it's very cumbersome. If you want to be able to track the user on every page on your Web site, you must include a query string with every hyperlink on your Web site. Every query string must contain the name of the user.

Another disadvantage of this method of retaining state is that it doesn't allow you to pass large amounts of data. Remember, query strings can't be too large. When a query string becomes larger than about 1,000 characters, certain browsers either truncate the query string or fail to create a functioning hyperlink at all.

Retaining State with Hidden Form Fields

If you need to pass a large amount of data from page to page without using session variables, you have no choice but to use an HTML form. You can hide the information you're passing by using a hidden form field, as in this example:

```
<HTML>
<HEAD><TITLE> Form State </TITLE></HEAD>
<BODY>
<%
UserName="Bill Gates"
%>
<FORM METHOD="Post" Action="/nextpage.asp">
<INPUT NAME="UserName" TYPE="HIDDEN" VALUE="<%=UserName%>">
<INPUT TYPE="SUBMIT" VALUE="Next Page">
</FORM>
</BODY>
</HTML>
```

This page includes an HTML form. The form has a hidden field named UserName that contains the value of the UserName variable. The form also contains one button. When the button is clicked, the page nextpage.asp is loaded and the data in the hidden form field is passed to the new page.

You can continue to pass data from page to page in this way indefinitely. On each page, you must use the Form collection of the Request object to retrieve the data in the hidden field. Next, you must create a new hidden field so the data can be passed to a new page again. Here's an example:

```
<HTML>
<HEAD><TITLE> Next Page </TITLE></HEAD>
<BODY>
<%
UserName=Request.Form("Username")
%>
<FORM METHOD="Post" Action="/nextpage.asp">
<INPUT NAME="UserName" TYPE="HIDDEN" VALUE="<%=UserName%>">
<INPUT TYPE="SUBMIT" VALUE="Next Page">
</FORM>
</BODY>
</HTML>
```

Combining Methods

Neither of these two methods of retaining state is particularly elegant. However, these are the only alternative methods of retaining state without using session variables and cookies. By using query strings and hidden form fields, you can preserve compatibility with all browsers.

If you need to track a user through every page on your Web site, you must include either a query string or a hidden form field on every page in your Web site. As soon as a user clicks a naked hyperlink—a hyperlink without a query string—you can no longer track the user.

> **NOTE**
>
> One significant disadvantage of using either query strings or hidden form fields to retain state is that both methods require information to be passed back and forth between the server and browser. This means that you should be cautious with passing private information such as passwords.

You can combine these two methods of retaining state. For example, on some pages you can use a query string to pass the name of the user, and on other pages you can use a hidden form field. If you do this, you don't need to check both the QueryString and Form collections on every page. If you call the Request method without specifying the collection, both collections are automatically checked. Look at this example:

```
<HTML>
<HEAD><TITLE> Next Page </TITLE></HEAD>
<BODY>
<%
UserName=Request("UserName")
%>
<FORM METHOD="Post" Action="/nextpage.asp">
<INPUT NAME="UserName" TYPE="HIDDEN" VALUE="<%=UserName%>">
<INPUT TYPE="SUBMIT" VALUE="Next Page">
</FORM>
<A HREF="/nextpage.asp?<%=Server.URLEncode(UserName)%>">Click Here</A>
</BODY>
</HTML>
```

In this example, the variable UserName is assigned the name of the user regardless of whether the name was passed by a hidden form field or a query string. The call to Request("UserName") retrieves the value of UserName from either the Form or the QueryString collection.

Summary

In this chapter, you learned how to work with sessions. You learned how to use the Session object to create session variables that can be used to store information over multiple Web pages. You learned how to create scripts that execute when a session starts and ends. You also learned about a close relative of sessions—how to create and read cookies. Finally, some alternative methods for retaining state without cookies were discussed.

CHAPTER 17

Working with Active Server Pages Applications

IN THIS CHAPTER

In this chapter, you learn how to work with applications. The first section provides an overview of applications. In the second section, you learn how to use the methods, collections, and events of applications. Finally, in the third section, two programming examples using applications are discussed. You learn how to create a simple multiuser chat program. You also learn how to create an Active Server Page that displays real-time usage statistics for your Web site.

What Is an Application?

Microsoft wants you to think of Active Server Pages in traditional programming terms. When you create a single Active Server Page, you're creating something like a procedure or subroutine. When you create a group of related Active Server Pages, you're creating an application.

However, an application is something more than a group of pages sitting on a hard drive. When Active Server Pages are joined together in an application, they have certain properties that they would otherwise lack. Following is a list of some features of an Active Server Pages application:

- Data can be shared among the pages in an application, and therefore among more than one user of a Web site.
- An application has events that can trigger special application scripts.
- An instance of an object can be shared among all the pages in an application.
- Separate applications can be configured with the Internet Service Manager to have different properties.
- Separate applications can be isolated to execute in their own memory space. This means that if one application crashes, the others won't also crash.
- You can stop one application (unloading all of its components from memory) without affecting other applications.

A Web site can have more than one application. Typically, you create separate applications when you have collections of pages related to separate tasks. For example, you might create one application containing all the pages meant for public consumption. You might create another application that's restricted to use by Web site administrators.

You can also create separate applications that correspond to distinct Web sites hosted on the same computer. For example, the same computer might host an application for Tom's Online Flower Shop and an application for Roger's Web Book Shop.

An *application* is defined by using the Internet Service Manager to specify a root directory for the application. An application consists of a particular directory and all of its subdirectories. If one of these subdirectories is also defined to be an application, then it constitutes a separate application. In other words, no two applications overlap.

When you first install Active Server Pages, a few applications are created by default. For example, an application is created for your default Web site. However, you can create as many additional applications as you need.

Follow these steps to define an Active Server Pages application:

1. Launch the Internet Service Manager from the Microsoft Internet Information Server program group.

2. Click the name of your default Web site in the navigation tree. (If you haven't changed anything, it will be named Default Web Site.)

3. You can select any existing directory, the default Web site, or create a new directory for your application. To create a new virtual directory, right-click the name of your default Web site and then choose New | Virtual Directory.

4. After you have chosen a directory for your application, you need to view its property sheet. You can do this by clicking the Properties icon or by right-clicking the name of the directory and choosing Properties.

5. In the property sheet, click the tab labeled either Virtual Directory or Home Directory.

6. In the Application Settings section, click the Create button.

NOTE

When you create an application, you can provide the application with a name. This name is used only within the Internet Service Manager. It doesn't affect your Active Server Pages scripts.

You have now successfully created a new application. After you create an application, you can set a number of its properties by selecting Configuration from the Application Settings panel (see Figure 17.1). For example, you can specify whether the application should use sessions or whether the application should buffer Active Server Pages.

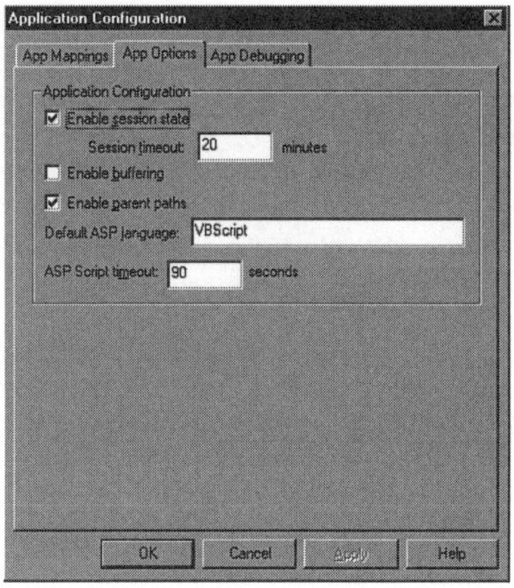

FIGURE 17.1.

Creating an application.

Furthermore, once you create an application, you can provide it with its own `Global.asa` file that contains application-wide scripts. You place this file in the root directory of the application. You learn more about using this file in the later section "Application Events."

Using the Application Object

The `Application` object has all the collections, methods, and events related to applications. In the following sections, you learn how to use the `Application` object to create application variables and application events.

An Introduction to Application Variables

An *application variable* contains data that can be used on all the pages and by all the users of an application. Application variables can contain any type of data, including arrays and objects. An application variable differs from a session variable in two ways:

- Unlike a session variable, an application variable doesn't depend on cookies. The Web server doesn't need to track user sessions to use application variables. This means that using them is risk-free, because they're compatible with all browsers.

- Unlike a session variable, the data in an application variable can be shared among multiple users. Data can be retrieved from one user and stored in an application variable to be read by another user.

> **NOTE**
>
> For information on session variables, see Chapter 16, "Working with Active Server Pages Sessions."

Following are some common uses for application variables:

- An application variable can be used to display transient information on every Web page. For example, you can use an application variable to display a "tip of the day" or a daily news update on every Web page.

- An application variable can be used to record the number of times that a banner advertisement on your Web site has been clicked. (You learn how to do this in Chapter 21, "Working with Advertisements.")

- An application variable can hold data retrieved from a database. For example, you can retrieve a list of items for sale at your Web site from a database and display this list on multiple pages using an application variable.

- An application variable can contain a running count of the number of visitors at your Web site. You learn how to do this in the later section "The WhosOn Page."

- An application variable can be used to enable communication between the users of your Web site. For example, you could use application variables to create multiuser games or multiuser chat rooms. An example of a chat page using application variables is provided in the later section "The Chat Page."

Creating and Reading Application Variables

Creating application variables is easy. To create a new application variable, you can simply pass the name of the new variable to the Application object, as in the following example:

```
<HTML>
<HEAD><TITLE> Application Example </TITLE></HEAD>
<BODY>
<%
Application("Greeting")="Welcome!"
%>
<%=Application("Greeting")%>
</BODY>
</HTML>
```

In this example, a new application variable named Greeting is created and assigned the value "Welcome!". Finally, the value of the new application variable is outputted to the browser retrieving the page.

Once an application variable has been assigned a value, the value can be displayed on all the pages in an application. For example, the following page would also display the greeting, even though the Greeting variable hasn't been assigned a value on this page:

```
<HTML>
<HEAD><TITLE> Another Page </TITLE></HEAD>
<BODY>
<%=Application("Greeting")%>
</BODY>
</HTML>
```

It's important to understand that, unlike session variables, application variables don't die when a user leaves. Once an application variable has been assigned a value, it retains that value until the Web server is shut down or the application is unloaded. If you're lucky, this could be weeks or even months.

Because application variables aren't destroyed automatically when a user leaves, you must be careful not to go wild with creating them. Application variables use memory; you should use them sparingly.

NOTE

How do you remove an application variable once it's created? You can't. Application variables remain in memory until the server is shut down, the Global.asa file is altered, or the application is unloaded.

17

WORKING
WITH ASP
APPLICATIONS

It's also important to understand that an application variable is not relative to a particular user. If one user requests a Web page that assigns one value to an application variable, and another user requests a page that assigns another value, the value of the variable will change for both users. Consider the following script:

```
<%
Randomize
If INT(2*RND)=1 THEN
  Application("FavoriteColor")="Blue"
ELSE
  Application("FavoriteColor")="Red"
END IF
%>
```

This script randomly assigns the value "Blue" or "Red" to the application variable named FavoriteColor. Suppose two users retrieve a page with this script. In that case, the value of the variable would be the same for the two users. The variable would have whatever value was assigned to it when the second user retrieved the page. Potentially, this could create a problem. Because more than one user can access an application variable at the same time, conflicts could arise. For example, suppose you're using an application variable to record the number of times a banner advertisement has been clicked. Every time the advertisement is clicked, a script like the following is executed:

```
<%
NumClicks=Application("BannerClicks")
NumClicks=NumClicks+1
Application("BannerClicks")=Numclicks
%>
```

The script simply increments the number stored in the application variable BannerClicks by 1. But suppose two users click an advertisement at the same time. The same script would be executed at the same time for both users. If this happens, the value of BannerClicks will be inaccurate. Both users will have incremented the variable to the same value.

Fortunately, the Application object has two methods that can help in precisely this type of situation. The Lock and Unlock methods are used to temporarily prevent other users from changing the value of an application variable. Here's the previous example, rewritten to prevent any potential conflicts:

```
<%
Application.Lock
NumClicks=Application("BannerClicks")
NumClicks=NumClicks+1
Application("BannerClicks")=Numclicks
Application.Unlock
%>
```

The first line in the script locks all the variables in the application object. When the variables are locked, other users can't modify them until they're unlocked. The application variables remain locked until the Unlock method is explicitly called (as in the preceding example) or until the end of the page is reached.

Notice that you can't lock application variables selectively; it's an all-or-none choice. The preceding script temporarily prevents other users from modifying all the application variables that may exist.

It's important to understand that locking the application variables doesn't permanently prevent other users from modifying the variables. Locking simply forces any modifications to take place in an orderly fashion. The application variables are modified serially rather than haphazardly.

Dumping Application Variables

Most application variables are actually stored in the `Contents` collection of the `Application` object. Whenever you create a new application variable, a new item is added to this collection. For example, the following two statements are equivalent:

```
<% Application("FavoriteColor")="Blue" %>
```

```
<% Application.Contents("FavoriteColor")="Blue" %>
```

Because application variables are stored in a collection, you can manipulate them by using all the collection methods previously discussed. You can retrieve a count of the number of application variables by using the `Count` method. You can display all the items contained in the `Contents` collection by using either a `FOR...EACH` loop or a `FOR...NEXT` loop. Here's an example using a `FOR...EACH` loop:

```
<%
FOR EACH thing IN Application.Contents
Response.Write("<BR>"&thing&"="&Application.Contents(thing))
NEXT
%>
```

This script displays all the application variables by looping through the `Application.Contents` collection.

Application Events

Like the `Session` object, the `Application` object has two events: `Application_OnStart` and `Application_OnEnd`. One event is fired when an Active Server Pages application starts; the other event is fired when it ends.

When does an application start? Not, as you might expect, immediately after you start the Web server. An application doesn't start until the first page is requested from the application.

An `Application_OnStart` event will always occur before a `Session_OnStart` event. However, unlike a `Session_OnStart` event, the `Application_OnStart` event is not fired whenever a new visitor requests a page from the application. The `Application_OnStart` event only fires once—when the first visitor arrives.

The `Application_OnEnd` event is fired when the Web server is shut down or the application is unloaded. For example, if you use the Internet Service Manager to turn off the Web service, the `Application_OnEnd` event will be fired. If you're running an application as a separate process, this event is also triggered when the application is unloaded using the Unload button. An `Application_OnEnd` event always occurs after the last `Session_OnEnd` event.

The `Application_OnStart` and `Application_OnEnd` events each trigger one and only one script. Both of these scripts must be located in the `Global.asa` file. These special scripts can't be called from any other Active Server Page.

The `Global.asa` file is a special file that resides in the root directory of an application. Each application can have only one of these files. The `Global.asa` file contains all the scripts and objects that are global to an application. The file has the following structure:

```
<SCRIPT LANGUAGE=VBScript RUNAT=Server>
SUB Application_OnStart
END SUB
</SCRIPT>

<SCRIPT LANGUAGE=VBScript RUNAT=Server>
SUB Application_OnEnd
END SUB
</SCRIPT>

<SCRIPT LANGUAGE=VBScript RUNAT=Server>
SUB Session_OnStart
END SUB
</SCRIPT>

<SCRIPT LANGUAGE=VBScript RUNAT=Server>
 SUB Session_OnEnd
 END SUB
</SCRIPT>
```

You learned about two of the `Global.asa` scripts in Chapter 16; the `Session_OnStart` and `Session_OnEnd` events are used with sessions. The remaining two scripts, however, are triggered by the two events of the `Application` object.

You are very restricted in what you can include in these `Application_OnStart` and `Application_OnEnd` scripts. You can't place any statements that output content. For example, you can't use HTML or the `Response.Write` method. Furthermore, you must be cautious with the object you use within the `Application_OnStart` or `Application_OnEnd` scripts.

> **NOTE**
>
> Exactly what objects can you include in the `Application_OnStart` and `Application_OnEnd` scripts? As this book goes to press, there's no definite answer to this question. With the current beta release, you can use almost any object within the Application scripts (including the ActiveX Data Objects). However, the current beta documentation suggests that the final release of IIS may have more stringent restrictions. The best strategy is to experiment and see what works.

The `Application_OnStart` script is valuable for initializing application-wide variables. For example, one common use of the `Application_OnStart` and `Session_OnStart` scripts is for tracking the total number of visitors since the application was started. Here's an example of how you can do this:

```
<SCRIPT LANGUAGE=VBScript RUNAT=Server>
SUB Application_OnStart
  Application("TotalUsers")=0
END SUB
</SCRIPT>

<SCRIPT LANGUAGE=VBScript RUNAT=Server>
SUB Session_OnStart
  Application.Lock
  Application("TotalUsers")=Application("TotalUsers")+1
  Application.Unlock
END SUB
</SCRIPT>
```

A single statement has been added to the `Application_OnStart` script. The statement initializes the application variable named `TotalUsers` to zero. This script is executed only when the Web server is first started.

The `Session_OnStart` script has been modified to increment `TotalUsers` whenever a new user arrives at the Web site. Notice how the application variable is first locked before it's modified. This prevents conflicts when more than one new user arrives at the same time.

After you've modified the `Global.asa` file, you can display the total number of visitors on any Active Server Page by including the following line:

```
<%=Application("TotalUsers") %>
```

The Chat Page

In this section and the next, you learn how to create two Active Server Pages projects by using the `Application` object—a chat page and a real-time Web site statistics program. These projects are intended to illustrate some of the topics discussed in this chapter, but I hope that you'll also find them useful for your Web site.

The best way to attract users back to your Web site again and again is to create a sense of community. One of the best ways to create a sense of community is to come up with a way for users to interact. The chat page will do this.

> **NOTE**
>
> You may experience problems with the chat page if you view it using Netscape Navigator 4.0 on the same machine as your Web server. However, the problem doesn't affect earlier versions of Netscape or any version of Internet Explorer.

The chat page discussed in this section allows real-time interaction between multiple participants. All the users who request the page can view the messages entered by others. Furthermore, they can add their own messages (see Figure 17.2).

FIGURE 17.2.
The chat page.

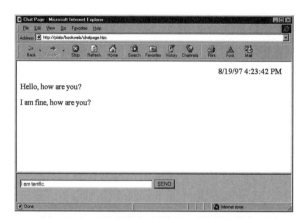

You need to create three files to create the chat page. The following list is an overview of the files that need to be created or modified in this project:

- The chat page. The chat page will have two frames; the top frame will display messages from other users and the bottom frame will allow new messages to be entered.

- The display page. This page will display all the messages entered by other users. Every five seconds or so, the contents of the frame will be updated with new messages.

- The message page. This page will allow a user to enter a new message. It contains a single text input box.

- The Global.asa file. The Application_OnStart script will be modified.

Creating the Chat Page

The first page that needs to be created is the chat page. The only purpose of this page is to act as a container for the other two pages. Because it doesn't contain any scripts, you should save it with the name ChatPage.htm, as shown in Listing 17.1.

Listing 17.1. chatpage.htm.

```
<HTML>
<HEAD><TITLE> Chat Page </TITLE></HEAD>
<FRAMESET ROWS="*,100">
<FRAME SRC="Display.asp">
<FRAME SRC="Message.asp">
</FRAMESET>
</HTML>
```

Why create frames at all? Because the display page is automatically refreshed every five seconds, a separate page is needed to enter new messages. Otherwise, the page might refresh when a user has entered only half a message (which would be irritating).

Modifying the Global.asa File

For the chat page to work, the Global.asa file must be modified. The following script is used to initialize the application variables needed for the chat page. The variables must be application variables so they can be accessed by all users. The first application variable is named Talk. It's an array that holds all the messages. The Talk array is created by assigning the TempArray to it. The second application variable is named TPlace (talk place). It's used to point to the current message in the Talk array. The following script initializes this variable to zero:

```
<SCRIPT LANGUAGE=VBScript RUNAT=Server>
SUB Application_OnStart
 Dim TempArray(5)
 Application("Talk")=TempArray
 Application("TPlace")=0
END SUB
</SCRIPT>
```

Creating the Message Page

The purpose of the message page is to allow a user to enter a new message (see Figure 17.3). The page includes an HTML form with a text input box and a submit button. When the submit button is clicked, the page reloads itself.

FIGURE 17.3.

The message page.

The script does two things. First, it checks whether there are more than four messages. If there are more than four messages, the application variable TPlace is reinitialized to zero. This prevents the Talk array from overflowing with too many messages.

Next, the script adds a new message to the Talk array and increments TPlace. TPlace will always point to the next place in the Talk array where a message can be entered.

Listing 17.2 shows the content of the message page.

Listing 17.2. message.asp.

```
<%
IF not Request.Form("message")="" THEN
  Application.LOCK
  IF Application("TPlace")>4 THEN
    Application("TPlace")=0
  END IF
    TempArray=Application("Talk")
    TempArray(Application("TPLACE"))=Request.Form("Message")
    Application("Talk")=TempArray
    Application("TPlace")=Application("TPlace")+1
  Application.Unlock
END IF
%>
<HTML>
<HEAD><TITLE> Message Page </TITLE></HEAD>
<BODY BGCOLOR="LIGHTBLUE">
<FORM METHOD="POST" ACTION="message.asp">
<INPUT NAME="message" TYPE="TEXT" SIZE=50>
<INPUT TYPE="SUBMIT" VALUE="SEND">
</FORM>
</BODY>
</HTML>
```

Creating the Display Page

The final page that needs to be created is the display page. This is the page where the messages from all the users are actually displayed (see Figure 17.4).

The page automatically refreshes itself every five seconds. It does this by using client-pull. The HTML <META> tag contains the command to do this. (It adds a REFRESH header to the Active Server Page.)

The first script in the following page is used to identify the current page. The full URL of the current page is retrieved from the ServerVariables collection and assigned to the variable named MySelf. MySelf is used with the <META> tag to indicate the page to be refreshed.

The main script is used to display the contents of the Talk array. The FOR...NEXT loop displays all the current messages. Listing 17.3 shows the display page.

Listing 17.3. display.asp.

```
<%
MyServer=Request.ServerVariables("SERVER_NAME")
MyPath=Request.ServerVariables("SCRIPT_NAME")
MySelf="HTTP://"&MyServer&MyPath
%>
<HTML>
<HEAD>
<META HTTP-EQUIV="REFRESH" CONTENT="5;<%=MySelf%>">
<TITLE>Display Page</TITLE>
</HEAD>
```

```
<BODY>
<P ALIGN=RIGHT><%=NOW%></P>
<%
TempArray=Application("Talk")
FOR i=0 to Application("TPlace")-1
  Response.Write("<P>"&Temparray(i))
NEXT
%>
</BODY>
</HTML>
```

FIGURE 17.4.

The display page.

Extending the Chat Page Project

There are a number of ways in which the chat page can be improved. For example, the maximum number of messages that the chat page can display at one time is five. This would be inadequate for heavy usage. You can change the maximum number of messages by modifying the size of the TempArray in the Global.asa file and by modifying the number at which TPlace reinitializes in the message page.

The chat page allows you to enter messages that include HTML formatting. However, it wouldn't be difficult to modify the message page to make this easier. For example, you could have message-formatting check boxes that allow you to specify the font and color of a message.

Finally, the chat page doesn't associate usernames with their messages. Again, this wouldn't be a difficult modification. You can add a logon page before the chat page that requests the username. This name can then be prefixed to all of the messages that the user sends.

> **NOTE**
>
> You can see working versions of many of the examples in this book by visiting the companion Web site to this book at http://www.aspsite.com.

17

WORKING
WITH ASP
APPLICATIONS

The WhosOn Page

Good Webmasters have a single purpose in life: They want more users to visit their Web sites. Part of this obsession involves accurately tracking the number of users currently online and determining what they're doing.

The project described in this section allows you to track the visitors to your Web site in real time. You can determine the number of visitors to your Web site at any moment. You can also learn the last page requested by each of your visitors (see Figure 17.5).

FIGURE 17.5.

The WhosOn Page.

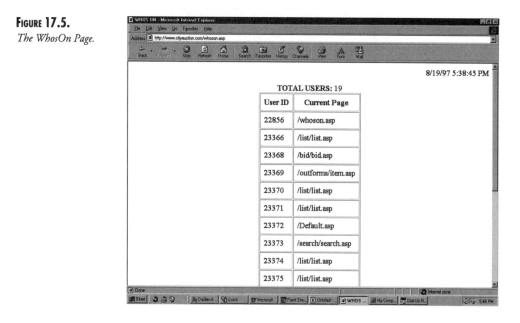

This project illustrates how to assign an object to an application variable. The Dictionary object will be used to store information about visitors. Whenever a user requests a page, the information in the Dictionary object will be updated. The following files need to be created or modified for this project:

■ The Global.asa file. Both the Application_OnStart and Session_OnEnd scripts need to be modified for this project.

■ The GrabStats file. This file updates the Dictionary object. You'll need to include this file in every page you want to track.

■ The WhosOn page. The WhosOn page displays the users currently at your Web site.

Modifying the Global.asa File

To create this project, you need to modify two scripts in the Global.asa file. First, you will need to create the Dictionary object, which is used to store the information about your visitors. Because this object needs to be created only once, this is accomplished in the `Application_OnStart` script:

```
<SCRIPT LANGUAGE=VBScript RUNAT=Server>
SUB Application_OnStart
Set Application("Stats") = Server.CreateObject("Scripting.Dictionary")
END SUB
</SCRIPT>
```

A single line has been added to the preceding script. The statement assigns an instance of the `Dictionary` object to the application variable named `Stats`. Once created, this variable can be used throughout your application.

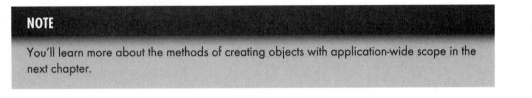

NOTE

You'll learn more about the methods of creating objects with application-wide scope in the next chapter.

The `Session_OnEnd` script in the `Global.asa` file also must be modified. The purpose of the following script is to remove a user from the `Dictionary` object when the user's session ends:

```
<SCRIPT LANGUAGE=VBScript RUNAT=Server>
SUB Session_OnEnd
   IF Application("Stats").Exists(Session.SessionID) THEN
     Application.Lock
     Application("Stats").Remove(Session.SessionID)
     Application.Unlock
  End IF
END SUB
</SCRIPT>
```

Users will be tracked by their session IDs. The keys in the dictionary named `Stats` correspond to these session IDs. The preceding script checks whether an entry with the session ID of the current user exists in the dictionary. If it does, the entry is removed.

Creating the GrabStats File

To determine the current page of your visitors, you need to include a file in every page you want to track. The file consists of a single-line script, as shown in Listing 17.4.

Listing 17.4. GrabStats.asp.

```
<%
Application("Stats").item(Session.SessionID)=
➡Request.ServerVariables("SCRIPT_NAME")
%>
```

This script adds the path of the current page to the `Dictionary` object. The path of the current page is determined by retrieving the `SCRIPT_NAME` server variable. Next, the value of this variable is assigned to the dictionary key that corresponds to the current user. (If the key doesn't exist, it's created automatically.)

Save the preceding file with the name `GrabStats.asp`. You should include this file in every Active Server Page that you want to track. Simply add the following line to the top of an Active Server Page:

```
<!-- #INCLUDE VIRTUAL="GrabStats.asp" -->
```

Creating the WhosOn Page

The WhosOn page is used to display the current visitors. The session ID of each visitor is displayed next to the last page that the visitor requested. Listing 17.5 shows the WhosOn page.

Listing 17.5. WhosOn.asp.

```
<!-- #INCLUDE VIRTUAL="GrabStats.asp" -->
<%
MyServer=Request.ServerVariables("SERVER_NAME")
MyPath=Request.ServerVariables("SCRIPT_NAME")
MySelf="HTTP://"&MyServer&MyPath
%>
<HTML>
<HEAD>
<META HTTP-EQUIV="REFRESH" CONTENT="20;<%=MySelf%>">
<TITLE>WHOSON</TITLE>
</HEAD>
<BODY>
<%
Application.Lock
Set TempStats=Application("Stats")
Application.UnLock
%>
<CENTER>
<B>TOTAL USERS:</B> <%=TempStats.Count%>
<TABLE BORDER=1 CELLPADDING=10>
<TR><TH>User ID</TH><TH>Current Page</TH></TR>
<%
TempItems=TempStats.items
TempKeys=TempStats.keys
For i=0 to UBOUND(TempKeys)
%>
<TR><TD><%=TempKeys(i)%></TD><TD><%=TempItems(i)%></TD></TR>
<%
NEXT
%>
</CENTER>
</TABLE>
</BODY>
</HTML>
```

The first line in this file includes the `GrabStats.asp` file that you created in the previous section. This allows you to know, when you are viewing this page, that you actually are viewing this page. The path of the WhosOn page will appear next to your session ID.

The first script is used to retrieve the path of the current page. The WhosOn page is automatically refreshed, using client-pull, every 20 seconds. The path of the current page is needed so the page can be refreshed.

The second script transfers the dictionary stored in the application variable to a temporary `Dictionary` object named `TempStats`. `TempStats` is automatically destroyed when the page ends.

The number of current visitors is retrieved by returning a count of the number of items in the dictionary. The final script displays all the entries in the dictionary by looping through its keys and items (see Figure 17.6).

FIGURE 17.6.

Tracking user ID and last page accessed.

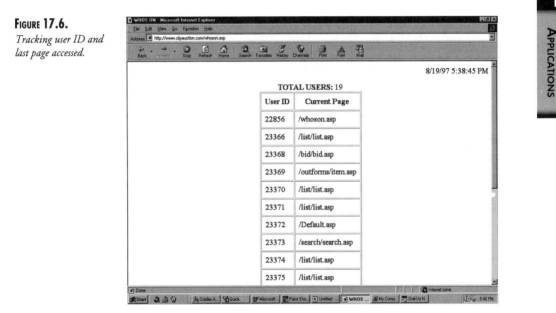

Extending the WhosOn Page

As it stands, the WhosOn page provides valuable information about the users of your Web site. By viewing the WhosOn page, you can gather a rough estimate of the number of users currently at your Web site. You can also see the last page each user requested.

There are a number of ways in which this project could be extended. For example, if your Web site requires users to register, you could display user names rather than session IDs. To do this, simply use visitor names as the keys in the dictionary rather than session IDs.

Furthermore, it would be useful to know how long each visitor has been online. You could modify the project in a number of ways to track this information. For example, you could simply create a second application variable that contains a second dictionary. In that case, you could track the length of each user's visit by storing this information in the second dictionary.

> **NOTE**
>
> You can view working versions of a number of examples in this book by visiting the book's companion Web site at http://www.aspsite.com.

Summary

In this chapter, you learned how to work with Active Server Pages applications. The first section provided an overview of applications. In the second section, you learned how to use the collections, properties, and events of the Application object. Finally, in the third and final section, two programming examples were discussed. You learned how to create a chat page and a page that allows you to track visitors at your Web site.

Working with Browsers

CHAPTER 18

This chapter introduces the first of the ActiveX components that are included with Active Server Pages. The first section provides an overview of the methods of integrating components into your Active Server Pages. In the next section, you learn how to use the Browser Capabilities component. Finally, in the last section, a sample application of the Browser Capabilities component is provided.

Using Components in Active Server Pages

Previous chapters explained how to use the built-in Active Server Pages objects, such as the `Request` and `Response` objects. Active Server Pages components are very similar to these objects. However, a component isn't as tightly integrated with Active Server Pages. Components are intended to extend the core functions provided by the built-in objects.

You can create components of your own, using such languages as Visual Basic, C++, Java, and Delphi. You learn how to do this in Chapter 28, "Extending Active Server Pages." You can also buy components from third-party companies. For example, the company Software FX sells components that allow you to generate charts and graphs easily with your Active Server Pages (see `http://www.softwarefx.com`). Finally, Microsoft bundles a number of free ActiveX components with Active Server Pages. You learn how to use these bundled components in this chapter and the following chapters.

Before you can use a component, you must first create an instance of it. You can automatically access the properties, collections, and methods of the built-in objects on every page. To use a component, on the other hand, you must create an instance of the component with a particular scope. In the following three sections, you learn how to create an instance of a component with page, session, and application scope.

Creating a Component with Page Scope

In most cases, you'll create an instance of a component with *page scope*. A component with page scope is created on a single page and dies when processing on the page ends. You can't use a component with page scope on any page where it wasn't explicitly created. To create an instance of a component with page scope, you use the `Server.CreateObject()` method.

> **NOTE**
>
> Don't use the `CreateObject` method of VBScript or the new statement of `JScript` to create an instance of a component. If you use either of these two methods of creating a component, weird and unpredictable things will happen. Always use the Active Server Pages `Server.CreateObject()` method instead.

Here's an example of creating a component with page scope:

```
<%
Set MyBrow=Server.CreateObject("MSWC.BrowserType")
%>
```

This script creates an instance of the Browser Capabilities component. It assigns the variable `MyBrow` to an instance of this component. Notice the use of the VBScript `Set` statement. Because you're assigning an instance of a component to a variable, you must use the `Set` statement.

> **NOTE**
>
> See Appendix A, "Quick ASP Object and Component Reference," for examples of how to create each ActiveX component.

The method for creating an instance of a component with page scope using JScript is very similar. However, you must use the `var` statement rather than the `Set` statement.

> **NOTE**
>
> Remember that JScript is case-sensitive. You must use var rather than Var or JScript won't recognize the statement.

The following example uses the `var` statement:

```
<%
var MyBrow=Server.CreateObject("MSWC.BrowserType")
%>
```

Microsoft recommends that you create the majority of your components with page scope. By creating components with page scope, you place less of a burden on the Web server. A page scope component releases any memory and other resources it requires when the processing of the page comes to an end.

Creating Components with Session Scope

Two methods are available for creating components with *session scope*. One method is to assign a component to a session variable by using the `Server.CreateObject()` method, as in the following example:

```
<%
Set Session("MyBrow")=Server.CreateObject("MSWC.BrowserType")
%>
```

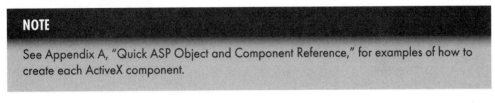

This script assigns the session variable named MyBrow to an instance of the Browser Capabilities component. The session variable is available on every page that a particular user requests. You can place this script in the Session_OnStart script of the Global.asa file or in any other Active Server Page.

This method of creating a component with session scope has a significant disadvantage. The Server.CreateObject() method immediately creates an instance of a component. Even if the instance of the component is never used, it still drains resources from the server.

Fortunately, there's a second way to create a component with session scope. You can create a component within the Global.asa file by using the Microsoft HTML <OBJECT> tag, like this:

```
<OBJECT RUNAT="Server" SCOPE="Session" ID="MyBrow"
PROGID="MSWC.BrowserType"></OBJECT>
```

This example shows how to create an instance of the Browser Capabilities component with the <OBJECT> HTML tag. The SCOPE attribute indicates that the component created should have session scope. The ID attribute provides the component with a unique identifier (a name), so you can refer to it in your Active Server Pages scripts. The PROGID is used to specify the component's registered name. This is the name the server uses to identify the component when it creates an instance of it. It's the same name you would pass to the Server.CreateObject() method.

When you use the <OBJECT> tag in the Global.asa file, you must place it outside any of the scripts. Do not use the <OBJECT> tag within the Session_OnStart, Session_OnEnd, Application_OnStart, or Application_OnEnd script.

> **NOTE**
>
> Instead of using a component's registered name, you can also use the component's registered number (CLASSID) when using the <OBJECT> tag, as in this example:
> ```
> <OBJECT RUNAT="Server" SCOPE="Session" ID="MyBrow"
> CLASSID="0ACE4881-8305-11CF-9427-444553540000"></OBJECT>
> ```

When a component is created with session scope in either of the two ways just described, any of its methods, collections, or properties are available on any page that a particular user requests. However, a particular instance of the component must be created for each user. Like a session variable, a component with session scope is created relative to a particular user session.

When would you need to create a component with session scope? In Chapter 21, "Working with Advertisements," you learn how to use the Ad Rotator component. The Ad Rotator component can be used to display different banner advertisements with different frequencies. If you want to display banner advertisements on a number of pages, it would make sense to assign the Ad Rotator component to a session variable.

Creating Components with Application Scope

When you create an instance of a component with *application scope*, you can treat it as if it were a built-in object. Once created, any methods, collections, or properties of the component can be accessed by any user on any page. The component remains available until the server shuts down, the Global.asa file is modified, or the application is unloaded.

> **NOTE**
>
> If a component is created with application scope, its `OnStartPage()` and `OnEndPage()` methods are not called. This may be relevant when you are using custom components.

You can create a component with application scope by using methods similar to those used to create a component with session scope. First, you can create a component with application scope by using the `Server.CreateObject()` method. Look at this example:

```
<%
Set Application("MyBrow")=Server.CreateObject("MSWC.BrowserType")
%>
```

Here, the Browser Capabilities component is assigned to an application variable. You can do this inside a script within the Global.asa file, such as the `Application_OnStart()` script. You could also create a component in this way within any of your Active Server Pages. After an instance of the Browser Capabilities component has been created with application scope, you can use its properties on any Active Server Page.

You can also create a component with application scope by using the Microsoft HTML `<OBJECT>` tag, like this:

```
<OBJECT RUNAT="Server" SCOPE="Application" ID="MyBrow"
 PROGID="MSWC.BrowserType"></OBJECT>
```

In this example, the `<OBJECT>` tag is used to create an instance of the Browser Capabilities component with application scope. The `SCOPE` attribute indicates that the component should have application rather than session scope. The `ID` attribute provides a name for the component. The `PROGID` attribute allows the server to identify the component.

You can place the `<OBJECT>` tag within the Global.asa file. However, it must be located outside of any of the scripts. Don't place the `<OBJECT>` tag within the `Session_OnStart`, `Session_OnEnd`, `Application_OnStart`, or `Application_OnEnd` script.

When would you need to create an object with application scope? In the WhosOn Page programming example in Chapter 17, "Working with Active Server Pages Applications," you learned how to track user page requests. This information was stored in a dictionary created with application scope. This component needed to be created with application scope. Otherwise, it could not be accessed by every user on every page.

18

WORKING WITH
BROWSERS

The Browser Capabilities Component

One explanation for the explosive growth of the Internet is the openness of its standards. HTML was designed to be platform- and browser-neutral. In theory, a Web page should appear the same way regardless of the browser and the computer being used. In reality, however, this was never quite true. From the beginning, Netscape introduced proprietary HTML tags. For example, Netscape Navigator version 1.0 could interpret an HTML tag for blinking text. To this day, the majority of non-Netscape browsers can't interpret this tag. Frames are another example of a Netscape extension to HTML.

As competition between Netscape and Microsoft has heated up, the situation has only worsened. Microsoft has introduced its fair share of proprietary tags. For example, the `<BGSOUND>` tag, which plays background sounds, and the `<MARQUEE>` tag, which displays a scrolling marquee, can be interpreted only by the Microsoft browser.

HTML is being fragmented steadily into multiple standards. With each new version of the Microsoft and Netscape browsers, the gap between what might be called "Netscape HTML" and "Microsoft HTML" widens. This creates a serious problem for the Web page designer.

On the one hand, there's pressure on the Web page designer to include the newest HTML tags. Never underestimate the "coolness factor." If you want users to return to your Web site, you need to push the limits of HTML.

On the other hand, there's pressure on the Web page designer to make Web pages universally accessible. No one appreciates a Web page that they can't see. As soon as you use proprietary HTML tags, you risk losing whole populations of potential users.

Caught between these contradictory pressures, what should a good Web page designer do? Microsoft's answer is to use the Browser Capabilities component, as described in the following section.

Using the Browser Capabilities Component

You can use the Browser Capabilities component to display different Web pages, depending on the capabilities of a browser. For example, some browsers support frames; others don't. Using the Browser Capabilities component, you can detect whether a browser supports frames, and display a framed version of a page only when appropriate.

> **NOTE**
>
> Depending on the version of the browscap.ini file installed on your computer, the Browser Capabilities component may detect more browser features than listed here. For details, see the later section "How the Browser Capabilities Component Really Works."

NOTE

You can also detect certain browser and computer features such as screen resolution and color depth by using the ServerVariables collection. This works only with some versions of Microsoft Internet Explorer. For more information, see Chapter 14, "Working with a Single Active Server Page."

By default, the Browser Capabilities component can detect the following features of a Web browser:

- browser. The type of the browser; for example, Internet Explorer or Netscape.
- version. The complete version of the browser.
- majorver. The major version of the browser (the number before the period).
- minorver. The minor version of the browser (the number after the period).
- frames. Indicates whether the browser supports frames.
- tables. Indicates whether the browser supports tables.
- cookies. Indicates whether the browser supports cookies.
- backgroundsounds. Indicates whether the browser supports the <BGSOUND> tag.
- vbscript. Indicates whether the browser supports client-side VBScript scripts.
- javascript. Indicates whether the browser supports client-side JavaScript scripts.
- javaapplets. Indicates whether the browser supports Java applets.
- ActiveXControls. Indicates whether the browser supports client-side ActiveX controls.
- beta. Indicates whether the browser is still a beta version.
- platform. Indicates the operating system of the browser. For example, Windows 95, Windows NT, or Mac PowerPC.
- Win16. Indicates whether the browser runs on Windows 3.x rather than Windows 95 or Windows NT.

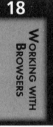

18

WORKING WITH BROWSERS

To use the Browser Capabilities component, you need to create an instance of it. Next, you can simply append the feature you want to detect to the name of the component instance. Here's an example that displays a number of browser features (continued on the next page):

```
<HTML>
<HEAD><TITLE> Browser Capabilities Example </TITLE></HEAD>
<BODY>
<%
Set MyBrow=Server.CreateObject("MSWC.BrowserType")
%>

Your browser has the following properties:
<P>
<TABLE BORDER=1 CELLPADDING=10>
```

```
<TR>
<TD>Browser Type</TD><TD><%=MyBrow.Browser%></TD>
</TR>
<TR>
<TD>Cookies</TD><TD><%=MyBrow.Cookies%></TD>
</TR>
<TR>
<TD>Frames</TD><TD><%=MyBrow.Frames%></TD>
</TR>
<TR>
<TD>Platform</TD><TD><%=MyBrow.Platform%></TD>
</TR>
<TR>
<TD>VBScript</TD><TD><%=MyBrow.vbscript%></TD>
</TR>
</TABLE>
</BODY>
</HTML>
```

This script detects and displays a number of browser features. For different browsers, different results will be displayed. Figure 18.1 shows sample output using Netscape Navigator 3.0; Figure 18.2 shows sample output using Microsoft Internet Explorer 4.0.

FIGURE 18.1.

Sample Browser Capabilities component output using Netscape Navigator 3.0.

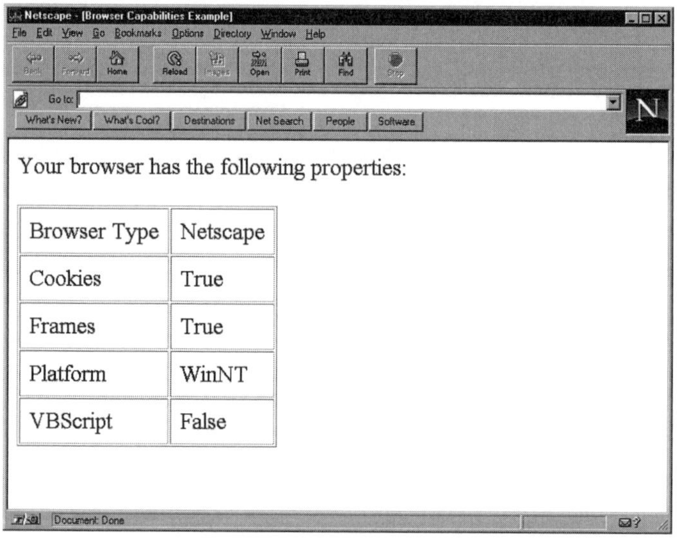

How the Browser Capabilities Component Really Works

It's important to understand how the Browser Capabilities component really works so you can understand some of its serious limitations. The component detects the features of a browser by using an HTTP request header and a special text file that contains browser information.

FIGURE 18.2.
Sample Browser Capabilities component output using Internet Explorer 4.0.

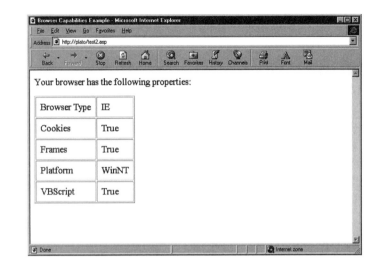

Whenever a browser makes a request, it includes a USER-AGENT header in the request. This header contains information about the type of browser being used and its version number. You can retrieve this header directly by using the ServerVariables collection of the Request object, like this:

```
<%=Request.ServerVariables("HTTP_USER_AGENT")%>
```

When used with Netscape Navigator 3.0, for instance, the value of the USER-AGENT header would be as follows:

```
Mozilla/3.0 (WinNT; I)
```

It's important to understand that this is the only information passed between the browser and the server. The Browser Capabilities component depends on the information in this header. The component doesn't detect any of the features of a browser directly.

The Browser Capabilities component retrieves the value of the USER-AGENT header and attempts to match it with a browser definition in a special file named browscap.ini. The browscap.ini file is located on the server. When you installed Active Server Pages, this file was automatically installed as well.

The browscap.ini file is nothing more than a normal text file. It contains a list of browsers and their features. For example, this is the browser definition in the browscap.ini file for Netscape Navigator version 2.0 (continued on the following page):

```
[Netscape 2.0]
browser=Netscape
version=2.0
majorver=2
minorver=0
frames=TRUE
tables=TRUE
```

18

WORKING WITH BROWSERS

```
cookies=TRUE
backgroundsounds=FALSE
vbscript=FALSE
javascript=TRUE
javaapplets=TRUE
beta=False
Win16=False
```

The Browser Capabilities component uses this definition when it reports the features of Netscape Navigator 2.0. You can modify this text file directly. For example, contrary to reality, you could specify that Netscape Navigator 2.0 can use the <BGSOUND> tag by changing backgroundsounds from FALSE to TRUE.

There are a number of browser features that the Browser Capabilities component should detect but doesn't. For example, it would be extremely useful if you could use the component to detect whether a certain browser can use the Secure Sockets Layer or cascading style sheets. Because this information isn't included in the browscap.ini file, however, you can't use the Browser Capabilities component to detect these features. However, you can add this information to the browscap.ini file yourself. For example, you can add the following two lines to the definition entry for Netscape Navigator 2.0:

```
SSL=TRUE
CSS=FALSE
```

Once these two lines are added, the Browser Component will report these features for Netscape Navigator 2.0. Whenever the component detects that a browser is Netscape Navigator 2.0 (using the USER-AGENT header), the component will assume that the browser has these properties. For example, the following script returns TRUE when included in a page retrieved by Netscape Navigator 2.0:

```
<%=MyBrow.SSL %>
```

You might notice that many of the browser definitions in the browscap.ini file look like this:

```
[Mozilla/2.0 (Win95; U)]
parent=Netscape 2.0
platform=Win95
```

When a browser definition has a parent parameter, the definition will inherit all the features of its parent. The preceding definition inherits all the features of the Netscape Navigator 2.0 browser. For instance, even though the definition doesn't specify whether the Windows 95 version of Netscape can use frames, the Browser Capabilities component will report that this version of Netscape Navigator can use frames because its parent can.

With the parent parameter, the same information doesn't have to be entered over and over. You can make one parent definition, and create a number of smaller child definitions that contain more specific information. Any browser feature specified in the child definition that conflicts with the parent definition will take precedence.

The Browser Capabilities component is only as accurate as the browscap.ini file. If someone is using a browser or a version of a browser that isn't included in the browscap.ini file, the Browser

Capabilities component won't be able to report its features accurately. When the Browser Capabilities component doesn't recognize a browser, it reports the features specified for the default browser. This is an example of the default browser definition:

```
[Default Browser Capability Settings]
browser=Default
Version=0.0
majorver=#0
minorver=#0
frames=False
tables=True
cookies=False
backgroundsounds=False
vbscript=False
javascript=False
javaapplets=False
activexcontrols=False
AK=False
SK=False
AOL=False
beta=False
Win16=False
Crawler=False
CDF=False
```

Again, if you don't like the default properties specified in the browscap.ini file, you can modify them directly. For example, you might not want to assume that all browsers can use tables. To change this assumption, simply change the value of the tables property in the definition for the default browser.

> **NOTE**
>
> You should check for updates to the browscap.ini file at the Microsoft site; Microsoft frequently updates this file. Check at http://www.microsoft.com/iis.
>
> A number of third-party updates to this file are also available. One example is at BrowsCap Central, located at http://www.cyscape.com/asp/browscap/.

A Sample Application of the Browser Capabilities Component

This section presents a possible application of the Browser Capabilities component. The purpose of this example is not only to show how to use the component, but also to show its limitations.

In the Active Server Page shown in Listing 18.1, the Browser Capabilities component is used to detect whether a browser can use frames. If the browser can use frames, a framed version of the page is displayed. If the browser can't use frames, the user is warned that he or she must have a frames-compliant browser to visit the Web site.

Listing 18.1. Checkframes.asp.

```
<%
Set MyBrow=Server.CreateObject("MSWC.BrowserType")
IF MyBrow.Frames THEN
%>
<HTML>
<HEAD><TITLE> Framed Page </TITLE></HEAD>
<FRAMESET COLS="100,*">
<FRAME SRC="menu.asp">
<FRAME SRC="body.asp">
</FRAMESET>
</HTML>
<% ELSE %>
<HTML>
<HEAD><TITLE> Frameless Page </TITLE></HEAD>
<BODY>

We have detected that your browser is incapable of using frames.
You are using a <%=MyBrow.browser%> browser
(version <%=MyBrow.version %>).
To download a more recent browser, please visit:
<P> <A HREF="http://www.microsoft.com">Microsoft</A>
<P> OR
<P> <A HREF="http://www.netscape.com">Netscape</A>
</BODY>
</HTML>
<% END IF %>
```

This Active Server Page conditionally displays two other pages. If the Browser Capabilities component detects that a user's browser can interpret the frame tags, the first page is displayed. This page displays two frames. Otherwise, the second page is displayed. Notice how the Browser Capabilities component is also used to report the name and version of the browser being used.

This example not only illustrates how the Browser Capabilities component can be used, but also why the component normally should not be used for this purpose. It illustrates a serious problem with the Browser Capabilities component.

The problem with this Active Server Page is that it will always display the second page when it doesn't recognize a browser. In other words, even if a browser can support frames, the second page will be displayed when the Browser Capabilities component doesn't recognize it. For example, as of the printing date of this book, the current version of the browscap.ini file didn't recognize the newest version of the Netscape browser. Therefore, even though this browser can use frames, the second page is displayed (see Figure 18.3).

The major shortcoming of the Browser Capabilities component is that it must depend on the information placed by Microsoft or you in the browscap.ini file. The speed at which new technologies and new browsers are introduced on the Internet undermines its usefulness.

FIGURE 18.3.

Bad results from the Browser Capabilities component.

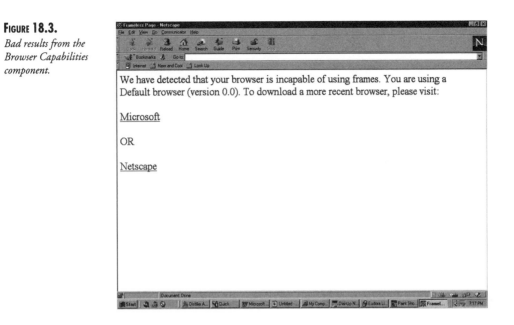

When possible, it's much better to use HTML itself to display different content, depending on the capabilities of a browser. For example, a better way to detect whether a browser can use frames is by using the <NOFRAMES> HTML tag, as described in Chapter 7, "Advanced HTML." The advantage of this approach is that it should continue to work with new browsers.

Summary

In this chapter, you learned how to integrate ActiveX components into your Active Server Pages. You learned how to create an instance of a component with page, session, and application scope, and how to use the Browser Capabilities component. Finally, an example of an Active Server Page using the Browser Capabilities component was provided. This example also demonstrated a significant limitation of this component.

18

WORKING WITH BROWSERS

CHAPTER 19

Working with Files, Drives, and Folders

IN THIS CHAPTER

This entire chapter is devoted to the Active Server Pages File Access component. By using this component within your Active Server Pages, you can gain complete control over your computer's file system. The first section of this chapter presents an overview of the objects used by this component. In the second section, you learn how to read and write to a text file. The third section shows how to work with the methods, properties, and collections of files. The final section investigates the methods for manipulating folders and drives.

Overview of the File Access Component

In previous releases of Internet Information Server, you had very restricted access to the file system. You were limited to doing nothing more than reading and writing from a text file. This limitation was sorely felt. For example, no direct method was available for doing something as simple as checking whether or not a file exists.

> **NOTE**
>
> As I write this, the File Access component is still very much in beta. Check the documentation included with Internet Information Server for the latest information on its features.

Fortunately, with the release of Internet Information Server 4.0, this situation has changed dramatically. The version of Active Server Pages included with this release has a rich set of methods, properties, and collections for working with files. By using Active Server Pages scripts, you now have complete control over almost all aspects of the file system.

To work with files, you use the File Access component. This component uses the following objects:

- `FileSystemObject`. This object includes all the basic methods for working with the file system. For example, you can use the methods of this object to copy and delete folders and files.
- `TextStream`. This object is used for reading and writing to a file.
- `File`. The methods and properties of this object enable you to work with individual files.
- `Folder`. The methods and properties of this object enable you to work with file folders.

After reading the following pages, you'll understand how to use the most valuable methods and properties of these objects. For a complete list of the methods, properties, and collections of these objects, see Appendix A, "Quick ASP Object and Component Reference," at the back of this book.

Reading and Writing to a File

This section describes how to read and write to a text file. There are many uses for a text file, including these common ones:

- **A custom log.** Use a text file to record the activities of the visitors to your Web site. You can record such information as their IP addresses, the browsers they used, and the amount of time they spent at your Web site.

- **Form data.** Use a text file to store the information collected from an HTML form. For example, if a user enters registration information into an HTML form, you can store that information in a text file.

- **Tip of the Day.** Store a list of tips for using your Web site in a text file, and randomly retrieve and display them on a Web page.

Writing to a Text File

To create and write to a text file, you can use the `FileSystemObject` and `TextStream` objects. First, you must create an instance of the `FileSystemObject` object. Next, you call the `CreateTextFile()` method of the `FileSystemObject` object to return an instance of a `TextStream` object. Finally, you use the `WriteLine()` method of the `TextStream` object to write data to the file. Here's an example:

```
<%
Set MyFileObject=Server.CreateObject("Scripting.FileSystemObject")
Set MyTextFile=MyFileObject.CreateTextFile("c:\mydir\test.txt")
MyTextFile.WriteLine("Hello There!")
MyTextFile.Close
%>
```

This example creates a file named `test.txt` with the path `c:\mydir\test.txt`. The `WriteLine()` method is used to send the single line of text `Hello There!` to the file. Finally, the instance of the `TextStream` object is closed to preserve system resources. Each of these steps is described in more detail in the following paragraphs.

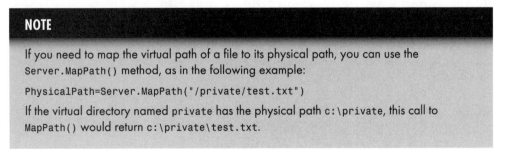

NOTE

If you need to map the virtual path of a file to its physical path, you can use the `Server.MapPath()` method, as in the following example:

`PhysicalPath=Server.MapPath("/private/test.txt")`

If the virtual directory named `private` has the physical path `c:\private`, this call to `MapPath()` would return `c:\private\test.txt`.

The `CreateTextFile()` method is used to create the new text file. When this method is called, a `TextStream` object is returned. This method has one required parameter and two optional ones (as shown on the following page):

■ *FileSpecifier*. Specifies the path of the file to create. If a directory in the path doesn't exist, the error File not found is returned.

■ *Overwrite*. This parameter is optional. By default, it has the value TRUE. A call to CreateTextFile() automatically overwrites any preexisting file with the same name. If this parameter is set to FALSE, an error occurs if the file already exists.

■ *Unicode*. This parameter is optional. By default, it has the value FALSE, which indicates that a file using the ASCII character set should be created. If set to TRUE, a file using the Unicode character set will be created.

After a file has been created with the CreateTextFile() method, you can use the TextStream object to write to the file. When using the TextStream object for writing, you can use the following methods:

■ Write(*string*). This method writes a string to the file.

■ WriteLine(*[string]*). This method writes a string to the file and adds a newline character. The *string* argument is optional. If no string is specified, a newline character is written to the file.

■ WriteBlankLines(*lines*). This method writes the specified number of blank lines (newline characters) to the file.

■ Close. This method is used to close an open TextStream file and free up resources.

For example, to create a text file containing the text Hello World! 32 times in a row, you would use the following script:

```
<%
Set MyFileObject=Server.CreateObject("Scripting.FileSystemObject")
Set MyTextFile=MyFileObject.CreateTextFile("c:\mydir\test.txt")
FOR i=1 to 32
  MyTextFile.WriteLine("Hello World!")
NEXT
MyTextFile.Close
%>
```

Reading and Appending Data from a Text File

To read from a text file, you first need to create an instance of the FileSystemObject object. Next, you use the OpenTextFile() method to return an instance of the TextStream object. Finally, you can use the ReadLine method of the TextStream object to read from the file. Here's an example:

```
<%
Set MyFileObject=Server.CreateObject("Scripting.FileSystemObject")
Set MyTextFile=MyFileObject.OpenTextFile("c:\mydir\test.txt")
WHILE NOT MyTextFile.AtEndOfStream
  Response.Write(MyTextFile.ReadLine)
WEND
MyTextFile.Close
%>
```

This script reads everything from the text file named test.txt. It outputs the contents of this file to the browser. If the file doesn't exist, the error File Not Found is returned. (In the next section, you learn how to detect whether a file exists.)

The WHILE...WEND loop in this example moves through the contents of the file until the end of the file is reached. The AtEndOfStream property has the value FALSE until the loop moves to the end of the file.

The following properties of the TextStream object are useful when reading from a text file:

- AtEndOfLine. This property indicates whether the end of a particular line in a text file has been reached. When the newline character is detected, this property has the value TRUE.

- AtEndOfStream. This property indicates whether the end of the entire text file has been reached. It can have the value TRUE or the value FALSE.

- Column. This property indicates the current character position in a line. The property returns an integer value.

- Line. This property indicates the current line in a file. The property returns an integer value.

Instead of using the ReadLine method to read through the contents of a file, you can use the Read() method. The Read() method returns a specified number of characters from an open text file. Following is an example of how to use this method:

```
<%
Set MyFileObject=Server.CreateObject("Scripting.FileSystemObject")
Set MyTextFile=MyFileObject.OpenTextFile("c:\mydir\test.txt")
WHILE NOT MyTextFile.AtEndOfLine
  Response.Write(MyTextFile.Read(1))
WEND
MyTextFile.Close
%>
```

This script retrieves the first line from a text file, one character at a time. The AtEndOfLine property detects when the end of the first line of the text file has been reached. The Read() method reads one character at a time from the text file.

The following methods are useful when reading data from a text file (continued on the next page):

- Read(*characters*). This method reads the specified number of characters from the text file.

- ReadLine. This method reads a single line from the text file. (The newline character is not returned.)

- ReadAll. This method retrieves the entire contents of the TextStream file.

- Skip(*characters*). This method skips the specified number of characters in an open text file.

- ▪ SkipLine. This method skips a single line in an open text file.

- ▪ Close. This method closes an open TextStream file and frees up resources.

Normally, the OpenTextFile() method is used for retrieving data from a text file. However, you can also use this method to append new data to a text file, like this:

```
<%
Set MyFileObject=Server.CreateObject("Scripting.FileSystemObject")
Set MyTextFile=MyFileObject.OpenTextFile("c:\mydir\browser.log", 8, TRUE)
MyTextFile.WriteLine(Request.ServerVariables("HTTP_USER_AGENT"))
MyTextFile.Close
%>
```

This script creates a log of the browsers being used at a Web site. Whenever the script is executed, the type of browser used to request the page is recorded in a text file. This browser information is retrieved from the ServerVariables collection.

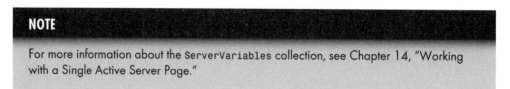

NOTE

For more information about the ServerVariables collection, see Chapter 14, "Working with a Single Active Server Page."

The preceding script appends the browser type to the end of the text file named browser.log. If the file browser.log doesn't exist when this script is first executed, the file is created automatically. This is accomplished by using two parameters of the OpenTextFile() method: the IOMode and the Create parameters.

The following list describes all the parameters of the OpenTextFile() method:

- ▪ *FileSpecifier*. Specifies the path to the file to open for reading or appending.

- ▪ *IOMode*. Optional parameter indicating whether the file should be opened for reading, writing, or appending. The default value is 1 for reading. To open a file for writing, set this value to 2. To open a file for appending, set this value to 8.

- ▪ *Create*. Optional parameter indicating whether the file should be created if it doesn't exist. By default, the value of this parameter is FALSE.

- ▪ *Format*. Optional parameter that specifies the format of the file. By default, a file uses the ASCII character set. However, you can use the Unicode character set by passing the value -1, or the system default by passing the value -2.

NOTE

You can't use constants with the OpenTextFile() method in the current release of Active Server Pages. For example, you must use the value 8 rather than the constant ForAppending with the *IOMode* parameter.

Sample Application

This section provides a sample application of the methods used for reading and writing to files. As I write this, Amazon.com (the online bookstore) is holding a competition to write a collaborative online story. The first part of the story was entered by John Updike. Each day, visitors to the Amazon.com Web site submit new sentences to add to the story. One sentence is selected every day, and the winner receives $1,000. The story is being written collaboratively.

This competition is a great idea. It attracts repeat visitors to the Amazon.com Web site, and it has generated a tremendous amount of publicity. You may want to add something similar to your Web site. Listing 19.1 shows a simple example of how you could do this.

Listing 19.1. Script for `story.asp`.

```
<%
IF NOT Request.Form("NextLine")="" THEN
Set MyFileObject=Server.CreateObject("Scripting.FileSystemObject")
Set MyTextFile=MyFileObject.OpenTextFile("c:\mydir\TheStory.txt", 8, TRUE)
MyTextFile.WriteLine(Request.Form("NextLine"))
MyTextFile.Close
END IF
%>
<HTML>
<HEAD><TITLE> Online Story </TITLE></HEAD>
<BODY>
<HR>
<%
Set MyFileObject=Server.CreateObject("Scripting.FileSystemObject")
Set MyTextFile=MyFileObject.OpenTextFile("c:\mydir\TheStory.txt")
WHILE NOT MyTextFile.AtEndOfStream
  Response.Write("  "&MyTextFile.ReadLine)
WEND
MyTextFile.Close
%>
<HR>
<H3>Enter a new line for the story: </H3>
<FORM METHOD="POST" ACTION="story.asp">
<INPUT NAME="NextLine" TYPE="TEXT" SIZE=70>
<INPUT TYPE="SUBMIT" VALUE="Submit Sentence">
</FORM>
</BODY>
</HTML>
```

This Active Server Page contains two scripts. The first script executes when a new sentence has been submitted. If a new sentence exists, it's appended to the file named `TheStory.txt`.

The second script is used to display the contents of the `TheStory.txt` file. Each line in the file is outputted (see Figure 19.1). The lines are separated by two nonbreaking space characters so that the sentences will be divided by spaces when displayed.

19

WORKING WITH
FILES, DRIVES,
AND FOLDERS

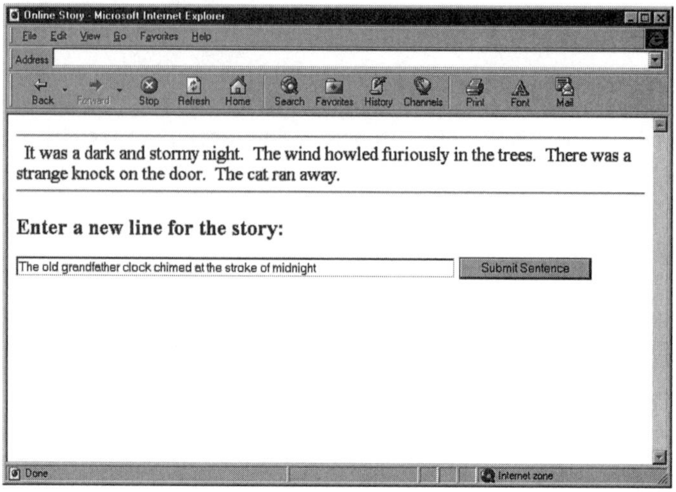

FIGURE 19.1.

An online collaborative story.

The remainder of the Active Server Page contains an HTML form for submitting the next line in the story. The Active Server Page posts the form contents to itself. For this to work, you must name the Active Server Page story.asp.

Before you use this Active Server Page for the first time, you need to create a text file named TheStory.txt. The first sentence of the story needs to be entered into this file. If you want to restart the story, simply clear this file and enter a new first sentence.

Working with Files

This section covers how to work with files—how to copy, move, and delete files; how to detect whether a file exists; and how to retrieve the attributes of a file.

Copying, Moving, and Deleting Files

There's more than one way to copy, move, or delete a file. To do this, you can use the methods of the FileSystemObject object or the methods of the File object. The methods of the FileSystemObject object are slightly more flexible because you're not restricted to working with a single file.

The following list describes the methods of the FileSystemObject for manipulating files:

■ CopyFile *source, destination,* [*Overwrite*]. This method copies a file from one location to another. You can use wildcards in the *source* parameter to copy more than one file at a time. The optional *Overwrite* parameter indicates whether to overwrite an existing file. It can have the value TRUE or the value FALSE.

■ MoveFile *source, destination*. This method moves a file from one location to another. You can use wildcards in the *source* parameter to move more than one file at a time. If the file already exists at the destination, an error is generated.

■ DeleteFile *FileSpecifier*. This method deletes the specified file. You can use wildcards to delete more than one file at a time. If you use wildcards and no matches are made, an error is generated.

Before you can use any of these methods, however, you first need to create an instance of the FileSystemObject object. The next example shows how each of the methods is used:

```
<%
'  Create an instance of the FileSystemObject object
Set MyFileObject=Server.CreateObject("Scripting.FileSystemObject")
'  Create a file to manipulate
Set MyFile=MyFileObject.CreateTextFile("c:\test.txt")
MyFile.Writeline("Hello")
MyFile.Close
' Copy the file
MyFileObject.CopyFile "c:\test.txt","c:\test2.txt"
' Move the file
MyFileObject.MoveFile "c:\test2.txt","c:\test3.txt"
' Delete both files
MyFileObject.DeleteFile "c:\test.txt"
MyFileObject.DeleteFile "c:\test3.txt"
%>
```

Instead of using the FileSystemObject object to copy, move, or delete files, you can also use the File object. These are the equivalent methods you can use with the File object:

■ Copy *newcopy*, *[Overwrite]*. This method creates a new copy of the current file. If the optional *Overwrite* parameter is set to TRUE, any preexisting file is overwritten.

■ Move *newcopy*. This method moves the current file. The current file will now refer to this file.

■ Delete. Deletes the current file.

Before you can use these methods, you must first create an instance of the File object. To create an instance of the File object, you can use the GetFile() method of the FileSystemObject object. Here's the preceding script, rewritten to use the methods of the File object:

```
<%
'  Create an instance of the FileSystemObject object
Set MyFileObject=Server.CreateObject("Scripting.FileSystemObject")
'  Create a file to manipulate
Set MyFile=MyFileObject.CreateTextFile("c:\test.txt")
MyFile.Writeline("Hello")
MyFile.Close
'  Create an instance of the File object.
Set afile=MyFileObject.GetFile("c:\test.txt")
' Copy the file
afile.Copy "c:\test2.txt"
' Move the file
afile.Move "c:\test3.txt"
' Delete the original file
afile.Delete
%>
```

Detecting Whether a File Exists

To detect whether or not a particular file exists, you can use the `FileExists()` method of the `FileSystemObject` object. Simply pass the physical path of a file to this method and it will return either `TRUE` or `FALSE`. Here's an example of how this method is used:

```
<HTML>
<HEAD><TITLE> FileExists Example </TITLE></HEAD>
<BODY>
<%
MySelf=Request.ServerVariables("PATH_TRANSLATED")
'  Create an instance of the FileSystemObject object
Set MyFileObject=Server.CreateObject("Scripting.FileSystemObject")
If MyFileObject.FileExists(Myself) THEN
  Response.Write("I exist!")
ELSE
  Response.Write("I do not exist.")
END IF
%>
</BODY>
</HTML>
```

This Active Server Page checks whether or not it exists. The server variable `PATH_TRANSLATED` is used to return the physical path of the current file. The `FileExists` method checks whether this file exists. In this example, necessarily, the method must always return `TRUE`. (In other words, A checks to see whether A itself exists, and of course it does, so it comes back `TRUE`.)

Retrieving the Attributes of Files

The `File` object includes a number of properties that are useful when working with files. The following list explains these properties:

- `Attributes`. This property returns the attributes of the current file (like the DOS `ATTRIB` command). For example, you can use this property to determine whether a file is hidden or read-only.

- `DateCreated`. This property returns the date and time the file was created.

- `DateLastAccessed`. This property returns the date and time the file was last accessed.

- `DateLastModified`. This property returns the date and time the file was last modified.

- `Drive`. This property returns the drive where the file is located.

- `Name`. This property returns the name of the file.

- `ParentFolder`. This property returns the folder in which the file is contained.

- `Path`. This property returns the path of the file.

- `Size`. This property returns the size of the file in bytes.

- `Type`. This property returns the type of the file—for example, `Text Document`, `ASP File`, or `Internet Document (HTML)`.

To use any of these properties, you must first create an instance of the `File` object. The next example displays all the properties for a file with the path `c:\test.txt` (see Figure 19.2):

```
<HTML>
<HEAD><TITLE>File Properties</TITLE></HEAD>
<BODY>
<%
'   Create an instance of the FileSystemObject object
Set MyFileObject=Server.CreateObject("Scripting.FileSystemObject")
'   Create an instance of the File object.
Set afile=MyFileObject.GetFile("c:\test.txt")
%>
<BR>Name: <%=afile.Name%>
<BR>Path: <%=afile.Path%>
<BR>Drive: <%=afile.Drive%>
<BR>Size: <%=afile.Size%>
<BR>Type: <%=afile.Type%>
<BR>Attributes: <%=afile.Attributes%>
<BR>Date Created: <%=afile.DateCreated %>
<BR>Date Last Accessed: <%=afile.DateLastAccessed%>
<BR>Date Last Modified: <%=afile.DateLastModified%>
</BODY>
</HTML>
```

FIGURE 19.2.

File properties.

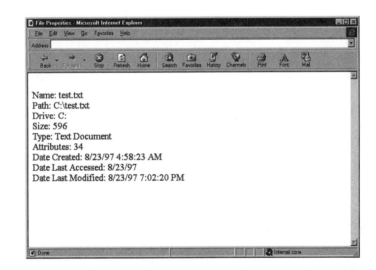

The Attributes property requires some explanation. This property returns a number corresponding to the sum of the file attributes that have been set. The following table lists the file attribute values.

Attribute	Value
Normal	0
Read-only	1
Hidden	2
System	4

continues

Attribute	*Value*
Volume	8
Directory	16
Archive	32
Alias	64
Compressed	128

The file shown in Figure 19.2 has its hidden and archive attributes set. The combination of the values 2 (for hidden) and 32 (for archive) equals 34. There's no danger of ambiguity, because every combination of attribute values yields a unique number.

Some of these properties not only can be read, but also can be set. You can set the read-only, hidden, system, and archive properties. For example, to make the file c:\test.txt hidden, you could use the following script:

```
<%
'  Create an instance of the FileSystemObject object
Set MyFileObject=Server.CreateObject("Scripting.FileSystemObject")
'  Create an instance of the File object.
Set afile=MyFileObject.GetFile("c:\test.txt")
'  Make it hidden
afile.attributes=2
%>
```

Working with Drives and Folders

This section explores the methods for working with drives and folders. You learn how to retrieve information about the drives on the current machine. You also learn how to create, copy, move, delete, and list the contents of folders.

Working with Drives

There are two objects that you can use to retrieve information about the drives on the local machine: the FileSystemObject object and the Drive object. For example, the following Active Server Page displays a list of all the drives on the server and their total size and available size (see Figure 19.3):

```
<HTML>
<HEAD><TITLE>Drive List</TITLE></HEAD>
<BODY>
<%
'  Create an instance of the FileSystemObject object
Set MyFileObject=Server.CreateObject("Scripting.FileSystemObject")
'  Loop through the Drives collection
FOR EACH thing in MyFileObject.Drives
%>
<BR>Drive Letter: <%=thing.DriveLetter%>
<BR>Drive Total Size: <%=thing.TotalSize%>
<BR>Drive Available Space: <%=thing.AvailableSpace%>
```

```
<HR>
<%
NEXT
%>
</BODY>
</HTML>
```

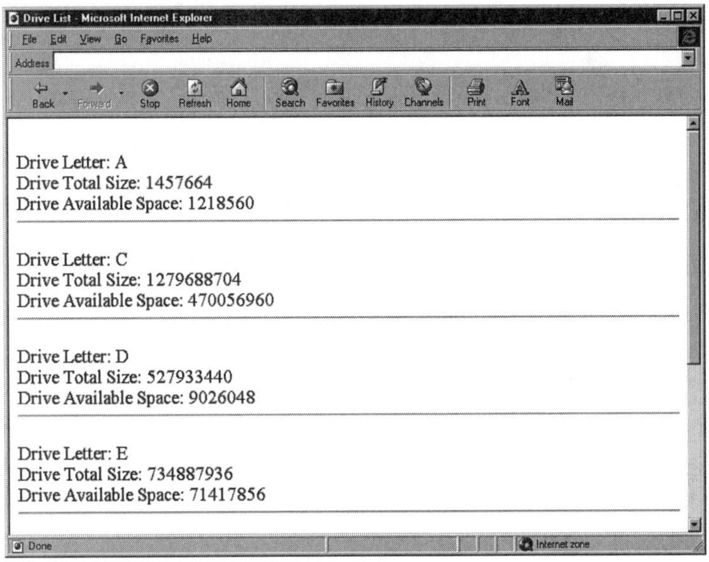

FIGURE 19.3.

Drives on the local machine.

The `Drives` collection of the `FileSystemObject` object contains the collection of all the available drives on the server. However, it contains only those drives that have been mapped to a drive letter.

These are the methods of the `FileSystemObject` object related to drives:

■ `DriveExists(DriveSpecifier)`. Returns TRUE if the specified drive exists.

■ `Drives`. Returns the collection of drives for the local machine.

■ `GetDrive(DriveSpecifier)`. Returns a `Drive` object that represents the drive specified.

■ `GetDriveName(Path)`. Returns a string that contains the drive for the path specified.

Not surprisingly, the `Drive` object also contains a number of methods and properties that are useful for working with drives (continued on the following page):

■ `AvailableSpace`. Returns the space available on the drive in bytes.

■ `DriveLetter`. Returns the letter of the drive—for example, C:, D:, or E:.

■ `DriveType`. Returns a number corresponding to the type of the drive—for example, a CD-ROM or removable drive.

■ `FreeSpace`. Returns the amount of free space on the drive in bytes (normally the same as `AvailableSpace`).

19

WORKING WITH
FILES, DRIVES,
AND FOLDERS

> **TIP**
>
> You may wonder when `FreeSpace` and `AvailableSpace` would differ. There's a hint that the system administrator will be able to allocate how much hard drive space each user of a server can use in the next version of NT. If so, the two values would differ.

- `IsReady`. Indicates whether a volume is ready to be used. This property is useful for indicating the state of removable drives.
- `Path`. Indicates the path of the drive.
- `RootFolder`. This property returns a `Folder` object representing the root folder on the drive.
- `SerialNumber`. Returns the serial number of the drive.
- `ShareName`. Returns the share name of the drive.
- `TotalSize`. Returns the total size of the drive in bytes.
- `VolumeName`. Returns a string representing the volume name of the drive.

To use these properties and methods, you need to create an instance of the `Drive` object. You can do this by using the `GetDrive()` method of the `FileSystemObject` object. The following example returns the volume name of the C: drive:

```
<%
'  Create an instance of the FileSystemObject object
Set MyFileObject=Server.CreateObject("Scripting.FileSystemObject")
'  Create an instance of the Drive object
Set MyDrive=MyFileObject.GetDrive("c:")
Response.Write(MyDrive.VolumeName)
%>
```

Working with Folders

This section shows how to manipulate folders and display their contents. To work with folders, you can use both the `FileSystemObject` object and the `Folder` object. This example displays all the files in a folder with the path `c:\myfolder`:

```
<HTML>
<HEAD><TITLE>Folder Contents</TITLE></HEAD>
<BODY>
<%
'  Create an instance of the FileSystemObject object
Set MyFileObject=Server.CreateObject("Scripting.FileSystemObject")
'  Create a folder object
Set MyFolder=MyFileObject.GetFolder("c:\myfolder")
'  Loop through the Files collection
FOR EACH thing in MyFolder.Files
  Response.Write("<P>"&thing)
NEXT
%>
</BODY>
</HTML>
```

In this example, a `Folder` object is created by using the `GetFolder()` method of the `FileSystemObject` object. Once the `Folder` object is created, the `FOR...NEXT` loop is used to loop through its `Files` collection. The page displays all the files in this collection (see Figure 19.4).

FIGURE 19.4.

Folder contents.

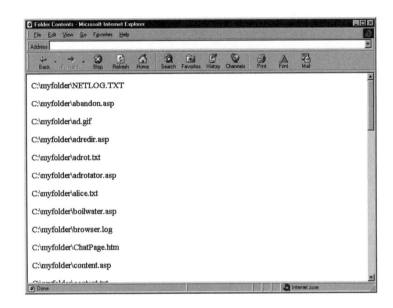

The `FileSystemObject` object includes a number of methods for working with folders. The following list provides a brief explanation of how these methods can be used:

- `CopyFolder source, destination, [Overwrite]`. This method copies a folder from one location to another. You can use wildcards in the *source* parameter to copy multiple folders at the same time. By default, if the folder already exists, it will be overwritten. Set *Overwrite* to FALSE to prevent this from happening.
- `CreateFolder FolderSpecifier`. Creates the specified folder.
- `DeleteFolder FolderSpecifier`. Deletes a folder and all its contents. You can use wildcards to delete multiple folders at the same time.
- `FolderExists(FolderSpecifier)`. Returns TRUE if the folder exists, FALSE otherwise.
- `GetFolder(FolderSpecifier)`. Returns a `Folder` object that represents the folder specified.
- `GetParentFolderName(Path)`. Returns a string containing the path of the parent folder.
- `MoveFolder source, destination`. Moves a folder from one location to another. You can use wildcards in the *source* parameter to move more than one folder at a time.

To use any of these methods, you need to first create an instance of the `FileSystemObject` object. The following example (next page) creates a folder, moves it, and then deletes it:

19

WORKING WITH
FILES, DRIVES,
AND FOLDERS

```
<%
'   Create an instance of the FileSystemObject object
Set MyFileObject=Server.CreateObject("Scripting.FileSystemObject")
'   Create a new folder
MyFileObject.CreateFolder "c:\newfolder"
'   Move the folder
MyFileObject.MoveFolder "c:\newfolder", "c:\oldfolder"
'   Delete the folder
MyFileObject.DeleteFolder "c:\oldfolder"
%>
```

The methods and properties of the Folder object can also be used to manipulate folders. Here's a brief explanation of the properties and methods of the Folder object:

- CopyFolder *newcopy*, [*Overwrite*]. Copies the current folder to a new location. If *Overwrite* is set to FALSE, an error occurs if the folder already exists.

- DeleteFolder. Deletes the current folder and any of its contents.

- Files. Returns the collection of Files contained in the folder. Hidden files are not revealed.

- IsRootFolder. Returns TRUE if the folder is a root folder.

- MoveFolder *FolderSpecifier*. Moves the folder from one location to another.

- Name. Returns the name of the folder.

- ParentFolder. Returns the parent folder.

- Size. Returns the size of a folder and all its subfolders in bytes.

- SubFolders. Returns the collection of subfolders of the current folder.

To use any of these methods, you need to first create an instance of the Folder object. This example returns a list of all the subfolders of the folder with the path c:\myfolder:

```
<%
'   Create an instance of the FileSystemObject object
Set MyFileObject=Server.CreateObject("Scripting.FileSystemObject")
'   Create an instance of the Folder object
Set MyFolder=MyFileObject.GetFolder("c:\myfolder")
FOR EACH thing IN MyFolder.SubFolders
 Response.Write(thing)
NEXT
%>
```

Summary

This chapter described how to use the objects of the File Access component. You learned how to read and write to text files and how to work with the methods and properties of the File object. Finally, you learned how to use the Folder and Drive objects to manipulate folders and retrieve information about the drives on your server.

Providing Site-Wide Navigation

CHAPTER 20

This chapter covers how to use two ActiveX components that are included with Active Server Pages. In the first section, you learn how to use the Content Linking component. This component can be used to make your site easier to navigate. The second section presents a detailed example that illustrates how to use this component. You learn how to use the Content Linking component to create a simple newsgroup. Finally, in the third section, you learn how to use the Permission Checker component. This component displays a link to a page only when the user has permission to access the page.

The Content Linking Component

The *Content Linking component* is useful in situations where you have a series of pages you need to link together. For example, you can use this component to link the pages of an online book, a slide show, or even the messages in a newsgroup. An example of how you can use this component to create a simple newsgroup is presented in the following section.

Normally, to link a series of pages, you need to insert a hypertext link in each page. The Content Linking component simplifies this process. Using this component, you can create a list of pages in a single file. Once this file is created, you can use the methods of the component to display appropriate links in each page.

The Content Linking component has the following methods:

- GetListCount*(Content Linking List File)*

  Returns the total number of pages contained in the Content Linking List file.

- GetListIndex*(Content Linking List File)*

  Returns the position of the current page in the Content Linking List file.

- GetNextDescription*(Content Linking List File)*

  Returns the description of the next page in the Content Linking List file.

- GetNextURL*(Content Linking List File)*

  Returns the path of the next page in the Content Linking List file.

- GetNthDescription*(Content Linking List File, Number)*

  Returns the description for a page with a particular index in the Content Linking List file.

- GetNthURL*(Content Linking List File, Number)*

  Returns the path of the page with a particular index in the Content Linking List file.

- GetPreviousDescription*(Content Linking List File)*

  Returns the description for the previous page in the Content Linking List file.

- GetPreviousURL*(Content Linking List File)*

  Returns the path of the previous page in the Content Linking List file.

For example, suppose you want to create a step-by-step guide to cooking pasta on your Web site. You want to devote a distinct Active Server Page to each step and display the steps in order. The Content Linking component makes this easy to do.

First, you need to create a special file called the *Content Linking List file*. The Content Linking List file is a normal text file that you can create with any text editor. It simply contains a list of the pages you want to link. Here's an example:

```
/pasta/grabpot.asp          Grab a pot from the cupboard.

/pasta/boilwater.asp        Boil some water in the pot.

/pasta/openbox.asp          Open box of pasta.

/pasta/dumpcontents.asp     Dump contents of box in pot.

/pasta/wait.asp             Wait ten minutes.

/pasta/home.asp             Return to home page.
```

Once you create the Content Linking List file, you can save the file with any name. For example, you could save the file as `pasta.txt`.

This sample file has two columns. The first column contains a list of the files to link. These can be Active Server Pages files or normal HTML files. The second column contains descriptions of these files. These two columns must be separated by a single tab character rather than spaces. The Content Linking component won't be able to distinguish the two columns otherwise.

> **NOTE**
>
> Any special formatting applied to the Content Linking List file, such as bold or italics, is ignored. The Content Linking List file is nothing more than a text file.

After you have created the Content Linking List file, you can use the Content Linking component to add navigational links to your Active Server Pages. For example, you might want to display a list of all the steps involved in preparing pasta on the home page of your Web site. You could do this with the following Active Server Page:

```
<HTML>
<HEAD><TITLE> Home Page </TITLE></HEAD>
<BODY>
<H2>Welcome To The Pasta Web Site!</H2>
<%
Set mylinks=Server.CreateObject("MSWC.NextLink")
%>
Here are the
<%=mylinks.GetListCount("pasta.txt")-1%>
steps for preparing pasta:
<OL>
<%
```

```
FOR i=1 TO mylinks.GetListCount("pasta.txt")-1
%>
<LI><A HREF="<%=mylinks.GetNthURL("pasta.txt",i)%>">
<%=mylinks.GetNthDescription("pasta.txt",i)%></A>
<%
NEXT
%>
</OL>
</BODY>
</HTML>
```

This Active Server Page displays a list of the links in the Content Linking List file (see Figure 20.1). This is accomplished by creating an instance of the Content Linking component. An instance of this component is assigned to the variable named `mylinks`.

FIGURE 20.1.

The Pasta Web site.

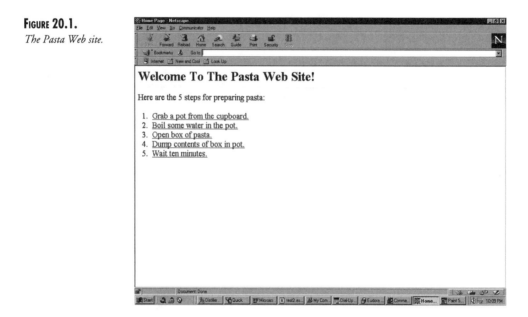

Three methods of the component are used:

- First, the `GetListCount()` method retrieves a count of the number of entries in the Content Linking List file. Whenever you call a method of the Content Linking component, you must pass the name of the Content Linking List file. In this example, the method is called by using `mylinks.GetListCount("pasta.txt")`.

> **NOTE**
>
> The last `FOR` loop goes from 1 to `GetListCount()-1`, leaving out the last list item. That's correct and intended (the last item in the list file is `Return to home page`).

■ Second, the GetNthURL() method retrieves the *n*th URL entry in the Content Linking List file. This method has two parameters. The first parameter indicates the name of the Content Linking List file. The second parameter indicates which entry to retrieve from this file. For example, if you call GetNthURL("pasta.txt",2), the URL listed as the second entry in the pasta.txt file is returned.

■ Third, the GetNthDescription() method is called to retrieve the page descriptions from the Content Linking List file. This method also takes two parameters. The first parameter specifies the name of the Content Linking List file. The second parameter indicates which entry to retrieve from this file. For example, if you call GetNthDescription("pasta.txt", 2), the description in the second entry in the pasta.txt file is returned.

The GetNthURL() and GetNthDescription() methods are used within a FOR...NEXT loop to display all the entries in the Content Linking List file. All the entries are displayed except the final one. This last entry is excluded because it points back to the home page.

In the preceding example, the methods of the Content Linking component are used to list a series of pages. You can also use the methods of this component to link the individual pages together, as in the following example:

```
<HTML>
<HEAD><TITLE> Step One </TITLE></HEAD>
<BODY>
<H1>Step 2: Boil Water </H1>
<H3>Boil some water in a pot.</H3>
<HR>
<%
Set mylinks=Server.CreateObject("MSWC.NextLink")
IF mylinks.GetListIndex("pasta.txt")>1 THEN
%>
<A HREF="<%=mylinks.GetPreviousURL("pasta.txt")%>">
Previous Step</A>
<% END IF %>
<P>
<A HREF="<%=mylinks.GetNextURL("pasta.txt")%>">
Next Step</A>
</BODY>
</HTML>
```

Two methods of the Content Linking component are used in this Active Server Page. The GetPreviousURL() method retrieves the path of the previous page. The GetNextURL() method retrieves the path of the next page. These methods create a link to the previous page and a link to the next page.

The GetPreviousURL() and GetNextURL() methods return different results depending on the current page. When these methods are called, the path of the current page is compared to the entries in the Content Linking List file. The GetPreviousURL() method returns the entry that's above the entry for the current page. The GetNextURL() method returns the entry that's below the entry for the current page.

If the current page isn't included in the Content Linking List file, the GetPreviousURL() method returns the first entry in the Content Linking List file. The GetNextURL() method retrieves the last entry.

Content Linking Component Sample Application

This section shows how to use the Content Linking component to create a simple newsgroup. Users of the newsgroup can post new messages and read postings from other users.

NOTE

Live versions of many of the examples in this book can be seen at this book's companion Web site at http://www.aspsite.com.

The Content Linking component is used in this example to organize the messages in the newsgroup. The component enables a user to view a list of all postings in the newsgroup, and lets the user move easily from one posting to the next (see Figure 20.2).

FIGURE 20.2.

A simple newsgroup.

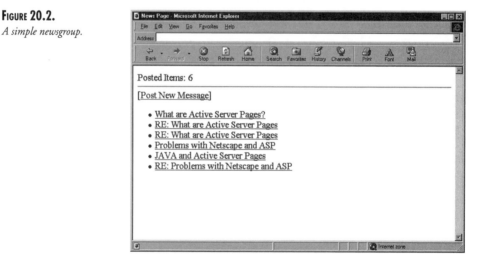

To create the newsgroup, you need to create the following four files:

- **The Post page.** This page is used to post new messages.
- **The Include file.** This file is included at the bottom of every message posted.
- **The New Item page.** This page is used to dynamically generate new Active Server Pages containing the postings.
- **The News page.** This page contains a list of all messages posted in the newsgroup.

The Post Page

The purpose of the Post page is to enable users to post new messages (see Figure 20.3). It's a normal HTML page containing an HTML form, as shown in Listing 20.1. The form has a subject line so that the user can enter a subject for his or her posting. The form also has a text area for entering a message. The WRAP=VIRTUAL attribute is used to allow word wrapping in the text area.

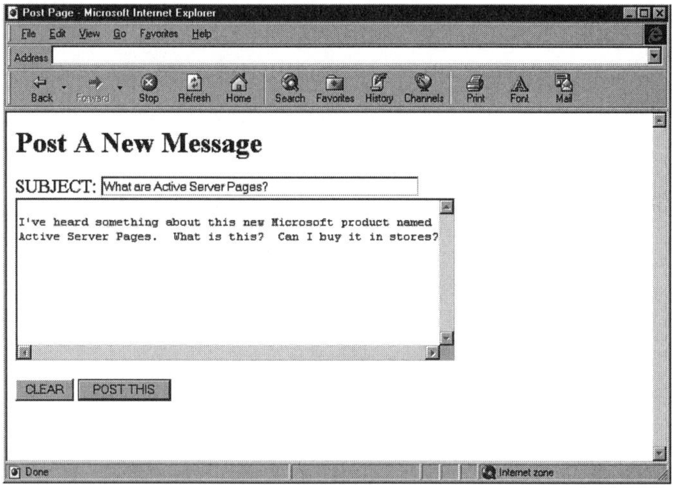

FIGURE 20.3.

The Post page.

Listing 20.1. Script for post.htm.

```
<HTML>
<HEAD><TITLE> Post Page </TITLE></HEAD>
<BODY>
<H2>Post A New Message</H2>
<FORM METHOD="POST" ACTION="newitem.asp">
SUBJECT: <INPUT NAME="subject" TYPE="TEXT" SIZE="50" MAXLENGTH=50>
<BR>
<TEXTAREA NAME="posting" COLS=60 ROWS=10 WRAP="VIRTUAL"></TEXTAREA>
<P>
<INPUT TYPE="RESET" VALUE="CLEAR">
<INPUT TYPE="SUBMIT" VALUE="POST THIS">
</FORM>
</BODY>
</HTML>
```

The Include File

Each message in the newsgroup will include a link to the previous and next messages, as Listing 20.2 shows. It will also include a link back to the News page (see Figure 20.4). These links are added to the message in the Include file. This file is automatically included in every new Active Server Page generated by the New Item page. You'll see how this is done in the next section.

FIGURE 20.4.

A message in the newsgroup.

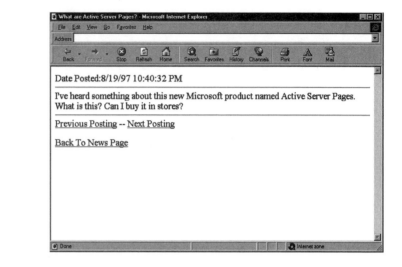

Listing 20.2. Script for `news.inc`.

```
<HR>
<%
Set MyLinks=Server.CreateObject("MSWC.NextLink")
IF mylinks.GetListIndex("news.txt")>1 THEN
%>
<A HREF="<%=mylinks.GetPreviousURL("news.txt")%>">
Previous Posting</A> --
<% END IF %>
<A HREF="<%=mylinks.GetNextURL("news.txt")%>">
Next Posting</A>
<P><A HREF="news.asp">Back To News Page</A>
```

The New Item Page

After a user posts a message, she is brought to the New Item page. The New Item page looks boring (see Figure 20.5). However, behind the scenes, the page actually does quite a lot.

The New Item page is used to dynamically generate new Active Server Pages. When a user posts a new message, that message is saved in a text file. However, the text file is no ordinary text file. It's an Active Server Page. The New Item page creates the Active Server Page from the information the user entered into the HTML form.

The New Item page also updates the Content Linking List file. The page appends new information about the new posting to this file. This enables the Content Linking component to reflect new postings accurately and automatically.

The listing for the New Item page is longer than any of the examples previously discussed. The approach here is to first present the listing for the page in its entirety (see Listing 20.3). Each section of the page is then discussed in detail.

FIGURE 20.5.

The New Item page.

Listing 20.3. The New Item page.

```
<%
' Create the posting
TheSubj=Server.HTMLEncode(Request.Form("subject"))
IF TheSubj="" THEN TheSubj="No Subject"
ThePost="<HTML><HEAD><TITLE>"&TheSubj&"</TITLE></HEAD><BODY>"
ThePost=ThePost&"Date Posted:"&NOW&"<HR>"
ThePost=ThePost&Server.HTMLEncode(Request.Form("posting"))
ThePost=ThePost&"<!-- #INCLUDE VIRTUAL=""news.inc"" -->"
ThePost=ThePost&"</BODY></HTML>"

' Create unique file name
Set mylinks=Server.CreateObject("MSWC.NextLink")
TheName="item"&mylinks.GetListCount("news.txt")+1&".asp"
TheNamePath=Server.MapPath(TheName)

' Save the new posting file
Set MyFileObj=Server.CreateObject("Scripting.FileSystemObject")
Set MyOutStream=MyFileObj.CreateTextFile(TheNamePath)
MyOutStream.Write ThePost
MyOutStream.Close

' Update the Content Linking List File
TheNews=Server.MapPath("news.txt")
Set MyNews=MyFileObj.OpenTextFile(TheNews,8,TRUE)
MyNews.Writeline TheName&vbTab&TheSubj
MyNews.Close
%>

<HTML>
<HEAD><TITLE>New Item</TITLE></HEAD>
<BODY>
<H1> Thank you for posting a new message! </H1>
```

continues

Listing 20.3. continued

```
<A HREF="news.asp">News Page</A>

</BODY>
</HTML>
```

In the first section of this page, a variable named ThePost is created. The value of this variable is actually an Active Server Page. The Active Server Page is created as one long string. Here's the portion of the page that does this:

```
' Create the posting
TheSubj=Server.HTMLEncode(Request.Form("subject"))
IF TheSubj="" THEN TheSubj="No Subject"
ThePost="<HTML><HEAD><TITLE>"&TheSubj&"</TITLE></HEAD><BODY>"
ThePost=ThePost&"Date Posted:"&NOW&"<HR>"
ThePost=ThePost&Server.HTMLEncode(Request.Form("posting"))
ThePost=ThePost&"<!-- #INCLUDE VIRTUAL=""news.inc"" -->"
ThePost=ThePost&"</BODY></HTML>"
```

The Active Server Page that's created includes the text the user entered into the HTML form. It also includes the current date and time. Finally, the INCLUDE directive is added to automatically include the news.inc file discussed earlier.

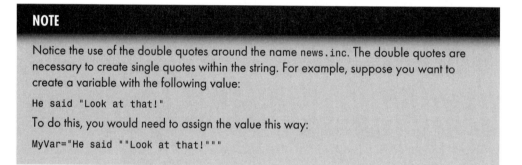

NOTE

Notice the use of the double quotes around the name news.inc. The double quotes are necessary to create single quotes within the string. For example, suppose you want to create a variable with the following value:

```
He said "Look at that!"
```

To do this, you would need to assign the value this way:

```
MyVar="He said ""Look at that!"""
```

The next section of the script provides the new Active Server Page with a unique name. You wouldn't want a message posted by one user to overwrite a message posted by a previous user. Before the Active Server Page can be saved, a unique name must be generated. This portion of the script creates the unique name:

```
' Create unique file name
Set mylinks=Server.CreateObject("MSWC.NextLink")
TheName="item"&mylinks.GetListCount("news.txt")+1&".asp"
TheNamePath=Server.MapPath(TheName)
```

To create a unique name, the Content Linking component is used. Each new posting will be included in the Content Linking List file. By retrieving a count of the number of entries in this file and adding one, a unique name for the new Active Server Page is generated. The first message posted will have the name item1.asp, the second message will have the name item2.asp, and so on. Each message posted corresponds to a unique Active Server Page.

The third section of the New Item page script saves the new Active Server Page. The value of `ThePost` is saved to a text file. This file is saved with the unique name contained in the variable `TheNamePath`. The `FileSystemObject` is used to save the file to disk:

```
' Save the new posting file
Set MyFileObj=Server.CreateObject("Scripting.FileSystemObject")
Set MyOutStream=MyFileObj.CreateTextFile(TheNamePath)
MyOutStream.Write ThePost
MyOutStream.Close
```

> **NOTE**
>
> For more information on how to use the `FileSystemObject` component, see Chapter 19, "Working with Files, Drives, and Folders."

The final section of the script updates the Content Linking List file. The path and name of the new Active Server Pages file is appended to the Content Linking List file. Here's the portion of the script that does the updating:

```
' Update the Content Linking List File
TheNews=Server.MapPath("news.txt")
Set MyNews=MyFileObj.OpenTextFile(TheNews,8,TRUE)
MyNews.Writeline TheName&vbTab&TheSubj
MyNews.Close
```

If the Content Linking List file doesn't exist, this script automatically creates it. The Content Linking List file that the script creates is named `news.txt`. When the first message is posted in the newsgroup, the Content Linking List file is created.

Notice how the VBScript constant `vbTab` is used in this script. The columns in the Content Linking List file must be separated by a single tab character. The `vbTab` constant is used to insert this tab character.

The News Page

The final page needed to create the newsgroup is the News page. The News page displays the number of messages in the newsgroup and lists all of the messages by their subject lines (see Figure 20.6). Listing 20.4 shows the script for the News page.

Listing 20.4. Script for news.asp.

```
<%
' Create the Content Linking component
Set mylinks=Server.CreateObject("MSWC.NextLink")

%>

<HTML>
<HEAD><TITLE> News Page </TITLE></HEAD>
```

20

continues

Listing 20.4. continued

```
<BODY>
Posted Items: <%=mylinks.GetListCount("news.txt")%>
<HR>
[<A HREF="post.htm">Post New Message</A>]
<UL>
<%
' Display the list of messages
FOR i=1 TO mylinks.GetListCount("news.txt")
%>
<LI>
<A HREF="<%=mylinks.GetNthURL("news.txt",i)%>">
<%=mylinks.GetNthDescription("news.txt",i)%></A>
<%
NEXT
%>
</UL>
</BODY>
</HTML>
```

Figure 20.6.

The News page.

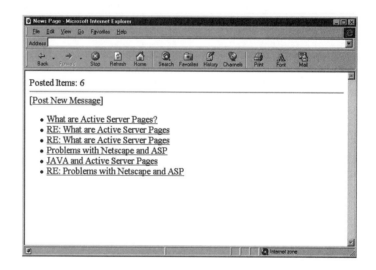

In this page, the Content Linking component is used to retrieve the number of entries in the Content Linking List file. This will correspond to the number of messages posted. Second, all the entries in the Content Linking List file are displayed. If a user clicks any of the entries, he'll be linked to the contents of the posting associated with the entry.

Extending the Newsgroup Example

The simple newsgroup discussed in the preceding sections could be used to track only a small number of postings for a small number of users. Problems would arise if multiple users attempted to post new messages at the same time. The Content Linking component wasn't designed for this purpose.

A much better approach to creating a newsgroup would be to store the messages in a database such as Microsoft SQL Server. To do this, you could use the ActiveX Data Objects (for details, see Chapter 22, "ActiveX Data Objects"). Unlike the Content Linking component, databases are designed to store and retrieve large amounts of information efficiently.

However, this sample application does illustrate how the Content Linking component can be used to easily link large numbers of Active Server Pages together. All the postings in the newsgroup are automatically linked in a series. The Content Linking component makes this easy to do.

Using the Permission Checker Component

The Permission Checker component can be used to display a link to a page only when a user is authorized to access the page. This component has a single property named HasAccess. When a user has access to a file, the property returns TRUE. If the user doesn't have access to the file or the file doesn't exist, the property returns FALSE. Following is an example of how this component is used:

```
<%
Set Permit=Server.CreateObject("MSWC.PermissionChecker")
%>
<HTML>
<HEAD><TITLE> Administration Page </TITLE></HEAD>
<BODY>
<%
IF Permit.HasAccess("DestroyAll.asp") THEN
%>
<A HREF="DestroyAll.asp">
Click here to delete all files on the hard drive.
</A>
<%
ELSE
%>
You cannot delete all the files on the hard drive.
<% END IF %>
</BODY>
</HTML>
```

> **NOTE**
>
> The Permission Checker component is not officially supported by Microsoft. However, it's included with the current (beta) version of Internet Information Server. You can also download the component from Microsoft at http://www.microsoft.com/iis.

In this example, the hypertext link to destroy all files on the hard drive is displayed only to those users who have permission to access it. Users who aren't authorized to access this file won't even see the hypertext link to the file.

When is a user authorized to access a file? This is determined by Windows NT security. When Windows NT is configured to use the NTFS file system, every file has an associated set of permissions. You can grant permission to read a file to a particular user or a group of users.

> **NOTE**
>
> Remember to allow Basic authentication when you want to be able to access password-protected pages using the Netscape browser.

To specify the permissions for a particular file, right-click the name of the file and choose Properties. Click the Security tab and then click the Permissions button. In the File Permissions dialog box that appears, you can specify the users or groups that have permission to access the file (see Figure 20.7).

FIGURE 20.7.

Setting file permissions with Windows NT.

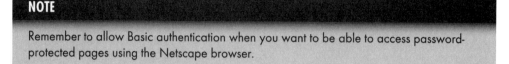

The Permission Checker component uses the permission settings to determine the users who have access to a file. However, the component can do this only when it knows the identity of the user. If the users of your Web site are never forced to log in, this component isn't useful.

There are two ways to force a user to log in at your Web site. The first way is to use the Internet Service Manager to enable either Basic or Windows NT Challenge/Response authentication. When either type of password authentication is enabled, you can force anonymous users to log in. By default, all anonymous users of your Web site use the same account. From the perspective of Windows NT, every visitor to your Web site is using the IUSR_*Machine* account. For example, if the name of your machine is Plato, all anonymous Web visitors use the IUSR_Plato account.

After enabling password authentication, you can force an anonymous Web user to log in when accessing a particular file. You do this by specifying that the IUSR_*Machine* account doesn't have permission to access the file. When an anonymous user attempts to access the file, the Password dialog box appears, forcing the user to log in and allowing the Permission Checker component to identify the user.

However, there's a second way in which you can force this to happen. You can cause the Password dialog box to appear by using a script, like this:

```
<%
LOGON=Request.ServerVariables("LOGON_USER")
If LOGON = "" OR ISNULL(LOGON) OR ISEMPTY(LOGON) Then
  Response.Status = "401 Unauthorized"
  Response.End
End if
Set Permit=Server.CreateObject("MSWC.PermissionChecker")
%>
<HTML>
<HEAD><TITLE> Administration Page </TITLE></HEAD>
<BODY>
<%
IF Permit.HasAccess("DestroyAll.asp") THEN
%>
<A HREF="DestroyAll.asp">
Click here to delete all files on the hard drive.
</A>
<%
ELSE
%>
You cannot delete all the files on the hard drive.
<% END IF %>
</BODY>
</HTML>
```

This example is the same as the previous one except for the first few lines of the script. The Status method of the Response object is used to send an Unauthorized status code to the browser. When this happens, the browser automatically displays the Password dialog box, forcing the user to log in.

> **NOTE**
>
> For more information on how to use the Status method, see Chapter 14, "Working with a Single Active Server Page."

After the user has logged in, the Permission Checker component can be used to determine the files that user has permission to access. Different users can be assigned different permissions, depending on their roles. The Permission Checker component can be used to display just the options appropriate for a particular role.

For example, your Web site may have multiple administrators with different permissions. You might want to allow certain administrators to have only the permission to delete messages from newsgroups. You might want a second group of administrators to have permission to do such things as delete all the files on the hard drive. By using the Permission Checker component, you can prevent people from being tempted to do things that they shouldn't do.

Summary

This chapter covered how to use two ActiveX components. You learned how to use the Content Linking component to link a series of Web pages together, and reviewed a sample application of this component. You also learned how to create a simple newsgroup by using the Content Linking component. Finally, you learned how to use the Permission Checker component to determine when a user has permission to access a file.

Working with Advertisements

CHAPTER 21

This chapter explores a number of additional ActiveX components. In the first section, you learn how to use the Ad Rotator component. This component can be used to display banner advertisements on your Web site. The second section discusses the Content Rotator component. This component randomly displays different HTML content on a Web page. Finally, in the third section, you learn how to use both the Counter and the Page Counter components. These two components can be used for tracking the number of visitors to your Web site.

The Ad Rotator Component

Many commercial Web sites are built on the assumption that they'll make money through banner advertisements. The assumption is that a Web site is very much like a magazine or a television show. Like a TV show, a Web site with compelling content attracts a population of viewers. Where viewers go, it's assumed, advertisers will soon follow with advertising dollars.

So far, however, this strategy hasn't worked for most Web sites. The problem is that very few corporations are paying for advertisements on the Internet. Even worse, the few corporations willing to advertise on the Internet tend to advertise only on the same select group of Web sites. Netscape and the Internet search engines such as Yahoo!, Infoseek, and Excite tend to draw all the advertising money. This leaves very few advertising dollars for the little guys.

> **NOTE**
>
> A recent Jupiter Communications survey showed that the top 1% of Web sites receive between 80% and 90% of all advertisement revenue (see `http://www.jup.com`).

Nevertheless, selling banner advertisements is the primary way of making money on the Internet. Unless you plan to generate revenue directly from your Web site's visitors—an even riskier proposition—you'll need to use banner advertisements. In this section, you learn how to incorporate banner advertisements into your Web pages.

Using the Ad Rotator Component

Using the *Ad Rotator component*, you can create a Web page that displays a different banner advertisement every time it's viewed. You can assign advertisements different weights so that they're displayed at different frequencies. You can also record the number of times an advertisement has been clicked to determine the advertisement's click-through rate.

NOTE

Advertisers typically measure the effectiveness of a Web site advertisement by its *click-through rate*. The click-through rate shows how often a viewer of an advertisement was interested enough in the advertisement to click it and learn more. The click-through rate is determined by dividing the number of times an advertisement has been displayed by the number of times it has been clicked. Typically, anything above 10% is good.

The Ad Rotator component has a single method. The GetAdvertisement() method is used to retrieve information about a banner advertisement. Here's an example of how it's used:

```
<HTML>
<HEAD><TITLE> Home Page </TITLE></HEAD>
<BODY>
<CENTER><H1>Welcome to our web site!</H1></CENTER>
<HR>
<%
Set MyAd=Server.CreateObject("MSWC.AdRotator")
%>
<CENTER><%= MyAd.GetAdvertisement("adrot.txt") %></CENTER>
</BODY>
</HTML>
```

This Active Server Page displays a banner advertisement at the bottom of the page (see Figure 21.1). Here, the script creates an instance of the Ad Rotator component by using the Server.CreateObject() method. Next, the banner advertisement is actually displayed by calling the GetAdvertisement() method.

FIGURE 21.1.

Banner advertisement example.

> **NOTE**
>
> The placement of a banner advertisement on a Web page can have a dramatic effect on its impact. A recent study showed that banner advertisements placed one-third of the way down a page generated a 77% higher click-through rate than advertisements placed on top of a page. Advertisements placed in the lower-right corner of a page are even more effective. They generated a 228% higher click-through rate (see `http://webreference.com/dev/banners/`).

Notice that the `GetAdvertisement()` method takes a parameter. This parameter specifies a file that contains the information about the advertisements to be displayed. In this example, the name of this file is `adrot.txt`. You learn how to create this file in the next section.

The Rotator Schedule File

Before you can use the Ad Rotator component, you need to create a special file called the *Rotator Schedule file*. The Rotator Schedule file contains all the information about the banner advertisements. It's a normal text file that you can create and edit with any text editor.

The Rotator Schedule file has two sections. In the first section, you provide general information about all the advertisements you want to display. In the second section, you specify the information for each advertisement. Listing 21.1 shows an example of this file.

Listing 21.1. The adrot.txt file.

```
REDIRECT /adredir.asp
WIDTH 200
HEIGHT 30
BORDER 0
*
bannerad.gif
http://www.aspsite.com
The Active Server Pages Site
80
http://www.collegescape.com/gifs/csad.gif
http://www.collegescape.com
Collegescape
20
```

The two sections of information in this file are divided by an asterisk (*). The first section contains four parameters that affect all the advertisements in the file. Here's an explanation of what these parameters do:

■ `REDIRECT`. Specifies a redirection file for the advertisements. When a banner advertisement is clicked, the user is redirected to this file.

■ `WIDTH`. The width of the banner advertisement image, specified in pixels. If you omit this parameter, the value of this parameter defaults to 440 pixels.

- **HEIGHT.** The height of the banner advertisement image, specified in pixels. If you omit this parameter, the value of this parameter defaults to 60 pixels.

- **BORDER.** The size of the border around the banner advertisement image. By default, the advertisement has a border that's one pixel thick.

In the adrot.txt file shown in Listing 21.1, the REDIRECT parameter points to the Active Server Page named adredir.asp. The WIDTH and HEIGHT parameters specify that the width of the banner advertisement image should be 200 pixels and the height should be 30 pixels. Finally, the BORDER parameter is set to 0, which results in no border being displayed.

The second section contains information specific to each advertisement. Here, the Rotator Schedule file contains information on two advertisements. The first banner advertisement is for the Active Server Pages site. The second advertisement is for a Web site named Collegescape.

For each advertisement, you provide four lines of information. The first line gives the path to the image for the advertisement. This image may be located on the local computer or anywhere else on the Internet.

The second line contains the URL for the advertiser's home page. When users click an advertisement, they can be redirected to this page (see the next section). If you place a hyphen (-) on this line, the advertisement won't function as a hyperlink.

The third line indicates alternative text to display when a browser doesn't support graphics. It's equivalent to the ALT attribute of the HTML <IMAGE> tag. You can place any non-HTML text here that you want.

Finally, the fourth line specifies how often a particular advertisement should be shown. It indicates the *relative weight* to be given to the advertisement. In the example, the first advertisement will be displayed 80% of the time, and the second advertisement will be displayed 20% of the time.

NOTE

By specifying different weights for each advertisement, you can sell advertisements at different rates. Normally, Web sites sell advertisements according to their cost per thousand impressions (CPM). In other words, buyers are charged a certain amount depending on the number of times their banner advertisements are viewed. The formula used to determine the cost of displaying an advertisement is (number of impressions/1,000) × CPM.

For example, suppose your Web site averages 100,000 visitors a month and you want to sell banner advertisement space at a CPM of $10.00. If a buyer purchases $100 dollars worth of advertisement impressions, the advertisement should be displayed 10,000 times. In other words, the banner advertisement should be shown 10% of the time. Using the Rotator Schedule file, you can specify that an advertisement should be shown at this frequency by indicating the relative weight of the advertisement.

The Redirection File

You can specify a *Redirection file* that applies to all the advertisements in a particular Rotator Schedule file. When users click a banner advertisement, they're brought to this file. This file can be an Active Server Pages file.

The main function of this file is to record the number of times a particular banner advertisement has been clicked. Once this information is recorded, the user is typically redirected to the advertiser's home page. Listing 21.2 shows an example.

Listing 21.2. The `adredir.asp` file.

```
<%
Response.AppendToLog Request.QueryString("url")
Response.Redirect Request.QueryString("url")
%>
```

This Redirection file contains a two-line Active Server Pages script. The first line records information about which advertisement has been clicked in the server log. Next, the script uses the `Redirect` method to send the user to the advertiser's home page.

Whenever the Redirection file is called, two query strings are passed. The `url` query string contains the path to the advertiser's home page. This is the same path that you entered as the path for the advertiser's home page in the Rotator Schedule file.

The second query string is named `image`. The `image` query string contains the path of the banner image. The value of this query string indicates the path you entered for the banner image in the Rotator Schedule file.

You actually can place anything you want in the Redirection file. For example, you could make the Redirection file a normal HTML file that displays your Web site's advertisement rates. Here's an example (see Figure 21.2):

```
<HTML>
<HEAD><TITLE> Ad Rates </TITLE></HEAD>
<BODY>
<H1> Advertisement Rates </H1>
To advertise at this Web site, please contact
<A HREF="mailto:admaster@mysite.com"> Ad Info </A>.
<P>
By advertising at this Web site, you will reach
thousands of developers a day.
We offer a number of advertising packages:
<OL>
<LI>The Gold Package: $30 CPM
<LI>The Silver Package: $20 CPM
<LI>The Bronze Package: $10 CPM
</OL>
</BODY>
</HTML>
```

FIGURE 21.2.

Advertisement information.

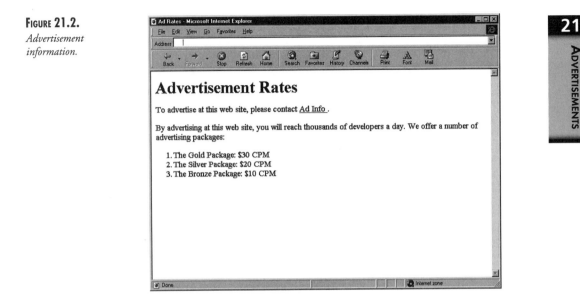

Ad Rotator Properties

The Ad Rotator component has three properties. Before calling the GetAdvertisment() method, you can set these properties to control how an advertisement is displayed. The following list explains each property:

- Border. This property overrides the BORDER parameter specified in the Rotator Schedule file. You can use this property to indicate the size of a banner advertisement's border (in pixels) for a particular page.

- Clickable. This property specifies whether the banner advertisement should function as a hyperlink. It can have the value True or False.

- TargetFrame. This property indicates the name of the frame into which the banner link should be loaded.

The TargetFrame property is particularly useful. If you set the TargetFrame property to the name of a new frame, when a user clicks a banner advertisement the advertiser's home page loads into the frame (see Figure 21.3). By doing this, you prevent the user from permanently leaving your Web site. Here's an example of how this property is used (continued on the following page):

```
<HTML>
<HEAD><TITLE> Home Page </TITLE></HEAD>
<BODY>
<CENTER><H1>Welcome to our web site!</H1></CENTER>
<HR>
<%
Set MyAd=Server.CreateObject("MSWC.AdRotator")
```

```
MyAd.TargetFrame("AdFrame")
%>
<CENTER><%= MyAd.GetAdvertisement("adrot.txt") %></CENTER>
</BODY>
</HTML>
```

FIGURE 21.3.

Using the TargetFrame
property.

The Content Rotator Component

The *Content Rotator component* is very similar to the Ad Rotator component. However, unlike the Ad Rotator component, this component is used to randomly display different HTML content on a Web page. Here are some ideas for how this component can be used:

- **Tip of the day.** You can use this component to randomly display different tips for using your Web site. For example, Visit our news group to exchange messages with other users.

- **News flash.** This component can be used to rotate through a list of news events. For example, Active Server Pages Unleashed now available in stores!

- **Random link.** You can use this component to display a random link drawn from a list of your favorite Web sites.

- **Banner advertisement.** Like the Ad Rotator component, this component can be used to display banner advertisements. However, using this component, you have greater flexibility over how the advertisement is displayed.

NOTE

This component isn't officially supported by Microsoft. However, it's included in the current (beta) release of Internet Information Server. You can also download the component from Microsoft at http://www.microsoft.com/iis.

To use the Content Rotator component to display an HTML content string, you use the component's ChooseContent() method. The ChooseContent() method retrieves an HTML string from a special file called the *Content Schedule file* and displays it in an Active Server Page, as shown in the following example:

```
<HTML>
<HEAD><TITLE> Home Page </TITLE></HEAD>
<BODY>
<%
Set MyContent=Server.CreateObject("MSWC.ContentRotator")
%>
<%=MyContent.ChooseContent("content.txt") %>
</BODY>
</HTML>
```

In this example, an instance of the component is first created by calling the CreateObject() method. Next, an HTML content string is retrieved from the Content Schedule file named content.txt and displayed on the Web page. Whenever the page is requested, a different HTML string may be displayed.

The Content Schedule File

The Content Schedule file is used to contain all the HTML content strings. This file is a normal text file, which can be created and edited with any text editor. It can also be given any name. Listing 21.3 shows an example.

Listing 21.3. The content.txt file.

```
%%#2 // Here is the first entry
<FONT COLOR="RED"> Visit Our News Group! </FONT>
%%#3 // Here is the second entry
<B> Don't Forget To Bookmark This Web Site. </B>
%%#5 // Here is the third entry
Download the following free software from our Download Page:
<UL>
<LI> ActiveX Components
<LI> Link Checker
<LI> HTML Validator
</UL>
```

This Content Schedule file contains three entries. The beginning of each entry is marked by a double percent sign (%%). Whenever the ChooseContent() method is called, one of these entries is retrieved.

In this example, each entry is given a certain *weight*. This determines the relative frequency at which a particular entry will be chosen by the ChooseContent() method. You indicate a weight by providing a number after the number sign (#). For example, the first entry is given a weight of 2.

The weight of an entry can be any number between 0 and 65,535. If an entry has a weight of 0, it's never shown (this is useful for temporarily disabling an entry). The higher the weight, the more likely an entry will be retrieved by the ChooseContent() method. If you don't specify a weight for an entry, the entry will have a weight of 1.

In this example, the first entry will be displayed 2 out of every 10 times that the ChooseContent() method is called. The second entry will be displayed 3 out of 10 times, and the third entry will be displayed 5 out of 10 times. To determine how often an entry will be displayed, divide the weight of that entry by the sum of the weights of all of the entries.

Each entry also includes a comment. For example, appropriately enough, the first entry includes the comment "Here is the first entry". To include a comment, simply use two slash characters (//) before the comment. The comment won't be displayed on the page when the HTML content string is retrieved.

Finally, each entry contains an HTML content string. This string can span multiple lines. It can include any HTML tags. For example, the first entry displays the string Visit Our News Group! in red. The last entry contains a list of software that can be downloaded from the Web site.

Both comments and weights are optional. A minimal Content Schedule file would contain nothing but HTML content strings that are separated with the %% characters. In that case, every content string would be displayed with the same frequency.

Dumping the Contents of the Content Schedule File

The Content Rotator component includes one additional method. By using the GetAllContent() method, you can retrieve all the HTML content strings from the Content Schedule file. Here's an example of how this method is used:

```
<HTML>
<HEAD><TITLE> Content Schedule File Contents </TITLE></HEAD>
<BODY>
<%
Set MyContent=Server.CreateObject("MSWC.ContentRotator")
%>
<%=MyContent.GetAllContent("content.txt") %>
</BODY>
</HTML>
```

When this Active Server Page is displayed, all the entries in the Content Schedule file named content.txt are included in the page. Entries are automatically separated by horizontal rules with the HTML <HR> tag.

Why would you want to do this? In a number of situations, this method may prove useful. For example, if you're using the Content Rotator component to randomly display links to Web sites, you may want to give the user an option to view all the links.

The GetAllContent() method is also useful for debugging a Content Schedule file. If you want to test the appearance of all the entries in this file, you can use this method to view its contents before the entries are displayed to the world.

Counting Visitors

Two components included with Active Server Pages can be used to create *page counters*. Using page counters, you can track the number of times that a particular page has been requested. You can display this information on the page itself, or you can keep track of this information for your own purposes.

The Counters Component

The *Counters component* can be used to count the number of times a page has been requested, but it can also be used to count anything else as well. For example, you can use it to count the number of visitors to your Web site, the number of times an advertisement has been clicked, or even the number of times someone has requested a Web page with the Netscape 2.0 browser.

You can create only one instance of this component. However, once you create an instance of the component, you can create as many individual counters as you need. The single Counters component can contain many individual counters with different names.

Because you can create only one Counters component, it's a good idea to create the Component within the Global.asa file. This will guarantee that only one instance of the Counters component is created when your Web server starts.

> **NOTE**
>
> For more information on using the Global.asa file, see Chapter 17, "Working with Active Server Pages Applications."

Here's an example of how you can create the component within the Global.asa file:

```
<OBJECT RUNAT="Server" SCOPE="Application" ID="MyCount"
PROGID="MSWC.Counters"></OBJECT>
```

The Microsoft extended HTML `<OBJECT>` tag is used here to create an instance of the Counters component named `MyCount` with application-wide scope. Remember to use the `<OBJECT>` tag outside any scripts within the `Global.asa` file. Once an instance of the Counters component has been created in this way, its methods can be accessed from any page within your specific application.

The Counters component has four methods. The following list details how each method is used:

- `Get(counter name)`. This method returns the current value of a counter. If the counter doesn't exist, it is created and set to 0.

- `Increment(counter name)`. This method adds 1 to the current value of a counter. If the counter doesn't exist, it is created and its value set to 1.

- `Remove(counter name)`. This method destroys a counter.

- `Set(counter name, integer)`. This method accepts two arguments. The first argument is the name of a counter, and the second argument is an integer value. The method adds the integer to the counter. If the counter doesn't exist, the counter is created with the specified value.

Once an instance of the Counters component has been created in the `Global.asa` file, you can increment and decrement individual counters within any Active Server Page. A counter created in one page can be incremented, decremented, or removed in another page. Following is an example of how you can use the Counters component to keep track of the number of times a particular page has been requested:

```
<HTML>
<HEAD><TITLE>Some Page</TITLE></HEAD>
<BODY>
This page has been requested
<%=MyCount.Increment("PageCnt") %>
times.
</BODY>
</HTML>
```

The first time this page is requested, a counter named `PageCnt` is created and set to the value 1. Subsequent requests increment the value of this counter by 1. The `PageCnt` counter reflects the number of times the page has been requested (see Figure 21.4).

What happens if your server is unexpectedly shut down? The counters you create with the Counters component are persistent. They're saved in a file named `counters.txt`. If the server shuts down, the counters still exist when it starts again.

Admittedly, the counter in Figure 21.4 is a little boring. Most counters you see on Web sites use images for their counters. You can do this as well:

```
<%
SUB ShowImageCnt(TheNum)
CntStr=CSTR(TheNum)
FOR i=1 TO LEN(CntStr)
CntPart=MID(CntStr,i,1)
%>
<IMG SRC="<%=CntPart%>.gif" ALT="<%=CntPart%>">
<%
NEXT
END SUB
%>
<HTML>
<HEAD><TITLE>Some Page</TITLE></HEAD>
<BODY>
This page has been requested
<%
ShowImageCnt MyCount.Increment("PageCnt")
%>
times.
</BODY>
</HTML>
```

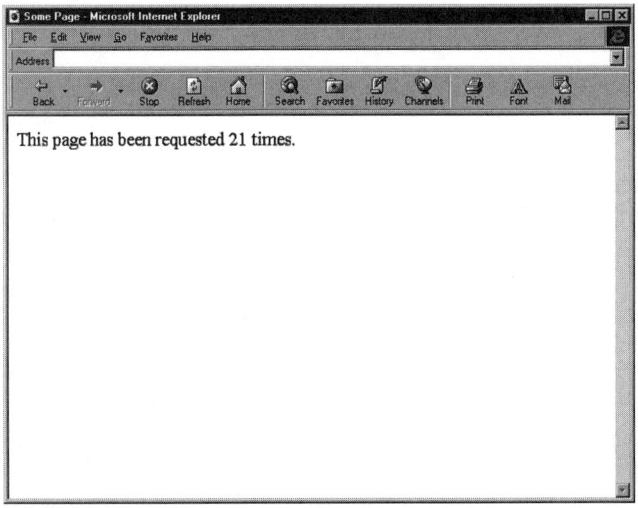

FIGURE 21.4.

A page with a counter.

This new Active Server Page also displays a page counter. However, the page count is displayed by using images rather than text (see Figure 21.5). The procedure named ShowImageCnt first converts the page count to a string. Next, a FOR...NEXT loop is used to walk through each numeral in the string and display a corresponding image.

FIGURE 21.5.

A page counter with images.

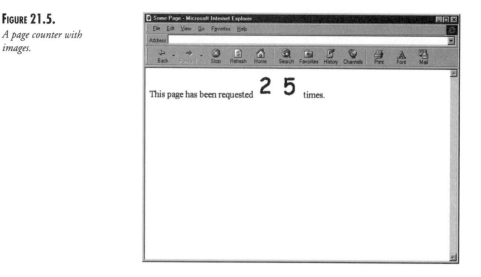

To use this example, you'll need 10 images named 0.gif, 1.gif, 2.gif, and so on. You can create these images yourself. However, a number of Internet sites have libraries of counter images that you can download freely (check the graphics section at your favorite Internet directory).

The Page Counter Component

There's a second component that you can use to display a page counter on a Web page. By using the *Page Counter component*, you can track the number of times a particular Web page has been opened.

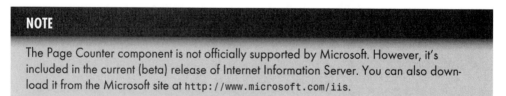

NOTE

The Page Counter component is not officially supported by Microsoft. However, it's included in the current (beta) release of Internet Information Server. You can also download it from the Microsoft site at http://www.microsoft.com/iis.

The Page Counter component is much less flexible than the Counters component. It can't be used to track anything other than a page's hit count. This component has the following two methods:

- Hits(*path*). This method returns the number of times a page with the specified path has been opened. If no path is provided, the method returns this value for the current page.
- Reset(*path*). This method resets the count to 0 for the page with the specified path. If no path is provided, the value for the current page is reset.

Unlike when using the Counters component, you don't need to create an instance of the Page Counter component within the Global.asa file. You can create an instance of the component in the same page in which you use it, like this:

```
<HTML>
<HEAD><TITLE> Page Counter Example </TITLE></HEAD>
<BODY>
<%
Set MyHits=Server.CreateObject("MSWC.PageCounter")
%>
This page has been viewed
<%=MyHits.Hits%>
times.
</BODY>
</HTML>
```

This Active Server Page simply displays the number of times the current page has been opened. The Hits method is called without any parameters, which results in the hit count for the current page being returned.

Summary

This chapter showed you how to incorporate advertisements into your Web pages. You learned how to use the Ad Rotator component to display a series of banner advertisements. You also learned how to use the Content Rotator component to randomly display different HTML content strings. Finally, you learned how to use two components that can be used to display a page counter on a Web page.

V
PART

The Database Component

ActiveX Data Objects

IN THIS CHAPTER

This chapter introduces the ActiveX Data Objects (ADO). The first section provides an overview of these objects. The second section gives you a step-by-step guide to using the ADO to retrieve and store data in a database. Finally, in the third section, you are formally introduced to a particularly important ADO object: the Connection object.

Overview of the ActiveX Data Objects

Using the *ActiveX Data Objects (ADO)*, you can store and retrieve data from a variety of data providers. For example, you can use the ADO to access information from Microsoft Access and the Microsoft SQL and Oracle database servers. You can even use the ADO to retrieve information from a Microsoft Excel spreadsheet.

In this book, you learn how to use the ADO with Microsoft SQL Server. All the examples assume that this database is being used. However, you should realize that much of what you learn in the following chapters is transferable to other databases as well.

In Part III, "Working with Data: SQL," you learned how to use Structured Query Language (SQL). Starting with this chapter, you put this knowledge to good use. The emphasis is on using SQL with the ADO to store and retrieve data from a database. This combination of the ADO and SQL is powerful.

> **NOTE**
>
> For a complete reference for all of the methods, properties, and collections of the ActiveX Data Objects, see Appendix A, "Quick ASP Object and Component Reference," at the back of this book.

The ActiveX Data Objects consists of seven independent objects. The following list names these objects and provides a brief explanation of their functions:

- Connection object. Represents a unique session with a data source. For example, you can use the Connection object to open a connection to Microsoft SQL Server.
- Recordset object. Represents records from a data provider. For example, you can use the Recordset object to alter the records contained in a SQL Server table.
- Field object. Represents an individual field in a Recordset.
- Command object. Represents a command. For example, you can use the Command object to execute a SQL stored procedure or a parameterized query.
- Parameter object. Represents an individual parameter in a SQL stored procedure or parameterized query.
- Property object. Represents data-provider-specific properties.
- Error object. Represents ADO errors.

When using the ADO, you'll be most directly interacting with the Connection, Recordset, and Command objects. This chapter provides a detailed overview of the Connection object. In the next two chapters, you learn how to use both the Recordset and Command objects. First, however, you must learn how to configure your server to use the ADO.

Using the ActiveX Data Objects

This section provides a step-by-step guide to using the ADO in your Active Server Pages. First you learn how to configure your server to use the ADO. Then the next section presents a basic example of how to use the ADO to store and retrieve data from a database. Finally, in case you encounter problems, a troubleshooting section is provided.

Configuring Your Server to Use the ActiveX Data Objects

This book assumes that you're using the ADO with Microsoft SQL Server. Before you continue, Microsoft SQL Server must be installed on either the same machine as your Web server or a machine that's located on the same network as your Web server. See Chapter 3, "Installing and Using SQL Server," for details on installing and configuring Microsoft SQL Server.

Before you can use the ADO, you must create a *data source*. A data source contains information about how to connect to a data provider. In this case, you'll use the data source to connect to Microsoft SQL Server. There are three types of data sources: You can create a *user data source*, a *system data source*, or a *file data source*. When creating a data source to use with a Web server, you should create a file data source. The advantage of creating a file data source is that the connection information is stored in an actual file. More than one user can access this file. Also, if you need to transfer your Web application from one Web server to another, you can simply transfer this file.

> **NOTE**
>
> Before creating a new data source, make sure that SQL Server is running. Use the SQL Service Manager from the Microsoft SQL Server program group to determine whether the SQL Service is running.

To create a new file data source, follow these steps:

1. Open the Windows NT Server Control Panel (choose Start | Settings | Control Panel).
2. Click the icon labeled ODBC.
3. Click the File DSN tab.
4. Click the Add button. The Create New Data Source dialog box appears.

5. In the dialog box, select the SQL Server driver and click the Next button. The Create a New Data Source dialog box opens.

6. Enter a name for your new file data source. For example, enter **MyData.dsn**. Click Next and then click Finish. The Create a New Data Source to SQL Server Wizard will be launched (see Figure 22.1).

FIGURE 22.1.

The Create a New Data Source to SQL Server Wizard.

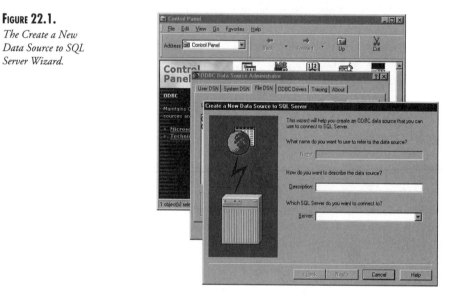

7. In the Description text box, enter a description such as **My Data Source**. In the Server text box, enter the name of the server where Microsoft SQL Server is installed. (You can use Local if Microsoft SQL Server is installed on the same machine as your Web server.) Click Next.

8. A series of dialog boxes asks you to configure different properties of the data source. You should specify a default database. Select the name of the database where your tables are located as your default database. Leave the other options with their default values, and click Next to move through each dialog box.

9. Finally, you'll be presented with the opportunity to test your new data source. If the test is successful, click OK to add the new data source.

You have created a new file data source named MyData.dsn, which you can use to connect to Microsoft SQL Server. The next section explains how to do this.

Using the ActiveX Data Objects to Store and Retrieve Data from a Database

This section provides an example of how to use the ADO to store and retrieve data from Microsoft SQL Server. This example has a dual purpose: It illustrates the basic methods of accessing Microsoft SQL Server from an Active Server Page, and you can use the example to test your server's configuration.

The Active Server Page in Listing 22.1 inserts the text Hello World! into a database table. Next, the text Hello World! is retrieved from the table and outputted to the browser.

Listing 22.1. Hello World!

```
<HTML>
<HEAD><TITLE> ADO Example </TITLE></HEAD>
<BODY>
<%
Set MyConn=Server.CreateObject("ADODB.Connection")
MyConn.Open "FILEDSN=d:\Program Files\Common Files\ODBC\Data Sources\MyData.dsn"
MyConn.Execute "INSERT MyTable (MyColumn) VALUES ('Hello World!')"
Set RS=MyConn.Execute("SELECT * FROM MyTable")
Response.Write(RS("MyColumn"))
MyConn.Close
%>
</BODY>
</HTML>
```

Before you can use this example, you need to create a table named MyTable. You can do this by using ISQL/w. Launch the program, select your default database, and execute the following SQL statement:

```
Create Table MyTable (MyColumn VARCHAR(255))
```

NOTE

For more information about creating tables, see Chapter 10, "Basic SQL."

The first line in this Active Server Page creates an instance of the Connection object. Next, the Open method of the Connection object is called to open a connection to the database. The file data source, which you created in the previous section, is used with the Open method to create the connection. (Replace the path of the file data source in this script with the path of this file on your machine.)

Once a connection is opened, you can execute SQL statements with the connection. The Execute method in this script is used to execute two SQL statements. First, a SQL INSERT statement is used to enter the string Hello World! into the database table. Next, the SQL SELECT statement is used to retrieve this string from the database table.

If your system is configured correctly, the string Hello World! should be displayed in your browser window. This string was inserted into the database table and retrieved once again. If all does not go well, see the next section.

Troubleshooting the ActiveX Data Objects

If you're having difficulties accessing Microsoft SQL Server with the ADO, this section should help. The Active Server Page described in the preceding section could fail for a variety of reasons. Following is a list of symptoms and possible causes for a number of common problems that you may encounter:

- **Symptom:** You get the error `Unable to create file buffer`.

  Cause: The file data source is inaccurate. You get this error if the file data source has an invalid path or invalid name, or doesn't exist. Make sure that the path of the file data source on your machine is the same as the path used for the `Open` method in the Active Server Page.

- **Symptom:** You get the error `Invalid object name 'MyTable'`.

  Cause: The table `MyTable` doesn't exist in your database. Create this table by using ISQL/w as described in the preceding section.

  Cause: The table `MyTable` isn't located in your default database. You need to specify a default database. Choose Start | Settings | Control Panel. Click the ODBC icon and then click the File DSN tab. Select the name of your file data source, click Configure, and then click Options. You can specify the name of your default database in the resulting dialog box.

- **Symptom:** You get the error `The server appears to be not available`.

  Cause: SQL Server isn't running. Launch the SQL Service Manager from the Microsoft SQL Server program group. Select MSSQLSERVER and click the green light.

- **Symptom:** You get the error `Login failed`.

  Cause: You are not using Windows NT Integrated Security, and the SQL Server login ID associated with the data source requires a password. If you want to use SQL Server Standard Security with a login ID that requires a password, you need to include both the login ID and password in the connection string. When opening a connection, use the connection string `"FILEDSN=MyDSN;UID=Login ID;PWD=Password"` where `MyDSN` refers to a file data source, `Login ID` refers to a valid SQL Server login ID, and `Password` refers to the login ID's password. For more information, see the section "Understanding SQL Server Security Options" in Chapter 3, "Installing and Using SQL Server."

- **Symptom:** You get the error `INSERT permission denied on object MyTable` or the error `SELECT permission denied on object MyTable`.

  Cause: The login ID you specified when creating the file data source doesn't have adequate permissions to access the table named `MyTable`. You need to change the login ID used with the file data source or you need to grant additional permissions to the user or group with this login within SQL Server.

To grant additional permissions on a table, launch the SQL Enterprise Manager from the Microsoft SQL Server program group. Navigate to the table named `MyTable` and right-click it.

Choose Permissions. You can now grant permissions on the table for different users or groups. Remember to click the Set button to finalize any changes in permissions.

Using the Connection Object

All communication with a database takes place through an open connection. Before you can insert or retrieve any information in a database, a connection with the database must be opened. This process of opening and closing a connection is often compared with the process of placing a telephone call. Before you can communicate with SQL Server, you must first call it.

This section describes how to use the ADO Connection object. First you learn how to open and close a connection to a database. Next, you learn how to execute SQL statements with an open connection. Finally, you learn how to use the Connection object to create transactions.

Opening and Closing a Database Connection

To open a connection with a database, you can create an instance of the Connection object. Once an instance of this object is created, you can call the Open method of the Connection object to actually open the connection. Here's an example:

```
<%
Set MyConn=Server.CreateObject("ADODB.Connection")
MyConn.Open "FILEDSN=d:\Program Files\Common Files\ODBC\Data Sources\MyData.dsn"
MyConn.Execute "INSERT MyTable (MyColumn) VALUES ('Hello World!')"
MyConn.Close
%>
```

In this example, an instance of the Connection object named MyConn is created. The Open method is called with the name of a file data source. Next, the Execute method of the Connection object is called to execute a SQL statement. Finally, the connection is closed.

Any sane person quickly grows tired of entering the name of the file data source every time a new connection needs to be opened. You should assign this string to a session variable or make it a constant in an Include file. This way, you only need to type the name of a variable rather than the whole name of the file data source. To create a session variable that contains the name of the file data source, you should create this variable within the Global.asa file. For example, you can add the following line to the Session_OnStart script of the Global.asa file:

```
Session("connectionstring")="FILEDSN=d:\Program Files\Common
➥Files\ODBC\Data Sources\MyData.dsn"
```

> **NOTE**
>
> For more information on using session variables, see Chapter 16, "Working with Active Server Pages Sessions."

After this session variable has been created, you can open a connection by using the following script:

```
<%
Set MyConn=Server.CreateObject("ADODB.Connection")
MyConn.Open Session("connectionstring")
%>
```

Another advantage of assigning the file data source name to a session variable is that you can easily change the data source in the future. If you need to use a different data source, you can simply change the value of a single session variable in the Global.asa file.

When you're finished using a connection, you should close it. This is like hanging up a phone so that you're no longer tying up the line. The Close method of the Connection object closes a connection. After a connection is closed, you can no longer use the connection to communicate with the database. Therefore, objects that depend on the connection can no longer communicate with the database.

Executing SQL Statements with an Open Connection

To execute a SQL statement with an open connection, you use the Execute method. This method has two forms: One form is used when retrieving results from a database, and the other form is used when no results are returned.

The following example shows how you can use the Execute method to execute a SQL statement that doesn't retrieve any results:

```
<%
Set MyConn=Server.CreateObject("ADODB.Connection")
MyConn.Open "FILEDSN=d:\Program Files\Common
➥Files\ODBC\Data Sources\MyData.dsn"
MyConn.Execute "INSERT MyTable (MyColumn) VALUES ('Hello World!')"
MyConn.Close
%>
```

In this example, the Execute method is used to execute a SQL INSERT statement. Because no results are returned, the Execute method doesn't use parentheses.

You can also use the Execute method to return results from a SQL query, as in this example:

```
<%
Set MyConn=Server.CreateObject("ADODB.Connection")
MyConn.Open "FILEDSN=d:\Program Files\Common
➥Files\ODBC\Data Sources\MyData.dsn"
Set RS=MyConn.Execute("SELECT * FROM MyTable")
MyConn.Close
%>
```

In this example, the Execute() method is used to return the results from a SQL SELECT query. Unlike the preceding example, parentheses are used with this Execute method. When returning results, you must remember to include the parentheses, or you'll get the error Expected end of statement.

The results of the SQL query are retrieved into an instance of a Recordset object named RS. This Recordset is automatically created by the Execute() method. You learn how to work with Recordsets in the next chapter.

The Execute method includes two optional parameters. You can provide a RecordsAffected parameter that indicates the number of records that the SQL statement affected. You can also include an Options parameter that provides information about the type of SQL statement being executed. This example uses both of these optional parameters:

```
<!-- #INCLUDE VIRTUAL="ADOVBS.inc" -->
<%
Set MyConn=Server.CreateObject("ADODB.Connection")
MyConn.Open "FILEDSN=d:\Program Files\Common
➡Files\ODBC\Data Sources\MyData.dsn"
MyConn.Execute "UPDATE MyTable Set
➡MyColumn='Goodbye!'", HowMany, adCMDText
Response.Write(HowMany)
MyConn.Close
%>
```

In this script, a SQL UPDATE statement is executed to change the values of all the rows in the MyTable table. The Execute method also has two additional parameters. The first parameter is the RecordsAffected parameter. In this example, the variable named HowMany is passed as the RecordsAffected parameter. After the SQL statement executes, this variable will contain the number of records that the SQL statement affected. For example, if 32 rows in the table are updated, the value of HowMany will be 32.

The second parameter included with this Execute method is the Options parameter. In this example, the Options parameter is specified as the constant adCMDText. This constant is used to warn the ADO that it should interpret the contents of the command string to be a textual command rather than the name of a table or a stored procedure. By warning the ADO about the contents of the string being executed, the constant makes ADO execute the command more efficiently. (For more on commands, see Chapter 24, "Working with Commands.")

You can use the following constants for the Options parameter:

- adCMDTable. The string being executed contains the name of a table.
- adCMDText. The string being executed contains a textual command.
- adCMDStoredProc. The string being executed contains the name of a stored procedure.
- adCMDUnknown. The contents of the string are unspecified. (This is the default value.)

Before you can use any of these constants in an Active Server Page, you must include a special file called the ADOVBS.inc file. The ADOVBS.inc file contains all the VBScript constants that are used with the ADO. The first line in the preceding example contains an INCLUDE directive to include the ADOVBS.inc file.

When you installed Active Server Pages, this file should have been installed automatically as well. Currently, the file is installed into the c:\Program Files\Common Files\System\ADO directory. However, you may have to use the Find command from the Windows NT Start menu to find the exact location of this file. After you find it, copy the file into your Active Server Pages directory.

> **NOTE**
>
> If you're using JScript rather than VBScript, the name of the ADO constants file will be ADOJAVAS.inc.

You can call the Execute method as many times as you need after a connection is open. For example, the following script enters 32 different strings into the table named MyTable:

```
<!-- #INCLUDE VIRTUAL="ADOVBS.inc" -->
<%
Set MyConn=Server.CreateObject("ADODB.Connection")
MyConn.Open "FILEDSN=d:\Program Files\Common
➥Files\ODBC\Data Sources\MyData.dsn"
FOR i=1 TO 32
MySQL="INSERT MyTable (MyColumn) VALUES ('This is entry "&i&"')"
MyConn.Execute MySQL, HowMany, adCMDText
NEXT
MyConn.Close
%>
```

This script uses a FOR...NEXT loop to insert 32 records into the MyTable table. The variable MySQL contains the SQL command string used with the Execute method. Notice how single quotes and double quotes are used when specifying the SQL string. The single quotes are used to represent the quotation marks that appear within the SQL statement. The double quotes specify the beginning and end of the string within VBScript.

You can use the Execute method to execute almost any SQL command. For example, the following script creates a table, populates it, truncates it, and then drops it:

```
<!-- #INCLUDE VIRTUAL="ADOVBS.inc" -->
<%
Set MyConn=Server.CreateObject("ADODB.Connection")
MyConn.Open "FILEDSN=d:\Program Files\Common
➥Files\ODBC\Data Sources\MyData.dsn"
' Create a new table
MySQL="CREATE TABLE NewTable (MyColumn VARCHAR(255))"
MyConn.Execute MySQL
' Populate the table
MySQL="INSERT NewTable (MyColumn) VALUES ('hello')"
MyConn.Execute MySQL
' Truncate the table
MySQL="TRUNCATE TABLE NewTable"
MyConn.Execute MySQL
' Drop the table
MySQL="DROP TABLE NewTable"
MyConn.Execute MySQL
MyConn.Close
%>
```

Creating Transactions

When a group of statements form a transaction, if one statement fails, they all fail. Transactions are useful when you need to update information in more than one table and you don't want one update to fail and the other to succeed.

For example, suppose whenever someone buys something from your Web site, the information about the purchase is stored in two tables. One table contains a list of credit cards to be debited. The second table contains a list of items to be shipped.

Now, suppose someone attempts to buy something from your Web site. The person's credit card number is entered into the first table. However, at that very moment, disaster strikes. A bolt of lightning hits your server and the second table doesn't get updated. In this situation, it would be much better if neither table is updated. You don't want to charge the person for buying an item that will never be shipped. Using transactions, you can prevent the credit card number table from being updated if the shipping table is never updated:

```
<%
Set MyConn=Server.CreateObject("ADODB.Connection")
MyConn.Open "FILEDSN=d:\Program Files\Common
➥Files\ODBC\Data Sources\MyData.dsn"
MyConn.BeginTrans
MyConn.Execute "INSERT CreditCard (CCNum) VALUES ('5555-55-555-55-5555')"
MyConn.Execute "INSERT Shipping (Address) VALUES ('Paris, France')"
MyConn.CommitTrans
MyConn.Close
%>
```

In this example, the `BeginTrans` and `CommitTrans` methods are used to mark the beginning and end of a transaction. After the `BeginTrans` method call, if anything goes wrong before `CommitTrans` is called, the tables are not updated. If lightning strikes after the first table is updated, this change is automatically rolled back.

You can also roll back a transaction explicitly. To do this, you use the `RollBackTrans` method. Consider the following script:

```
<%
Set MyConn=Server.CreateObject("ADODB.Connection")
MyConn.Open "FILEDSN=d:\Program Files\Common
➥Files\ODBC\Data Sources\MyData.dsn"
MyConn.BeginTrans
MyConn.Execute "INSERT CreditCard (CCNum) VALUES ('5555-55-555-55-5555')"
MyConn.Execute "INSERT Shipping (Address) VALUES ('Paris, France')"
IF WEEKDAYNAME(WEEKDAY(DATE))="Sunday" THEN
  MyConn.RollBackTrans
ELSE
  MyConn.CommitTrans
END IF
MyConn.Close
%>
```

In this example, the `RollBackTrans` method is used to explicitly roll back the transaction on Sunday. On Sunday, neither the `CreditCard` table nor the `Shipping` table will be updated.

Summary

This chapter introduced the ActiveX Data Objects. The first section gave you an overview of the ADO. In the second section, you learned how to configure your server to use the ADO. Finally, you were introduced to one of the most important of the ADO objects: the `Connection` object.

Working with Recordsets

23

CHAPTER

In Chapter 22, "ActiveX Data Objects," you learned how to use the ActiveX Data Objects (ADO) Connection object to open a database connection. You also learned how to use an open connection to execute SQL commands and return Recordsets. However, the methods for manipulating the Recordset object were not discussed.

This chapter explains how to use the Recordset object. In the first section, you learn the basic methods for displaying data with this object. In the second section, you learn how to open a Recordset with different cursor and locking types. Finally, the third section describes a number of advanced methods for working with the records in a Recordset.

Using a Recordset to Display Records

A *Recordset* can be used to represent the records in a database table. Like a table, a Recordset contains one or more *records* (rows). Each record contains one or more *fields* (columns). At any given moment, only one record is the *current record*.

To create a new instance of a Recordset object, you can use the Execute() method of the Connection object. When you use the Execute() method to return results from a database query, a new Recordset is created automatically. Here's an example:

```
<%
Set MyConn=Server.CreateObject("ADODB.Connection")
MyConn.Open "FILEDSN=d:\Program Files\Common Files\ODBC\Data Sources\MyData.dsn"
Set RS=MyConn.Execute("SELECT * FROM MyTable")
RS.Close
MyConn.Close
%>
```

In this example, a SQL SELECT statement is used to retrieve all the records from a table named MyTable. The Execute() method returns a Recordset. In this script, the Recordset is assigned to the variable named RS. The Recordset is then closed. Finally, the connection is closed.

Each record in the RS Recordset corresponds to a record in the MyTable table. To display all the records in the Recordset, you can simply loop through the records, as in the following example:

```
<%
Set MyConn=Server.CreateObject("ADODB.Connection")
MyConn.Open "FILEDSN=d:\Program Files\Common Files\ODBC\Data Sources\MyData.dsn"
Set RS=MyConn.Execute("SELECT * FROM MyTable")
WHILE NOT RS.EOF
  Response.Write("<BR>"&RS("MyColumn"))
  RS.MoveNext
WEND
RS.Close
MyConn.Close
%>
```

In this example, the WHILE...WEND loop is used to move through each record contained in the RS Recordset. The MyColumn field of each record is outputted to the browser. This script displays all the records contained in the MyTable table.

When a Recordset is first populated with records, the current record is always the first record. In the preceding example, the MoveNext method of the Recordset object is used to move to the next record. When all the records have been displayed, the EOF property of the Recordset object has the value True and the WHILE...WEND loop is exited.

A Recordset object has a Fields collection that contains one or more Field objects. A Field object represents a particular column in a table. For example, in the preceding script, the column MyColumn is displayed by using the expression RS("MyColumn"). Actually, you can display the value of a column in a number of ways. Each of the following expressions displays the value of the column named MyColumn:

```
RS("MyColumn")

RS(0)

RS.Fields("MyColumn")

RS.Fields(0)

RS.Fields.Item("MyColumn")

RS.Fields.Item(0)
```

Notice that you can refer to a particular field either by its name or by its ordinal number. For example, you can refer to the MyColumn field either by using RS("MyColumn") or by using RS(0). Either method works because the field named MyColumn corresponds to the first column in the table (the first field is the zero field).

Referring to a field by its ordinal number is useful when you don't know the names of the fields in a Recordset. For example, the following Active Server Page script (continued on the next page) displays all the columns and all the rows in a table (see Figure 23.1):

```
<HTML>
<HEAD><TITLE> Show All Rows And Columns </TITLE></HEAD>
<BODY>
<%
Set MyConn=Server.CreateObject("ADODB.Connection")
MyConn.Open "FILEDSN=d:\Program Files\Common Files\ODBC\Data Sources\MyData.dsn"
Set RS=MyConn.Execute("SELECT * FROM MyTable")
%>
<TABLE BORDER=1>
<TR>
<% FOR i = 0 to RS.Fields.Count - 1 %>
    <TH><% = RS(i).Name %></TH>
<% Next %>
</TR>
<% While Not RS.EOF %>
```

```
<TR>
<% FOR i = 0 TO RS.Fields.Count - 1 %>
  <TD><% = RS(i) %></TD>
<% Next %>
</TR>
<%
RS.MoveNext
WEND
RS.Close
MyConn.Close
%>
</TABLE>
</BODY>
</HTML>
```

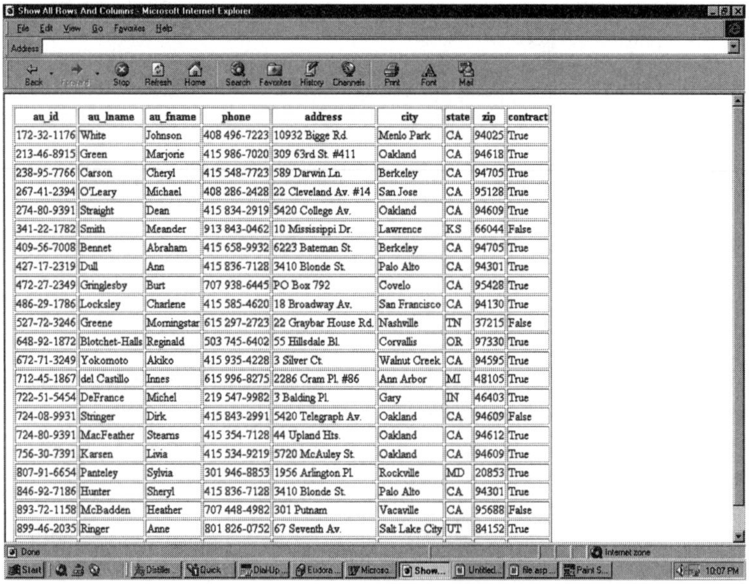

au_id	au_lname	au_fname	phone	address	city	state	zip	contract
172-32-1176	White	Johnson	408 496-7223	10932 Bigge Rd.	Menlo Park	CA	94025	True
213-46-8915	Green	Marjorie	415 986-7020	309 63rd St. #411	Oakland	CA	94618	True
238-95-7766	Carson	Cheryl	415 548-7723	589 Darwin Ln.	Berkeley	CA	94705	True
267-41-2394	O'Leary	Michael	408 286-2428	22 Cleveland Av. #14	San Jose	CA	95128	True
274-80-9391	Straight	Dean	415 834-2919	5420 College Av.	Oakland	CA	94609	True
341-22-1782	Smith	Meander	913 843-0462	10 Mississippi Dr.	Lawrence	KS	66044	False
409-56-7008	Bennet	Abraham	415 658-9932	6223 Bateman St.	Berkeley	CA	94705	True
427-17-2319	Dull	Ann	415 836-7128	3410 Blonde St.	Palo Alto	CA	94301	True
472-27-2349	Gringlesby	Burt	707 938-6445	PO Box 792	Covelo	CA	95428	True
486-29-1786	Locksley	Charlene	415 585-4620	18 Broadway Av.	San Francisco	CA	94130	True
527-72-3246	Greene	Morningstar	615 297-2723	22 Graybar House Rd.	Nashville	TN	37215	False
648-92-1872	Blotchet-Halls	Reginald	503 745-6402	55 Hillsdale Bl.	Corvallis	OR	97330	True
672-71-3249	Yokomoto	Akiko	415 935-4228	3 Silver Ct.	Walnut Creek	CA	94595	True
712-45-1867	del Castillo	Innes	615 996-8275	2286 Cram Pl. #86	Ann Arbor	MI	48105	True
722-51-5454	DeFrance	Michel	219 547-9982	3 Balding Pl.	Gary	IN	46403	True
724-08-9931	Stringer	Dirk	415 843-2991	5420 Telegraph Av.	Oakland	CA	94609	False
724-80-9391	MacFeather	Stearns	415 354-7128	44 Upland Hts.	Oakland	CA	94612	True
756-30-7391	Karsen	Livia	415 534-9219	5720 McAuley St.	Oakland	CA	94609	True
807-91-6654	Panteley	Sylvia	301 946-8853	1956 Arlington Pl.	Rockville	MD	20853	True
846-92-7186	Hunter	Sheryl	415 836-7128	3410 Blonde St.	Palo Alto	CA	94301	True
893-72-1158	McBadden	Heather	707 448-4982	301 Putnam	Vacaville	CA	95688	False
899-46-2035	Ringer	Anne	801 826-0752	67 Seventh Av.	Salt Lake City	UT	84152	True

FIGURE 23.1.
Displaying all the records and rows in a table.

In this example, the `Count` property of the `Fields` collection is used to return a count of the number of fields in the Recordset. The `Name` property is used to retrieve the name of each field. Both of the `FOR...NEXT` loops are used to walk though all the fields in the Recordset. No matter how many columns and rows the table contains, they'll all be displayed.

Recordset Cursor and Locking Types

You can open a Recordset with one of four types of *cursors*. A cursor determines the types of operations you can perform with a Recordset. The cursor also determines what types of changes other users can make in an open Recordset. The following list describes the cursor types and their restrictions:

- adOpenForwardOnly. Using a *forward-only cursor*, you can only move forward through the records in a Recordset.

- adOpenKeyset. Using a *keyset cursor*, you can move both forward and backward in a Recordset. If a record is deleted or changed by another user, this is reflected in the Recordset. However, if a new record is added by another user, the new record won't appear in the Recordset.

- adOpenDynamic. Using a *dynamic cursor*, you can move both forward and backward in a Recordset. Any changes made to records by other users are reflected in the Recordset.

- adOpenStatic. Using a *static cursor*, you can move both forward and backward in a Recordset. However, a static cursor doesn't reflect changes in the records made by other users.

By default, when you open a Recordset, it's opened with a forward-only cursor. This means that you can only move forward through the records in the Recordset, using the MoveNext method. Other types of operations with the Recordset are not fully supported.

The advantage of a forward-only cursor is that it's fast. Whenever you can get away with it, you should use a forward-only cursor. However, if you need to open a Recordset with a richer type of cursor, you can use a script like the following:

```
<!-- #INCLUDE VIRTUAL="ADOVBS.inc" -->
<%
Set MyConn=Server.CreateObject("ADODB.Connection")
Set RS=Server.CreateObject("ADODB.RecordSet")
MyConn.Open "FILEDSN=d:\Program Files\Common Files\ODBC\Data Sources\MyData.dsn"
RS.Open "SELECT * FROM MyTable", MyConn, adOpenDynamic
RS.Close
MyConn.Close
%>
```

To open a Recordset with a specific type of cursor, you must explicitly create the Recordset and open it with the cursor type. To do this, you first create an instance of the Recordset object. Next, you use the Open method to open the Recordset with a particular connection and cursor type. In this script, the RS Recordset is opened using the MyConn Connection object and a dynamic cursor.

When opening a Recordset, you can also specify the type of *locking* to use. The locking type determines how the database will handle situations in which more than one user attempts to change a record at the same time. You can specify any one of the following four locking types:

- adLockReadOnly. Indicates that you can't modify the records in a Recordset.

- adLockPessimistic. Indicates that a record should be locked immediately upon editing.

- adLockOptimistic. Indicates that a record should be locked only when the Recordset's Update method is called.

- adLockBatchOptimistic. Indicates that the records will be batch-updated.

By default, a Recordset uses read-only locking. To specify a different locking type, you include one of these locking constants when you open the Recordset. Here's an example of how you can do this:

```
<!-- #INCLUDE VIRTUAL="ADOVBS.inc" -->
<%
Set MyConn=Server.CreateObject("ADODB.Connection")
Set RS=Server.CreateObject("ADODB.RecordSet")
MyConn.Open "FILEDSN=d:\Program Files\Common Files\ODBC\Data Sources\MyData.dsn"
RS.Open "SELECT * FROM MyTable", MyConn, adOpenDynamic, adLockPessimistic
RS.Close
MyConn.Close
%>
```

This script is the same as the preceding script except for the addition of the locking type. When the RS Recordset is opened, it's opened using a pessimistic lock. This means that the records in the Recordset can be modified. (You learn how to do this in the next section.)

Finally, when you open a Recordset, you can specify an Options parameter. The Options parameter indicates the type of command string being used to open the Recordset. Warning the ADO about the contents of the string being executed helps ADO to execute the command more efficiently.

You can use the following constants for the Options parameter:

- adCMDTable. The string being executed contains the name of a table.
- adCMDText. The string being executed contains a textual command.
- adCMDStoredProc. The string being executed contains the name of a stored procedure.
- adCMDUnknown. The contents of the string are unspecified. (This is the default value.)

In the following script, the Options parameter is used to warn the ADO that the content of the command string is a textual command:

```
<!-- #INCLUDE VIRTUAL="ADOVBS.inc" -->
<%
Set MyConn=Server.CreateObject("ADODB.Connection")
Set RS=Server.CreateObject("ADODB.RecordSet")
MyConn.Open "FILEDSN=d:\Program Files\Common Files\ODBC\Data Sources\MyData.dsn"
RS.Open "SELECT * FROM MyTable", MyConn,
  adOpenDynamic, adLockPessimistic, adCMDText
RS.Close
MyConn.Close
%>
```

Advanced Methods for Working with Recordsets

Up to this point, you've learned only how to use SQL to modify the records in a Recordset. However, you can also use a number of Recordset methods to modify the records in a Recordset. The following list briefly explains each method:

- AddNew. Adds a new record to a Recordset.
- CancelBatch. Cancels a batch update when a Recordset is in batch-update mode.
- CancelUpdate. Cancels any changes made to the current record before the Update method is called.
- Delete. Deletes a record from a Recordset.
- Update. Saves any changes made to the current record.
- UpdateBatch. Saves all changes made to one or more records when a Recordset is in batch-update mode.

For example, you can use the AddNew method to add a brand new record to an open Recordset, like this:

```
<!-- #INCLUDE VIRTUAL="ADOVBS.inc" -->
<%
Set MyConn=Server.CreateObject("ADODB.Connection")
Set RS=Server.CreateObject("ADODB.RecordSet")
MyConn.Open "FILEDSN=d:\Program Files\Common Files\ODBC\Data Sources\MyData.dsn"
RS.Open "SELECT MyColumn FROM MyTable",
 MyConn, adOpenDynamic, adLockPessimistic, adCMDText
RS.AddNew
RS("MyColumn")="A new column"
RS.Update
RS.Close
MyConn.Close
%>
```

In this script, the AddNew method is used to create a new record. Next, the MyColumn field of the new record is given the value A new column. Finally, the Update method is called to save the new record. To use these methods, the Recordset must be opened with a locking type other than read-only.

Instead of using the AddNew method to add a new record to a table, however, you can use the SQL INSERT method instead. In general, it's better to use SQL than the methods just described because SQL is much more flexible. For the remainder of this book, SQL is used to manipulate the data in a database table.

Navigating a Recordset

The Recordset object includes a number of methods for moving through the records in a Recordset. Many of these methods can be used only when a Recordset is opened with a particular type of cursor. This list (continued on the following page) includes some of these methods and an explanation of their functions:

- Move *NumRecords*. Moves the specified number of records forward or backward in a Recordset.
- MoveFirst. Moves to the first record in a Recordset.

- MoveNext. Moves to the next record in a Recordset.
- MovePrevious. Moves to the previous record in a Recordset.
- MoveLast. Moves to the last record in a Recordset.

The Recordset object also includes a number of properties that are useful for navigating through a set of records. Again, many of the properties require particular cursor types:

- AbsolutePosition. Used to set or read the ordinal position of the current record in the Recordset.
- BOF. Indicates that the current record position is before the first record in the Recordset.
- EOF. Indicates that the current record position is after the last record in the Recordset.
- RecordCount. Indicates the total number of records in a Recordset.

For example, suppose you want to move backward through the records in a Recordset. You could do this by using the MoveLast and MovePrevious methods and the BOF property. The following Active Server Page illustrates how:

```
<HTML>
<HEAD><TITLE> Backwards Recordset </TITLE></HEAD>
<BODY>
<!-- #INCLUDE VIRTUAL="ADOVBS.inc" -->
<%
Set MyConn=Server.CreateObject("ADODB.Connection")
Set RS=Server.CreateObject("ADODB.RecordSet")
MyConn.Open "FILEDSN=d:\Program Files\Common Files\ODBC\Data Sources\MyData.dsn"
RS.Open "SELECT MyColumn FROM MyTable", MyConn, adOpenStatic
RS.MoveLast
WHILE NOT RS.BOF
  Response.Write("<BR>"&RS("MyColumn"))
RS.MovePrevious
WEND
RS.Close
MyConn.Close
%>
</BODY>
</HTML>
```

In this example, the Recordset is opened with a static cursor. This stratagy is required for both the MoveLast and the MovePrevious methods to work. Once the Recordset is opened, each record in the Recordset is displayed until the beginning of the Recordset is reached. The BOF property is used to detect when this happens.

You can use these methods to move backward through a Recordset. However, it's difficult to think of a legitimate reason why you would need to do this. It's much more efficient to use the SQL language itself to order the results of a query. When you can, you should order your records by using a SQL ORDER BY clause. (See Chapter 10, "Basic SQL," for more information on using the ORDER BY clause.)

Retrieving a Record Count

You can use the RecordCount property of the Recordset object to determine the number of records contained in a Recordset. However, you should resist using this property. The problem is that this property is extremely inefficient in most situations.

You can't use the RecordCount property with a Recordset that uses a forward-only cursor. You must open a less efficient cursor, as in this example:

```
<!-- #INCLUDE VIRTUAL="ADOVBS.inc" -->
<%
Set MyConn=Server.CreateObject("ADODB.Connection")
Set RS=Server.CreateObject("ADODB.RecordSet")
MyConn.Open "FILEDSN=d:\Program Files\Common Files\ODBC\Data Sources\MyData.dsn"
RS.Open "SELECT MyColumn FROM MyTable", MyConn,adOpenStatic
Response.Write(RS.RecordCount)
RS.Close
MyConn.Close
%>
```

This script outputs the number of records in the table named MyTable. The RecordCount property is used to return this number. For the RecordCount property to be used, the Recordset is opened with a static cursor.

Normally, the only reason you need a record count is to determine whether at least one record fits certain criteria. For example, you might want to check whether a person has entered a valid password. In this situation, you may be tempted to query a password table and use the RecordCount property to determine whether the password exists. If RecordCount is greater than 0, the password exists; otherwise, it doesn't, and the password is invalid.

However, it's far better to use the EOF property to check whether a query has returned any results. You can use the EOF property when using a Recordset with a forward-only cursor. Here's an example:

```
<!-- #INCLUDE VIRTUAL="ADOVBS.inc" -->
<%
Set MyConn=Server.CreateObject("ADODB.Connection")
Set RS=Server.CreateObject("ADODB.RecordSet")
MyConn.Open "FILEDSN=d:\Program Files\Common Files\ODBC\Data Sources\MyData.dsn"
RS.Open "SELECT * FROM Password_Table
  WHERE Password="&Request.Form("Password"), MyConn
IF RS.EOF THEN
  Response.Write("The password you entered is invalid.")
ELSE
  Response.Write("Welcome to our web site!")
END IF
RS.Close
MyConn.Close
%>
```

In this example, the EOF property is used to test whether any results were returned from the query. If the EOF property is TRUE, the password that the user entered doesn't exist in the password table.

In some situations, you really do need to retrieve a record count. For example, you might want to display the total number of registered users at your Web site. Again, however, you should avoid using the RecordCount property. Instead, you can perform a SQL COUNT(*) query, as in the following lines:

```
<%
Set MyConn=Server.CreateObject("ADODB.Connection")
Set RS=Server.CreateObject("ADODB.RecordSet")
MyConn.Open "FILEDSN=d:\Program Files\Common Files\ODBC\Data Sources\MyData.dsn"
RS.Open "SELECT COUNT(*) MyCount FROM Password_Table", MyConn
%>
There are <%=RS("MyCount")%> registered users at this web site.
<%
RS.Close
MyConn.Close
%>
```

Notice how the column alias MyCount is used in this SQL query. By providing the aggregate function COUNT(*) with a name, you can use this name when outputting the results of the query.

> **NOTE**
>
> The next chapter discusses an additional method of retrieving a record count using a SQL stored procedure. See the section "Using Return Status Values with the Command Object."

Paging Through a Recordset

Suppose you want to display a list of products for sale at your Web site. However, you're selling hundreds of items. In that case, you probably wouldn't want to display all the items within a single Active Server Page. It would be better if you could allow the user to page through the list of items.

The Recordset object has three properties for this very purpose. You can use these properties to divide the records in a Recordset into logical pages. By dividing the records in a Recordset into different pages, you can display only portions of a Recordset at a time. Here's a list of these properties:

- ■ AbsolutePage. Specifies the current page of records.
- ■ PageCount. Returns the number of pages in the Recordset.
- ■ PageSize. Specifies the number of records in an individual page. The default value is 10.

To divide a Recordset into multiple pages, you use the PageSize property to specify the number of records in a single page. You then can use the AbsolutePage property to move to a particular page of records. Finally, the PageCount property can be used to return the total number of pages. Listing 23.1 shows how these properties can be used (see Figure 23.2 on the following page).

Listing 23.1. Script for pages.asp.

```
<HTML>
<HEAD><TITLE> Recordset With Pages </TITLE></HEAD>
<BODY>
<!-- #INCLUDE VIRTUAL="ADOVBS.inc" -->
<%
' Figure out the current page
IF Request.QueryString("MOVE")="NEXT" THEN
  Session("CurrentPage")=Session("CurrentPage")+1
END IF
IF Request.QueryString("MOVE")="PREV" THEN
  Session("CurrentPage")=Session("CurrentPage")-1
END IF
IF Session("CurrentPage")="" THEN
  Session("CurrentPage")=1
END IF
%>
<H1>Current Page: <%=Session("CurrentPage")%></H1>
<HR>
<%
' Open a Connection and Recordset
Set MyConn=Server.CreateObject("ADODB.Connection")
Set RS=Server.CreateObject("ADODB.RecordSet")
MyConn.Open "FILEDSN=d:\Program Files\Common Files\ODBC\Data Sources\MyData.dsn"
' Retrieve the list of products
RS.Open "SELECT ProductName FROM Products", MyConn, adOpenStatic
' Set the number of records in a page
RS.PageSize=5
' Set the current page
RS.AbsolutePage=Session("CurrentPage")
' Show the records for the current page
WHILE NOT RS.EOF AND NumRows<RS.PageSize
%>
<BR>Product Name: <%=RS("ProductName")%>
<%
RS.MoveNext
NumRows=NumRows+1
WEND
%>
<HR>
<% IF Session("CurrentPage")>1 THEN %>
<A HREF="pages.asp?MOVE=PREV"> [PREV] </A>
<% END IF %>
<% IF Session("CurrentPage")<RS.PageCount THEN %>
<A HREF="pages.asp?MOVE=NEXT"> [NEXT] </A>
<% END IF %>
```

continues

Listing 23.1. continued

```
<%
RS.Close
MyConn.Close
%>
</BODY>
</HTML>
```

FIGURE 23.2.

Paging through the records in a Recordset.

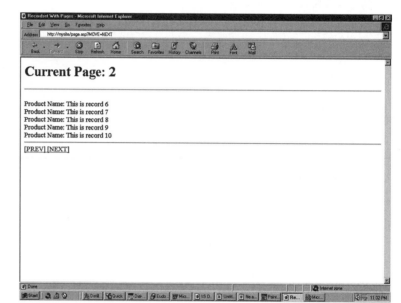

This Active Server Page displays the records in the Products table five records at a time. A session variable named CurrentPage is used to keep track of the current page within the Recordset. When the user clicks NEXT, the next page of records is displayed. When the user clicks PREV, the previous page is displayed.

Retrieving Records into an Array

In certain situations, you'll need to retrieve the records of a Recordset into an array. For example, if you need to alter the data represented by a Recordset, but you don't want to change the records in the Recordset itself, you can retrieve the records into an array.

To assign the records in a Recordset to an array, you use the GetRows() method of the Recordset object. Here's an example:

```
<%
Set MyConn=Server.CreateObject("ADODB.Connection")
Set RS=Server.CreateObject("ADODB.RecordSet")
MyConn.Open "FILEDSN=d:\Program Files\Common Files\ODBC\Data Sources\MyData.dsn"
```

```
RS.Open "SELECT MyFirstCol, MySecondCol FROM MyTable", MyConn
MyArray=RS.GetRows()
RS.Close
MyConn.Close
%>
```

In this script, all the records contained in the Recordset named RS are assigned to the array named MyArray. This array is automatically created and populated by the GetRows() method. The GetRows() method creates a two-dimensional array. The first subscript identifies the field and the second subscript indicates the record number.

The following script can be used to display all the contents of MyArray:

```
<%
FOR i=0 TO UBOUND(MyArray,2)
%>
<BR> First Column:  <%=MyArray(0,i)%>
<BR> Second Column: <%=MyArray(1,i)%>
<%
NEXT
%>
```

The VBScript UBOUND() function is used to determine the size of the second dimension of the array. The FOR...NEXT loop is used to iterate through all of its elements. This array represents a Recordset with two columns. When the first index of the array has the value 0, the first column is represented. When the first index of the array has the value 1, the second column is represented.

Specifying the Maximum Size of a RecordSet

Suppose you want to display the last 10 messages posted on your Web site, but no more than 10 messages. Or imagine that you want to display three links and no more than three links to your favorite Web sites. How can you limit the records that you retrieve into a Recordset? A property of the Recordset object is available for this purpose. You can limit the number of records retrieved into a Recordset from a database query by using the MaxRecords property, as in the following example:

```
<%
Set MyConn=Server.CreateObject("ADODB.Connection")
Set RS=Server.CreateObject("ADODB.RecordSet")
MyConn.Open "FILEDSN=d:\Program Files\Common Files\ODBC\Data Sources\MyData.dsn"
RS.MaxRecords=10
RS.Open "SELECT MyColumn FROM MyTable", MyConn
WHILE NOT RS.EOF
  Response.Write("<BR>"&RS("MyColumn"))
  RS.MoveNext
WEND
RS.Close
MyConn.Close
%>
```

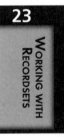

In this script, the MaxRecords property is set to 10. When the RS Recordset is opened, no more than 10 records will be retrieved from the query. Even if the table contains 10,000 records, only 10 will be retrieved.

When you use the MaxRecords property, you must set the property before you open the Recordset. After a Recordset is open, the property is read-only.

Summary

This chapter explored the Recordset object. You learned how to use a Recordset to display data from a database table in your Active Server Pages. You also learned how to open a Recordset with different types of cursors and locking. Finally, you learned a number of advanced methods of the Recordset object.

Working with Commands

CHAPTER 24

This final chapter on the ActiveX Data Objects covers how to use the Command object. First you learn how to use the Command object to execute SQL stored procedures with parameters. The remainder of this chapter is devoted to two sample applications of the ADO. First you learn how to create an advanced feedback page for your Web site. Then you learn how to create a custom password-protection system.

Using the Command Object

The Command object represents a command (for example, a SQL query or a SQL stored procedure). Chapter 22, "ActiveX Data Objects," and Chapter 23, "Working with Recordsets," respectively, show how to use the Execute method of the Connection object and the Open method of the Recordset object to execute a command string. Consider these two examples:

```
RS.Open "SELECT * FROM MyTable", MyConn

MyConn.Execute "UPDATE MyTable SET MyColumn='Hello'"
```

Both of these examples use a SQL command string. In the first example, the command string is used to open the Recordset. In the second example, the command string is executed.

Instead of using a command string, you can use the Command object. The Command object can be used to explicitly represent a command. You can use an instance of the Command object to return a Recordset or to execute a SQL command that doesn't return a Recordset. Here's an example:

```
<!-- #INCLUDE VIRTUAL="ADOVBS.inc" -->
<%
Set MyConn=Server.CreateObject("ADODB.Connection")
Set MyCommand=Server.CreateObject("ADODB.Command")
MyConn.Open "FILEDSN=d:\Program Files\Common Files\ODBC\Data Sources\MyData.dsn"
Set MyCommand.ActiveConnection=MyConn
MyCommand.CommandText="UPDATE MyTable SET MyColumn='Hello'"
MyCommand.CommandType=adCMDText
MyCommand.Execute
MyConn.Close
%>
```

In this example, an instance of the Command object is created. Next, the ActiveConnection property associates the Command with an open connection. (This is accomplished with the Set statement, because you're assigning an object.) The CommandText property specifies which SQL statement will be executed. The CommandType property indicates that the command is a textual definition of a command. Finally, the Execute method is called to execute the Command.

In this example, the Command object isn't used to return a Recordset. However, there are two ways in which you can use the Command object to return a Recordset. This is the first way:

```
<!-- #INCLUDE VIRTUAL="ADOVBS.inc" -->
<%
Set MyConn=Server.CreateObject("ADODB.Connection")
```

```
Set MyCommand=Server.CreateObject("ADODB.Command")
MyConn.Open "FILEDSN=d:\Program Files\Common Files\ODBC\Data Sources\MyData.dsn"
Set MyCommand.ActiveConnection=MyConn
MyCommand.CommandType=adCMDText
MyCommand.CommandText="SELECT * FROM MyTable"
Set RS=MyCommand.Execute()
RS.Close
MyConn.Close
%>
```

In this script, the `Execute()` method of the `Command` object is used to return a Recordset. Notice that parentheses are used because the method is being used to return results. After you have created a new instance of a Recordset with the `Command` object, you can manipulate it in the normal ways.

You can also use the `Command` object with a preexisting Recordset, like this:

```
<!-- #INCLUDE VIRTUAL="ADOVBS.inc" -->
<%
Set MyConn=Server.CreateObject("ADODB.Connection")
Set MyCommand=Server.CreateObject("ADODB.Command")
Set RS=Server.CreateObject("ADODB.RecordSet")
MyConn.Open "FILEDSN=d:\Program Files\Common Files\ODBC\Data Sources\MyData.dsn"
Set MyCommand.ActiveConnection=MyConn
MyCommand.CommandText="SELECT * FROM MyTable"
MyCommand.CommandType=adCMDText
RS.Open MyCommand,,adOpenStatic,adLockOptimistic
RS.Close
MyConn.Close
%>
```

The advantage of passing a `Command` object to a preexisting Recordset is that you can specify the Recordset's cursor and locking type. In this example, the `Command` object is used to open a Recordset that uses a static cursor and optimistic locking. Notice that you don't include a reference to the `Connection` object when using the `Open` method with a `Command` object. The connection is determined by the `Command` object instead.

These examples illustrate *how* you can use the `Command` object. However, they don't illustrate *why* you should use a `Command` object. Why should you explicitly create a `Command` object rather than use a command string?

Using a `Command` object has one main advantage. You can use the `Command` object with a SQL stored procedure.

24

WHY USING SQL STORED PROCEDURES IS GOOD

Chapter 12, "Advanced SQL," explains how to create SQL stored procedures. When you have finished developing a Web site, it's a good idea to transfer as many SQL commands

continues

continued

as possible to stored procedures. Instead of issuing SQL queries from within your Active Server Pages, you should call stored procedures that contain the queries.

There are a number of good reasons for using SQL stored procedures:

■ SQL stored procedures typically execute much faster than textual SQL commands. When a SQL statement is contained in a stored procedure, the server doesn't need to parse and compile the statement every time it's executed.

■ You can call the same stored procedure from multiple Active Server Pages. This makes your Web site easier to maintain. If any changes need to be made to a SQL statement, you only have to do it once.

■ You can also use stored procedures to exploit the full power of Transact-SQL. A stored procedure can contain multiple SQL statements. You can use variables and conditionals. This means that you can use a stored procedure to create very complex queries and update the database in very complicated ways.

■ Finally, and perhaps most importantly, you can use parameters with a stored procedure. You can both pass and return parameters from a stored procedure. You can also retrieve a return value (from a SQL RETURN statement).

In short, always use stored procedures when you can. The advantages of stored procedures are significant.

Using the Command Object to Call a Stored Procedure

Suppose you want to retrieve all the records in a table named MyTable and display them in an Active Server Page. Furthermore, suppose that you want to retrieve the records from this table in the most efficient way possible. In that case, you should use a stored procedure.

To create a new stored procedure, launch ISQL/w from the Microsoft SQL Server program group. Next, enter the following text in the query window:

```
CREATE PROCEDURE sp_myproc AS
SELECT * FROM MyTable
```

Click the Execute Query button (it shows a green triangle) and the stored procedure will be created. The new stored procedure is named sp_myproc.

To call sp_myproc from an Active Server Page, you can use an instance of the Command object. Here's an example:

```
<!-- #INCLUDE VIRTUAL="ADOVBS.inc" -->
<%
Set MyConn=Server.CreateObject("ADODB.Connection")
Set MyCommand=Server.CreateObject("ADODB.Command")
MyConn.Open "FILEDSN=d:\Program Files\Common Files\ODBC\Data Sources\MyData.dsn"
Set MyCommand.ActiveConnection=MyConn
```

```
MyCommand.CommandType=adCMDStoredProc
MyCommand.CommandText="sp_myproc"
Set RS=MyCommand.Execute()
WHILE NOT RS.EOF
  Response.Write("<BR>"&RS("MyColumn"))
  RS.MoveNext
WEND
RS.Close
MyConn.Close
%>
```

This script displays all the records in the table named MyTable. The records are retrieved by calling the sp_myproc stored procedure. When you use a Command object to call a stored procedure, you should set its CommandType property to adCMDStoredProc. You use the CommandText property to specify the stored procedure to call.

Using Return Status Values with the Command Object

You can use the Command object to retrieve the *return status value* from a stored procedure. For example, suppose you want a count of the number of records in a table. The absolutely most efficient way to do this is to create a stored procedure, as in the following example:

```
CREATE PROCEDURE sp_CountMyTable AS
RETURN(SELECT COUNT(*) FROM MyTable)
```

This stored procedure returns the number of records in the table named MyTable. The SQL COUNT() aggregate function counts the number of records in the table. The RETURN statement returns this count.

To retrieve the return status value of a stored procedure, you must create a parameter for the Command object. The Command object has a collection named Parameters. The Parameters collection is a collection of Parameter objects.

You create a parameter by using the CreateParameter() method of the Command object. Next, you use the Append method of the Command object to append the parameter to the Command object's Parameters collection. Here's an example:

```
<!-- #INCLUDE VIRTUAL="ADOVBS.inc" -->
<%
Set MyConn=Server.CreateObject("ADODB.Connection")
Set MyCommand=Server.CreateObject("ADODB.Command")
MyConn.Open "FILEDSN=d:\Program Files\Common Files\ODBC\Data Sources\MyData.dsn"
Set MyCommand.ActiveConnection=MyConn
MyCommand.CommandType=adCMDStoredProc
MyCommand.CommandText="sp_CountMyTable"
Set MyParam=MyCommand.CreateParameter("RetVal",adInteger,adParamReturnValue)
MyCommand.Parameters.Append MyParam
MyCommand.Execute
%>
There are <%=MyCommand("RetVal")%> records in MyTable.
<%
MyConn.Close
%>
```

24

WORKING WITH COMMANDS

In this script, a new `Parameter` object is created by using the `CreateParameter()` method. The `CreateParameter()` method has three arguments in this example:

- The first argument specifies a name for the new parameter.
- The second argument indicates the datatype.
- Finally, the last argument specifies the type of the parameter. In this example, the constant `adParamReturnValue` indicates that the parameter is a return parameter.

After any new parameter is created, it must be appended to the `Parameters` collection of the `Command` object. The `Append` method is used to add a new parameter to this collection.

After the `Command` executes, the value of the parameter can be retrieved. Because the parameter is a member of the `Command` object's `Parameters` collection, the value of the parameter can be returned by using `MyCommand("RetVal")`. Actually, you can also retrieve this value by using any of the following expressions:

```
MyCommand("RetVal")
```

```
MyCommand(0)
```

```
MyCommand.Parameters("RetVal")
```

```
MyCommand.Parameters(0)
```

```
MyCommand.Parameters.Item("RetVal")
```

```
MyCommand.Parameters.Item(0)
```

All these methods of retrieving the value of a parameter work because a parameter is part of a `Command` object's `Parameters` collection. Notice that, as with all collections, you can specify a parameter either by name or by ordinal number.

Using Output Parameters with the Command Object

The example in the preceding section illustrates how you can retrieve a return status value. The procedure for retrieving *output parameters* from a stored procedure is very similar. The advantage of using output parameters is that there can be more than one of them. Also, an output parameter can be of any datatype.

Imagine that you have a table named `WebUsers` that contains the list of registered user names for your Web site. This table has a single column named `UserName`. Now suppose you want to retrieve both the alphabetically highest and lowest name from this table. You can use the following stored procedure to do this:

```
CREATE PROCEDURE sp_HighAndLow
(@HighUser VARCHAR(30) OUTPUT, @LowUser VARCHAR(30) OUTPUT)
AS
SELECT @HighUser=MAX(UserName) FROM WebUsers
SELECT @LowUser=MIN(UserName) FROM WebUsers
```

This stored procedure has two output parameters named @HighUser and @LowUser. @HighUser contains the name of the user with the alphabetically highest name (for example, Zeek Zimmerman). @LowUser contains the name of the user with the alphabetically lowest name (for example, Anne Arnold).

To call this stored procedure in an Active Server Page, you could use the following script:

```
<!-- #INCLUDE VIRTUAL="ADOVBS.inc" -->
<%
Set MyConn=Server.CreateObject("ADODB.Connection")
Set MyCommand=Server.CreateObject("ADODB.Command")
MyConn.Open "FILEDSN=d:\Program Files\Common Files\ODBC\Data Sources\MyData.dsn"
Set MyCommand.ActiveConnection=MyConn
MyCommand.CommandType=adCMDStoredProc
MyCommand.CommandText="sp_HighandLow"
Set MyFirstParam=MyCommand.CreateParameter("HighUser",adVarChar,adParamOutput, 30)
MyCommand.Parameters.Append MyFirstParam
Set MySecondParam=MyCommand.CreateParameter("LowUser",adVarChar,adParamOutput, 30)
MyCommand.Parameters.Append MySecondParam
MyCommand.Execute
%>
<P>The person with the alphabetically highest name is
<%=MyCommand("HighUser")%>
<P>The person with the alphabetically lowest name is
<%=MyCommand("LowUser")%>
<%
MyConn.Close
%>
```

The structure of this script is very similar to the preceding one. In this script, two Parameter objects are created with the CreateParameter() method. They're both created with VARCHAR data types. To indicate that they're output parameters, the constant adParamOutput is used. Finally, the maximum size of each parameter, 30, is included in the CreateParameter() method. When you create parameters with variable-size data such as VARCHAR or CHAR, you must supply a maximum-size argument.

Using Input Parameters with the Command Object

One more type of parameter has yet to be discussed. A SQL stored procedure can accept *input parameters*. Input parameters enable you to pass data to a stored procedure.

For example, imagine you have a table containing user names and passwords. Now suppose you want to create a stored procedure that checks passwords. You could check whether a user has supplied a valid password with the following stored procedure:

```
CREATE PROCEDURE sp_CheckPass
(@CHKName VARCHAR(30),@CHKPass VARCHAR(30),@ISValid CHAR(4) OUTPUT)
AS
IF EXISTS(SELECT UserName FROM WebUsers
WHERE UserName=@CHKName AND UserPass=@CHKPass)
 SELECT @ISValid="Good"
ELSE
 SELECT @ISValid="Bad"
```

This stored procedure accepts two input parameters. The @CHKName input parameter passes a user name to the procedure. The @CHKPass input parameter inputs a password to the procedure. If a user with the specified password exists, the output parameter returns the value Good. Otherwise, the value Bad is returned.

The method for using an input parameter is very similar to the method for using output parameters. The crucial difference is that an input parameter must be assigned a value before the Command is executed. Here's an example:

```
<!-- #INCLUDE VIRTUAL="ADOVBS.inc" -->
<%
Set MyConn=Server.CreateObject("ADODB.Connection")
Set MyCommand=Server.CreateObject("ADODB.Command")
MyConn.Open "FILEDSN=d:\Program Files\Common
  Files\ODBC\Data Sources\MyData.dsn"
Set MyCommand.ActiveConnection=MyConn
MyCommand.CommandType=adCMDStoredProc
MyCommand.CommandText="sp_CheckPass"
Set MyFirstParam=MyCommand.CreateParameter("UserName",
➥adVarChar,adParamInput,30)
MyCommand.Parameters.Append MyFirstParam
Set MySecondParam=MyCommand.CreateParameter("UserPass",
➥adVarChar,adParamInput,30)
MyCommand.Parameters.Append MySecondParam
Set MyThirdParam=MyCommand.CreateParameter("RetValue",
➥adChar,adParamOutPut,4)
MyCommand.Parameters.Append MyThirdParam
MyCommand("UserName")="Bill Gates"
MyCommand("UserPass")="Billions"
MyCommand.Execute
%>
The Password is <%=MyCommand("RetValue")%>.
<%
MyConn.Close
%>
```

In this example, the name Bill Gates with the password Billions is passed to the stored procedure. If this name-and-password combination exists in the WebUsers table, the password is reported as Good. Otherwise, the password is reported as Bad.

In this script, the two input parameters are indicated by using the constant adParamInput. Notice that both of these input parameters are assigned a value before the Command is executed.

Retrieving Parameter Information

You may discover that you need to use a stored procedure, but don't know the parameters that the procedure requires. For example, you may not know the datatypes of the parameters or their sizes. How can you determine this information?

You can retrieve information about the parameters used in a stored procedure by using the following script:

```
<!-- #INCLUDE VIRTUAL="ADOVBS.inc" -->
<%
Set MyConn=Server.CreateObject("ADODB.Connection")
Set MyCommand=Server.CreateObject("ADODB.Command")
MyConn.Open "FILEDSN=d:\Program Files\Common
  Files\ODBC\Data Sources\MyData.dsn"
Set MyCommand.ActiveConnection=MyConn
MyCommand.CommandType=adCMDStoredProc
MyCommand.CommandText="sp_myproc"
MyCommand.Parameters.Refresh
%>
<HTML>
<HEAD><TITLE>Parameter Information</TITLE></HEAD>
<BODY>
<TABLE BORDER=1>
<CAPTION>Parameter Information</CAPTION>
<TR>
 <TH>Parameter Name</TH>
 <TH>Datatype</TH>
 <TH>Direction</TH>
 <TH>Size</TH>
</TR>
<%For Each thing in MyCommand.Parameters %>
<TR>
 <TD><%=thing.name %></TD>
 <TD><%=thing.type %></TD>
 <TD><%=thing.direction %></TD>
 <TD><%=thing.size %></TD>
</TR>
<%
Next
MyConn.Close
%>
</TABLE>
</BODY>
</HTML>
```

This example displays all the parameter information for the procedure named sp_myproc. The name, datatype, direction, and size for each parameter is displayed in a table. (The *direction* indicates whether the parameter is an input parameter, output parameter, or return status value.) To display information about another stored procedure, simply substitute the procedure's name for sp_myproc.

The important statement in this example is MyCommand.Parameters.Refresh. When this statement is executed, information about the stored procedure's parameters is retrieved from the database.

This script doesn't return constants. Instead, it returns raw values. To interpret the values returned by this script, you need to examine the ADOVBS include file. In this file, the raw numerical values are associated with the correct constants.

24

WORKING WITH
COMMANDS

Sample Application: An Advanced Feedback Page

It's a good idea to include a feedback page on your Web site. A feedback page allows users to comment on problems, suggest improvements, and provide compliments. You can use this information to intelligently adapt your site to the requirements of your audience.

The simplest way to create a feedback page is to use an HTML form that sends the feedback to an e-mail account. For example, the following HTML page e-mails the information entered into a form to the webmaster@yoursite.com e-mail account:

```
<HTML>
<HEAD><TITLE> Feedback </TITLE></HEAD>
<BODY>
<H2> Please enter any suggestions for improving
this web site in the form below: </H2>
<FORM ACTION="MAILTO:webmaster@yoursite.com">
<TEXTAREA NAME="Feedback" COLS=30 ROWS=10 WRAP=VIRTUAL></TEXTAREA>
<P><INPUT TYPE="SUBMIT" VALUE="Submit Feedback">
</FORM>
</BODY>
</HTML>
```

This feedback form would work fine for small Web sites. All feedback is sent to a single e-mail account. However, if your Web site has multiple administrators, you may want all the administrators to be able to view the feedback. Also, you may want to store any feedback so it can be retrieved and analyzed in the future. In that case, you should store user feedback in a database table.

This section describes how to use the ADO to store and retrieve user feedback. You learn how to create an advanced feedback form. The following table and files are used in this project:

- Feedback table. A SQL Server database table used to store user feedback.
- Feedback page. An HTML page where users enter feedback on your Web site.
- Acknowledgment page. An Active Server Page that thanks the user for entering feedback and stores the feedback in the database.
- Display page. An Active Server Page that displays user feedback by retrieving it from the database.

Creating the Feedback Table

The Feedback table has four columns: one column each for the e-mail address, the IP address, the date the feedback was created, and the contents of the feedback. To create this table, launch ISQL/w from the Microsoft SQL Server program group. Next, enter the following text in the query window and execute it:

```
CREATE TABLE Feedback (Feed_Email VARCHAR(50),
  Feed_IP VARCHAR(20),
  Feed_Date DATETIME Default GetDATE(),
  Feed_Contents TEXT)
```

Creating the Feedback Page

The Feedback page is a normal HTML page (see Figure 24.1). It contains a text field where users can enter their e-mail address and a text area where users can enter feedback. It also has a single submit button for submitting the feedback. When the feedback is submitted, the user is brought to the Acknowledgment page. Listing 24.1 shows the script for the Feedback page.

FIGURE 24.1.

The Feedback page.

Listing 24.1. Script for feedback.htm.

```
<HTML>
<HEAD><TITLE> Feedback </TITLE></HEAD>
<BODY BGCOLOR=#FFFFFF>
<H2> Please enter any suggestions for improving
this web site in the form below: </H2>
<FORM METHOD="POST" ACTION="acknowledge.asp">
Please enter your email address:
<BR><INPUT NAME="Email" TYPE="TEXT" SIZE="30" MAXLENGTH="50">
<P><TEXTAREA NAME="Contents" COLS=30 ROWS=10 WRAP=VIRTUAL></TEXTAREA>
<P><INPUT TYPE="SUBMIT" VALUE="Submit Feedback">
</FORM>
</BODY>
</HTML>
```

24

WORKING WITH
COMMANDS

Creating the Acknowledgment Page

The Acknowledgment page has a dual purpose. First, it's used to thank the user for providing feedback (see Figure 24.2). Second, and more importantly, this page is used to actually store the feedback in the Feedback table. The feedback is added to this table with the SQL INSERT statement, as shown in Listing 24.2.

FIGURE 24.2.

The Acknowledgment page.

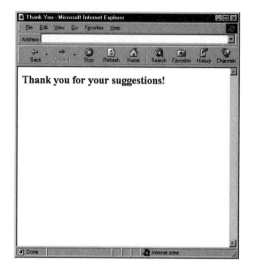

Listing 24.2. Script for `acknowledge.asp`.

```
<%
' Retrieve form fields into variables
Email=Replace(Request.Form("Email"),"'","'''")
Contents=Replace(Request.Form("Contents"),"'","'''")

' Check for empty content
IF Email="" THEN Email="Unknown"
IF Contents="" THEN Contents="None"

' Grab the user's IP address
UserIP=Request.ServerVariables("REMOTE_ADDR")

' Create the SQL command string
MySQL="INSERT Feedback (Feed_Email,Feed_IP,Feed_Contents)
  VALUES ('"&Email&"','"&UserIP&"','"&Contents&"')"

' Insert the form data into the Feedback table
Set MyConn=Server.CreateObject("ADODB.Connection")
MyConn.Open "FILEDSN=d:\Program Files\Common
  Files\ODBC\Data Sources\MyData.dsn"
MyConn.Execute MySQL
%>
<HTML>
<HEAD><TITLE> Thank You </TITLE></HEAD>
<BODY>
<H2> Thank you for your suggestions! </H2>
</BODY>
</HTML>
```

NOTE

Notice how the VBScript `Replace()` function is used in this script. The `Replace()` function replaces every single quote with two single quotes. This is necessary to prevent SQL Server from thinking that it has reached the end of a SQL string. If the `Replace()` function isn't used and a user enters feedback that includes a single quote, the `INSERT` statement would cause an error.

Creating the Display Page

The Display page is used to display the feedback that users have entered (see Figure 24.3). The feedback is retrieved from the `Feedback` table. Because a Web site may receive thousands of feedback messages, the Display page doesn't show all the records from this table. Only the last 25 feedback messages entered are displayed. This is accomplished by using the `MaxRecords` property of the `Recordset` object.

FIGURE 24.3.

The Display page.

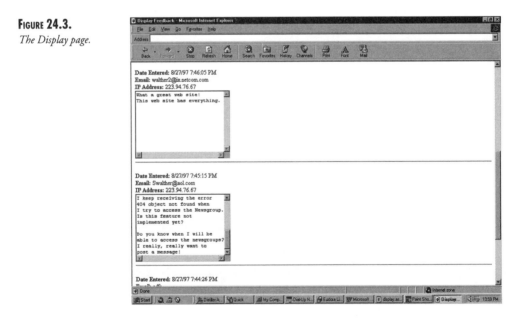

To show the contents of each feedback message, a text area is used. The advantage of using text areas is that they have scroll bars. If a really long feedback message is entered, it won't dominate the Display page. Listing 24.3 (on the next page) shows the script for `display.asp`.

Listing 24.3. Script for `display.asp`.

```
<%
' Create ADO objects
Set MyConn=Server.CreateObject("ADODB.Connection")
Set RS=Server.CreateObject("ADODB.RecordSet")
MyConn.Open "FILEDSN=d:\Program Files\Common Files\ODBC\Data Sources\MyData.dsn"

' Set the maximum number of records to return
RS.MaxRecords=25

' Retrieve the records
RS.Open "SELECT * FROM Feedback ORDER BY Feed_Date DESC", MyConn
%>

<HTML>
<HEAD><TITLE>Display Feedback</TITLE></HEAD>
<BODY>
<FORM>
<%
' Display the records
WHILE NOT RS.EOF
%>
<BR><B>Date Entered:</B> <%=RS("Feed_Date")%>
<BR><B>Email:</B> <%=RS("Feed_Email")%>
<BR><B>IP Address: </B><%=RS("Feed_IP")%>
<BR><TEXTAREA COLS=30 ROWS=10><%=RS("Feed_Contents")%></TEXTAREA>
<HR>
<%
RS.MoveNext
WEND
%>

</FORM>
</BODY>
</HTML>
<%
' Close the Recordset and Connection
RS.Close
MyConn.Close
%>
```

Sample Application: Creating a Custom Password System

This section shows how to use the ADO to password-protect your Web site. You learn how to create a registration page that new visitors can use to register for your Web site. You also learn how to prevent visitors from viewing pages that they don't have permission to access.

Why is a custom password-protection system necessary? You can configure IIS to use either Basic or Windows NT Challenge/Response authentication. By using either authentication system, and changing permissions on files, you can force users to enter a password before they can access certain pages.

NOTE

For more information on using Basic or NT Challenge/Response authentication with your Active Server Pages, see the section "Using the Permission Checker Component" in Chapter 20, "Providing Site-Wide Navigation."

There is a problem, however, with using either Basic or Windows NT Challenge/Response authentication. Both of these authentication systems are integrated with Windows NT security. This means that you have to manually add a user every time a new user registers. It also means that you can't easily access and modify passwords and usernames from your Active Server Pages.

If you merely want to password-protect certain pages of your Web site for yourself and other administrators, either of the authentication systems provided by IIS is appropriate. However, suppose you want to automatically register new users of your Web site after they provide such information as a telephone number or credit card number? In that case, you need to create a custom password-authentication system.

In this section, you learn how to use the ADO to create a custom password-authentication system. You need to create the following database table and two files:

- WebUsers table. This database table contains registration information.
- Registration page. This Active Server Page contains a registration form. By completing the form, a new user can gain access to your Web site.
- Password Include file. This file must be included in every Active Server Page that you want to password-protect.

Creating the WebUsers Table

The WebUsers table is a SQL Server table that contains only three columns. The first column holds user names, the second column holds user passwords, and the third column holds user telephone numbers.

To create this table, launch ISQL/w from the Microsoft SQL Server program group. Next, type the following text into the query window and execute it:

```
CREATE TABLE WebUsers (UserName VARCHAR(30),
  UserPass VARCHAR(30),
  UserPhone VARCHAR(30))
```

Whenever a new visitor attempts to access a password-protected page, the user's name and password are checked against this table.

Creating the Registration Page

The Registration page is used to allow new visitors to your Web site to register (see Figure 24.4). If someone who doesn't have a valid password attempts to access a password-protected page, he or she will be redirected to this page.

FIGURE 24.4.

The Registration page.

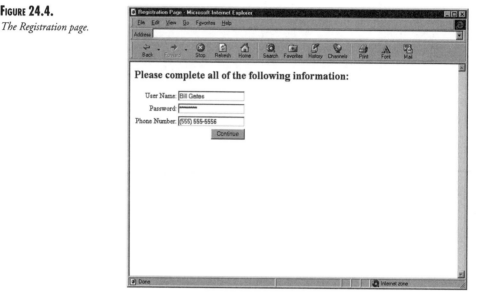

The Registration page uses one big conditional. If all the fields in the HTML form haven't been completed, the HTML form appears. Otherwise, if all the information has been entered, three things happen:

- First, the registration information is inserted into the WebUsers database table.
- Second, the session variables named UserName and UserPass are assigned the new user-name and password.
- Finally, the user is redirected back to the page where that user originated (if this is unknown, the user is sent to the home page).

The Registration page requests very little information from the user. However, you can easily extend this example to ask the user anything you want. For example, you may require the user to enter a credit card number or an address before using your Web site. To do this, just add the extra fields to the HTML form and the WebUsers database table. Listing 24.4 shows the script for the Registration page.

> **NOTE**
>
> If you ask for sensitive information such as a credit card number in your registration form, you should use the Secure Sockets Layer to encrypt the information. To find out more about the Secure Sockets Layer, see Chapter 2, "Installing and Using Internet Information Server."

Listing 24.4. Script for `register.asp`.

```asp
<%
CONST HomePage="/default.asp"

'   Check If Registration Information Is Incomplete
IF Request.Form("UserName")="" OR Request.Form("UserPass")=""
➡OR Request.Form("UserPhone")="" THEN
%>
  <HTML>
  <HEAD><TITLE>Registration Page</TITLE></HEAD>
  <BODY BGCOLOR=#FFFFFF>
  <H2>Please complete all of the following information:</H2>
  <FORM METHOD="POST"
   ACTION="<%=Request.ServerVariables("SCRIPT_NAME")%>">
  <TABLE>
  <TR>
  <TD ALIGN=RIGHT>User Name:</TD>
  <TD><INPUT NAME="UserName" TYPE="TEXT"
      VALUE="<%=Request.FORM("UserName")%>"></TD>
  </TR><TR>
  <TD ALIGN=RIGHT>Password:</TD>
  <TD><INPUT NAME="UserPass" TYPE="PASSWORD"
      VALUE="<%=Request.FORM("UserPass")%>"></TD>
  </TR><TR>
  <TD ALIGN=RIGHT>Phone Number:</TD>
  <TD><INPUT NAME="UserPhone" TYPE="TEXT"
      VALUE="<%=Request.FORM("UserPhone")%>"></TD>
  </TR><TR>
  <TD ALIGN=RIGHT COLSPAN=2><INPUT TYPE="SUBMIT" VALUE="Continue">
  </TD>
  </TR>
  </TABLE>
  </FORM>
  </BODY>
  </HTML>
<%
ELSE
  ' Ready Database Objects
  Set MyConn=Server.CreateObject("ADODB.Connection")
  MyConn.Open "FILEDSN=d:\Program Files\Common
     Files\ODBC\Data Sources\MyData.dsn"
```

continues

Listing 24.4. continued

```
' Insert The Registration Information Into WebUsers
MySQL="INSERT WebUsers (UserName,UserPass,UserPhone) VALUES ("
MySQL=MySQL&"'"&Request.FORM("UserName")&"'"
MySQL=MySQL&",'"&Request.FORM("UserPass")&"'"
MySQL=MySQL&",'"&Request.FORM("UserPhone")&"')"
MyConn.Execute MySQL
MyConn.Close

' Create Session Variables
Session("UserName")=Request.FORM("UserName")
Session("UserPass")=Request.FORM("UserPass")

' Redirect The User To The Appropriate Page
IF Session("GoBack")="" THEN Session("GoBack")=HomePage
Response.Redirect Session("GoBack")
END IF
%>
```

Creating the Password Include File

The Password Include file is included in every Web page that you want to password-protect. It checks whether the session variables UserName and UserPass exist. If they don't exist, the user is asked to enter a name and password (see Figure 24.5). This name and password are checked against the WebUsers table. If the password is invalid, the user is redirected to the registration page. Listing 24.5 shows the script.

FIGURE 24.5.

The Password Include file.

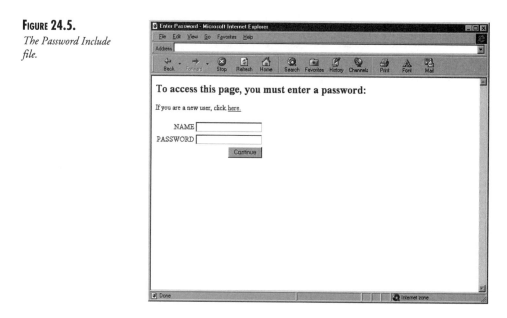

Listing 24.5. Script for pass.inc.

```
<%
IF Session("UserName")="" OR Session("UserPass")="" THEN
  IF Request.FORM("UserName")="" OR Request.FORM("UserPass")="" THEN
%>
<HTML>
<HEAD><TITLE>Enter Password</TITLE></HEAD>
<BODY>
<H2>To access this page, you must enter a password: </H2>
If you are a new user, click
<A HREF="register.asp"> here. </A>
<FORM METHOD="POST"
ACTION="<%=Request.ServerVariables("SCRIPT_NAME")%>">
<TABLE>
<TR>
<TD ALIGN=RIGHT>NAME</TD>
<TD><INPUT NAME="UserName" TYPE="TEXT"></TD>
</TR><TR>
<TD ALIGN=RIGHT>PASSWORD</TD>
<TD><INPUT NAME="UserPass" TYPE="PASSWORD"></TD>
</TR><TR>
<TD ALIGN=RIGHT COLSPAN=2>
<INPUT TYPE="SUBMIT" VALUE="Continue"></TD>
</TR>
</TABLE>
</FORM>
</BODY>
</HTML>
<%
Response.End
  ELSE
' Ready Database Objects
  Set MyConn=Server.CreateObject("ADODB.Connection")
  MyConn.Open "FILEDSN=d:\Program Files\Common
    Files\ODBC\Data Sources\MyData.dsn"

  ' Check The Password
  MySQL="SELECT UserName FROM WebUsers
  WHERE USERNAME='"&Request.FORM("UserName")
  MySQL=MySQL&"' AND USERPASS='"&Request.FORM("UserPass")&"'"
  SET RS=MyConn.Execute(MySQL)

  ' If the password is bad, redirect to the Registration Page
  IF RS.EOF THEN
    RS.CLOSE
    Session("GoBack")=Request.ServerVariables("SCRIPT_NAME")
    Response.Redirect "register.asp"
    Response.END
  END IF
  RS.CLOSE
  END IF
END IF
%>
```

24

WORKING WITH
COMMANDS

Testing the Custom Password System

To implement this password-protection system on your Web site, you need to include the file named pass.inc in every Active Server Page you want to password-protect. (You can't include this file in normal HTML pages.) Listing 24.6 shows a simple example of how it's done.

Listing 24.6. Script for testpass.asp.

```
<!-- #INCLUDE VIRTUAL="pass.inc" -->
<HTML>
<HEAD><TITLE> Restricted </TITLE></HEAD>
<BODY>
Only registered users can see this sentence!
</BODY>
</HTML>
```

This Active Server Page is displayed only to registered users. While testing the pages in this section, you can use the Session.Abandon method to drop your session variables. After the UserName and UserPass session variables are dropped, you have to enter a password again to access a password-protected page.

Summary

This chapter explored how to use the Command object to execute SQL stored procedures. You learned how to pass and retrieve input parameters, output parameters, and return values. The second section of this chapter presented two sample applications that utilized the ADO. You learned how to create an advanced feedback page. You also learned how to password-protect your Web site.

This is the final chapter on the objects and components included with Active Server Pages. In the next part of this book, "Using Microsoft Visual Studio," you learn how to use a number of programs included with Visual Studio. These programs allow you to create and extend your Active Server Pages easily.

VI
PART

Using Microsoft Visual Studio

Using Visual
InterDev

CHAPTER

25

Microsoft Visual InterDev is a software development environment for creating and managing World Wide Web sites. It's part of the Microsoft Visual Studio suite of development tools and, as such, enables you to easily incorporate Visual InterDev and other projects with a single workspace GUI.

In addition, Visual InterDev enables you to incorporate advanced features into your Web sites that go a long way beyond the use of HTML. Client-side (ActiveX) and server-side (Active Server) scripts, database access, and more are readily available to you through Microsoft's Active Platform technologies, fully supported by Visual InterDev.

Integration with other Microsoft products, including FrontPage and Visual SourceSafe, enables you to work in teams on the same Web site project. Integration with Internet Information Server and Personal Web Server provides the option of working on your Web site either online or offline. Many of the built-in features of InterDev make it one of the most powerful development environments for creating interactive Web sites.

Visual InterDev Architecture

A complex, interactive Web site is typically composed of a number of separate components. These components may all be developed or run on the same computer, or they may be spread over a number of different computers such as the following:

- Development workstation (runs the Visual InterDev software)
- Web server (with FrontPage Server Extensions)
- Web browser (views the completed Web pages)
- Database server (optional)

Visual InterDev greatly simplifies the task of interacting with all these components and allows the author to integrate them in a seamless manner. The development workstation is used to create and edit content, and the content is automatically uploaded to the Web server. If the project includes a database connection, Visual InterDev allows the author to view and interact with the data on the database server. The Microsoft Web browser is integrated with Visual InterDev for use by the author to view the Web pages during development and by users once the Web site has been completed.

Development Workstation

Visual InterDev on the development workstation provides a number of different ways to view your Web site and to access its components during development:

- The File View tab enables you to see all the files and subfolders in a project in a hierarchy, similar to that used in Windows Explorer. Simple point-and-click (or right-click) features let you create, edit, and delete any of these files and directories.
- The Data View tab displays all the database connections available to the Web project. Database elements such as tables and queries can be created and edited through this view.

- The Info View tab gives you access to the extensive help files and additional information provided with Visual InterDev. Search facilities let you quickly find the appropriate page, or you can browse through the Info View menu.

- Finally, using the Link View option, you can view the hyperlinks within the project and repair any pages that have broken or misdirected hyperlinks.

The File View, Data View, and Link View tabs are located at the bottom of the left-hand pane. In a manner similar to that for the tabs in many dialog boxes, you can bring any of the three views to the top (and therefore visible to the user) by simply clicking the appropriate tab.

To access Link View, highlight the file you want to view in the File view and choose the Links command from the View menu. Alternatively, right-click the appropriate file name and choose the View Links command.

You can see examples of a project in File View, Data View, and Info View in the later section "Web Projects and Workspaces." You can find out more about Link View in the section "Displaying Your Web Project's Links."

Web Server

The Web server stores the content that comprises the Web site under development. When Visual InterDev updates this content after it has been created or modified on the development workstation, it uses the FrontPage Server Extensions to update the final Web site on the Web server.

Other authors can access the Web server for development purposes from their own workstation, using either Visual InterDev or FrontPage. The Web server is also responsible for delivering the final content to users browsing the site via the World Wide Web.

Web Browser

Any Web browser can be used during the development process to view Web pages after they have been created or modified. Users of the completed Web site also use a Web browser to view the pages. It's recommended that you use different Web browsers during the development of a Web site to ensure compatibility between various programs, such as Internet Explorer and Netscape Navigator.

Database Server

Data connections can be made from Web projects to databases stored on a database server. Visual InterDev enables the author to create a new database and to create and edit database elements transparently from his or her workstation. Database tables can be defined and modified on the server, and queries can be designed and tested.

When the Web pages are browsed on the Web server, the Web server makes an independent connection to the database server to execute queries and extract the data.

Installing Visual InterDev

All sites on the WWW run on a Web server. To develop Web sites using Visual InterDev, the Web server must also be running FrontPage Server Extensions, which are available for various Web servers and operating systems.

The Web servers supported by FrontPage Server Extensions include Windows NT Server running Microsoft Internet Information Server (IIS) and a number of UNIX-based servers.

You can develop and maintain Web sites that are running on any properly configured Web server in the world (running FrontPage Server Extensions) if your development computer is connected to the Web server computer via the Internet or an intranet. This online development enables members of a team to work on the same online project from multiple locations.

If your computer doesn't maintain a connection to the Internet or to a Web server via an intranet, you can develop your Web sites offline. By installing Personal Web Server for Windows 95 or Peer Web Services for Windows NT Workstation 4.0, you can develop your Web site hosted from a Web server running on your own local computer. When development is finished, you can upload your Web site to any properly configured Web server for public Internet or intranet access.

Web Server Configuration

If you're developing your Web site on a separate Windows NT server, the following hardware and software configurations are recommended. Note that you can also run Microsoft SQL Server on a database server that's separate from the Web server computer.

- Pentium-compatible server (32MB RAM or more)
- Windows NT Server 4.0
- Internet Information Server 4.0
- Visual InterDev server components
- SQL Server 6.5 with Service Pack 1 for SQL Server 6.5 (SQL Server is optional)

To install the Microsoft Visual InterDev server components, follow these steps:

1. Run the Visual InterDev Master Setup program, `setup.exe`.
2. Open the installation instructions for the server components from the Master Setup. These instructions will help you with the rest of the installation process.
3. Install Personal Web Server for Windows 95. (Install this component only if you want to develop your Web site locally on your Windows 95 machine. You can also develop against the Peer Web Services in Windows NT Workstation 4.0.)
4. Install Active Server Pages.
5. Install Microsoft FrontPage 97 Server Extensions.
6. Choose Exit to close the Master Setup screen.

Development Workstation Configuration

The following hardware and software configuration is recommended for your development workstation:

- Pentium-compatible workstation (32MB RAM or more for Windows NT or 24MB RAM or more for Windows 95)
- Windows NT Workstation 4.0 or Windows 95
- Visual InterDev client components

To install the Microsoft Visual InterDev client components, follow these steps:

1. Run the Visual InterDev Master Setup program, `setup.exe`.
2. Open the installation instructions for the client components from the Master Setup. These instructions will help you with the rest of the installation process.
3. Install Visual InterDev client.
4. Install Microsoft Image Composer (optional).
5. Install Media Manager (optional).
6. Install Music Producer (optional).

> **NOTE**
>
> These four programs appear as buttons or hyperlinks on the main menu of the Master Setup program. Each uses a wizard to complete the installation. The wizards are easy to use; just follow the instructions as they appear in the wizard.

7. Choose Exit to close the Master Setup screen.

If you don't have Internet Explorer 3.01 installed, the setup process will also install this component for you. Internet Explorer (IE) is used as a component for viewing the HTML help topics integrated into Visual InterDev, as well as for viewing your finished Web pages. You can use other Web browsers for viewing your Web pages during development, but IE still needs to be installed for Visual InterDev to function correctly.

What Are All Those Extra Server Files?

When Visual InterDev creates a new Web on a Web server, it also creates a number of extra directories and files. These are all created directly under the root directory of the new Web site. Generally they have names with _vit and contain a number of DLLs and configuration files.

These files are used to maintain information about the files on your Web site, such as who last modified the file and what type of file it is. This information is updated by Visual InterDev and FrontPage Server Extensions. The files shouldn't be modified directly in any way.

These directories and files aren't visible to the author in the Visual InterDev development environment. Rather, Visual InterDev uses the information in these files when it presents dialog boxes and options to the author during the development process.

Using Visual InterDev

When you are working on a Web site with Visual InterDev, all the files that comprise your Web site are stored on the Web server. This is either a separate Web server computer, which your workstation can access via the Internet or an intranet, or your own machine's Web server if you're running Personal Web Server (Windows 95) or Peer Web Services (Windows NT). The files you create will be stored in the Internet publishing directory that you nominated during Web server setup.

When you add files to the Web site, or edit any of the existing files, Visual InterDev creates a second copy of the files on your local computer. This is called the *working copy*. If you're running a local Web server, Visual InterDev still creates a working copy of the files for editing. These copies are stored in Visual InterDev's designated projects folder—by default, that's `c:\Program Files\DevStudio\MyProjects`. Whenever these working copies are saved, Visual InterDev updates the file on the Web server as well.

The files in your Web site can be stored on any Web server to which you have access, as long as that Web server has FrontPage Server Extensions installed. Visual InterDev keeps track of where the files are stored on which Web server by using another local file called a *project file*. This file has an extension of `.dsp` and is stored in your `MyProjects` folder with your other local files. The project file enables you to connect to your Web site on the Web server every time you want to work on your Web site. Thus, a Web project is made up of the files stored on the Web server, plus the project file stored in your local folder.

Web Projects and Workspaces

To organize your work on multiple Web sites, Visual InterDev creates workspaces for you to use. A *workspace* is a container for your Web project; it also enables you to create new Web projects or to connect to existing Web projects on the Web server by generating a new project file. A workspace can contain more than one project and more than one type of project.

After you've created a Web project within your workspace, the directory that contains your local project file becomes your working directory for the entire project. Whenever a file is added to the project or copied from the Web server for editing, its working copy is added to this directory. Its location exactly matches the location of the file on the Web server, in relation to the root directory of the Web project. If a file is stored in a subdirectory on the Web server, that same subdirectory is automatically created in your local working directory.

If you're working on a Web site that's on a Web server on your local workstation (Personal Web Server or Peer Web Services), the process is identical. The project file is created in a working directory created by Visual InterDev. Files added to the project or copied for editing are also added to this working directory. Subdirectories are created to match the files' locations on the Web server. You end up with two copies of the files you're working on, but this system makes the development process identical for any Web server on which the Web site is hosted.

Multiple Projects in a Workspace

As mentioned earlier, a workspace can contain more than one project. Several Web projects can be contained within a single workspace, even if they're on different Web servers. The project files for each project keep track of which server the files are located on.

A workspace can also contain projects of different types. For example, a workspace can contain one or more Web or database projects. A workspace can also contain Visual C++ or Visual J++ projects.

Visual InterDev allows only one workspace at a time to be open. When you open a new workspace, the previous one—including all its projects—will be closed. If you want to work on more than one Web project at a time, add those projects to the same workspace. When you have multiple projects within a workspace, it's also easier to move files between the projects.

Opening a Workspace

To open an existing workspace in Visual InterDev, use the Open Workspace command on the File menu. By default, this command displays all the directories contained in the MyProjects folder. Each workspace has a local file with a .dsw extension. Double-clicking this file opens the workspace you created previously. For example, if you have created a workspace named MyWorkspace, a directory named MyWorkspace is in your MyProjects folder, and this directory will be displayed in the Open Workspace dialog box. Within this directory, you'll find the MyWorkspace.dsw file. Double-clicking this file opens your MyWorkspace workspace. All the projects you have added to the MyWorkspace workspace will be retrieved from their respective Web servers and opened as well.

The File menu also includes a Recent Workspaces command, which lists the last four workspaces that you've worked on. You can directly open any of these workspaces by using this menu command, without having to go through the Open Workspace dialog box.

If you want to create a brand new workspace, choose File | New. This action opens the New dialog box (see Figure 25.1), which provides many options for creating new files, projects, and workspaces. To create a blank workspace, click the Workspaces tab at the top of the dialog box, enter a name for your workspace in the blank Workspace Name field, and click OK. By default, your workspace will be created in the MyProjects folder, but you can change its location and store the workspace anywhere on your local workstation.

FIGURE 25.1.

Create a new workspace with the Workspaces page in the New dialog box.

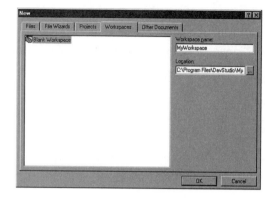

After you have created or opened a workspace, it's displayed in the left pane of the Visual InterDev window. By using the File View tab at the bottom of this pane, you can view all the projects and files contained within the workspace, listed hierarchically in their directories and subdirectories. With the Data View tab, you can view all the database connections contained within your workspace; you can access the extensive Visual InterDev help files with the Info View tab (see Figure 25.2). By default, the Info View tab is available when you launch Visual InterDev, whether or not you open any workspaces.

FIGURE 25.2.

Visual InterDev provides three different views of your project.

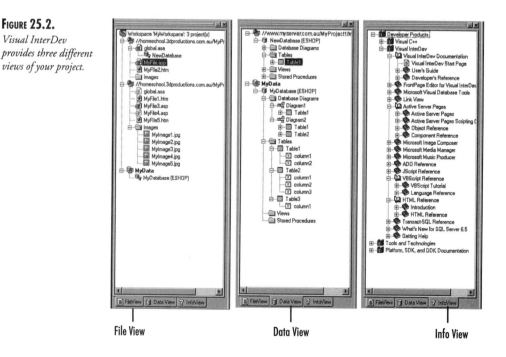

File View   Data View   Info View

Opening a Project

When you create a new workspace, it's displayed as a blank workspace containing `'0'` Projects. To create or edit a Web site, you must add a project to your workspace. As mentioned earlier, you can add multiple projects or projects of different types to a single workspace. This enables you to work on more than one Web site at a time.

To add an existing project to your workspace, you can use the menu command Project | Insert Project Into Workspace, or right-click the workspace name and choose the same command from the pop-up menu. This presents a dialog box, open by default to your `MyProjects` folder, to allow you to find the project you want to add to your workspace. A project is designated by its project file, which has a `.dsp` extension. Double-clicking this file adds the project to your workspace.

You can also add a new project to your workspace by choosing File | New or right-clicking the workspace name and choosing Add Project To Workspace from the pop-up menu. In either case, you get the New dialog box, which provides many options for creating files, projects, or workspaces. To create your new project, click the Projects tab. This displays a list of wizards to assist you in creating the project.

As when you created a workspace, you can give your project a name and change its location from the default `MyProjects` folder. Remember, this location will become your working directory when you start to add or edit files. If you intend to add the new project to your currently open workspace, you must also select the Add to Current Workspace option (as opposed to the Create New Workspace option, which is selected by default).

Depending on which wizard you choose, you'll have to follow a number of steps to complete the project. The next section discusses the process of creating a new Web project with the Web Project Wizard. The later section "Using Data Connections" covers the process of creating a new database project with the New Database Wizard.

Creating a New Web Project

As mentioned earlier, creating a new Web project involves Visual InterDev connecting to a Web server, either on a remote machine via the network or a Web server running on your local workstation (such as Personal Web Server or Peer Web Services). Visual InterDev creates a Web on the Web server, or connects to an existing Web and also creates a local project file and working directory.

The easiest way to accomplish this is to use Visual InterDev's Web Project Wizard. This automates all the tasks necessary to create and edit a Web on any Web server to which you have access, as long as the server has FrontPage Server Extensions correctly installed. Follow these steps:

1. Start the Web Project Wizard by choosing File | New or by right-clicking the name of the workspace and choosing Add Project to Workspace. In the New dialog box

(see Figure 25.3), click the Projects tab and then select Web Project Wizard from the list of available wizards.

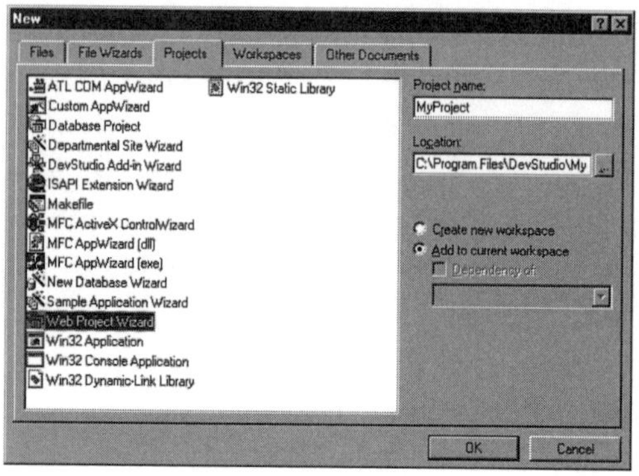

FIGURE 25.3.

Create a new workspace using the Projects tab in the New dialog box.

2. Specify a name for your Web project in the Project Name box. If you choose an invalid name, or a name that has been used previously, you'll get an error message and will be asked to choose a different name.

3. If desired, select the location for your Web project in the Location box. By default, this will be the MyProjects folder, but you can choose to save your Web project in any other location on your workstation. Remember that your project file will be stored in this location; it will also become your working directory when you start to add or edit files in your Web project.

4. If you want to add your Web project to a workspace that's already open in Visual InterDev, select the Add To Current Workspace option. You can then have multiple projects open within the same workspace, if you want. Alternatively, you can create a new workspace to contain your new Web project by selecting the Create New Workspace option. The new workspace will be created with the same name as your new project. (This option is selected by default.)

5. After you're satisfied that all the information is correct, click OK.

6. Specify the server where your new Web project will be hosted (see Figure 25.4). This can be any Web server to which you have access, either via the Internet or an intranet, as long as FrontPage Server Extensions is correctly installed. Type the name of the server using either its name (for example, **www.myserver.com.au**) or its IP address (for example, **192.168.1.1**). If you want to use a Web server running on your local workstation, such as Personal Web Server or Peer Web Services, type the name of your own computer (for example, **MyComputer**).

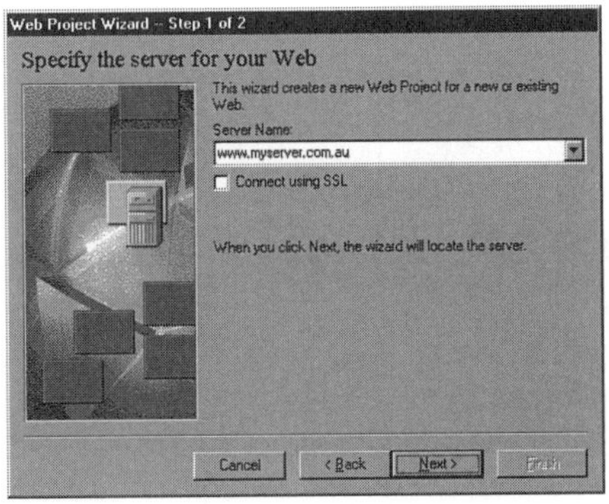

FIGURE 25.4.

Choose the server where your Web project will be hosted.

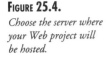

7. If you're connecting to an SSL (Secure Sockets Layer) Web server, select the Connect Using SSL check box. *SSL encryption* is a low-level protocol that enables secure communications between the server and a browser. If you access a Web site through the HTTP protocol (that is, your Web site address is `http://web.site.address`), the server is not SSL. If you use the HTTPS protocol (your Web site address is `https://web.site.address`), the server is SSL. If you're unsure whether the Web server to which you're connecting is SSL, check with the server administrator.

8. Click Next. Visual InterDev attempts to contact the specified Web server. This may take a few seconds. If Visual InterDev can't establish a connection to the Web server, you get an error message. This may occur if FrontPage Server Extensions hasn't been set up correctly on the server, or if you don't have proper access to the server. You can either change the Web server or cancel the operation.

9. If Visual InterDev is successful in establishing a connection to the Web server, it retrieves a list of existing Webs on that server (see Figure 25.5). You can choose to connect directly to an existing Web (selected from the drop-down list box) or create a new Web on that server. You can also specify whether you want Visual InterDev to index your Web site automatically for text searches.

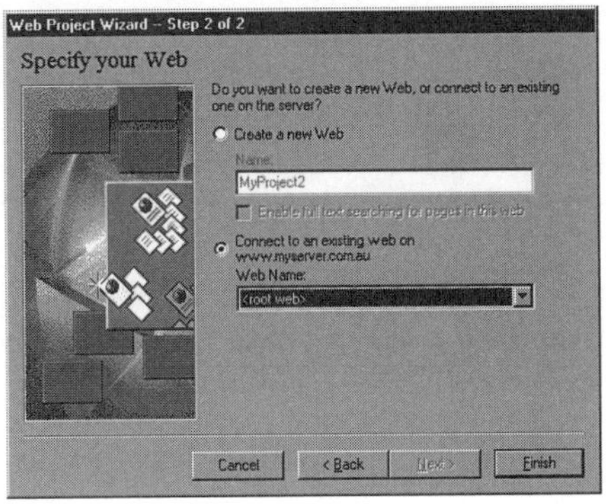

FIGURE 25.5.

Choose to connect to one of the existing Webs, or create a new one on the server.

25

USING VISUAL INTERDEV

10. Click Finish. Visual InterDev creates your project file and working directory and opens the new Web project in the workspace you specified in step 1.

You can click the File View tab at the bottom of the workspace to view all the files and subdirectories in your Web project or the Data View tab to view the data connections (if any). If you need help from Visual InterDev at any stage, click the Info View tab to bring up extensive help documents.

Whenever you want to open your Web project again, just open the workspace that contains the project. Visual InterDev connects to the server again to verify the current status of the Web project, and redisplays it in your workspace.

Adding Files to a Web

After you've created your workspace and added a Web project to it, you can then add, delete, move, or edit any of the files within that project. Any files that you alter in these ways will be copied into your local working directory. Whenever any of these files are saved, the copies on the Web server will also be updated.

With a new Web project, Visual InterDev creates a Global.asa file and, if you selected the full-text search option, a search.htm file within your project. An images directory will also be created for your images. But no other files will be in your Web project.

If you have connected to an existing Web, you may have a variety of files and subdirectories already within your project. You can view these with the hierarchical File View tab in a manner similar to viewing files in Windows Explorer.

To add files to any project, you can either add existing files from another source, including existing HTML, ASP, or multimedia files (images, animations, sounds, and so on), or create new files within Visual InterDev (such as .htm files or .asp files).

Adding Existing Files to a Web Project

You can add existing files to your Web project one at a time, or add the contents of an entire folder directly. Use the Project | Add To Project command and select either Files or Folder Contents. Browse through your local system or network, select the files or folder that you want to add to your project, and click OK. The files or folder will be added to your project in the location highlighted when you first selected the menu command.

Alternatively, you can simply right-click the project name and select Add Files or Add Folder Contents. Again, once you have browsed and found the files or folder you want to add, click OK. If you want to add them to a folder within your project other than the root directory, simply highlight where you want the files or folder added, and right-click that location.

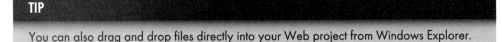

TIP

You can also drag and drop files directly into your Web project from Windows Explorer.

Whenever you add files or folders in any of these ways, Visual InterDev automatically copies them to the Web server and places copies in your local working directory.

Creating New Files for a Web Project

Instead of adding existing files to a Web project, Visual InterDev will help you create new files automatically. You can choose File | New or choose Projects | Add to Project | New. Both of these commands open the New dialog box. Make sure that the Add to Project option is checked at the upper-right corner of the dialog box.

You can then choose to create one of several file types, including .htm and .asp files, from the Files tab at the top of the dialog box. You can also choose to use one of the wizards from the File Wizards tab or create a document of another type from the Other Documents tab. Creating an HTML layout and using the Data Form Wizard are covered later in this chapter.

After selecting the type of file you want to create, give the file a name and click OK. Again, you can select a different location in which to save the file, although keeping all the project files together in your working directory is recommended.

Visual InterDev automatically creates the file with the appropriate headers and footers for that file type and opens the file in the working pane to the right of the workspace, allowing you to edit the file. If you close the file or choose File | Save, the file is saved both to your local working directory and to the Web server.

Previewing the Files

After you have saved a file, you can preview the file and see how it's displayed in a Web browser. Three methods are available:

- Highlight the file you want to browse and choose File | Preview in Browser, or right-click the file and choose Preview in Browser from the pop-up menu. Either action opens the file in the default browser installed on your workstation. When using Visual InterDev, this is often Internet Explorer.

- Right-click the file, choose Browse With from the pop-up menu, select any browser that you have installed on your workstation (such as Netscape Navigator), and click Open.

- Open the file with the Info Viewer, which displays the file in the working pane of Visual InterDev, in the same way that Info View files are opened for you to read. Use the Browse With command as just mentioned, but choose Info Viewer instead of a Web browser.

TIP

You can change which browser is set as the default by using the Browse With command. Select the browser you want to use and click the Set as Default button before you click Open. From then on, every time you use the Preview in Browser command, the file will be displayed in the specified default browser.

NOTE

Most browsers—including the Info Viewer and Internet Explorer—cache files by default. Be sure to click Refresh to update the version of the page you're viewing.

When viewing ASP pages, you'll notice that the page you're viewing has been stripped of all the server-side scripting. You can check this by using the View Source command from the browser. Only the HTML code is sent to the browser, which enables you to view ASP pages in any standard browser.

It's also possible to view the changes that you make to your files directly from the Web server. After you save the changes, the file on the Web server is automatically updated as well. You can then enter the URL of the online version of your Web project and view the final result. This is especially useful when you're developing a Web site with frames and you need to see how the page appears within the frameset layout.

Working Copies of Files

When you open a Web project, some of the file icons in the project hierarchy may be colored; others are gray. The colored icons indicate that you have a current working copy in your local working directory. If you try to edit a file whose icon is gray, Visual InterDev attempts to get a working copy from the Web server and copy it into your working directory for editing.

The request for a working copy will always succeed. Visual InterDev makes no effort to determine whether someone else has a working copy of your file and is currently editing it. However, if the copy of the file on the Web server is different from the local working copy, Visual InterDev asks whether you want to retain your local working copy or update to the master copy from the Web server. This may happen if someone else has edited the file since you last worked on the Web project.

When used in conjunction with Visual SourceSafe, on the other hand, Visual InterDev won't allow you to get a working copy of a file unless no one else currently has his or her own working copy for editing. This ensures that two people can't edit and update the same file at the same time.

You can retrieve working copies of a file or files at any time by highlighting the file(s) in the File View hierarchy and selecting the Get Working Copy command that appears when you right-click (see Figure 25.6).

FIGURE 25.6.
If you get a working copy of a file, its icon changes from gray to colored.

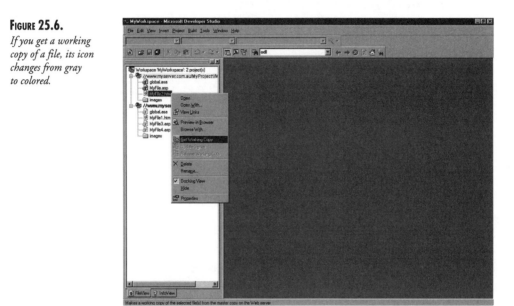

You can release the working copy of a file (or files) at any time by right-clicking the file(s) and selecting Release Working Copy. This command returns the icon to gray.

Some operations can be performed only after you release the working copy of a file—such as renaming it or moving it within the Web project. Releasing the working copy also enables another person to get a working copy and edit the file when the project is controlled by Visual SourceSafe.

Creating HTML Layouts

An HTML layout page is a file with an .alx extension. It appears in Visual InterDev as a blank grid on which you can position a variety of ActiveX controls, such as drop-down lists, radio buttons, command buttons, and so on. Using the HTML toolbar and the grids provided, you can place these controls on the page exactly where you want them to appear.

25

USING VISUAL INTERDEV

An HTML layout page can easily be created and added to your project by following the procedure for creating a new `.htm` or `.asp` page. From the New dialog box, select the HTML Layout from the Files tab, give the file a name, and click OK. The HTML Layout page will be created, added to your project, added to the Web on the Web server, and opened in the working pane to the right of the workspace.

Editing HTML Layouts

When Visual InterDev opens your HTML layout page in the working pane, it also opens the HTML Layout toolbox and HTML Layout toolbar. All the elements you can add to the HTML layout are available in the toolbox. Simply click the element you want to add and then click in the layout grid to position the element.

After you add an element to the layout, you can move or resize that element with the Arrow tool from the toolbox. Click the element with the Arrow tool; small sizing handles will appear in the corners and along all four sides. By dragging these sizing handles, you can precisely adjust the size, shape, and position of the element on the page.

Double-clicking any element brings up the Properties page, a list of various properties that you can set to customize the page. Right-clicking the element enables you to access the Script Wizard, which you can use to add scripts to give the elements various functionality triggered by different events.

When you're satisfied with your HTML layout (although, of course, you can edit it later), choose File | Save or close and save the file.

Inserting an HTML Layout into an HTML Page

After an HTML layout page has been created and saved, it can be inserted into any `.htm` or `.html` page quite easily. Simply open the HTML page for editing by double-clicking its filename in the File View hierarchy.

First, position your cursor where you want the HTML layout to appear. This must be between the `<BODY>` and `</BODY>` tags in the HTML file. Then choose Insert | Into HTML | HTML Layout or simply right-click the open HTML page and select Insert HTML Layout. You will then be able to choose which HTML layout page you want to insert into the page.

Visual InterDev automatically generates the code needed to insert the layout. After saving the file, you can preview it in your browser to make sure that the layout has been inserted correctly.

Displaying Your Web Project's Links

An extremely useful feature of Visual InterDev is the Link View facility, which enables you to view all the link relationships to and from any file that you select. This includes links to other HTML or ASP files, images and multimedia files, HTML layouts—even ActiveX controls and Java applets.

To view the links to and from a particular file, highlight that file in the File View hierarchy and choose View | Links. Alternatively, right-click the file and choose View Links. Either command opens the Link View in the working pane to the right of the workspace. The specified file is at the center of the view; all other files linked to it are arranged around it on the page (see Figure 25.7). Arrows indicate which way the hyperlink goes and whether it's two-way (that is, whether the linked page also links back to the center page). Broken links (that is, links to files that can't be found at the specified location) are depicted in red.

Figure 25.7.

Link View graphically displays all the hyperlinks contained within the file.

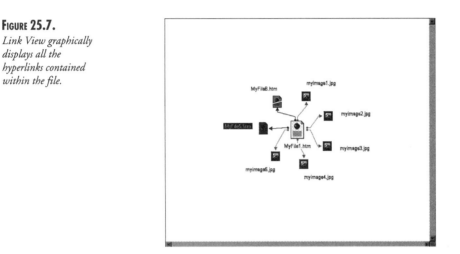

If you click any of the other files displayed, an additional set of links is overlaid in the Link View, showing the hyperlink relationship between that file and any others on the page. In this way, you can easily get a comprehensive, visual idea of the hyperlink structure between all files in your Web project.

If the Link View gets too crowded to be useful, you can filter out some of the detail. For instance, if you're only interested in hyperlinks to other HTML pages, choose the View | Filters command to turn the various options on and off. If you turn off all the multimedia files, more space is available for clearly viewing the HTML hyperlinks.

Double-clicking a file opens that file for editing. Right-clicking a file lets you make that file the center of the Link View, open it for editing, or preview it in a browser.

Displaying Links from Other Sites

Link View can also be used to display the hyperlink relationship from any site on the WWW. Choose Tools | View Links on WWW and enter the URL of the site you want to view. Visual InterDev retrieves the link information from the URL and displays it in the same way that it displays the link relationships from your own Web project.

Again, right-clicking any of the linked files enables you to make that file the center of the Link View, open it for editing, or preview it in a browser.

Updating Links

Visual InterDev can also update and repair any hyperlinks within your project that need to be altered when you rename or move a file. By default, whenever you rename or move a file you're asked whether you want Visual InterDev to check and update any hyperlinks referencing that file. You can choose Yes or No, but you can also choose to have Visual InterDev do this automatically each time without asking you (by selecting the check box at the bottom of this Renaming or Moving dialog box).

You can also set this option by choosing Tools | Options. Specify the Link Repair option on the Web Projects page, and hyperlinks will be updated automatically each time.

Editing Files

After you create files in your Web project, you can edit and manipulate them in many ways. Some of the easiest ways of doing this are outlined in the following sections.

Using the Source Editor

Visual InterDev contains its own *Source Editor*, a text editor for editing pages such as ASP and HTML files. It color codes much of the text in these files—highlighting code, HTML tags, keywords, comments, text, and so on in different colors for easy identification (see Figure 25.8).

To open a file in the Visual InterDev Source Editor, simply double-click its filename in the File View hierarchy. Alternatively, you can highlight the filename and choose File | Open or right-click the filename and choose Open. This is assuming that Visual InterDev has retained its default editor setting from its installation (changing the default editor is described in the next section).

With the file open in the Source Editor, it's easy to type HTML tags, text, scripts, or other components into the open file. The File | Save command saves all changes and automatically updates the changes to the Web server.

You can also add HTML layouts, ActiveX controls, design-time ActiveX controls, VBScript, JavaScript, and so on easily by using the commands on the Insert menu or by right-clicking in the file at the insertion point and using one of the commands that appears. These commands include Insert HTML Using Wizard, Insert HTML Layout, Insert ActiveX Control, and Script Wizard.

You can set many options with the Source Editor, including editing methods, color tags, interface, and so forth. Choose Tools | Options and change the settings as desired to customize the Source Editor to your particular style of working.

FIGURE 25.8.

The Source Editor enables you to edit the actual text of your files, including all tags and code.

```
<%@ LANGUAGE="VBSCRIPT" %>

<HTML>
<HEAD>
<META NAME="GENERATOR" Content="Microsoft Visual InterDev 1.0">
<META HTTP-EQUIV="Content-Type" content="text/html; charset=iso-8859-1">
<TITLE>Document Title</TITLE>
</HEAD>
<BODY>

<!-- Insert HTML here -->

<% Code and Script is Coloured Yellow in the Default Settings %>

This text will be displayed on the page when viewed in a browser.

</BODY>
</HTML>
```

Using the FrontPage Editor

In case you prefer to edit your HTML pages in a WYSIWYG editor, Visual InterDev comes with a cut-down version of FrontPage called *FrontPage for Visual InterDev*. This lets you edit your files in much the same manner as with a normal word processor, without having to type HTML tags for formatting. This greatly simplifies tasks such as inserting and editing tables, bookmarks, hyperlinks, bulleted lists, and the like.

FrontPage is best used for editing .htm and .html files only. If you use it to edit .asp or .alx files, the results may be unpredictable. The FrontPage for Visual InterDev editor tries to interpret the code elements that are part of .asp and .alx files; this can result in the code being changed in unexpected ways.

Opening Your HTML Page

If Visual InterDev still retains its default settings, you can open an .htm or .html file in FrontPage by highlighting the filename in the File View hierarchy and choosing File | Open With. Alternatively, right-click the filename and choose Open With from the pop-up menu that appears. FrontPage for Visual InterDev should appear on the list of editors that you can use to open the file. Just select it and click Open. FrontPage launches and displays the file (see Figure 25.9).

You're free to edit the file in any way. Whenever you save the changes, Visual InterDev automatically updates both the local working copy of the file and the copy on the Web server.

FIGURE 25.9.

With the FrontPage Editor for Visual InterDev, you edit HTML files in a WYSIWYG environment.

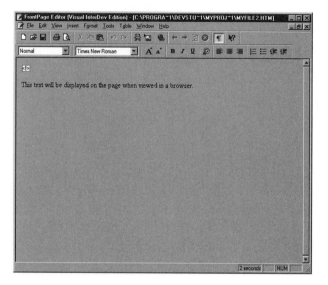

If you want to make FrontPage the default editor for editing `.htm` or `.html` files, use the Open With dialog box. After selecting FrontPage in the list of editors, simply click the Set as Default option before clicking Open. From then on, every time you double-click a file of that type in Visual InterDev, FrontPage is used to open the file.

> **NOTE**
>
> This setting applies only to files with that same extension. If you set FrontPage as the default editor for `.htm` files, `.html` files will still be opened in the Source Editor until you set the default for that file type as well.

Formatting Text

FrontPage uses many features to format and arrange text in a way similar to that of Microsoft Word. You can type text, highlight it, and use the various commands on the Format menu to obtain the desired results.

Many of these commands are also duplicated on the Formatting toolbar, with easy-to-use toolbar buttons for increasing or decreasing font size, changing font and font style, paragraph alignment, indenting and bulleting text, and many other features.

Inserting Other Elements

It's also easy to insert other elements into your HTML files using FrontPage. Commands on the Insert menu let you insert images and other multimedia files, hyperlinks, bookmarks, line breaks and horizontal lines, and so on. You can even insert other files, marquees, scripts, or components such as ActiveX controls and Java applets.

A couple of these most common tasks are outlined briefly in the following sections. However, if you prefer this style of editing (in which you don't have to worry about HTML tags), it's well worth further investigation of the advanced features of FrontPage for Visual InterDev.

Inserting an Image

To insert an image into your HTML file, position the cursor where you want the image to appear and choose Insert | Image. You can use the Browse button to find an image on your local workstation or network, or type the URL of an image that exists elsewhere on the Internet. FrontPage displays the image on the page for you to see.

It's a good idea to add the image to your project (the Images folder is a good place to keep all of your images) before adding it to your HTML file. You can then enter a relative URL in the From Location box (for example, `images/imagename.jpg`). If you have a local copy of the image, it's displayed in FrontPage for you to see. Otherwise, FrontPage places a reference to a local file on your hard drive, which won't work when other people view the page.

Inserting and Editing a Table

You can use the commands on the Table menu to insert and edit tables in much the same way that you do in Microsoft Word. To insert a table, choose Table | Insert Table. You can specify values for the table such as the number of columns and rows, alignment, border size, and so forth.

After the table is inserted, you can type text, insert images, and so on directly into the appropriate cells in the table. You can also edit the cell, row, column, or table properties by right-clicking that part of the table and selecting the appropriate command. All the text within the table can be formatted in the same way as normal text.

Creating and Following a Hyperlink

To create a hyperlink, type the text that you want to display the hyperlink in the finished file. Highlight that text and choose Insert | Hyperlink. You can then type the URL of the file to which you want to direct the link. The tabs at the top of the dialog box simplify the process of selecting a URL from the World Wide Web, linking to another file that you already have open, or linking to a new file that hasn't yet been created. If you want to link to another file in your Web project, just type the relative URL (for example, `subfolder/filename.html`).

You can follow hyperlinks that you have created in FrontPage by right-clicking the hyperlink and choosing the Follow Hyperlink command. This opens the target file in FrontPage for you to view or edit.

Changing the Background Color

You can change the background color, include a background image, and change the text color and other features of your page by using the Format | Background command. You can type the name of an image to use for the background, or browse to find the image on your local system.

> **NOTE**
>
> The choice of text and background colors can make a great deal of difference to the
> impact and readability of your page. Some text/background color combinations are
> extremely difficult to read or annoying to viewers.

Viewing the Results

After making the changes to your HTML file, you can save the file by choosing File | Save.
This updates the file in your local working directory and on the Web server. You can then view
the file by choosing Preview in Browser, either from FrontPage itself or from Visual InterDev.

Working with Third-Party Content Editors

If you prefer to edit your files in a different editor than the ones provided by Visual InterDev,
choose File | Open With from the menu or by right-clicking the filename. If your installed
editor isn't listed in the Open With dialog box, you can add it by clicking the Add button.
This enables you to type the path and filename of your preferred editor, or to browse through
your local system to find the correct path and filename.

After you've added the editor to the list, use the Open With command every time you want to
open a file in that editor, or set the editor as default for certain file types.

Use this strategy to edit your files in a different text editor than Source Editor (such as Notepad,
Programmer's File Editor, and so on), to use a different HTML editor than FrontPage, to add
different browsers for viewing completed files, or to add your preferred image, sound, or animation editors for use with multimedia files.

Whichever editor you choose, whenever you save the file Visual InterDev still automatically
updates the file copy on the server, as well as your local working copy. If you're using Visual
SourceSafe, you are also assured that no one else can access these files while you're editing the
working copies in your favorite editor.

Adding Graphics and Multimedia

The ability to use third-party editors, as well as the multimedia editors that can be installed
with Visual InterDev (Microsoft Image Composer for graphics and Microsoft Music Producer
for sound), enable you to create truly fantastic Web sites with superb images, animation, and
sound relatively easily.

Further information about these programs is available through the Info View help files in
Visual InterDev or from the software documentation.

Before adding any multimedia file to your Web site, it's best to add the file to your project, as
described earlier. The Images folder is always a good place to store images and other multimedia

files. You can then add the multimedia elements to your Web pages using any of your preferred HTML editors, FrontPage, or the Source Editor.

After opening a file in the Source Editor, position the cursor where you want to insert the image or other multimedia file. You can then type the appropriate HTML tags, such as `<IMG SRC>` or `<BGSOUND>`. You can also insert ActiveX controls to handle your multimedia, such as the ActiveMovie control.

You can also insert ActiveX controls into your HTML layout files using the HTML Layout editor, which will then appear on HTML pages that reference those HTML layouts.

Opening Multimedia Files

You can open any of the multimedia files that have been added to your Web project at any time to view them or edit them. Double-clicking the filename in the File View hierarchy opens the file in the default program assigned to that file type.

Alternatively, you can use the Open With command and choose an editor with which to open the file. You can also set your preferred editor as the default for files of that type by selecting the Set As Default option in the Open With dialog box. In this way you can use any preferred graphics, animation, sound, or video editor to view and edit your multimedia files.

Using Data Connections

One of the most powerful features of Visual InterDev is its capability to simplify the task of designing, connecting, and manipulating databases. Databases can truly make your Web sites interactive and much more useful to the people viewing and using the pages.

This section briefly covers these tasks:

- Creating a new SQL database with the New Database Wizard
- Connecting to an existing database by adding a new database connection to your Web project
- Viewing the various elements of a database with Data View
- Creating, editing, and deleting database objects with the Database Designer
- Designing and editing database queries with the Query Designer

Using the New Database Wizard

The New Database Wizard can be used to create a new database on any SQL server to which you have access. To access the New Database Wizard, choose File | New, select the Projects tab, and click the New Database Wizard.

This wizard will create a new project to contain your database. You should therefore decide whether you want to add the database project to your existing workspace or create a new workspace for it. Then specify a name for your database project. When you're satisfied with the settings for these options, click OK.

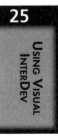

The first screen of the wizard asks you to specify the SQL server to host your database. It also asks for a user ID and password to access the SQL server. If you're unsure about any of these details, contact the server administrator. When you have typed the server name, user ID, and password, click Next. Visual InterDev attempts to establish a connection to the SQL server. If this fails for any reason, you're given the option to reenter your details or cancel the operation.

If Visual InterDev succeeds in connecting to the SQL server, you get further options as to the location and size of your new database. Again, if you're unsure, contact the server administrator. After entering these details on each page, click Next. After the fourth page of the wizard, click Finish. Visual InterDev creates the database for you.

The database project is opened in your existing workspace or the new workspace, depending on what you specified in the first step. You can then use the Data View tab to view the various elements of the database. You can also establish data connections to the new database from your existing Web projects.

Adding a Database Connection

After creating a Web project and a database, you can establish a connection from one to the other. This will allow your forms and script to access and update all the data contained within the database. To create this database connection, follow these steps:

1. Choose Projects | Add to Project | Database Connection, or right-click the project name in the File View hierarchy and choose Add Data Connection.

2. You will be prompted for a DSN (data source name). Select one from the list or create a new one by clicking New. If you create a new DSN, you can also select the type of drivers needed to connect to your database.

3. Click OK.

4. Make sure that the server name, user ID, and password are correct. If you're unsure about any of these details, contact the server administrator.

5. Click the Options button to display further options, including a drop-down list of all the databases stored on the SQL server. Specify which database you want to connect to.

6. Click OK. Visual InterDev creates the data connection between your Web project and your database. It stores the server, user ID, and password information, although some servers (for security reasons) require that you enter this information every time your Web project connects with the database.

Data source information is also inserted into the Session_OnStart event procedure in your Global.asa file. The runtime properties of the database (right-click the database connection in File View and choose Properties) include the user ID and password. You can change these settings to create different security permissions for users when running your Web application, as opposed to the security permissions available to developers while creating the Web project.

The database connection is inserted into your project under the Global.asa and can be viewed there in File View. The connection and all the database elements can also be viewed using the Data View tab (described in the next section).

Working in Data View

In a way similar to that with which File View presents a hierarchical list of all the files, folders, subdirectories, and other elements contained within a Web project, Data View presents a hierarchical view of all the elements contained within a database (see Figure 25.10). When you have established a connection to the database, click the Data View tab at the bottom of your workspace. You can then view any database diagrams, tables, views, and stored procedures that have been created.

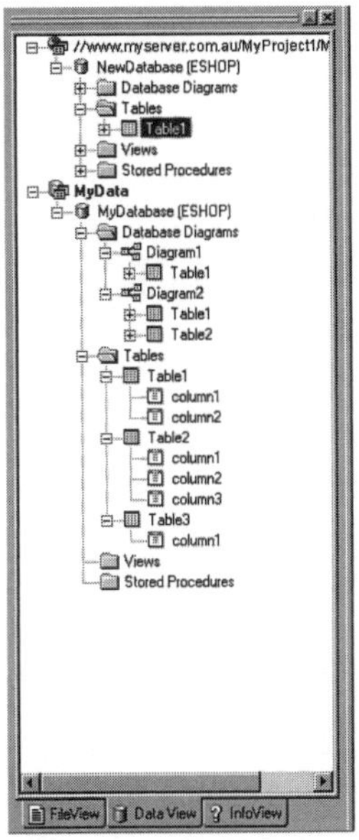

FIGURE 25.10.

The Data View tab shows all of the database elements hierarchically.

Further functions are available by double-clicking any of the individual database elements, some of which are briefly covered in the following sections. Or you can right-click the elements to gain further information.

Creating and Editing Tables with the Database Designer

The *Database Designer* provides an easy-to-use graphical interface to perform many of the functions of setting up and maintaining your database. You can create and edit tables, including table columns and properties and table relationships. Features such as drop-down lists simplify tasks such as changing a data field type. You can also create database diagrams for the tables in your database.

> **NOTE**
>
> You must have appropriate permissions to create or edit tables in your database. If you think permissions are causing problems, consult the SQL server administrator.

You can create a new table in your database by selecting the database in Data View and choosing Insert | New Database Item. Alternatively, right-click the `Tables` folder from the Data View hierarchy and select the New Table command. Choose a name for your new table and click OK. The Database Designer opens in your working pane, to the right of the workspace. You can type names for as many columns as you want the table to contain. Clicking the Datatype box provides a drop-down list of datatypes from which to choose (see Figure 25.11).

FIGURE 25.11.

The Database Designer provides a graphical interface for creating and editing tables.

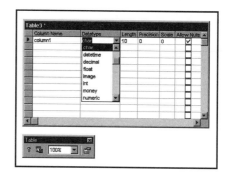

Once you've selected a datatype, the other fields will adopt default values, but you can edit these if you choose. You can also edit the table properties and create index keys from the Table toolbar. When finished, close the Database Designer and save your table.

You can edit the properties of any table by highlighting the table name in Data View and choosing View | Design. Alternatively, right-click the table name in Data View and select the Design command. This command reopens the Database Designer and enables you to edit any of the columns or fields in the table.

You can also add and edit records contained within the table. Simply highlight the table name in Data View and choose File | Open, right-click the table name and choose Open, or double-click the table name. This opens the table and enables you to create and edit any of the records contained in it.

Creating a Database Diagram

In addition to creating and editing tables, the Database Designer can also create and edit *database diagrams*. These diagrams make it easy to establish connections and relationships between all the tables in your database.

To create a new database diagram, select the Database Diagrams folder in Data View and choose Insert | New Database Item, or right-click the folder name in Data View and select the New Database Diagram command.

The Database Designer opens with a blank working space. You can drag and drop any of your tables onto the Database Designer and then drag and drop columns from your tables into each other (see Figure 25.12). The Database Designer prompts you to specify the type of relationship that you want to create.

FIGURE 25.12.

The Database Designer enables you to create and edit database diagrams.

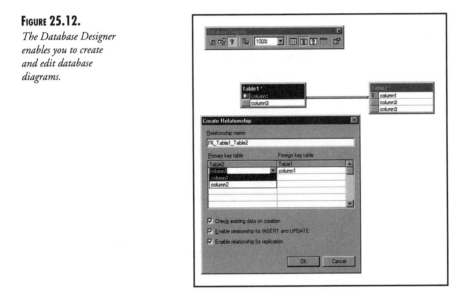

When you have set up the relationships to your satisfaction, close the Database Designer, remembering to save the changes. You must also indicate that you want to update the tables changed in your database diagram.

After creating a relationship in this way, you can edit it by clicking the line joining the tables and selecting Properties on the Relationship Property page.

Using the Query Designer

In the same way that the Database Designer simplifies the process of creating and editing database elements such as tables and diagrams, the Query Designer simplifies the creation and editing of database queries, without need for SQL coding.

The Query Designer is started from either a data range header control (see the next section) or a data command design-time ActiveX control. Simply right-click in the code representing the control and select Properties. You can then choose the SQL Builder button (see the next section for details on setting the properties).

Once you have specified or edited your query, the design-time ActiveX control automatically generates and updates the script needed to perform the query on your database. It also handles the returned results, generating a dynamic Web page based on the results of the query by generating a standard HTML script to allow the page to be viewed in any Web browser.

A number of these design-time ActiveX controls, two of which are briefly discussed in the following sections, are available with Visual InterDev. Third-party developers can also create and use their own design-time ActiveX controls.

Adding a Data Range Header Control

You can add a *data range header control* to your page to enable you to build SQL queries in the Query Designer. It automatically generates the script to cause the server to display the returned results in HTML.

First, open your .asp file in the Source Editor. Position the cursor where you want to insert the control. Choose Insert | Into HTML | ActiveX Control. Alternatively, you can right-click at the insertion point and choose the Insert ActiveX Control command. Select the Data Range Header Control from the Design-Time page. This will display the Properties page of the Data Range Header Control. Choose the database from the drop-down list of the data connections currently in your Web project. Various other options can also be set; these are explained in detail in the Info View topic page titled "Data Range Header Control."

Building the Query

After you've set all the options in the Properties page of the data range header control, click the SQL Builder button to start the Query Designer (see Figure 25.13). Drag and drop the tables that you want to query onto the blank workspace in the Query Designer.

FIGURE 25.13.

The Properties page from a data range header or data command control lets you access the Query Designer.

Select the columns you want to query. You can sort a column easily using the icons on the Query toolbar. Toolbar functions also include building an INSERT query, UPDATE query, or DELETE query.

The SQL generated by the Query Designer appears in the SQL window in the Query Designer and is updated as you build your query (see Figure 25.14). You can test your query at any time by using the Run button on the SQL toolbar. When you're happy with the query, close the Query Designer, remembering to save the changes. Click Yes when prompted to update your database connections.

FIGURE 25.14.

The Query Designer helps you to build SQL queries.

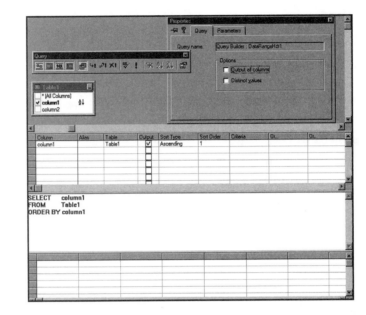

The Query Designer generates the script needed to perform the query from your Web page. You can edit existing ActiveX design-time controls by opening your file in the Source Editor, right-clicking in the generated code, and selecting Edit Design-Time Control.

Adding the Records to Display

After adding the data range header control, you must add the records that you want to display. Bring up the Properties page for the data range header control as described earlier, and click the Copy Fields button. This prompts you to select which fields from the returned results you want to display on the Web page.

Visual InterDev copies the correct script to display those fields onto the Clipboard. Close the data range header control and position the cursor after the code generated by the data range header control in the file. Choose Edit | Paste; the script is pasted into the file from the Clipboard.

Adding a Data Range Footer Control

After you're happy with your query and with the fields that you're displaying from the results returned, you must add another design-time ActiveX Control. The *data range footer control* is added in the same manner as the data range header control, positioned after the code that has been generated so far.

The default properties can generally be accepted for the data range footer control, although you can edit them if required. Close the Properties page and the Control Editor, and the data range footer control generates the script and automatically inserts it into the file. You can then close and save the file and view the results in your browser.

Using the Data Form Wizard

Another feature of Visual InterDev is that it enables you not only to display the results of a query to a database, but to generate forms with which users of your Web site can add to or edit information in the database via Web browser.

The easiest way to accomplish this is with the Data Form Wizard. Choose File | New and select the File Wizards tab in the New dialog box (see Figure 25.15). Click Data Form Wizard, specify a filename and location, and click OK.

FIGURE 25.15.

Create a new data form by using the File Wizards tab in the New dialog box.

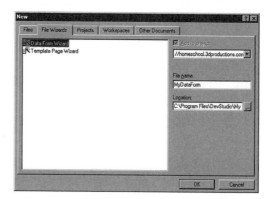

From the first page of the wizard, select the database to which you want to connect in the drop-down list. (Alternatively, you can choose to create a new database connection, in which case you go through the procedure outlined previously.) You must also specify a title to appear at the top of your form.

The second page of the wizard asks you to choose whether a table, a view, a stored procedure, or a SQL statement will be used to generate the record set for this data form.

The third page asks you to specify which fields will be displayed on the data form. You can also rearrange the order using the up and down arrows.

The fourth page asks you to assign the level of security privileges you want users to have. You can choose to let users browse the form only, modify existing records, add or delete records, and return feedback. You can also allow information to be filtered.

The fifth page allows you to choose whether you want your form displayed in List View, Form View, or both. You can also choose whether or not to display a status line.

The sixth page gives you the option of giving your data form one of the themes included with Visual InterDev. The theme assigns a background image, text colors, and other formatting of your data form to an arrangement designed to be pleasing to the eye.

When you're satisfied with your selections on each page, click Next to proceed to the next one. On the seventh page, click Finish to exit the wizard.

If you selected both List View and Form View, the Data Form Wizard generates three .asp pages named FormNameList.asp, FormNameAction.asp, and FormNameForm.asp. You can preview the results of your data form by viewing FormNameForm.asp in your browser.

Using Client-Side Scripting

Visual InterDev can be used to insert client-side script into your HTML pages in a number of ways, including inserting ActiveX controls, VBScript, or JavaScript elements by using the Script Wizard. Of course, you can simply edit files in the Source Editor and type all the script yourself.

Inserting ActiveX Controls

Visual InterDev makes it easy to insert ActiveX Controls into your HTML files using either the Source Editor or FrontPage. Simply open the HTML file in the editor and position the cursor where you want to insert the control.

If you are using Source Editor, choose Insert | Into HTML | ActiveX Control. Alternatively, you can right-click at the insertion point and select the Insert ActiveX Control command when it appears.

You'll be asked to select the name of the ActiveX Control (or design-time ActiveX control) from the available list. Click OK. This will present you with the Properties page for the ActiveX control. After you set the properties, close the Properties page and the Control Editor. The necessary code is generated and inserted into your file at the appropriate point.

In FrontPage, choose Insert | Other Components | ActiveX Control. You can choose an ActiveX control from the Pick a Control box, or type the control's class ID number. If you want to set the properties for the control, click Properties. The ActiveX control is inserted into the page when you close the Properties dialog box.

In both of these cases, the ActiveX control is inserted between <OBJECT> and </OBJECT> tags in your HTML file.

Using the Script Wizard

You can also add VBScript and JavaScript to your HTML files with the Script Wizard. This is an easy way of generating the script to add with a simple, visual programming interface. You can start the Script Wizard from either the Source Editor or the HTML Layout Editor by choosing View | Script Wizard. Alternatively, you can right-click in the open file and choose the Script Wizard command.

The Script Wizard lets you work on your VBScript or your JavaScript in either List View or Code View. List View provides a simplified, point-and-click interface for your programming. You can associate methods and properties listed in the Action pane with objects in the Events pane. Script Wizard automatically updates the script generated. Code View just lists the code and lets you edit it directly.

The script inserted is placed between `<SCRIPT>` and `</SCRIPT>` tags.

Using Server-Side Scripting

Active Server Pages (ASP pages, with the extension `.asp`) are easy to create in Visual InterDev. Active Server Pages contain code that's executed on the server when the page is accessed by a user, and dynamically generates an HTML page for the user to browse. Unlike client-side script, Active Server script is embedded between `<%` and `%>` tags. Script can be added to `.asp` pages in a number of languages, including VBScript, JavaScript, and Perl.

ASP pages can also contain HTML code and client-side script (described in the preceding section) that isn't processed by the server.

Creating an Active Server Page

Many of Visual InterDev's controls and wizards create `.asp` pages automatically. You can create your own `.asp` page by choosing File | New. In the New dialog box, select the Files tab and click `.asp` Page. After specifying a filename and location, click OK; a new `.asp` page is generated and opened in the Source Editor.

You can close and save this blank `.asp` file; it will be added to the files on the Web server. Or you can type your script into the file before saving and closing. The file can then be previewed in your browser.

Working with Design-Time ActiveX Controls

Another method for adding script to your ASP page is to use one of the design-time ActiveX controls to generate this server-side script for you. Insert your design-time ActiveX control in the same way that you would insert any other ActiveX control, and view the Properties page that opens.

After setting the properties for your design-time ActiveX control, close the Properties page; the Control Editor and Visual InterDev insert the script into your .asp file.

Each of the design-time ActiveX controls performs a different task, generating different script for your ASP file. You can find out more about the design-time ActiveX controls through the Info View files in Visual InterDev.

Managing Your Site

There are many more features to Visual InterDev that can assist you in the creation and maintenance of your Web sites. These are further documented in Info View. Various functions let you move, rename, add, and delete elements; automatically repair and update links throughout your site; and generate powerful server-side and client-side scripts.

Working in Teams

Visual InterDev enables you to work effectively in teams with other people on the same Web site project. By allowing programmers, HTML authors, graphic designers, and copywriters to work on the same project, a much higher-quality and more extensive Web site can be created than by any one of these people alone.

Even without Visual SourceSafe protection, Visual InterDev will notify all users if a file has been edited or changed by another person.

Visual SourceSafe

By putting a Web project under Visual SourceSafe protection, Visual InterDev protects files from potential editing conflicts, preserves backup copies to undo unwanted revisions, and negotiates between all of the people working on the project.

FrontPage 97 Compatibility

By interoperating with FrontPage 97, Visual InterDev allows programmers and HTML authors to work together on the same project. Any Web created by FrontPage 97 can be opened and edited by Visual InterDev, and any project created by Visual InterDev can be opened and edited by FrontPage 97.

Moving a Web

It's possible to move a Web site from one server to another with Visual InterDev. This might be done once a Web site has been completely developed and needs to be hosted on its destination server. Choose Project | Copy Web and enter the new server name. This command works via the HTTP protocol, so you can move Web sites through firewalls.

Summary

As this chapter shows, Visual InterDev enables you to easily perform many of the complex programming and database tasks required in the creation of a Web site, as well as the incorporation of HTML formatting and layouts, graphics, and other multimedia components. Its architecture allows for fully distributed development among a team of people, independent of their physical locations. This means that content developers, graphic designers, multimedia artists, HTML authors, database engineers, and programmers can all work on the same Web site project. The combination of these various skills can create a more sophisticated, visually exciting, and interactive Web site than any of the individuals could create alone.

Using Microsoft
Image Composer

CHAPTER 26

Microsoft Image Composer is an application that enables you to easily create graphic compositions consisting of new or existing images. You can retrieve images into Microsoft Image Composer from various sources, such as an existing graphics file, a TWAIN-compliant (see sidebar) scanning device, or a photo CD. The file formats that Microsoft Image Composer supports include TIFF (.tif), CompuServe GIF (.gif), Targa (.tga), JPEG (.jpg), Windows bitmap (.bmp), and Adobe Photoshop 3.0 (.psd).

WHY USE TWAIN ?

The standard *TWAIN* (Technology Without an Interesting Name) describes a software protocol—an application programming interface (API) for communication between image applications and image acquisition hardware. The great advantage of TWAIN is that application programmers only need to write code for one device in order to support many devices, and the device vendor's product is more widely supported when supplying a TWAIN driver for the acquisition hardware. This standard applies to flatbed scanners, frame grabbers (interfaces to CCD cameras), and image databases.

Microsoft Image Composer is an ideal application for use in conjunction with your Web pages and Web page applications. In just moments you can create that certain effect you're looking for to make your site look sharp.

The best part of Microsoft Image Composer is its simplicity, or ease of use. The interface is very user-friendly, and, as with most Microsoft software, the menus are straightforward and in standard Windows format, making it easy to get the job done.

This chapter starts by going over the features of Microsoft Image Composer, beginning with the visible features located on the user interface and then going into detail about the menu options. While you begin to understand where all the "controls" are located, you can apply what you're learning to a few example images along the way.

Features of Microsoft Image Composer

Before you can use Microsoft Image Composer, you need to install it! You can obtain a copy with FrontPage 98 or with Visual InterDev. You'll need about 16MB for a minimal install. That means installing just the Image Composer and the Impressionist Plug-In. If you add the tutorial and help files, make it 28MB.

TIP

A full install would require 292MB, but most of that is art samples, and they're better left on the install CD. You can access the art from the CD at any time, opening the art and inserting it into current images. There's no sense wasting hard disk space when you don't have to.

After installing Microsoft Image Composer, start the program (see Figure 26.1).

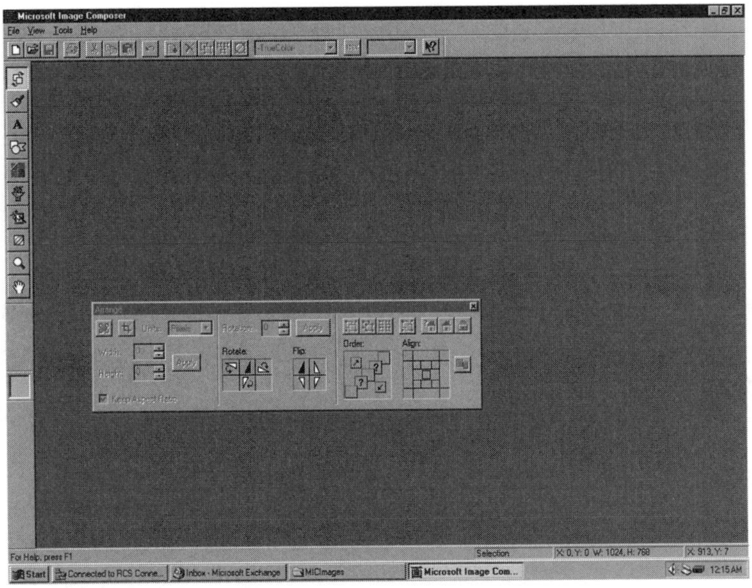

FIGURE 26.1.

The Microsoft Image Composer user interface.

You should become familiar with the three general control areas in Image Composer:

- The active feature control area
- The feature palette control area
- The menu/toolbar control area

The following paragraphs go over each area and its features to help you better understand what options are available to you, and try out some features along the way to make them easier to understand.

TIP

As with any software product that you're unfamiliar with, you shouldn't try to do actual work with Image Composer as soon as you install it. You'll get frustrated and perhaps end up blaming the product and hating it. Always experiment with new software and learn the features before you need to apply it for working purposes. With this approach, you'll be more productive and much more successful in your endeavors—not to mention avoiding wasted time and frustration.

You should also be familiar with the following terms before starting to work with Image Composer:

- **Sprite.** In this case, a sprite isn't a refreshing soft drink; instead, it's the basic image component of Image Composer. You can move sprites using the click-and-drag method with your mouse, the same way you move icons and other visible items on the Windows 95 desktop. When you insert an image onto an Image Composer workspace, it's automatically converted into a sprite. That doesn't mean that the source file from which the image was obtained was altered—just the working copy of the image.

- **Palette.** A palette is something you use to paint with. It contains the colors that are available to you in creating an image, whether in real life or onscreen. Image Composer has eight different feature palettes with specific controls that depend on the feature selected.

- **ToolTip.** As with most Microsoft controls, placing the mouse pointer over a control or option in Image Composer displays a small yellow tag called a ToolTip. This gives you a hint about what the command or tool actually does.

The following sections describe the controls and their associated palettes.

The Toolbox

The *toolbox*, shown in Figure 26.2, displays the current (active) control as a "pressed" toolbar button. There are 10 tool controls, 8 of which have associated control palettes that appear when the tool is selected. Table 26.1 shows the individual tools; the following sections describe each tool and its use in detail.

FIGURE 26.2.

The toolbox.

Table 26.1. Tools in the Image Composer toolbox.

Tool	Name
	Arrange
	Paint
	Text

Tool	Name
	Shapes
	Patterns and Fills
	Warps and Filters
	Art Effects
	Color Tuning
	Zoom
	Pan

The Arrange Tool

The *Arrange tool* (shown in Figure 26.3) is the default tool that's selected when you start an Image Composer session. This tool is used for arranging and positioning image sprites on your workspace. When selected, the sprite appears to have a highlighted border and eight sizing handles (see Figure 26.4). If you deselect the image, the palette controls are deactivated.

FIGURE 26.3.

Use the Arrange tool to arrange and position image sprites.

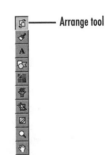

──── Arrange tool

FIGURE 26.4.

A selected sprite with sizing handles.

Controlling Size and Location

The sizing handles—white boxes with arrows pointing away from the image—enable dynamic resizing of the image sprite. If you click a handle and drag it, the image distorts to the shape you stretch it into. If you want to make certain the shape retains its *aspect ratio* (the way it looks without distortion), hold down the Shift key while resizing. This forces the image to retain its aspect ratio.

The handle in the upper-right corner shows a different type of arrow. This circular arrow allows dynamic rotation of the image. Also, when a sprite is selected, certain sprite attributes are displayed on the Arrange palette (see Figure 26.5). The Arrange palette gives you control of the image's size, location, grouping, and more, as described in this section and the following sections.

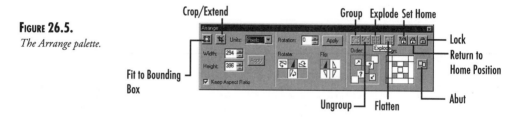

Figure 26.5.

The Arrange palette.

The Width and Height boxes show the current sprite's size measured either by pixels or original percentage, depending on the setting in the Units drop-down list. When you change either the width or the height, the Apply button is activated, enabling you to apply your recent changes. You can use the spin arrows located directly to the right of the Height and Width boxes to change the values, or simply type the new value into the appropriate text box.

If the Keep Aspect Ratio check box is selected when you make a change to either the width or the height, the item opposite the one you changed is also changed automatically, to reflect a proper image based on the image's aspect ratio. This ensures that any changes made won't distort the image (just like using the Shift key when dragging the image with the sizing handles).

To the left of the Units option are two buttons. The button on the left, Fit to Bounding Box, resizes the image to fit the box in which it is bound or contained. This isn't necessary unless you change the image's bounding box by using the button on the right, Crop/Extend. The Crop/Extend button crops the currently selected image—eliminating unnecessary image space—or extends the bounding box for enlarging the image. If you extend the box and then want to return the bounds to just the image, use the Fit to Bounding Box button.

Rotating and Flipping

If you change the setting in the Rotation box, the Apply button in that section of the palette becomes active. Clicking Apply rotates the selected image inside its bounding box *x* degrees to the right, where *x* represents the value you type, from 1–360 (degrees in a circle). Keep in mind that 360 and 0 do the same thing—nothing. If you type 360, Image Composer makes you wait as if it's going to do something. If you type 0 and click Apply, no action is taken.

Using Microsoft Image Composer

CHAPTER 26

671

26

USING
MICROSOFT
IMAGE COMPOSER

The Rotate and Flip boxes enable you to instantly manipulate the image, depending on which white area you select. For rotation, the options are to rotate 90 degrees to the left, rotate 90 degrees to the right, and rotate 180 degrees (which doesn't require a direction, because rotating 180 degrees in either direction gives the same result). For flipping, the options are to flip horizontally, flip vertically, or flip both ways.

Working with Sprite Groups

The last section of the Arrange palette has seven buttons at the top. Left to right, the first three are for grouping, the middle button is for flattening, and the last three are for anchoring and home positions.

If you want to create a sprite group, select each sprite by Shift-clicking each image. That is, hold down the Shift key while clicking each image. To deselect a sprite, Shift-click it again. After the items are selected, click the first grouping button, named Group. Vòila! You have just created your first group. To ungroup this item, simply click the next button, Ungroup. The sprites are all still selected, but you can see that they have been separated from the group. One reason for grouping sprites is that, when creating *composite images* (images made up of one or more sprites), you may need to move them together while arranging. Grouping is one way to make sure that you get all the pieces of the composite moved at the same time. Grouping simply turns many images into one—a composite image.

Using the Explode button to the right of the Ungroup button is the same as clicking Ungroup, but it keeps any subgroups that may be contained in the main group intact and separated. If you're happy with a group that you have created and want to make sure that you or others don't ungroup it by accident, you may choose to *flatten* the group, creating a single sprite from it. This is accomplished by using the Flatten button, directly to the right of the Explode button. Once this is done, it can only be undone by immediately choosing Edit | Undo command from the menu (or pressing Ctrl+Z). Be certain you want to flatten a group before you do it.

The home and anchoring buttons to the right of the Flatten button make it possible to set a *home position* for a sprite and to lock down a sprite so you don't accidentally move it when moving other sprites. The Set Home button (the one with the question mark) allows you to declare the original (home) position for the currently selected sprite. If you subsequently move the sprite and decide you want it moved back to its original position, click the button to the right of the Set Home button, called Return to Home Position. That will return your sprite to its declared home position. The Lock button to the right of the Return to Home Position button enables you to anchor your sprite so that it won't be moved accidentally while performing other tasks. This is useful when you have made up your mind that the image belongs just where it is.

The Order and Align options display graphical representations of how the sprite appears onscreen. The Order setting controls the Z-order positioning (layering) of your sprite (front to back). *Z-order* is the position of the image sprite in relation to other image sprites in the current composition. Where X is the horizontal position of your image and Y is the vertical position, Z is the "front-to-back" position. The Align option controls alignment of your sprite with respect to other sprites currently on the screen. First select a sprite, then move your mouse cursor over a white region in the Order or Align area; the ToolTips that appear will describe the options available to you. Just click the option that suits you.

Last but not least is the Abut button. When a sprite is selected, this command allows you to align the left side of the selected sprite to the right side of the subsequent sprite selection. This can be handy when you have two images that need to be edge-aligned on opposite sides of each image—for example, when using two images to create a mirror-image effect.

The Paint Tool

The *Paint tool* (shown in Figure 26.6) is used to enhance your images through various artistic means. When the tool is selected, the Paint palette becomes visible (see Figure 26.7).

FIGURE 26.6.

Use the Paint tool to "paint" parts of the image with various colors and textures.

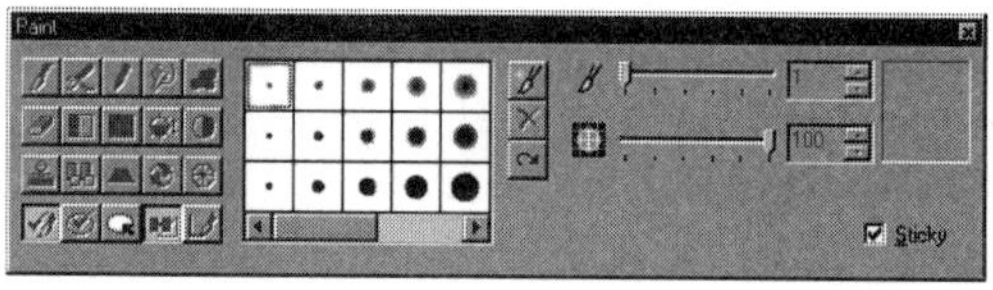

—— Paint tool

FIGURE 26.7.

The Paint palette.

The Paint palette consists of three areas. At the left side of the palette are 20 buttons that you can use to select the specific type of paint tool you want to use. The top three rows are brush types; the bottom row is brush modifiers. In the center of the palette, you can select or create the size of brush you need. With the options on the right side of the palette, you can make additional changes to the brush size and opacity.

First, I'll discuss the types of paint tools. Imagine that the 20 buttons in this section of the Paint palette are labeled 1–20, in four rows of five. The first row would be 1–5, the second row 6–10, and so on, left to right and then top to bottom. This should make it easier to discuss.

The default Paint tool type is a paintbrush (button 1). When selected, the paintbrush distributes the color of paint currently selected. The color is displayed in the large box below the last toolbox tool, on the toolbox bar. Clicking once with the mouse enables you to change the color or palette by displaying the Color Picker dialog box, shown in Figure 26.8.

FIGURE 26.8.

*The Color Picker
dialog box.*

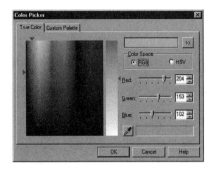

There are four ways to choose your color:

- Using red-blue-green combination values (RGB, the default Color Space option)
- Using hue-saturation-value combinations (HSV, an optional Color Space option)
- Using your mouse pointer to select a color by clicking the color panel
- Using the Eyedropper button (near the bottom center of the Color Picker dialog box) to select a color from one of the sprites in the active composition

Using the RGB Color Space option, you can hand-type the separate values for red, green, and blue in the text boxes provided, use the spin buttons directly to the right of each text box, or use the slider controls. If you'd rather use the HSV Color Space option, follow the same steps for adjusting the RGB option.

NOTE

If you select the HSV option, the other options change from Red, Green, and Blue to Hue, Saturation, and Value.

Just above the Color Space option you can see two blocks of color, with a button to the right labeled >>. The blocks of color represent the original color you selected when opening the Color Picker dialog box (on the left) and the new or current color selected in the Color Picker dialog box (on the right). If you want to revert to the original color you selected, press the >> button.

TIP

Remember to take advantage of the ToolTips (moving your mouse over areas and controls to get some instant help) while using palettes and dialog boxes. It will save time and help you get your work done faster.

Back to the Paint palette and the 20 tool type buttons—the following paragraphs give brief overviews of each style.

> **NOTE**
>
> If you select the Sticky option (located in the lower-right corner of the Paint palette), when you switch from sprite to sprite the same paint tool type stays selected. Otherwise, you need to select a paint tool type when you change the active sprite.

> **NOTE**
>
> What if you open graphics files that have transparent color sets? When painting to these file images, only the visible color areas are painted.

As you select different paint styles, the area to the right of the 20 buttons may change to provide other modifying features for that particular style. I'll note when you can expect this to happen.

The following table describes the buttons in row 1 (buttons 1–5).

Button	Name	Description
	Paintbrush	The Paintbrush style can be considered the normal painting tool. As when using a real paintbrush, you get strokes that depend on the size of the brush selected. After selecting the paintbrush style, select the size and opacity. The size determines the width of the brush stroke. The opacity determines how much of the current image shows through when you paint. The closer the opacity level is to 100, the less the current image shows through. Where available, the opacity and brush size have the same effect on each brush style.
	Airbrush	The Airbrush style is much like using an airbrush. The painting has a light and feathered effect.
	Pencil	Like a normal (sharpened!) pencil, the Pencil style gives you precise pixel drawing power. The default brush size of the pencil style is set to 1. For a thicker pencil, change the brush size to a larger number. To use the pencil tool well, you may want to zoom in closer for accuracy. (The Zoom tool is discussed later in this chapter.)

Button	Name	Description
	Smear	The Smear style does exactly what it implies. It enables you to smear—dragging pixels across other pixels in any direction, and producing a smearing effect.
	Impression	This is a rather unique tool. It enables you to be creative with the image by diffusing the color wherever the tool comes in contact. The best way to describe this feature might be using clay and a coin. If you press a coin into the clay, it makes an impression of the coin's ridges and reliefs. Similarly, if you apply this tool to the image, it makes an impression based on the modifiers you select for it.

The following table describes the buttons in row 2 (buttons 6–10).

Button	Name	Description
	Erase	This style does exactly what it says—it becomes an eraser. Using the opacity modifier produces partial erasure and give the image a "ghosted" effect.
	Tint	The Tint style enables you to tint the image with whatever color is currently on the color palette. Unlike the Colorize style, the tint is applied to the entire image.
	Colorize	The Colorize style allows you to apply whatever color is currently on the color palette to the "colored" areas of your image. Unlike the Tint style, the color is applied only to parts of the image that have a color value, not to white areas.
	Dodge-Burn	Here's a style you may not have heard of. When you select the Dodge-Burn tool, notice that the opacity modifier changes to a Dodge-Burn modifier, and its value should read 0 (zero). If you move the Dodge-Burn slider control to the left, the number becomes a negative number; moving it to the right causes an increasingly positive number. If the number is in the negative range, the tool applies a "burn" effect to the colored areas of the image—darkening the color. If the number is in the positive rage, the tool applies a "dodge" effect—brightening the colored areas of the image, almost like a whitewash effect.

continues

Button	Name	Description
	Contrast	The Contrast style does exactly the opposite of the Dodge-Burn tool. The opacity modifier is replaced with the contrast modifier, initially set to 0 (zero). Moving the Contrast slider control to the left produces a negative number for the contrast modifier, yet brightens up the entire image when applied. The opposite is true when the contrast number is set to a positive number—the entire image is darkened.

The following table describes the buttons in row 3 (buttons 11–15).

Button	Name	Description
	Rubber Stamp	The Rubber Stamp style is one of the coolest options I've seen in a while. I'm not sure who thought this up, but it's really interesting. This style takes a portion of an image and lets you "stamp" it all over the place. First select the Rubber Stamp style by clicking the button. With the special mouse cursor that appears, click the exact center of the area you want to replicate. After the first click, subsequent clicks "stamp" that image selection wherever you click. To deactivate this tool, simply select any other tool. Really neat.
	Transfer	Did I speak too soon? The Transfer style is another incredible option that enables you to begin drawing a selected image concentrically, anywhere within another image, starting with an epicenter area that you define. Select the Transfer style by clicking the button. Then, with the special mouse cursor that appears, select the center of the area where you'd like Image Composer to start replicating. After the first click, each subsequent click-and-drag begins drawing the entire image from the spot you selected. To deactivate this tool, simply select any other tool.
	Mesa	The Mesa style makes the image either convex (bubble upward) or concave (bubble downward), depending on how you set the warp direction. When you select the Mesa style, notice that the opacity modifier becomes a radius factor. This is the percentage of pixels that are affected when the style tool is applied. Also, the warp direction modifier appears. The warp direction determines the manner in which the image is "distorted"— warped in or warped out.

Using Microsoft Image Composer

CHAPTER 26

677

26

USING
MICROSOFT
IMAGE COMPOSER

Button	Name	Description
	Vortex	The Vortex style creates a swirl or whirlpool effect on the image. After selecting the Vortex style, notice that the opacity modifier changes to the angle modifier. The angle modifier determines the angle of swirl to be applied when using the tool. If you click in the same spot while applying this style, the affected section appears to spin in increments of the degree determined by the angle modifier.
	Spoke Inversion	The Spoke Inversion style inverts the image and creates a spoked wheel effect in a certain region of the image. After you click the Spoke Inversion button, the opacity modifier becomes a value modifier. This value determines the percentage of the image selection affected by the Spoke Inversion style when it's applied.

The fourth row of style buttons is unique in that each button can be used only during certain instances of the other 15 buttons. The following table describes the buttons in row 4 (buttons 16–20).

Button	Name	Description
	Use Brush	When selected (the default setting), the current brush style selected is the method that Image Composer uses to apply the active color on the current palette.
	Use Template	When selected, the active color is applied in the shape of the currently selected template.
	Pick Template	When selected, Image Composer enables you to chose a sprite to use as a template for painting with the selected brush style.
	Over	When selected, and when your image contains transparent pixels, both transparent and nontransparent pixels are "painted over." When not selected (the default setting), only nontransparent pixels are painted over.
	Continuous Strokes	When selected (the default setting), the current brush style strokes are continuous. If unselected, the painting method resembles "footprints" of the current brush style.

If you prefer to design your own brush shapes, click the New Brush button in the center of the Paint palette (shown in Figure 26.9) to open the Brush Designer dialog box (shown in Figure 26.10).

New Brush button

FIGURE 26.9.

Click the New Brush button to open the Brush Designer dialog box.

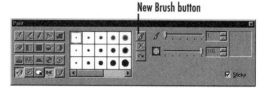

FIGURE 26.10.

The Brush Designer dialog box.

By adjusting the slider controls, you can interactively design a personal brush shape. The following list describes the options:

- **Diameter.** Controls the brush width.
- **Aspect.** This option controls brush obliqueness or horizontal shift. *Obliqueness* can be thought of like perspective. If you look at a building straight on from the side, you would call that an *elevation* or *view*—for example, a "right elevation." If you walk around the building, toward the back, the view begins to look oblique or elongated, until you get completely behind the building, and then have a "rear elevation." This obliqueness is also known as a *perspective* or *three-point view.* When using this feature, ask yourself, "How am I shifting the horizon?"
- **Rotation.** The degree of rotation to apply to the brush.
- **Softness.** 0 is soft and fuzzy; 100 is hard lines and solid.

Below the New Brush button are two other buttons. The button with the X enables you to delete the currently selected brush. The button showing the curved arrow restores all default brushes, in case you just deleted a basic brush shape. If you choose to restore brush defaults, note that any custom brushes are deleted at the same time.

The Text Tool

The *Text tool* (shown in Figure 26.11) is used for placing text throughout your Image Composer composition. Different fonts, point sizes, and styles can dramatically enhance images when used creatively. For example, you can create a 3-D text effect by laying a contrasting copy of the same text over another copy and offsetting the text slightly in any direction, depending on the desired effect. (An example of this type of technique is shown later in this chapter.)

FIGURE 26.11.
*Use the Text tool
to add text to your
composition.*

Text tool

Clicking the Text tool displays the Text palette shown in Figure 26.12. Near the top of the
Text palette are labels that indicate the current font, size, and style. In the Text box, you type
the text that you want to place in your composition. As you type the text, it appears in the
recessed display box on the right exactly as it will appear in your composition. If you want to
change the font, size, or style of the text, click the Select Font button to display the Font dialog
box (see Figure 26.13).

FIGURE 26.12.
The Text palette.

FIGURE 26.13.
The Font dialog box.

Using the Font dialog box, choose the desired characteristics for your text. The Font Style and
Size selections change with different font selections. When you're finished, click OK to confirm your selection or Cancel to ignore any changes.

To the right of the Select Font button on the Text palette is the familiar opacity modifier. This
allows you to create watermark-type images by making the text almost completely transparent.
As with the Paint opacity options, you can change the font opacity by using the slider control,
typing the new value in the text box, or using the spin buttons to increase or decrease the value.
Remember, the lower the opacity value, the more transparent the text.

The Shapes Tool

The Shapes tool (shown in Figure 26.14) is quite handy when you want to incorporate rectangles, ovals, splines, or polygons into your composition. A *spline* is a shape with curved lines, and a *polygon* is a shape that contains multiple straight lines. Clicking the Shapes tool displays the Shapes - Geometry palette shown in Figure 26.15.

FIGURE 26.14.

Use the Shapes tool to add various shaped objects to your composition.

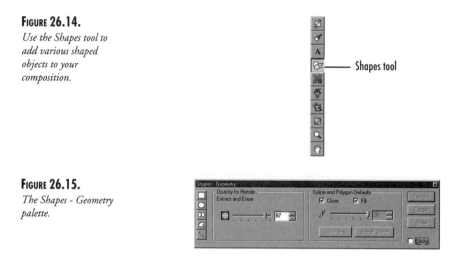

Shapes tool

FIGURE 26.15.

The Shapes - Geometry palette.

The Shapes - Geometry palette has four areas that warrant discussion. The first is a vertical column of shape control buttons on the left side of the palette. The first four buttons from top to bottom are shape selectors—respectively, Rectangle, Oval, Spline, and Polygon. The last button, Color Lift, is a bit different. If you have ever used a graphics product that allows you to select an entire area of the same color pixel, this will be quite familiar to you. In other programs, this may be referred to as a "magic wand." Unlike with some programs, however, you have considerable control over this wand in Image Composer. Clicking this button displays the Shapes - Color Lift palette shown in Figure 26.16.

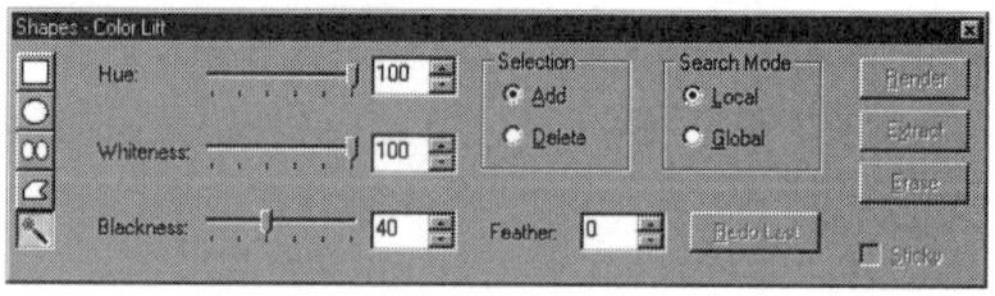

FIGURE 26.16.

The Shapes - Color Lift palette.

The following options are available during color lift:

- **Hue.** Adjusts the amount of color that can be applied to the current sprite.
- **Whiteness.** Adjusts the whiteness of the current sprite.
- **Blackness.** Adjusts the blackness of the current sprite.

Using Microsoft Image Composer

CHAPTER 26

681

26

USING
MICROSOFT
IMAGE COMPOSER

- **Selection.** Add or delete the current selection.
- **Search Mode.** Choose between Local (only adjacent same-colored pixels) and Global (all same-colored pixels).
- **Feather.** The level of softness of the selection border.

You also have the Sticky option (check box, lower-right corner) that was discussed earlier. Just in case you've forgotten, the Sticky option enables you to use the same features of the current palette on a different image sprite. That way, you don't have to reset your palette every time you switch between images.

The Redo Last button allows the last action taken to be re-executed.

I'll talk about the Render, Extract, and Erase buttons shortly; meanwhile, back to the Shapes - Geometry palette. Click any button above the Color Lift button to change the Shapes palette back to the Geometry version.

The Opacity for Render area of the palette should be a familiar control by now—the opacity slide control. In the shape scenario, opacity is used during rendering, erasing, and extracting.

The third area of interest in the Shapes - Geometry palette is the Spline and Polygon Defaults section, consisting of the Close and Fill check boxes, which allow rendered images to be closed and filled by default. (If the object is to be filled, the default color on the color palette is used as the fill color.) If you deselect either the Close or the Fill box, the spline line with slide control, located directly beneath these options, becomes active. The value of this control is the actual width of the spline line in pixels. The width can be from 1 to 19 pixels. After drawing a spline when the Close box is unchecked, the Edit Points button becomes active. This button enables you to drag, pull, and distort anchor points of the spline, creating a new shape. After you have a new shape, you can click the Render button to fill in the shape, if Fill is selected. In any case, you might want your spline or shape line back so you can build onto your drawing. Simply click the Recall Spline button to achieve this goal.

Last but not least is what I call the "action button area." Once an image is drawn, it's simply a template that you fill in when you're ready. After you're satisfied with the shape, click the Render button to complete the image's creation. Using the Extract button while a new shape is overlaying another image causes a differentiation effect. Wherever the other shape is drawn, the new one won't be drawn. Clicking the Erase button after a new shape is drawn removes it from your composition. Don't forget about the Sticky option in the lower-right corner!

The Patterns and Fills Tool

The Patterns and Fills tool (shown in Figure 26.17) enables you to add pattern and fill effects to your images. Clicking the tool displays the Patterns and Fills palette, shown in Figure 26.18. This palette has three areas of interest. Not all areas are shown by default; the options vary, depending on the patterns and fills option selected.

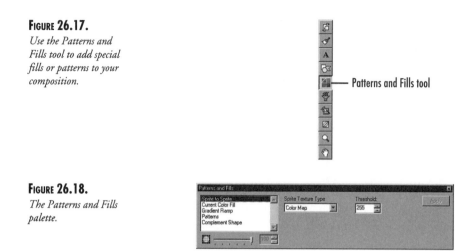

FIGURE 26.17.
Use the Patterns and Fills tool to add special fills or patterns to your composition.

— Patterns and Fills tool

FIGURE 26.18.
The Patterns and Fills palette.

The list box in the upper-left portion of the Patterns and Fills palette contains five options. The following sections go over each option briefly to give you an idea of how much fun this tool can be. (By the way, below this list of options you'll notice the familiar opacity slider control.)

Sprite to Sprite

When the Sprite to Sprite option is selected, the option Sprite Texture Type appears. The Sprite to Sprite transfer takes selected attributes of the source sprite and transfers them to the target sprite. The nine options in the drop-down list box define the transfer process that will take place:

- **Transfer Shape.** Transfers the shape of one sprite to another.
- **Transfer Full.** Transfers one entire sprite into another.
- **Glue.** "Glues" the shape of the image on the area selected.
- **Snip.** Snips the overlaid section of the source sprite from the destination sprite.
- **Tile.** Creates a "tile" in the image of the source sprite from the shape of the destination sprite. (The Intertile X and Y subsettings are used to determine at what point on the image selected—X,Y—the effect starts.)
- **Intensity Map.** Transfers the intensity or contrast map from one sprite to another (Threshold setting 0–255).
- **Color Map.** Transfers the color map or palette from one sprite to another (Threshold setting 0–255).
- **Transparency Map.** Transfers the transparent pixel map from one sprite to another.
- **Saturation Map.** Transfers the saturation or hue map from one sprite to another.

In this list, the words in parentheses refer to subsettings available where noted. If subsettings are available, they appear to the right of the Sprite Texture Type drop-down list box.

Current Color Fill

The Current Color Fill option fills the destination sprite with the color currently on the color palette. Easy enough.

Gradient Ramp

The Gradient Ramp setting is pretty interesting; it gives you the option of blending colors to create color transitioning effects, as in a sunset. When this setting is selected, a preview square appears with tiny squares near each corner. Clicking a tiny square enables you to change the color of that section of the entire preview square. You also get a Color Selection dialog box from which to choose a color. You can also select from the Ramp Name drop-down list that appears to the right of the preview square. There are 19 different built-in ramp effects. You can create and save your own effects as well. You also have the option to delete current ramps.

> **CAUTION**
>
> I am unaware of any undo for deletes, so be cautious with the Delete button!

Patterns

The Patterns option lets you apply patterns to the destination sprite. There are nine built-in patterns: Color Array, Grayscale Array, Color Bars, Hue/Blackness, Hue/Whiteness, Color Noise, Gray Noise, Checkerboard, and Stripes. The last two, Checkerboard and Stripes, have options for spacing and width.

Complement Shape

The last option, Complement Shape, does just that. It fills the complementary area of the shape with the active color. The *complement* of the shape is the area that the shape doesn't occupy—the inverse of the shape.

Clicking the Apply button in the upper-right corner of the Patterns and Fills palette causes the selected option to be applied to the selected destination image sprite.

The Warps and Filters Tool

The Warps and Filters tool (shown in Figure 26.19) lets you create special effects, as the name subtly implies. The Warps and Filters palette (shown in Figure 26.20) has several areas that change, depending on which options are selected.

FIGURE 26.19.

Use the Warps and Filters tool to create special effects for your composition.

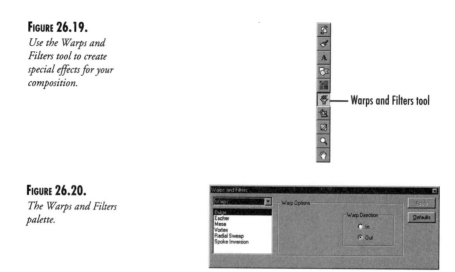

Warps and Filters tool

FIGURE 26.20.

The Warps and Filters palette.

The drop-down list box in the upper-left corner of the Warps and Filters palette lists five major options. When you select an item in this list, the minor options in the list box below change to display the minor options for that major selection.

Directly to the right of the major and minor options lists is the option's modifier area. This area changes as major and minor options are selected and deselected.

The Apply button applies the current option setting to the selected sprite, and the Defaults button changes the options setting to reflect Image Composer's defaults for that option (if you changed them).

The Art Effects Tool

The Art Effects tool (shown in Figure 26.21) enables you to apply many different art effects to the currently selected image. Clicking the tool displays the Art Effects palette shown in Figure 26.22, which enables you to control the type of effect and the qualities of that effect.

FIGURE 26.21.

Use the Art Effects tool to apply other effects to your composition.

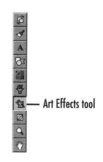

Art Effects tool

FIGURE 26.22.

The Art Effects palette.

The available effects are Paint, Sketch, Graphic, Exotic, and Utility. After you select an effect from the drop-down list, the type list box located directly below the drop-down list displays the available types for the selected effect. Depending on which effect type you select, modifiers appear directly to the right of the list; you use these settings to adjust the quality of that effect type. After you select the appropriate settings, click the Apply button to apply the effect to the selected image. If it wasn't the effect you wanted, click the Undo button on the toolbar or press Ctrl+Z.

The Color Tuning Tool

The Color Tuning tool (shown in Figure 26.23) adjusts the quality of the color in the selected image. Clicking this tool displays the Color Tuning palette in Figure 26.24.

FIGURE 26.23.

Adjust the color in your composition with the Color Tuning tool.

Color Tuning tool

FIGURE 26.24.

The Color Tuning palette.

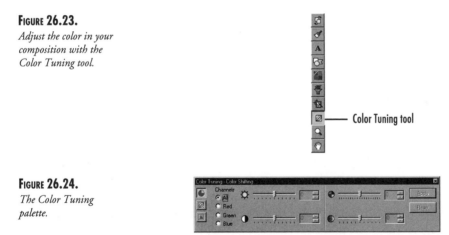

The three toggle buttons on the left side of the palette, top to bottom, are Color Shifting, Highlight and Shadow, and Dynamic Range:

- The Color Shifting option controls the brightness, contrast, hue, and color saturation levels for the currently selected image. You can tune (or adjust) all channels or an individual color channel.

- When the Highlight and Shadow button is selected, the threshold of the highlights and shadows of the current image may be changed. You can change the highlights and shadows of all color channels, or select an individual channel to work with.

■ Finally, when the Dynamic Range button is selected, you can control the intensity ranges on the current image sprite. The horizontal axis represents intensity levels— increasing the intensity as you move to the right. The vertical axis represents the number of pixels that fall into that intensity range. On the horizontal range are two solid vertical bars, one on each end. The first bar represents the source intensity; the second represents the destination intensity. Changing the ranges alters the current intensity ranges, based on your selection.

The Zoom Tool

The Zoom tool (shown in Figure 26.25) controls the actual view size of your composition. The upper-right corner of the composition window displays the actual size of the image displayed in the Zoom Percent drop-down list. After selecting the Zoom tool and clicking the image, it becomes 100% larger every time you click. To reset the image back to its 100% mode, click the button labeled 100% to the left of the Zoom Percent drop-down list.

FIGURE 26.25.

Zoom in on the image with the Zoom tool.

—— Zoom tool

The Pan Tool

The Pan tool (shown in Figure 26.26) moves the composition around in the current *viewport* (the bordered area in which you can see the current image, also known just as "the window"). Simply select the Pan tool, click the area of the image you want to "grab," and drag it in the direction of your choice. The image is moved around just as if you were dragging a piece of paper around your workspace or desk.

FIGURE 26.26.

Pan the image with the Pan tool to place it in the window for best viewing.

—— Pan tool

The Toolbar

The Image Composer toolbar (shown in Figure 26.27) includes several special controls in addition to the standard application toolbar buttons (New, Open, Save, Print, Cut, Copy, Paste, Undo, in order from left to right on the toolbar). Table 26.2 lists the special controls and provides a brief description of each.

FIGURE 26.27.

The Image Composer toolbar.

Table 26.2. Special buttons on the Image Composer toolbar.

Button	Name	Description
	Insert Image File	Enables you to insert a file from disk. After you click this button, the Insert from File dialog box opens, allowing you to select an existing file for insertion into your composition.
	Duplicate	Creates an exact duplicate of the currently selected sprite.
	Select All	Selects all sprites in the current composition. This is useful if you want to create a group or move all sprites to a certain location in the composition.
	Clear Selection	Deselects any sprites that are currently selected.
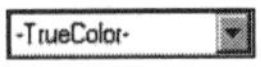	Color Format	Displays the color palette to use for your composition. The color palette options are True Color, Balanced Ramp, Gray Ramp, and Black and White. Depending on how many image sprites are loaded into your composition, their names appear here as well, allowing you to apply the color palette for each image to the entire image.
	Actual Size	Allows you to return your composition to its actual size on demand. This is handy if you have been zooming in and out and want to return to the actual size quickly.
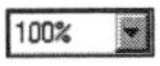	Zoom Percent	Enables you to zoom in or out on the composition, simply by selecting a percentage from this list. The percentages shown are all relative to the composition's actual size.

The Menu

The following sections list and describe each item on the Image Composer menu, along with the submenu options for each. Many menu items correlate directly with the toolbox items discussed in the preceding section; I note those where applicable.

The File Menu

The File menu in any Windows application usually contains functions relevant to opening, saving, and closing files. Printing functions and "last file open" options are available, too—the last few files you have opened are listed at the bottom of the File menu. The following list describes each option:

- **New.** Creates a new Image Composer composition.
- **Open.** Opens an existing image file.
- **Close.** Closes the current Image Composer composition.
- **Exit.** Terminates the Image Composer session. If any changes were made, Image Composer prompts you to save the changes.
- **Save.** Saves the current Image Composer composition.
- **Save As.** Allows you to save the current image to another file name or format.
- **Save Selection As.** Allows you to save individual selected sprites or sprite groups as separate images.
- **Composition Properties.** Displays information about the entire current composition. When you select this option, Image Composer displays the Composition Properties dialog box (see Figure 26.28). This dialog box details the properties of the composition, such as the type of image, resolution, alpha content (transparent pixels), and a list of the individual sprites that make up the composition. If you double-click a sprite in the sprite list near the bottom of the dialog box, the Sprite Properties dialog box appears (see Figure 26.29). This dialog box shows information on the specific sprite you have selected.
- **Scan, Select Scan Source, and Acquire Scan.** These three options together allow for input into Image Composer from any TWAIN-compliant device, such as a scanner or digital camera. You use the Select Scan Source menu item first, to select a source from which to scan. Then you use the Acquire Scan menu item to retrieve or scan the information into Image Composer.
- **Print.** Prints the current composition to the currently selected printer, or to another printer that your machine can access.
- **Print Setup.** Enables you to select options such as the paper size and source for your printing needs, before you print.
- **Send.** If you have an e-mail application that's MAPI-compliant installed on your system, this menu item appears, allowing you to send the current composition as an attachment to an e-mail message.

FIGURE 26.28.

*The Composition
Properties dialog box.*

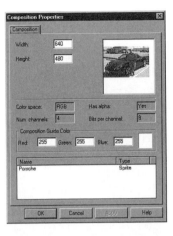

FIGURE 26.29.

*The Sprite Properties
dialog box.*

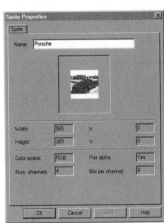

The Edit Menu

The Edit menu contains the standard Windows Edit menu features plus a few enhancements:

■ **Undo.** Essentially "undoes" the last action—or group of actions if using a tool such as a paintbrush.

■ **Cut.** Removes the currently selected item or items from the composition and places them on the Windows Clipboard (in memory) for pasting at a later time if needed.

■ **Copy.** Copies and places the currently select item or items on the Windows Clipboard for pasting at a later time.

■ **Delete.** Deletes the currently selected sprite(s).

■ **Select All.** Selects all sprites on the current working desktop.

■ **Clear Selection.** Clears the currently selected area on the selected sprite.

■ **Duplicate.** Like the Duplicate button discussed earlier, the Duplicate option generates another copy of the currently selected image(s).

■ **Copy, Paste, and Broadcast Channels.** These items are related to "color-separated"
versions of an image. If the image is in color, it consists of different *channels*—colors
creating a single image—that is, the channels red, green, blue, and alpha (transparent).
Just like the standard Copy and Paste commands, the Copy Channel and Paste
Channel items copy and paste the image, but only in the channel selected. The
Broadcast Channel replaces all channels of the current selection, with the broadcast
channel selected. The Broadcast Channel—red, green, or blue—is the "mask" that
defines how that specific channel (red, green, or blue) is arranged within the image.
All three channels combined create the full color image. It's like color separation.

■ **Properties.** Selecting this option while a sprite is selected displays the Properties
dialog box for that sprite (refer to Figure 26.29).

The View Menu

The View menu contains items that affect the way you see items in Image Composer:

■ **Go to Composition Guide.**

■ **Center on Selection.** Centers the current composition on the selected sprite, making
the selected sprite the "center of attention."

■ **Toolbars.** Displays the Toolbars dialog box, enabling you to determine which
toolbars are visible while using Image Composer.

■ **Toggle Palette View.** Allows you to hide the current tool palette. Operates as a
toggle.

■ **Zoom In, Zoom Out, and Actual Size.** These items control the current viewing size
of the composition. As with the buttons on the toolbar, you can use these options to
zoom in, zoom out, or show the actual size on demand.

The Insert Menu

The Insert menu has options for inserting images into your composition (you can also use OLE
or DDE, of course):

■ **From File.** Allows insertion of an existing image from a file into your current
composition.

■ **From Photo CD.** Allows insertion of an image from a photo CD.

The Tools Menu

The Tools menu activates tools from the toolbox discussed earlier:

■ **Color Picker.** Displays the Color Picker dialog box (refer to Figure 26.8). This dialog
box enables you to select the current color for painting.

- **Options.** Displays Image Composer's Options dialog box (see Figure 26.30), which controls the Image Composer environment options.

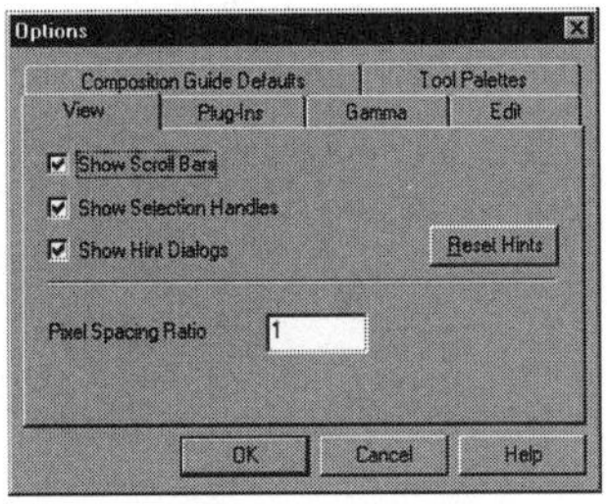

FIGURE 26.30.
The Options dialog box.

- **Microsoft GIF Animator.** Starts the Microsoft GIF Animator program (if you installed it during setup).

The Arrange Menu

The Arrange menu works exactly like the items on the Arrange palette discussed earlier (refer to Figure 26.5). See the earlier section "The Arrange Tool" for details on these menu items.

The Plug-Ins Menu

Plug-ins are program features that are provided through Microsoft or a third party to enhance the features of your application. Image Composer comes with the Impressionist plug-in. The Plug-Ins menu has the following options:

- **Repeat Last Plug-in.** After executing a plug-in feature, this option allows you to repeat the last command executed from that plug-in.

- **Impressionist.** The Impressionist plug-in comes with Image Composer, and is shown only if you elected to install it with the setup program. The Impressionist plug-in enables you to apply many different effects to the currently selected image(s). After you select this item, the Impressionist dialog box opens, as shown in Figure 26.31.

  You can apply a plethora of artistic effects to your image. I won't go into detail here because there are 17 styles that you can apply. The styles have, on average, at least 5 types or style modifiers from which to choose. You can control the brush size, amount of coverage, and brush pressure. Clicking the Run Demo button cycles through each style to give you an example of what each style would look like if applied to your image. (To quit the demo, press Esc.) I encourage you to play with this tool for a while, trying out each style and modifier so you are familiar with the effects that can be accomplished using the Impressionist plug-in feature.

The Window Menu

As with other multiple-document interface (MDI) programs, you can use the Window menu to arrange and switch between child windows in the current application.

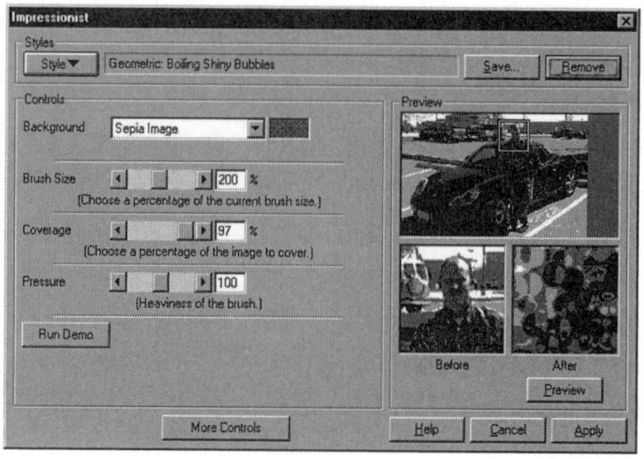

FIGURE 26.31.

The Impressionist dialog box.

The Help Menu

This is where you can find some help!

- **Microsoft Image Composer Help Topics.** Launches the Image Composer help program.

- **Sample Sprites Catalog.** Allows you to load sample sprites from a sample catalog.

- **Microsoft on the Web.** Sends you to Microsoft's Web page for possible software updates, enhancements, or other goodies. You must have an Internet service provider and a Web browser installed to use this option.

- **About the Microsoft Image Composer.** Shows the current version number of Image Composer and your registration information. You need this information if you call Microsoft support services for any reason.

A Quick Walk in the Park...

Now that you're familiar with Image Composer's many options, it's time to open an image and perform some quick magic. This section is a quick walkthrough of many options to give you a feel of the many things Image Composer can help you create.

Creating a Banner for Your Web Site

We'll start out with a simple example—making what's known as a *banner* for a Web page. Sometimes, when designing a Web site, companies or people keep their interface consistent by using standard components on each page, such as banners, toolbars, footers, or sidebars. The banner created in this section is for the CyberLan Software company. (I made up this company name—but if it exists, it's purely coincidental!)

Follow these steps:

1. Start out by creating a new workspace. Choose File | New (or click the New button—the first button on the toolbar). A default image workspace (composition) will be created.

2. Now change the size to match the size of the banner you want to create. Choose File | Composition Properties (see Figure 26.32).

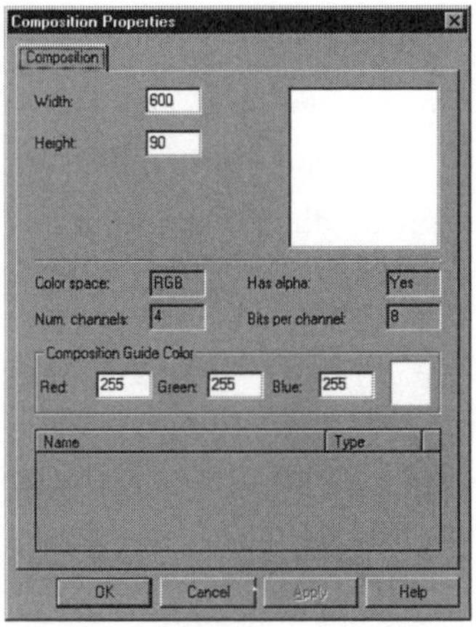

FIGURE 26.32.

Setting the composition properties.

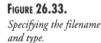

3. Change the Width setting to **600** and the Height setting to **90**. This is a good size for a banner, whether for a header or footer.

4. Now, make a cool background on which to place some text and images. Even though you have a white area to work with, you won't be able to draw on it until you save it. (Seems silly, but saving turns this blank area into a sprite.) Choose File | Save As. In the Save As dialog box, type a name for the banner. In this case, use **Banner.gif** and save the file as type CompuServe GIF (*.gif), as shown in Figure 26.33. Then click Save.

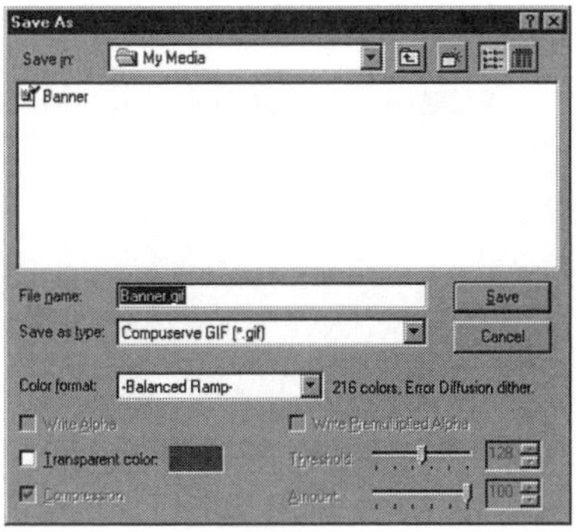

FIGURE 26.33.

Specifying the filename and type.

5. Close the current workspace by choosing File | Close.

6. Open the File menu. You should see the name of your new file, directly after the Open option and menu item separator, named `C:\Multimedia Files\...\Banner` or simply `Banner`. This is the file you just saved. (I asked you to do this to illustrate the Last Files Open feature on the File menu.) Select this option to open your new composition, containing a blank banner sprite.

There are different things you can do to make this banner sprite a good background item. For example, you could select the Patterns and Fills tool, and select the Gradient Ramp option to create a gradient background. Try it:

1. Select the banner sprite image.

2. Click the Patterns and Fills tool (fifth button down in the toolbox).

3. Select the Gradient Ramp option in the Patterns and Fills palette.

4. Select a ramp name modifier. For this example, use Cool Steel.

5. Click Apply. You should get a sprite that looks similar to the one in Figure 26.34.

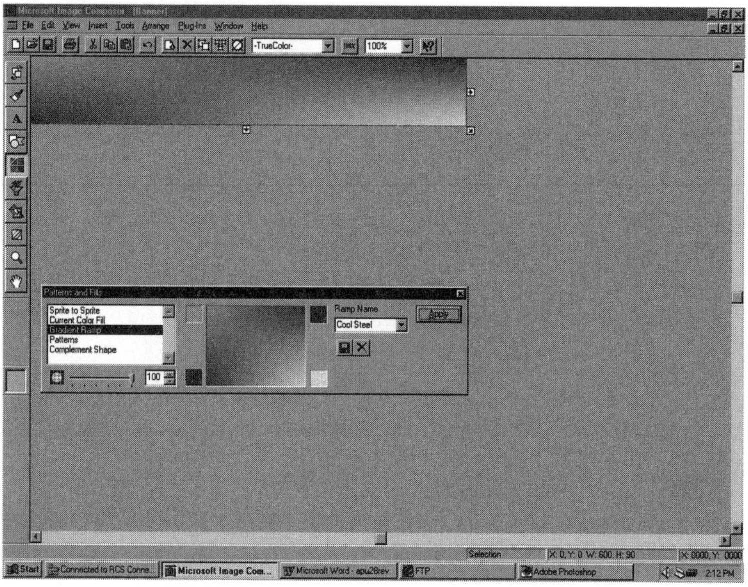

FIGURE 26.34.

The banner sprite with the Cool Steel gradient ramp effect applied.

Next, let's put the company name on the banner:

1. Click the Text tool in the toolbox (third button down). In the Text palette, select the Arial Black font, size 36.

2. Type the company name, in this case **CyberLAN**.

3. Click the color swatch under the toolbox to open the Color Picker (refer to Figure 26.8) and set the color values as follows: Red = **61**, Green = **67**, Blue = **67**.

4. Click the Apply button. You now have the shadow part of your text image (see Figure 26.35).

Using Microsoft Image Composer

CHAPTER 26

695

26

USING
MICROSOFT
IMAGE COMPOSER

FIGURE 26.35.
*The banner sprite with
the new shadow text
element.*

FIGURE 26.35. [image of banner sprite]

Creating the overlay to give the 3-D effect is easy:

1. Using the Color Picker, change the color swatch to a light value of the same tone. Set Red = **204**, Green = **206**, Blue = **206**.

2. Click the Apply button. You will then have a lighter version or overlay of the text image shown in Figure 26.36.

FIGURE 26.36.
*The banner sprite with
overlay text element
added.*

3. Select the overlay and drag it slightly above and to the left of the shadow text element. You now have a 3-D text graphic (see Figure 26.37).

FIGURE 26.37.
*The banner sprite with
its 3-D text graphic.*

To make sure you don't mess up this effect by moving only part of the image in the future, group the text items into one object:

1. Select both the overlay and shadow text elements. (Not the banner sprite!)

2. Click the Arrange tool in the toolbox (top button).

3. Click the Group button on the Arrange palette (above the Order box). You have now grouped the text items.

4. To secure this group so no one can ungroup them later, click the Flatten button, just above the Align option on the Arrange palette. This is now a complete single sprite.

Now let's draw a border box for the text to sit on:

1. Before drawing the box, select a darker color, such as blue. Click the current color swatch and change it to these values: Red = **28**, Green = **12**, and Blue = **192**.

2. Click the Shapes tool in the toolbox (fourth button down) to open the Shapes - Geometry palette.

3. On the palette, make sure that opacity is set at **100**, and select the Close and Fill options.

4. Click the top button on the left side of the palette to begin creating a rectangle.

5. Starting from the left side of your banner, click and draw to the right, creating a small, thin rectangle.

Now that the box is drawn, you'll need to send it behind the text, or it will cut off the bottom of the *y* in CyberLAN (see Figure 26.38).

FIGURE 26.38.
The new box graphic paints over the y.

The bottom of the *y* is missing

While the blue box is still selected, follow these steps:

1. Click the Arrange tool in the toolbox (top button) to open the Arrange palette.

2. In the Order box, click the arrow pointing up and to the right (Send Backward). The box now resides behind the *y* in the text, yet in front of the banner sprite. This gives a nice overlay effect, as shown in Figure 26.39.

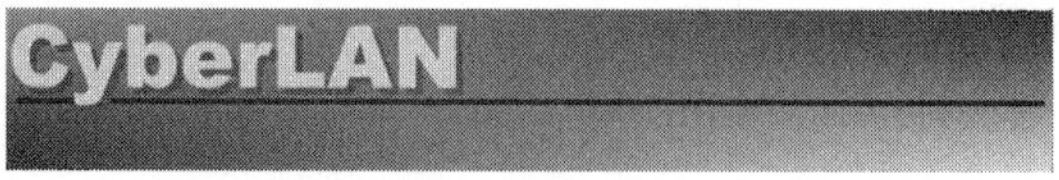

FIGURE 26.39.
The same box graphic, sent behind the CyberLAN *text.*

Now let's make a simple logo for this fictitious company. We'll start out with a circle:

1. Change the current color swatch to Red = **16**, Green = **0**, and Blue = **242**. This is a brighter blue than we used for the box.

2. Click the Shapes tool in the toolbox (fourth button down).

3. On the Shapes - Geometry palette, make sure that opacity is set to **100**, and the Close and Fill boxes are checked.

4. Click the second button down on the left side of the palette (it shows an oval).

5. Draw a circle, about half an inch in diameter. A transparent box outline shows how big the circle will be when rendering. (To get a perfect circle, hold down the Shift key while drawing.) Then click the Render button. You should see something like Figure 26.40.

FIGURE 26.40.
A new circle graphic.

Repeat the preceding steps, creating a white circle on top of the previous circle. (First change the color swatch colors: Red = **255**, Green = **255**, and Blue = **255**. This should be white.) Then use the Arrange tool to group and flatten the circles, as shown in Figure 26.41.

FIGURE 26.41.

The new grouped and flattened circle sprite.

Now let's get a little "artsy"—we want the logo to be unique:

1. With the new grouped circle sprite selected, click the Art Effects tool in the toolbox (seventh button down) to open the Art Effects palette.

2. Select the Sketch effect and the Rough Pastels option.

3. Set the stroke length to **6** and the stroke detail to **7**.

4. Click the Apply button. You should now have an interesting effect applied to your circle, as shown in Figure 26.42.

FIGURE 26.42.

The circle sprite with the Rough Pastels effect applied.

You now have a banner that can be used for your Web page. When you save your composition, all of the sprites are flattened—become one image—and you won't be able to move them around independently any longer when you reopen the file, so make certain that everything is in place before you save and close your composition.

Summary

Many types of images can be created using the Microsoft Image Composer, with the only limits being your imagination (and disk space, of course)! The best way to make the most of this product is to experiment and try techniques that may seem odd or unusual; you may surprise yourself. Make notes of style combinations or techniques you invent. This will be a useful resource in your future compositions.

Most of all, have fun with Image Composer!

Using Microsoft Music Producer

CHAPTER 27

Microsoft Music Producer (MP) is a new product that enables you to create music compositions relatively painlessly to add to your Web pages or multimedia presentations. In literally minutes you can produce professional-sounding MIDI (Musical Instrument Digital Interface) or WAV files that will correctly convey the mood of your presentation, whether it be Web or multimedia. You can even use it for hold or background announcement music if you're developing a Telephony application. Using Microsoft Music Producer is so easy that even my grandmother can use it—and she has!

After you've created the music file, it's easily incorporated into your presentation using OLE linking or embedding, or into your Web page simply by referencing it in your HTML code.

The best thing about MP is the flexibility to save files in multiple formats, which can definitely have advantages. If disk space or file size is a concern, you may choose to save your files as `.mid` files. These files can be 95% smaller than a comparable `.wav` file. If you're using the music for a Web page, this could reduce the time it takes to download your page content to the user's browser, which always makes for a good first impression.

Anywhere you can use a MIDI or WAV file, you can use the music you create with Microsoft Music Producer.

To use Microsoft Music Producer, you need a sound card installed in your computer and at least 10.5MB available on your computer's hard drive.

Switching the Output Device

Microsoft Music Producer uses the synthesizer to produce output. This synthesizer is an electronic component located on your computer's sound card (Sound Blaster, AdLib, and so on). You may have various sound output capabilities, depending on your sound card. To control which features of the card Microsoft Music Producer uses, or which devices are available to you from the sound card, use the Setup Sound Device command. For example, if the default device MP uses on your machine is being used by another application, you need to switch Music Producer's musical output device in order to produce output.

To switch the output device for MP, follow these steps:

1. Choose Options | Setup Sound Device.
2. In the Setup Sound Device dialog box, select the sound device that you want MP to use (see Figure 27.1).

Using the Feature Settings

Microsoft Music Producer uses six different features to help you compose music: Style, Personality, Band, Tempo, Key, and Shape. Each feature contains selections or modifiers that enable you to customize that feature to portray a particular characteristic you want. Each feature has a label above it in the main program dialog box making the feature's options easy to identify (see Figure 27.2). The following sections cover each of these features and describe ways to use them to enhance your musical compositions.

FIGURE 27.1.
Sound device setup.

FIGURE 27.2.
Microsoft Music Producer's main screen.

Preview button

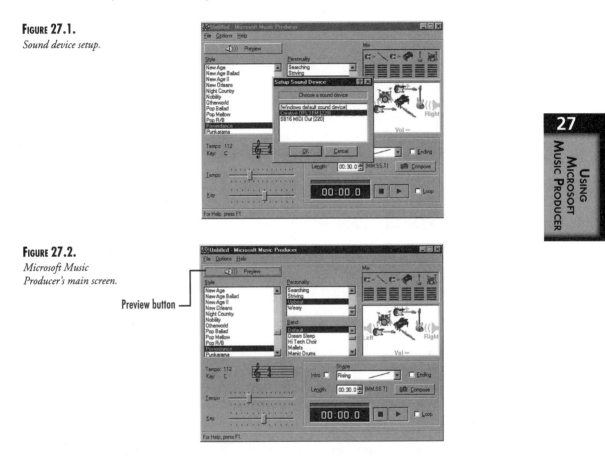

One thing to remember about features: Whenever you make changes to any features or feature modifiers, you can get a preview of the composition content by clicking the Preview button. To stop the preview, simply click the preview button once again (which should now read "Stop Preview"). You will be able to change features while the preview is playing in "real time." This is useful, as you don't have to stop the music between previews. Once you start composing, the only feature you can change is the band—so get your composition features worked out in the preview mode before you start to compose!

Choosing a Style

The Style settings (see Figure 27.3) can be considered one of the key features for defining the character of your composition. There are over 100 different styles you can select, all the way from a Ballad to an Upbeat Rave that would make even Madonna jealous.

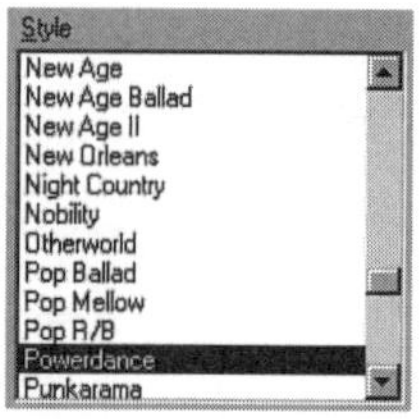

FIGURE 27.3.

Style settings.

When you select each style, notice how the other MP features are affected. The Personality, Tempo, Key signature, Band, and Mix items all seem to change a bit. If you notice how the Style description changes the other features, you can get an idea of which items are affecting others and create similar custom styles of your own.

Although you can't add custom names to the Style list box, you can create your own styles by modifying the other features available to you.

Giving the Music "Personality"

The Personality settings (see Figure 27.4) give your music its mood. A good way to describe the Personality feature is the way the band is feeling when they're playing. If you want the band to sound slightly drunk, then you might choose Weary. If you want the band to sound as if they have had too much coffee, you might select Upbeat.

FIGURE 27.4.

Personality settings.

Setting Up the Band

Not unlike the actual definition of the word, the Band feature shown in Figure 27.5 can be thought of as a group of instruments that work together to give a certain effect. Each of the Microsoft Music Producer bands contains six "musicians" on different output channels, which together produce a unique instrument sound.

FIGURE 27.5.

Band settings.

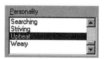

For each different band selected in the Band box, a different group of instruments appears in the Mix box (see Figure 27.6).

FIGURE 27.6.
Mix settings.

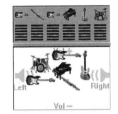

The Mix box includes the indicators Vol + (at the top), Vol – (bottom), Left, and Right. Using your mouse or pointer, if you click and drag an instrument toward or away from any of these indicators, the sound of that particular instrument is altered (see Figure 27.7).

FIGURE 27.7.
*You balance the mix
with these settings.*

You need to be in Preview mode to hear the changes in sound you're making while you're making them. (Click the Preview button.) Raising and lowering the instrument in the Mix box raises and lowers that instrument's volume. Moving the instrument to the left increasingly shifts its sound to the left speaker. Conversely, moving it to the right shifts the sound to the right speaker. To balance the sound, place the instrument right in the middle.

Toward the top of the Mix box are icons of instruments (at least six) with six black horizontal bars under each, as shown in Figure 27.8. These six horizontal bars comprise one vertical bar (a meter), which represents the *volume units* (VU or level) for each instrument that's currently displayed on the Mix grid. While in Preview or Compose mode, the black bars may seem to dance with red accents, indicating the actual level of intensity during play.

FIGURE 27.8.
*You control the volume
with these settings.*

If you see two instruments that appear to be identical, don't think that this represents a mini duet. Holding the cursor over the instrument on the actual mix grid or above the VU meters, you'll notice that a "tag" (ToolTip) pops up describing that instrument specifically (for example, Timpani or String quartet). Two instruments that are different may appear identical, simply because Microsoft has classified each instrument (for example, Marimba and Tubular Bells) as the same visual image.

Controlling the Tempo

Toward the lower-left corner of the Microsoft Music Producer window are the Tempo and the Key signature slider controls. Use the Tempo slider control to change the playing speed (*tempo*) of your composition (see Figure 27.9).

FIGURE 27.9.

Tempo control.

Moving the control to the left decreases the playing speed; moving the control to the right increases the speed. The range of tempo that's available is 10 beats per minute (bpm), which is when the slide control is completely left, through 350 bpm, which is represented when the slide control is completely right.

As a former disc jockey (DJ), I can safely say that most high-energy dance or club-type music sits around the 110–135 bpm setting, while slower, soft, mood-setting tunes are around 70–80 bpm, very much like the beat of your own heart. DJs use beats per minute to decide which tracks (tunes, songs) will mix easily with other tracks, usually with a discrepancy of 10–20 beats, depending on the DJ's plan. Some DJs actually use harmonics as well to make the mixes not only unnoticeable, but attractive to the ear. To get the harmonics straight, you'll need a key signature (see the next section).

No, you aren't losing your mind if, after you change the tempo, the screen still displays 4/4 time. The program continues to display this time signature after the tempo has actually been changed.

Changing the Key

If you want to change the key, more commonly known as the *key signature*, use the Key slider control shown in Figure 27.10.

FIGURE 27.10.

Change the key with this setting.

Moving the control toward the left causes a decrease in the key signature, lowering the tonal pitches. Moving the control toward the right causes an increase in tonal pitches. Try it, and watch the key signature—that is, the number of sharps or flats that appear with each change.

I won't go into a theory lesson here—just some simple reminders for you to think about. Think of this as a simple keystroke, moving up and down a piano keyboard in half steps—up the scale, C, C sharp, D, D sharp, and down the scale, C, B, B flat, A, A flat, G, and so on. Remember that some notes have more than one name: B flat can be considered A sharp. Although D sharp is actually E flat, it's more commonly known as E flat.

When you change each key, you'll see the key signature noted toward the right of the word Key in the dialog box (see Figure 27.11).

FIGURE 27.11.
The key signature indicator.

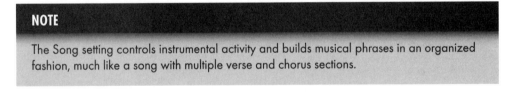

Harmonics and keys are a great way to express feelings in a track. Flat pitches seem to convey sincere, serious, or sullen tones; sharp pitches seem to have a more poignant or exciting effect.

Defining the Shape

You define the content of your composition with the Shape setting shown in Figure 27.12. The Shape feature basically tells Microsoft Music Producer how to build the content of your composition. For example, if you select Rising, your composition will build in intensity throughout the entire period you define. If you select Falling, the content will gradually drop off in intensity until the composition ends. This is a pretty easy concept to grasp. The options available for this feature are Rising, Falling, Peaking, Level, Loud, Quiet, Song, Loopable, and Random.

> **NOTE**
>
> The Song setting controls instrumental activity and builds musical phrases in an organized fashion, much like a song with multiple verse and chorus sections.

FIGURE 27.12.
Control the shape with this setting.

Introducing and Ending Compositions

Sometimes it may be important to create an introduction to a composition. To accomplish this, click the Intro check box located to the left of the Shape drop-down list. Conversely, you may require an ending. In the same manner, click the Ending check box.

Specifying the Length of the Composition

By default, Microsoft Music Producer produces a composition 30 seconds in length. You may decide to keep this setting and use a shape that's looping. On the other hand, if you want some sort of techno-all-over-the-place tune that lasts a bit longer, you can change the Length setting (see Figure 27.13).

FIGURE 27.13.

Setting the composition length.

The Length setting is shown in MM:SS:TT (minutes, seconds, tenths of a second). Microsoft Music Producer has a maximum output capacity of 1,000 measures of music. The number of measures or amount of sound produced is directly related to the tempo. The greater the tempo value, the less the maximum composition period. Remember, 1,000 measures—that's all you get.

Creating the Composition

Okay, you have your features set. How do you create your composition? Easy—click the Compose button. Pressing this button will seem to do nothing. What it actually does is reset your "music cache" or clear your working slate and get ready to start a new session. To hear the music being composed, you actually need to click the Play button (see Figure 27.14).

You can loop your composition endlessly on playback by selecting the Loop check box, located just to the right of the Play button. The Loop option works best when the shape selected is Loopable.

FIGURE 27.14.

Control the play with these settings.

Period chronometer   Stop button   Play button   Select the Loop option to loop the playback endlessly

After you click the Play button, your work comes to life, and the Play button becomes a Pause button. While playing, the period chronometer advances until the allotted time period specified in the Length setting is displayed and achieved. During this period, you can click and drag the instruments in the Mix box (refer to Figure 27.6) to satisfy your sound effect needs. See the earlier section "Setting Up the Band" to learn how to move the instruments around to create various sound qualities.

You have now created a fantastic customized sound file!

Saving the Composition

You can save your composition in one or more of three different formats: .wav, .mid, and .mmp. If you plan to edit this musical composition in the future, save it first as an .mmp file (the native format for Microsoft Music Producer); then save it to the desired format, .wav or .mid.

NOTE

If you don't save a copy in .mmp format, you won't be able to edit this composition in the future. Not with Microsoft Music Producer, that is. Music Producer only allows editing of files saved in its native .mmp format—always remember that.

Adding Your Sounds to Your Web Pages

To use your new Music Producer sounds in your Web pages, you need to reference the sound files using HTML tags. The tag commonly associated with sound is <BGSOUND> with the LOOP and SRC attributes. This tag works only with Microsoft Internet Explorer.

The <BGSOUND> tag identifies information that will be associated with background sound. The first attribute, SRC, tells the browser where the source of the referenced sound is located. The second attribute, LOOP, indicates the number of times you want the sound file to play after the page is loaded. (This is also called *iterations*.) If you want the music to play virtually forever, simply set the LOOP attribute to INFINITE.

Here's how you code the HTML line in your HTML document:

```
<BGSOUND SRC=C:\MUSIC\Caribe.mid LOOP=1>
```

This tag indicates to the browser that the source file is C:\MUSIC\Caribe.mid and you only want it played once.

If you want this music to play for as long as the current page is displayed, use this HTML line:

```
<BGSOUND SRC=C:\MUSIC\Caribe.mid LOOP=INFINITE>
```

Try these two examples and see how this works. You always learn from experience which settings are right for your specific needs. Experiment with the LOOP attribute by changing the value up or down to make the music last just long enough.

TIP

If you have a sound file with a "laser blast" effect in it, you can give the effect of multiple laser blasts simply by changing the LOOP value, therefore eliminating the need to use a separate file or create one.

Another way of playing a sound file on your Web page is by referencing the file with a standard hyperlink. This is probably one of the easier ways to implement sound in a Web page. For example, this type of HTML text could look like this:

```
<A HREF=laserblast.mid>Laser Blast</A>
```

The Web browser simply displays a hyperlink for the file, like this:

```
Laser Blast
```

If properly referenced, clicking this link activates the sound file. If it doesn't work, check your syntax and spelling. If it still doesn't work, make sure that you have a sound card on the machine you're using, and the volume is turned up and not muted.

I find it unnecessary to enclose the filename in quotes, but for some browsers it may be required. If you're using a long filename such as `Sallys Voice.wav`, quotes will probably be necessary. However, I suggest reverting to the MS-DOS short filename to ensure that the file plays when requested. You can pretty much rely on the short filename to work. The MS-DOS short filename for `Sallys Voice.wav` would be `Sallys~1.wav`, unless of course you had other files in that directory beginning with the same six letters. (Then it could be `Sallys~2.wav`, and so on.)

> **NOTE**
>
> The MS-DOS short filename is normally the first six letters of a filename, followed by a tilde (~), then a sequential number designating the number of files that match the first six letters of the file in question. If files exist that match the first six letters of a new file you're saving in the same location, the new file will be assigned the next sequential number after the current count of files.

If you have multiple files and you want to be certain of a file's MS-DOS short filename, in Windows 95, right-click the file and select the Properties menu item to display the property sheet, as shown in Figure 27.15.

FIGURE 27.15.

The property sheet for a sound file.

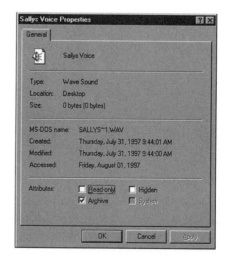

In the second section, look at the MS-DOS Name setting (roughly four lines down in the dialog box). Whatever is displayed for this setting is the MS-DOS short filename for your file.

The advantage of using a hyperlink over a `<BGSOUND>` tag is that hyperlinks are the HTML standard, and work with most browsers. Another advantage is that the sound file is played on demand, when the user wants to hear it, and not loaded automatically when the page is first hit. This could save the user time and frustration, especially if he or she hates music—or just hates *your* music.

Some disadvantages include the fact that the user has to perform some action before the music is played. Maybe you need the music to play when the user first opens the page. If this is the case, the hyperlink method clearly won't work for you. You need to use the `<BGSOUND>` tag, or, if your users won't all be using Internet Explorer, you could use this `<META>` tag:

```
<META HTTP-EQUIV="REFRESH" CONTENT="1;http://mysite/Laserblast.mid">
```

This `<META>` example redirects the browser to the listed sound file. Unfortunately, it keeps on redirecting, and it does cause a bit of page flicker—which can be annoying if there's a lot of text to be read. This is especially so with smaller sized fonts.

The best way to find out which HTML tag will work best for your particular needs is to experiment. Try each method in your Web page and see which example seems to work the most effectively without degrading performance of your Web page.

A more complex way to add sounds is by using Microsoft's `<EMBED>` tag. Although this tag has many options, you only need to use a few to actually get the job done. For a brief rundown of the `<EMBED>` tag attributes, see Table 27.1.

> **NOTE**
>
> Remember that these tags are proprietary and, of course, will work only in Microsoft's browser.

Table 27.1. EMBED tag attributes.

Attribute	Description
`ACCESSKEY=string`	Specifies an accelerator for the element. (The accelerator is the key pressed at the same time as the Alt key to activate the embedded object.)

continues

Table 27.1. continued

Attribute	Description
ALIGN=*setting*	Specifies the alignment for the control-like element. (This is used only if the embedded object is visible. You only need to use this if you actually have an ActiveX control embedded to play your sound.) Specify ABSBOTTOM, ABSMIDDLE, BASELINE, BOTTOM, LEFT, MIDDLE, RIGHT, TEXTTOP, or TOP for *setting*.
HEIGHT=*string*	Along with WIDTH, specifies the size at which the element is drawn. (Same as ALIGN, use only if visible.)
HIDDEN=*string*	Forces the embedded element to be invisible. (Use this for sound without an ActiveX association.)
ID=*string*	An SGML identifier used as the target for hypertext links or for naming particular elements in associated style sheets.
SRC=*string*	Specifies a source URL for the associated file. (This one is important—it's the name and location of your file.)
STYLE=*string*	Specifies an inline style sheet for the tag. (Only if visible, and this doesn't apply to sound.)
TITLE=*string*	Provides advisory information. If your browser is configured to ignore graphics, for example, and this has a graphic, the graphic will be replaced with a text bar labeled whatever you named this item.
WIDTH=*string*	Returns the calculated width of the element in pixels. In HTML, this attribute may be initially set in pixels or percentages.
event = *script*	Explained in the following paragraphs.

Although the <EMBED> tag enables you to embed documents of any type, you and the user need to have an application server object that can activate the data installed correctly on your machines.

> **NOTE**
>
> An *application server object* is a MIDI player, or MIDI out-of-process server. Don't worry, if you installed your sound drivers, it's probably there.

Because the <EMBED> tag takes advantage of Active technology, it supports certain events. An event occurs when the user performs an action on the control. The following list shows the possible events that can be triggered by this tag:

OnAfterUpdate	OnKeyUp
OnBeforeUpdate	OnLoad
OnBlur	OnMouseDown
OnClick	OnMouseMove
OnDblClick	OnMouseOut
OnFocus	OnMouseOver
OnHelp	OnMouseUp
OnKeyDown	OnReadyStateChange
OnKeyPress	

The events are for the most part self-explanatory. For example, the OnClick event occurs when a user clicks the object, and so on.

The <EMBED> tag is a block element tag, meaning that it has to be delimited. Although the starting tag is required (<EMBED>), the ending tag (</EMBED>) is optional.

For more information on tags like this, visit the Microsoft site developers' Web page at www.microsoft.com/sitebuilder. Look under the technologies section, Active Platform area.

When placing the sound HTML tags in my HTML code, I sometimes find it helpful to place the multimedia tags that are not ordinal-specific toward the end of the page if they are used with an autoload-type tag (<BGSOUND>, and so on). This gives the browser a chance to process the page completely and most likely display faster, if the MIDI or WAV files are a little larger.

> **TIP**
>
> Always keep the user in mind. Don't make your music files so large that your users leave before the sound begins. Use the looping features to create that extended effect, and use MIDI files where possible to keep the file size to a minimum.

Some Practical Examples

Why would someone want music on a Web page? Simply put, your expressions through music can show others how you want them to feel while viewing your graphics and text. Let's examine a familiar example of how you would properly portray an actual image. Then we'll discuss some Web-type examples.

Start by visualizing Darth Vader with his feathering black satin robes proceeding down the cathedral-like chambers of his immense star destroyer. What type of sounds would you use to portray this? Of course, you might be well familiar with John Williams' idea of the "Imperial

March," which was more than impressive, but I'm going to give you a few settings to try with Microsoft Music Producer. Keep in mind that I'm no John Williams, but I might come off sounding like a slight protégé if I can get my message across with sound!

First, let's think of key and tempo. A key with a lot of flats might sound a bit villainous, and a tempo a bit slower but not dragging might give a bit of zip while still containing the "you never know what will happen next" mood. For the key signature, let's try an old favorite of mine, A flat. That's about the third tick mark on the Key slider control. For the tempo, a slower pace but enough tempo to keep the flow. Let's try 88. Great.

In the Style box, select the style named Dark Techno. That's actually a perfect name for that style, too. You'll see once you start your preview.

In the Personality box, select Searching, which will give the effect of wandering things—well, like the cape.

Finally, in the Band box, select Lush, which might describe the rather ominous surroundings.

You know the drill now—click the Preview button. Sounds pretty cool, right? I admit it, John Williams I am not, but I think I have a good grasp on this scene.

For fun, select the Intro and Ending options, then for the sound shape, select Random. Leave the length at the default setting of 30 seconds, click the Compose button, and then click the Play button.

You have now created a sound file with a purpose! It's much easier to design a Web page and then do your sounds. As the old saying goes, get the machine working, then throw in the bells and whistles. Well, these are your bell and whistles!

Now that you have a little experience creating music for setting a scene, let's try another example.

Let's say you have a friend, Ann, who needs you to design a Web system for her travel agency. Ann offers travel to many different countries, and you'd like to put the Web page user in the correct mood for each different area.

Ann has packages for each different region or country of the world, which will make it a little easier on you, and is probably a good idea on her part, as you can group regions or country packages together on the same page.

The first page you're ready to jazz up is the Caribbean island getaways. Using Music Producer, your work is almost finished before you start. Under the Style selection, choose Caribbean, then click the Preview key. Vòila! So easy! And it sounds pretty good without any modification. But don't forget about the other features of Music Producer that enable you to modify this style to make it a style of your own.

For example, you may want to change the band to Bright & Punchy to make the music a little more sassy. The default tempo for Caribbean is 96, and the key signature is set to C. Slowing down the tempo may give the effect of a relaxed tropical breeze blowing through the trees.

Other countries Ann might offer could include Italy, Argentina, China, India, or Eastern Europe. All of these named styles and many others can be found in Music Producer with default settings that I would deem appropriate for most uses.

> **TIP**
>
> Keep the volume in mind. You don't want to alarm users by having them leap from a soft gentle breeze to a wild Italian accordionfest. Use similar volumes on each page and be consistent.

If you have the ideas at hand, it will prove much easier to create your musical compositions. Everyone is different in approaching the same task, however. You may find it easier for your specific task to do the contrary. It's up to you—I'm simply showing ways to approach and formulate easy design methods.

Summary

Microsoft Music Producer is a fantastic application that enables non-musicians (or the non-music-oriented) to add sound features to their applications or presentations easily. Although it's true that Microsoft Music Producer is nothing fancy, it's a great way to spice and jazz up any computerized display with ease and with a very small learning curve.

The best way to make the most of Microsoft Music Producer is to sit down and play. Make note of your favorite feature names or settings, and incorporate them together.

Imagine what Mozart could have done with Microsoft Music Producer. Better yet, imagine what Music Producer can do for you!

Extending Active Server Pages

CHAPTER 28

One of Internet Information Server's most powerful features is its extensibility. Because IIS uses Microsoft's Component Object Model (COM), it's possible to build a component in virtually any language, and then add that component to IIS.

What sorts of components are useful? Your imagination is the limit. The following list is just a few possibilities:

- Create a complex pricing algorithm.
- Add a smart-card authentication routine.
- Extract images from a database.
- Call the Windows API from ASP.
- Use as a VBScript replacement.

Replacing scripts with components sounds like lots of work for little return. But there's a commercial reason to do this: If you're in the business of developing and selling ASP sites, there's no other way to "compile" (hide) your code.

Because COM itself is language-independent, you're free to use virtually any language that supports DLL compilation. These languages include Visual Basic, C, Java, and COBOL. COBOL is one of the most interesting languages mentioned here. By rewriting legacy code as a DLL, it's possible to port legacy code to the Internet!

> **NOTE**
>
> This chapter contains several examples that illustrate how you can build powerful components in Visual Basic and Java. But the chapter isn't a tutorial about either language. For an excellent tutorial on these two topics, see *Visual Basic 5 Developers Guide* by Tony Mann or *Developing Enterprise Apps with Visual J++* by Michael Mitchell.

> **NOTE**
>
> This is a chapter about creating server-side components. Unfortunately, Microsoft named both client and server components ActiveX for marketing reasons. Judging from the constant stream of questions on Microsoft's mailing lists and newsgroups, the naming convention is less than optimal.

Threading Models: Who Cares?

When a visitor accesses your Web site, he or she is really logging on as a user (usually named IUSR_*MACHINE*, where *MACHINE* is the name of your computer). This presents a new challenge: If multiple visitors are all doing the same thing at the same time (and as the same user), your software can't make any assumptions about the order of events. For example, you can't write a component that updates a database based on the most-recently-read record. If two people are accessing the database at the same time, and your component assumes that the record to be updated is the last record that it read, then Bad Things will happen.

As a component developer, it's your responsibility to understand threading models, and how the threading model affects your application! As you'll see in a moment, Visual Basic's threading model is not the same as Java's.

Microsoft's Component Object Model introduces the notion of *thread safety*. In the old days, everyone ran single-user Windows workstations that were used by one person at a time. Windows NT and the Internet changed everything. Web servers process multiple requests at a time, and, in order to optimize server efficiency, code and data connections are *pooled*. That is, one Web request may execute a portion of code, then another Web request will ask that same code module to do something different. It's the code's responsibility to assume nothing about who or what requested an operation. This model is called *free-threaded*.

Not all objects are free-threaded. Visual Basic and Microsoft Access, for example, are not. VB 5 uses the apartment model (see Table 28.1), and Access is effectively single-threaded. The way you use a component must take into account its threading model. However, truly "unsafe" objects can be bundled inside Microsoft Transaction Server packages to provide a higher level of isolation, which in turn leads to thread safety.

Table 28.1. Threading models.

Model	Description
Single-threaded	Designed as a single-user application, where all processes are handled in a linear fashion. Do not use for Web applications.
Apartment-threaded	Can run as a multiple-use component, but with only a single thread at a time. Do not use as a system-wide object (for example, at the application level) because you'll create a bottleneck. VB 5 uses this model.
Free-threaded	Runs as a multiple-use component, with more than one thread at a time. J++ and C++ are able to create these components, but programmers need to be aware that the issues involved require a fundamental understanding of thread safety.
Both	Able to operate as both free-threaded and apartment-threaded. This is the best of all worlds. By default, Java uses this model in the Microsoft environment.

The remainder of this chapter is devoted to three "cookbook" examples that show you how to build a component. The examples assume that you've already installed Visual Basic 5 or a Java compiler, and that you know your way around the integrated development environment (IDE).

We'll jump right into Java, which is more complex than Visual Basic. It's also more powerful because Java is analogous to C, in that it exposes a lower level of the Windows API.

The second two examples use Visual Basic, which is the easiest way to build almost anything. But our second VB example digs into the Windows API to demonstrate several advanced concepts.

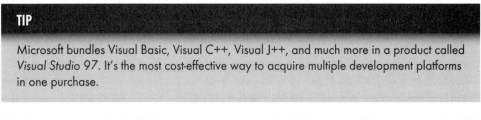

TIP

Microsoft bundles Visual Basic, Visual C++, Visual J++, and much more in a product called *Visual Studio 97*. It's the most cost-effective way to acquire multiple development platforms in one purchase.

Our first two examples build the same component in both languages. The component itself is not as complex as a typical production component for two reasons:

- Production code requires extra error-handling code that gets in the way of the example.

- A truly robust example is difficult to read because code complexity obscures the lesson.

The component accepts a state abbreviation as input, and then returns all soaring (glider) clubs in that state, in formatted table format. Couldn't this be done in VBScript, without the hassle of writing a component? Of course it could. The advantage is that our code is compiled, which protects our intellectual investment.

Because the component runs as a session-level object (one instance per user), the apartment-threading model is appropriate. Both Visual Basic and Java are able to create apartment-threaded objects, so either tool is an appropriate choice.

Setting Up the Development Environment

This chapter uses a Web site with four directories, as follows:

```
SSA
\Root
\Components
\Images
\Scripts
```

Only the `Scripts` and `Components` directories are actually used here, but the real site needs all four. Our Java component will be installed in `\WinNt\Java\TrustLib` for security reasons associated with Java, but the VB components will be placed in the `\Components` subdirectory shown here.

> **NOTE**
>
> All the code examples in this chapter are contained on the CD included with this book.

Chapter 2, "Installing and Using Internet Information Server," describes how to set up Internet Information Server. If you haven't already set up a Web site, review the chapter now and set up the site tree just shown. Pay particular attention to the section in Chapter 2 called "Application Development Settings."

Creating Server-Side Components with J++

J++ is close to C++ in that it's an object-oriented language. Java's biggest differentiation is that it is platform-independent, although one can argue that Internet product life cycles are so short that you'll never have time to compile your component on two platforms before it's obsolete! C++ still holds a speed advantage over J++, although the difference is narrowing.

This chapter uses Visual J++ 1.1 as a development environment. Because Java is portable, almost any Windows-based Java compiler will work. The only "unusual" aspect is that your component must be registered as a COM object, which involves importing the COM type libraries and using `javareg` to register the component with Windows NT.

> **NOTE**
>
> COM is a Microsoft technology, and for this reason Java code written for IIS components won't run on other platforms. This isn't likely to be an issue, however, because IIS runs only on NT.

Java component development includes the following steps:

1. Install type libraries, if needed.
2. Write the source code.
3. Build the project.
4. Register your component.
5. Reference the component from an ASP page.

> **NOTE**
>
> Marketing hype alert! This section describes how to build components in Java, which is very different from JavaScript or JScript. Both JavaScript and JScript are interpreted scripting languages, and have little or nothing to do with Java or J++. The only similarity is in the minds of the marketing folks who promote their client's favorite product line.

Installing Type Libraries

To write Java applications for ASP, you must first generate the type libraries. Any reference to `import asp;` will fail unless you've completed this step. (`import.asp`) is a Java type library, which is analogous to C's `include` files that end in `.h`.

Within the Visual J++ IDE, choose Tools | Java Type Library Wizard, then select Microsoft Active Server Pages 1.0 Library. Click OK to generate the libraries.

Built-in Object Interfaces

The type libraries that you installed in the preceding section support access to ASP's intrinsic objects via the `IScriptingContext` interface. Table 28.2 lists the interfaces exposed by the type libraries, and additional information about each exposed object is described in Part Three, Section B—Active Server Objects.

Table 28.2. Built-in object interfaces.

Interface	Purpose
IApplicationObject	Calls the `Application` object's methods and properties.
IRequest	Calls the `Request` object's methods and properties.
IResponse	Calls the `Response` object's methods and properties.
IReadCookie	Returns the contents of the `Cookies` collection (read-only).
IRequestDictionary	Indexes the collections in the `Request` object via the `IRequest` interface.
IScriptingContext	Returns an interface to the `Application`, `Request`, `Response`, `Server`, or `Session` object.
IServer	Calls the `Server` object's methods and properties.
ISessionObject	Calls the `Session` object's methods and properties.
IStringList	Returns string values from collections such as `QueryString`, `Form`, and `ServerVariables`.
IWriteCookie	Sets cookie contents.

Building the Component

Using Explorer, create an empty folder named `AspUnleashed`. This example assumes it's on drive `C:`, in the format `C:\AspUnleashed`.

Start Visual Studio or J++, as appropriate for your installation. Choose File | New to display the workspace dialog box. Click the Workspaces tab, enter **Chapter28** as the workspace name, and set the location to **C:\AspUnleashed\Chapter28**, as shown in Figure 28.1. (If you already tried the Visual Basic example, this workspace exists.)

FIGURE 28.1.

Step 1: Create the `Chapter28` *workspace.*

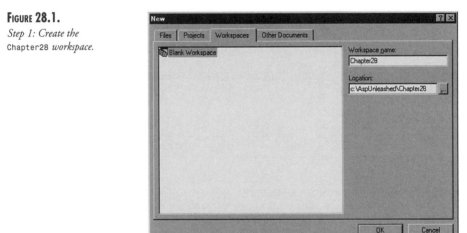

28

EXTENDING ACTIVE
SERVER PAGES

Within the workspace, a Java project is required. Choose File | New, click the Projects tab, select Java Project from the list, and then enter **JavaSoaringSites** as the project name, as shown in Figure 28.2. Be sure to select the Add to Current Workspace option.

FIGURE 28.2.

Step 2: Create the JavaSoaringSites *project inside the* Chapter28 *workspace.*

Finally, create a Java source file. Once again, choose File | New. Click the Files tab, select Java Source File from the list, and then enter **JSoaringSites** as the filename, as shown in Figure 28.3.

FIGURE 28.3.

Step 3: JSoaringSites *is the only file created in this project.*

Listing 28.1 is a simple Java Calendar component. Error-trapping is omitted from the example, in order to focus on the concept. The same algorithm is also shown later (in Listing 28.4) as a Visual Basic component.

Listing 28.1. JSoaringSites.java.

```java
// JSoaringSites
// This small Java example demonstrates how to create an
// ASP component in Java

import com.ms.com.*;
import asp.*;

class JSoaringSites
{
    IResponse m_iResponse = null;
    IRequest m_iRequest = null;

    String m_sReturnString = "";

    public void OnStartPage(IScriptingContext objScriptContext)
    {
        m_iResponse = objScriptContext.getResponse();
        m_iRequest = objScriptContext.getRequest();
    }

    public void OnEndPage()
    {
        m_iResponse = null;
```

```
        m_iRequest = null;
    }

    public void ListSoaringSites(String sState)
    {
        Variant vOutput = new Variant();
        vOutput.putString("Requested State: "+sState);
        m_iResponse.Write(vOutput);

        m_sReturnString = "<P>";
        if (sState.equalsIgnoreCase("WA"))
        {
            m_sReturnString += "Arlington, WA<BR>";
            m_sReturnString += "Burlington, WA<BR>";
            m_sReturnString += "Pullman, WA<BR>";
            m_sReturnString += "Richland, WA<BR>";
            m_sReturnString += "Wenatchee, WA<BR>";
            m_sReturnString += "Yakima, WA<BR>";
        }
        else if (sState.equalsIgnoreCase("WI"))
            m_sReturnString += "<BR>West Bend, WI<BR>";
        else m_sReturnString += "No sites found for "+sState;
        vOutput.putString(m_sReturnString);
        m_iResponse.Write(vOutput);
    }
}
```

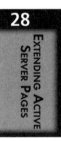

Two lines of code are elements unique to Java. The `import com.ms.com.*` and `import asp.*` statements are analogous to `include` files in C. These two statements reference COM and ASP type libraries that you installed a moment ago.

`OnStartPage` and `OnEndPage` are special events that automatically execute whenever the component initializes or terminates. ASP calls these routines for you, so no special consideration is needed in your code. In fact, this component could easily skip including the references, but they're in the example in case you want to extend it for other purposes. For example, you might add a database open event that executes as soon as the component initializes when the page opens.

By using `equalsIgnoreCase` we're able to match all case combinations as valid input. So wa, Wa, and WA all work as state abbreviations for Washington.

Our example has information for two states only, scientifically picked to exclude lots of typing. In real life it's unlikely that you'd build a massive `if` statement to list soaring sites. This component should be rewritten to use database queries, but we're keeping the example as small as possible in order to present basic concepts.

After you've typed in the code or copied it from the CD, build the Java component by pressing F7. Then copy the component to the `\WinNt\java\TrustLib` directory. Finally, register the component as follows (make certain you're in the `TrustLib` directory, at a shell prompt):

```
"\Program Files\DevStudio\VJ\bin\javareg" /register /class:JSoaringSites
➥/progid:Chapter28.JSoaringSites
```

NOTE

If you've already registered the component, don't forget to unregister the previous instance by typing the following commands *before* registering the newest component version:

```
"\Program Files\DevStudio\VJ\bin\javareg" /unregister
➥/class:JSoaringSites /progid:Chapter28.JSoaringSites
```

Make sure that there are no registered instances by using `OleView.exe`, which is in your `Java\bin` directory. For some reason—probably related to the inability of Visual J++ 1.1 to register from any directory—unregistering a class doesn't always work. If you find references to this class inside OleView, the only alternative is to search the Registry for all instances of the class, then manually delete them. There will be three references per class.

TIP

OleView is an excellent debugging tool. Sometimes it's difficult to isolate problems; are they a registration/configuration issue, or are they an ASP issue? When you double-click a class in OleView, you're actually creating an instance of the COM object.

If the object is properly registered, OleView displays the COM interfaces associated with the component. If OleView reports an error, the problem is likely to be a configuration/registration issue. (This undocumented tip is from a well-known Microsoft ASP support tech.)

NOTE

With Java 1.1 or higher, you aren't required to copy your component to a common directory, because the registration process maps a path to wherever you registered it from. You'll save lots of pain if all components are kept in a common directory, as no tool is available to show you which directory the component was in when it was registered.

Murphy's Law dictates that just before your site goes live, you'll accidentally register a component in the wrong location, and then be stuck poking through the Registry to manually eradicate it.

The following two ASP pages make use of the component. The first page is a simple form that accepts the user's choice of states. The second form processes the request and passes it to the Java component. Because only two states (Washington and Wisconsin) are in the Java component, most queries simply return a `No sites found` reply.

Listing 28.2 illustrates how the Soaring Sites component is used. The HTML code asks the user to choose a state in which to search for a soaring site. Then the user's request is passed to Listing 28.3 by using HTML's FORM object.

Listing 28.2. JavaSoaringSites.asp.

```
<!DOCTYPE HTML PUBLIC "-//W3C//DTD HTML 4.0 Final//EN">
<HTML>
<HEAD>
    <TITLE>Soaring Sites Results</TITLE>
</HEAD>

<BODY BGCOLOR="#FFFFFF">
<FONT SIZE="2" FACE="Verdana, Arial, Helvetica">

<CENTER><H1>Soaring Sites</H1></CENTER>
<HR Color="Red">

<FORM ACTION="JavaSoaringSitesAction.asp">
    Enter a state abbreviation to search for a site:  
    <INPUT NAME="State" SIZE="2"><BR>
    <INPUT TYPE="SUBMIT">
</FORM>

</BODY>
</HTML>
```

Listing 28.3 is where our JSoaringSites component is actually used. The HTML code retrieves the user's request from the REQUEST object (an intrinsic ASP component), then passes the information to the custom component by calling the ListSoaringSites method. The component itself returns HTML code to the page, which contains a formatted answer.

Listing 28.3. JavaSoaringSitesAction.asp.

```
<% Option Explicit %>
<!DOCTYPE HTML PUBLIC "-//W3C//DTD HTML 3.2 Final//EN">
<HTML>
<HEAD>
    <TITLE>Soaring Sites Results</TITLE>
</HEAD>

<BODY BGCOLOR="#FFFFFF">
<FONT SIZE="2" FACE="Verdana, Arial, Helvetica">

<CENTER><H1>Soaring Sites</H1></CENTER>
<HR Color="Red">

<%
Dim SoaringSites
Set SoaringSites = Server.CreateObject("Chapter28.JSoaringSites")
SoaringSites.ListSoaringSites Request("State")
Set SoaringSites = Nothing
%>

</BODY>
</HTML>
```

> **TIP**
>
> You can skip component registration altogether. Microsoft has implemented the capability to refer to Java components by their monikers, in the following form:
>
> ```
> Set SoaringSites = Server.CreateObject("Java:Chapter28.JSoaringSites")
> ```
>
> As this book goes to press, this functionality was not yet implemented, so the examples in this chapter don't make use of the enhanced syntax.

Creating Server-Side Components with Visual Basic

Visual Basic is the easiest and fastest way to develop a component. The disadvantage is that free-threaded objects can't be written in VB, which means that application-wide components aren't well suited to this environment. Either VB 4 Professional Level or VB 5 is appropriate as a tool. Our examples use VB 5.

The following three steps are all that are required to build a component. This is one less step than the Java example, because Visual Basic doesn't require type libraries.

1. Write the source code.
2. Build the project.
3. Register your component.
4. Reference the component from an ASP page.

Writing the Source Code

Start a new VB 5 ActiveX DLL project. Because we're building a DLL, no user interface exists. VB displays a default code window named Class1. Press F4 and change the property sheet settings as follows:

```
(Name) VBSoaringSites
Instancing 5 - MultiUse
```

If you're using VB 4, set Public to True.

Choose Project | Project 1 Properties on the menu. Change the project name to **SoaringSites** and select the Unattended Execution option.

Finally, click the Make tab of the dialog box and select Auto Increment. Click OK to save these settings.

You can add ASP.DLL as a reference to your project. Choose Projects | References and then select Microsoft Active Server Pages 1.0 Library, as shown in Figure 28.4. Our VB component differs a little from the Java component in that we don't use `OnStartPage` and `OnEndPage` events, so we could skip this reference. It's included as part of the example because you may find it useful for other components.

FIGURE 28.4.

Adding ASP.DLL *as a reference.*

The code in Listing 28.4 takes a different approach than the Java example. The Java example writes to the client directly; this example returns a string to the ASP page, and then the ASP page displays the results.

Enter the source code in the `SoaringSites` code window, as shown in Listing 28.4. Note the addition of `Option Explicit` in the declarations section. Because this statement requires variable declaration, it helps you find typographical errors before they become bugs.

Listing 28.4. VbSoaringSites source code.

```
Option Explicit

Public Function ListSoaringSites(sState As String) As String
    Dim sOutput        As String

    sOutput = "Requested State: " & sState
    sOutput = sOutput & "<P>"

    If UCase(sState) = "WA" Then
        sOutput = sOutput _
            & "Arlington, WA<BR>" _
            & "Burlington, WA<BR>" _
            & "Pullman, WA<BR>" _
            & "Richland, WA<BR>" _
            & "Wenatchee, WA<BR>" _
            & "Yakima, WA<BR>"
    ElseIf UCase(sState) = "WI" Then
        sOutput = sOutput _
            & "<BR>West Bend, WI<BR>"
    Else
        sOutput = sOutput & "No sites found for " & sState
    End If

    ListSoaringSites = sOutput

End Function
```

After all these steps are completed, your project should look like Figure 28.5. Pay particular attention to module and project names, because the operating system uses the names that you entered when you registered your component. A typo will cause extensive head scratching later.

FIGURE 28.5.

The VB project after all settings are completed and code has been keyed.

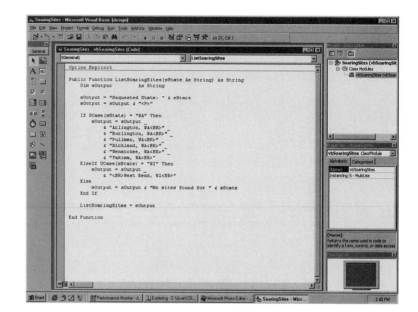

Building the DLL

Save your work to disk. The example on the CD uses \AspUnleashed\Chapter28\VbSoaringSites for a target path, but you can save it in any location that suits your environment.

Choose File | Make VbSoaringSites DLL to build the DLL. The component is saved to the same directory in which you just saved your work.

Copy the DLL to the Components directory of the SSA site. Use the Microsoft Management Console to make certain that this directory's properties include Run in Separate Memory Space, in order to be sure that you can install various versions of the DLL without having to restart the entire computer. (See Chapter 2 for additional information.)

Register the DLL from a command prompt with the following two commands (substitute as needed):

```
cd \ssa\Components
RegSvr32 VbSoaringSites.dll
```

> **CAUTION**
>
> If this isn't your first VbSoaringSites DLL registration, unregister the old DLL *before* copying the new one to the Components directory. Failure to do this will result in multiple entries in the Registry, which in turn will require a tedious RegEdit session to clean out the bad references.
>
> The following commands unregister the old DLL:
>
> ```
> cd \ssa\Components
> RegSvr32 /unregister VbSoaringSites.dll
> ```

Using the Component in a Page

The only difference between the code in Listing 28.5 and its Java counterpart is that this listing calls a different ASP page than the Java example. Listing 28.6 contains more code differences because we're retrieving a string and then using it. That's because this VB DLL doesn't write directly to the client.

Listing 28.5. VBSoaringSites.asp.

```
<!DOCTYPE HTML PUBLIC "-//W3C//DTD HTML 3.2 Final//EN">
<HTML>
<HEAD>
    <TITLE>Soaring Sites Results</TITLE>
</HEAD>

<BODY BGCOLOR="#FFFFFF">
<FONT SIZE="2" FACE="Verdana, Arial, Helvetica">

<CENTER><H1>Soaring Sites</H1></CENTER>
<HR Color="Red">

<FORM ACTION="VBSoaringSitesAction.asp">
    Enter a state abbreviation to search for a site:  
    <INPUT NAME="State" SIZE="2"><BR>
    <INPUT TYPE="SUBMIT">
</FORM>

</BODY>
</HTML>
```

Listing 28.6. VBSoaringSitesAction.asp.

```
<% Option Explicit %>
<!DOCTYPE HTML PUBLIC "-//W3C//DTD HTML 3.2 Final//EN">
<HTML>
```

continues

Listing 28.6. continued

```
<HEAD>
    <TITLE>Soaring Sites Results</TITLE>
</HEAD>

<BODY BGCOLOR="#FFFFFF">
<FONT SIZE="2" FACE="Verdana, Arial, Helvetica">

<CENTER><H1>Soaring Sites</H1></CENTER>
<HR Color="Red">

<%
Dim oSoaringSites
Dim sSiteList

Set oSoaringSites = Server.CreateObject("SoaringSites.vbSoaringSites")

' Set the string to return value of function
sSiteList = oSoaringSites.ListSoaringSites(Request("State"))

Response.Write sSiteList          ' Display the result

Set oSoaringSites = Nothing        ' De-reference the object
%>


</BODY>
</HTML>
```

Listing Printers on a Server

The two examples in the previous sections are useful illustrations, but are far from compelling reasons to write a component, unless you simply need to hide your work in a compiled format. Imagine that your corporate intranet server will print reports from the killer Web app that you're building. Users need to select a printer before they print, and the component described in this section lists the printers on your system. You can enhance the code to actually select a printer and send print jobs to it.

Component Logic

This component was written "the hard way" in order to demonstrate how to call the Windows API from Visual Basic. The same results can be achieved if you use the printers collection that's part of VB 5.

The component calls the EnumPrinters function used by Windows NT. The function returns a list of printers in one of five formats, depending on the "level" that you specify. In this case, we're using level four, which enumerates just the names and locations of the printers attached to our NT server (either directly or by a network connection).

NOTE

The component code shown here works only with Windows NT. If you're running Personal Web Server on Windows 95, use level five; Windows 95 handles network printers as if they're local. That is, the local print engine prints to remote printers.

Level five print structures differ slightly from level four. Use the VB 5 API Browser to copy the `PRINTER_INFO_5` structure into your code.

This is a powerful API call, with many different options. The help file that ships with Visual C provides details about how to use `EnumPrinters`, but translating the C syntax to VB may be challenging. Download Microsoft Knowledge Base article Q166008 from www.microsoft.com for additional details about the translation.

We're storing the returned data in a long array because it's easier to manipulate and inspect than other low-level storage structures. By using the `PtrToStr` and `StrLen` calls, we're able to translate the long array to strings, which are easiest to use in high-level VB.

After determining how many printers are attached to the system, we `redim` two arrays (`m_aDeviceName` and `m_aServerName`) to the number of printers found. If no printers are found, the code will die because error-handling code was left out to preserve clarity.

Writing the Source Code

Again, start a new VB 5 ActiveX DLL project. VB displays a default code window named Class1. Press F4 and change the property sheet settings as follows:

```
(Name) WebPrinters
Instancing 5 - MultiUse
```

If you're using VB 4, set Public to `True`.

Choose Projects | Project 1 Properties, change the project name to **WebUtils**, and select Unattended Execution. Finally, click the Make tab of the dialog box and select Auto Increment. Click OK to save these settings.

Listing 28.7 contains the source code for our printer component. The component only enumerates the printers on your system—you'll need to enhance the code in order to actually print to a printer. Unlike the previous VB component, this example makes use of VB's `Get` and `Let` properties. Discussion of these properties is beyond the scope of this example, but Microsoft's Visual Books Online (bundled with VB 5) contains an in-depth explanation of these two procedures.

28

EXTENDING ACTIVE
SERVER PAGES

Listing 28.7. WebUtils.WebPrinters source code.

```
Option Explicit

Private Declare Function EnumPrinters Lib "winspool.drv" _
    Alias "EnumPrintersA" _
    (ByVal flags As Long, ByVal name As String, _
    ByVal Level As Long, pPrinterEnum As Long, _
    ByVal cdBuf As Long, pcbNeeded As Long, pcReturned As Long) _
    As Long

Private Declare Function PtrToStr Lib "Kernel32" Alias "lstrcpyA" _
        (ByVal RetVal As String, ByVal Ptr As Long) As Long

Private Declare Function StrLen Lib "Kernel32" Alias "lstrlenA" _
        (ByVal Ptr As Long) As Long

Private Type PRINTER_INFO_4
    pPrinterName As String
    pServerName As String
    Attributes As Long
End Type

Private Const PRINTER_ENUM_LOCAL = &H2
Private Const PRINTER_ENUM_CONNECTIONS = &H4
Private Const PRINTER_ENUM_NAME = &H8
Private Const PRINTER_ENUM_NETWORK = &H40
Private Const PRINTER_ENUM_REMOTE = &H10
Private Const PRINTER_ENUM_SHARED = &H20

Private m_iPrinterCount        As Integer
Private m_aDeviceName()        As String
Private m_aServer()            As String

Private Property Let PrinterCount(iValue As Integer)
    m_iPrinterCount = iValue
End Property

Public Property Get PrinterCount() As Integer
    PrinterCount = m_iPrinterCount
End Property

Private Property Let DeviceName(iIndex As Integer, sValue As String)
    m_aDeviceName(iIndex) = sValue
End Property

Public Property Get DeviceName(iIndex As Integer) As String
    DeviceName = m_aDeviceName(iIndex)
End Property

Private Property Let Server(iIndex As Integer, sValue As String)
    m_aServer(iIndex) = sValue
End Property

Public Property Get Server(iIndex As Integer) As String
    Server = m_aServer(iIndex)
End Property
```

```
Private Sub Class_Initialize()
    Dim bReturn             As Boolean
    Dim lFlags              As Long
    Dim sName               As String
    Dim lLevel              As Long
    Dim lBuffer()           As Long
    Dim lCdBuf              As Long
    Dim lPcbNeeded          As Long
    Dim lEntries            As Long
    Dim i                   As Integer
    Dim lTemp               As Long
    Dim sTempString         As String

    lFlags = PRINTER_ENUM_CONNECTIONS Or PRINTER_ENUM_LOCAL
    sName = vbNullString
    lLevel = 4
    lCdBuf = 3072
    ReDim lBuffer((lCdBuf \ 4) - 1) As Long

    bReturn = EnumPrinters(lFlags, sName, lLevel, lBuffer(0), lCdBuf,
    ➥lPcbNeeded, lEntries)
    PrinterCount = lEntries              ' Number Printers Found

    ReDim m_aDeviceName(PrinterCount) As String
    ReDim m_aServer(PrinterCount) As String
    ReDim m_aPaperBin(PrinterCount) As String
    ReDim m_aPaperSize(PrinterCount) As String

    For i = 0 To PrinterCount - 1
        ' Set the Device Name
        sTempString = Space(StrLen(lBuffer(i * 3)))
        lTemp = PtrToStr(sTempString, lBuffer(i * 3))
        DeviceName(i) = sTempString

        ' Set the Server Name
        sTempString = Space(StrLen(lBuffer(i * 3 + 1)))
        lTemp = PtrToStr(sTempString, lBuffer(i * 3 + 1))
        Server(i) = sTempString
    Next i
End Sub
```

Building the DLL

Save your work to disk. The example on the CD uses \AspUnleashed\Chapter28\Utils.

Choose File | Make WebUtils DLL to build the DLL. The component is saved to the same directory in which you just saved your work.

Copy the DLL to the Components directory of the SSA site. Use the Microsoft Management Console to make certain that this directory's properties include Run in Separate Memory Space, in order to be sure that you can install various versions of the DLL without having to restart the entire computer. (See Chapter 2 for additional information.)

Register the DLL from a command prompt with the following two commands (substitute as needed, and don't forget to unregister any previous builds first):

```
cd \ssa\Components
RegSvr32 WebUtils.dll
```

Using the Component in a Page

The ASP code shown in Listing 28.8 lists all printers attached to your system. By rewriting the sample code, you can implement drop-down list boxes that let users select a printer, then pass their choice to your own custom component that sends a report to the printer that they selected.

Listing 28.8. Printers.asp.

```asp
<% Option Explicit %>
<!DOCTYPE HTML PUBLIC "-//W3C//DTD HTML 3.2 Final//EN">
<HTML>
<HEAD>
    <TITLE>System Printers</TITLE>
</HEAD>

<BODY BGCOLOR="#FFFFFF">
<FONT SIZE="2" FACE="Verdana, Arial, Helvetica">

<CENTER><H1>Web Server Printers</H1></CENTER>
<HR Color="Red">

<%
Dim oSystemPrinters
Dim i

Set oSystemPrinters = Server.CreateObject("WebUtils.WebPrinters")
%>
There are <%=oSystemPrinters.PrinterCount%> Server printers<BR>

<%
    i = oSystemPrinters.PrinterCount
    If i > 0 Then
      For i = 0 to i - 1
%>
Printer <% =cstr(i + 1) %>: <%=oSystemPrinters.deviceName(cint(i))%><BR>
<%
        Next
    End If
Set oSystemPrinters = Nothing         ' De-reference the object
%>

</BODY>
</HTML>
```

Summary

Components are incredibly powerful, and separate Microsoft's vision of the Web from all contenders. Take the time to learn how to build them; no ordinary HTML coder can compete with your new skill set!

Additional information about components is available at `www.microsoft.com/iis`, and on various newsgroups such as `news://news.extencia.com/aspdeveloper` and the many Microsoft newsgroups at `news://msnews.microsoft.com`.

28

EXTENDING ACTIVE
SERVER PAGES

VII
PART

Bringing It All Together

Creating an Online Career Services Web Site

IN THIS CHAPTER

This chapter shows you how to create a fully functional Web site from start to finish—in this case, a career services Web site. In particular, you learn how to build the Active Server Pages Job Site.

The process of constructing this Web site illustrates two things. First, it illustrates some of the programming challenges that arise only in the course of creating a full-blown Web site. In earlier chapters, you learned how to use Active Server Pages objects and components one by one. In this chapter, you learn how to integrate multiple objects and components to create a complete Web site.

Second, building this Web site illustrates the tremendous flexibility and power of Active Server Pages. The Web site discussed in this chapter has a number of advanced features. However, using Active Server Pages, it's easy to create. After reading this chapter, you should be able to use Active Server Pages to easily create advanced Web sites of your own.

Overview of the ASP Job Site

The purpose of the Active Server Pages Job Site is to allow people to exchange information about Web development jobs. Web developers who visit the site can search job listings and post their résumés. Employers who visit the site can post new job listings and search the résumés of consultants. The goal of the site is to connect consultants who have very specialized skills with employers who have very specialized needs.

The Web site has six sections (see Figure 29.1). Each section corresponds to a possible action of a consultant or employer.

FIGURE 29.1.
ASP Job Site sections.

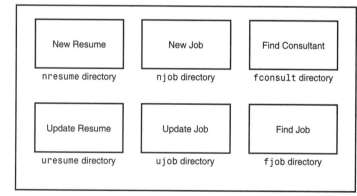

ASPJob directory

The following list explains the purpose of each section:

- **The New Resume section.** In this section, consultants can post their résumés.
- **The Update Resume section.** In this section, consultants can update their résumés as their skills change.

- **The New Job section.** In this section, employers can post new job listings.
- **The Update Job section.** In this section, employers can update the information for a job.
- **The Find Consultant section.** In this section, employers can search for consultants by geography and skills.
- **The Find Job section.** In this section, consultants can search job listings by geography and required skills.

Each of these sections contains either two or three Active Server Pages. In all, the ASP Job Site contains 17 Active Server Pages. It also uses two database tables named `resumes` and `jobs`.

Important Features

The ASP Job Site illustrates how to solve a number of advanced programming problems. You likely will encounter many of these same problems when completing your own Web project. After creating this Web site, you will know how to do the following tasks:

- **Create required form fields.** In many situations, you need to force a user to enter data into a form field before continuing. If the user doesn't answer a required question, you want the form to be redisplayed. The challenge is to do this gracefully. For example, if the user neglects to answer one question in a long HTML form, he or she shouldn't have to completely start over. The form should be redisplayed with the previous answers intact. In this chapter, you learn how to repopulate the fields automatically in an HTML form.
- **Maintain state without sessions or cookies.** Active Server Pages sessions are potentially very useful. However, many browsers don't support them. This project doesn't use either sessions or cookies. You learn how to live without them.
- **Automatically insert the contents of an HTML form into a database table.** If you have a large HTML form with many fields, creating a SQL statement to insert all the form fields into a database table can be tedious. In this chapter, you learn how to have Active Server Pages automatically generate the SQL `INSERT` statement for you.
- **Password-protect an Active Server Page.** At the Active Server Pages Job Site, consultants can post résumés and employers can post job listings. You learn how to use passwords to prevent unauthorized users from altering either the résumés or job listings. You also learn how to generate password codes for users automatically.
- **Populate the fields of an HTML form from a database.** Automatically displaying data in the fields of an HTML form is surprisingly difficult. For example, placing check marks in the right check boxes can be tricky. You learn how to take command of check boxes.

■ **Search a database table.** Visitors to the Active Server Pages Job Site can search résumés and job postings according to different criteria. You learn how to generate SQL statements dynamically to search a database table.

Viewing the Source Code

The Active Server Pages Job Site contains too many pages to list them all in this chapter. The approach is to list only the most important sections of each page. To see the complete source of all of the Active Server Pages discussed in this chapter, you have two options.

The first—and easiest—option is to visit the companion Web site to this book. At `http://www.aspsite.com/aspjobsite`, you'll find a fully functional version of the Active Server Pages Job Site. On the upper-right corner of each page, you can click View Source to view the source code for the Active Server Page.

Second, all the Active Server Pages discussed in this chapter are included on the CD-ROM at the back of this book. You can use any text editor to load and view a page as you read about it in this chapter. If you want, you can also install the Active Server Pages Job Site on your Web server. To do this, follow these steps:

1. Create a directory named `ASPJob` on your hard drive.

2. Copy the files from the CD to this directory. When you do this, make sure you retain all the subdirectories.

3. Use the Internet Service Manager to create a virtual directory that corresponds to the `ASPJob` directory.

4. Use the Internet Service Manager to create an application for this directory. See Chapter 17, "Working with Active Server Pages Applications," for more information on creating applications.

5. Use ISQL/w to open the file named `maketables.sql` from the `ASPJob` directory. Choose your default database and execute the query. Executing the `maketables.sql` file creates two tables named `resumes` and `jobs`.

6. Use any text editor to open the `Global.asa` file from the `ASPJob` directory. You need to assign the name of a valid file data source to the `Application` variable named `ConnectionString`. See Chapter 22, "ActiveX Data Objects," for more information about creating and using a file data source.

The Home Page

The home page of the Active Server Pages Job Site is the first page visitors see when they arrive at the site (see Figure 29.2). It provides information about the purpose of the site. It also has links to all the sections.

FIGURE 29.2.

The home page.

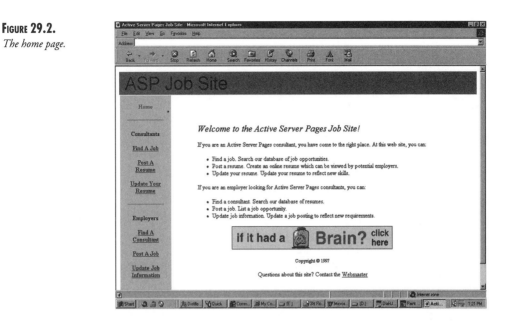

The home page is named `default.asp`. When you provide the page with this name, the page acts as the default page for the directory. For example, you can retrieve the home page by typing `http://www.aspsite.com/aspjobsite` instead of `http://www.aspsite.com/aspjobsite/default.asp`.

NOTE

You can use the Internet Service Manager to specify the filenames of the default pages of a directory.

The home page is an Active Server Page. This is necessary because the Ad Rotator component is used to display a rotating banner advertisement. Otherwise, the page contains only HTML. Listing 29.1 shows the script for the home page.

Listing 29.1. Script for `default.asp`.

```
<HTML>
<HEAD><TITLE> Active Server Pages Job Site </TITLE></HEAD>
<BODY BGCOLOR="#FFFFFF" ALINK="#FF0000">

<!-- Create Top Table For The Title Banner -->
<TABLE BGCOLOR="#00AAff" WIDTH="100%">
<TR><TD VALIGN=CENTER>
<FONT FACE=ARIAL SIZE=+4>  ASP Job Site</FONT></TD></TR>
</TABLE>
```

continues

29

CREATING AN
ONLINE CAREER
SERVICES SITE

Listing 29.1. continued

```
<!-- Create Main Body Table -->
<TABLE HEIGHT="100%" CELLPADDING=20>
<TR>

<!-- The Left Cell Of The Body Table
Contains The Navigation Strip -->
<TD ALIGN=CENTER VALIGN=TOP BGCOLOR="#D0D0D0" WIDTH=100>
<B>
<P><FONT COLOR="#808080">Home</FONT>
<P><HR>
<P>Consultants
<P><A HREF="/fjob/fjob1.asp">Find A Job</A>
<P><A HREF="/nresume/nresume1.asp">Post A Resume</A>
<P><A HREF="/uresume/uresume1.asp">Update Your Resume</A>
<P><HR>
<P>Employers
<P><A HREF="/fconsult/fconsult1.asp">Find A Consultant</A>
<P><A HREF="/njob/njob1.asp">Post A Job</A>
<P><A HREF="/ujob/ujob1.asp">Update Job Information</A>
</B>
</TD>

<!-- The Right Cell Of The Body Table
Contains The Page Contents -->
<TD ALIGN=CENTER VALIGN=CENTER>

<!-- Create Nested Table -->
<TABLE HEIGHT="100%" ALIGN=CENTER CELLSPACING=50>
<TR><TD>
<FONT SIZE=+2><I>Welcome to the Active Server Pages Job Site!</I></FONT>
<P>If you are an Active Server Pages consultant,
you have come to the right place.  At this web site, you can:
<UL>
<LI> Find a job.  Search our database of job opportunities.
<LI> Post a resume.  Create an online resume
which can be viewed by potential employers.
<LI> Update your resume.  Update your resume to reflect new skills.
</UL>
<P>If you are an employer looking for Active Server Pages
consultants, you can:
<UL>
<LI> Find a consultant.  Search our database of resumes.
<LI> Post a job.  List a job opportunity.
<LI> Update job information.  Update a job posting to reflect
new requirements.
</UL>


<!-- Create Page Footer Containing Banner Advertisement -->
<P>
<CENTER>
<% Set MyBrow=Server.CreateObject("MSWC.ADRotator") %>
<%=MyBrow.GetAdvertisement("adrot.txt")%>
<P><FONT SIZE=-1>Copyright &copy; 1997 </FONT>
<P>Questions about this site? Contact the
<A HREF="MAILTO:webmaster@aspsite.com">Webmaster</A>
</CENTER>
```

```
</TD></TR>

<!-- Close The Nested Table -->
</TABLE>
</TD></TR>

<!-- Close The Main Body Table -->
</TABLE>

</BODY>
</HTML>
```

The home page, like all the pages contained in the Active Server Pages Job Site, is divided into three sections, which is accomplished by using tables. The same effect could have been accomplished by using frames. However, there are a number of good reasons to avoid frames when possible (see the section "Final Thoughts on Frames" in Chapter 7, "Advanced HTML").

The first section contains the table for the title banner. The title banner is the blue strip across the top of the page. It's used to show the name of the Web site and the name of the current section.

The second section contains a navigation strip. This navigation strip appears down the left side of every page. It contains links to all the other sections. When you include the navigation strip on every page, the user is only one click away from every other section. The navigation strip is created with a table.

Finally, a third table contains the contents of the page. The home page contains some brief text explaining the purpose of the Active Server Pages Job Site. It also contains the Ad Rotator component, which is used to display an advertisement.

The New Resume Section

The New Resume section is in a subdirectory named nresume. It contains two Active Server Page files (see Figure 29.3). These two pages are used to post a new résumé. At the first page, the user enters résumé information. At the second page, this information is confirmed and inserted into the database.

FIGURE 29.3.
*The New Resume
section.*

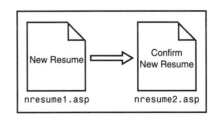

New Resume

The New Resume Page

The source file for the New Resume page is named `nresume1.asp`. The bulk of the New Resume page is made up of an HTML form (see Figure 29.4). This form contains sections where the user can enter information, such as work goals and a list of skills. For example, here's the source of the HTML form for entering contact information:

```
<BLOCKQUOTE>
<BR>*Your Full Name:
<BR><INPUT NAME="FullName" TYPE=TEXT SIZE=30
VALUE="<%=Server.HTMLEncode(Request.Form("FullName"))%>" MAXLENGTH="50">
<P>*Your Email:
<BR><INPUT NAME="Email" TYPE=TEXT SIZE=30
VALUE="<%=Server.HTMLEncode(Request.Form("Email"))%>" MAXLENGTH="50">
<P>Your Phone:
<BR><INPUT NAME="Phone" TYPE=TEXT SIZE=30
VALUE="<%=Server.HTMLEncode(Request.Form("Phone"))%>" MAXLENGTH="30">
</BLOCKQUOTE>
```

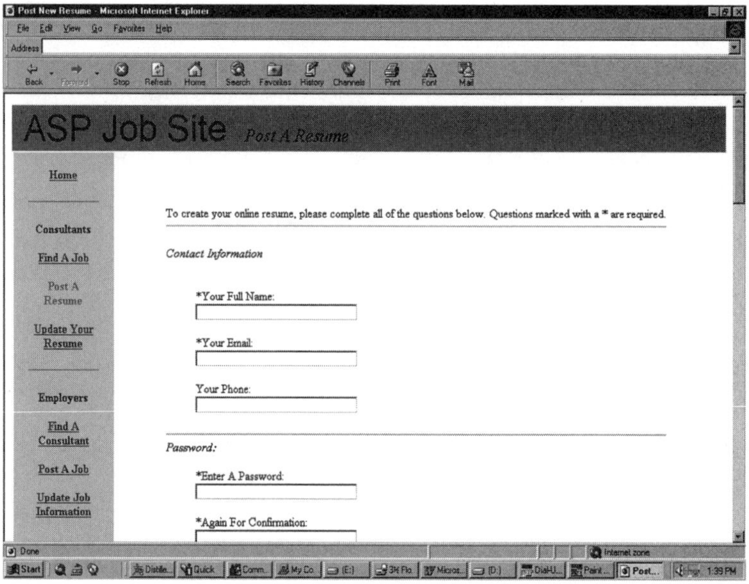

FIGURE 29.4.

The New Resume page.

Notice that each form field has a MAXLENGTH attribute. The data entered into each of the fields will be inserted into the columns of a database table. A table column has a maximum size. The MAXLENGTH attribute prevents the user from entering more information than a particular table column can hold. If you didn't use the MAXLENGTH attribute, you might receive an error from SQL Server when the contents of the form are inserted into the database.

Notice also that the VALUE attribute of each form field is used. For example, the VALUE attribute of the FullName field is assigned the value "<%=Server.HTMLEncode(Request.Form("FullName"))%>.

When this HTML form is first displayed, `Request.Form("FullName")` returns an empty string. In other words, the VALUE attribute accomplishes nothing. The purpose of the VALUE attribute is revealed in the next section.

The Confirm New Resume Page

When the user clicks the Submit Resume button on the New Resume page, he is brought to the Confirm New Resume page. The name of the file for the Confirm New Resume page is `nresume2.asp`.

Depending on the contents of the form that the user submitted, the Confirm New Resume page may display any one of a number of different pages (see Figure 29.5).

FIGURE 29.5.

The Confirm New Resume page.

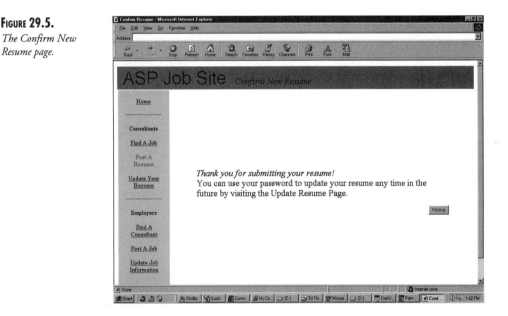

The page is used to verify the contents of a form before it's inserted into the database. Listing 29.2 contains the complete code for this page.

Listing 29.2. The code for `nresume2.asp`.

```
<%
'  Replaces Single Quotes With Double Quotes
FUNCTION KillQuotes(theString)
  KillQuotes=Replace(theString,"'","''")
END FUNCTION

'  Create All Of The Hidden Fields
SUB HiddenFields
```

continues

Listing 29.2. continued

```
 FOR EACH thing IN Request.Form
 %>
 <INPUT NAME="<%=Thing%>" TYPE="HIDDEN"
VALUE="<%=Server.HTMLEncode(Request.Form(Thing))%>">
 <%
 NEXT
END SUB
%>
<HTML>
<HEAD><TITLE> Confirm Resume </TITLE></HEAD>
<BODY BGCOLOR="#FFFFFF"    ALINK="#FF0000">

<!-- Create Title Banner Table -->
<TABLE BGCOLOR="#00aaff" WIDTH="100%">
<TR><TD VALIGN=CENTER>
<FONT FACE=ARIAL SIZE=+4>  ASP Job Site</FONT>
<FONT SIZE=+2>   <I> Confirm New Resume </I></FONT>
</TD></TR>
</TABLE>

<!-- Create Main Body Table -->
<TABLE HEIGHT="100%" CELLPADDING=20>
<TR>

<!-- The Left Cell Of The Body Table
Contains The Navigation Strip -->
<TD ALIGN=CENTER VALIGN=TOP BGCOLOR="#D0D0D0" WIDTH=100>
<B>
<P><A HREF="../default.asp">Home</A>
<P><HR>
<P>Consultants
<P><A HREF="/fjob/fjob1.asp">Find A Job</A>
<P><FONT COLOR="#808080">Post A Resume</FONT>
<P><A HREF="/uresume/uresume1.asp">Update Your Resume</A>
<P><HR>
<P>Employers
<P><A HREF="/fconsult/fconsult.asp">Find A Consultant</A>
<P><A HREF="/njob/njob1.asp">Post A Job</A>
<P><A HREF="/ujob/ujob1.asp">Update Job Information</A>
</B>
</TD>

<!-- The Right Cell Of The Body Table
Contains The Page Contents -->
<TD ALIGN=CENTER VALIGN=CENTER>
<TABLE HEIGHT="100%" ALIGN=CENTER CELLSPACING=50>
<TR><TD>

<%
'  Check Whether Passwords Match
IF UCASE(Request.Form("Password"))<>UCASE(Request.Form("CHKPass")) THEN
%>
<FONT SIZE=+2><I>The two passwords you entered do not match.</I>
<BR>Click Back to return to the previous page.</FONT>
<P>
 <FORM METHOD="POST" ACTION="nresume1.asp">
```

```
 <% HiddenFields %>
 <INPUT TYPE="SUBMIT" VALUE="Back">
 </FORM>
<%
ELSE

'  Check For Required Fields
IF Request.Form("FullName")="" or
➥Request.Form("Email")="" or
➥Request.Form("Password")="" THEN
%>
<FONT SIZE=+2><I>In order to submit your resume,
you must complete all required fields.</I>
<BR>Click Back to return to the previous page.</FONT>
<P>
<FORM METHOD="POST" ACTION="nresume1.asp">
<% HiddenFields %>
<INPUT TYPE="SUBMIT" VALUE="Back">
</FORM>
<%
ELSE
' Create ADO Objects
Set MyConn=Server.CreateObject("ADODB.Connection")
MyConn.Open Application("ConnectionString")

' Check If Email Already Exists
SET RS=MyConn.Execute("SELECT FullName FROM resumes WHERE
➥EMAIL='"&Request.Form("Email")&"'")
IF NOT RS.EOF THEN
%>
<FONT SIZE=+2><I>The email address you entered already exists.</I>
<BR>To update your resume, please visit our Update Resume Page.
Otherwise, click Back to return to the previous page and
enter a different email address.</FONT>
<P>
 <FORM METHOD="POST" ACTION="nresume1.asp">
 <% HiddenFields %>
 <INPUT TYPE="SUBMIT" VALUE="Back">
 </FORM>
<%

ELSE
' IF Email Does NOT Exist, Then Do SQL INSERT

'  Create SQL Insert String
FOR EACH thing IN Request.FORM
IF Request.Form(thing)<>"" and UCASE(thing)<>"CHKPASS" THEN
 MyCols=MyCols&thing&","
 IF Request.Form(thing)="CHECKED" THEN
   MyVals=MyVals&"1,"
 ELSE
   MyVals=MyVals&"'"&KillQuotes(Request.Form(thing))&"',"
 END IF
END IF
NEXT
MyCols="INSERT resumes ("&MyCols&"EntryDate) "
```

continues

Listing 29.2. continued

```
MyVals="VALUES ("&MyVals&"'"&NOW&"')"
MySQL=MyCols&MyVals
MyConn.Execute MySQL
%>
<FONT SIZE=+2><I>Thank you for submitting your resume!</I>
<BR>You can use your password to update your resume
any time in the future by visiting the Update Resume Page.</FONT>
<P>
<FORM ACTION="../default.asp">
<P ALIGN=RIGHT><INPUT TYPE="SUBMIT" VALUE="Home">
</FORM>
<%
END IF ' For Email Exists
RS.Close
MyConn.Close
END IF ' For Required Fields
END IF ' For Matching Passwords
%>
</TD></TR>

<!-- Close Nested Table -->
</TABLE>
</TD></TR>

<!-- Close Body Table -->
</TABLE>

</BODY>
</HTML>
```

The Active Server Page checks three things before submitting the HTML form contents:

- First, it checks whether the two passwords the user entered into the HTML form match.
- Second, it checks whether data was entered into all the required fields.
- Finally, it checks whether the e-mail address the user entered already exists in the database.

If any of these three conditions fails, the user is presented with an error message. He can click a button labeled Back to return to the New Resume page. For example, here's the section of code for displaying the error that appears when the user hasn't completed a required form field:

```
'  Check For Required Fields
IF Request.Form("FullName")="" or
➥Request.Form("Email")="" or
➥Request.Form("Password")="" THEN
%>
<FONT SIZE=+2><I>In order to submit your resume,
you must complete all required fields.</I>
<BR>Click Back to return to the previous page.</FONT>
<P>
<FORM METHOD="POST" ACTION="nresume1.asp">
```

```
<% HiddenFields %>
<INPUT TYPE="SUBMIT" VALUE="Back">
</FORM>
```

This code fragment checks whether the user entered a name, e-mail address, and password. If he failed to enter any one of these items, the error message and HTML form are displayed. Notice the call to the subroutine named HiddenFields. This procedure call is placed within the HTML form. What does it do?

Suppose someone completes all of a résumé but forgets to enter an e-mail address. He submits the form and is presented with an error message and a button back to the previous page. The user would be justifiably upset if he returned to the previous page only to discover that all the information he already entered into the form had been lost. How can this be prevented?

By passing all the data back to the page again inside hidden fields, the form can be repopulated with the data the user previously entered. For example, suppose someone enters a lengthy essay on his job goals in the New Resume page, but forgets to enter an e-mail address. To pass the essay back to the New Resume page from the Confirm New Resume page, you could use the following code:

```
<FORM METHOD="POST" ACTION="nresume1.asp">
<INPUT NAME="Goals" TYPE="HIDDEN" VALUE="<%=Request.FORM("Goals")%>">
<INPUT TYPE="SUBMIT" VALUE="Back">
</FORM>
```

Remember from the previous section that all the HTML form fields in the New Resume page contain a VALUE attribute. For example, the text area form field for Goals looks like this:

```
<BLOCKQUOTE>
Enter a brief description of your work goals:
<BR><TEXTAREA NAME="Goals" COLS=40 ROWS=10
WRAP="VIRTUAL"><%=Request.Form("Goals")%></TEXTAREA>
</BLOCKQUOTE>
```

When the user first arrives at the New Resume page, nothing is shown in the Goals text area. However, suppose an error occurs when he submits the form. When he clicks the Back button on the Confirm New Resume page to return to the New Resume page, any data entered into the Goals text area reappears. The data has been passed back through a hidden form field.

However, it would be very tedious to list every form field from the New Resume page in the Confirm New Resume page as a hidden field. Fortunately, you don't have to do this. The HiddenFields subroutine does it automatically. Here's the code for this subroutine:

```
'  Create All Of The Hidden Fields
SUB HiddenFields
 FOR EACH thing IN Request.Form
 %>
 <INPUT NAME="<%=Thing%>" TYPE="HIDDEN"
VALUE="<%=Server.HTMLEncode(Request.Form(Thing))%>">
 <%
 NEXT
END SUB
```

This subroutine creates a hidden field for each of the items in the Form collection. If the HTML form submitted from the New Resume page contained 500 form fields, this procedure would automatically create 500 hidden form fields in the Confirm New Resume page. When the user clicks the Back button, all these hidden form fields would be passed back to the New Resume page.

The information entered into all the HTML form elements is preserved. Text boxes, text areas, and even check boxes are repopulated with the correct data from hidden form fields. Check boxes create a special problem in this regard. Here's the code used in the New Resume page to provide a check box with the right value:

```
<BR><INPUT NAME="IIS" TYPE="CHECKBOX"
VALUE="CHECKED" <%=Request.Form("IIS")%>>Internet Information Server
```

Notice that the VALUE attribute of the check box is set to CHECKED. If the check box is checked when the form is submitted, the value of the IIS form field will be CHECKED. If the user returns to the page after an error, this value is displayed within the INPUT tag. By displaying the attribute CHECKED, the check box is checked again.

Now suppose there are no problems with the form contents. In that case, the data is inserted into the database table named resumes. A SQL INSERT statement is used to insert the data into the resumes table. In the preceding listing, the SQL INSERT statement is generated dynamically from the Form collection. The name of each item in the Form collection corresponds to the name of a column in the resumes table. By looping through the Form collection, the SQL INSERT statement is generated.

Following is the section of the preceding listing used to dynamically generate the SQL INSERT string:

```
'  Create SQL Insert String
FOR EACH thing IN Request.FORM
IF Request.Form(thing)<>"" and UCASE(thing)<>"CHKPASS" THEN
 MyCols=MyCols&thing&","
 IF Request.Form(thing)="CHECKED" THEN
   MyVals=MyVals&"1,"
 ELSE
   MyVals=MyVals&"'"&KillQuotes(Request.Form(thing))&"',"
 END IF
END IF
NEXT
MyCols="INSERT resumes ("&MyCols&"EntryDate) "
MyVals="VALUES ("&MyVals&"'"&NOW&"')"
MySQL=MyCols&MyVals
MyConn.Execute MySQL
%>
```

The Update Resume Section

The Update Resume section is contained in a subdirectory named uresume. It contains three Active Server Page files (see Figure 29.6). These three pages are used to update an existing résumé.

At the first page, the user enters an e-mail address and password to verify her identity. At the second page, she can update an existing résumé. At the third page, this information is confirmed and inserted into the database.

FIGURE 29.6.

The Update Resume section.

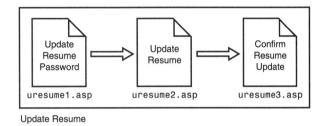

Update Resume

The Update Resume Password Page

The Update Resume Password page contains an HTML form where the user can enter an e-mail address and password (see Figure 29.7). This information is used to verify her identity. When the form is submitted, she is brought to the Update Resume page.

FIGURE 29.7.

The Update Resume Password page.

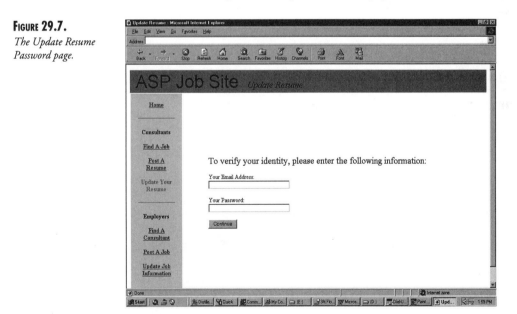

29

CREATING AN
ONLINE CAREER
SERVICES SITE

The Update Resume Page

The Update Resume page does two things. First, it checks the resumes table to see whether the e-mail address and password combination the user entered is valid. If the information is valid, the appropriate résumé is retrieved from the resumes table and displayed in an HTML form (see Figure 29.8).

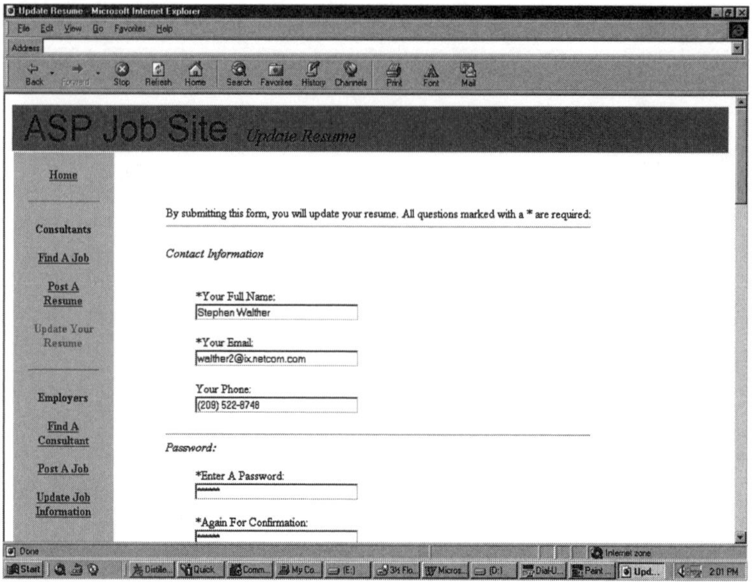

FIGURE 29.8.

The Update Resume page.

Here's a fragment of the code for displaying the data from the database table:

```
<BLOCKQUOTE>
<BR>*Your Full Name:
<BR><INPUT NAME="FullName" TYPE=TEXT SIZE=30
VALUE="<%=TheValue("FullName")%>" MAXLENGTH="50">
<P>*Your Email:
<BR><INPUT NAME="Email" TYPE=TEXT SIZE=30
VALUE="<%=TheValue("Email")%>" MAXLENGTH="50">
<P>Your Phone:
<BR><INPUT NAME="Phone" TYPE=TEXT SIZE=30
VALUE="<%=TheValue("Phone")%>" MAXLENGTH="30">
</BLOCKQUOTE>
```

Notice how the VALUE attribute is used. This attribute is assigned to a function named TheValue(). The data for each field is retrieved from this function. This is the listing for the function:

```
FUNCTION TheValue(theVar)
IF Request.Form("error")<>"" THEN
  TheValue=Server.HTMLEncode(Request.Form(TheVar))
ELSE
  IF NOT ISNULL(RS(TheVar)) THEN TheValue=Server.HTMLEncode(RS(TheVar))
END IF
END FUNCTION
```

This function returns either the value of a form field or the value of a database field. When the form field named error has a value, the function returns the form field. When error doesn't have a value, the function returns the database field. What's the purpose of this function?

When the user first arrives at the Update Resume page, the form field named error doesn't have a value. Because error doesn't have a value, all the form fields are retrieved from the database.

Suppose she makes extensive changes to her résumé and submits the updated version. Now suppose she inadvertently deletes the e-mail address. In that case, she'll be redirected back to the same page.

When the user is redirected back to the Update Resume page, the form fields shouldn't be retrieved from the database. Remember, she made extensive changes. It would be upsetting to lose these changes. Instead, the data should be passed back through hidden form fields.

The function named TheValue() retrieves the values for the HTML form fields from the database only when there has not been an error. When a user has been redirected back to the Update Resume page, the hidden field named error is assigned a value. This causes all the fields in the Update Resume page to be retrieved from hidden form fields. All changes the user made are preserved, so she has no reason to be upset.

The Confirm Resume Update Page

The Confirm Resume Update page is very similar to the Confirm New Resume page. The purpose of this page is to check the contents of the submitted form. If nothing is wrong with the form contents, the resumes table is updated (see Figure 29.9).

FIGURE 29.9.
The Confirm Resume Update page.

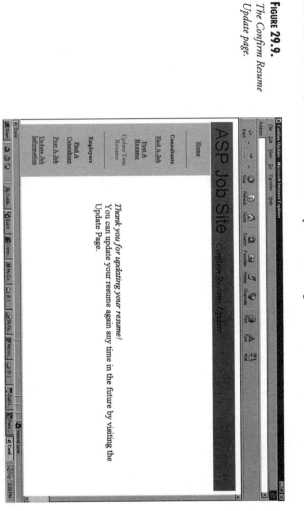

The database table is not updated using the SQL UPDATE statement. Instead, the following series of SQL statements is used:

```
    Replace Resume As A Transaction
MyConn.BeginTrans
MyConn.Execute "DELETE resumes WHERE UserID="&Request.Form("UserID")
```

```
MyConn.Execute MySQL
MyConn.CommitTrans
```

This script creates a transaction that first deletes the old résumé information and then inserts the new résumé information. Why couldn't a SQL UPDATE statement be used?

If I was allowed to change only one aspect of HTML, it would be the behavior of check boxes. The problem is that you can't use a check box to detect the *absence* of a value. When a check box is not checked, nothing is passed when the form is submitted.

Suppose that when a user initially submits a résumé, she checks the check box labeled VBScript. By checking this check box, the user indicates that VBScript is one of her skills. However, suppose she changes her mind. She uses the Update Resume page to uncheck this check box. When the HTML form is submitted, no value for the check box will be passed. The change will not be detected.

Using a SQL INSERT statement avoids this problem. Unlike an UPDATE statement, an INSERT statement replaces the complete record. If the check box isn't checked, the value of the VBScript column will be FALSE when the new record is inserted.

In short, if you use check boxes in an HTML form, don't use the SQL UPDATE statement. If you use an UPDATE statement, once a check box is checked, it can never be unchecked.

The New Job Section

The New Job section is contained in a subdirectory named njob. It contains two Active Server Pages files (see Figure 29.10). These two pages are used to create a new job posting. At the first page, a user enters information about the job into an HTML form. At the second page, this information is confirmed and entered into a database table named jobs.

Figure 29.10.
The New Job section.

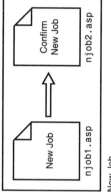

New Job

The New Job Page

Except for some differences in the HTML form fields, the New Job page is almost exactly the same as the New Resume page (see Figure 29.11). At this page, the user can enter the information for a new job listing.

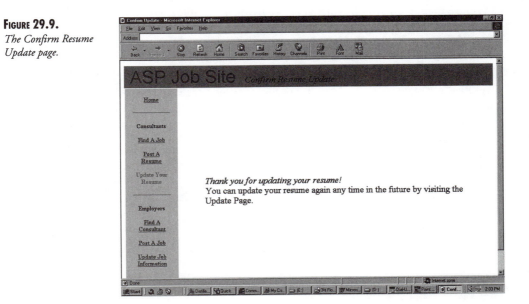

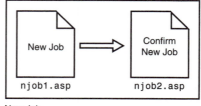

FIGURE 29.11.
The New Job page.

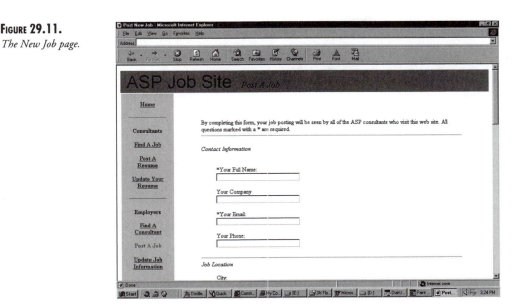

Unlike the New Resume page, the user doesn't enter a password. Each job is assigned a randomly generated secret Job Code instead. The combination of the Job Code and the e-mail address of the user uniquely identifies each job. Following is the script used to generate the random Job Code:

```
'  Create Random Secret Code
FUNCTION SecretCode()
  RANDOMIZE
  SecretCode=INT(9000*RND+1000)
END FUNCTION
```

This script creates a random number that has four digits. When the user wants to update the job listing, he or she must enter this secret Job Code. The Job Code acts like a password for a job listing.

The Confirm New Job Page

The Confirm New Job page is almost identical to the Confirm New Resume page (see Figure 29.12).

One interesting feature of this page is the way it detects whether the browser's Back button or Refresh button has been used. By using the Refresh or Reload button on a browser, a user can resubmit the same form over and over. This could be a problem.

Suppose someone completes a job listing and submits it. A new record is added to the database table named jobs. Now suppose the user clicks the browser's Refresh or Reload button. Another new record will be added. There's nothing to prevent the user from doing this forever.

A malicious user could wreak havoc with your database tables this way. Even worse, an innocent user could do the same thing by accident. How can you prevent this from happening?

Because the random Job Code is generated at the New Job page, the Job Code will be the same every time a user refreshes or reloads the Confirm New Job page. By checking whether the combination of the Job Code and e-mail address already exists in the database, you can detect whether the Confirm New Job page has been reloaded or refreshed. A particular e-mail address and Job Code combination can only be entered once into the jobs database table.

FIGURE 29.12.

The Confirm New Job page.

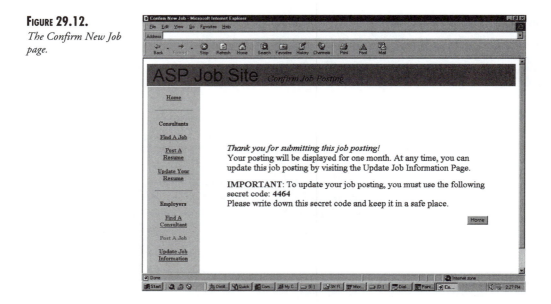

The Update Job Section

The Update Job section is contained in a subdirectory named ujob. It contains three Active Server Pages files (see Figure 29.13). These three pages are used to update an existing job posting. At the first page, the user enters an e-mail address and Job Code to verify his identity (see Figure 29.14). At the second page, he can update an existing job posting (see Figure 29.15).

FIGURE 29.13.

The Update Job section.

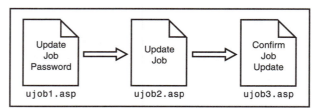

FIGURE 29.14.
The Update Job Password page.

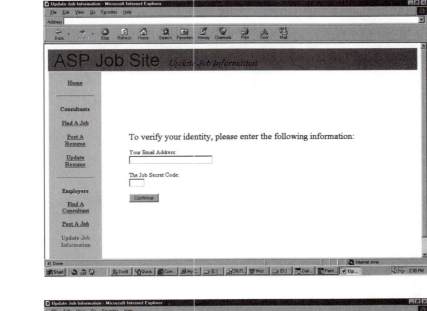

FIGURE 29.15.
The Update Job page.

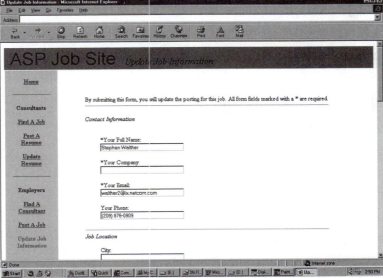

29

CREATING AN ONLINE CAREER SERVICES SITE

At the third page, this information is confirmed and inserted into the database (see Figure 29.16).

FIGURE 29.16.
The Confirm Job Update page.

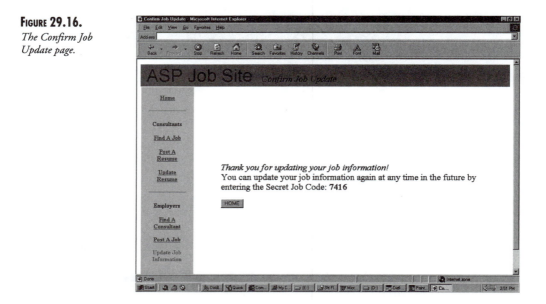

The three Active Server Pages in this section function similarly to the three pages in the Update Resume section. The crucial difference is that the `jobs` database table is updated rather than the `resumes` table. Because the pages in this section are so similar to the pages in the Update Resume section, they won't be discussed in detail.

The Find Consultant Section

The Find Consultant section is contained in a subdirectory named `fconsult`. It contains three Active Server Pages files (see Figure 29.17). At the first page, a user can enter search criteria to find a consultant. At the second page, the results of the search are displayed. Finally, at the third page, the user can view the résumés returned by the search.

FIGURE 29.17.
The Find Consultant section.

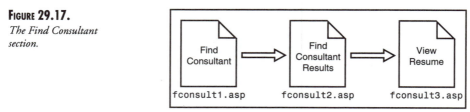

The Find Consultant Page

The Find Consultant page contains an HTML form that can be used to enter search criteria (see Figure 29.18). A user can search for consultants based on their geographical location. For example, you can search only for consultants who live in Fresno, California. Or you can search only for consultants in France.

Furthermore, a user can search for only those consultants who have particular skills. The form can be used to specify up to three skills. For example, you can search for consultants who know how to program using Delphi and JScript.

You can also use the form to specify different Boolean operators. For example, you can search only for those consultants who know both Delphi AND JScript or those consultants who know either Delphi OR JScript.

FIGURE 29.18.

The Find Consultant page.

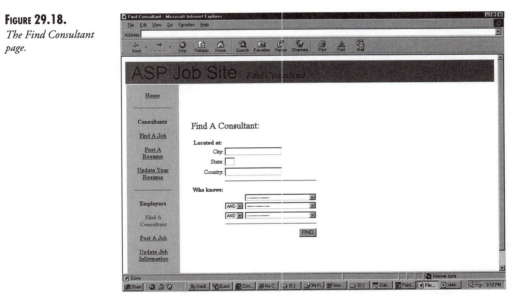

The Find Consultant Results Page

The results of a search are displayed in the Find Consultants Results page (see Figure 29.19). All the work is done in this Active Server Page. In this page, a SQL query string is generated dynamically to search the resumes table.

Figure 29.19.
The Find Consultant Results page.

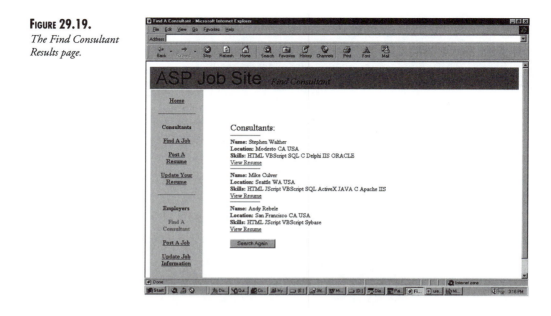

Listing 29.3 shows the complete listing for the Find Consultant Results page.

Listing 29.3. Script for `fconsult2.asp`.

```
<%
CONST adBoolean=11
'  Shows Matching Job Skills In Red
SUB ShowSkills
DIM SkillA,SkillB,SkillC
SkillA=Request.Form("SkillA")
SkillB=Request.Form("SkillB")
SkillC=Request.Form("SkillC")
 FOR i=0 TO RS.Fields.Count-1
  IF RS(i).type=adBoolean THEN
    IF RS(i) THEN
     IF RS(i).NAME=SkillA OR RS(i).NAME=SkillB or RS(I).NAME=SkillC THEN
       Response.Write("<FONT COLOR=""#FF0000""><B>"
        ➥&RS(i).Name&"</B></FONT> ")
     ELSE
       Response.Write(RS(i).Name&" ")
     END IF
    END IF
  End IF
 NEXT
END SUB
%>
<HTML>
<HEAD><TITLE> Find A Consultant </TITLE></HEAD>
<BODY BGCOLOR="#FFFFFF" ALINK="#FF0000">
```

```
<!-- Create Title Banner Table -->
<TABLE BGCOLOR="#00aaff" WIDTH="100%">
<TR><TD VALIGN=CENTER>
<FONT FACE=ARIAL SIZE=+4>  ASP Job Site</FONT>
<FONT SIZE=+2>   <I> Find Consultant </I></FONT>
</TD></TR>
</TABLE>


<!-- Create Main Body Table -->
<TABLE HEIGHT="100%" CELLPADDING=20>
<TR>

<!-- The Left Cell Of The Body Table Contains The Navigation Strip -->
<TD ALIGN=CENTER VALIGN=TOP BGCOLOR="#D0D0D0" WIDTH=100>
<B>
<P><A HREF="../default.asp">Home</A>
<P><HR>
<P>Consultants
<P><A HREF="/fjob/fjob1.asp">Find A Job</A>
<P><A HREF="/nresume/nresume1.asp">Post A Resume</A>
<P><A HREF="/uresume/uresume1.asp">Update Your Resume</A>
<P><HR>
<P>Employers
<P><FONT COLOR="#808080">Find A Consultant</FONT>
<P><A HREF="/njob/njob1.asp">Post A Job</A>
<P><A HREF="/ujob/ujob1.asp">Update Job Information</A>
</B>
</TD>

<!-- The Right Cell Of The Body Table Contains The Page Contents -->
<TD ALIGN=CENTER VALIGN=CENTER>
<TABLE HEIGHT="100%" ALIGN=CENTER CELLSPACING=50>
<TR><TD>
<%
'   Create The Search String
MySQL="SELECT * FROM resumes "
IF Request.Form("City")<>"" THEN Loc="City=
➥'"&Request.Form("City")&"' AND "
IF Request.Form("State")<>"" THEN Loc=Loc&"State=
➥'"&Request.Form("State")&"' AND "
IF Request.Form("Country")<>"" THEN Loc=Loc&"Country=
➥'"&Request.Form("Country")&"' AND "

IF LEFT(Request.Form("SkillA"),1)<>"" THEN
  Match=Request.Form("SkillA")&"=1 "
END IF
IF LEFT(Request.Form("SkillB"),1)<>"" THEN
  IF Match<>"" THEN Match=Match&Request.Form("AndOrB")&" "
  Match=Match&Request.Form("SkillB")&"=1 "
END IF
IF LEFT(Request.Form("SkillC"),1)<>"" THEN
  IF Match<>"" THEN Match=Match&Request.Form("AndOrC")&" "
  Match=Match&Request.Form("SkillC")&"=1 "
END IF
```

continues

Listing 29.3. continued

```
IF Loc<>"" OR Match<>"" THEN
 MySQL=MySQL&"WHERE "&Loc
 IF Match<>"" THEN
  MySQL=MySQL&"("&Match&")"
 ELSE
  MySQL=LEFT(MySQL,LEN(MySQL)-4)
 END IF
 MySQL=MySQL&" ORDER BY EntryDate DESC"
END IF

' Create ADO Objects
Set MyConn=Server.CreateObject("ADODB.Connection")
MyConn.Open Application("ConnectionString")
Set RS=MyConn.Execute(MySQL)

' Check For No Matches
IF RS.EOF THEN
%>
<FONT SIZE=+2><I>No consultants matched your criteria.</I></FONT>
<P>
<FORM ACTION="fconsult1.asp">
<INPUT TYPE="SUBMIT" VALUE="Search Again">
</FORM>
<%
ELSE
%>
<FONT SIZE=+2>Consultants:</FONT>
<%
' Show All Matches
WHILE NOT RS.EOF
%>
<HR WIDTH=80 ALIGN=LEFT>
<B>Name: </B><%=RS("FullName")%>
<BR><B>Location: </B>
<%=RS("City")&" "&UCASE(RS("State"))&" "&RS("Country")%>
<BR><B>Skills: </B><%ShowSkills%>
<BR><A HREF="fconsult3.asp?UserID=<%=RS("UserID")%>">View Resume</A>
<%
RS.MoveNext
WEND
%>
<P>
<FORM ACTION="fconsult1.asp">
<INPUT TYPE="SUBMIT" VALUE="Search Again">
</FORM>
<%
END IF ' For No Match
RS.Close
MyConn.Close
%>
```

```
</TD></TR></TABLE>
</TD></TR>
</TABLE>
</BODY>
</HTML>
```

The SQL query string used to search the `resumes` table is created in the section of code labeled `Create The Search String`. The query string is built out of the information the user entered into the HTML form in the Find Consultant page.

The query string is used to return a Recordset. If the Recordset is empty, the user is told that no consultants matched the specified criteria. Otherwise, the list of matching consultants is displayed.

When the consultants are listed, their skills are also displayed. The consultant skills that match the search criteria are listed in red. Other skills are listed in black. This is accomplished by using the `ShowSkills` subroutine.

The `ShowSkills` subroutine uses a trick. It automatically detects the skill columns from the `resumes` table by detecting the datatypes of the columns. The `Type` property of the ADO `Field` object returns the datatype of a column. In the `resumes` table, the skills are all contained in `BIT` columns (known to VBScript as `vbBoolean` columns). A consultant either has the skill or not. Therefore, the `ShowSkills` subroutine only displays the names and values of `BIT` columns.

For each consultant listed, a `View Resume` hyperlink is also listed. This link is created by the following line of code:

```
<BR><A HREF="fconsult3.asp?UserID=<%=RS("UserID")%>">View Resume</A>
```

The text `View Resume` links to the Active Server Page named `fconsult3.asp`. This is the View Resume page. When the user clicks the `View Resume` link for a particular consultant, the UserID of the consultant is passed to the View Resume page in a query string.

The View Resume Page

The View Resume page displays a résumé (see Figure 29.20). The page retrieves the résumé of the user who matches the UserID passed in the UserID query string. If this page is retrieved without a query string, the user is warned away.

Listing 29.4 contains the complete listing for the View Resume page.

FIGURE 29.20.

The View Resume page.

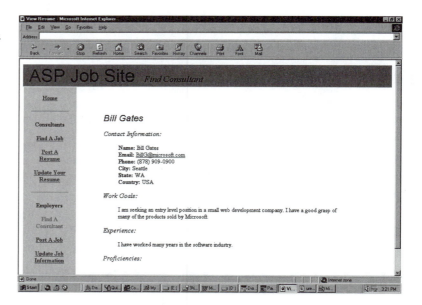

Listing 29.4. The View Resume page, `fconsult3.asp`.

```asp
<%
CONST adOpenDynamic=2
CONST adBoolean=11
'   Shows A Part Of A Resume Only If It Exists
SUB ShowIt(theCol,theVar)
  IF RS(theVar)<>"" THEN
%>
<B><%=theCol%></B> <%=RS(theVar)%><BR>
<%
  END IF
END SUB


'   Loops Through All Skills In Resume
SUB ShowSkills
 FOR i=0 TO RS.Fields.Count-1
  IF RS(i).type=adBoolean THEN
    IF RS(i) THEN Response.Write("<LI>"&RS(i).Name)
  End IF
 NEXT
END SUB
%>
<HTML>
<HEAD><TITLE> View Resume </TITLE></HEAD>
<BODY BGCOLOR="#FFFFFF" ALINK="#FF0000">

<!-- Create Title Banner Table -->
<TABLE BGCOLOR="#00aaff" WIDTH="100%">
<TR><TD VALIGN=CENTER>
<FONT FACE=ARIAL SIZE=+4>  ASP Job Site</FONT>
<FONT SIZE=+2>   <I> Find Consultant </I></FONT>
```

```
</TD></TR>
</TABLE>

<!-- Create Main Body Table -->
<TABLE HEIGHT="100%" CELLPADDING=20>
<TR>

<!-- The Left Cell Of The Body Table
Contains The Navigation Strip -->
<TD ALIGN=CENTER VALIGN=TOP BGCOLOR="#D0D0D0" WIDTH=100>
<B>
<P><A HREF="../default.asp">Home</A>
<P><HR>
<P>Consultants
<P><A HREF="/fjob/fjob1.asp">Find A Job</A>
<P><A HREF="/nresume/nresume1.asp">Post A Resume</A>
<P><A HREF="/uresume/uresume1.asp">Update Your Resume</A>
<P><HR>
<P>Employers
<P><FONT COLOR="#808080">Find A Consultant</FONT>
<P><A HREF="/njob/njob1.asp">Post A Job</A>
<P><A HREF="/ujob/ujob1.asp">Update Job Information</A>
</B>
</TD>

<!-- The Right Cell Of The Body Table
Contains The Page Contents -->
<TD ALIGN=CENTER VALIGN=CENTER>
<TABLE HEIGHT="100%" ALIGN=CENTER CELLSPACING=50>
<TR><TD>
<%
' Create ADO objects
Set MyConn=Server.CreateObject("ADODB.Connection")
MyConn.Open Application("ConnectionString")

'  Create SQL SELECT String
MySQL="Select * FROM resumes WHERE UserID="&Request.QueryString("UserID")
Set RS=Server.CreateObject("ADODB.RecordSet")

'  A Non Forward-Only Cursor Must Be Used To Retrieve The TEXT fields
RS.Open MySQL,Myconn,adOpenDynamic

'  Checks For Leap To Page From Nowhere
IF RS.EOF THEN
%>
<FONT SIZE=+2><I>You cannot retrieve this page directly.</I>
<BR>Click the Back button to return to the Find Consultant Page.</FONT>
<P>
<FORM ACTION="fconsult1.asp">
<INPUT TYPE="SUBMIT" VALUE="BACK">
</FORM>

<% ELSE %>

<!-- Show The Resume -->
<FONT SIZE=+2 FACE="Arial"><I><%=RS("FullName")%></I></FONT>
```

29

continues

Listing 29.4. continued

```
<P>
<FONT SIZE=+1><I>Contact Information:</I></FONT>
<BLOCKQUOTE>
<% ShowIt "Name:","FullName" %>
<B>Email:</B>
<A HREF="MAILTO:<%=RS("Email")%>"><%=RS("Email")%></A><BR>
<% ShowIt "Phone:","Phone" %>
<% ShowIt "City:","City" %>
<% ShowIt "State:", "State" %>
<% ShowIt "Country:","Country" %>
</BLOCKQUOTE>

<% IF RS("Goals")<>"" THEN %>
<P>
<FONT SIZE=+1><I>Work Goals:</I></FONT>
<BLOCKQUOTE>
<%=RS("Goals")%>
</BLOCKQUOTE>
<% END IF %>

<% IF RS("Experience")<>"" THEN %>
<P>
<FONT SIZE=+1><I>Experience:</I></FONT>
<BLOCKQUOTE>
<%=RS("Experience")%>
</BLOCKQUOTE>
<% END IF %>

<P>
<FONT SIZE=+1><I>Proficiencies:</I></FONT>
<BLOCKQUOTE>
<UL>
<% ShowSkills %>
</UL>
</BLOCKQUOTE>
<% IF RS("MoreScript")<>"" THEN %>
<P>
<FONT SIZE=+1><I>Scripting Language Experience:</I></FONT>
<BLOCKQUOTE>
<%=RS("MoreScript")%>
</BLOCKQUOTE>
<% END IF %>

<% IF RS("MoreProg")<>"" THEN %>
<P>
<FONT SIZE=+1><I>Programming Language Experience:</I></FONT>
<BLOCKQUOTE>
<%=RS("MoreProg")%>
</BLOCKQUOTE>
<% END IF %>

<% IF RS("MoreWeb")<>"" THEN %>
<P>
<FONT SIZE=+1><I>Web Server Experience:</I></FONT>
<BLOCKQUOTE>
<%=RS("MoreWeb")%>
```

```
</BLOCKQUOTE>
<% END IF %>

<% IF RS("MoreData")<>"" THEN %>
<P>
<FONT SIZE=+1><I>Database Experience:</I></FONT>
<BLOCKQUOTE>
<%=RS("MoreData")%>
</BLOCKQUOTE>
<% END IF %>


<%
END IF
RS.Close
MyConn.Close
%>
</TD></TR>
</TABLE>
</TD></TR>
</TABLE>
</BODY>
</HTML>
```

The résumé of the user is retrieved from the resumes table. A Recordset is opened that contains a single record corresponding to the user's résumé. Notice that this Recordset is not opened with a forward-only cursor. If you attempt to retrieve TEXT fields when using a forward-only cursor, strange and unpredictable things will happen.

The View Resume page uses the same trick as the previous page to list the skills from a résumé. The BIT columns in the record are detected using the Type property of the ADO Field object. All the skills listed in the résumé are automatically displayed by the ShowSkills subroutine.

The Find Job Section

The Find Job section is contained in a subdirectory named fjob. It contains three Active Server Pages files (see Figure 29.21). These three pages are used to search the job postings. At the first page, a user enters search criteria for a job (see Figure 29.22). At the second page, the results from this search are displayed (see Figure 29.23). At the third page, the user can view the detailed job posting (see Figure 29.24).

FIGURE 29.21.
The Find Job section.

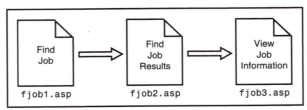

Find Job

FIGURE 29.22.
The Find Job page.

FIGURE 29.23.
The Find Job Results page.

FIGURE 29.24.
The View Job Information page.

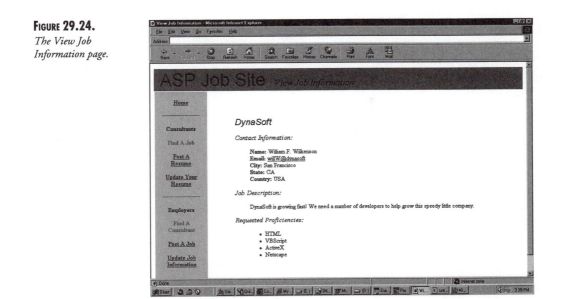

These three Active Server Pages function almost identically to the pages contained in the Find Consultant section. The only difference is that the jobs database table is searched rather than the resumes table. Because the pages in this section are so similar to the pages in the Find Consultant section, they won't be discussed in detail.

Summary

This chapter showed you how to create the Active Server Pages Job Site. You learned how to handle a number of advanced programming challenges. For example, you learned how to use hidden form fields to gracefully repopulate an HTML form. You also learned a number of methods for dynamically generating SQL strings. You should now be fully prepared to create almost any Web site, no matter how advanced.

CHAPTER 30

Web Site Promotion and Marketing

IN THIS CHAPTER

Web site promotion and marketing is like any promotion and marketing in that the goal is to increase awareness and sales or traffic. However, it's unlike traditional marketing in that new tools and technologies enable you to reach people in a more targeted way, and in a way that allows them to effortlessly follow your marketing to your site.

The actual design and implementation of your site is part of the marketing, so you should understand this chapter before you finish designing your Web site. Not only do search engines use the words on your page to decide when to show your site as a search result, but also you can design your site to encourage others to do your marketing for you.

This chapter explains the most important features of Web site marketing and promotion, and then goes into detail on how to use each of the methods described to get the best results for your site. You've put a lot of work into creating it; now it's time to bring on the audience.

> **NOTE**
>
> This chapter assumes that your Web site is intended for the public.

What Is Web Site Marketing?

In its most basic terms, Web site marketing is

- Figuring out who the customer is
- Bringing your customer to the site the first time
- Getting your customer to come back to the site
- Getting your customer to bring friends to the site

Most people focus most of their attention on getting customers to the site; however, your long-term success depends much more on the other three points. *Only the successful site can keep people coming back over and over again.*

Creating repeat business and referrals can be accomplished only by design. Your site needs to be designed to achieve these goals. All the methods you employ should be coordinated to build, support, and leverage your member base so that it feeds on itself and creates a lasting community.

Once you understand the dynamic of how your customer base should be built, you can design and market your site in a way that works.

Components of Web Marketing Campaigns

An effective and powerful Web marketing campaign involves each of the following components: bringing in new customers, leveraging your customer base, and creating repeat business.

While the primary focus of many Web marketing campaigns is bringing new customers to a Web site, it's important to remember that bringing customers to your Web site is only the first step in your marketing plan to build a comprehensive customer base. The ability to leverage your customer base as well as create recurrent site visits plays a critical role in the long-term viability and success of your Web site. All Web marketing activities should be based on a clear understanding of your target customer. Each step in the process has its own areas of concentration:

- Attracting new customers
    - Search engines
    - Specialized directories
    - Press coverage
    - Newsgroups
    - Targeted e-mail
    - Chats
    - Online services
    - Leveraging technology companies
    - Advertising
    - Contests and prizes
- Leveraging the customer base
    - Customer referral programs
    - Reciprocal links
    - Mailing lists
    - Web rings
    - Banner exchanges
- Creating repeat business
    - Customer mailing lists
    - Loyalty programs
    - Personalization

A high-quality Web site marketing program is a balance of all three types of programs, based on a strong analysis of who the customer is.

Attracting New Customers

Bringing new customers to your site is the first step in building a strong customer base and a successful Web site. The following sections describe the basic steps you should take to create your customer base. These tactics, wherever possible, should be tailored to the characteristics of your target customer.

30

WEB SITE
PROMOTION AND
MARKETING

Search Engines

Search engines are often the main source of customers for a site, with Yahoo! being at the top of most sites' lists. This is critical to getting new customers to your site. There are three steps to achieving success with search engines:

1. Figure out what phrases your target customers are likely to type into a search box.
2. Design the site with search engines in mind.
3. Submit the site properly to each individual search engine and directory.

Unfortunately, you aren't the only person who has found this out. Everyone is trying to reach the top of the search results page, and some employ tactics to "fool" a search engine into ranking a certain page highly—even when it's not relevant to the user's search. This is called *search engine spamming*, or *spam-dexing*.

For a while it seemed that the search engines were going to put tools in the hands of Web sites to give them full control over how they were indexed. The search engines have reacted to spamming by shutting down a lot of the Web site marketer's ability to affect search engine ranking.

There are literally hundreds of search engines, but the vast majority of traffic comes from the top: Yahoo!, Infoseek, Excite, Alta Vista, Lycos, WebCrawler, and HotBot.

These are the steps to effective search-engine-oriented site design:

1. Determine likely search phrases for people looking for sites like yours.
2. Include the words in your site in such a way as to maximize the relevance of your site.

After explaining these two components of search engine strategy, I'll give an example of how one search engine (Infoseek) calculates relevance. Then I'll explain Yahoo!, which is in a class by itself among search engines and directories.

First, what are some likely search phrases? You can guess at this if you *pretend you're a user and think of words you would be likely to type*. However, if you're the engineer of your Web site, you're probably more likely to type logically constructed search phrases than your average user. A better but more difficult way to determine likely search phrases is to *survey your target users*. Send e-mail to people you think are in your target market, and ask them something like this: "If you were looking for a job search site, what words would you type into a search engine to find it?"

Let's say that your survey finds the following answers:

Response 1:	`job search`
Response 2:	`jobs`
Response 3:	`employment`
Response 4:	`jobs in medicine`
Response 5:	`help wanted`
Response 6:	`computer programming jobs`

You have a difficult task. It's apparent from the responses that some people look for a job search site by designating industry- or job-specific terms. However, the important thing to learn from this step is that the preceding sets of words are likely to be typed by your target customers. You can infer from the responses that similar sets of terms, such as "financial analysis jobs" or "jobs in marketing" would also be used in the real world.

What about the "top 200 search words" and similar lists? There's much talk about the top 200 search words, available for reference on several Web sites. You can also use WebCrawler to see a real-time sampling of search phrases that people type. However, any legitimate Web site is in the business of bringing the *right* viewers to the front door—not just *any* viewers. In addition, so many people read the top 200 lists that the word sex is found on about 1.2 million Web pages, and the phrase Pamela Anderson is found on nearly 7,000 Web pages. You're not going to get on the top of any searches by adding either phrase to your site. *The goal, after all, is to find viewers who are looking for something that you offer.*

If you view the phrases that came to you in response to your search-word survey as entire phrases rather than sets of words, then you can be more effective at getting responses. For example, if you see some people typing **computer programming jobs**, then it isn't enough to have those three words on your site; you should have the entire phrase on your site. That way, if someone puts the phrase in quotes (a way to search for words together on many search engines), you'll end up on the list.

The features of a site that affect its ranking in search engines are as follows:

- Page title
- Page text
- Frames
- <META> tag description
- <META> tag keywords
- <ALT> text of images
- robots.txt

Of all these, *the title is the most important text on the page.* If two pages both say job search but one has it in the title and one has it in the body, the one with the phrase in the title usually comes up first.

Frames can work against your site. The way frames work, only the text of the main page is indexed. *The text within a frame is not indexed on most search engines.* This is a major reason not to use frames.

<META> tag descriptions and keywords were created to make life easier for the search engines and site authors, so that sites would be easier to index correctly. However, so much abuse of these devices has happened that many search engines no longer use them. The search engines that still use them include Infoseek and Alta Vista, though, so it's still worth working on them.

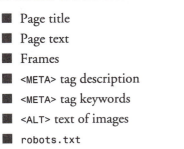

For those unfamiliar with them, the format of these <META> tags is as follows:

```
<META NAME="Keywords" CONTENT="insert keywords separated by commas">
<META NAME="Description" CONTENT="insert site description">
```

There are limits on the amount of text used by the search engines in these tags. In general, *keep your description under 200 characters and your keywords under 1,000 characters.* (These guidelines are provided by Infoseek.)

Capitalization is very important! If you use the keyword jobs, it would result in a match for someone searching for **jobs** but *not* **JOBS** or **Jobs**. If you use the keyword JOBS, it's a match for **jobs** and **JOBS** but not **Jobs**. The reason is that search engines interpret a lowercase search word as non-case-sensitive, but any other capitalization as case-sensitive. Therefore, use either all caps or first letter capitalization for your keywords—whichever of the two is more likely to be used as a search phrase by your users. *In no case should your keywords be lowercase.*

One issue to watch out for is *keyword dilution.* Many search engines calculate the percentage of a page made up of relevant words, so that a page consisting of three copies of the entire dictionary would not come up at the top of every search. Therefore, you may want to keep only relevant words and a minimum of other words on the welcome page of your site.

Most search engines index the <ALT> text of images. Therefore, you may want to be clever about what words you use in those fields.

robots.txt *files are a good way to regulate which pages of a site are indexed.* robots.txt files determine which files in your Web site will be spidered by search engines. For example, you may not want the search engines to index your help pages. A robots.txt file is the right way to prevent that from happening. The robots.txt file is stored in the main directory of your Web site, and specifies which pages to exclude from robot searches. Because the standards for robots.txt files are evolving, you should check for the latest robots.txt protocol on WebCrawler at this address:

http://info.webcrawler.com/mak/projects/robots/robots.html

If you have only one page that's indexed by the search engines, you won't get a whole lot of traffic from the search engines, no matter what you do. For Yahoo! it will work, but with the others it won't have much effect. The reason is that a broad range of phrases are typed into search engines, and if you rank #1 on one type of search, you probably won't be #1 on another. The way to solve this problem is to *create a number of indexable pages that each individually rank #1 on some type of search phrase* that your target customers might type to reach your kind of site.

To be more specific, let's go back to the job listing site discussed earlier. The survey showed that some people use the phrase **jobs in medicine** or **jobs in computer programming** or other such phrases with industry names in them. To rank highly on the search engines for these people, you should have individual pages within your site that list jobs in medicine, jobs in computer programming, and other industries. The title of each page should include the likely search phrase.

Without considering the effect on search engines, you might be inclined to design the site so that the computer programming page, for example, is the result of setting a session variable to the value `computer programming`. The URL to reach such a page might be something like this:

```
http://www.jobsearchpage.com/industry.asp?IND="comp_programming"
```

This may work well for you as a programming construct, but it doesn't work with search engines. Most search engines won't index any page with a question mark in the middle.

Another way you might be tempted to design your site is to have one large page with hyperlinks to sections pertaining to individual industries. This doesn't work with search engines because the wide variety of content dilutes the relevance of the page to any single search phrase.

To rank highly in the search engines for all the search phrases your customers are likely to type, you have to create a wide variety of pages, each at a static location. In this example, you could change the structure so that the computer programming jobs are located at this address:

```
http://www.jobsearchpage.com/industry/computer_programming.asp
```

Every other industry would also have its own static page location.

The implication of this approach is that *your customers could arrive at your site at many different points.* To keep them from feeling lost, every possible entry point should have a link to an explanation of what your site is all about, and a link to your site's main page.

I had the opportunity to hear Steve Kirsch speak about the way Infoseek indexes pages. In general terms, Infoseek uses a *dot product* to determine which page is most relevant, with *each search phrase and each Web page viewed as a vector.*

In simpler terms, if you search for **job listings**, Infoseek treats that phrase as one mention of **job** and one mention of **listings**. If a Web page contains two mentions of **job**, one mention of **listings**, and many other words, the Web page is treated as one mention of **listings**, two mentions of **job**, and so on. When you multiply corresponding terms, you get 1×2 for **job**, and 1×1 for **listings**. Infoseek then adds them all up and gets a total index of 3. Every Web page is treated the same way, and the highest total is the top result.

Infoseek has added various corrections to this system, and they aren't as easily understood. For example, Infoseek doesn't keep track of more than three mentions of a word on a particular page, and counts mentions of a word in a title or `<META>` tag as essentially the same as three mentions elsewhere on the page. Infoseek, like most major search engines, also uses spam filters to eliminate sites that use the technique of *spam-dexing.*

Spam-dexing is the practice of loading up a page with irrelevant words (most commonly, the word sex mentioned hundreds of times), usually words in the same color text as the page background. These words are invisible to users, and are designed to fool search engines into thinking that a page is more relevant than it is. This technique is so well known and overused that search engines have developed sophisticated ways to block sites that use these techniques. The stakes are too big to risk spam-dexing. *If your site is designed to be spamming the search engines, they won't list your site at all.* It's much better to avoid spamming and to stick to relevant words strategically placed on your site.

Yahoo! is often responsible for the largest individual portion of a Web site's new customers. For whatever reason, many Webmasters claim that 30–50% of their traffic comes from Yahoo!. If you can get a prominent or favorable listing in Yahoo!, it's worth whatever trouble you had to go through to get it. After all, unlike advertising, your listing in Yahoo! doesn't cost anything after you've paid with your effort to get it.

Yahoo! is indexed by human beings, not by robots. Your site will be judged by a site reviewer who looks at it and determines whether it merits placement in their directory. For that reason, *be nice to Yahoo! reviewers.* Don't create useless work for them by submitting the same site to many different Yahoo! categories. You're not the first person to try this. Yahoo! will look at all your submissions at once and figure out where you belong. If you submit to too many places, they'll pick one for you. You're better off submitting to only two Yahoo! categories.

It sometimes takes several weeks to get a response from Yahoo!. However, they have a phone number to call to check on your submission. If after two weeks you don't see your listing in Yahoo!, try calling them at (408) 731-3300. Select the option for customer support to get to the Web site reviewing team. If your site has not been reviewed for two weeks, they'll be able to help you. Again, don't call before two weeks are up, and be patient. (Imagine if your job were to index all relevant Web pages.)

Several sites, such as Scott Banister's Submit It!, promise to submit your site to hundreds of search engines. These are the problems with such sites:

- They treat the submission process as "one size fits all."
- The traffic from small search engines is almost negligible.

If you're spending significant resources creating your site, *you should spend the time to submit it manually to the six major search engines.* If you want to use Submit It! or a similar service to submit to the rest, it won't take you much time and it's not going to get you a lot of traffic.

Specialized Directories

Every industry segment has some sites that are used as directories of all the resources pertaining to a particular group of people. For example, there are directories that list all the auctions on the Internet. For CityAuction, an online auction site I developed (http://www.cityauction.com), one of our first tasks was to get listed in these directories. For your industry segment, there are probably directories and resources that you would like to be a part of.

To find the specialized directories or "super sites" for your industry, you need to do some homework. The first stop is usually Yahoo!, where the directories within any segment are separated into their own section. At the top of the page, there's often a line called Indices. If you follow that link, you'll see a listing of sites that are themselves directories. As an example, let's look at Yahoo! Sports. Under Sports is an Indices heading, under which are 36 entries, many of which are simply collections of links to interesting sports sites. If you were launching your own sports site, one of the first things you would want to do is to write a short note to the Webmaster of each index to ask whether your site could be included in the collection.

Press Coverage

You should use the press as much as possible, because they're the cheapest way to get your name in front of the public. Also, even when the press coverage doesn't generate a lot of direct business to your site, it provides articles you can link to from your site, and coverage that *gives you credibility* among potential partners, financing sources, and customers.

How do you get press coverage? The press wants to cover interesting stories. They have to fill lots of paper every day, and they're starving for ideas for articles that their readership might want to read. Your job is to position your story as something in which their readers might be interested.

To get your foot in the door, it helps to know who you want to talk to. Instead of sending out a mass e-mail to thousands of press contacts, you should find out something about each person to whom you write. Read some of their articles to get a sense of what they do. If they don't write articles about your industry, don't waste their time or yours. *Find reporters who cover your industry and then approach them with a personalized message* that lets them know you're familiar with their work.

> **NOTE**
>
> I don't mean to imply that e-mail is the best way to contact the press. In fact, it's probably less effective than a phone call. However, it's more considerate of the reporter's time to try e-mail first.

To get the e-mail address of the reporter, first look in the publication. Many computer magazines include the e-mail address of the writer of an article at the end of the article. Even magazines that don't include e-mail addresses sometimes have them in back issues; check a library.

If you don't get the e-mail addresses from the publication, try the publicly available e-mail directories on the Web. Here are some of the best:

- Yahoo! advanced e-mail search

    `http://www.yahoo.com/search/people/advemail.html`

- WhoWhere?

    `http://www.whowhere.com`

- Switchboard

    `http://www.switchboard.com`

Internet Address Finder

`http://www.iaf.net/`

Media directories are also available, but many are outdated. One of the best that's kept reasonably up-to-date is Steve O'Keefe's site, Internet Publicity Resources, at `http://www.olympus.net/okeefe/pubnet/`.

Newsgroups

Using newsgroups to promote your commercial Web site is a touchy subject. Many newsgroups are dominated by users who view commercialization of the Internet as a bad thing. However, if you follow the charter of each newsgroup and post only relevant articles of interest to a newsgroup's readership, you shouldn't have any major problems. People will still object—some of them strongly—but if you followed all the rules you should be able to defend yourself successfully.

First of all, *before you post to any newsgroup, read the other posts.* This strategy gives you an idea of what kinds of things are accepted there, and occasionally you'll run across a copy of the group's charter. In the charter you'll see a statement of what posts are okay for the group. In many cases, however, the newsgroup has drifted away from its original charter, so it's often more relevant to look at the other posts than at the charter. The charter is best used as a defense against the attacks of newsgroup readers who object to your posts.

To find the right newsgroups for you, several tools are available that can save time. Whenever I use the newsgroups, I first search Alta Vista (`http://altavista.digital.com`) for newsgroups with other relevant articles. For example, if I'm looking for the right newsgroup in which to post a job listing for a C++ programmer, I search like this:

```
+"C++ programming" +job
```

I make sure I click Usenet rather than The Web. Alta Vista returns a list of all newsgroup posts that include the phrases I'm searching for. By looking at all the posts, I can see which ones are like mine, and on which newsgroups they tend to be posted.

Often, one newsgroup has a slightly different function than another, similar newsgroup. For example, there's a newsgroup for PDA Programming and another newsgroup for PDA Marketplace. If you're selling Newtons, you should post on the PDA Marketplace newsgroup. Posting to the wrong one is inviting the wrath of the newsgroup police.

To many newsgroup users, excessive posting or cross-posting of articles (posting of the same message to several groups simultaneously) is spamming. It's also spamming to post too many articles on the same day.

TIP

For a good reference on Usenet etiquette, see `http://www.landfield.com/usenet/`.

Some newsgroups are moderated and some aren't. Moderated newsgroups usually are much more useful to read, because they don't contain the "get rich quick" schemes and other trash that seem to seep into many of the unmoderated groups. In a moderated group, all posts automatically go to the moderator, who then filters out the useless or irrelevant articles and posts only the appropriate messages to the group.

Even in the unmoderated groups, though, some people take on the role of newsgroup police. They perform a very useful function; without them, newsgroups would decay into a useless mass of irrelevant articles. These are often people with no authority, but who take it upon themselves to keep newsgroups clean. They are your friends, because they keep the discussions relevant, keeping readers using the newsgroups. Newsgroups with good policing get much higher readership than those without.

CAUTION

If you post inappropriately, the newsgroup police flame you—even worse, they use a cancelbot against you. A *cancelbot* is a program that cancels your posts.

Don't be afraid to shoot for links from big sites. Sometimes they'll give them to you! As with the smaller sites, a phone call is the most effective means, and with the bigger sites you should probably *try the phone first.* It's critical that you have a good argument for how you'll provide value to their site, including a link back from your site. They'll want to know traffic numbers for your site in order to put a value on the reciprocal link. Therefore, the high-level sites are *best approached after you have launched and established somewhat of a following.*

Targeted E-mail

Targeted e-mail is a controversial subject. For many people who have been using the Internet for years, the idea of commercial e-mail of any kind is repulsive. However, it can also be *one of the most effective techniques to build traffic* in the beginning of a Web site's life.

The wrong way to do e-mail marketing is to spam. Spam e-mail is often referred to as *unsolicited commercial e-mail* (*UCE*), but so much mail of all kinds is unsolicited that to refer to all unsolicited e-mail as spam would be overbroad. Most people view spam as the junk that has nothing to do with them, and was sent by a machine to millions of recipients in the hopes that a few would respond positively. This is extremely disrespectful of the recipient's time.

Following are some typical ploys of spammers:

- Forged headers to hide the real return address
- Relayed mail through other people's mail servers
- No e-mail contact—just a P.O. box for sending checks
- Advertisement for a pyramid scheme, multilevel marketing, or pornographic Web site

- E-mail that's several screens long
- Multiple identical e-mails to the same address

All these tactics are disrespectful and in some cases potentially illegal. Also, because the spammers use these techniques, you must be extra careful to make your legitimate e-mail marketing not look like theirs. Be aware that many people get upwards of 15–20 spam e-mails a day, many of them advertising the same thing over and over and over.

The right way to do targeted e-mail marketing is to *take the time to do it right*. You need to pick your audience carefully, and to respect their time enough to send them only something that you have very good reason to think might appeal to them personally. *Do not* send them something because they're on the Internet. That's not enough of a reason to think they're in the target market. You need to know that they have expressed interest in something specific that you're offering.

For example, if your Web site is a listing of financial analyst jobs, it's probably okay to send mail to people who have listed their e-mail addresses on a Web site with résumés, looking for financial analyst jobs. It is *not* okay to send your financial analyst jobs listing to everyone looking for a job.

A good general guideline is that if the targeting and drafting of the e-mail takes you just as long per recipient as it takes a recipient to quickly read and discard it (about 10 seconds), then you're probably doing things right. If you've found a way to send out 1 million e-mail solicitations in an hour, you're definitely doing things the wrong way. *Time efficiency is NOT the goal; proper targeting is.*

When you're done creating a list of target recipients, compose an e-mail to each recipient individually. This doesn't mean that you have to write a whole page for each individual person, but you do have to write something more than `Dear Internet Enthusiast`. You should tell each person why he or she was specifically targeted. If someone posted a résumé looking for a financial analyst job in Connecticut, say that! Start with `I'm writing because I saw you were looking for a financial analyst job in Connecticut, and . . . .` After you have targeted properly and let the recipient know how he or she was chosen, you can present your case.

TIP

Several software packages enable you to mail-merge e-mail. You can personalize each e-mail you send out without having to write each copy individually. The program I use is Campaign by Arial Software. It offers several versions, one of which ties directly into a SQL database to select which records to send the e-mail to, and to pull out fields to insert into the e-mail. The URL for Arial Software is `http://www.arialsoftware.com`.

You can find other e-mail software at `http://www.shareware.com` or `http://www.windows95.com` for 32-bit Windows applications.

Your message *should not be wider than 65 characters*, and you *should include hard line breaks*. Some mail readers don't word-wrap, and the recipients of your mail won't be able to read your e-mail without scrolling horizontally (a bad thing). A 65-character line is the least common denominator of most popular e-mail client programs.

The message should be short. *If it's longer than two screens, it's too long.* Find a way to condense your message, and use a Web page for further information.

When you compose your e-mail, you should *have in mind what action you want the recipient to take*. If you have a clear goal for what you want the recipient to do, you can *craft a message that leads the reader to that action*. For example, if your goal is to get the reader to simply view your site, you should give enough information about your site to intrigue the reader and show that the site is worth his or her time, but you shouldn't give away the whole content of the site.

The tone of your e-mail should be familiar and *not* marketing talk! *If you speak in marketing talk, the recipient will feel spammed.* Treat the e-mail as if you were a third party who thought the recipient might be interested in your Web site. Give the facts, not exclamation points.

Another feature of tone is formatting. *If you send out e-mail with HTML formatting, it might look nice but it also looks like a sales job.* People don't send fancy HTML e-mail—machines do. If possible, you should avoid using HTML in your e-mail.

Unlike spammers, you should give personal contact information in your e-mail. If you do, people see a telltale sign that what you're sending is not spam. Use your real return address. That way, people who are interested in your product can contact you. If the cost of dealing with upset recipients is higher than the value of the leads your e-mail generates, you probably weren't selective enough with your targeting, or the tone of your e-mail was marketing-speak.

In e-mail campaigns where I've given out my phone number in the e-mail, I have received fewer than 1% phone responses, and no negative phone responses. Giving out your personal contact information is an important signal to the recipient that a real person is on the other end of the e-mail they're receiving. In the majority of cases, they won't need to use the direct response mechanism you provide, but they'll appreciate the fact that they can.

If you send out any promotion of your site via e-mail, *you will get some strong negative responses*. Some people are so fed up with e-mail abuse (and rightfully so) that they react immediately to all marketing e-mail with a nasty note to the postmaster of the sender of the e-mail, as well as notes to the postmasters of the service providers upstream from the sender's ISP. In some cases, the recipient researches other e-mail addresses of the sender and reports the e-mail as e-mail abuse to the postmasters of other ISPs where the sender has an account.

The first rule for you to follow to defend yourself is to *document everything you do*. Most ISPs are very understanding of marketing e-mail sent out from one person to another. They're not very understanding of indiscriminate spamming. They interpret the sending of 1 million e-mail messages as spamming, because how could any one person target 1 million people personally? It makes a mockery of the word *targeting*.

> **CAUTION**
>
> If the ISP feels that you're spamming, the ISP will sometimes warn you, and then shut down your account if you don't respond to the warnings.

One nice thing is that if you do this right, you will undoubtedly get more positive reactions than negative ones. It's sometimes surprising to me that people take the time to reply at such length about an issue you raise.

Most people who talk about direct marketing talk about 1–2% response rates. If you're in that range on e-mail, you're probably spamming. If you get response rates of 10–30%, you're probably targeting correctly. Most people think that these response rates are unrealistic; however, if you properly target and personalize your message, you should expect to hear from a significant number of recipients.

Chats

Chats can be a good way to promote some types of sites; however, there are two downsides:

- The chat crowd is not a great demographic.
- It takes a lot of time for the effect you generate.

If your target market is 15–25 year olds, chat is a wonderful tool to reach them. If you want to get an idea of who is chatting on the Internet, go to the Webchat Broadcasting System at `http:/ /www.wbs.net`. You'll see lots of chat rooms with different topics, some of which may be relevant to your site. However, the rooms with most of the volume are the pure chat rooms, and those are generally populated by a younger crowd or people who are busy looking for romance rather than a cool new Web site.

To promote your site through chat, *you need to schedule a chat event.* You could use IRC (Internet Relay Chat), or sites such as WBS will schedule chats for you. However, America Online's traffic on chat is much higher than either IRC or WBS. To schedule a chat event on AOL or WBS, you should talk directly to them and arrange for pre-chat publicity and chat-event support.

Online Services

The online services—America Online, Prodigy, and CompuServe—are promotional opportunities separate from the Internet. Forums on each are open only to members and provide the opportunity to reach people who don't venture out onto the Internet, or who find easy-to-use resources within their online service.

As most people know, *America Online has the largest audience* of all the online services. At the time of this writing, they have between 8 and 10 million active users. CompuServe is in second place with about 3 million, and Prodigy is in third place with a little over 2 million. CompuServe's niches are international and computer-centric. Because CompuServe provides a lot of support forums for different computer products, they tend to attract people who use computer products in their day-to-day work. Also, CompuServe has local access numbers all over the world, and has had them for longer than America Online.

It's worth getting an AOL account just for promotional purposes, and if your target market is international or computer-centric, you might consider a CompuServe account. With AOL you can get a special account that gives you TCP/IP access for half the regular unlimited-use price. That way, you can have a window open to AOL at the same time that you're using Eudora and your other tools. For promotional purposes, this type of account is all you need.

On every online service are *forums that pertain to narrow interest groups*: forums on parenting, model trains, skiing, computing, and so on. To promote your site, you should find the forums that relate most closely to the topic of your site.

After you've found the right forum, the best places to go are *the message boards*. That's where members post articles for other users to read. While advertising is flashing in front of the user, the focus of the user's attention is on the content of the forum. If you can *integrate your promotion into the topic of discussion*, you'll get not only the eyes but the minds of the readers.

For example, let's look at the job search site. In AOL we use Find to get a list of 13 resources about Jobs. One of them is About Work, which includes a message board. To promote your job search Web site, an appropriate post to the About Work message boards would be very effective.

In addition to forums, the online services provide classified advertising. Recently they have been trying to charge money for them, but *the best one is the America Online original (free) classifieds*. If you go to keyword Classifieds you'll see only the paid classifieds that they're trying to promote. The paid classifieds have far fewer items than the free classifieds. To find the free classifieds, go to keyword Classifieds, then click Using AOL Classifieds, and then click Buy & Sell Bulletin Boards.

> **NOTE**
>
> It's a shame that they're trying to turn classifieds into a pay service, because the value of it has always been that so many things were listed that you could always find something interesting. If they cancel the free classifieds, they run the risk of the classifieds becoming just a place for businesses to sell things to consumers on an ongoing basis.

With CityAuction, we placed classified ads in the AOL free classifieds for individual items that were being sold on our site. *More response came from the AOL classifieds than from any other single source.*

Classifications in the AOL Classifieds are as follows:

- Business
- Collectibles

- Computing
- Employment
- General
- Personals
- Real Estate
- Travel
- Vehicle

For many Web sites, classified ads are an inappropriate way to advertise. However, for others they're a great way to reach AOL's members without being part of AOL (other than being an individual subscriber).

Leveraging Technology Companies

Battles often go on between technology companies trying to gain market share on the Internet. Often, they enlist the support of content companies to help encourage the content company's customers to switch to their technology. For example, when Microsoft and Netscape were initially battling for market share, Microsoft was enlisting content companies to participate in the launch of Internet Explorer 3. Companies that participated in the launch were asked to make something special on their sites for Internet Explorer users. Many of these companies were listed among Internet destinations on the Microsoft home page, and many of them sold advertising to Microsoft. They were also included in the massive public relations campaign that accompanied the Internet Explorer 3 launch.

Technology companies are interested in content companies for the audiences they bring, so if you don't yet have an audience or proof of a captive audience, it's not worth your time to attempt this route. However, if you're growing and have a large customer base, note that *technology companies will often go out of their way to trade publicity for your choosing their technology.*

It can't hurt to *talk to each company providing key technology to your site* to find out whether they will provide public relations (PR) or promotional support to you in order to publicize the use of their technology. If you're known as a "cool site," you're like the Michael Jordan of the Internet. Instead of Nike wanting to show everyone that the best basketball player uses Nike shoes, technology companies want to show everyone that your cool site uses their technology.

The right technology companies to approach are those that are in a high-profile battle for market share. In the past, that battle has been in the browsers, but in the future it may be "push" or other client technology.

One caveat is that if the technology you use makes it difficult for your customers to use your site, it may not be worth the trade-off. However, if you can add a feature that's not essential to the use of your site, it may be worth the trade.

Advertising

The issue of advertising is complex, and would take an entire book to explain. This section is intended to answer questions that a small Web site operator may have about how to use advertising to publicize a Web site.

ADVERTISING TERMINOLOGY

The following table provides brief definitions of important advertising terminology that you'll need to understand.

Term	Definition
Ad deliveries	The number of times a particular ad is fully delivered to a viewer. Partial downloads of an ad normally are not counted.
Click-through rate	The ratio of the number of times an ad is clicked to the number of times an ad is fully delivered.
CPM	Cost per thousand.
Hits	A meaningless term because of the ambiguous ways in which people use it. It's a shame, because it's a good word, but at this point it's useless.
Page views	The number of times a full page is viewed. This is used as a measure of the readership of a site.
Run-of-site	An ad delivery scheme in which ads are delivered wherever a site has space available. This is cheaper than ads that must be delivered on a particular page or part of a site.
Sessions	The number of user sessions a site experiences. For game sites and other sites with very high page views, you want to know the number of sessions. Sometimes a very small number of users causes a very large number of page views.

Advertising for Web sites is usually best done on the Internet. Web sites are having a lot of trouble selling advertising space, and a well-placed ad can bring customers directly to your site. For Web sites that don't use ad agencies, buying ads can be intimidating at first. Where do you buy them? What's a fair price? How do you target? How can you trust the seller's statistics? I provide answers to these questions as well as a list of places where small Web sites can buy ads in small quantities at reasonable rates.

Where do you buy ads? Some sites sell their own ads. If you know of *a particularly good site that appeals to your target market*, you'd be well advised to contact them directly. Often they'll sell you ads even when none are listed on their site. The problem is that if you buy ads directly from a small site, you're likely to buy impressions to the same viewers over and over, with the *later impressions too stale to provide any value*. Also, small sites don't have the technology to give you accurate and up-to-date audited reporting. *However, you may find a great deal on the right audience.*

It's tempting to think that large sites offer the best advertising space—sites such as Yahoo! and the search engines. However, they're also the sites with the highest ad rates. The best comparison of ad sites is click-through rates (the number of times someone clicks an ad and goes to the destination site compared to the number of times the ad is fully delivered). *Click-through rates on the large sites are no higher than those of the small sites.* The best argument for advertising on the large search engines is the ability to target a specific search term. However, when you buy a search term, the rates go up, so you might be better off just buying the smaller sites that appeal to the same narrowly targeted audience.

What's a fair price? The definition of a fair price is the highest price a willing buyer is ready to pay. With so much ad inventory on the Internet going unused, you can negotiate a great deal with sites.

Rates are quoted in terms of CPM (cost per thousand). The rates on banner advertising *range from $1 to $250 CPM.* Don't believe the rates quoted in the press by the large sites, because they use the public statements they make about rates as a way to get their advertisers to feel good about the deals they've struck.

Advertising rates on *Yahoo!* at the time of this writing are about *$15–20 CPM for run-of-site* advertising (ads that run everywhere on Yahoo! without any real targeting). *Targeted ads can run as high as $60 CPM.* However, *only about 25–40% of their ad space sells.* The rest of the pages either show no ad at all, or are used to overdeliver the ads they did sell.

Advertising rates on *small targeted sites* range all over the board, but a typical selling price is about *$10 CPM.* However, they often quote rates of $20–50 CPM based on their targeting. They typically sell even less of their inventory than Yahoo! does, so you have lots of room to negotiate.

How do you target? On smaller sites, you target by selecting sites that meet your target audience criteria. You find them by using Yahoo! or other directories. They may be sites that you approached about reciprocal links; they may be sites that have approached you about getting links from your site. Or they may be sites you found by looking at Focalink's MarketMatch (`http://www.focalink.com`).

As of this writing, most sites on MarketMatch languish on the list for weeks or months without getting a nibble. However, that shouldn't keep you from using it to find places to advertise.

Another place you can go to purchase small volumes of targeted advertising is Flycast (`http://www.flycast.com`). At Flycast, you can browse through lots of different sites, and place orders for advertising online. It's a new concept, but one that might offer you great targeting at a reasonable price.

To purchase advertising via auction, try AdBot. The prices of advertising on AdBot range from a low of $0.55 to $5 CPM, depending on the site and/or category. AdBot offers targeting by channel, or by individual site in some cases. See AdBot at `http://www.adbot.com`.

LinkExchange (discussed in the later section "Banner Exchanges") is another option. While not as cheap as AdBot or some of the sites on Flycast, LinkExchange offers the ability to target a narrow channel for a reasonable price, and because of the large number of sites in the LinkExchange network, your ads won't get as stale as they might on a smaller network. See LinkExchange at `http://www.linkexchange.com`.

For some sites, untargeted advertising is the way to go. If the appeal of your site is broad, and you don't need to pay for the privilege of advertising to a small segment of the population, you can buy blocks of untargeted ads very, very inexpensively. *Even some sites with a narrow target audience are better off with untargeted ads because of the extremely low price.* On AdBot, the price of untargeted ads is about *$1.30–$1.50 CPM*, and on Flycast the cost of untargeted ads is about *$2 CPM*. Even if the response rates are 25% of those on a good targeted ad buy, you may still get more response per dollar spent.

Some networks such as AdBot are offering blocks of click-throughs rather than ad deliveries. The cost of click-throughs runs from *a low of $0.08 to a high of $2 or so.* Yahoo! currently quotes $1 for run-of-site ad click-throughs, while the high bid in the most recent AdBot auction was $0.08 per click-through on blocks of 50,000.

This may be a great way to buy ads, but I don't think the model will last long. Think of it—you can design an ad that appeals only to your narrow target market, and clearly screens out people who wouldn't want to go to your site. Because the goal of your ad is not to increase click-through but to get the most out of every click-through that happens, you're really trying to *decrease* click-throughs. As both sides discover techniques to make the most of the pricing model, I suspect that people will gravitate back toward CPM pricing or a hybrid of the two.

If you can buy click-throughs, by all means try it. Design an ad that will bring only the perfect viewer to your site, and buy all the click-throughs you can.

CAUTION

Flawed data. Data on ad deliveries is not 100% reliable. Two factors stand out as the biggest sources of error: caching and robots. *Caching by services such as AOL results in a lower number of reported ad deliveries than actually happened.* For you, the ad purchaser, the effect is positive; you get more ad deliveries than you paid for. For the site on which the ads appear, the effect is negative, because they don't get credit every time an ad is shown.

Robots are another source of error, but this one goes against the ad purchaser. *Robots from search engines and browsers that pre-load sites for the viewers to see are causing an increasing percentage of hits on ad banners.* Some report as much as 10% of hits are a result of robots of various types. For networks such as LinkExchange, where there are a large number of sites, each contributing a small number of page views, the effect is larger than with big sites like Yahoo!.

Contests and Prizes

Many sites have been promoted by using contests and prizes. However, the legal restrictions on contests and prizes are complicated enough that you should *consult an attorney* regarding this option before proceeding. Many states have laws about what kinds of contests they allow, and all contests must provide an alternative way to enter, other than becoming a customer.

The effect of contests and prizes has diminished since the early days of the Web, when one million-dollar giveaway by WebCrawler was a big event covered by the media. These days, a contest with cash prizes probably won't get media attention the way it would have a year or two ago.

Leveraging Your Customer Base

Once you have established a customer base, you are in a position to build a network of references to your site that generate traffic. Banner exchanges, reciprocal links, referrals, Web rings, and mailing lists are all tools that can help you drive traffic to your site.

Banner Exchanges

One way small sites have been promoting themselves for a long time is *banner exchanges*. Unquestionably, the largest and most successful banner exchange is LinkExchange, with over 200,000 sites in its network. The way it works is that sites in LinkExchange insert code into their pages so that LinkExchange banners appear on them. For every banner shown on a member site's pages, the site gets 1/2 credit. A whole credit is worth one ad delivery of the site's ad on another site in the network. In other words, for every 100 times you show an ad on your site, LinkExchange shows your ad 50 times on other sites in its network. There is no minimum volume, so even the small sites can participate.

About a month ago, the value of LinkExchange to its member sites went up when it introduced targeting. The idea is that each site self-categorizes, and then prescribes which category it wants its ads to appear on. For example, you may categorize your site as a Classified Ad site, but target your ads to Antiques & Collectibles sites. Some member sites have been reporting increases in click-through rates from 0.5% to 3% from this change.

One drawback to banner exchanges is that they make a site look a little more like a home page and a little less like a professional Web site. This perception may change in the future, though.

Other banner exchanges launch and go out of business regularly. For a complete list of banner exchanges, see Mark Welch's page at `http://www.markwelch.com`. You'll also see a review of advertising networks on Mark's site.

Reciprocal Links

Getting other sites to provide a link to your site is good not only for the direct traffic it generates, but for raising your ranking in some search engines. When search engines find lots of links to your site, they infer that your site is more relevant to its users than sites with no links to them.

The most valuable links are those from sites with complementary content. For example, if your site offers job listings for computer programmers, good places for links to your site to appear include programming-tips pages, pages that explain legal issues to independent contractors, job advice pages, classified ad pages, and so on.

To get other sites to give you links, you need to approach them on the right level. A professional site such as Pathfinder from Time Warner won't respond to the same type of communication as Joe's Home Page. Sometimes the best sites from which to get a link are sites that are relatively non-commercial but that receive big traffic. There are many sites like this. You may not have heard of them, but if you see a site listed prominently in Yahoo!, you can assume that it gets good traffic.

You can also find good reciprocal link sites by participating in relevant discussion lists and newsgroups. If you're trying to promote a gardening Web site, try participating in newsgroups that pertain to gardening. You'll see other people's signatures, which tell you about their Web sites. After you've participated in a discussion with someone, it's much easier to approach him or her to ask for a link.

Once you've located the sites you want to target, *the first step is to send them e-mail.* Because most Web professionals are busy people, send them a short note complimenting their site and suggesting a place on their site where you think a link to your site would be valuable to their site's readers. Include your URL! Don't ask for a link location that wouldn't benefit the other person's site.

If you don't get a response to your e-mail, you may want to call the Webmaster on the phone. Because we're in an age and industry where many people rely almost exclusively on e-mail, *the power of a phone call is extremely strong.* People aren't used to someone making the effort to make an actual phone call. If you're polite and ask for something reasonable, you may get much quicker service with a phone call.

What about offering a link from your site to theirs? Use your best judgment. Sometimes you'll have to give a link in exchange for the one you get, and sometimes you won't. It's best to create a Cool Links page or something similar on which to place your relevant links. On CityAuction (`http://www.cityauction.com`), we have a Local Content Sites area where we provide links to sites that give links back to CityAuction.

EXAMPLE OF A GOOD LINK-SOLICITATION NOTE

```
To: Joe Webmaster

From: You

Subject: Gardening site

Joe--

I just saw your Gardening in the West Web site. I liked it a lot, especially
the Java-based daffodil animation. I've never seen anything like it.

I have a site that enables people to order daffodil bulbs online, and
thought it may be valuable for your viewers to be able to buy bulbs after
seeing your site. Would you be willing to provide a link to my bulb-ordering
site from yours?

The URL for Bulbs Online is http://www.bulbs-online.com.

Thanks, and please write or call if you have any questions. I look forward
to hearing from you.

Your Name

Your Phone Number
```

Referrals

One technique to generate traffic to your site is to *enable current users to refer their friends and associates to your site.* ZDNet uses an innovative way of doing this on publications such as AnchorDesk, by providing a button on pages for you to e-mail an article to a friend. While it's always possible for readers to copy and paste an article into an e-mail program and send it, by providing this button ZDNet suggests and enables pass-along readership of their site.

Another way to do this is to give users a URL to promote their own presence on your site. If you provide customized content (such as classified ads, personals, or even user profiles), you can give each user his or her own URL to promote. The users will put these URLs in their signatures or America Online profiles, and extend the reach of your site. It's important to *think of ways that you can involve your users in your site—in a way that gives them a reason to tell their friends.*

One site that I've developed is CityAuction (`http://www.cityauction.com`), an online auction site. The way we approached referrals with CityAuction was to provide sellers with a URL for their own listings. That way, they can post to individual newsgroups or send e-mail to people with the URL of their auction. That brings new users to our site by using the initiative of the current users.

Web Rings

Web rings are groups of Web sites that provide links to each other. They typically have a common theme—say, job search resources. Every site provides a link somewhere on the page that leads viewers to the next site in the ring. It's called a *Web ring* because it leads viewers around to all the sites in the ring. The biggest plus to Web rings is that *they provide targeting*. Because there's a common theme, the people who come from one of the Web-ring links are usually qualified rather than random viewers. One downside to Web rings is that they tend to lead your viewers to your competitors. If you're not confident that your subject matter will be more appealing than your competitor's, you may want to consider staying out of a themed Web ring until you improve your position.

To find out more about Web rings, check out `http://www.webring.org`. It's a good resource for finding the right Web ring for your subject matter.

Mailing Lists

Mailing lists (also called *Listservs*) are groups of people who subscribe to a regular e-mail newsletter on a particular subject. Usually the content is provided by subscribers who submit articles that are then reviewed by the moderator of the list, and, if they're appropriate, are included in that day's or week's mailing to the membership. Discussions on topics of interest to the group sometimes become heated. Because mailing lists are pushed out to the membership, and because everyone on the list has subscribed, you get a *highly targeted and responsive group of readers.*

Promoting your site on mailing lists is best done by participating in them. You can also buy ads; however, you can get nearly the same effect by participating, and you don't have the cost of buying ads.

To participate in a mailing list, you first have to find it. The best universal list of mailing lists is Liszt, at `http://www.liszt.com`. You'll find a large number of mailing lists organized by subject matter. When you find the right list, first subscribe to the list (using the procedure outlined on Liszt) and then *read a few issues before attempting to participate.*

Another way to find lists is to ask people in your industry which lists they read. You might be surprised to know how many people read mailing lists, and they're the right people to let you know about lists that pertain to your niche. Your current customers are also a great source of information on targeted lists that fit your customer profile.

By the way, *mailing lists are generally free.* I know of none that charge a subscription that are of any value compared to the free ones.

The key is your signature. It's considered rude to submit a plug for your Web site into a list when it's not relevant to the topic of discussion. Rather, you should participate in the discussion at hand, and rely on the e-mail signature at the end of your submission to advertise your site. Also, if mentioning your site in response to a question someone on the list has raised, it's perfectly fine to describe your site and to explain how it could solve the problem posed to the group.

To design a good signature, read a few of the posts in the mailing lists relevant to your industry or area of interest. *Design a signature that's consistent with the standards of the group*; however, in most cases more than six lines is considered too long. Try to *keep your message contained in the 4–6 lines*, and make sure you put the URL of your site in the sig (with the preceding http:// so that e-mail readers will make it a hyperlink).

Creating Repeat Business

A one-time customer doesn't make a business. As you establish your customer base, you should develop programs that keep the customer involved with the site. By creating a sense of community around your site through customer-aware programs, you'll generate repeat visits and repeat business.

Customer Mailing Lists

Just like the mailing lists for your industry (described in the preceding section), you can create a mailing list that helps to create community for your users. Software to manage your mailing list can come from a variety of sources, but Liszt contains a set of references to list management software. Majordomo is one of the most popular. To see the list of software, see Liszt at http:// www.liszt.com.

LinkExchange is one company that has made great use of a customer mailing list to create repeat business and community for their member sites. Out of about 200,000 sites in the LinkExchange network, nearly 30,000 subscribe to the LinkExchange mailing list. It has become one of the best sources for discussion of how small Web sites can promote and advertise their sites.

If your site has a registration process, you should make subscribing to your mailing list part of the registration. No one wants to be included on a list without asking, so you should ask every time before putting someone on your list. There's no reason not to. If your site doesn't have a registration process, put a plug on the main page that encourages people to register. However, if you don't have a registration process, getting your number of subscribers up to a reasonable level may take a long time. Lists with fewer than 300–500 members usually have a hard time maintaining a reasonable level of activity. You may want to wait until your site reaches a certain traffic level before launching a mailing list that doesn't have a chance of succeeding, but when you reach that point, it may be one of your most valuable tools in creating and maintaining customer loyalty.

Forums

If a mailing list isn't right for your site, perhaps a forum would be. You can create a place on your site where users can post messages on topics of interest to your other viewers, and lively discussions can take place on your site. This obviously brings people back, and *provides a way for your users to get to know each other. Creating community in this way is a great way to encourage repeat visits to your site.* The best software to conduct a forum is probably your own, created using Active Server Pages and a database of customer submissions.

Personalization

Personalizing your site so that each viewer sees your site in a way he or she designed is *a way to make your users feel some ownership of your site.* If they feel ownership, they're more likely to come back over and over. The technical and user interface hurdles are high, but if you can manage to create a simple way for people to personalize your site in the way they want, you can probably manage to create a loyal group of customers. In addition, *by analyzing which options users choose, you can figure out which features of your site are more valuable* than the others, and which are so unpopular that you should remove them.

Many big sites have created personalized versions. Here are two examples:

- My Yahoo!

    `http://my.yahoo.com`
- E*Trade Securities (requires opening an account)

    `http://www.etrade.com`

Resources

These are the resources I use every day to learn about Web site marketing and promotion:

- Mailing lists
    - LinkExchange Digest

        `http://www.ledigest.com`
    - Online Ads discussion list

        `http://www.o-a.com/`
    - I-Advertising

        `http://www.exposure-usa.com/i-advertising/`
    - WebPromote

        `http://www.webpromote.com`
- Newsgroups
    - LinkExchange newsgroups (from news server `news2.linkexchange.com`)
        - `le.discuss`—a discussion about Web site creation
        - `le.test`—a discussion of Web site promotion and advertising

Summary

This chapter explained some of the top techniques for promoting and marketing your own Web site. It's tempting to try to rank them, but a better way of looking at it is that your site needs *a cohesive marketing campaign, with components that combine to establish, build, and maintain your market presence.* After you've determined who your target customer is, you can use techniques such as search-engine-conscious site design from the first part of this chapter to bring people to your site the first time. Then use techniques such as customer referrals or link exchanges from the second part of the chapter to build your customer base. Finally, use techniques from the last part to build a strong sense of loyalty to your site and bring people back time after time. If you accomplish all three goals, your Web site has a good chance to succeed. If you ignore part of the program, your efforts won't produce the maximum possible effect.

VIII
PART

Appendixes

Quick ASP Object and Component Reference

APPENDIX A

NOTE

The information for this appendix was extracted from the Internet Information Server online documentation. For more information on any of the following objects, please consult the Microsoft documentation.

Built-in Active Server Pages Objects

You can use all the following built-in objects without explicitly creating an instance of them in your scripts.

The Application Object

The Application object can be used to store and retrieve information that can be shared among all users of an application.

Collections

Application.Contents(Key)

Collection of all the data and objects declared at the application level without using the <OBJECT> tag. Key is the name of the application item.

Application.StaticObjects(Key)

Collection of all objects declared at the application level using the <OBJECT> tag. Key is the name of the application item.

Events

Application.OnEnd

Triggered by the Web server being shut down or by the unloading of the application. Occurs after all user sessions have ended.

Application.OnStart

Triggered by the first request for a Web page in the application. Occurs before the start of any user sessions.

Methods

Application.Lock

Prevents all other users from modifying any variable in the Application object.

Application.Unlock

Allows other users to modify variables in the Application object.

The `ObjectContext` Object

Used to control Active Server Pages transactions. The transactions are managed by the Microsoft Transaction Server (MTS).

Events
`ObjectContext.OnTransactionAbort`

Triggered by an aborted transaction. Doesn't occur until after the script finishes processing.

`ObjectContext.OnTransactionCommit`

Triggered by a committed transaction. Doesn't occur until after the script finishes processing.

Methods
`ObjectContext.SetAbort`

Explicitly aborts a transaction.

`ObjectContext.SetComplete`

Overrides any previous calls to the `ObjectContext.SetAbort` method.

The `Request` Object

The `Request` object can be used to access all information sent in a request from a browser to your server.

Collections
`Request.ClientCertificate(Key[SubField])`

Collection of information from client certificate. For `Key`, this collection has the following keys:

`Subject`	The subject of the certificate. Contains information about the recipient of the certificate. Can be used with all the `SubField` suffixes (see the following list).
`Issuer`	The issuer of the certificate. Contains information about the certificate authority. Can be used with all of the `SubField` suffixes except `CN`.
`ValidFrom`	The date the certificate was issued. Uses VBScript formatting.
`ValidUntil`	The date when the certificate will no longer be valid.
`SerialNumber`	Contains the serial number of the certificate.
`Certificate`	Contains the binary stream of the entire certificate content in ASN.1 format.

For *SubField*, the `Subject` and `Issuer` keys can be appended with the following *SubFields* (for example, `SubjectOU` or `IssuerL`):

C	Country of origin.
O	Company or organization name.
OU	Organizational unit.
CN	Common name of the user.
L	Locality.
S	State (or province).
T	Title of the person or organization.
GN	Given name.
I	Initials.

When the file `cervbs.inc` (for VBScript) or `cerjavas.inc` (for JScript) is included in your Active Server Page by using the `#INCLUDE` directive, the following two flags can be used:

`ceCertPresent`	Indicates whether a client certificate is present. Has the value TRUE or FALSE.
`ceUnrecognizedIssuer`	Indicates whether the issuer of the last certification in this chain is unknown. Has the value TRUE or FALSE.

Request.Cookies(*Cookie*[(*Key*).*Attribute*]

Collection of cookies. Allows access to browser cookies. *Cookie* specifies which cookie to return. *Key* is used with cookie dictionaries to return a cookie with a particular key. For *Attribute*, you can use the attribute `HasKeys` to determine whether a cookie has keys. `HasKeys` has the value TRUE or FALSE.

Request.Form(*Parameter*)[(*Index*).Count]

Collection of data entered into HTML forms. *Parameter* is the name of an element in an HTML form. *Index* is used when a parameter can have more than one value (for example, when MULTIPLE is used with the <SELECT> tag). When a parameter has multiple values, *Count* provides a count of the number of values.

Request.QueryString(*Variable*)[(*Index*).Count]

Collection of values from a query string. *Variable* is the name of a variable in a query string. *Index* is used when a variable can have more than one value. When a variable has multiple values, *Count* provides a count of the number of values.

Request.ServerVariables(*Server Environment Variable*)

Collection of environmental variables. Allows access to HTTP headers. You can retrieve any header by using `HTTP_` prefixed to the header name. For example, `HTTP_USER_AGENT` retrieves the user agent HTTP header (the browser type). In addition, you can use any of the following variables for *Server Environment Variable*:

ALL_HTTP	All HTTP headers sent from the client to the server. The results are prefixed by HTTP_.
ALL_RAW	All HTTP headers sent from the client to the server. The results appear exactly as sent—possibly without being prefixed by HTTP_.
APPL_MD_PATH	The metabase path of the application.
APPL_PHYSICAL_PATH	The physical path corresponding to the metabase path of the application.
AUTH_PASSWORD	Authentication password that's entered by users in the Password dialog box for Basic authentication.
AUTH_TYPE	Authentication type used to validate users when they attempt to retrieve a protected script.
AUTH_USER	Authentication user name.
CERT_COOKIE	Unique client certificate ID.
CERT_FLAGS	Client certificate flags. Bit 0 is set to 1 if the certificate is present and bit 1 is set to 1 if the certifying authority is not recognized.
CERT_ISSUER	Client certificate ISSUER field.
CERT_KEYSIZE	Number of bits in the SSL connection key.
CERT_SECRETKEYSIZE	Number of bits in the server certificate private key.
CERT_SERIALNUMBER	Client certificate SERIAL NUMBER field.
CERT_SERVER_ISSUER	Server certificate ISSUER field.
CERT_SERVER_SUBJECT	Server certificate SUBJECT field.
CERT_SUBJECT	Client certificate SUBJECT field.
CONTENT_LENGTH	Content length according to the client.
CONTENT_TYPE	Content type of posted form contents or HTTP PUT.
GATEWAY_INTERFACE	Gateway interface used by the server.
HTTPS	Returns ON if an SSL request and OFF otherwise.
HTTPS_KEYSIZE	Number of bits in the SSL connection key.
HTTPS_SECRETKEYSIZE	Number of bits in the server certificate private key.
HTTPS_SERVER_ISSUER	Server certificate ISSUER field.
HTTPS_SERVER_SUBJECT	Server certificate SUBJECT field.

INSTANCE_ID	The ID for the IIS instance.
INSTANCE_META_PATH	The metabase path for the IIS instance.
LOCAL_ADDR	The server address used in the request.
LOGON_USER	The Windows NT account of the user.
PATH_INFO	Path information according to the client.
PATH_TRANSLATED	Path that has been translated with virtual-to-physical mappings.
QUERY_STRING	Query string contents.
REMOTE_ADDR	The IP address of the user.
REMOTE_HOST	Host performing the request.
REQUEST_METHOD	Request method such as GET, POST, HEAD.
SCRIPT_NAME	Name of the script being executed.
SERVER_NAME	Server's hostname, DNS address, or IP address.
SERVER_PORT	The server port that received the request.
SERVER_PORT_SECURE	If request is on a secure port, the value of this variable is 1.
SERVER_PROTOCOL	The name and revision of the protocol being used by the server.
SERVER_SOFTWARE	The name and revision of the software being executed on the server.
URL	Provides the base URL.

Methods
Request.BinaryRead(*Count*)
Retrieves raw contents of an HTML form. When this method is called, *Count* specifies how many bytes to retrieve. After the method is called, *Count* indicates how many bytes were actually retrieved.

Properties
Request.TotalBytes
The size of the body of the request, measured in bytes.

The Response Object
The Response object is used to send information back to a browser.

Collections
Response.Cookies(*Cookie*)[*Key.Attribute*]
Allows you to add a cookie to a browser. *Cookie* is the name of the cookie to add. *Key* is used when creating cookie dictionaries. *Attribute* specifies one of the following cookie attributes:

Domain	Specifies that the cookie should be sent only to this domain. For example, `"aspsite.com"`.
Expires	The expiration date of the cookie. For example, `"July 4, 1998"`. If this attribute isn't specified, the cookie expires immediately after the user leaves the Web site.
HasKeys	Specifies whether the cookie is a cookie dictionary. Has the value TRUE or FALSE.
Path	Specifies that the cookie should be sent only to this path. For example, `"/wwwroot/news/"`.
Secure	Specifies whether a cookie is secure. Has the value TRUE or FALSE.

Methods

Response.AddHeader *Name*, *Value*

Adds a new HTTP header to the response. *Name* is the name of the new header. *Value* is the value of the header variable. You can add a header with any name and any value.

Response.AppendToLog *String*

Appends a string to an entry in the log of the Web server. *String* is the string to append to the log.

Response.BinaryWrite *Data*

Sends non-string information in the response. *Data* is the data to send.

Response.Clear

Clears the buffered response. Doesn't clear headers.

Response.End

Forces the Web server to stop any further processing of a script and send the current results.

Response.Flush

Sends all contents of the buffer in the case of a buffered response.

Response.Redirect *URL*

Attempts to redirect a browser to a new page. *URL* is the Internet address of the new page.

Response.Write *Variant*

Sends a string to a browser. *Variant* is a string or a variable that has a string as its value.

Properties

Response.Buffer

Buffers an Active Server Page. The response is not sent until the end of the page or until the `Response.Flush` or `Response.End` method is called.

Response.CacheControl

Specifies whether proxy servers should cache the Active Server Page. By default, this property is FALSE.

Response.CharSet(*Charsetname*)

Specifies the character set to be used for the current page. A possible value is "ISO-LATIN-1".

Response.ContentType

Specifies the content of the response. Possible values include text/plain and image/GIF.

Response.Expires

The length of time that a browser should cache the current page, measured in minutes.

Response.ExpiresAbsolute

The date and time after which a browser should no longer cache the current page.

Response.IsClientConnected

Indicates whether a browser is still connected to the server. Has the value TRUE or FALSE.

Response.PICS(*PICSLabel*)

Used to add a PICS rating for a page. A *PICS rating* indicates a content rating for the page, such as the degree of violence or profanity.

Response.Status

Specifies the status line that's returned by a server.

The Server Object

Allows use of various utility functions on the server.

Methods

Server.CreateObject(*ProgID*)

Creates an instance of an object for use within the current Active Server Page. *ProgID* indicates the type of object to create. For example:

```
<% Set MyBrow=Server.CreateObject("MSWC.BrowserType") %>
```

Server.HTMLEncode(*String*)

Converts a string to use special HTML characters. See Appendix D, "Quick HTML Reference," for a list of these characters. *String* is the string to encode.

Server.MapPath(*Path*)

Maps a relative or virtual path to a physical path. *Path* is the relative or virtual path to convert.

Server.URLEncode(*String*)

Converts a string to URL-encoded form. *String* is the string to convert.

Properties
Server.ScriptTimeOut

Determines the amount of time a script is allowed to execute before it's terminated. The time is measured in seconds, and the default value is **90**.

The Session Object

The Session object can be used to store and retrieve information about particular user sessions.

Collections
Session.Contents(*Key*)

Collection of all the data and objects declared at the session level without using the <OBJECT> tag. *Key* is the name of the session item.

Session.StaticObjects(*Key*)

Collection of all objects declared at the session level using the <OBJECT> tag. *Key* is the property to return.

Methods
Session.Abandon

Used to terminate a user session. Destroys all data and objects contained in the user session.

Properties
Session.CodePage

Specifies which server code page to use when displaying dynamic content.

Session.LCID

Specifies which location identifier to use when displaying dynamic content.

Session.SessionID

A unique identifier for a user session.

Session.Timeout

The length of time in minutes before an idle session will be terminated automatically. This property has the default value of 20 minutes.

Active Server Pages Installable Components

These are the standard ActiveX components that are bundled with Active Server Pages. You must create an instance of each component before you can use it.

Using VBScript:

```
<% Set MyComponent=Server.CreateObject("ComponentName")%>
```

Using JScript:

```
<% var MyComponent=Server.CreateObject("ComponentName")%>
```

The Ad Rotator Component

Used to display banner advertisements on a Web page. You can use this component to rotate through a number of different advertisements.

```
<% Set MyAd=Server.CreateObject("MSWC.AdRotator") %>
```

Files
Redirection File

When you click a banner advertisement, you're sent to this Active Server Page.

Rotator Schedule File

This text file includes all the information about the advertisements. It has two sections, divided by an asterisk (*), which specify global parameters and advertisement-specific information. Global parameters:

REDIRECT	Supply a path to the redirection file after this parameter.
WIDTH	Supply the width of the advertisement after this parameter.
HEIGHT	Supply the height of the advertisement after this parameter.
BORDER	Supply the size of the advertisement border after this parameter.

If using advertisement-specific information, for each advertisement you can list the location of the banner image file, the location of the home page of the advertiser, alternative advertisement text, and a number that indicates how often an advertisement should be displayed:

```
http://www.mysite.com/GSbanner.gif
http://www.greatsoftware.com
Check out our great software!
20
```

Quick ASP Object and Component Reference

APPENDIX A

811

A

ASP OBJECT
AND COMPONENT
REFERENCE

Methods
GetAdvertisement(*Rotator Schedule File*)

Use to actually display an advertisement on a page. *Rotator Schedule File* is the path to the Rotator Schedule file.

Properties
Border(*Size*)

Used to specify the border size of the advertisement. *Size* is the size of the border.

Clickable(*Value*)

Specifies whether a banner advertisement is a hyperlink. *Value* can be either TRUE or FALSE.

TargetFrame(*Frame*)

Specifies the frame in which to display the banner advertisement. *Frame* is the name of a frame.

The Browser Capabilities Component

Use this component to access information about the capabilities of different browsers:

```
<% Set MyBCap=Server.CreateObject("MSWC.BrowserType") %>
```

Files
Browscap.ini

Text file that contains information about browsers. You can list any set of properties for each browser. Here's the entry for the Netscape 4.00 browser:

```
[Netscape 4.00]
browser=Netscape
version=4.00
majorver=4
minorver=00
frames=TRUE
tables=TRUE
cookies=TRUE
backgroundsounds=FALSE
vbscript=FALSE
javascript=TRUE
javaapplets=TRUE
ActiveXControls=FALSE
```

The Content Linking Component

Use this component to link a series of Web pages together:

```
<% Set MyContent=Server.CreateObject("MSWC.NextLink") %>
```

Files
Content Linking List File

Text file containing a list of HTML files. Each line specifies a particular HTML file, a description for the Web page, and an optional comment. The elements of a line are separated by the tab character:

```
Chapter1.htm      Installing and Using Windows NT Server
Chapter2.htm      Installing and Using Internet Information Server
Chapter3.htm      Installing and Using SQL Server
```

Methods
GetListCount(*Content Linking List File*)

Returns the total number of pages contained in the Content Linking List file. *Content Linking List File* lists the path or address of the Content Linking List file.

GetListIndex(*Content Linking List File*)

Returns the position of the current page in the Content Linking List file. *Content Linking List File* indicates the path of the Content Linking List file.

GetNextDescription(*Content Linking List File*)

Returns the description of the next page in the Content Linking List file. *Content Linking List File* is the path of the Content Linking List file.

GetNextURL(*Content Linking List File*)

Returns the Internet address of the next page in the Content Linking List file. *Content Linking List File* is the path of the Content Linking List file.

GetNthDescription(*Content Linking List File, Number*)

Returns the description for a page with a particular index in the Content Linking List file. *Content Linking List File* is the path of the Content Linking List file. *Number* is the index number of a particular item in the Content Linking List file.

GetNthURL(*Content Linking List File, Number*)

Returns the Internet address for a page with a particular index in the Content Linking List file. *Content Linking List File* is the path of the Content Linking List file. *Number* is the index number of a particular item in the Content Linking List file.

GetPreviousDescription(*Content Linking List File*)

Returns the description for the previous page in the Content Linking List file. *Content Linking List File* is the path of the Content Linking List file.

GetPreviousURL(*Content Linking List File*)

Returns the Internet address for the previous page in the Content Linking List file. *Content Linking List File* is the path of the Content Linking List file.

The Content Rotator Component

This component can be used to randomly display different HTML content on a page:

```
<% Set MyContent=Server.CreateObject("MSWC.ContentRotator") %>
```

Files
Content Schedule File

Text file that contains a list of HTML strings. The component rotates through these strings when displaying HTML content on a page. Each entry is marked by a double percentage sign (%%). The %% sign can be followed by a number that indicates how often the HTML string should be displayed (marked with the # sign) and one or more optional comments (marked by //):

```
%% #2 // This HTML string is displayed 1/2th of the time
<HR COLOR="RED">
We sell shoes at half the normal price!
<HR COLOR="RED">
%% #1 // This HTML string is displayed 1/4 of the time
<FONT SIZE=+1>
Our shoes last forever!
</FONT>
%% #1 // This HTML string is displayed 1/4 of the time
<FONT COLOR="RED">
Don't buy your shoes anywhere else!
</FONT>
```

Methods
ChooseContent(*Content Schedule File*)

Returns an HTML string from the Content Schedule file to be displayed in a Web page. Different strings are randomly retrieved with a frequency determined by the Content Schedule file. *Content Schedule File* is the path of the Content Schedule file.

GetAllContent(*Content Schedule File*)

Returns all HTML strings from the Content Schedule file and displays them on a Web page separated by horizontal rules. *Content Schedule File* is the path or address of the Content Schedule file.

The Counters Component

Used to create one or more counters that can be used to track such information as the number of visits to a Web page or Web site. You're allowed to create only one Counters component, but the component may have more than one counter.

Create only one Counters component for your application by including this line in the `Global.asa` file:

```
<OBJECT RUNAT=Server SCOPE=Application ID=Counter
➥PROGID="MSWC.Counters"></OBJECT>
```

Files

Counters.txt

Text file containing all the individual counters.

Methods

Get(*Counter Name*)

Returns the current value of a particular counter. *Counter Name* is the name of an individual counter.

Increment(*Counter Name*)

Adds 1 to the current value of a particular counter, or creates a new counter with value 1. *Counter Name* is the name of an existing (or soon to exist) counter.

Remove(*Counter Name*)

Destroys a counter by removing it from the `Counters.txt` file. *Counter Name* is the name of an individual counter that soon will no longer exist.

Set(*Counter Name*, *Number*)

Sets the value of a counter to a particular integer value. *Number* is the new integer value of the counter. *Counter Name* is the name of a counter. If the counter doesn't exist, this method creates it with the specified value.

The Page Counter Component

You can use the Page Counter component as a hit counter. This component can be used to keep track of how many times each page on your Web site has been visited:

```
<% Set MyCNT=Server.CreateObject("MSWC.PageCounter") %>
```

Files
Hit Count Data File

Text file that stores the number of hits each page in an application has received.

Methods
Hits([*Web Page Path*])

Returns the number of times a Web page has been hit. *Web Page Path* (optional) is the path of a particular Web page. If no path is supplied, the method returns the number of hits for the current page.

Reset([*Web Page Path*])

Resets to zero the number of times a Web page has been hit. *Web Page Path* (optional) is the path of a particular Web page. If no path is supplied, the method resets the current page.

The Permission Checker Component

This component checks whether a user has permission to access a particular file. The component uses Internet Information Server's password authentication protocols to determine permissions.

```
<% Set MyPermit=Server.CreateObject("MSWC.PermissionChecker") %>
```

Methods
HasAccess(*File Path*)

Checks whether a user has permission to access a particular file. Returns TRUE if the user has permission. Returns FALSE if the user doesn't have permission or the file doesn't exist. *File Path* is the path to a particular file.

The File Access Component

The File Access component contains a collection of objects that provides complete control over a computer's file system. For example, you can use these objects to read and write to files and manipulate file folders and disk drives.

The Drive Object

The Drive object is used to retrieve information about the properties of a computer's drives or network shares.

```
<%
Set fs = Server.CreateObject("Scripting.FileSystemObject")
Set d = fs.GetDrive("c:")
%>
```

Properties
AvailableSpace
Returns the space available on a particular drive or network share.

DriveLetter
Returns the drive letter of a particular drive or network share.

DriveType
Returns a number specifying the type of a particular drive. This property can have the values shown in the following table.

Value	Description
0	Unknown
1	Removable
2	Fixed
3	Remote
4	CD-ROM
5	RAM disk

FileSystem
Returns the file system used by a particular drive. Possible values include NTFS and FAT.

FreeSpace
Returns the space available on a particular drive or network share.

IsReady
Indicates whether a particular drive, such as a CD-ROM or removable disk drive, is ready. Returns either TRUE or FALSE.

Path
Returns the path of a particular drive.

RootFolder
Returns a Folder object representing the root folder of a particular drive.

SerialNumber
Returns the unique serial number of a disk volume.

ShareName
Returns the network share name of a particular drive.

Quick ASP Object and Component Reference

APPENDIX A

817

A

ASP OBJECT
AND COMPONENT
REFERENCE

TotalSize
Returns the total space of a drive or network share in bytes.

VolumeName
Specifies the volume name of a particular drive. This property can be both read and set.

The Drives Collection
The Drives collection contains all available drives:

```
<%
Set fs = Server.CreateObject("Scripting.FileSystemObject")
Set dc = fs.Drives
%>
```

Properties
Count
Returns the number of drives in the Drives collection.

Item(*Key*)
Used to specify a particular drive in the Drives collection. *Key* specifies the drive.

The File Object
The File object enables you to access and manipulate the properties of an individual file:

```
<%
Set fs = Server.CreateObject("Scripting.FileSystemObject")
Set f = fs.GetFile("c:\somefile")
%>
```

Methods
Copy *Destination* [,*Overwrite*]
Copies a file to a new destination. *Destination* is a file path. *Overwrite* can be either TRUE or FALSE. If TRUE, an existing file at the destination will be overwritten. If FALSE and a file already exists, an error occurs. Overwrite is TRUE by default.

Delete [*Force*]
Deletes a file. *Force* specifies whether to delete a file with the read-only attribute set. By default, *Force* is FALSE.

Move *Destination*
Moves a file to a new destination. *Destination* is a particular file path.

OpenAsTextStream([*iomode* [,*format*]])

Opens a file for reading, writing, or appending.

iomode determines the type of operation to be performed on the file. *iomode* can have the values shown in the following table.

Constant	Value	Description
ForReading	1	Opens a file for reading.
ForWriting	2	Opens a file for writing.
ForAppending	8	Opens a file for appending.

format determines the character set of the file. *format* can have the values shown in the following table.

Constant	Value	Description
TristateUseDefault	-2	Use the system default.
TristateTrue	-1	Open the file as Unicode.
TristateFalse	0	Open the file as ASCII.

Properties

Attributes

Specifies the attributes of a file. This property can have the values shown in the following table.

Constant	Value	Description
Normal	0	No attributes set.
ReadOnly	1	Read/write attribute.
Hidden	2	Read/write attribute.
System	4	Read/write attribute.
Volume	8	Read-only attribute.
Directory	16	Read-only attribute.
Archive	32	Read/write attribute.
Alias	64	Read-only attribute.
Compressed	128	Read-only attribute.

DateCreated
Returns the date on which the file was created. This property is read-only.

DateLastAccessed
Returns the date on which the file was last accessed. This property is read-only.

DateLastModified
Returns the date on which the file was last modified. This property is read-only.

Drive
Returns the drive where the file is located. This property is read-only.

Name
Specifies the name of a file. This property can be both read and set.

ParentFolder
Returns the `Folder` object that represents the folder containing the file.

Path
Returns the path of the file.

ShortName
Returns the short name of a file (pre-Windows 95 short file name).

ShortPath
Returns the short path of a file (pre-Windows 95 short path).

Size
Returns the size of a file in bytes.

Type
Returns the file type. Possible values include `Text Document`, `ASP File`, and `Internet Document` (`HTML`).

The Files Collection
The `Files` collection contains all files within a folder:

```
<%
Set fs = Server.CreateObject("Scripting.FileSystemObject")
Set f = fs.GetFolder("c:\somefolder")
Set fc = f.Files
%>
```

Properties
Count
Returns the number of files in the `Files` collection.

Item(*Key*)
Returns the file in the `Files` collection specified by *Key*.

The FileSystemObject Object
Allows general access to a computer's file system.

```
<%
Set fs = Server.CreateObject("Scripting.FileSystemObject")
%>
```

Methods
BuildPath(*Path*, *Name*)
Used for building file paths. Adds a name to an existing path.

CopyFile *Source*, *Destination* [,*Overwrite*]
Copies one or more files from *Source* to *Destination*. The path specified as *Source* can contain wildcards. Using wildcards, you can copy multiple files at once. However, if you use wildcards and no files match, an error occurs.

Overwrite specifies whether to overwrite existing files. *Overwrite* can be either TRUE or FALSE. By default, it's TRUE. This method never overwrites files with their read-only attribute set to TRUE.

CopyFolder *Source*, *Destination* [,*Overwrite*]
Copies one or more folders from *Source* to *Destination*. The path specified as *Source* can contain wildcards. Using wildcards, you can copy multiple folders at once. However, if you use wildcards and no folders match, an error occurs.

Overwrite specifies whether to overwrite existing folders. *Overwrite* can be either TRUE or FALSE. By default, it's TRUE.

CreateFolder *Foldername*
Creates a new folder with the name specified by *Foldername*. If the folder already exists, an error occurs.

CreateTextFile(*Filename* [,*Overwrite* [,*Unicode*]])
Creates a file and returns a `TextStream` object. *Filename* specifies the name of the new file. *Overwrite* indicates whether existing files should be overwritten. It can have the value TRUE or FALSE (by default, it's FALSE). If *Unicode* is TRUE, the file is created as Unicode. If FALSE, the file is created as ASCII (the default).

DeleteFile *Filespec* [*,Force*]

Deletes one or more files. *Filespec* specifies the file to delete. Filespec can contain wildcards. If it contains wildcards, more than one file can be deleted at a time.

Force indicates whether to force the deletion of files with their read-only attributes set. Force can be either TRUE or FALSE. By default, *Force* is FALSE.

DeleteFolder *Folderspec* [*,Force*]

Deletes one or more folders. *Folderspec* specifies the folders to delete. *Folderspec* can contain wildcards. If it contains wildcards, more than one folder can be deleted at a time.

Force indicates whether to force the deletion of folders with their read-only attributes set. Force can be either TRUE or FALSE. By default, *Force* is FALSE.

DriveExists(*Drivespec*)

Returns TRUE if the drive specified by *Drivespec* exists, FALSE otherwise.

FileExists(*Filespec*)

Returns TRUE if the file specified by *Filespec* exists, FALSE otherwise.

FolderExists(*Folderspec*)

Returns TRUE if the folder specified by *Folderspec* exists, FALSE otherwise.

GetAbsolutePathName(*Pathspec*)

Returns a complete file path from the partial path specified in *Pathspec*.

GetBaseName(*Path*)

Returns nothing but the filename (without the file extension) from a full path.

GetExtensionName(*Path*)

Returns nothing but the file extension (without the filename) from a full path.

GetFile(*Filespec*)

Returns a File object representing the file specified by *Filespec*.

GetFileName(*Pathspec*)

Returns nothing but the filename and extension from a full path.

GetFolder(*Folderspec*)

Returns a Folder object that represents the folder specified in *Folderspec*.

GetParentFolderName(*Path*)

Returns the name of the folder containing the folder or file specified in *Path*.

GetSpecialFolder(*Folderspec*)

Returns the folder specified by *Folderspec*. *Folderspec* can be any one of the values shown in the following table.

Constant	Value	Description
WindowsFolder	0	Windows operating system folder
SystemFolder	1	System folder
TemporaryFolder	2	Temp folder

GetTempName

This method returns a randomly generated unique filename. This filename can be used with methods such `CreateTextFile()` or `CreateFolder()` to create a temporary file or folder with a unique name.

MoveFile *Source, Destination*

Moves one or more files from *Source* to *Destination*. *Source* can contain wildcards. If *Source* contains wildcards, more than one file can be moved at a time.

MoveFolder *Source, Destination*

Moves one or more folders from *Source* to *Destination*. *Source* can contain wildcards. If *Source* contains wildcards, more than one folder can be moved at a time.

OpenTextFile(*Filename* [,*iomode* [,*create* [,*format*]]])

Opens a file for reading or appending and returns a `TextStream` object. The file to be opened is specified by *Filename*.

iomode determines the type of operation to be performed on the file. *iomode* can have the two values shown in the following table.

Constant	Value	Description
ForReading	1	Opens a file for reading.
ForAppending	8	Opens a file for appending.

create specifies whether to create a file if it doesn't exist. If TRUE, a new file is created. If FALSE, no file is created. By default, *create* is FALSE.

format determines the character set of the file. *format* can have the values shown in the following table.

Quick ASP Object and Component Reference

APPENDIX A

823

A

ASP OBJECT
AND COMPONENT
REFERENCE

Constant	Value	Description
TristateUseDefault	-2	Use the system default.
TristateTrue	-1	Open the file as Unicode.
TristateFalse	0	Open the file as ASCII.

Properties
Drives
Returns the Drives collection for the local machine (see the earlier section "The Drives Collection").

The Folder Object
The properties and methods of the Folder object are used to return information and perform operations on individual folders:

```
<%
Set fs=Server.CreateObject("Scripting.FileSystemObject")
Set f=fs.GetFolder("c:\myfolder")
%>
```

Methods
Copy *Destination* [*,Overwrite*]
Copies the folder to the path specified by *Destination*. If Overwrite is TRUE, existing files or folders are overwritten. If *Overwrite* is FALSE (the default), nothing is overwritten.

CreateTextFile(*Filename* [*,Overwrite* [*,Unicode*]])
Creates a file and returns a TextStream object. *Filename* specifies the name of the new file. *Overwrite* indicates whether existing files should be overwritten. It can have the value TRUE or FALSE (by default, it's FALSE). If *Unicode* is TRUE, the file is created as Unicode. If FALSE, the file is created as ASCII (the default).

Delete *Force*
Deletes the folder. If *Force* is TRUE, the folder will be deleted even if its read-only attribute is set to TRUE. By default, *Force* is FALSE.

Move *Destination*
Moves the folder to the new path specified by *Destination*.

Properties
Attributes

Specifies the attributes of a folder. This property can have the values shown in the following table.

Constant	Value	Description
Normal	0	No attributes set.
ReadOnly	1	Read/write attribute.
Hidden	2	Read/write attribute.
System	4	Read/write attribute.
Volume	8	Read-only attribute.
Directory	16	Read-only attribute.
Archive	32	Read/write attribute.
Alias	64	Read-only attribute.
Compressed	128	Read-only attribute.

DateCreated

Returns the date on which the folder was created. This property is read-only.

DateLastAccessed

Returns the date on which the folder was last accessed. This property is read-only.

DateLastModified

Returns the date on which the folder was last modified. This property is read-only.

Drive

Returns the drive where the folder is located. This property is read-only.

IsRootFolder

Returns TRUE if the current folder is the root folder and FALSE otherwise.

Name

Specifies the name of a folder. This property can be both read and set.

ParentFolder

Returns the Folder object that represents the folder containing the current folder.

Path

Returns the path of the folder.

Quick ASP Object and Component Reference

APPENDIX A

825

A

ASP OBJECT
AND COMPONENT
REFERENCE

ShortName
Returns the short path of a folder (with pre-Windows 95 short filenames).

ShortPath
Returns the short path of a folder (with pre-Windows 95 short path).

Size
Returns the size of all files and folders contained in the current folder, in bytes.

SubFolders
Returns the `Folders` collection containing all folders contained in the current folder.

The Folders Collection

The `Folders` collection consists of a collection of folders contained in a particular folder:

```
<%
Set fs = Server.CreateObject("Scripting.FileSystemObject")
Set f = fs.GetFolder("c:\myfolder")
Set fc = f.SubFolders
%>
```

Methods
AddFolder *FolderName*
Adds a new folder to the `Folders` collection with the name specified by *FolderName*.

Properties
Count
Returns the number of folders in the `Folders` collection.

Item(*Key*)
Returns the folder in the `Folders` collection specified by *Key*.

The TextStream Object

The `TextStream` object has a number of methods and properties that are useful for returning information and performing operations on individual files:

```
<%
Set fs = Server.CreateObject("Scripting.FileSystemObject")
Set f = fs.CreateTextFile("c:\myfile.txt", True)
%>
```

Methods
Close
Closes a `TextStream` file that's open.

Read(*characters*)

Retrieves a certain number of characters from a TextStream file into a string.

ReadAll

Retrieves an entire TextStream file into a (potentially very long) string.

ReadLine

Reads a single line from a TextStream file into a string. Doesn't include the newline character.

Skip(*characters*)

Skips the specified number of characters in a TextStream file.

SkipLine

Skips a single line in a TextStream file.

Write(*String*)

Writes a string to a TextStream file without a newline character.

WriteBlankLine(*Lines*)

Writes the specified number of blank lines (newline characters) to the TextStream file.

WriteLine([*String*])

Writes a string to a TextStream file with a newline character. If *String* is omitted, only the newline character is written.

Properties

AtEndOfLine

Returns TRUE if a newline character is reached, FALSE otherwise.

AtEndOfStream

Returns TRUE if the end of a TextStream file has been reached, FALSE otherwise. Used only with a TextStream file opened for reading.

Column

Returns the current column position in a TextStream file.

Line

Returns the current line position in a TextStream file.

The ActiveX Data Objects (ADO)

The ADO is a collection of objects that enable you to store and retrieve data in a database. These objects can be used to perform SQL queries and execute stored procedures with Microsoft SQL Server (as well as many other data providers).

A number of the ADO methods and properties accept constants. Microsoft recommends that you refer to constants by name rather than by value because the values may change in a future version. To do this, you need to include a file in every Active Server Page that uses the ADO constants. You include files by using the #INCLUDE directive (see the later section "Server-Side Includes"). For VBScript, include the file named Adovbs.inc. For JScript, include the file named Adojavas.inc.

The Command Object

Using the Command object, you can execute stored procedures, SQL queries, and SQL statements with parameters. You can use the Command object to retrieve a Recordset object.

```
<% Set MyCMD=Server.CreateObject("ADODB.Command") %>
```

Collections
Parameters

The Parameters collection is a collection of Parameter objects (see the later section "The Parameter Object"). Parameter objects can be used when performing parameterized SQL queries or when passing and retrieving parameters from a SQL stored procedure.

Properties

The Properties collection is a collection of Property objects (see the later section "The Property Object"). Different data providers such as Microsoft SQL Server and Microsoft Access have different properties that are exposed in a Command object's Properties collection. These properties affect the ways in which a Command object can be used.

Methods
CreateParameter([*Name*], [*Type*], [*Direction*], [*Size*], [*Value*])

Creates a new parameter to use with the Command object. *Name* is the name of the new parameter. *Type* is the datatype of the parameter. You can use any of the datatype constants described in the following table.

Constant	Value	Description
adBigInt	20	8-byte signed integer
adBinary	128	Binary value
adBoolean	11	Boolean value
adBSTR	8	Null-terminated string (Unicode)
adChar	129	String value
adCurrency	6	Currency value
adDate	7	Date value
adDBDate	133	Date value (yyyymmdd)
adDBTime	134	Time value (hhmmss)
adDBTimeStamp	135	Date-time stamp (yyyymmddhhmmss plus a fraction in billionths)
adDecimal	14	Exact numeric value with a fixed precision and scale
adDouble	5	Double-precision floating-point value
adEmpty	0	No value was specified
adError	10	32-bit error code
adGUID	72	Globally Unique Identifier
adIDispatch	9	Pointer to an IDispatch interface on an OLE object
adInteger	3	4-byte signed integer
adIUnknown	13	Pointer to an IUnknown interface on an OLE object
adLongVarBinary	205	Long binary value
adLongVarChar	201	Long string value
adLongVarWChar	203	Long null-terminated string
adNumeric	131	Exact numeric value with a fixed precision and scale
adSingle	4	Single-precision floating-point value
adSmallInt	2	2-byte signed integer
adTinyInt	16	1-byte signed integer
adUnsignedBigInt	21	8-byte unsigned integer
adUnsignedInt	19	4-byte unsigned integer
adUnsignedSmallInt	18	2-byte unsigned integer
adUnsignedTinyInt	17	1-byte unsigned integer
adUserDefined	132	User-defined variable
adVarBinary	204	Binary value

Quick ASP Object and Component Reference

APPENDIX A

829

A

ASP OBJECT
AND COMPONENT
REFERENCE

Constant	Value	Description
adVarChar	200	String value
adVariant	12	OLE Automation Variant
adVarWChar	202	Null-terminated Unicode string
adWChar	130	Null-terminated Unicode string

`Direction` determines whether the parameter is an input or output parameter or the return value from a stored procedure. The following table describes the constants you can use.

Constant	Value	Description
adParamInput	1	Input parameter (default)
adParamOutput	2	Output parameter
adParamInputOutput	3	Input/output parameter
adParamReturnValue	4	Return value

`Size` is the maximum length of the parameter measured in characters or bytes. `Value` is the value of the parameter.

Execute [*RecordsAffected*], [*Parameters*], [*Options*] or Execute([*RecordsAffected*], [*Parameters*], [*Options*])

Executes the SQL query, SQL statement, or SQL stored procedure contained in the `CommandText` property. Use parentheses, the second form of the `Execute` method, when returning a Recordset.

After the command executes, the value of the *RecordsAffected* variable will contain the number of records that the command affected. *Parameters* is the array of input parameters that override parameters previously added to the `Command` object. You can make the command more efficient by warning the data provider (for example, SQL Server) about the type of command being executed, using *Options*. You can use the options described in the following table.

Constant	Description
adCmdText	Evaluate `CommandText` as a textual definition of a command, such as a SQL statement.
adCmdTable	Evaluate `CommandText` as a table name.
adCmdStoredProc	Evaluate `CommandText` as a stored procedure.
adCmdUnknown	Unknown command (default value).

Properties

ActiveConnection

A string or the name of a `Connection` object that specifies a connection to a data provider.

CommandText

Set this property to specify the SQL statement, SQL query, stored procedure, or table that will be used when the `Command` object's `Execute` method is called.

CommandTimeOut

Specifies the amount of time in seconds that the `Command` object will wait for a response from the data provider after issuing a command. The default value is 30 seconds. If this value is set to `0`, the `Command` object will wait forever.

CommandType

Makes the command more efficient by warning the data provider (for example, SQL Server) about the type of command being executed. The `adRunAsync` option executes the command asynchronously. You can use the options described in the following table.

Constant	Description
adCmdText	Evaluate `CommandText` as a textual definition of a command, such as a SQL statement.
adCmdTable	Evaluate `CommandText` as a table name.
adCmdStoredProc	Evaluate `CommandText` as a stored procedure.
adCmdUnknown	Unknown command (default value).

Name

Specifies a name for the command.

Prepared

Specifies that a prepared (compiled) version of the command should be created by the data provider before the command is first executed. This slows down the first execution of the command, but speeds up later executions. This property has the value TRUE or FALSE.

State

Returns the current state of the `Command` object. This property can have the values described in the following table.

Constant	Description
adStateClosed	The object is closed (default value).
adStateOpen	The object is open.

The Connection Object

Creates the actual connection with the data provider:

```
<% MyConn=Server.CreateObject("ADODB.Connection") %>
```

Collections

Errors

Collection of `Error` objects (see the later section "The `Error` Object"). This collection can be examined to determine whether an error with the `Connection` object has occurred.

Properties

The `Properties` collection is a collection of `Property` objects (see the later section "The `Property` Object"). Different data providers such as Microsoft SQL Server and Microsoft Access have different properties that are exposed in a `Connection` object's `Properties` collection. These properties affect the ways in which a `Connection` object can be used.

Methods

BeginTrans

Begins a database transaction. Updates are not committed until the `CommitTrans` method is called, and can be rolled back by the `RollBackTrans` method.

Close

Closes an open connection to a data source. If a `Recordset` object is open, closes the `Recordset` object as well.

CommitTrans

Commits any pending changes within a transaction. Delimits the end of a transaction.

Execute *CommandText*, *[RecordsAffected]*, *[Options]* or
Execute(*CommandText*, *[RecordsAffected]*, *[Options]*)

Executes the SQL query, SQL statement, or SQL stored procedure contained in the `CommandText` property. Use parentheses, the second form of the `Execute` method, when returning a Recordset.

After the command executes, the value of the *RecordsAffected* variable will contain the number of records that the command affected. You can make the command more efficient by warning the data provider (for example, SQL Server) about the type of command being executed, using *Options*. You can use the options described in the following table.

Constant	*Description*
adCmdText	Evaluate `CommandText` as a textual definition of a command, such as a SQL statement.
adCmdTable	Evaluate `CommandText` as a table name.

continues

Constant	Description
adCmdStoredProc	Evaluate CommandText as a stored procedure.
adCmdUnknown	Unknown command (default value).

Open [*ConnectionString*], [*UserID*], [*Password*]

Opens a connection to a data source. *ConnectionString* specifies a data source name (DSN) or a connection string that includes argument and value pairs separated by semicolons. For example, this works with SQL Server:

```
dsn=MyDatabase;uid=MyLoginName;pwd=MyPassword
```

You can use the argument and value pairs from the following table in the connection string.

Argument	Value
Provider	Name of the data provider.
Data Source	Name of the data source (for example, an ODBC data source for SQL Server).
User	Username to use when opening connection.
Password	Password to use when opening connection.
File Name	Name of provider-specific file that has preset connection information.

UserID is the username to use when opening the connection. *Password* is the password to use when opening the connection.

OpenSchema(*QueryType*,[*Criteria*])

Used to retrieve information about the general structure of a database (for example, the tables and columns it contains). The schema information is retrieved into a Recordset object. *QueryType* is the schema query to execute (see the following table). *Criteria* is an array of constraints on the schema query (see the following table).

QueryType	Criteria
adSchemaAsserts	CONSTRAINT_CATALOG
	CONSTRAINT_SCHEMA
	CONSTRAINT_NAME
adSchemaCatalogs	CATALOG_NAME
adSchemaCharacterSets	CHARACTER_SET_CATALOG
	CHARACTER_SET_SCHEMA
	CHARACTER_SET_NAME

QueryType	*Criteria*
adSchemaCheckConstraints	CONSTRAINT_CATALOG
	CONSTRAINT_SCHEMA
	CONSTRAINT_NAME
adSchemaCollations	COLLATION_CATALOG
	COLLATION_SCHEMA
	COLLATION_NAME
adSchemaColumnDomainUsage	DOMAIN_CATALOG
	DOMAIN_SCHEMA
	DOMAIN_NAME
	COLUMN_NAME
adSchemaColumnPrivileges	TABLE_CATALOG
	TABLE_SCHEMA
	TABLE_NAME
	COLUMN_NAME
	GRANTOR
	GRANTEE
adSchemaColumns	TABLE_CATALOG
	TABLE_SCHEMA
	TABLE_NAME
	COLUMN_NAME
adSchemaConstraintColumnUsage	TABLE_CATALOG
	TABLE_SCHEMA
	TABLE_NAME
	COLUMN_NAME
adSchemaConstraintTableUsage	TABLE_CATALOG
	TABLE_SCHEMA
	TABLE_NAME
adSchemaForeignKeys	PK_TABLE_CATALOG
	PK_TABLE_SCHEMA
	PK_TABLE_NAME
	FK_TABLE_CATALOG
	FK_TABLE_SCHEMA
	FK_TABLE_NAME

continues

QueryType	Criteria
adSchemaIndexes	TABLE_CATALOG
	TABLE_SCHEMA
	INDEX_NAME
	TYPE
	TABLE_NAME
adSchemaKeyColumnUsage	CONSTRAINT_CATALOG
	CONSTRAINT_SCHEMA
	CONSTRAINT_NAME
	TABLE_CATALOG
	TABLE_SCHEMA
	TABLE_NAME
	COLUMN_NAME
adSchemaPrimaryKeys	PK_TABLE_CATALOG
	PK_TABLE_SCHEMA
	PK_TABLE_NAME
adSchemaProcedureColumns	PROCEDURE_CATALOG
	PROCEDURE_SCHEMA
	PROCEDURE_NAME
	COLUMN_NAME
adSchemaProcedureParameters	PROCEDURE_CATALOG
	PROCEDURE_SCHEMA
	PROCEDURE_NAME
	PARAMETER_NAME
adSchemaProcedures	PROCEDURE_CATALOG
	PROCEDURE_SCHEMA
	PROCEDURE_NAME
	PARAMETER_TYPE
adSchemaProviderTypes	DATA_TYPE
	BEST_MATCH
adSchemaReferentialConstraints	CONSTRAINT_CATALOG
	CONSTRAINT_SCHEMA
	CONSTRAINT_NAME

QueryType	*Criteria*
adSchemaSchemata	CATALOG_NAME
	SCHEMA_NAME
	SCHEMA_OWNER
adSchemaSQLLanguages	none
adSchemaStatistics	TABLE_CATALOG
	TABLE_SCHEMA
	TABLE_NAME
adSchemaTableConstraints	CONSTRAINT_CATALOG
	CONSTRAINT_SCHEMA
	CONSTRAINT_NAME
	TABLE_CATALOG
	TABLE_SCHEMA
	TABLE_NAME
	CONSTRAINT_TYPE
adSchemaTablePrivileges	TABLE_CATALOG
	TABLE_SCHEMA
	TABLE_NAME
	GRANTOR
	GRANTEE
adSchemaTables	TABLE_CATALOG
	TABLE_SCHEMA
	TABLE_NAME
	TABLE_TYPE
adSchemaTranslations	TRANSLATION_CATALOG
	TRANSLATION_SCHEMA
	TRANSLATION_NAME
adSchemaUsagePrivileges	OBJECT_CATALOG
	OBJECT_SCHEMA
	OBJECT_NAME
	OBJECT_TYPE
	GRANTOR
	GRANTEE

continues

QueryType	Criteria
adSchemaViewColumnUsage	VIEW_CATALOG
	VIEW_SCHEMA
	VIEW_NAME
adSchemaViewTableUsage	VIEW_CATALOG
	VIEW_SCHEMA
	VIEW_NAME
adSchemaViews	TABLE_CATALOG
	TABLE_SCHEMA
	TABLE_NAME

RollbackTrans

Prevents all database changes from being committed in the current transaction. Usually preceded by the `BeginTrans` method call.

Properties

Attributes

Specifies an attribute of a transaction. The constants in the following table can be read or set.

Constant	Description
adXactCommitRetaining	Specifies that calling the `CommitTrans` method should automatically begin a new transaction.
adXactAbortRetaining	Specifies that calling the `RollbackTrans` method should automatically begin a new transaction.

CommandTimeOut

Specifies the amount of time in seconds that all objects that depend on a `Connection` (`Commands` and `Recordsets`) will wait for a response from the data provider. By default, this property has the value 30. If you set this property to 0, the ADO will wait forever for a response from the server.

ConnectionString

Specifies a data source name (DSN) or a connection string that includes argument and value pairs separated by semicolons. For example, this works with SQL Server:

```
dsn=MyDatabase;uid=MyLoginName;pwd=MyPassword
```

You can use the argument and value pairs from the following table in the connection string.

Argument	*Value*
Provider	Name of the data provider.
Data Source	Name of the data source (for example, an ODBC data source for SQL Server).
User	Username to use when opening connection.
Password	Password to use when opening connection.
File Name	Name of provider-specific file that has preset connection information.

ConnectionTimeOut

Specifies the amount of time in seconds that a Connection object will wait when attempting to open a connection to a data provider. By default, the value of this property is 15 seconds. If you set this property to 0, the Connection object will keep attempting to open a connection forever.

CursorLocation

Specifies which cursor library to use. This property can have the values shown in the following table.

Constant	*Description*
adUseClient	Use client-side cursors.
adUseServer	Use server or driver cursors (default value).

DefaultDatabase

Specifies the default database to use with a Connection. When there's a default database, you don't need to include the database name in all your SQL strings.

IsolationLevel

Specifies the isolation level of a connection. A change in this property doesn't take effect until the BeginTrans method is called. This property has the values shown in the following table.

Constant	*Description*
adXactUnspecified	Property returns this value when the data provider is using a different isolation level than the one specified.
adXactChaos	Indicates that you can't overwrite changes that are pending from more isolated transactions.

continues

Constant	Description
adXactBrowse	Indicates that you can view uncommitted changes in other transactions.
adXactReadUncommitted	Same as adXactBrowse.
adXactCursorStability	Indicates that you can't view uncommitted changes in other transactions (the default value).
adXactReadCommitted	Same as adXactCursorStability.
adXactRepeatableRead	Same as adXactCursorStability except allows requerying to retrieve new Recordsets.
adXactIsolated	Indicates that all transactions are performed in isolation of other transactions.
adXactSerializable	Same as adXactIsolated.

Mode

Specifies available permissions for changing data in a connection. This property can have the values shown in the following table.

Constant	Description
adModeUnknown	Undetermined (default value).
adModeRead	Read-only permissions.
adModeWrite	Write-only permissions.
adModeReadWrite	Read and write permissions.
adModeShareDenyRead	Prevents others from opening connections with read permissions.
adModeShareDenyWrite	Prevents others from opening connections with write permissions.
adModeShareExclusive	Prevents others from opening connections with either read or write permissions.
adModeShareDenyNone	Prevents others from opening connections with any permissions.

Provider

Specifies the name of the provider for a connection. By default, this property has the value MSDASQL (Microsoft ODBC Provider for OLEDB).

State

Used when a `Connection` object is executing asynchronously (with the `adRunAsync` option). Returns the current state of the `Connection` object. This property can have the values shown in the following table.

Constant	Description
adStateClosed	The object is closed.
adStateOpen	The object is open.

Version

Returns the current version of ADO as a string.

The Error Object

This object is used to contain errors and warnings. This object only has properties.

Properties
Description

A string describing the error.

HelpContext

Indicates the help topic in a help file associated with an error.

HelpFile

Indicates the help file associated with an error.

NativeError

Shows an error provided by a data provider (for example, an error from SQL Server).

Number

Indicates the error number.

Source

The object to blame for the error (for example, `ADODB.Command` or `ADODB.Recordset`).

SQLState

Five-character string error code generated by SQL Server when processing a SQL statement that results in an error.

The Field Object

The `Field` object represents a particular column in a Recordset.

Collections
Properties

The Properties collection is a collection of Property objects (see the later section "The Property Object"). Different data providers such as Microsoft SQL Server and Microsoft Access have different properties that are exposed in a Field object's Properties collection. These properties affect the ways in which a Field object can be used.

Methods
AppendChunk *Data*

Used to add a big chunk of binary or character data to a field. For example, this method can be used to add a really long string to a field that represents a Text column in a SQL Server table. To use this method, the adFldLong attribute of the field's Attributes property must be set to TRUE.

Data is the data that's added to the field. The first time this method is called on a field, the contents of the field are overwritten with the data. Subsequent calls to this method append the data to the field until the method is called on another Field object.

GetChunk(*Number*)

Returns data from a field when the field represents a SQL Text column or another column that holds large amounts of data. *Number* is the number of characters or bytes of data to retrieve. When the method is first called, the data is retrieved starting from the first byte or character. Subsequent calls retrieve the next number of bytes or characters. If the method is called on another field, data is retrieved from the beginning again.

Properties
ActualSize

The size of the data contained a field. If the size can't be determined, the constant adUnknown (the value -1) is returned.

Attributes

The attributes of a Field object. Can be any of the constants shown in the following table.

Constant	Description
adFLDMayDefer	The value of this field is not retrieved with the whole record, but only when explicitly accessed.
adFldUpdatable	You can write to the field.
adFldUnknownUpdatable	Whether you can write to the field is unknown.
adFldFixed	The field contains fixed-length data.
adFldIsNullable	You can write NULL values to the field.
adFldMayBeNull	You can read NULL values from the field.

Constant	Description
adFldLong	You can use the AppendChunk and GetChunk methods with the field.
adFldRowID	The field represents an Identity column.
adFldRowVersion	The field represents a Timestamp column.
adFldCacheDeferred	The field value is cached and read from the cache.

DefinedSize
Returns the defined size of the data in a field. This may vary from the actual size of the data as represented by the ActualSize property.

Name
The name of the Field object.

NumericScale
Indicates the number of digits after the decimal point that a numeric field can represent.

OriginalValue
The original value of a field before it was changed by the Recordset object's Update or UpdateBatch method.

Precision
Indicates the number of digits that a numeric field can represent.

Type
The datatype of a field. Can be any one of the datatype constants listed in the following table.

Constant	Value	Description
adBigInt	20	8-byte signed integer
adBinary	128	Binary value
adBoolean	11	Boolean value
adBSTR	8	Null-terminated string (Unicode)
adChar	129	String value
adCurrency	6	Currency value
adDate	7	Date value
adDBDate	133	Date value (yyyymmdd)
adDBTime	134	Time value (hhmmss)
adDBTimeStamp	135	Date-time stamp (yyyymmddhhmmss plus a fraction in billionths)

continues

Constant	*Value*	*Description*
adDecimal	14	Exact numeric value with a fixed precision and scale
adDouble	5	Double-precision floating-point value
adEmpty	0	No value was specified
adError	10	32-bit error code
adGUID	72	Globally Unique Identifier
adIDispatch	9	Pointer to an IDispatch interface on an OLE object
adInteger	3	4-byte signed integer
adIUnknown	13	Pointer to an IUnknown interface on an OLE object
adNumeric	131	Exact numeric value with a fixed precision and scale
adSingle	4	Single-precision floating-point value
adSmallInt	2	2-byte signed integer
adTinyInt	16	1-byte signed integer
adUnsignedBigInt	21	8-byte unsigned integer
adUnsignedInt	19	4-byte unsigned integer
adUnsignedSmallInt	18	2-byte unsigned integer
adUnsignedTinyInt	17	1-byte unsigned integer
adUserDefined	132	User-defined variable
adVariant	12	OLE Automation Variant
adWChar	130	Null-terminated Unicode string

UnderlyingValue

Returns the current value of the field from the database.

Value

The value of a field.

The Parameter Object

The Parameter object represents the parameters used with a parameterized SQL query or stored procedure, or the return value from a stored procedure:

```
<% Set MyParam=Server.CreateObject("ADODB.Parameter") %>
```

Collections
Properties

The `Properties` collection is a collection of `Property` objects (see the later section "The `Property` Object"). Different data providers such as Microsoft SQL Server and Microsoft Access have different properties that are exposed in a `Parameter` object's `Properties` collection. These properties affect the ways in which a `Parameter` object can be used.

Methods
AppendChunk *Data*

Used to add a big chunk of binary or character data to a parameter. To use this method, the `adParamLong` attribute of the `Parameter` object's `Attributes` property must be `TRUE`.

Data is the data added to the parameter. The first time this method is called on a parameter, the contents of the parameter are overwritten with the data. Subsequent calls to this method append the data to the parameter until the method is called on another `Parameter` object. Using the `AppendChunk` method with a `NULL` value results in an error.

Properties
Attributes

This property can accept any of the constants in the following table as values.

Constant	Description
adParamSigned	Parameter accepts signed values (default value).
adParamNullable	Parameter accepts null values.
adParamLong	Parameter accepts long data (you can use the AppendChunk method with it).

Direction

Determines whether the parameter is an input or output parameter or the return value from a stored procedure. You can use any of the constants shown in the following table.

Constant	Value	Description
adParamInput	1	Input parameter (default)
adParamOutput	2	Output parameter
adParamInputOutput	3	Input/output parameter
adParamReturnValue	4	Return value

Name

The name of the `Parameter` object.

NumericScale

Indicates the number of digits after the decimal point that a numeric parameter can represent.

Precision

Indicates the number of digits that a numeric parameter can represent.

Size

Indicates the maximum size of the data that can be stored in a parameter.

Type

The datatype of the parameter. You can use any of the datatype constants shown in the following table.

Constant	Value	Description
adBigInt	20	8-byte signed integer
adBinary	128	Binary value
adBoolean	11	Boolean value
adBSTR	8	Null-terminated string (Unicode)
adChar	129	String value
adCurrency	6	Currency value
adDate	7	Date value
adDBDate	133	Date value (yyyymmdd)
adDBTime	134	Time value (hhmmss)
adDBTimeStamp	135	Date-time stamp (yyyymmddhhmmss plus a fraction in billionths)
adDecimal	14	Exact numeric value with a fixed precision and scale
adDouble	5	Double-precision floating-point value
adEmpty	0	No value was specified
adError	10	32-bit error code
adGUID	72	Globally Unique Identifier
adIDispatch	9	Pointer to an IDispatch interface on an OLE object
adInteger	3	4-byte signed integer
adIUnknown	13	Pointer to an IUnknown interface on an OLE object
adLongVarBinary	205	Long binary value
adLongVarChar	201	Long string value
adLongVarWChar	203	Long null-terminated string
adNumeric	131	Exact numeric value with a fixed precision and scale

Constant	Value	Description
adSingle	4	Single-precision floating-point value
adSmallInt	2	2-byte signed integer
adTinyInt	16	1-byte signed integer
adUnsignedBigInt	21	8-byte unsigned integer
adUnsignedInt	19	4-byte unsigned integer
adUnsignedSmallInt	18	2-byte unsigned integer
adUnsignedTinyInt	17	1-byte unsigned integer
adUserDefined	132	User-defined variable
adVarBinary	204	Binary value
adVarChar	200	String value
adVariant	12	OLE Automation Variant
adVarWChar	202	Null-terminated Unicode string
adWChar	130	Null-terminated Unicode string

Value

The value of a parameter.

The Property Object

Different data providers, such as Microsoft SQL Server and Microsoft Access, have different properties that are exposed in Property objects. Property objects are used with other ADO objects to represent information specific to a particular data provider. The Property object has properties of its own, described in the following section.

Properties
Attributes

The Attributes property can have any of the constants in the following table as a value.

Constant	Description
adPropNotSupported	The data provider doesn't support this property.
adPropRequired	The data source requires this property before being initialized.
adPropOptional	The data source doesn't require this property before being initialized.
adPropRead	The property can be read by the user.
adPropWrite	The property can be set by the user.

Name

The name of the Property object.

Type

The datatype of the property. Can be any one of the datatype constants shown in the following table.

Constant	Value	Description
adBigInt	20	8-byte signed integer
adBinary	128	Binary value
adBoolean	11	Boolean value
adBSTR	8	Null-terminated string (Unicode)
adChar	129	String value
adCurrency	6	Currency value
adDate	7	Date value
adDBDate	133	Date value (yyyymmdd)
adDBTime	134	Time value (hhmmss)
adDBTimeStamp	135	Date-time stamp (yyyymmddhhmmss plus a fraction in billionths)
adDecimal	14	Exact numeric value with a fixed precision and scale
adDouble	5	Double-precision floating-point value
adEmpty	0	No value was specified
adError	10	32-bit error code
adGUID	72	Globally Unique Identifier
adIDispatch	9	Pointer to an IDispatch interface on an OLE object
adInteger	3	4-byte signed integer
adIUnknown	13	Pointer to an IUnknown interface on an OLE object
adNumeric	131	Exact numeric value with a fixed precision and scale
adSingle	4	Single-precision floating-point value
adSmallInt	2	2-byte signed integer
adTinyInt	16	1-byte signed integer
adUnsignedBigInt	21	8-byte unsigned integer

Constant	Value	Description
adUnsignedInt	19	4-byte unsigned integer
adUnsignedSmallInt	18	2-byte unsigned integer
adUnsignedTinyInt	17	1-byte unsigned integer
adUserDefined	132	User-defined variable
adVariant	12	OLE Automation Variant
adWChar	130	Null-terminated Unicode string

Value

The value of the Property object.

The Recordset Object

Used to represent a database table. The Recordset object is the primary interface between your Web application and SQL Server:

```
<% Set MyRS=Server.CreateObject("ADODB.Recordset") %>
```

Collections

Fields

The Fields collection is a collection of Field objects (refer to the earlier section "The Field Object"). The Fields collection represents all the columns in a table.

Properties

The Properties collection is a collection of Property objects (refer to the earlier section "The Property Object"). Different data providers such as Microsoft SQL Server and Microsoft Access have different properties that are exposed in a Recordset object's Properties collection. These properties affect the ways in which a Recordset object can be used.

Methods

AddNew [*Fields*], [*Values*]

Adds a new record to a Recordset. *Fields* is the name of one of the fields in a Recordset. You can also specify multiple fields by using an array of field names. In either case, you can indicate a field by ordinal position rather than by name. *Values* is the value of the field for the new record. If you have specified multiple fields, the value is an array of values.

CancelBatch [*AffectRecords*]

Used to cancel any pending updates when the Recordset is in batch-update mode. *AffectRecords* specifies which records the CancelBatch method will cancel. You can use the constants from the following table.

Constant	Description
adAffectCurrent	Cancels batch update only for the current record.
adAffectGroup	Cancels batch update only for records that satisfy the Filter property setting.
adAffectAll	Cancels batch update for all records (default value).

CancelUpdate

Cancels any changes to the current record or cancels the adding of a new record. If a record hasn't been updated or no new record has been added, an error is generated.

Clone

Returns an exact duplicate of the Recordset. You can clone a Recordset only when it supports bookmarks.

Close

Closes the Recordset and releases all the data it contains.

Delete [*AffectRecords*]

Deletes the current record. *AffectRecords* determines which records to delete. You can use the two constants shown in the following table.

Constant	Description
adAffectCurrent	Delete only the current record (default value).
adaffectGroup	Delete all records that satisfy the Filter property setting.

GetRows([*Rows*], [*Start*], [*Fields*])

Retrieves records into a two-dimensional array. The array is created automatically. The array's first index indicates the field; the second index identifies the record. *Rows* indicates how many rows to retrieve from the Recordset. By default, all rows are retrieved. *Start* specifies where to start retrieving rows from the Recordset, using a bookmark. To use this argument, the Recordset must support bookmarks. *Fields* is a single field name or array of field names that restricts which fields are retrieved into the array.

Move *NumRecords*, [*Start*]

Moves forward or backward through the records of a Recordset. If *NumRecords* is positive, the current record becomes the record that's *NumRecords* forward in the Recordset. If *NumRecords* is negative, the current record becomes the record that's *NumRecords* backward in the Recordset.

Start is a bookmark. Causes the move to be made relative to a bookmark rather than the current record. To use this argument, the Recordset must support bookmarks.

MoveFirst

Makes the current record the first record in a Recordset.

MoveLast

Makes the current record the last record in a Recordset. The Recordset must support bookmarks to use this method.

MoveNext

Makes the current record the next record in a Recordset.

MovePrevious

Makes the current record the previous record in a Recordset. The Recordset must support bookmarks or backward cursor movement to use this method.

NextRecordSet([*RecordsAffected*])

When an Open or Execute method returns multiple Recordsets, the NextRecordSet method clears the current Recordset and opens the next one. *RecordsAffected* returns the number of records affected by the NextRecordSet method.

Open [*Source*], [*ActiveConnection*], [*CursorType*], [*LockType*], [*Options*]

Opens a cursor on a Recordset. The cursor represents records from either a table or the results of a SQL query. *Source* is the name of a Command object, a SQL statement, a table name, or a stored procedure. *ActiveConnection* is the name of a Connection object or a connection string. *CursorType* can be any one of the constants shown in the following table.

Constant	Description
adOpenForwardOnly	Allows only forward movement through the records in a Recordset (default value).
adOpenKeyset	Reflects changes and deletions to records by other users. However, doesn't reflect new records added by other users.
adOpenDynamic	Reflects changes and deletions to records by other users, including new records added.
adOpenStatic	Doesn't reflect changes, deletions, or additions by other users.

LockType specifies the type of locking the data provider should use when opening the Recordset. You can use any of the constants from the following table.

Constant	Description
adLockReadOnly	The data can't be changed (default value).
adLockPessimistic	Typically, the data provider locks a record once you begin to edit the record.
adLockOptimistic	The data provider locks a record only when the Update method is called.
adLockBatchOptimistic	Required for batch updating.

Options makes the command represented by the *Source* argument more efficient by warning the data provider (for example, SQL Server) about the type of command being executed. Use this argument when *Source* isn't the name of a Command object. You can use the options from the following table.

Constant	Description
adCmdText	Evaluate *Source* as a textual definition of a command, such as a SQL statement.
adCmdTable	Evaluate *Source* as a table name.
adCmdStoredProc	Evaluate *Source* as a stored procedure.
adCmdUnknown	Unknown command (default value).

Requery
Refreshes all the records in a Recordset by re-executing the command that created the Recordset.

Resync [*AffectRecords*]
Resynchronizes the records in a Recordset with the records in the database. Doesn't reflect any new records added to the database. *AffectRecords* specifies which records the method will affect. It can be any of the three constants shown in the following table.

Constant	Description
adAffectCurrent	Affects only the current record.
adAffectGroup	Affects all records that match the Filter property setting.
adAffectAll	Affects all records in the Recordset (default value).

Supports(*CursorOption*)

Returns a value (TRUE or FALSE) indicating whether a Recordset supports a given cursor option. You can use the constants from the following table.

Constant	Description
adAddNew	The Recordset supports the AddNew method.
adApproxPosition	The Recordset supports the AbsolutePosition and AbsolutePage properties.
adBookmark	The Recordset supports the Bookmark property.
adDelete	The Recordset supports the Delete method.
adHoldRecords	The Recordset supports retrieving more records or changing the next retrieve position without committing all pending change and releasing all currently held records.
adMovePrevious	The Recordset supports using MovePrevious or the Move method to move backward without using bookmarks.
adResync	The Recordset supports the Resync method.
adUpdate	The Recordset supports the Update method.
adUpdateBatch	The Recordset supports batch updating.

Update [*Fields*], [*Values*]

Saves any new records added or any changes made with the current record. *Fields* is the name of one of the fields in a Recordset. You can also specify multiple fields by using an array of field names. In either case, you can indicate a field by ordinal position rather than by name. *Values* is a new value for the field. If you have specified multiple fields, the value is an array of values.

UpdateBatch [*AffectRecords*]

Saves any new records added or any changes made to the records in a Recordset when using batch-update mode. *AffectRecords* specifies which records the method affects. Can be any of the three constants shown in the following table.

Constant	Description
adAffectCurrent	Affects only the current record.
adAffectGroup	Affects all records that match the Filter property setting.
adAffectAll	Affects all records in the Recordset (default value).

Properties
AbsolutePage

Returns the number of the current page or moves to a new page when a Recordset has been divided into pages. You can use the constants in the following table with this property.

Constant	Description
adPosUnknown	Indicates that the current Recordset is empty, the page number is unknown, or the Recordset doesn't support the AbsolutePage property.
adPosBOF	The BOF property is TRUE.
adPosEOF	The EOF property is TRUE.

AbsolutePosition

The absolute position of the current record in a Recordset. Returns a number representing the absolute position of the current record, or moves to a record with the specified absolute position. You can use the constants from the following table with this property.

Constant	Description
adPosUnknown	Indicates that the current Recordset is empty, the page number is unknown, or the Recordset doesn't support the AbsolutePage property.
adPosBOF	The BOF property is TRUE.
adPosEOF	The EOF property is TRUE.

ActiveConnection

Specifies a connection string or name of a Connection object. When a Recordset has been opened or the Source property of the Recordset is a Command object, this property may only be read. Otherwise, a new connection can be created by setting this property.

BOF

Returns TRUE if the current record position is before the first record in a Recordset. Returns FALSE otherwise.

Bookmark

When this property is read, it returns a bookmark that identifies the current record. When this property is set to a bookmark, the current record becomes the record identified by the bookmark.

CacheSize

Specifies the number of records from a Recordset held in a local memory cache. For a forward-only cursor, the default value is 1. For all other cursors, the default value is 10.

CursorLocation

Specifies which cursor library to use. This property can have the values shown in the following table.

Constant	Description
adUseClient	Use client-side cursors.
adUseServer	Use server or driver cursors (default value).

CursorType

Can be any one of the constants shown in the following table.

Constant	Description
adOpenForwardOnly	Allows only forward movement through the records in a Recordset (default value).
adOpenKeyset	Reflects changes and deletions to records by other users. However, doesn't reflect new records added by other users.
adOpenDynamic	Reflects changes and deletions to records by other users, including new records added.
adOpenStatic	Doesn't reflect changes, deletions, or additions by other users.

EditMode

Returns a constant indicating the editing status of the current record (see the following table).

Constant	Description
adEditNone	No editing is in progress.
adEditInProgress	Current record has been edited, but not yet saved.
adEditAdd	The AddNew method has been called.

EOF

Returns TRUE if the current record position is after the last record in a Recordset. Returns FALSE otherwise.

Filter

Specifies a filter for the data in a Recordset. You can create a filter by supplying a criteria string, an array of bookmarks, or one of the constants shown in the following table.

Constant	Description
adFilterNone	Removes the current filter.
adFilterPendingRecords	Used only while in batch-update mode to view records that have been changed but not sent to the server.
adFilterAffectedRecords	Filters to records affected by the last Delete, Resync, UpdateBatch, or CancelBatch method call.
adFilterFetchedRecords	Filters to the last records returned from the database (records in the current cache).

LockType

Specifies the type of locking that the data provider should use when opening the Recordset. You can use any of the constants shown in the following table.

Constant	Description
adLockReadOnly	The data can't be changed (default value).
adLockPessimistic	Typically, the data provider locks a record once you begin to edit the record.
adLockOptimistic	The data provider locks a record only when the Update method is called.
adLockBatchOptimistic	Required for batch updating.

MarshalOptions

Specifies the records to be marshaled back to the server. The two constants shown in the following table can be used with this property.

Constant	Description
adMarshalAll	All rows are returned to the server (default value).
adMarshalModifiedOnly	Only modified rows are returned to the server.

MaxRecords
Specifies the number of records to return when the Recordset is opened. The default value is 0, which indicates that all records should be returned.

PageCount
Returns the number of pages of records in a Recordset when the Recordset has been divided into pages.

PageSize
Specifies the number of records that constitute an individual page. Used to divide the records in a Recordset into logical pages.

RecordCount
Returns the number of records in a Recordset. The value -1 is returned when the number of records can't be determined.

Source
The name of a Command object, a SQL statement, a table name, or a stored procedure. Used to specify the data source for a Recordset.

State
Returns the current state of the RecordSet object. This property can have the values shown in the following table.

Constant	Description
adStateClosed	The object is closed.
adStateOpen	The object is open.

Status
Returns the status of the current record when using batch updating. One or more of the constants shown in the following table are returned.

Constant	*Description*
adRecOK	The record was successfully updated.
adRecNew	The record is new.
adRecModified	The record was modified.
adRecDeleted	The record was deleted.
adRecUnmodified	The record wasn't modified.
adRecInvalid	The record wasn't saved because of an invalid bookmark.
adRecMultipleChanges	The record wasn't saved because doing so would affect more than one record.
adRecPendingChanges	The record wasn't saved because it refers to a pending insert.
adRecCanceled	The record wasn't saved because operation was canceled.
adRecCantRelease	The record wasn't saved because of existing record locks.
adRecConcurrencyViolation	The record wasn't saved because optimistic concurrency was in use.
adRecIntegrityViolation	The record wasn't saved because the user violated integrity constraints.
adRecMaxChangesExceeded	The record wasn't saved because there were too many pending changes.
adRecObjectOpen	The record wasn't saved because of a conflict with an open storage object.
adRecOutOfMemory	The record wasn't saved because the computer is out of memory.
adRecPermissionDenied	The record wasn't saved because the user has insufficient permissions.
adRecSchemaViolation	The record wasn't saved because it would violate the structure of the underlying database.
adRecDBDeleted	The record has already been deleted from the data source.

Active Server Pages Processing Directives

Active Server Pages processing directives (@ directives) specify how a particular Active Server Page should be processed. The directive should appear as the first line in the Active Server Page file.

@CODEPAGE

`<%@CODEPAGE=Code Page %>`

Used to specify a code page. This directive is useful when you need to specify a different human language with a different character set to use within an Active Server Page (for example, Japanese or Arabic).

@ENABLESESSIONSTATE

`<%@ENABLESESSIONSTATE=Boolean Value %>`

@ENABLESESSIONSTATE can be set to either TRUE or FALSE. If sessions are used anywhere within your Web application, this places some overhead on every Active Server Page. You can turn off session tracking for a particular page by setting @ENABLESESSIONSTATE to FALSE.

@LANGUAGE

`<%@LANGUAGE=Script Engine %>`

Specifies the script engine that should be used to interpret the scripts within a particular Active Server Page. By default, the script engine is VBScript.

@LCID

`<%@LCID=Locale Identifier %>`

Used to specify a locale identifier (LCID). An LCID is used to identify one of the system-defined locales.

@TRANSACTION

`<%@TRANSACTION=Value %>`

Used to specify that the Active Server Page should be treated as a transaction by Microsoft Transaction Server. Value can be any of the values shown in the following table.

Value	Description
Required	The page is processed as a transaction.
Requires_New	The page is processed as a transaction.
Supported	The page is not processed as a transaction.
Not_Supported	The page is not processed as a transaction.

Server-Side Includes

You can use any of the following server-side includes with Internet Information Server. However, only the #INCLUDE directive can be used with Active Server Pages. To use any of the other directives, the name of your file must end with the extension .stm, .shtm, or .shtml.

Except for the #INCLUDE directive itself, the IIS server-side includes are no longer particularly useful. The same functions can be performed with greater flexibility by using Active Server Pages. The server-side includes are presented here primarily for the sake of completeness.

#CONFIG

```
<!-- #CONFIG OUTPUT="String" -->
```

Specifies how to format error messages, dates, and file sizes. OUTPUT can be any one of the following parameters:

■ ERRMSG

Specifies the message to display when an error occurs during the processing of a server-side include. The string is the error message to display.

■ TIMEFMT

Specifies how dates and times should be formatted. You can use the formatting tokens from the following table in the string.

Token	Description
%a	Abbreviated day-of-week name
%A	Full day-of-week name
%b	Abbreviated month name
%B	Full month name
%c	Locale-specific date and time formatting
%d	Decimal representation of the day of the month
%H	24-hour format
%I	12-hour format

Token	Description
%j	Decimal representation of the year
%m	Decimal representation of the month
%M	Decimal representation of the minute
%p	AM or PM for current locale
%S	Decimal representation of seconds
%U	Decimal representation of the week of the year
%w	Decimal representation of the day of the week
%W	Decimal representation of the week of the year, with Monday as the first day of the week
%x	Date representation for the current locale
%X	Time representation for the current locale
%y	Decimal representation of the year (without century)
%Y	Decimal representation of the year (with century)
%z or %Z	Time zone name or abbreviation
%%	Percent sign

■ SIZEFMT

If the string is `"ABBREV"`, file sizes are displayed in kilobytes. If the string is `"BYTE"`, file sizes are displayed in bytes.

#ECHO

```
<!-- #ECHO var="Variable Name" -->
```

Displays the value of an environment variable (HTTP header). For `Variable Name`, you can substitute any of the variables shown in the following table.

Variable	Description
ALL_HTTP	Displays all headers that aren't displayed by any of the other environment variables that follow.
AUTH_TYPE	Authentication type used to validate users.
AUTH_PASSWORD	Authentication password entered by users in the Password dialog box for Basic authentication.
AUTH_USER	Authentication name entered by users in the Password dialog box for Basic authentication.

continues

Variable	Description
CONTENT_LENGTH	Content length according to the client.
CONTENT_TYPE	Content type of posted form contents or HTTP PUT.
DOCUMENT_NAME	The name of the current document.
DOCUMENT_URI	The virtual path to the current document.
DATE_GMT	The current date using Greenwich Mean Time.
DATE_LOCAL	The current date using the local time zone.
GATEWAY_INTERFACE	The version of the CGI specification used by the Web server.
HTTP_ACCEPT	Comma-separated list of MIME types.
LAST_MODIFIED	The date the current document was last modified.
PATH_INFO	The path after the script name but before the query string, according to the client.
QUERY_STRING	The query string (URL-encoded).
QUERY_STRING_UNESCAPED	The query string (not URL-encoded).
REMOTE_ADDR	The IP address of the client.
REMOTE_HOST	The hostname of the client.
REMOTE_USER	The username supplied by the client.
REQUEST_METHOD	The HTTP request method.
SCRIPT_NAME	The name of the current script program.
SERVER_NAME	The hostname or IP address of the server.
SERVER_PORT	The port where the request was received.
SERVER_PORT_SECURE	Returns 1 if the port is secure and 0 otherwise.
SERVER_PROTOCOL	The protocol of the request.
SERVER_SOFTWARE	The name and version of the current Web server software.
URL	Returns the base URL.

#EXEC

```
<!-- #EXEC CommandType="Command Description" -->
```

Executes an application, script, or shell command. For *CommandType*, you can use the two command types shown in the following table.

Command Type	Description
CGI	Executes an ASP script or a CGI or ISAPI program. *Command Description* is the virtual path to the application.

Command Type	Description
CMD	Executes a DOS shell command. `Command Description` is the path of the command. By default, this command type is disabled. To use it, you need to change the `SSIEnableCMDDirective` Registry entry (see Chapter 2, "Installing and Using Internet Information Server").

#FLASTMOD

`<!-- #FLASTMOD PathType="FileName" -->`

Returns the time at which the specified file was last modified. For `PathType`, you can specify either one of the path types shown in the following table.

Path Type	Description
FILE	The path is relative to the directory of the current document.
VIRTUAL	The path is a full path relative to a virtual directory.

#FSIZE

`<!-- #FSIZE PathType="FileName" -->`

Returns the size of a file. For `PathType`, you can specify either one of the path types shown in the following table.

Path Type	Description
FILE	The path is relative to the directory of the current document.
VIRTUAL	The path is a full path relative to a virtual directory.

#INCLUDE

`<!-- #INCLUDE PathType="FileName" -->`

Includes another file in the current document. For `PathType`, you can specify either one of the path types shown in the following table.

Path Type	Description
FILE	The path is relative to the directory of the current document.
VIRTUAL	The path is a full path relative to a virtual directory.

Quick JScript Reference

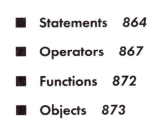

IN THIS APPENDIX

This appendix contains a quick reference of all the JScript statements, operators, functions, objects, and constants. The information for this appendix was extracted from the Microsoft JScript online documentation. For the latest information, check the documentation.

Statements

break

```
break [label];
```

Breaks out of the current loop. The optional *label* argument indicates the label of the statement you're terminating.

@cc_on

```
@cc_on
```

Turns on conditional compilation support.

Comment

```
//comment
```

Allows single-line comments to be ignored by the parser.

```
/*
comment
*/
```

Allows multiple-line comments to be ignored by the parser.

continue

```
continue[label];
```

Used inside `while`, `for`, or `for...in` loop, stops the loop's current iteration and starts from the loop's beginning. The optional *label* points to the statement to which `continue` applies.

do...while

```
do
 statement
while (expression);
```

Continues executing *statement* until *expression* is FALSE. Always executes *statement* at least once.

for

```
for (initialization;test;increment)
statement
```

After the *initialization* expression is executed, executes *statement* for as long as *test* is TRUE. The increment expression executes after every loop.

for...in

```
for (variable in [object¦array])
statement
```

Loop in which *variable* is assigned each element of the object or array in turn, and *statement* is executed for each.

function

```
functionfunctionname([argument1[,argument2[,...argumentn]]])
{
statements
}
```

Declares a new function with the name *functionname*.

@if

```
@if (condition1)
 text1
[@elif (condition2)
 text2]
[else
 text3]
@end
```

Conditionally executes, depending on the value of *condition*.

if...else

```
if (condition)
statement1
[else
statement2]
```

Executes statements conditionally. If *condition* evaluates to TRUE, *statement1* is executed. Otherwise, *statement2* is executed.

Label

```
label:
 statement
```

Provides a unique label to be used with the break and continue statements.

return

```
return [expression];
```

Exits the current function and, optionally, returns a value.

@set

```
@set @varname [=term]
```

Creates a numeric or Boolean variable that can be used in conditional compilation statements.

switch

```
switch (expression) {
 case label:
  statementlist
 case label:
  statementlist
 ...
 default:
  statementlist
}
```

Conditionally executes different statements when *expression* matches *label*. When no labels match, the statements following default are executed.

this

```
this.property
```

Usually used in object constructors; refers to the current object. When used without context in client versions of JScript, refers to the window object.

var

```
var variable[=value][,variable2[=value2],...]
```

Declares *variable* and can assign initial value.

while

```
while (expression)
statement
```

Executes *statement* until *expression* is FALSE.

with

```
with (object)
statement
```

Specifies a default object for *statement*.

Operators

new Operator

```
new constructor[(arguments)]
```

Creates and initializes a new object by calling the object's `constructor`. The `arguments` can be used to initialize the new object.

Computational Operators

- Operator

```
result = number1 - number2
```

Subtraction.

```
-number
```

Sign of `number`.

++ Operator

```
result = ++variable
```

Increments `variable` by one before assignment to `result`.

```
result = variable++
```

Increments `variable` by one after assignment to `result`.

- - Operator

```
result = --variable
```

Decrements `variable` by one before assignment to `result`.

```
result = variable--
```

Decrements `variable` by one after assignment to `result`.

* Operator

```
result = number1*number2
```

Multiplies two numbers.

/ Operator

```
result = number1 / number2
```

Divides two numbers.

% Operator

```
result = number1 % number2
```

Divides two numbers and returns only the remainder.

+ Operator

```
result = expression1 + expression2
```

Sum or string concatenation.

Logical Operators

! Operator

```
result = !expression
```

Logical negation.

Comparison Operators (=, <, >, <=, >=, ==, !=)

```
result = expression1 < expression2
```

Less than.

```
result = expression1 > expression2
```

Greater than.

```
result = expression1 <= expression2
```

Less than or equal to.

```
result = expression1 >= expression2
```

Greater than or equal to.

```
result = expression1 == expression2
```

Equality.

```
result = expression1 != expression2
```

Inequality.

&& Operator

```
result = expression1 && expression2
```

Logical conjunction (`result` is TRUE only if both expressions are TRUE; `result` is FALSE if either expression is FALSE).

¦¦ Operator

```
result = expression1 ¦¦ expression2
```

Logical disjunction (`result` is TRUE if either expression is TRUE or both expressions are TRUE).

?: Operator

```
test ? statement1 : statement2
```

Shortcut for if...else statement.

, Operator

```
expression1 , expression2
```

Executes expressions in left-to-right order and allows sequential expressions to be treated as a single expression.

Bitwise Operators

~ Operator

```
result = ~expression
```

Performs bitwise negation on `expression`'s binary representation (replaces any digit 1 with 0 and 0 with 1).

<< Operator

```
result = expression1 << expression2
```

Shifts the bits of `expression1` left by the number of bits designated by `expression2`.

>> Operator

```
result = expression1 >> expression2
```

Shifts the bits of `expression1` right by the number of bits designated by `expression2` while maintaining the sign.

>>> Operator

```
result = expression1 >>> expression2
```

Shifts the bits of `expression1` right by the number of bits designated by `expression2` without maintaining the sign.

& Operator

```
result = expression1 & expression2
```

Performs bitwise AND on the expressions' binary representations. (Where both expressions have digit 1, *result* will have digit 1. Everywhere else, *result* will have digit 0.)

^ Operator

```
result = expression1 ^ expression2
```

Performs bitwise exclusive OR on the expressions' binary representations. (Where one and only one expression has digit 1, *result* will have digit 1. Everywhere else, *result* will have digit 0.)

¦ Operator

```
result = expression1 ¦ expression2
```

Performs bitwise OR on the expressions' binary representations. (Where either expression has digit 1, *result* will have digit 1. Everywhere else, *result* will have digit 0.)

Assignment Operator

= Operator

```
result = expression
```

Assigns a value to a variable.

Compound Assignment Operators

+= Operator

```
result += expression
```

Increments (shortcut for *result = result + expression*).

-= Operator

```
result -= expression
```

Subtraction (shortcut for *result = result - expression*).

*= Operator

```
result *= expression
```

Multiplication (shortcut for *result = result * expression*).

/= Operator

`result /= expression`

Division (shortcut for `result = result / expression`).

%= Operator

`result %= expression`

Division returning only the remainder (shortcut for `result = result % expression`).

<<= Operator

`result <<= expression`

Shifts the bits of `result` left (shortcut for `result = result << expression`).

>>= Operator

`result >>= expression`

Shifts the bits of `result` right while maintaining the sign (shortcut for `result = result >> expression`).

>>>= Operator

`result >>>= expression`

Shifts the bits of `result` right without maintaining the sign (shortcut for `result = result >>> expression`).

&= Operator

`result &= expression`

Bitwise AND (shortcut for `result = result & expression`).

¦= Operator

`result ¦= expression`

Bitwise OR (shortcut for `result = result ¦ expression`).

^= Operator

`result ^= expression`

Bitwise exclusive OR (shortcut for `result = result ^ expression`).

Functions

ScriptEngine

```
ScriptEngine();
```

Returns the name of the current scripting language.

ScriptEngineBuildVersion

```
ScriptEngineBuildVersion();
```

Returns the build version for the current script engine.

ScriptEngineMajorVersion

```
ScriptEngineMajorVerion();
```

Returns the major version of the current script engine.

ScriptEngineMinorVersion

```
ScriptEngineMinorVersion();
```

Returns the minor version of the current script engine.

Objects
The Array Object

```
new Array()
new Array(size)
new Array(element0, element1,...,elementn)
```

Used to represent an array of any datatype.

Methods
concat

```
array1.concat(array2)
```

Concatenates two arrays into one.

join

```
arrayobj.join(separator)
```

Joins all of the elements together in an array. *separator* is a string used to separate each element in the resulting string.

reverse

```
arrayobj.reverse()
```

Reverses all the elements in an Array object.

slice

```
arrayobj.slice(start,[end])
```

Returns a subarray from an array. Retrieves elements from *start* to *end*.

sort

```
arrayobj.sort(sortfunction)
```

Sorts the elements in an Array object according to the function *sortfunction*.

toString

```
arrayobj.toString()
```

Returns a string representation of the Array object.

valueOf

```
arrayobj.valueOf()
```

Returns the elements of the array as one string. Elements within the string are separated by commas.

Properties
constructor

arrayobj.constructor

Specifies the Array object's creation function.

length

numVar=arrayObj.length;

Returns an integer value one greater than the highest index value of the array.

prototype

arrayobj.prototype

Refers to the prototype of the Array object.

The Boolean Object

var *variablename*=new Boolean(*boolvalue*)

Wrapper for the Boolean datatype. *boolvalue* is the initial value of the new Boolean object.

Methods
toString

boolobj.toString()

Returns the string "true" or "false".

valueOf

boolobj.valueOf()

Returns the Boolean value.

Properties
constructor

boolobj.constructor

Designates the creation function for the Boolean object.

prototype

boolobj.prototype

Refers to the prototype for a class of Boolean objects.

The Date Object

```
var newDateObj=new Date()

var newDateObj=new Date(dateVal)

var newDateObj=new Date(year, month, date [,hours[, minutes[, seconds [ms]]]])
```

The Date object is used to represent and manipulate dates and times.

Methods

getDate

objDate.getDate()

Returns the day of the month stored in the Date object.

getDay

objDate.getDay()

Returns the day of the week stored in the Date object.

getFullYear

objDate.getFullYear()

Returns the year stored in the Date object.

getHours

objDate.getHours()

Returns the hours stored in a Date object.

getMilliseconds

objDate.getMilliseconds()

Returns the milliseconds stored in a Date object.

getMinutes

objDate.getMinutes()

Returns the minutes stored in the Date object.

getMonth

objDate.getMonth()

Returns the month stored in the Date object.

getSeconds

objDate.getSeconds()

Returns the number of seconds stored in the Date object.

getTime

objDate.getTime()

Returns the time stored in the Date object.

getTimezoneOffset

objDate.getTimezoneOffset()

Returns the difference between the time according to the host computer and Universal Coordinated Time, in minutes.

getUTCDate

objDate.getUTCDate()

Returns the date of the month stored in the Date object according to Universal Coordinated Time.

getUTCDay

objDate.getUTCDay()

Returns the day of the week stored in the Date object according to Universal Coordinated Time.

getUTCFullYear

objDate.getUTCFullYear()

Returns the year stored in the Date object according to Universal Coordinated Time.

getUTCHours

objDate.getUTCHours()

Returns the hours stored in the Date object according to Universal Coordinated Time.

getUTCMilliSeconds

objDate.getUTCMilliseconds()

Returns the milliseconds stored in the Date object according to Universal Coordinated Time.

getUTCMinutes

objDate.getUTCMinutes

Returns the minutes stored in the Date object according to Universal Coordinated Time.

getUTCMonth

objDate.getUTCMonth()

Returns the month stored in the Date object according to Universal Coordinated Time.

getUTCSeconds

objDate.getUTCSeconds

Returns seconds stored in the Date object according to Universal Coordinated Time.

B

getVarDate

objDate.getVarDate()

Returns the VT_DATE stored in the Date object.

getYear

objDate.getYear()

Returns the year stored in the Date object.

parse

Date.parse(*dateVal*)

Returns the number of milliseconds between *dateVal* and midnight, January 1, 1970.

setDate

objDate.setDate(*numDate*)

Sets the day of the month for the Date object.

setFullYear

objDate.setFullYear(*numYear*[,*numMnth*[,*numDate*]])

Sets the year of the Date object.

setHours

objDate.setHours(*numHours*[,*numMin*[,*numSec*[,*numMilli*]]])

Sets the hour of the Date object.

setMilliseconds

objDate.setMilliseconds(*numMilli*)

Sets the milliseconds of the Date object.

setMinutes

objDate.setMinutes(*numMinutes*[,*numSeconds*[,*numMilli*]])

Sets the minutes of the Date object.

setMonth

objDate.setMonth(*numMonth*[,*dateval*])

Sets the month of the Date object.

setSeconds

objDate.setSecond(*numSeconds*[, *numMilli*])

Sets the seconds of the Date object.

setTime

objDate.setTime(*milliseconds*)

Sets date and time of the Date object in milliseconds since midnight, January 1, 1970 GMT.

setUTCDate

objData.setUTCDate(*numDate*)

Sets the day of the month of the Date object according to Universal Coordinated Time.

setUTCFullYear

objDate.setUTCFullYear(*numYear*[,*numMonth*[,*numDate*]])

Sets the year of the Date object according to Universal Coordinated Time.

setUTCHours

objDate.setUTCHours(*numHours*[,*numMin*[,*numSec*[,*numMilli*]]])

Sets the hour of the Date object according to Universal Coordinated Time.

setUTCMilliseconds

objDate.setUTCMilliseconds(*numMilli*)

Sets the milliseconds of the Date object according to Universal Coordinated Time.

setUTCMinutes

objDate.setUTCMinutes(*numMinutes*[,*numSeconds*[,*numMilli*]])

Sets the minutes of the Date object according to Universal Coordinated Time.

setUTCMonth

objDate.setUTCMonth(*numMonth*[,*dateVal*])

Sets the month of the Date object according to Universal Coordinated Time.

setUTCSeconds

objDate.setUTCSeconds(*numSeconds*[, *numMilli*])

Sets the seconds of the Date object according to Universal Coordinated Time.

setYear

objDate.setYear(*numYear*)

Sets the year of the Date object.

toGMTString

objDate.toGMTString()

Converts the date to a string using Greenwich Mean Time.

toLocaleString

objDate.toLocaleString()

Converts the date to a string using the current locale.

toString

objDate.toString()

Returns a string representation of the Date object.

toUTCString

objDate.toUTCString()

Converts the date to a string using Universal Coordinated Time.

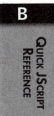

UTC

Date.UTC(*year*, *month*, *day*[,*hours*[,*minutes*[,*seconds*[,*ms*]]]])

Returns the time since midnight, January 1, 1970, in milliseconds.

valueOf

objDate.valueOf()

Returns the time since midnight, January 1, 1970, in milliseconds using Universal Coordinated Time.

Properties
constructor

objDate.constructor

Designates the creation function for a Date object.

prototype

objDate.prototype

Refers to the prototype for a class of Date objects.

The Dictionary Object

Set mydict=Server.CreateObject("Scripting.Dictionary")

Creates a dictionary of key and item pairs.

Methods
Add

object.Add(*key*, *item*)

Adds a key and item to a Dictionary object.

Exists

object.Exists(*key*)

Returns true if *key* exists in the Dictionary object and false otherwise.

Items

object.Items()

Returns all the items in a Dictionary object in the form of an array.

Keys

object.Keys()

Returns all the keys in a Dictionary object in the form of an array.

Remove

object.Remove(*key*)

Removes a particular key and item pair from a Dictionary object.

RemoveAll

object.RemoveAll()

Removes every key and item from a Dictionary object.

Properties

Count

object.Count

Returns the number of items in the Dictionary object.

Item

object.Item(*key*)

Returns or sets the item that corresponds to *key*.

Key

object.Key(*key*)

Sets a particular key in the Dictionary object.

The Enumerator Object

new Enumerator(*collection*)

Enables you to access the members of a collection.

Methods

atEnd

MyEnum`.atEnd()`

Returns `true` if the current item is the last in the collection, the collection is empty, or the current item is undefined.

item

myEnum`.item()`

Returns the current item.

moveFirst

myEnum`.moveFirst()`

Moves to the first item in the collection.

moveNext

myEnum`.moveNext()`

Moves to the next item in the collection.

The Global Object

The `Global` object is automatically created when the scripting engine is initialized.

Methods

escape

`escape(`*charstring*`)`

Encodes a string with Unicode format.

eval

`eval(`*codestring*`)`

Evaluates and executes the JScript code in *codestring*.

isFinite

`isFinite(`*number*`)`

Returns `true` if *number* is finite.

isNaN

`isNaN(`*numvalue*`)`

Determines whether a value is not a number.

parseFloat

```
parseFloat(numstring)
```

Converts a string into a floating-point number.

parseInt

```
parseInt(numstring, [radix])
```

Converts a string into an integer.

unescape

```
unescape(charstring)
```

Decodes a string that has been encoded in Unicode format.

Properties
NaN

```
NaN
```

Has the initial value of NaN (Not a Number).

Infinity Property

```
Infinity
```

Has the initial value of POSITIVE_INFINITY.

The Function Object

Syntax 1:

```
function functionname(
 [argname1 [,...argnameN]])
{
 body
}
```

Syntax 2:

```
var functionname=new Function([argname1, [...argnameN,]] body);
```

Declares a new function.

Methods
toString

```
functionname.toString()
```

Returns a string representing the function.

valueOf

`functionname.valueOf()`

Returns the value of the function.

Properties

arguments

`functionname.arguments[]`

An array of all the arguments passed to the function.

caller

`functionname.caller`

Refers to the function that called the current function.

constructor

`functionname.constructor`

Designates the function's creation function.

prototype

`functionname.prototype`

Refers to the prototype for a class of functions.

The Math Object

`Math[.{property ¦ method }]`

Methods

abs

`Math.abs(number)`

Returns an absolute value.

acos

`Math.acos(number)`

Returns the arccosine of *number*.

asin

`Math.asin(number)`

Returns the arcsine of *number*.

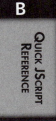

atan

`Math.atan(number)`

Returns the arctangent of *number*.

atan2

`Math.atan2(y,x)`

Returns the angle from the X axis to the point y,x in radians.

ceil

`Math.ceil(number)`

Returns the smallest integer greater than or equal to *number*.

cos

`Math.cos(number)`

Returns the cosine of *number*.

exp

`Math.exp(number)`

Returns *e* to the power of *number*.

floor

`Math.floor(number)`

Returns the greatest integer less than or equal to *number*.

log

`Math.log(number)`

Return the natural logarithm of *number*.

max

`Math.max(number1,number2)`

Returns the larger of two numbers.

min

`Math.min(number1,number2)`

Returns the smaller of two numbers.

pow

`Math.pow(base,exponent)`

Returns the value of *base* raised to a specified power.

random

```
Math.random()
```

Returns a pseudo-random number between 0 and 1.

round

```
Math.round(number)
```

Rounds *number* to the nearest integer.

sin

```
Math.sin(number)
```

Returns the sine of *number*.

sqrt

```
Math.sqrt(number)
```

Returns the square root of *number*.

tan

```
Math.tan(number)
```

Returns the tangent of *number*.

Properties

E

```
Math.E
```

Returns Euler's constant.

LN2

```
Math.LN2
```

Returns the natural logarithm of 2.

LN10

```
Math.LN10
```

Returns the natural logarithm of 10.

LOG2E

```
objname.LOG2E
```

Returns the Base 2 logarithm of *e*.

LOG10E

```
objname.LOG10E
```

Returns the Base 10 logarithm of *e*.

PI

`Math.PI`

Returns the ratio of the circumference of a circle to its diameter.

SQRT1_2

`Math.SQRT1_2`

Returns 1 divided by the square root of 2.

SQRT2

`Math.SQRT2`

Returns the square root of 2.

The Number Object

`new Number(value)`

An object that represents the `number` datatype. Also used as a placeholder for numeric constants.

Methods
toString

`numobject.toString`

Converts a number to a string.

valueOf

`numobject.valueOf()`

Returns the numeric value.

The Object Object

`new Object([value])`

This object has methods and properties common to all objects.

Methods
toString

`objectname.toString()`

Returns a string representation of an object.

valueOf

`objectname.valueOf()`

Returns the object itself.

Properties
constructor

objectname.constructor

Designates the creation function of an object.

prototype

objectname.prototype

Refers to the prototype for a class of objects.

The RegExp Object

RegExp.*propertyname*

Stores the result of a regular expression search.

Properties
$1..$9

RegExp.$*n*

Indicates the nine most recently memorized portions matched during pattern searching.

index

RegExp.index

Specifies the location of the first match in a searched string.

input

Syntax 1:

RegExp.input

Syntax 2:

RegExp.$_

Returns the string being searched.

lastIndex

RegExp.lastIndex

Specifies the location of the last match in a searched string.

lastMatch

Syntax 1:

RegExp.lastMatch

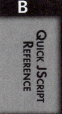

Syntax 2:

```
RegExp.$&
```

Specifies the location of the last matched characters.

lastParen

Syntax 1:

```
RegExp.lastParen
```

Syntax 2:

```
RegExp.$+
```

Designates the last parenthesized substring match.

leftContext

Syntax 1:

```
RegExp.leftContext
```

Syntax 2:

```
RegExp.$'
```

Designates the input string up to the most recent match.

multiline

Syntax 1:

```
RegExp.multiline
```

Syntax 2:

```
RegExp.$*
```

Designates whether searching is continued across line breaks.

rightContext

Syntax 1:

```
RegExp.rightContext
```

Syntax 2:

```
RegExp.$'
```

Designates the input string past the most recent match.

The Regular Expression Object

Syntax 1:

```
/pattern/[switch]
```

Syntax 2:

```
new regularexpression=new RegExp("pattern",["switch"])
```

Represents a regular expression pattern.

Methods
compile

```
rgexp.compile(pattern)
```

Compiles a regular expression.

exec

```
rgexp.exec(string)
```

Executes a search for a match in the *string* specified.

test

```
rgexp.text(string)
```

Returns `true` if a pattern exists in *string*.

Properties
global

```
rgexp.global
```

Returns `true` if the global (g) switch is used with a regular expression.

ignoreCase

```
rgexp.ignoreCase
```

Returns `true` if the ignore case (i) switch is used with a regular expression.

lastIndex

```
rgexp.lastIndex
```

Designates the index at which to start the next match.

source

```
rgexp.source
```

Returns the text of the regular expression pattern.

The String Object
Methods
anchor

strVariable.anchor(*anchorstring*)

"String Literal".anchor(*anchorstring*)

Creates a named anchor.

big

strVariable.big()

"String Literal".big()

Surrounds the text with an HTML <BIG> tag.

blink

strVariable.blink()

"String Literal".blink()

Surrounds the text with an HTML <BLINK> tag.

bold

strVariable.bold()

"String Literal".bold()

Surrounds the text with an HTML <B> tag.

charAt

strVariable.charAt(*index*)

"String Literal".charAt(*index*)

Returns the character at the index position specified.

charCodeAt

strVariable.charCodeAt(*index*)

Returns the character at the index position specified with Unicode encoding.

concat

string1.concat(*string2*)

Returns *string1* and *string2* joined into one string.

fixed

strVariable.fixed()

"String Literal".fixed()

Surrounds the text with an HTML <TT> tags.

fontcolor

strVariable.fontcolor(*colorval*)

"String Literal".fontcolor(*colorval*)

Surrounds the text with an HTML <FONT> tag with the COLOR attribute specified by *colorval*.

fontsize

strVariable.fontsize(*intSize*)

"String Literal".fontsize(*intSize*)

Surrounds the text with an HTML <FONT> tag with the SIZE attribute specified by *intSize*.

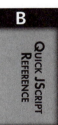

fromCharCode

String.fromCharCode(*code1,...codeN*)

Creates a string from a series of Unicode character codes.

indexOf

strVariable.indexOf(*substring*[,*startindex*])

"String Literal".indexOf(*substring*[,*startindex*])

Returns an integer indicating the beginning of the *substring* in the string.

italics

strVariable.italics()

"String Literal".italics()

Surrounds the text with an HTML <I> tag.

lastIndexOf

strVariable.lastIndexOf(*substring*, *startindex*)

"String Literal".lastIndexOf(*substring*, *startindex*)

Returns an integer indicating the last occurrence of *substring* in the string.

link

strVariable.link(*linkstring*)

"String Literal".link(*linkstring*)

Surrounds the text with a hypertext anchor with the HREF attribute specified by *linkstring*.

match

stringObj.match(*rgExp*)

Searches the string by using the regular expression *rgExp*.

replace

stringObj.match(*rgExp*,*replaceText*)

Returns the text in *stringObj* replaced with *replaceText* wherever a match is made with *rgExp*.

search

stringObj.search(*rgExp*)

Returns true if a match is made with the regular expression *rgExp*.

slice

stringObj.slice(*start* [,*end*])

Returns a portion of a string.

small

strVariable.small()

"String Literal".small()

Surrounds the text with an HTML <SMALL> tag.

split

stringObj.split(*rgExp*)

Removes text from *stringObj* wherever *rgExp* matches.

strike

strVariable.strike()

"String Literal".strike()

Surrounds the text with an HTML <STRIKE> tag.

sub

strVariable.sub()

"String Literal".sub()

Surrounds the text with an HTML <SUB> tag.

substr

strVariable.substr(*start* [,*length*])

Returns a substring starting at *start* and having length *length*.

substring

strVariable.substring(*start, end*)

"String Literal".substring(*start, end*)

Returns a substring from a string starting at *start* and ending at *end*.

sup

strVariable.sup()

"String Literal".sup()

Surrounds the text with an HTML <SUP> tag.

toLowerCase

strVariable.toLowerCase()

"String Literal".toLowerCase()

Converts to lowercase characters.

toString

strObject.toString()

Returns the value of the String object.

toUpperCase

strVariable.toUpperCase()

"String Literal".toUpperCase()

Converts to uppercase characters.

valueOf

strObject.valueOf()

Returns the string value.

Properties
constructor

strObject.constructor

Designates the creation function for the object.

length

strVariable.length

"String Literal".length

Returns the length of the string.

prototype

strObject`.prototype`

Refers to the prototype for the class of `String` objects.

The VBArray Object

`new VBArray(`*safeArray*`)`

Allows access to Visual Basic safe arrays.

Methods

dimensions

safeArray`.dimensions()`

Returns the number of dimensions in a `VBArray` object.

getItem

safeArray`.getItem(`*dimension1*`[,`*dimension2*`,...],`*dimensionN*`)`

Returns the element from the `VBArray` at the location specified.

lbound

safeArray`.lbound(`*dimension*`)`

Returns the lowest index value of the *dimension*.

toArray

safeArray`.toArray()`

Converts `VBArray` to a JScript array.

ubound

safeArray`.ubound(`*dimension*`)`

Returns the highest index value of the *dimension*.

Constants

The following special characters can be used in regular expressions for creating patterns to be matched. See both the RegExp and Regular Expression objects.

Character	Description
\	Marks the next character as special.
^	Matches the beginning of the input or line.
$	Matches the end of the input or line.
*	Matches the preceding character zero or more times.
+	Matches the preceding character one or more times.
?	Matches the preceding character zero or one time.
.	Matches any single character except the newline.
(pattern)	Matches *pattern* and remembers the match.
x|y	Matches either *x* or *y*.
{n}	Matches exactly *n* times.
{n,}	Matches at least *n* times.
{n,m}	Matches at least *n* and at most *m* times.
[xyz]	Matches any one of the enclosed characters.
[~xyz]	Matches any character not enclosed.
\b	Matches a word boundary.
\B	Matches a non-word boundary.
\d	Matches a digit character.
\D	Matches a non-digit character.
\f	Matches a form feed character.
\n	Matches a line feed character.
\r	Matches a carriage return.
\s	Matches white space.
\S	Matches any nonwhite space.
\t	Matches a tab character.
\v	Matches a vertical tab character.
\w	Matches any word character including an underscore.
\W	Matches any non-word character.
\num	Matches the positive integer *num*.
/n/	Matches the octal, hexadecimal, or decimal escape value.

Quick VBScript Reference

IN THIS APPENDIX

This appendix contains a quick reference of all the VBScript statements, functions, operators, objects, and constants. Many of the VBScript functions make use of constants. See the end of this appendix for a list of these constants.

> **NOTE**
>
> The information for this appendix was extracted from the Microsoft VBScript online documentation. For the latest information, check the documentation.

Statements

Call

```
[Call] name [argumentlist]
```

Transfers control to a function or subroutine. Using `Call` when calling a function or subroutine is always optional. However, if the optional `Call` keyword is used, *argumentlist* must be enclosed in parentheses.

Const

```
[Public ¦ Private] Const constantname=expression
```

Used to declare a constant. You can declare multiple constants within a single line by separating each constant assignment with a comma.

Dim

```
Dim varname[([subscripts])][, varname[([subscripts])]] . . .
```

Creates a new variable and allocates storage space.

Do...Loop

Syntax 1:

```
Do [{While ¦ Until} condition]
[statements]
[Exit Do]
[statements]
Loop
```

Syntax 2:

```
Do
[statements]
[Exit Do]
[statements]
Loop [{While ¦ Until} condition]
```

Both forms of the statement repeat *statements* while *condition* is TRUE or until it becomes TRUE.

Erase

```
Erase array
```

Erases *array*, reinitializing elements of fixed-size arrays and recovering storage space of dynamic arrays.

Exit

```
Exit Do
```

Exits a Do...Loop statement.

```
Exit For
```

Exits a For...Next or For Each...Next loop.

```
Exit Function
```

Exits a function.

```
Exit Sub
```

Exits a subroutine.

For...Next

```
For counter = start To end [Step step]
[statements]
[Exit For]
[statements]
Next
```

Repeats a group of *statements* the number of times designated by the loop counter.

For Each...Next

```
For Each element In group
[statements]
[Exit For]
[statements]
Next [element]
```

For each element in the array or collection, repeats the group of *statements*.

Function

```
[Public ¦ Private] Function name [(arglist)]
[statements]
[name = expression]
[Exit Function]
[statements]
[name = expression]
End Function
```

Defines a function, assigning a name, arguments, and code.

If...Then...Else

Syntax 1:

```
If condition Then statements [Else elsestatements]
```

Syntax 2:

```
If condition Then
statements
[ElseIf condition-n Then
[elseifstatements]] . . .
[Else
[elsestatements]]
End If
```

Both forms of the statement conditionally execute groups of statements.

On Error

```
On Error Resume Next
```

When an error occurs, this statement executes the statement immediately following the statement that caused the runtime error, or executes the statement immediately following the most recent call out of the procedure containing the On Error Resume Next statement.

Option Explicit

```
Option Explicit
```

Forces the explicit declaration of all variables using the Dim, Private, Public, or ReDim statements.

Private

```
Private varname[([subscripts])][, varname[([subscripts])]] . . .
```

Creates private variables (variables available only to the script in which they were declared) and allocates storage space.

Public

```
Public varname[([subscripts])][, varname[([subscripts])]] . . .
```

Creates public variables (variables available to all procedures in all scripts in all projects) and allocates storage space.

Randomize

```
Randomize [number]
```

Gives the Rnd function's random-number generator a new seed value.

ReDim

```
ReDim [Preserve] varname(subscripts) [, varname(subscripts)] . . .
```

Revises dimension subscripts, sizing or resizing a dynamic array. `Preserve` protects data in the existing array.

Rem

Syntax 1:

```
Rem comment
```

Syntax 2:

```
' comment
```

Both forms of this statement keep comments from being parsed. If `Rem` follows other statements on a line, it must be separated by a colon.

Select Case

```
Select Case testexpression
[Case expressionlist-n
[statements-n]] . . .
[Case Else expressionlist-n
[elsestatements-n]]
End Select
```

Executes statements paired with any `expressionlist` that matches `testexpression`. If `testexpression` doesn't match any `expressionlist`, the statements paired with `Case Else` are executed.

Set

```
Set objectvar = {objectexpression ¦ Nothing}
```

Sets the object reference for the variable or the property. `Nothing` dissociates `objectvar` from any specific object.

Sub

```
[Public ¦ Private] Sub name [(arglist)]
[statements]
[Exit Sub]
[statements]
End Sub
```

Defines a subroutine, assigning a name, arguments, and code.

While...Wend

```
While condition
[statements]
Wend
```

Continues to execute the series of `statements` as long as `condition` is TRUE.

Functions

Abs(*number*)
Returns an absolute value.

Array(*arglist*)
Creates an array.

Asc(*string*)
Returns ANSI code for the first letter in *string*.

Atn(*number*)
Returns the arctangent.

CBool(*expression*)
Converts to variant of subtype Boolean.

CByte(*expression*)
Converts to variant of subtype Byte.

CCur(*expression*)
Converts to variant of subtype Currency.

CDate(*date*)
Converts to variant of subtype Date.

CDbl(*expression*)
Converts to variant of subtype Double.

Chr(*charcode*)
Converts ANSI code to the corresponding keyboard character.

CInt(*expression*)
Converts to variant of subtype Integer.

CLng(*expression*)
Converts to variant of subtype Long.

Cos(*number*)

Returns the cosine.

CreateObject(*servername.typename*)

Creates an Automation object.

CSng(*expression*)

Converts to variant of subtype `Single`.

CStr(*expression*)

Converts to variant of subtype `String`.

Date

Returns the date according to the system.

DateAdd(*interval,number,date*)

Adds the time interval to *date*. The *interval* argument accepts the values shown in the following table.

Setting	Description
yyyy	Year
q	Quarter
m	Month
y	Day of year
d	Day
w	Weekday
ww	Week of year
h	Hour
m	Minute
s	Second

DateDiff(*interval,date1,date2[,firstdayofweek [,firstweekofyear]]*)

Returns the number of intervals between two dates. See the later section "Date and Time Constants" for values of *firstdayofweek* and *firstweekofyear*. The *interval* argument accepts the values shown in the following table.

Setting	Description
yyyy	Year
q	Quarter
m	Month
y	Day of year
d	Day
w	Weekday
ww	Week of year
h	Hour
m	Minute
s	Second

DatePart(*interval,date*[,*firstdayofweek* [,*firstweekofyear*]])

Returns the designated part of the date. See the later section "Date and Time Constants" for values of *firstdayofweek* and *firstweekofyear*. The *interval* argument accepts the values shown in the following table.

Setting	Description
yyyy	Year
q	Quarter
m	Month
y	Day of year
d	Day
w	Weekday
ww	Week of year
h	Hour
m	Minute
s	Second

DateSerial(*year,month,day*)

Converts to variant of subtype Date.

DateValue(*date*)

Converts to variant of subtype Date.

Day(*date*)

Returns the day of the month according to the argument.

Exp(*number*)

Raises *e* to the power of *number*.

Filter(*InputStrings,Value[,Include[,Compare]]*)

Creates a new array according to the filter criteria. See the later section "Comparison Constants" for values of *Compare*.

Fix(*number*)

Converts to integer (rounds up for a negative number).

FormatCurrency(*Expression[,NumDigitsAfterDecimal [,IncludeLeadingDigit[,UseParensForNegativeNumbers [,GroupDigits]]]]*)

Formats as currency. See the later section "Tristate Constants" for values of *IncludeLeadingDigit*, *UseParensForNegativeNumbers*, *GroupDigits*.

FormatDateTime(*Date[,NamedFormat]*)

Formats dates and times. See the later section "Date Format Constants" for values of *NamedFormat*.

FormatNumber(*Expression[,NumDigitsAfterDecimal [,IncludeLeadingDigit[,UseParensForNegativeNumbers [,GroupDigits]]]]*)

Formats numbers. See the later section "Tristate Constants" for values of *IncludeLeadingDigit*, *UseParensForNegativeNumbers*, *GroupDigits*.

FormatPercent(*Expression[,NumDigitsAfterDecimal [,IncludeLeadingDigit[,UseParensForNegativeNumbers [,GroupDigits]]]]*)

Formats percentages. See the later section "Tristate Constants" for values of *IncludeLeadingDigit*, *UseParensForNegativeNumbers*, *GroupDigits*.

GetObject([*pathname*][,*class*])

Returns the specified Automation object from the specified file.

Hex(*number*)

Returns the hexadecimal value of *number*.

Hour(*time*)

Returns the hour according to the *time* argument.

InputBox(*prompt*[,*title*][,*default*][,*xpos*][,*ypos*] [,*helpfile*,*context*])

Prompts and returns user input.

InStr([*start*,]*string1*,*string2*[,*compare*])

Returns the first appearance of *string2* within *string1*. See the later section "Comparison Constants" for values of *compare*.

InStrRev(*string1*,*string2*[*start*[,*compare*]])

Returns the last appearance of *string2* within *string1*. See the later section "Comparison Constants" for values of *compare*.

Int(*number*)

Returns an integer (rounds down for a negative number).

IsArray(*varname*)

Determines whether the variable is an array.

IsDate(*expression*)

Determines whether *expression* can be converted to date format.

IsEmpty(*expression*)

Determines whether the variable has been initialized.

IsNull(*expression*)

Determines whether *expression* is null.

IsNumeric(*expression*)
Determines whether *expression* is a number.

IsObject(*expression*)
Determines whether *expression* is an Automation object.

Join(*list[,delimiter]*)
Joins substrings in an array separated by the character indicated by *delimiter*.

LBound(*arrayname[,dimension]*)
Returns the lower limit of the array dimension. This function always returns zero with the current version of VBScript.

LCase(*string*)
Formats as lowercase.

Left(*string,length*)
Returns the left string portion of the designated length.

Len(*string,varname*)
Returns the length of the string or the byte size of the variable.

LoadPicture(*picturename*)
Loads a picture object.

Log(*number*)
Returns the natural logarithm of the number.

LTrim(*string*)
Removes extra left spaces.

Mid(*string,start[,length]*)
Returns a string portion of the designated length.

Minute(*time*)
Returns the minute according to the argument.

Month(date)

Returns the month represented by the number.

MonthName(month[,abbreviate])

Returns the month represented by the name.

MsgBox(prompt[,buttons][,title][helpfile,context])

Prompts the user to choose a button and indicates which button the user has chosen. See the later section "MsgBox Constants" for *button* and return values.

Now

Returns the current date and time according to the system.

Oct(number)

Returns the octal value of *number*.

Replace(expression,find,replacewith[,start[,count [,compare]]])

Replaces the designated substring *find* with the substring *replacewith* the designated number of times. See the later section "Comparison Constants" for values of *compare*.

Right(string,length)

Returns the right string portion of the designated length.

Rnd([number)])

Generates a pseudo-random number.

Round(number[,numdecimalplaces])

Rounds *number* to the specified number of decimal places.

RTrim(string)

Removes extra right spaces.

ScriptEngine

Returns the name of the scripting language in use.

ScriptEngineBuildVersion

Returns the name of the script engine in use.

ScriptEngineMajorVersion

Returns the major version number of the script engine in use.

Second(*time*)

Returns the second of the minute according to the argument.

Sgn(*number*)

Returns the sign of *number*.

Sin(*number*)

Returns the sine of *number*.

Space(*number*)

Creates a string with the specified number of spaces.

Split(*expression*[,*delimiter*[,*count*[,*compare*]]])

Splits a string and converts it into an array. See the later section "Comparison Constants" for values of *compare*.

Sqr(*number*)

Returns the square root of the specified number.

StrComp(*string1*,*string2*[,*compare*])

String comparison. See the later section "Comparison Constants" for values of *compare*.

StrReverse(*string1*)

Reverses the characters of a string.

String(*number*,*character*)

Creates a string with *character* repeated the specified number of times.

Tan(*number*)

Returns the tangent of the number.

Time

Returns the current time according to the system.

TimeSerial(*hour,minute,second*)

Returns Date Variant.

TimeValue(*time*)

Returns Date Variant containing time.

Trim(*string*)

Removes extra spaces at left and right.

TypeName(*varname*)

Returns the subtype by name. See the later section "VarType Constants" for return values.

UBound(*arrayname[,dimension]*)

Returns the upper bound of the array dimension. If no dimension is specified, the first dimension is assumed.

UCase(*string*)

Formats the string as uppercase.

VarType(*varname*)

Returns the subtype by value. See the later section "VarType Constants" for return values.

Weekday(*date,[firstdayofweek]*)

Returns the day of the week by number. See the later section "Date and Time Constants" for values of *firstdayofweek*.

WeekDayName(*weekday,abbreviate,firstdayofweek*)

Returns the day of the week by name. See the later section "Date and Time Constants" for values of *firstdayofweek*.

Year(*date*)

Returns the year according to the argument.

Operators

+ Operator

```
result = expression1 + expression2
```

Sum. Can be used for string concatenation, but & is less ambiguous.

And Operator

```
result = expression1 And expression2
```

Logical conjunction. Also performs bitwise comparison, returning digit 1 only where both expressions have digit 1.

& Operator

```
result = expression1 & expression2
```

String concatenation.

/ Operator

```
result = number1/number2
```

Divides two numbers and returns a floating-point number.

Eqv Operator

```
result = expression1 Eqv expression2
```

Logical equivalence. Also performs bitwise comparison, returning digit 1 only where bits in the two expressions are identical.

^ Operator

```
result = number^exponent
```

Raises *number* to the power of *exponent*.

Imp Operator

```
result = expression1 Imp expression2
```

Material implication. Also performs bitwise comparison. The following table illustrates logical implication.

expression1	expression2	result
TRUE	TRUE	TRUE
TRUE	FALSE	FALSE
TRUE	NULL	NULL
FALSE	TRUE	TRUE
FALSE	FALSE	TRUE
FALSE	NULL	TRUE
NULL	TRUE	TRUE
NULL	FALSE	NULL
NULL	NULL	NULL

The following table illustrates the bitwise comparison associated with the Imp operator.

expression1	expression2	result
0	0	1
0	1	1
1	0	0
1	1	1

\ Operator

`result = number1\number2`

Divides two numbers and returns an integer.

Is Operator

`result = object1 Is object2`

Checks whether two variables refer to the same object and returns TRUE or FALSE.

Mod Operator

`result = number1 Mod number2`

Divides two numbers and returns only the remainder.

* Operator

`result = number1*number2`

Multiplication.

- Operator

`result = number1-number2`

Subtraction.

`-number`

Sign of number.

Not Operator

`result = Not expression`

Logical negation. Also performs bitwise negation.

Or Operator

`result = expression1 Or expression2`

Logical disjunction. `result` is TRUE if either expression is TRUE or both expressions are TRUE. The Or operator also performs bitwise comparison, returning digit 0 only where both expressions have digit 0. Elsewhere digit 1 is returned.

Xor Operator

`result = expression1 Xor expression2`

Logical exclusion. `result` is TRUE if one and only one expression is TRUE. The Xor operator also performs bitwise comparison, returning digit 1 only where one and only one expression has digit 1. Elsewhere digit 0 is returned.

Objects
The Dictionary Object
Methods
Add *Key, Item*
Adds *Key* and associated *Item* to a Dictionary object.

Exists(*Key*)
Checks whether the specified *Key* already exists in the Dictionary object and returns either TRUE or FALSE.

Items
Returns all *Items* in the Dictionary object as an array.

Keys
Returns all existing *Keys* in the Dictionary object as an array.

Remove(*Key*)
Removes *Key* and associated item from the Dictionary object.

RemoveAll
Removes all keys and their associated items from the Dictionary object.

Properties
CompareMode
Specifies how items in the dictionary should be compared. See the later section "Comparison Constants" for possible values.

Count
Counts items in the Dictionary object (read-only).

Item(*Key*)
Returns the item associated with the designated *Key* in the Dictionary object or associates a new value with the key.

Key(*Key*)
Sets the specified *Key* in the Dictionary object.

The Err Object
Methods
Clear
Explicitly clears the Err object of all property settings.

Raise *number source*

Returns a runtime error. *number* identifies the type of error. VBScript errors are numbered in the range 0–65535. *source* indicates the object or application that originally generated the error.

Properties

Description

Returns or sets a brief description of an error.

HelpContext

Sets or returns the identifier for a topic within the Help file that's appropriate for the Err object.

HelpFile

Sets or returns the fully qualified path to the Help file that's appropriate for the Err object.

Number *errornumber*

Returns a number identifying the error or, if *errornumber* is included, associates the error with either a VBScript error number or an SCODE error value.

Source *object*

Identifies the source of the error, usually by class name or programmatic ID of the object or application that generated the error (*object* is the Err object).

Constants

In the following sections, the constants (left column of each table) can be used in place of the values (in the center column).

Color Constants

Constant	Value	Description
vbBlack	&h00	Black
vbRed	&hFF	Red
vbGreen	&hFF00	Green
vbYellow	&hFFFF	Yellow
vbBlue	&hFF0000	Blue
vbMagenta	&hFF00FF	Magenta
vbCyan	&hFFFF00	Cyan
vbWhite	&hFFFFFF	White

Comparison Constants

Constant	Value	Description
vbBinaryCompare	0	Binary comparison
vbTextCompare	1	Textual comparison
vbDatabaseCompare	2	Comparison based on information in the database

Date and Time Constants

Constant	Value	Description
vbSunday	1	Sunday
vbMonday	2	Monday
vbTuesday	3	Tuesday
vbWednesday	4	Wednesday
vbThursday	5	Thursday
vbFriday	6	Friday
vbSaturday	7	Saturday
vbFirstJan1	1	Week of Jan 1 (default)
vbFirstFourDays	2	First week (of the year) that has at least four days
vbFirstFullWeek	3	First full week of the year

Constant	Value	Description
vbUseSystem	0	Use the date format of the computer's regional settings
vbUseSystemDayOfWeek	0	Use the first day of the week according to the system settings

Date Format Constants

Constant	Value	Description
vbGeneralDate	0	Display the date and/or time according to the system settings
vbLongDate	1	Display the date in long date format
vbShortDate	2	Display the date in short date format
vbLongTime	3	Display the time in long time format
vbShortTime	4	Display the time in short time format

MsgBox Constants

These constants are used with the MsgBox function to specify buttons and icons displayed in the message box and to identify the default icon.

Constant	Value	Description
vbOKOnly	0	Show only the OK button.
vbOKCancel	1	Show OK and Cancel buttons.
vbAbortRetryIgnore	2	Show Abort, Retry, and Ignore buttons.
vbYesNoCancel	3	Show Yes, No, and Cancel buttons.
vbYesNo	4	Show Yes and No buttons.
vbRetryCancel	5	Show Retry and Cancel buttons.
vbCritical	16	Show Critical Message icon.
vbQuestion	32	Show Warning Query icon.
vbExclamation	48	Show Warning Message icon.
vbInformation	64	Show Information Message icon.
vbDefaultButton1	0	The first button is the default.
vbDefaultButton2	256	The second button is the default.
vbDefaultButton3	512	The third button is the default.
vbDefaultButton4	768	The fourth button is the default.

The constants in the following table specify modality.

Constant	Value	Description
vbApplicationModal	0	The current application won't continue until the user responds to the message box.
vbSystemModal	4096	No applications will continue until the user responds to the message box.

The constants in the following table identify which button has been pressed.

Constant	Value	Description
vbOK	1	OK button
vbCancel	2	Cancel button
vbAbort	3	Abort button
vbRetry	4	Retry button
vbIgnore	5	Ignore button
vbYes	6	Yes button
vbNo	7	No button

String Constants

Constant	Value	Description
vbCr	Chr(13)	Carriage return
vbCrLf	Chr(13) & Chr(10)	Combination carriage return and line feed
vbFormFeed	Chr(12)	Form feed
vbLF	Chr(10)	Line feed
vbNewLine	Chr(13) & Chr(10) or Chr(10)	Newline character appropriate for platform
vbNullChar	Chr(0)	Character of value 0
vbNullString	string having value 0	Null string
vbTab	Chr(9)	Horizontal tab
vbVerticalTab	Chr(11)	Vertical tab

Tristate Constants

Constant	Value	Description
TristateTrue	-1	TRUE
TristateFalse	0	FALSE
TristateUseDefault	-2	Use the default setting

VarType Constants

Constant	Value	Description
vbEmpty	0	Uninitialized (default)
vbNull	1	Contains no valid data
vbInteger	2	Integer subtype
vbLong	3	Long subtype
vbSingle	4	Single subtype
vbDouble	5	Double subtype
vbCurrency	6	Currency subtype
vbDate	7	Date subtype
vbString	8	String subtype
vbObject	9	Object
vbError	10	Error subtype
vbBoolean	11	Boolean subtype
vbVariant	12	Variant (only used for arrays of variants)
vbDataObject	13	Data access object
vbDecimal	14	Decimal subtype
vbByte	17	Byte subtype
vbArray	8192	Array

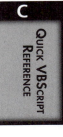

Quick HTML Reference

IN THIS APPENDIX

APPENDIX D

This appendix provides a quick reference of HTML, cascading style sheets, HTML character codes, and HTML colors. The HTML tags are listed alphabetically with a description of their attributes. When a tag is either Internet Explorer-specific or Netscape-specific, this is noted next to the tag's description.

HTML is evolving rapidly. For the latest information, visit `http://w3.org`.

Standard HTML Tags

In the following pages, note that the following abbreviations are used:

ASP	Active Server Pages
IE	Microsoft Internet Explorer
NS	Netscape Navigator

> **NOTE**
>
> Browsers that support style sheets have two additional attributes for most tags. These browsers support the ID attribute, which provides a unique identifier for a tag, and the CLASS attribute, which is used to associate a style with a class of tags.

`<!-- -->`

Specifies comments. Used to document HTML and for hiding client-side scripts and style sheets from non-compliant browsers.

`<!DOCTYPE>`

Specifies the version of HTML. Should appear as the first line in every HTML file, but is seldom used. Here's an example:

```
<!DOCTYPE HTML PUBLIC "-//W3C//DTD HTML 3.2 Final//EN">
```

`<A>...</A>`

Creates a hypertext anchor. Used for creating hypertext links and targets for hypertext links. The following table describes the attributes for this tag.

Attribute	Description
HREF=*URL*	The location where you are taken if you click the link.
NAME=*string*	The name used for named anchors.
REL=*forward link*	Specifies the forward link type. This attribute is seldom used.

Attribute	Description
REV=*reverse link*	Specifies reverse relationship. This attribute is seldom used.
TARGET=*name*	Used for named frame or window [NS2,IE3].

\<ADDRESS\>...\</ADDRESS\>

Formats address information (typically in italics).

\<APPLET\>...\</APPLET\>

Specifies a Java applet. The following table describes the attributes for this tag.

Attribute	Description
ALIGN=*setting*	Aligns the Java applet against the surrounding text. The settings are left, right, top, texttop, middle, absmiddle, baseline, bottom, and absbottom.
ALT=*text*	Alternative text to display for browsers that aren't smart enough to understand Java.
ARCHIVE=*archiveURL*	Allows you to specify a zipped but uncompressed file for the Java applet [NS3].
CODE=*applet file*	Name of the Java applet.
CODEBASE=*directory*	Specifies the directory where the Java applet is located.
HEIGHT=*number*	Specifies the height of the Java applet display area in pixels.
HSPACE=*number*	Specifies the space to the left and right of the Java applet display area in pixels.
MAYSCRIPT	Determines whether Java can use JavaScript [NS3].
NAME=*string*	Provides a name that identifies the Java applet.
VSPACE=*number*	Specifies the space above and below the Java applet display area, in pixels.
WIDTH=*number*	Specifies the width of the Java applet display area.

D

\<AREA\>

Specifies an area for a client-side image map. This tag is contained in the \<MAP\> tag (see the later section on \<MAP\>). The following table describes the attributes for this tag.

Attribute	*Description*
ALT=*text*	Alternative text to display for text-only browsers.
COORDS=*number,number...*	Defines a region on which to click in the image map.
HREF=*URL*	The Internet address where you arrive if you click an area.
NOHREF	Specifies a dead zone in the image map.
SHAPE=rect¦circle¦poly	Specifies the shape of the clickable area of the image map.
TARGET=*name*	Specifies the name of a frame or window to target [NS2,MS3].

<B>...</B>

Formats text as bold.

<BASE>

Provides the full URL for the current document. This tag must appear in the <HEAD> section. The following table describes the attributes for this tag.

Attribute	*Description*
HREF=*URL*	The full URL of the current document.
TARGET=*name*	Specifies the name of a frame or window to target [NS2,IE3].

<BASEFONT>

Specifies the base font size for the whole document. The following table describes the attributes for this tag.

Attribute	*Description*
COLOR=*color*	Specifies what color to make all the text in the document [IE3].
FACE=*typeface*	Specifies the typeface to use for all the text in the document [IE3].
SIZE=*number*	A number between 1 and 7 that specifies the size to make the font.

<BGSOUND>

Plays a background sound [IE3]. The following table describes the attributes for this tag.

Attribute	Description
LOOP=*number* ¦ INFINITE	Number of times to play the background sound. If INFINITE, it never stops.
SRC=*URL*	Source for the sound file.

`<BIG>...</BIG>`

Formats text in large font.

`<BLINK>...</BLINK>` [NS1]

Works only with Netscape. Makes text blink on and off.

`<BLOCKQUOTE>...</BLOCKQUOTE>`

Indents a block of text.

`<BODY>...</BODY>`

Contains all tags and text displayed in the browser window. The following table describes the attributes for this tag.

Attribute	Description
ALINK=*active hyperlink color*	Specifies the color for all active hypertext links.
BACKGROUND=*image*	Specifies the URL for an image that's tiled repeatedly across the background.
BGCOLOR=*color*	Specifies the background color for the document.
BGPROPERTIES=*fixed*	Determines whether the background image scrolls with the document or remains fixed [IE3].
LEFTMARGIN=*number*	Specifies the left margin for the entire document in pixels [IE3].
LINK=*color*	Specifies the color for all unvisited hypertext links in the document.
TEXT=*color*	Specifies the text color for the entire document.
TOPMARGIN=*number*	Specifies the top margin for the entire document in pixels [IE3].
VLINK=*color*	Specifies the color for all visited hypertext links in the document.

\<BR\>

Creates a line break. The following table describes the attribute for this tag.

Attribute	Description
CLEAR=LEFT¦RIGHT¦ALL	Moves below the floating images on the left, right, or either side.

\<CAPTION\>...\</CAPTION\>

Provides a table with a caption (see the later section on \<TABLE\>). The following table describes the attribute for this tag.

Attribute	Description
ALIGN=top¦bottom¦left¦right	Aligns the caption against the table.

\<CENTER\>...\</CENTER\>

Centers text.

\<CITE\>...\</CITE\>

Formats text as citation or reference, typically with italics.

\<CODE\>...\</CODE\>

Formats text as program code.

\<COL\> [IE3]

Used within a \<TABLE\> tag to specify properties for one or more columns. The following table describes the attributes for this tag.

Attribute	Description
ALIGN=left¦center¦right	Specifies text alignment for cells within the column.
SPAN=number	Specifies the number of columns that the property spans over.

\<COLGROUP\> [IE3]

Used within a \<TABLE\> tag to specify properties for one or more columns. The following table describes the attributes for this tag.

Attribute	Description
HALIGN=left¦center¦right	Specifies the horizontal alignment for the cells in the column group.
SPAN=*number*	Specifies the number of columns that the property spans over.
VALIGN=top¦middle¦bottom	Specifies the vertical alignment for the cells in the column.
WIDTH=*number*	Specifies the width of the columns in the column group.

`<COMMENT>...</COMMENT>` [obsolete]

Alternative method of inserting a comment. All text within this tag is ignored, except HTML.

`<DD>`

Definition of a term. Displayed in the right-hand column of a definition list. See the later section on <DL>.

`<DFN>...</DFN>`

Formats text as a definition.

`<DIR>...</DIR>`

Displays a directory list, typically with indented text.

`<DIV>...</DIV>`

Creates document divisions. Can be used with style sheets and for aligning blocks of text. The following table describes the attributes for this tag.

Attribute	Description
ALIGN=LEFT¦CENTER¦RIGHT	Aligns text within a division. Can be used instead of the <CENTER> tag. IE4 also recognizes JUSTIFY as a value.
NOWRAP	Specifies that text within the division shouldn't wrap to a new line automatically [IE4].

`<DL>...</DL>`

Creates a definition list. The following table describes the attribute for this tag.

Attribute	Description
COMPACT	Formats definition items with less spacing.

<DT>

Specifies a term in a definition list. Appears in the left-hand column.

<EM>...</EM>

Emphasizes text by formatting it as italic.

<EMBED> [NS2,IE3]

Indicates an embedded object. The following table describes the attributes for this tag.

Attribute	Description
ALIGN=left¦right¦top¦bottom	Aligns an embedded object [NS2].
BORDER=*number*	Size of the border in pixels [NS2].
FRAMEBORDER=*no*	Specifies that the frame has no border [NS2].
HIDDEN=true¦false	Determines whether the plug-in is visible [NS2].
HSPACE=*number*	Pixels specifying empty space on left and right [NS1].
HEIGHT=*number*	Specifies the height of the object on the page in pixels.
NAME=*name*	Provides a name for the embedded object.
PALETTE=*color*¦*color*	Sets the color palette to the foreground or background color.
PLUGINSPAGE=*URL*	Internet address of page that provides information about the plug-in [NS2].
SRC=*URL*	The Internet address of the object.
TYPE=*MIME type*	Specifies the MIME type [NS2].
UNITS=pixels¦ens	Specifies the units of measurement to use with the HEIGHT and WIDTH attributes [IE3].
VSPACE=*number*	Space above and below in pixels [NS1].
WIDTH=*number*	Specifies the width of the object on the page in pixels.

<FONT>...</FONT>

Formats text with a particular font. The following table describes the attributes for this tag.

Attribute	Description
COLOR=*color*	Color of the font, specified by a color constant or RGB value [NS3,IE3].
FACE=*typeface*	Typeface of the font [NS3,IE3].
SIZE=*absolute¦relative number*	Size of the font. Either a number between 1 and 7 or a relative value such as +1 or -1.

<FORM>...</FORM>

Encloses a fill-out form. See the later section on the <INPUT> tag for form contents. The following table describes the attributes for this tag.

Attribute	Description
ACTION=*URL*	The address of the server-side program that will process the form, or the e-mail address that specifies where to send the form contents.
ENCTYPE=*form encoding*	The content encoding to use for the form contents. For a file upload button to function properly, you should use multipart/form-data as the value of this attribute.
METHOD=post¦get	The method of sending the form contents.
TARGET=*name*	Specifies to return the results of the form submission to the targeted window or frame.

<FRAME>

Defines a particular frame in a set of frames. The following table describes the attributes for this tag.

Attribute	Description
ALIGN=top¦bottom¦left¦center¦right	Sets the alignment of the frame. [IE3]
BORDERCOLOR=*color*	Specifies the color of the frame border [NS3].
FRAMEBORDER=0¦1	Specifies whether the frame should have a border [IE3].
MARGINHEIGHT=*number*	Specifies the margin height for the frame in pixels.

continues

Attribute	*Description*
MARGINWIDTH=*number*	Specifies the margin width for the frame in pixels.
NAME=*name*	The name for the frame.
NORESIZE	Prevents the frame from being resized.
SCROLLING=yes¦no¦auto	Specifies whether the contents of the frame should scroll.
SRC=*URL*	The Internet address of the document that the frame holds.

<FRAMESET>...</FRAMESET>

Holds the collection of frames. The following table describes the attributes for this tag.

Attribute	*Description*
BORDER=*number*	Size of the frame borders in pixels [NS3].
BORDERCOLOR=*color*	Specifies the color of the frame borders [NS3].
COLS=*cols-width*	Specifies the division of frames into columns.
FRAMEBORDER=1¦0	Specifies whether the frames should have a border.
FRAMESPACING=*number*	Places space between the frames, measured in pixels [IE3].
ROWS=*rows-width*	Specifies the division of frames into rows.

<H#>...</H#>

Creates headings of different levels of importance from H1 (most important) to H6 (least important). The following table describes the attribute for this tag.

Attribute	*Description*
ALIGN=LEFT¦CENTER¦RIGHT	Aligns the heading.

<HEAD>...</HEAD>

Contains tags that aren't displayed in the main browser window but specify information about the document.

<HP#>...</HP#> [obsolete]

Used to indicate highlighted phrases.

<HR>

Creates a horizontal rule. The following table describes the attributes for this tag.

Attribute	Description
ALIGN=LEFT¦CENTER¦RIGHT	Aligns the horizontal rule.
COLOR=*color*	Specifies a particular color [IE3].
NOSHADE	Removes the groove and makes the horizontal rule a solid line.
SIZE=*number*	The vertical size of the horizontal rule in pixels.
WIDTH=*absolute¦relative number*	The width of the horizontal rule, measured in pixels or as a percentage of the screen.

<HTML>...</HTML>

Contains all other HTML tags.

<I>...</I>

Formats text as italic.

<IFRAME>...</IFRAME> [IE3]

Creates a floating frame. The following table describes the attributes for this tag.

Attribute	Description
ALIGN=top¦middle¦bottom¦left¦right	Aligns the floating frame.
FRAMEBORDER=0¦1	Specifies whether the frame has a border.
HEIGHT=*number*	Indicates the height of the frame in pixels.
MARGINHEIGHT=*number*	Specifies the margin height in pixels.
MARGINWIDTH=*number*	Specifies the margin width in pixels.
NAME=*name*	Provides a name for the floating frame.
NORESIZE	Prevents the frame from being resized.
SCROLLING=yes¦no¦auto	Controls whether the contents of the frame will scroll.

continues

D

QUICK HTML
REFERENCE

Attribute	Description
SRC=*URL*	Provides the Internet address of the document contained in the frame.
WIDTH=*number*	Specifies the width of the frame in pixels.

`<ILAYER>...</ILAYER>` [NS4]

Creates an *inflow layer* (a layer of content placed within the layout context of other screen elements).

`<IMG>`

Specifies an image to appear in the document. The following table describes the attributes for this tag.

Attribute	Description
ALIGN=TOP¦MIDDLE¦BOTTOM¦LEFT¦CENTER¦RIGHT	Aligns the image. Netscape Navigator also recognizes TEXTTOP, BASELINE, and ABSMIDDLE.
ALT=*string*	Alternative text to display when the browser has graphics turned off. On certain browsers, a balloon with this text appears over the image.
BORDER=*number*	Size of the image border.
CONTROLS	Determines how VCR controls appear for controlling dynamic media such as video clips [IE3,NS3].
DYNSRC=*URL*	Specifies the Internet address for a dynamic source, such as a video clip or VRML world [IE3].
HEIGHT=*number*	Height of the image in pixels.
HSPACE=*number*	The horizontal space on the left and right of the image in pixels.
ISMAP	Specifies that the image is a server-side image map.
LOOP=*number*¦INFINITE	Specifies the number of times a video clip will play again. If the loop is INFINITE, it will never, ever stop [IE3].

Attribute	Description
LOWSRC=*URL*	Displays a lower-resolution image while a higher-resolution image is loading [NS3].
SRC=*URL*	The Internet address of the image.
START=FILEOPEN¦MOUSEOVER	Determines when the media referenced by DYNSRC will start [IE3,NS3].
USEMAP=*URL*	Specifies the map name for a client-side image map.
VSPACE=*number*	The vertical space on the top and bottom of the image.
WIDTH=*number*	Width of the image in pixels.

<INPUT>

Creates a fill-in form input element. The following table describes the attributes for this tag.

Attribute	Description
ACCEPT=*MIME type*	The MIME types that a file upload button will accept.
ALIGN=top¦middle¦bottom¦left¦right	Aligns the form element against the surrounding text.
CHECKED	Determines whether a check box is checked when the form first appears.
MAXLENGTH=*number*	Specifies the maximum number of characters a TEXT or PASSWORD input element will accept.
NAME=*name*	Specifies the name for an input element.
SIZE=*number*	Specifies the displayed width of the input element.
SRC=*image*	Specifies the image URL for the image submit button.
TABINDEX=*number*	Specifies the place of the input element in the tabbing order [IE3].

continues

D

QUICK HTML
REFERENCE

Attribute	*Description*
TYPE=TEXT¦PASSWORD¦CHECKBOX¦RADIO¦ SUBMIT¦RESET¦FILE¦HIDDEN¦IMAGE	Specifies an input widget for a fill-in form element. The list following this table describes the types.
VALUE=*initial value*	Specifies the initial value of a TEXT, HIDDEN, or PASSWORD form element. Specifies the text displayed on a SUBMIT or RESET button. Specifies the value submitted by a CHECKBOX or RADIO button.

Types for the TYPE attribute of the <INPUT> command:

TEXT	Text box (default).
PASSWORD	Password box in which input is hidden.
CHECKBOX	Clickable off and on value.
RADIO	Multiple related check boxes.
SUBMIT	Submit form button.
RESET	Button that clears the form.
FILE	File upload button. [NS2]
TEXTAREA	Multiple-line text area. [IE3]
HIDDEN	Undisplayed form field.
IMAGE	Submit form image.

<ISINDEX>

Creates a search field for searching the document. This is not a form element, and this tag is rarely used. The following table describes the attributes for this tag.

Attribute	*Description*
ACTION=*URL*	Internet address of the program that will receive the search string.
PROMPT=*string*	Prompt that appears before the search field.

<KEYGEN> [NS3]

Generates public/private key pair. Must be used within the <FORM> tag. The following table describes the attributes for this tag.

Attribute	Description
NAME=*name*	Specifies a name.
CHALLENGE=*string*	Specifies the challenge string to be packaged with the public key.

<KBD>...</KBD>

Formats text as if typed from the keyboard.

<LAYER>...</LAYER> [NS4]

Creates a document layer. Use style sheets as a more universal method of creating layers. The following table describes the attributes for this tag.

Attribute	Description
LEFT=*number*	Position of the layer from the left side of the screen.
TOP=*number*	Position of the layer from the top of the screen.

<LI>

A list item contained in an ordered, unordered, menu, or directory list. The following table describes the attributes for this tag.

Attribute	Description
TYPE=A¦a¦I¦i¦1	The numbering style to use with the list item in an ordered list.
VALUE=*number*	The number that appears before this list item in an ordered list.

<LINK>

Defines the relationship between the current document and other documents such as style sheets. The following table describes the attributes for this tag.

Attribute	Description
HREF=*URL*	Provides the Internet address of the linked document.
REL=*link type*	Provides the forward link type.

continues

D

Attribute	Description
REV=*reverse relationship*	Indicates the reverse link.
TITLE=*title*	Provides an advisory title.
TYPE=*type*	Specifies the media type for a linked style sheet.

Here's an example:

```
<LINK TITLE="MyStyleSheet" REL=stylesheet HREF="/style.css" TYPE="text/css">
```

<LISTING>...</LISTING> [obsolete]

Creates preformatted text.

<MAP>...</MAP>

Specifies a client-side image map. Used with the <AREA> tag. The following table describes the attribute for this tag.

Attribute	Description
NAME=*name*	Provides a name for the image map. This name is case-sensitive.

<MARQUEE>...</MARQUEE>[IE3]

Creates a scrolling marquee. The following table describes the attributes for this tag.

Attribute	Description
ALIGN=left¦center¦right¦top¦bottom	Aligns the marquee with the text.
BEHAVIOR=scroll¦slide¦alternate	Determines how the text behaves within the marquee.
BGCOLOR=*color*	Specifies the background color for the marquee.
DIRECTION=left¦right	Indicates which direction to scroll. The default is from left to right.
HEIGHT=*absolute¦relative number*	Specifies the height of the marquee in either absolute number of pixels or percentage of screen.
HSPACE=*number*	Specifies space on the left and right of the marquee in pixels.

Attribute	*Description*
LOOP=*number*¦INFINITE	Specifies how many times the marquee will loop. If INFINITE, it never stops.
SCROLLAMOUNT=*number*	Specifies how far the text jumps across the marquee when scrolling.
SCROLLDELAY=*number*	Specifies how fast the text in the marquee should scroll in milliseconds.
VSPACE=*number*	Indicates the space above and below the marquee in pixels.
WIDTH=*absolute*¦*relative number*	The width of the marquee as either an absolute number of pixels or a percentage of the screen.

\<MENU>...\</MENU>

Formats text as a menu list.

\<META>

Provides meta-information about a document, such as the document author's name, the document expiration date for caches, and descriptions and keywords for search engines. Can also be used to perform client-pull.

```
NAME="value"
CONTENT="value"
HTTP-EQUIV="value"
```

Following are some examples.

Document author name:

```
<META NAME="author" CONTENT="creator of web site">
```

Document expiration:

```
<META HTTP-EQUIV="Expires" CONTENT="Wed, 01 Jan 2000 00:00:00 GMT">
```

Description for search engines:

```
<META NAME="DESCRIPTION" CONTENT="trading card web site">
```

Keywords for search engines:

```
<META NAME="KEYWORDS" CONTENT="trading cards, cards, buy">
```

Client-pull reloads page after five seconds:

```
<META HTTP-EQUIV="REFRESH" CONTENT="5;http://website/newpage.htm">
```

<MULTICOL>...</MULTICOL> [NS3]

Creates multiple-text columns (like newspaper columns). The following table describes the attributes for this tag.

Attribute	Description
COLS=*number*	Specifies the number of text columns to display.
GUTTER=*number*	Specifies the space between columns in pixels.
WIDTH=*number*	Specifies the width of each column in pixels.

<NOBR>...</NOBR>

Prevents text from wrapping to a new line. Also see <WBR>.

<NOEMBED>...</NOEMBED> [NS3]

Used to display text to browsers that can't interpret embedded objects.

<NOFRAMES>...</NOFRAMES> [IE3,NS3]

Displays content for non-frames-compliant browsers.

<NOLAYER>...</NOLAYER> [NS4]

Displays content for non-layer-compliant browsers.

<NOSCRIPT>...</NOSCRIPT> [NS3]

Displays alternative text for browsers that can't use a script.

<OBJECT>...</OBJECT> [IE3]

Specifies an object. The following table describes the attributes for this tag.

Attribute	Description
ALIGN=*setting*	Indicates alignment for the object. Settings are left, texttop, middle, textmiddle, baseline, textbottom, center, and right.
BORDER=*number*	If the object is a hyperlink, specifies the border size.
CLASSID=*URL*	Identifies the implementation of the object.

Attribute	Description
CODEBASE=*URL*	Specifies the code base for the object.
CODETYPE=*type*	Specifies the media type for the object.
DATA=*URL*	Identifies the data for the object.
DECLARE	Declares the object without instantiating it.
HEIGHT=*number*	Indicates the height of the object in pixels.
HSPACE=*number*	Specifies the amount of space to the left and right of the object in pixels.
NAME=*URL*	Creates a name for the object when submitted as part of a form.
NOTAB	Prevents tabbing into the object when tabbing through the document.
PROGID=*progid*	Specifies the identifier associated with a class identifier.
RUNAT=*server*	Specifies the server object [ASP].
SCOPE=application¦session	Specifies whether the object will be available at the session or application level [ASP].
SHAPES	Specifies that the object has a shaped hyperlink.
STANDBY=*message*	Displays a standby message while object is loading.
TABINDEX=*number*	Specifies the location of the object in the document tabbing order.
TYPE=*type*	Indicates the Internet media type of the object.
USEMAP=*URL*	Specifies the image map associated with the object.
VSPACE=*number*	Specifies the amount of space above and below the object in pixels.
WIDTH=*number*	Indicates the suggested width of the object in pixels.

Here's an example:

```
[ASP]
<OBJECT ID="myconnection" RUNAT="server" SCOPE="session">
PROGID="ADODB.Connection"
</OBJECT>
```

<OL>...</OL>

Creates an ordered list with numbered list items. The following table describes the attributes for this tag.

Attribute	Description
COMPACT	Formats the list items with less spacing.
START=*number*	Specifies the number of the first list item.
TYPE=1¦a¦A¦i¦I	Specifies the type of numerals.
<OPTION>	Specifies an item for a drop-down or scrolling list box. See the <SELECT> tag.
SELECTED	Specifies that this item is selected by default in the list box.
VALUE=*value*	Indicates the value for this item when the form is submitted.

<P>...</P>

Creates a paragraph. The end tag is not required. The following table describes the attribute for this tag.

Attribute	Description
ALIGN=LEFT¦CENTER¦RIGHT	Aligns the contents of the paragraph.

<PARAM>

Used with objects and Java applets to pass parameters. The following table describes the attributes for this tag.

Attribute	Description
NAME=*name*	Specifies a name for the parameter.
TYPE=*type*	Indicates the Internet media type [IE3].
VALUE=*value*	Specifies a value for the parameter.
VALUETYPE=data¦ref¦object	Specifies how the value should be interpreted [IE3].

<PLAINTEXT>...</PLAINTEXT> [obsolete]

Displays text without interpreting HTML.

<PRE>...</PRE>

Creates preformatted text with a monospaced font and preserves spacing. The following table describes the attribute for this tag.

Attribute	Description
WIDTH	Specifies the width of the preformatted text.

<S>...</S>

Formats text as strikethrough.

<SAMP>...</SAMP>

Formats text as sample program output.

<SCRIPT>...</SCRIPT>

Contains a client or server-side script. The following table describes the attributes for this tag.

Attribute	Description
EVENT=*string*	Indicates the event for which the script is being written.
FOR=*string*	Specifies an object to which the script is bound.
LANGUAGE=VBScript¦JScript¦JavaScript	The default browser language is JavaScript (use JavaScript instead of JScript when executing a client-side JScript program). The default ASP language is VBScript.
RUNAT=*server*	Specifies that a script should be executed on the server rather than the client. A very important attribute for Active Server Pages [ASP].
SRC=*filename*	An external source for the script.

<SELECT>...</SELECT>

Creates a drop-down or scrolling list box with a selection of options. Contains <OPTION> tags; see the <OPTION> section. Must appear in a form. The following table describes the attributes for this tag.

D

QUICK HTML
REFERENCE

Attribute	Description
SIZE=*number*	The number of options to display. By default, results in a drop-down list box. A number greater than 1 results in a scrolling list box.
MULTIPLE	If this attribute is present, more than one option can be selected at a time.
NAME=*name*	The name of the drop-down or scrolling list box.

<SERVER>...</SERVER> [NS]

Runs a server-side script (LiveWire script).

<SMALL>...</SMALL>

Formats text in small font.

<SPACER>

Creates a spacing rectangle to allow you to control document spacing [NS3]. The following table describes the attributes for this tag.

Attribute	Description
ALIGN=*setting*	Applies only when the spacer is a block spacer. Settings are left, right, top, absmiddle, absbottom, texttop, middle, baseline, and bottom.
HEIGHT=*number*	Applies only when the spacer is a block spacer, and indicates block height in pixels.
SIZE=*number*	When the spacer is a block spacer, indicates the absolute width and height of the spacer block. When the spacer is horizontal or vertical, indicates the extra spaces between words.
TYPE=horizontal¦vertical¦block	Specifies the type of spacer. When the spacer is horizontal, extra space is added between words. When the spacer is vertical, extra space is added between text lines. When the spacer is a block, creates a block of space.
WIDTH=*number*	Width of the spacer when the spacer is a block.

<SPAN>...</SPAN>

Used with style sheets to indicate the span of a style.

<STRIKE>...</STRIKE>

Formats text as strikethrough.

<STRONG>...</STRONG>

Emphasizes text by formatting it as bold.

<STYLE>...</STYLE>

Contains style sheet (see the section "Cascading Style Sheets"). Must be located in the document head.

<SUB>...</SUB>

Formats text as subscript.

<SUP>...</SUP>

Formats text as superscript.

<TABLE>...</TABLE>

Creates a table that can be used to display a table of data or to control the layout of your Web page. The following table describes the attributes for this tag.

Attribute	*Description*
ALIGN=LEFT¦CENTER¦RIGHT	By default, tables are aligned left.
BACKGROUND=*URL*	Specifies the background image to use with the table [NS4,IE3].
BGCOLOR=*color*	Indicates the color to use as the background color.
BORDER=*number*	The size of the table borders measured in pixels.
BORDERCOLOR=*color*	Specifies the border color [IE3].
BORDERCOLORDARK=*color*	Specifies the color for the dark color in a three-dimensional border [IE3].
BORDERCOLORLIGHT=*color*	Specifies the color for the light color in a three-dimensional border [IE3].
CELLSPACING=*number*	The amount of space to place between table cells, measured in pixels.

continues

Attribute	*Description*
CELLPADDING=*number*	The amount of space to place within a cell, measured in pixels.
COLS=*number*	Indicates the number of columns in a table. Can speed up processing on large tables [IE3, NS4].
FRAME=*frame-type*	Determines which outer table borders will appear. The frame type has the following values [IE3]:

	BORDER	Displays a border on all sides of the table frame. This is the default.
	VOID	Removes all outside table borders.
	ABOVE	Displays a border on the top side of the table frame.
	BELOW	Displays a border on the bottom side of the table frame.
	HSIDES	Displays a border on the top and bottom sides of the table frame.
	LHS	Displays a border on the left-hand side of the table frame.
	RHS	Displays a border on the right-hand side of the table frame.
	VSIDES	Displays a border on the left and right sides of the table frame.
	BOX	Displays a border on all sides of the table frame.

HSPACE=*number*	Specifies the horizontal width in which the table must fit [NS].
RULES=*rule-type*	Determines which inner table borders will appear [IE3]. *rule-type* has the following values:

	NONE	Removes all interior table borders. This is the default.
	GROUPS	Displays horizontal borders between all table groups. Groups are specified by the THEAD, TBODY, TFOOT, and COLGROUP elements.
	ROWS	Displays horizontal borders between all table rows.

Attribute		Description
	COLS	Displays vertical borders between all table columns.
	ALL	Displays a border on all rows and columns.
VSPACE=*number*		Specifies the vertical width in which the table must fit [NS].
WIDTH=*absolute¦ relative number*		Specifies the width of the table either as pixels or as a percentage of the screen.

<TBODY>...</TBODY> [IE3]

Divides the table body into different sections.

<TD>...</TD>

Indicates table data in a table. Use within a <TABLE> tag. The following table describes the attributes for this tag.

Attribute	Description
ALIGN=left¦center¦right	Alignment of the contents of the table cell.
BACKGROUND=*URL*	Specifies a background picture to appear in the table cell [NS4, IE4].
BGCOLOR=*color*	Specifies a background color for a table cell.
BORDERCOLOR=*color*	Specifies the border color for the table cell [IE3].
BORDERCOLORDARK=*color*	Specifies the dark color for the three-dimensional border [IE3].
BORDERCOLORLIGHT=*color*	Specifies the light color for the three-dimensional border [IE3].
COLSPAN=*number*	Number of columns for the table cell to span.
HEIGHT=*number*	Specifies the height of the table cell in pixels.
NOWRAP	Stops the table columns from wrapping if they extend past the end of the page.
ROWSPAN=*number*	Number of rows for the table cell to span.
VALIGN=middle¦top¦bottom¦baseline	Specifies the vertical alignment of cell contents.
WIDTH=*number*	Indicates the width of a table cell.

<TEXTAREA>...</TEXTAREA>

Creates an input box that can accept multiple lines of text. Place default text between the start and end tags. A text area must appear within a form. The following table describes the attributes for this tag.

Attribute	Description
COLS=*number*	The width of the text area in characters.
NAME=*name*	The name of the text area.
ROWS=*number*	The vertical height of the text area in characters.
WRAP=virtual¦physical¦off	Determines how word wrap functions in the text area. Netscape also uses the keywords soft and hard instead of virtual and physical [IE3, NS].

<TFOOT>...</TFOOT> [IE3]

Used to specify the rows that should be used as a table footer. The following table describes the attributes for this tag.

Attribute	Description
ALIGN=left¦center¦right	Specifies the horizontal alignment.
BGCOLOR=*color*	Determines the background color.
VALIGN=baseline¦bottom¦center¦top	Specifies the vertical alignment.

<TH>...</TH>

Creates a heading in a table. Has the same attributes as the <TD> tag.

<THEAD>...</THEAD>

Specifies the rows in the header of a table. The following table describes the attributes for this tag.

Attribute	Description
ALIGN=center¦left¦right	Specifies the horizontal alignment.
BGCOLOR=*color*	Determines the background color.
VALIGN=baseline¦bottom¦center¦top	Specifies the vertical alignment.

<TITLE>...</TITLE>

Provides a title for the document in the browser title bar and for bookmarks.

<TR>...</TR>

Designates a table row. Used with the <TABLE> tag. The following table describes the attributes for this tag.

Attribute	*Description*
ALIGN=center¦left¦right	Specifies alignment for the text in the row.
BGCOLOR=*color*	Indicates the background color for the row.
BORDERCOLORDARK=*color*	Specifies the color for the dark color of a three-dimensional border [IE3].
BORDERCOLORLIGHT=*color*	Specifies the color for the light color of a three-dimensional border [IE3].
NOWRAP	Stops table rows from wrapping to a new line if they extend longer than the page.
VALIGN=top¦middle¦bottom¦baseline	Specifies the vertical alignment of cell contents in rows.

<TT>...</TT>

Formats text as teletype or monospaced.

<U>...</U>

Formats text as underlined.

<UL>...</UL>

Creates an unordered list with bulleted list items. The following table describes the attributes for this tag.

Attribute	*Description*
TYPE=disc¦square¦circle	Specifies the shape of the bullet. Doesn't work with IE3.
COMPACT	Formats the list items with less spacing.

<VAR>...</VAR>

Formats text as variable.

<WBR>

Used with <NOBR> to specify the location of a possible line break.

<XMP>...</XMP> [obsolete]

Creates a sequence of literal characters.

Cascading Style Sheets

This section provides a quick reference for the Cascading Style Sheets (level 1) specification. This reference is not comprehensive, but covers the properties and values that are the most useful in everyday life. For more information, see http://w3.org.

The property and value descriptions in the following subsections use the following notational convention. When multiple values are separated by a single bar (¦), that means that only one of the values can be used at a time. When multiple values are separated by a double bar (¦¦), that means that more than one of the values can be used at the same time.

Many of the following properties accept a *length* value. This value may be specified by using inches (in), points (pt), pixels (px), centimeters (cm), picas (pc), millimeters (mm), or ems (em). When specifying the unit, use the unit's abbreviation.

Many of the following properties also accept a *percentage* value. To specify a percentage value, simply supply a value such as 12% or 87%.

Font Properties

{font-family: *family-name*¦¦*generic-family* }

This property selects a particular typeface or generic family of typefaces. For example, *family-name* can have the value "Arial" or "Comic Sans MS".

Instead of specifying a particular typeface, you can select a generic family of typefaces. *generic-family* can have the value serif, sans-serif, cursive, fantasy, or monospace.

You can list multiple alternative typefaces by separating each value with a comma. Providing alternative typefaces is useful because not all computers have all typefaces installed.

{font-style: normal¦italic¦oblique }

This property allows you to select an italic or oblique font.

{font-variant: normal¦small-caps }

This property selects a font that appears in small caps.

{font-weight: normal¦bold¦bolder¦lighter¦ 100¦200¦300¦400¦500¦600¦700¦800¦900 }

This property selects a font that appears with different degrees of boldness. The numbers allow for fine-grain control over the weight of the font.

{font-size: *absolute-size*¦*relative-size*¦ *length*¦*percentage* }

This property selects the size of a font. The value *absolute-size* can be xx-small, x-small, small, medium, large, x-large, or xx-large. The value *relative-size* can be either larger or smaller.

The size also can be specified by using either a length or a percentage. For example, the size can be set as 14pt; or 200%.

{font: *font-style*¦¦*font-variant*¦¦*font-weight*¦¦ *font-size*¦¦/*line-height*¦¦*font-family* }

This property allows you to specify multiple font properties at once (in addition to line height). Notice the forward slash (/) before *line-height*. This character must appear when you specify the line height, like this:

```
P {font: italic small-caps  bold 14pt/20pt Arial }
```

Text Properties

{color: *color* }

This property selects the color of text. The value *color* can be any of the standard 16 colors from the later section "HTML Colors." You also can supply an RGB color value for *color*, like this:

```
P {color: rgb(12,12,12) }
```

{word-spacing: normal¦*length* }

This property selects the amount of blank space that appears between words. See the beginning of this section for allowable units for *length*.

{letter-spacing: normal¦*length* }

This property selects the amount of blank space that appears between letters. See the beginning of this section for allowable units for *length*.

`{text_decoration: none¦[underline¦¦overline¦¦`
`line-through¦¦blink] }`

This property selects different ways that text can appear, such as blinking or strikethrough.

`{vertical-align: baseline¦sub¦super¦top¦`
`text-top¦middle¦bottom¦text-bottom¦`*`percentage`* `}`

This property selects the alignment of text relative to the baseline. For example, sub aligns the text below the baseline as subscript.

`{text-transform: capitalize¦uppercase¦lowercase¦none }`

This property converts the selected text to the value specified. For example, capitalize capitalizes the first letter in each word selected.

`{text-align: left¦right¦center¦justify}`

This property aligns text.

`{text-indent: `*`length`*`¦`*`percentage`* `}`

This property indents a line of text by the specified amount. See the beginning of this section for possible units of *length*.

`{line-height: normal¦`*`length`*`¦`*`percentage`* `}`

This property specifies the distance between baselines of lines of text. See the beginning of this section for possible units of *length*.

Margin Properties

`{margin-top: `*`length`*`¦`*`percentage`*`¦auto }`

This property specifies the top margin. See the beginning of this section for possible units of *length*. The value auto indicates that the browser will automatically calculate the margin.

`{margin-right: `*`length`*`¦`*`percentage`*`¦auto }`

This property specifies the right margin. See the beginning of this section for possible units of *length*. The value auto indicates that the browser will automatically calculate the margin.

`{margin-bottom: `*`length`*`¦`*`percentage`*`¦auto }`

This property specifies the bottom margin. See the beginning of this section for possible units of *length*. The value auto indicates that the browser will automatically calculate the margin.

{margin-left: *length*¦*percentage*¦auto }

This property specifies the left margin. See the beginning of this section for possible units of *length*. The value auto indicates that the browser will automatically calculate the margin.

{margin: *length*¦*percentage*¦auto }

This property specifies all the margins. If only one value is supplied, it's applied to all four margins. If four values are supplied, they're applied to the top, right, bottom, and left margins, in that order. If two or three values are supplied, the missing values are taken from the opposite side. The value auto indicates that the browser will automatically calculate the margins.

Border Properties

{border-color: *color* }

This property selects the color of a border. The value *color* can be any of the standard 16 colors from the later section "HTML Colors." You can also supply an RGB color value for *color*, like this:

```
P {border-color: rgb(12,12,12) }
```

If one value is supplied, the value is applied to all four borders. If four values are supplied, they're applied to the top, right, bottom, and left borders. If two values are supplied, the first value specifies the color of the top and bottom borders and the second value specifies the color of the left and right borders. Finally, if three values are supplied, the first value specifies the color of the top border, the second specifies the left and right borders, and the third specifies the bottom border.

{border-style: none¦dotted¦dashed¦solid¦double¦ groove¦ridge¦inset¦outset }

This property selects a border style. See Chapter 7, "Advanced HTML," for examples of how these different border styles appear.

{border-top-width: thin¦medium¦thick¦*length* }

This property selects the width of the top border.

{border-right-width: thin¦medium¦thick¦*length* }

This property selects the width of the right border.

{border-bottom-width: thin¦medium¦thick¦*length* }

This property selects the width of the bottom border.

{border-left-width: thin¦medium¦thick¦*length* }

This property selects the width of the left border.

{border-width: thin¦medium¦thick¦*length* }

This property specifies the width of all four borders. If one value is supplied, the value is applied to all four borders. If four values are supplied, they're applied to the top, right, bottom, and left borders. If two values are supplied, the first value specifies the color of the top and bottom borders and the second value specifies the color of the left and right borders. Finally, if three values are supplied, the first value specifies the color of the top border, the second specifies the left and right borders, and the third specifies the bottom border.

{border-top: *border-top-width*¦¦*border-style*¦¦*color* }

This property specifies the appearance of the top border. It combines the effects of the `border-top-width`, `border-style`, and `border-color` properties.

{border-right: *border-right-width*¦¦*border-style*¦¦*color* }

This property specifies the appearance of the right border. It combines the effects of the `border-right-width`, `border-style`, and `border-color` properties.

{border-left: *border-left-width*¦¦*border-style*¦¦*color* }

This property specifies the appearance of the left border. It combines the effects of the `border-left-width`, `border-style`, and `border-color` properties.

{border: *border-width*¦¦*border-style*¦¦*color* }

This property specifies the appearance of all four borders. It combines the effects of the previous border properties.

Background Properties

{background-color: *color*¦transparent }

Sets the background color of a screen element. The value is a color specified by keyword (see the table of the 16 standard HTML colors in the later section "HTML Colors") or by RGB value like this:

```
P {background-color: rgb(255,255,255) }
```

{background-image: *url*¦none }

Sets the background image of a screen element. *url* provides the path to an image, like this:

```
BODY {background-image: url("myimage.gif") }
```

{background-repeat: repeat¦repeat-x¦repeat-y¦no-repeat }

Specifies how a background image will be tiled. For example, repeat-x tiles the image horizontally.

{background-attachment: scroll¦fixed }

This property specifies whether a background image will scroll or remain fixed.

{background-position: [percentage¦length]¦ [top¦center¦bottom]¦¦[left¦center¦right] }

This property specifies the initial position of a background image. The following two examples both situate the image in the center of the screen:

```
BODY {background-position: 50% 50% }

BODY {background-position: center }
```

{background: background-color¦¦ background-image¦¦background-repeat¦¦ background-attachment¦¦background-position }

This property combines the effects of the background properties previously described.

HTML Colors

Most browsers should recognize the 16 standard keywords presented in the following sections. Both the Microsoft and Netscape browsers recognize many more color keywords (the Microsoft color keywords are presented in the next section). To be safe, you can use RGB values instead of color keywords. The RGB values are compatible with more browsers.

Standard Colors and RGB Values

Color	RGB Value
Black	000000
Green	008000
Silver	C0C0C0
Lime	00FF00
Gray	808080
Olive	808000
White	FFFFFF
Yellow	FFFF00

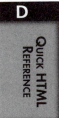

D

QUICK HTML REFERENCE

continues

Color	RGB Value
Maroon	800000
Navy	000080
Red	FF0000
Blue	0000FF
Purple	800080
Teal	008080
Fuchsia	FF00FF
Aqua	00FFFF

Microsoft Colors and RGB Values

Color	RGB Value
ALICEBLUE	F0F8FF
ANTIQUEWHITE	FAEBD7
AQUA	00FFFF
AQUAMARINE	7FFFD4
AZURE	F0FFFF
BEIGE	F5F5DC
BISQUE	FFE4C4
BLACK	000000
BLANCHEDALMOND	FFEBCD
BLUE	0000FF
BLUEVIOLET	8A2BE2
BROWN	A52A2A
BURLYWOOD	DEB887
CADETBLUE	5F9EA0
CHARTREUSE	7FFF00
CHOCOLATE	D2691E
CORAL	FF7F50
CORNFLOWERBLUE	6495ED
CORNSILK	FFF8DC
CRIMSON	DC143C

Color	*RGB Value*
CYAN	00FFFF
DARKBLUE	00008B
DARKCYAN	008B8B
DARKGOLDENROD	B8860B
DARKGRAY	A9A9A9
DARKGREEN	006400
DARKKHAKI	BDB76B
DARKMAGENTA	8B008B
DARKOLIVEGREEN	556B2F
DARKORANGE	FF8C00
DARKORCHID	9932CC
DARKRED	8B0000
DARKSALMON	E9967A
DARKSEAGREEN	8FBC8F
DARKSLATEBLUE	483D8B
DARKSLATEGRAY	2F4F4F
DARKTURQUOISE	00CED1
DARKVIOLET	9400D3
DEEPPINK	FF1493
DEEPSKYBLUE	00BFFF
DIMGRAY	696969
DODGERBLUE	1E90FF
FIREBRICK	B22222
FLORALWHITE	FFFAF0
FORESTGREEN	228B22
FUCHSIA	FF00FF
GAINSBORO	DCDCDC
GHOSTWHITE	F8F8FF
GOLD	FFD700
GOLDENROD	DAA520
GRAY	808080
GREEN	008000

D

QUICK HTML
REFERENCE

continues

Color	*RGB Value*
GREENYELLOW	ADFF2F
HONEYDEW	F0FFF0
HOTPINK	FF69B4
INDIANRED	CD5C5C
INDIGO	4B0082
IVORY	FFFFF0
KHAKI	F0E68C
LAVENDER	E6E6FA
LAVENDERBLUSH	FFF0F5
LAWNGREEN	7CFC00
LEMONCHIFFON	FFFACD
LIGHTBLUE	ADD8E6
LIGHTCORAL	F08080
LIGHTCYAN	E0FFFF
LIME	00FF00
MAROON	800000
NAVY	000080
OLIVE	808000
PURPLE	800080
RED	FF0000
SILVER	C0C0C0
TEAL	008080
WHITE	FFFFFF
YELLOW	FFFF00

HTML Character Codes

ISO-Latin-1 Character Set

Character	Numeric Entity	Hex Value	Character Entity (if any)	Description
	&#00;–&#08;	00–08		Unused
	&#09;	09		Horizontal tab
	&#10;	0A		Line feed
	&#11;–&#31;	0B–1F		Unused
	&#32;	20		Space
!	&#33;	21		Exclamation mark
"	&#34;	22	&quot;	Quotation mark
#	&#35;	23		Number sign
$	&#36;	24		Dollar sign
%	&#37;	25		Percent sign
&	&#38;	26	&amp;	Ampersand
'	&#39;	27		Apostrophe
(	&#40;	28		Left parenthesis
)	&#41;	29		Right parenthesis
*	&#42;	2A		Asterisk
+	&#43;	2B		Plus sign
,	&#44;	2C		Comma
-	&#45;	2D		Hyphen
.	&#46;	2E		Period (fullstop)
/	&#47;	2F		Solidus (slash)
0–9	0–9	30-39		Digits 0–9
:	&#58;	3A		Colon
;	&#59;	3B		Semicolon
<	&#60;	3C	&lt;	Less than
=	&#61;	3D		Equal sign
>	&#62;	3E	&gt;	Greater than
?	&#63;	3F		Question mark
@	&#64;	40		Commercial at

D

QUICK HTML
REFERENCE

continues

Character	Numeric Entity	Hex Value	Character Entity (if any)	Description
A–Z	A–Z	41–5A		Letters A–Z
[	&#91;	5B		Left square bracket
\	&#92;	5C		Reverse solidus (backslash)
]	&#93;	5D		Right square bracket
^	&#94;	5E		Caret
—	&#95;	5F		Horizontal bar
`	&#96;	60		Grave accent
a–z	a–z	61–7A		Letters a–z
{	&#123;	7B		Left curly brace
|	|	7C		Vertical bar
}	&#125;	7D		Right curly brace
~	&#126;	7E		Tilde
	&#127;–	7F–A0		Unused
¡	&#161;	A1		Inverted exclamation point
¢	&#162;	A2		Cent sign
£	&#163;	A3		Pound sterling
¤	&#164;	A4		General currency sign
¥	&#165;	A5		Yen sign
¦	&#166;	A6		Broken vertical bar
§	&#167;	A7		Section sign
¨	&#168;	A8		Umlaut (dieresis)
©	&#169;	A9	© (NHTML)	Copyright
ª	&#170;	AA		Feminine ordinal
‹	&#171;	AB		Left angle quotation, guillemot left

Character	Numeric Entity	Hex Value	Character Entity (if any)	Description
¬	&#172;	AC		Not sign
-	&#173;	AD		Soft hyphen
®	&#174;	AE	® (HHTM)	Registered trademark
¯	&#175;	AF		Macron accent
°	&#176;	B0		Degree sign
±	&#177;	B1		Plus or minus
²	&#178;	B2		Superscript two
³	&#179;	B3		Superscript three
´	&#180;	B4		Acute accent
µ	&#181;	B5		Micro sign
¶	&#182;	B6		Paragraph sign
·	&#183;	B7		Middle dot
¸	&#184;	B8		Cedilla
¹	&#185;	B9		Superscript one
º	&#186;	BA		Masculine ordinal
»	&#187;	BB		Right angle quotation, guillemot right
¼	&#188;	BC		Fraction one-fourth
½	&#189;	BD		Fraction one-half
¾	&#190;	BE		Fraction three-fourths
¿	&#191;	BF		Inverted question mark
À	&#192;	C0	&Agrave;	Capital A, grave accent
Á	&#193;	C1	&Aacute;	Capital A, acute accent
Â	&#194;	C2	&Acirc;	Capital A, circumflex accent

continues

Character	Numeric Entity	Hex Value	Character Entity (if any)	Description
Ã	&#195;	C3	&Atilde;	Capital A, tilde
Ä	&#196;	C4	&Auml;	Capital A, dieresis or umlaut mark
Å	&#197;	C5	&Aring;	Capital A, ring
Æ	&#198;	C6	&AElig;	Capital AE dipthong (ligature)
Ç	&#199;	C7	&Ccedil;	Capital C, cedilla
È	&#200;	C8	&Egrave;	Capital E, grave accent
É	&#201;	C9	&Eacute;	Capital E, acute accent
Ê	&#202;	CA	&Ecirc;	Capital E, circumflex accent
Ë	&#203;	CB	&Euml;	Capital E, dieresis or umlaut mark
Ì	&#204;	CC	&Igrave;	Capital I, grave accent
Í	&#205;	CD	&Iacute;	Capital I, acute accent
Î	&#206;	CE	&Icirc;	Capital I, circumflex accent
Ï	&#207;	CF	&Iuml;	Capital I, dieresis or umlaut mark
Ð	&#208;	D0	&ETH;	Capital Eth, Icelandic
Ñ	&#209;	D1	&Ntilde;	Capital N, tilde
Ò	&#210;	D2	&Ograve;	Capital O, grave accent
Ó	&#211;	D3	&Oacute;	Capital O, acute accent
Ô	&#212;	D4	&Ocirc;	Capital O, circumflex accent
Õ	&#213;	D5	&Otilde;	Capital O, tilde

Character	Numeric Entity	Hex Value	Character Entity (if any)	Description
Ö	&#214;	D6	&Ouml;	Capital O, dieresis, or umlaut mark
×	&#215;	D7		Multiply sign
Ø	&#216;	D8	&Oslash;	Capital O, slash
Ù	&#217;	D9	&Ugrave;	Capital U, grave accent
Ú	&#218;	DA	&Uacute;	Capital U, acute accent
Û	&#219;	DB	&Ucirc;	Capital U, circumflex accent
Ü	&#220;	DC	&Uuml;	Capital U, dieresis or umlaut mark
Ý	&#221;	DD	&Yacute;	Capital Y, acute accent
Þ	&#222;	DE	&THORN;	Capital THORN, Icelandic
β	&#223;	DF	&szlig;	Small sharp s, German (sz ligature)
à	&#224;	E0	&agrave;	Small a, grave accent
á	&#225;	E1	&aacute;	Small a, acute accent
â	&#226;	E2	&acirc;	Small a, circumflex accent
ã	&#227;	E3	&atilde;	Small a, tilde
ä	&#228;	E4	&aauml;	Small a, dieresis or umlaut mark
å	&#229;	E5	&aring;	Small a, ring
æ	&#230;	E6	&aelig;	Small ae dipthong (ligature)
ç	&#231;	E7	&ccedil;	Small c, cedilla

continues

D

QUICK HTML
REFERENCE

Character	Numeric Entity	Hex Value	Character Entity (if any)	Description
è	&#232;	E8	&egrave;	Small e, grave accent
é	&#233;	E9	&eacute;	Small e, acute accent
ê	&#234;	EA	&ecirc;	Small e, circumflex accent
ë	&#235;	EB	&euml;	Small e, dieresis or umlaut mark
ì	&#236;	EC	&igrave;	Small i, grave accent
í	&#237;	ED	&iacute;	Small i, acute accent
î	&#238;	EE	&icirc;	Small i, circumflex accent
ï	&#239;	EF	&iuml;	Small i, dieresis or umlaut mark
ð	&#240;	F0	&eth;	Small eth, Icelandic
ñ	&#241;	F1	&ntilde;	Small n, tilde
ò	&#242;	F2	&ograve;	Small o, grave accent
ó	&#243;	F3	&oacute;	Small o, acute accent
ô	&#244;	F4	&ocirc;	Small o, circumflex accent
õ	&#245;	F5	&otilde;	Small o, tilde
ö	&#246;	F6	&ouml;	Small o, dieresis or umlaut mark
÷	&#247;	F7		Division sign
ø	&#248;	F8	&oslash;	Small o, slash
ù	&#249;	F9	&ugrave;	Small u, grave accent

Character	Numeric Entity	Hex Value	Character Entity (if any)	Description
ú	ú	FA	ú	Small u, acute accent
û	û	FB	û	Small u, circumflex accent
ü	ü	FC	ü	Small u, dieresis or umlaut mark
ý	ý	FD	ý	Small y, acute accent
þ	þ	FE	þ	Small thorn, Icelandic
ÿ	ÿ	FF	ÿ	Small y, dieresis or umlaut mark

INDEX

I

X-Y-Z

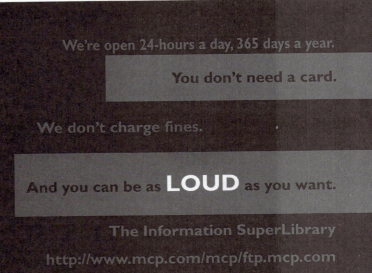

MACMILLAN COMPUTER PUBLISHING USA

A VIACOM COMPANY

Technical ---- Support:

If you need assistance with the information in this book or with a CD/Disk accompanying the book, please access the Knowledge Base on our Web site at **http://www.superlibrary.com/general/support**. Our most Frequently Asked Questions are answered there. If you do not find the answer to your questions on our Web site, you may contact Macmillan Technical Support **(317) 581-3833** or e-mail us at **support@mcp.com**.

What's on the Disc

The companion CD-ROM contains the authors' source code and samples from the book and many third-party software products.

Windows 95 Installation Instructions

1. Insert the CD-ROM disc into your CD-ROM drive.
2. From the Windows 95 desktop, double-click the My Computer icon.
3. Double-click the icon representing your CD-ROM drive.
4. Double-click the icon titled SETUP.EXE to run the installation program.
5. Installation creates a program group named Active Server Pages Unleashed. This group contains icons to browse the CD-ROM.

> **NOTE**
>
> If Windows 95 is installed on your computer and you have the AutoPlay feature enabled, the SETUP.EXE program starts automatically whenever you insert the disc into your CD-ROM drive.

By opening this package, you are agreeing to be bound by the following agreement:

Visual Basic Control Creation Edition was reproduced by Sams Publishing under a special arrangement with Microsoft Corporation. For this reason, Sams Publishing is responsible for the product warranty and for support. If your disk is defective, please return it to Sams Publishing, which will arrange for its replacement. PLEASE DO NOT RETURN IT TO MICROSOFT CORPORATION. Any product support will be provided, if at all, by Sams Publishing. PLEASE DO NOT CONTACT MICROSOFT CORPORATION FOR PRODUCT SUPPORT. End users of this Microsoft program shall not be considered "registered owners" of a Microsoft product and therefore shall not be eligible for upgrades, promotions, or other benefits available to "registered owners" of Microsoft products.

You may not copy or redistribute the entire CD-ROM as a whole. Copying and redistribution of individual software programs on the CD-ROM are governed by terms set by individual copyright holders. The installer and code from the author are copyrighted by the publisher and the author. Individual programs and other items on the CD-ROM are copyrighted by their various authors or other copyright holders. This software is sold as is without warranty of any kind, either expressed or implied, including but not limited to the implied warranties of merchantability and fitness for a particular purpose. Neither the publisher nor its dealers or distributors assumes any liability for any alleged or actual damages arising from the use of this program. (Some states do not allow for the exclusion of implied warranties, so the exclusion may not apply to you.)

NOTE: This CD-ROM uses long and mixed-case filenames, requiring the use of a protected-mode CD-ROM driver.

Installing the CD-ROM

This CD-ROM contains the Microsoft® Visual Basic® Control Creation Edition. Some of the features of Visual Basic 5 discussed in this book may not be possible with the use of the Control Creation Edition. The Control Creation Edition is provided to allow you to get familiar with the Visual Basic Environment and to create your own ActiveX controls.

The following are the minimum system requirements for the Visual Basic® Control Creation Edition:

- Personal computer with a 486 or higher processor
- Microsoft Windows® 95 or Windows NT® Workstation 4.0 or later
- 8MB of memory (12 recommended) if running Windows NT Workstation
- Hard disk space:
    - Typical installation: 20MB
    - Minimum installation: 14MB
    - CD-ROM installation (tools run from the CD): 14MB
    - Total tools and information on the CD: 50MB
- CD-ROM drive
- VGA or higher resolution monitor (SVGA recommended)

e. Support Services. Microsoft may provide you with support services related to the SOFTWARE PRODUCT ("Support Services"). Use of Support Services is governed by the Microsoft policies and programs described in the user manual, in "online" documentation, and/or in other Microsoft-provided materials. Any supplemental software code provided to you as part of the Support Services shall be considered part of the SOFTWARE PRODUCT and subject to the terms and conditions of this EULA. With respect to technical information you provide to Microsoft as part of the Support Services, Microsoft may use such information for its business purposes, including for product support and development. Microsoft will not utilize such technical information in a form that personally identifies you.

f. Software Transfer. You may permanently transfer all of your rights under this EULA, provided you retain no copies, you transfer all of the SOFTWARE PRODUCT (including all component parts, the media and printed materials, any upgrades, this EULA, and, if applicable, the Certificate of Authenticity), **and** the recipient agrees to the terms of this EULA. If the SOFTWARE PRODUCT is an upgrade, any transfer must include all prior versions of the SOFTWARE PRODUCT.

g. Termination. Without prejudice to any other rights, Microsoft may terminate this EULA if you fail to comply with the terms and conditions of this EULA. In such event, you must destroy all copies of the SOFTWARE PRODUCT and all of its component parts.

3. UPGRADES. If the SOFTWARE PRODUCT is labeled as an upgrade, you must be properly licensed to use a product identified by Microsoft as being eligible for the upgrade in order to use the SOFTWARE PRODUCT. A SOFTWARE PRODUCT labeled as an upgrade replaces and/or supplements the product that formed the basis for your eligibility for the upgrade. You may use the resulting upgraded product only in accordance with the terms of this EULA. If the SOFTWARE PRODUCT is an upgrade of a component of a package of software programs that you licensed as a single product, the SOFTWARE PRODUCT may be used and transferred only as part of that single product package and may not be separated for use on more than one computer.

4. COPYRIGHT. All title and copyrights in and to the SOFTWARE PRODUCT (including but not limited to any images, photographs, animations, video, audio, music, text, and "applets" incorporated into the SOFTWARE PRODUCT), the accompanying printed materials, and any copies of the SOFTWARE PRODUCT are owned by Microsoft or its suppliers. The SOFTWARE PRODUCT is protected by copyright laws and international treaty provisions. Therefore, you must treat the SOFTWARE PRODUCT like any other copyrighted material except that you may install the SOFTWARE PRODUCT on a single computer provided you keep the original solely for backup or archival purposes. You may not copy the printed materials accompanying the SOFTWARE PRODUCT.

5. DUAL-MEDIA SOFTWARE. You may receive the SOFTWARE PRODUCT in more than one medium. Regardless of the type or size of medium you receive, you may use only one medium that is appropriate for your single computer. You may not use or install the other medium on another computer. You may not loan, rent, lease, or otherwise transfer the other medium to another user, except as part of the permanent transfer (as provided above) of the SOFTWARE PRODUCT.

6. U.S. GOVERNMENT RESTRICTED RIGHTS. The SOFTWARE PRODUCT and documentation are provided with RESTRICTED RIGHTS. Use, duplication, or disclosure by the Government is subject to restrictions as set forth in subparagraph (c)(1)(ii) of the Rights in Technical Data and Computer Software clause at DFARS 252.227-7013 or subparagraphs (c)(1) and (2) of the Commercial Computer Software—Restricted Rights at 48 CFR 52.227-19, as applicable. Manufacturer is Microsoft Corporation/One Microsoft Way/Redmond, WA 98052-6399.

7. EXPORT RESTRICTIONS. You agree that neither you nor your customers intend to or will, directly or indirectly, export or transmit (i) the SOFTWARE or related documentation and technical data or (ii) your software product as described in Section 1(b) of this License (or any part thereof), or process, or service that is the direct product of the SOFTWARE, to any country to which such export or transmission is restricted by any applicable U.S. regulation or statute, without the prior written consent, if required, of the Bureau of Export Administration of the U.S. Department of Commerce, or such other governmental entity as may have jurisdiction over such export or transmission.

MISCELLANEOUS

If you acquired this product in the United States, this EULA is governed by the laws of the State of Washington.

If you acquired this product in Canada, this EULA is governed by the laws of the Province of Ontario, Canada. Each of the parties hereto irrevocably attorns to the jurisdiction of the courts of the Province of Ontario and further agrees to commence any litigation which may arise hereunder in the courts located in the Judicial District of York, Province of Ontario.

If this product was acquired outside the United States, then local law may apply.

Should you have any questions concerning this EULA, or if you desire to contact Microsoft for any reason, please contact the Microsoft subsidiary serving your country, or write: Microsoft Sales Information Center/One Microsoft Way/Redmond, WA 98052-6399.

LIMITED WARRANTY

NO WARRANTIES. Microsoft expressly disclaims any warranty for the SOFTWARE PRODUCT. The SOFTWARE PRODUCT and any related documentation is provided "as is" without warranty of any kind, either express or implied, including, without limitation, the implied warranties or merchantability, fitness for a particular purpose, or noninfringement. The entire risk arising out of use or performance of the SOFTWARE PRODUCT remains with you.

NO LIABILITY FOR DAMAGES. In no event shall Microsoft or its suppliers be liable for any damages whatsoever (including, without limitation, damages for loss of business profits, business interruption, loss of business information, or any other pecuniary loss) arising out of the use of or inability to use this Microsoft product, even if Microsoft has been advised of the possibility of such damages. Because some states/jurisdictions do not allow the exclusion or limitation of liability for consequential or incidental damages, the above limitation may not apply to you.

END-USER LICENSE AGREEMENT FOR MICROSOFT SOFTWARE
Microsoft Visual Basic, Control Creation Edition

IMPORTANT—READ CAREFULLY: This Microsoft End-User License Agreement ("EULA") is a legal agreement between you (either an individual or a single entity) and Microsoft Corporation for the Microsoft software product identified above, which includes computer software and may include associated media, printed materials, and "online" or electronic documentation ("SOFTWARE PRODUCT"). By installing, copying, or otherwise using the SOFTWARE PRODUCT, you agree to be bound by the terms of this EULA. If you do not agree to the terms of this EULA, do not install or use the SOFTWARE PRODUCT; you may, however, return it to your place of purchase for a full refund.

SOFTWARE PRODUCT LICENSE

The SOFTWARE PRODUCT is protected by copyright laws and international copyright treaties, as well as other intellectual property laws and treaties. The SOFTWARE PRODUCT is licensed, not sold.

1. GRANT OF LICENSE. This EULA grants you the following rights:

   a. Software Product.

   Microsoft grants to you as an individual, a personal, nonexclusive license to make and use copies of the SOFTWARE for the sole purposes of designing, developing, and testing your software product(s) that are designed to operate in conjunction with any Microsoft operating system product. You may install copies of the SOFTWARE on an unlimited number of computers provided that you are the only individual using the SOFTWARE. If you are an entity, Microsoft grants you the right to designate one individual within your organization to have the right to use the SOFTWARE in the manner provided above.

   b. Electronic Documents. Solely with respect to electronic documents included with the SOFTWARE, you may make an unlimited number of copies (either in hardcopy or electronic form), provided that such copies shall be used only for internal purposes and are not republished or distributed to any third party.

   c. Redistributable Components.

   (i) Sample Code. In addition to the rights granted in Section 1, Microsoft grants you the right to use and modify the source code version of those portions of the SOFTWARE designated as "Sample Code" ("SAMPLE CODE") for the sole purposes of designing, developing, and testing your software product(s), and to reproduce and distribute the SAMPLE CODE, along with any modifications thereof, only in object code form provided that you comply with Section d(iii), below.

   (ii) Redistributable Components. In addition to the rights granted in Section 1, Microsoft grants you a nonexclusive royalty-free right to reproduce and distribute the object code version of any portion of the SOFTWARE listed in the SOFTWARE file REDIST.TXT ("REDISTRIBUTABLE SOFTWARE"), provided you comply with Section d(iii), below.

   (iii) Redistribution Requirements. If you redistribute the SAMPLE CODE or REDISTRIBUTABLE SOFTWARE (collectively, "REDISTRIBUTABLES"), you agree to: (A) distribute the REDISTRIBUTABLES in object code only in conjunction with and as a part of a software application product developed by you that adds significant and primary functionality to the SOFTWARE and that is developed to operate on the Windows or Windows NT environment ("Application"); (B) not use Microsoft's name, logo, or trademarks to market your software application product; (C) include a valid copyright notice on your software product; (D) indemnify, hold harmless, and defend Microsoft from and against any claims or lawsuits, including attorney's fees, that arise or result from the use or distribution of your software application product; (E) not permit further distribution of the REDISTRIBUTABLES by your end user. The following **exceptions** apply to subsection (iii)(E), above: (1) you may permit further redistribution of the REDISTRIBUTABLES by your distributors to your end-user customers if your distributors only distribute the REDISTRIBUTABLES in conjunction with, and as part of, your Application and you and your distributors comply with all other terms of this EULA; and (2) you may permit your end users to reproduce and distribute the object code version of the files designated by ".ocx" file extensions ("Controls") only in conjunction with and as a part of an Application and/or Web page that adds significant and primary functionality to the Controls, and such end user complies with all other terms of this EULA.

2. DESCRIPTION OF OTHER RIGHTS AND LIMITATIONS.

   a. Not for Resale Software. If the SOFTWARE PRODUCT is labeled "Not for Resale" or "NFR," then, notwithstanding other sections of this EULA, you may not resell, or otherwise transfer for value, the SOFTWARE PRODUCT.

   b. Limitations on Reverse Engineering, Decompilation, and Disassembly. You may not reverse engineer, decompile, or disassemble the SOFTWARE PRODUCT, except and only to the extent that such activity is expressly permitted by applicable law notwithstanding this limitation.

   c. Separation of Components. The SOFTWARE PRODUCT is licensed as a single product. Its component parts may not be separated for use by more than one user.

   d. Rental. You may not rent, lease, or lend the SOFTWARE PRODUCT.